NAPOLEON

NAPOLEON

THE MYTH OF THE SAVIOUR

Jean Tulard
translated by Teresa Waugh

WEIDENFELD AND NICOLSON
LONDON

First published in Great Britain in 1984 by
George Weidenfeld & Nicolson Limited
91 Clapham High Street London SW4 7TA

ISBN 0 297 78439 0

Printed and bound in Great Britain by
Redwood Burn Limited
Trowbridge

D'ici à cinquante ans, il faudra
refaire l'histoire de Napolèon tous
les ans . . .

Stendhal, *Vie de Napolèon*, preface

CONTENTS

ILLUSTRATIONS

Endpapers: a letter from Napoleon to Josephine written during the Italian Campaign. Note its fiery tone and the almost illegible handwriting. (*Mansell*)

INTRODUCTION

THE CHOICE

When, at the end of *The Magic Flute*, Mozart, only a few months before his death, had the forces of the Queen of Night beaten by Sarastro's troops in the Temple of the Sun, he was foretelling the victory of 'enlightenment' over obscurantism. It was 1791, the French Revolution had begun, but the success of 'enlightenment' remained uncertain.

Ten years later, when Mozart's work was finally performed for the first time in Paris, the triumph of new ideas seemed more certain, but among the public who applauded *The Magic Flute*, now called *The Mysteries of Isis* (with the libretto by Morel and arranged by Lachnith), how many people could discern in Sarastro, the features of General Bonaparte, First Consul of the Republic and the last bulwark of the revolutionary conquests?

An unexpected matching of an individual to a moment of political upheaval. On the one hand there was an officer, a dreamer, serving a monarchy in the capacity of a mercenary, with the mentality of an exile, suicidal tendencies and an ennui which dogged him from garrison to garrison. On the other was the Revolution, or rather—when one considers the diversity of their aims—the revolutionaries. Chateaubriand noticed that it was the aristocracy which struck the first blows at the structure of the monarchy. By means of the royal finances crisis they attempted to reopen the question of the principles of absolutism. This was the objective assigned, more or less openly, to the meeting of the States-General. At heart, the nobility longed for the revenge of the Fronde, an end to political humiliation and a return to the fundamental laws already put forward by Cardinal de Retz in his *Mémoires* and by Fénelon in his last works. These were the real aspirations of the liberal nobility, masked by great words and inspired by the hastily read works of the *philosophes,* by the pamphlets of a marginal like the Comte d'Antraigues, and by the American War of

Independence in which a La Fayette and a Noailles had generously participated. The 14th of July and the Great Fear swept away these illusions. With Pandora's box imprudently opened the old nobility was swallowed up, titles were suppressed, feudal rights abolished, properties confiscated.

Another upheaval had come to the fore. *Jacquerie* had succeeded the Fronde. Thus disordered movements of the peasants dedicted to destruction enthused a great part of France and took on an original character. Anarchic revolt turned to revolution. A stocktaking took place. Precise objectives appeared in the dossier of complaints: the end of the feudal regime and of land appropriation was called for. Revision of the property registers undertaken by an increasingly indebted nobility played the part of a catalyst. On the other hand political formulas were non-existent. Despite the weight of taxation and statute labour, insurrections were not against the King but against the feudal lords. The Revolution was appeased. The decrees on the night of 4 August which abolished feudalism; the sale of Church property, the price rises which devalued farm rents, and the increase of journeymen's salaries (which admittedly happened slowly), combined to transform the French peasantry, or at least part of it, into a conservative block, which was certainly attached to the gains of revolution but which was soon to make up the battalions charged with crushing the proletarian insurrections of the nineteenth century.

The King could have used the peasantry against the nobility in a revolt. A Louis XI or a Louis XIV was needed. Louis XVI lacked authority and could not even be excused as a sceptic or a sensualist. Others were to profit from the troubles of the countryside: the bourgeoisie—or some of them. The *rentiers,* who lived off unearned incomes, holders of sinecures; commerce in the ports and the luxury goods trade all suffered badly. The bank ceased to function properly, thus limiting operations. The most audacious were often the humblest members of the lower middle class. One cannot forget Monsieur Grandet:

> As soon as the French Republic put church property up for sale around Saumur, the cooper, by then forty years old, had married the daughter of a rich timber merchant. Bearing all the ready money from his wife's dowry, Grandet went to that district and in con-sideration of two hundred double louis given by his father-in-law to the fierce republican in charge of the sale of national property, he

acquired, legally if not legitimately, for a piece of bread, the finest vineyards of the region, an old abbey and several farms. He prudently protected the aristocrats and did all in his power to prevent the sale of émigré properties. With a sound commercial sense, he supplied the republican armies with one or two thousand barrels of white wine and had himself paid in beautiful fields belonging to a convent and which had been kept back as a last lot. Under the Consulate, the good Grandet became mayor, he administered wisely and harvested his grapes even more wisely; under the Empire he became Monsieur Grandet.

There were many Grandets in the provinces, but it was in Paris that speculation over army supplies and the depreciation of *assignats* had taken on the greatest proportions. The nobility disappeared and the reign of the notables began. A new bourgeoisie developed; it was one which had been able to buy national property during a period of inflation or which had had a monopoly in supplies to the state. It had sidled into administration and knew the law; finally it had been able to free the guilds from shackles and, under the protection of the Directory, it had been able to develop factories and workshops.

What did the bourgeoisie want in 1789? Sieyès expounded his ideas in the famous pamphlet *Qu'est ce que le Tiers État?* More concisely, Napoleon summarized their aspirations in a phrase which may be apocryphal: 'Vanity; liberty,' he added, 'was merely a pretext.' The feudal reaction which was to close the ranks, or threaten to close the ranks, of the nobility to an ascendant bourgeoisie in an expanding France, pushed the bourgeois into opposition with social institutions. Besides, the first to revolt were not always to be those who were eventually to benefit from the destruction of the Ancien Régime. Bourgeois property was often to be victim of the abolition of feudalism. The fact remains, and it has frequently been stressed, that the peasants and the bourgeois found themselves engaged in the same fight against feudalism. In the end they were to triumph and become, to a certain extent, interdependent. They did, after all, represent quantity and talent.

A fourth element remained separate: the urban proletariat. Initially, unemployment and famine put artisans, journeymen, servants and low-paid workers on the streets of the towns, especially Paris. The fact that there were so few large enterprises, and the archaic structure of the workshops and working conditions—which brought employers and workers into close proximity—prevented the occurrence of severe social problems; and the idea of striking was restricted to one company or to only a few members of any one profession. Social aspirations, influenced by Rousseau, were limited to a world of 'small producers and small, independent merchants'; the sans-culottes dreamt of a kind of 'universal body of employers'. This urban proletariat was the spearhead of the Revolution during the Terror. But the Constituent Assembly wanted to ensure for their developing industry a cheap labour force, and by the Le Chapelier law of 4 June 1791 all grouping together of workers was forbidden. The disappearance of the guilds even favoured the exploitation of children in factories. Wishing to ensure the maintenance of order and the consolidation of property (their own), the Thermidorians, in their turn, urgently disarmed the suburbs. The new bourgeoisie crushed the sans-culottes movement; the peasants, meanwhile, remained indifferent to this failure.

After the *coup d'état* of Brumaire, Bonaparte claimed: 'I am the Revolution', only to contradict himself immediately: 'The Revolution is over.' The Revolution was thought to be over on 5 August 1789, or at the time of the breaking up of the Constituent Assembly, when the Convention celebrated the Supreme Being, or when Robespierre's head rolled into the basket. There were three possible ways of putting an end to the Revolution: a return to the monarchic and aristocratic system (with the old dynasty, or a new one); the consolidation of peasant and bourgeois gains; or the satisfaction of the demands of the Parisian sans-culottes—in fact, a return to the past, a continuation of the present or a preparation for the future.

The Napoleonic adventure depended on a choice, the choice which Bonaparte made in 1799.

THE FACTIONS FACE TO FACE
October 1799. The outcome of the Revolution was still undecided.

The Royalists had only just failed, in Vendémiaire and Fructidor, in their attempt to take power. They were, it is true, divided; there were the partisans of a constitutional monarchy, and the intransigent monarchists who grouped themselves around the Comte d'Artois, Louis XVIII's brother, and demanded a return to the Ancien Régime. They were strongest in the west and in the south. To many, a restoration seemed inevitable, but when, and in what guise?

On the left were the neo-Jacobins. They had triumphed at the elections of Year VI because of the preponderance in the towns' electoral assemblies of artisans and shopkeepers who made up their clientele. The Directory quashed these elections but the neo-Jacobins were to triumph again in Year VII. Their influence in the Council of the Five Hundred was important, but it was weaker in the second assembly, the Council of Ancients. Their programme, which was more moderate than that of the *Babouvistes,* some of whom joined them after Gracchus Babeuf's failure, brought them closer to the former 'terrorists'. They demanded a regime that would be more democratic than the oligarchic constitution of 1795 then in power; they attacked non-juror priests; finally they demanded a strengthening of the assemblies against the encroachment of the Directory. The renewal of war, in 1799, and the military disasters suffered by France had made it possible to pass the hostage law which made the relations of émigrés responsible for outrages committed against officials, and instituted a compulsory loan, levied on the rich. Neo-Jacobinism leant for support on generals like Bernadotte, Jourdan and Augereau, and it was all the more powerful for being a gathering of the discontented. But it was more of a coalition than a party and therefore lacked coherence. Furthermore the redressment of the situation abroad, thanks to the victories of Brune at Bergen and Masséna at Zurich on 26 September 1799, weakened their position by making the politics of terror, which they advocated, unpopular. In August, Fouché, who had become Minister of Police, closed, without any problems, the Jacobin Society known as the 'constitutional society', which had formerly caused the Directory to tremble. The neo-Jacobins had no more solid support in the army than in the administration.

The choice lay between a constitutional monarchy and a clear-cut stark republic.

The Thermidorians, veterans of the Revolutionary Assemblies who had held power since the fall of Robespierre—Sieyès, Cambacérès, Merlin, Fouché, Quinette and others—wanted neither the restoration of the King (most of them voted for the death of Louis XVI) nor anarchy, in so far as they represented the interests of the new land-owners who had benefited from the sale of national property. Aware of their unpopularity, which arose from their abuse of power and their indifference to the poverty of the people, they only held their position as a result of a string of illegalities, from the Decree of the Two-Thirds which put the Royalists out of the way, the the Floréal *coup d'état* against the Jacobins, and had sacrificed along the way those of their number who were most compromised. Barras, the Directory's man since its foundation, symbolized all the compromises which surrounded them.

The objectives of the Thermidorians were vague (they were content with a bourgeois republic) but they had a very definite following of *nantis*—the rich—who had something to lose should a change of regime bring about a return to the monarchy or the revenge of the hungry. Nevertheless they could be divided into two sections. In the heart of the Directory, at the seat of executive power, General Moulin and Gohier, the former Minister of Justice during the Terror, were in favour of upholding the Constitution. On the other hand, Sieyès, supported by one Roger Ducos, despised the Constitution, which he had not drawn up. Since all revision of the constitution necessitated a delay of nine years, the former Abbé's only option was an internal *coup d'état*, depending on the sword. So he envisaged applying to General Joubert, until the latter was killed at Novi on 15 August 1799. In this operation he made sure of the support of the representatives of the French intelligentsia, the descendants of the *philosophes*—Daunou, Cabanis, Destutt de Tracy, Garat and Volney, who like Sieyès belonged to the National Institute of Sciences and Arts which was founded by the Thermidorian convention and which replaced the Academies. The fifth Director, Barras, was hesitant. Royalist, not to say Orleanist, sympathies were attributed to him. Sympathies which were equally imputed to Sieyès when he was not alleged to be working for a 'foreign prince'.

To these divisions could be added two more causes for the weakening of the Directory; a catastrophic economic predicament and a disastrous military situation with renewal of war on the continent.

The military situation was so disastrous that the Directory who had been considering calling back to Paris the only as yet unbeaten general, Bonaparte, whom they had sent to Egypt with the excuse of preparing the conquest of British India, but really in order to rid themselves of an embarrassing person. A letter to this effect had been prepared on 18 September 1799, but the successes of Brune and Masséna made it useless. It was at this moment that news of Bonaparte's return reached Paris. This return altered the situation. Gohier wrote, quite rightly, in his *Mémoires* that General Bonaparte, made famous by his victories in Italy and in Egypt, was going to attract 'all the men of no allegiance, all the discontented'.

The Royalists immediately attributed ulterior motives to him, which favoured their cause. The moderates saw him as the president of a bourgeois republic. There was no one, even among the Jacobins, if Jourdan's *Mémoires* are to be believed, who did not imagine a counter-coup directed by Bonaparte which would avert a *coup d'état* which was being plotted by Sieyès and which Briot had denounced from the platform of the Five Hundred. The ideologues noticed that Bonaparte had been elected to the Institut before leaving for Egypt and Barras remembered that he had protected the general in his early days.

Strong in the prestige which arose from the public's fascination with victorious generals, strong also in the unity of the army with which he was perhaps wrongly credited, Bonaparte found himself in the position of arbitrator.

In 1799, prompted by self-interest as well as realism, and despite a strong feeling in the country, he had dismissed a restoration of the monarchy which would have immediately caused a civil war. Now he was able to choose between a government of public safety supported by the Jacobins (even though the preceding one had left bad memories), the consolidation of the Directory, and the *coup d'état* dreamt of by Sieyès. His purpose was to bring about his own revision of the constitution in favour of the *nantis*.

WHICH SIDE TO CHOOSE?

On 9 October 1799 Napoleon landed in the Bay of Saint-Raphael. It is not surprising that his arrival caused much curiosity, which led to his ship being exempted from quarantine, normally obligatory for all vessels coming from the East. By midday Bonaparte was on French soil, six hours later he was on the road for Paris. He had to hurry in order to forestall any inopportune decision of the Directory who might consider his return as a desertion of duty. The surprise element was essential. It failed. By 10 October the news had already reached Paris. This contretemps helped Bonaparte in the long run. At Avignon he became aware of the popularity which the mysterious and distant Egyptian expedition had afforded him. 'The crowd was enormous. Its enthusiasm reached a peak at the sight of the great man. The air echoed with cheers and with cries of "Long live Bonaparte", and this crowd and these shouts accompanied him right to the hotel where he stayed. It was an electrifying sight.' How can this movement be explained? 'From this moment he was considered as having been called to save France from the crisis into which it had been thrown by the pitiful government of the Directory and by the reverses of our armies.' Perhaps Boulard in his *Mémoires,* quoted above, exaggerates the political significance of the demonstration in Avignon. It was apparently a spontaneous movement. Then the demonstrations rapidly adopted an official air. The Municipality of Nevers asked to be received by the General on 15 October in the Hôtel du Grand-Cerf where he was staying. Undoubtedly this return was taking on a more and more favourable complexion. Bonaparte reached Paris on the 16th at about six o'clock in the morning and the first person he visited that evening was Gohier, the President of the Directory. He was cordially welcomed. Somewhat relieved, the young general took himself the next day to see the five representatives of executive power for an official reception. His dress caused a sensation: a round hat, an olive cloth frock-coat with a Turkish scimitar at his waist. His conversation pleasantly surprised the Directors: he would only draw his sword—in this instance a scimitar—in the defence of the Republic and of his government. Perhaps he was sincere and either believed himself to be, or wished to be, the saviour of a Directory which he had been told was at bay.

His hotel in the rue de la Victoire was besieged by visitors who came to discuss the political situation. He spoke with Talleyrand, Roederer, Maret—a future eminence grise—and Fouché. They all showed Bonaparte a Directory in a state of collapse and tried to draw him towards the opposition. Bonaparte has been blamed for his hesitations. He came back to Paris on 16 October and was master of France on 10 November. He could hardly have moved faster.

The political game was complex. The supporters of the status quo (the Directors, Gohier and Moulin) who had the law on their side (the power of legality was evident when Robespierre was outlawed) were opposed by Barras, who was being accused more than ever of intending to restore the monarchy, and by the neo-Jacobins who had won the last elections and who could still count on numerous deputies and the republican generals. Finally they were opposed by the Thermidorians who hoped to entrust Sieyès with the revision of the 1795 Constitution in order to make it more effective and to forestall the return of the King as much as the progress of anarchy, in fact anything which would ensure their maintaining power. They could take advantage of an intellectual guarantee, that of the 'ideologues'—the supporters of the philosophy of 'enlightenment' who reigned over the Institut of which Bonaparte was also a member.

Today the vague nature of all these plans strikes us: no one knew how to end the Revolution once and for all.

Bonaparte seems, initially, to have limited his objectives to becoming a member of the Directory. But he was excluded by the minimum age restriction of forty, and Gohier, perhaps on the occasion of a dinner given on 22 October, was immovable.

The Jacobin temptation was no less great. The author of *Le Souper de Beaucaire* and friend of Augustin de Robespierre must have been attracted to this camp. Neo-Jacobinism, which was strong in provincial administrations and in the army (Bernadotte, Jourdan), had advocated a government of public safety since year VII. The vote for a compulsory loan had, anyway, horrified large sections of the bourgeoisie and of the well-to-do peasantry. Furthermore, Bonaparte came up against Bernadotte. Their characters were opposed to each other, they had different views of the Republic and there was, of course, the rivalry over Desirée Clary, Bonaparte's one-time fiancée whom Bernadotte had married. The Jacobin card was a hard one to play.

As far as Barras was concerned, Bonaparte felt nothing but contempt for him. Everything about Barras annoyed him, the ostentation of the Luxembourg Palace, the cynicism of the man, and his favourites. Here again, a woman played a part—Josephine was the former mistress of the corrupt Director.

There remained Sieyès. The inscrutable ex-Abbé was content simply to let it be known that the time had come to apply the plan for the new constitution which he had been hatching for several years. The political prestige of the author of *Qu'est-ce que le Tiers État?* was considerable. It was thought that it was he who would close the chasm of the Revolution by means of this constitution which had been announced so often, which was so eagerly awaited and which would reassure all those who were disturbed by threats to the sacred principles of property and of equality under the law. 'Ideology' could serve as a link between two members of the Institut who, it is true, did not belong to the same faction.

A first meeting between Bonaparte and Sieyès on 23 October produced nothing. Perhaps the General's Jacobin past worried the former Abbé who would have preferred Moreau, even if the latter, on the other hand, was suspected of monarchist sympathies. The decisive interview took place on either 1 or 6 November. In fact Sieyès did not have a free hand. The revision of the Constitution was legally impossible—a complicated procedure and a delay of nine years being indispensable to any modification of the articles. It was therefore necessary to have recourse to force, to have another *coup d'état*. Sieyès saw the plan would bring about the fall of the Legislative Body. The councils would then designate a commission charged with drawing up a new constitution which would bear in mind the weakness of the preceding one; in order to intimidate the Legislative Body, some troop movements would be necessary. A sword would be brandished, only to be returned immediately to the scabbard.

The void in the Directory was easily created: Sieyès and his acolyte Roger Ducos left it. With the bribing of a third man, Barras, everything would be settled. A Jacobin opposition could be feared from the heart of the Council of the Five Hundred; on the pretext of a plot, the assemblies were to be removed from Paris in order to deny them the possible support of the suburbs. High finance was reticent with the exception of Perrégaux, and the several millions necessary would have to be furnished by a supply officer from the Army of Italy, Collot.

Bonaparte had entered the game by 6 November. It appears that he had been promised the position of Provisional Consul; he would have, in addition, the right of looking over the constitution, which would be submitted to the assemblies for approval. Sieyès's concessions were all the more important in that it was to be a parliamentary *coup d'état*, in which the military were only to be extras. The description '*coup d'état*' was even an exaggeration since everything was to take place with relative legality. It was an imperative inherited from the Revolution, not to confront the law face to face. Already Bonaparte's equivocal attitude had lessened his popularity, if the newspapers are to be believed.

THE COUP D'ÉTAT

Sieyès's operation began without difficulty. During the night of 8–9 November (17–18 Brumaire), military positions were taken up, proclamations were sent to the Demonville printers, and members of the Council of Ancients were summoned. Constitutionally this council determined where the Legislative Body should sit; furthermore it numbered in its midst, unlike the Five Hundred, a strong faction in favour of Sieyès.

On 9 November (18 Brumaire), at seven-thirty in the morning, the game began at the Tuileries. The Ancients, as yet barely awake and surprised by the troop movements, learnt from one of their number, Cornet, the deputy for the Loiret, that the Republic was threatened. In a pathetic address, Régnier from Lorraine changed their perplexity to

panic. He advised them to leave Paris for the suburbs, and, taking the circumstances into consideration, suggested the Château de Saint-Cloud. 'There, sheltered from surprises and from sudden attack, you will be able in calm and safety to consider ways of doing away with the dangers and also of destroying causes of possible future dangers.'
A decree was passed:

Article 1—The Legislative Body is transferred to the Commune of Saint-Cloud. The two councils will be seated in the two wings of the Palace.
Article 2—They will be there by midday tomorrow, 19 Brumaire. All continuation of their functions is forbidden elsewhere and before that time.
Article 3—General Bonaparte is charged with the application of this decree; he will take all the measures necessary to the safety of the nation's representatives.
Article 4—General Bonaparte is summoned to the heart of the council in order to receive a duplicate of the decree and in order to swear an oath.

Half past eight. Bonaparte was advised that the decree had been voted. Immediately, he mounted his horse and, accompanied by a brilliant escort of officers, he made his way to the Tuileries. Admitted to the Council of Ancients he explained the situation in a few words:

Citizens, Representatives, the Republic was perishing, you knew it and by your decree you have just saved it. Woe betide those who wish for trouble and disorder! I will arrest them, helped by General Lefebvre, General Berthier and all my companions in arms . . . Your wisdom has yielded this decree; we will be able to implement it. We want a republic founded on real liberty, civil liberty and national representation; we will have it, I swear, in my name and in the name of my companions in arms.

'We swear it,' echoed in chorus the generals who surrounded Bonaparte—Berthier, Lefebvre, Marmont, and others. Several movements were rapidly stifled. The intrusion of these noisy and arrogant soldiers had shocked some deputies.
Bonaparte went down into the Tuileries gardens where he noticed Bottot, Barras's secretary. He dragged him to where the troops were stationed around the palace and addressed him as follows:

In what condition did I leave France, and in what condition do I find it! Behind me I left peace, and I find war! Behind me I left conquests and now the enemy is crossing our frontiers! I left our arsenals full and now there are no arms. I left the Italian millions and everywhere I find spoliatory laws and poverty! This state of affairs cannot last; it would lead us within three months to despotism. But we want the Republic, the Republic built on foundations of equality, of morality, of civil liberty and of political tolerance. Under a good administration all individuals will forget the factions to which they had to belong, in order to become French. It is finally time for the country's defenders to be trusted as they are so justly entitled to be!

To judge by some agitators we will soon all be the enemies of the Republic, we who have consolidated it with our work and with our courage! There is no one more patriotic than the brave men who have been wounded in the service of the Republic!

This explosion which was no part of the conspirators' plan, served a very precise end. It excited the enthusiasm of the soldiers whose deepest beliefs were unknown, and discredited in their minds not only the Directory, but the Jacobins (by the allusion to spoliatory laws). Bonaparte's success was total. The soldiers acclaimed their general. And the army was prepared to sweep aside civil power. Bonaparte, who was thinking, perhaps, of a future confrontation with Sieyès, knew that he would be able to count on the troops stationed in Paris.

Eleven o'clock. The news of the decree passed by the Ancients reached the Council of the Five Hundred. Protestations were heard, but no resistance was formed against the removal to Saint-Cloud. Such resistance would have been illegal.

The void at the head of the executive had still to be created. Sieyès and Ducos immediately resigned from their offices, but what about Barras? Talleyrand, assisted by Bruix, had to obtain his resignation. They presented themselves at the Luxembourg Palace when the Director was at table. A table designed for thirty people but which had attracted only one guest, the financier, Ouvrard. Barras had already understood. He listened distractedly to Talleyrand, opened a window, saw the soldiers and did not insist. He signed a rapid note in which he declared that it was 'with joy that he rejoined the ranks of the ordinary citizens'. Talleyrand kissed his hands and affirmed that Barras had once again saved the Republic. Talleyrand apparently kept the millions with which Bonaparte is said to have entrusted him in order to bribe

Bonaparte's former protector, Barras. Barras set out for Grosbois. The retirement of this uncouth fighter proved the excellence of their plans to the conspirators. Moulin and Gohier, the last Directors to refuse to resign were confined to the Luxembourg Palace, guarded by General Moreau. The Directory had ceased to exist.

Night fell on a Paris which had not stirred and which appeared to be indifferent. The first round had been won. Bonaparte reputedly confided to his secretary, before going to bed, 'Today has not been too bad. Tomorrow we shall see.' In fact, for Sieyès, nothing was over. He guessed that the Council of Five Hundred, where the neo-Jacobins were active, would not let itself be walked over. Were he to arraign Bonaparte, would the troops, excited as they were when the Convention outlawed Robespierre, abandon their leader? Would it not be better to arrest, or remove instantly under any pretext, the forty most energetic deputies? But Bonaparte had always opposed this, whether through concern for lawfulness or because of a determination to break with revolutionary methods which would then prevent the national unity of which he dreamed. Or had he a last spark of sympathy for the Jacobins? Perhaps it was a tactical manoeuvre aimed at complicating the whole operation in order to allow Bonaparte to play a more important role than the one which Sieyès had reserved for him.

The second act took place in the Château de Saint-Cloud on 19 Brumaire. The meeting of the councils was planned for midday. The troops had to be allowed to move, but this left the deputies time in which to connive. Bonaparte arrived towards the end of the morning with Berthier, Gardanne, Lefebvre and Leclerc. It is said that the Château was surrounded by six thousand men under the command of Murat. Sebastiani and his dragoons had also to be taken into account. Lannes remained in Paris with other troops. According to eye-witnesses the soldiers launched themselves into hostile attacks against 'lawyers and speechifiers', whom they held responsible for the delay in pay, the holes in their shoes and the shortage of tobacco. Tempted by the diatribe against Bottot, the psychological reaction to Bonaparte developed effectively among the ranks.

The sitting of the Council of Ancients, in Apollo's gallery, decorated by Mignard, opened at one o'clock in the afternoon, presided over by Lemercier. Several representatives who intentionally had not been summoned the evening before, asked questions. Those who were part of the conspiracy replied in embarrassed tones. In order to respect legal form, Bonaparte waited in another room whilst the

Legislative Body took note of the resignation of the Directory and informed the Council of Five Hundred of it. This was the first step towards the designation of a provisional government. The discussions dragged on. Suddenly Bonaparte could stand it no longer. 'It must be done with,' he declared. His appearance in the middle of the debate caused a sensation. According to Bourrienne:

> Bonaparte's entry was sudden and angry; this did not give me a good opinion of what he was about to say. Many different speeches have been attributed to Bonaparte since his coming to power. This is inevitable. He made no speech to the Ancients, unless a conversation held without nobility and without dignity can be called a speech. Only these words could be heard: 'brothers-in-arms', 'plain speaking of a soldier'. The questions of the president came rapidly, they were quite clear. Nothing was more confused or worse articulated than Bonaparte's ambiguous and twisted replies. He spoke at random of volcanoes, secret agitations, victories and the violated constitution; he even reproached 18 Fructidor of which he had been the prime mover and strongest supporter. He claimed to have known nothing until the Council of Ancients had called him to the rescue of the country. Then came 'Caesar, Cromwell, tyrant'. He repeated several times: 'That is all I have to say to you', and he was saying nothing . . . I noticed the bad effect that this gabbling was having on the assembly, and Bonaparte's increasing discountenance. I pulled at his coat-tails, said to him in a low voice: 'Leave the room, General, you no longer know what you are saying.'

No doubt Bourrienne's *Mémoires* bear the stamp of ill will, but all evidence agrees in underlining the embarrassment of the General.

Once outside, Bonaparte regained his calm and it was with an assured step that he strode towards the Five Hundred who had been hastily installed in the Orangery. The debates which took place there were agitated. The conspirators did not have the majority in this assembly and they had to confront a vigorous opposition. The legality of Barras's resignation was questioned. Suddenly the sound of arms interrupted the speaker on the tribune; Bonaparte had entered.

The most diverse accounts have been given of the events which followed. As soon as he appeared, Bonaparte was questioned, surrounded and jostled by the deputies. On all sides cries went up of 'Outlaw the dictator! Long live the Republic and the Constitution of Year VII. We'll die in office!' Destrem has been attributed with the famous remark: 'General, is it for this then that you conquered?'

Lucien Bonaparte who presided over the council was unable to restore order. Some soldiers from Bonaparte's entourage made an effort to release Napoleon and protected him on his way out. The general was choking, he was pale and his face was slightly bleeding.

The game was lost. Bonaparte appeared to have missed his chance. As Sieyès had feared, some deputies demanded the general's dismissal. Bertrand, from Calvados, requested that the command of the grenadiers and of the parliamentary guard be taken away from him. Tarlot suggested that the council return to Paris, and suddenly someone shouted: 'Put the outlawing of General Bonaparte to the vote!' A terrible threat. Certainly the agreement of the Ancients was needed, but in the excitement everybody forgot this constitutional necessity. If an energetic general, like Barras in Thermidor, took command of the troops, the conspiracy would be ended. Lucien perceived the danger. In order to gain time, and having tried in vain to justify his brother, he put down the seals of his office and left the assembly stupefied. Outside he mounted his horse and made an improvised harangue to the Guards of the Court of Honour: 'The president declares that the vast majority of this council is for the moment living in terror of several representatives with stilettos who are besieging the tribune, confronting their colleagues with death and sending up the most dreadful threats . . . these brigands are no longer the representatives of the people, but of the dagger.' Lucien is said to have then indicated his brother whose face was smeared with blood. So the legend of the daggers was born. Then with a theatrical but effective gesture, he took a sword and swore that he would thrust it into his brother were his brother to become a traitor.

The soldiers of the parliamentary guard were shaken and felt, above all, behind them, the impatience and anger of the troops brought by Bonaparte. The drums began o beat. Murat led the grenadiers and marched towards the Orangery. Leclerc joined him. 'Kick all those people out of here!' shouted Murat. In five minutes the Orangery, where the Five Hundred were sitting, was emptied to the sound of the drum. There was no longer any question of parliamentary manoeuvres; Sieyès's plan was overthrown. The entry on the scene of the army altered the development of the operation planned by the former Abbé. Sieyès was one of the great losers in the affair. To maintain some continuity it was essential, in haste and confusion, to bring a certain number of Ancients together with any members of the

Five Hundred who could be found in the gardens of Saint-Cloud and convince them of the necessity for such a meeting. This improvised assembly took note of the void in the executive and replaced the Directory by a consular triumvirate consisting of Bonaparte, Sieyès and Roger Ducos. The Legislative Body was adjourned; two commissions were charged with drawing up a new constitution within six weeks. Finally sixty-one deputies (Jacobins) were excluded from the national representatives. At eleven o'clock in the evening, Bonaparte, who had regained his self-control and who took on the role of leader of the conspiracy, signed a proclamation in which he recounted, in his own way, the development of the *coup d'état*, drawing especial attention to the assassination attempt of which he was supposedly victim in the Council of the Five Hundred. He would not have been saved but for the intervention of the Legislative Body's grenadiers: 'Intimidated, the agitators dispersed and went away. The majority, protected from their blows, came freely and peacefully back to the council room; propositions necessary to the safety of the public were heard. The salutory resolution which is to become the new and provisional law of the Republic was discussed and prepared.'

Paris did not move. Since Germinal and Prairial the revolutionary spirit seemed to have been broken in a capital which had anyway been disarmed. All spirit of criticism had been crushed; without a word, the parisians accepted the version of events which was put before them. In the provinces there was a timid reaction. The departmental administrations, in the hands of the Jacobins, attempted to organize some resistance. In vain. Public opinion was too weary to consider another civil war.

'One of the worst conceived and worst conducted *coups d'état* imaginable, which succeeded only by virtue of the all-powerful nature of its causes—the state of mind of the public and the disposition of the army. Perhaps more because of the first than the second.' Thus Tocqueville described the 18 Brumaire.

In Paris the three new Consuls installed themselves provisionally in the Luxembourg Palace in place of the Directors. Who was to preside? Roger Ducos is supposed to have turned towards Bonaparte: 'It is useless to vote for the presidency. It is yours by right.' The Brumaire conspiracy had changed its leader if not its meaning.

Confronted by pressure from the neo-Jacobins and threats from the Royalists, the Thermidorians had the feeling that the new *coup d'état* would keep them in power. After the fall of Robespierre they had lacked popularity and authority—General Bonaparte brought them the former: he was the man who had created the peace of Campo-Formio and who had led the mysterious campaign in Egypt; as to authority, they would acquire it with the revision of the Constitution advocated by Sieyès.

Jacques Bainville was right to stress that Brumaire was no different from other *coups d'état*. It appeared to contemporaries as the victory of a political faction which had already been ruling France for five years; it gave rise to few questions and even less enthusiasm. At least it was known that it would not change the principles of the Revolution of which the ideologues set themselves up as guardians, neither would it harm the interests of the new bourgeoisie—those who had acquired national property. No doubt Benjamin Constant had warned Sieyès, on the evening of 20 Brumaire when the adjournment of the councils became known:

> This step appears disastrous to me in that it destroys the only barrier against a man whom you associated with yesterday but who is, nevertheless, all the more threatening to the Republic. His proclamations, in which he only speaks of himself and says that his return has given rise to the hope that he will put an end to France's troubles, have convinced me more than ever that in everything he does he sees only his own advancement. Nevertheless, the generals, the soldiers, the aristocratic riff-raff and all who welcome with enthusiasm the appearance of strength are on his side. On its side, the Republic has yourself which is certainly a great deal and representatives who, good or bad, will always be ready to put a curb to the plans of an individual.

The army had played a greater part than had been planned, but the alliance between Bonaparte and the 'Thermidorians' turned 'Brumairians' seemed solid since the General had closed the door to Royalists and Jacobins despite prejudices in favour of some of them. The 'bourgeois' revolution was on the path to consolidation. 'It will be agreed,' wrote the economist Francis d'Ivernois, a few months after Brumaire, 'that the French have managed to protect their purse strings quite well.' For his part, one of the architects of the *coup*, Regnault de Saint-Jean-d'Angély noted:

> From the time of the Constituent Assembly, a faction was created which attacked property. Instead of being crushed, the faction was

appeased; where the whole should have been courageously defended, a part was cravenly conceded. Since when, this faction, the enemy of social order, has destroyed all guarantees of property. Each small revolution within the big one has taken place at the cost of another blow to property. Only the revolution of Brumaire has a different character, it is a revolution which favours property.

PART I

THE BIRTH OF A SAVIOUR

Why did Bonaparte succeed where La Fayette, Dumouriez and Pichegru had failed? How did he become the arbiter of the political situation in 1799?

There was nothing about his Corsican origins which destined him for this, except perhaps the fact that the island, barely conceded to the Government of Versailles by the Republic of Genoa, found itself swept up by the Revolution that gripped France.

The mainland was dividing itself into rival factions. And Corsica, too, was shaken by factional struggles: aristocrats, partisans of the 1768 annexation (Buttafuoco) against Paolists, and Paolists in favour of the Convention (Salicetti) against anglophile Paolists (Pozzo di Borgo). Struggles as yet little known but which marked social divisions as extreme as the ideological conflicts. At a very early age, tracked down, exiled and arrested, Napoleon discovered in France and in Corsica the horror of civil war. Thence was born the dominant theme of Bonapartism: to be above party politics, set yourself up as a national reconciler.

But such a role demands great prestige. Bonaparte was the first general, perhaps since Caesar, to have understood the importance of propaganda. It is not enough to win battles, victory must be enshrined in an aura of legend. Bonaparte did not triumph at Fleurus, nor at Geisberg or Zurich, yet from the time of the Directory he was more popular than Jourdan, Hoche, Masséna or Moreau. This is because he knew how, by means of the press and popular imagery, to transform his campaign in Italy into a veritable *Iliad*.

Despite the final failure of the Egyptian expedition it was turned by Napoleon's chroniclers into an Eastern epic whose hero equalled

Alexander or Caesar. Bonaparte fascinates, irritates, captivates—in short leaves no one indifferent.

There was a third reason for his success: he appeared just as the Revolution was dying down, when the bourgeoisie, at last victorious, was able to contemplate complete rule. The attempts of La Fayette and Dumouriez were premature; since Thermidor the country had been wanting a return to order. This order could not be established by Pichegru despite the brilliance of his military successes for he was over-compromised with the Royalists as well as being the prisoner of a political faction. Bonaparte reassured everyone: he had been a friend of Augustin de Robespierre, but he belonged to the old nobility; he had been the protégé of Barras, but yet had managed to prove his independence from the Directory. Everything was in his favour even his strange appearance and his authoritarian character. Prevost-Paradol observed: 'The French Revolution has founded a society, but is still searching for a government.' 'Everyone,' wrote Stendhal, 'recognized the need for a strong government; and we got a strong government.'

1

THE FOREIGNER

The real name of Bonaparte is Buonaparte; he signed it this way himself throughout his Italian campaign and up until the age of thirty-three. Then he frenchified it and ever afterwards signed 'Bonaparte': I will leave him with the name which he adopted, the immortal name which he carved out for himself and which he has left as his own indestructible monument. Did Bonaparte falsify his date of birth by one year in order to have been born a Frenchman, that is, so that his birth did not precede the date of the union of Corsica and France? Bonaparte was born on 5 February 1768 and not on 15 August 1769 despite the positive assertion to the contrary of M. Bourrienne. This is why the conservative Senate in its proclamation of 3 April 1814 described Napoleon as a 'foreigner'.

Two characters in Chateaubriand's *Mémoires d'outre-tombe* are distorted: Napoleon and Chateaubriand himself. Let us ignore the latter, and turn to the former: golden legend may see him born on a carpet woven with scenes from the *Iliad,* but black legend, whose chief exponent was in fact Chateaubriand, is not far behind. It is established that Napoleon was born on 15 August 1769, but Chateaubriand's assessment of Napoleon's early years is not entirely inaccurate. There is in fact something of the 'outsider' about Napoleon and Chateaubriand is not wrong in speaking of an 'existence fallen from on high, belonging to all times and to all nations'. The fact remains that Napoleon was born at Ajaccio on 15 August 1769 in a Corsica still agitated by its annexation to France.

CORSICA IN THE EIGHTEENTH CENTURY

The island of Corsica was not unknown to eighteenth-century Europe. Her strategic position in the Mediterranean, between France and Italy, had made her the envied prey of the imperialists which confronted each other in the western part of this sea. She was also, in enlightened circles, the symbol of resistance to the oppressor. Several decades before American Independence, the attention of thinkers and writers like Vasco, Gorani or Boswell had been drawn to her by the revolt of the islanders against Genoese domination in 1729, the right to liberty which was proclaimed by the leaders of the uprising, and by the social reforms envisaged at the time. In his *Contrat Social*, Rousseau writes, 'There is still in Europe a country capable of legislation. It is the island of Corsica. These gallant people have regained and defended their liberty with a courage and perseverance which merit the advice of a wise man on how to conserve it. I have a certain premonition that one day this little island will astound Europe.'

In about 1764, at the request of Buttafuoco, a Corsican aristocrat, the philosopher undertook the drawing up of a constitution which was destined never to be administered.

Besides, how would he have been able to bring peace? The Treaty of Corte in 1732 resulted from the popular uprising of 1729 which had prompted an Austrian intervention, but two years later Genoa had forgotten all her concessions and a new revolt broke out. The affair rapidly took on international proportions and there were two French military interventions on the island, on behalf of Genoa. The Corsicans found in Pascal Paoli, the son of one of the heroes of 1729, the commander-in-chief they lacked. Paoli drove the Genoese away from coastal strongholds, and undertook a work of political and social reorganization which held the attention of Europe. Having chosen Corte as his capital because of its central position, he convened a Constituent Assembly there in November 1755. The outcome of this was a democratic constitution which entrusted the legislative powers to a council elected by universal suffrage; executive legislation was entrusted to Paoli who presided over a Council of State comprising nine members. Having devised the constitution, Paoli set to work on draining the marshes, building roads, opening quarries, constructing the Île-Rousse bridge (in order to be able to compete with Calvi in trade with Genoa), and forming a mercantile fleet which flew a chocolate-brown flag. As for the social reforms, Napoleon exaggeraed them in the dissertation which he presented to the Académie de Lyon in 1791:

> Paoli divided the land of each village into two categories: first there
> were the lowlands suitable for pasturing and crops. The second
> category comprised mountainous land suitable for olives, vineyards,
> sweet chestnuts and all kinds of trees. The land in the first category
> was called *Piage* and became public property with private life
> interest. Every three years the *Piage* of each village was divided
> among the inhabitants. The lands in the second category, liable to
> individual cultivation, remained under the domination of private
> greed.

In reality it was a matter of survival from the communal regime and not
of innovations introduced by Paoli. However this mistake bears
witness to the general feeling: the *Babbo* had introduced more social
justice during his advent to power. This consideration was to weigh
heavily in 1793, causing the popular movement to be channelled
towards Paoli to the detriment of Salicetti and the Bonapartes—who
were nevertheless partisans of the Montagnard Convention. Paoli's
effective action could only give rise to misgivings as much among the
Corsican nobility of the interior as around the coast where the last
bastions of Genoese Republic were feeling threatened. Under the first
Treaty of Compiègne, 14 August 1756, French troops occupied Calvi,
Saint-Florent and Ajaccio. War on the mainland obliged the French to
withdraw their forces. The Second Treaty of Compiègne in 1764,
brought them back to the island. Finally, Genoa, by the Treaty of
Versailles signed on 15 May 1768, conceded her Corsican rights to
France, but only provisionally until the Republic had repaid the debt
which she owed to France. Paoli refused to accept a treaty over which
the Corsicans had not been consulted. War broke out. The royal
troops met with the support of a French party which had greatly
developed since it was first encouraged by Cardinal Fleury. Paoli was
beaten at Ponte Novo on 8 May 1769 and was obliged to flee to
England. Corsica did not rank with the other provinces; she remained
from 1770 until 1786 under the military command of first the Comte de
Vaux, and then Monsieur de Marbeuf. However from 1775 the island
was assured of a relative autonomy by the Provincial Estates.

THE BONAPARTES
The most fantastical origins have been suggested for the Bonaparte
family. On St Helena, Napoleon was still laughing at the idea that he

was a descendant of the Iron Mask and of the daughter of M. Bonpart, the Governor of the Saint Margaret Islands. Kings of England, the Comneni, the Paleologues and even the Julian tribe have been attributed to Napoleon as ancestors. In return, black legend made Napoleon the descendant of a footman and a goat girl. In fact the Bonapartes were scions of a Tuscan family. As early as 1616 a Bonaparte is recorded as a member of the Council of Ancients of Ajaccio. Subsequently in the seventeenth and eighteenth centuries, several Bonapartes were members of this council. Considerable respect was paid to the position of a member of the Council of Ancients since after the annexation this status was seen as the equivalent of a French title. Thus Napoleon Bonaparte was a nobleman, even if, as was asserted by a Restoration pamphlet, everyone in Corsica was born a nobleman in order to avoid paying taxes.

His father, Charles Bonaparte, was a person of considerable standing. He had been part of Paoli's entourage, and Paoli had entrusted him with various responsibilities. Won over to the French party after 1768 he was an advocate in the Upper Council of Corsica and then, in 1777, deputy for the nobility; in this capacity he was sent to Versailles in 1778 to be received with other Corsican representatives by Louis XVI. It is said that he owed his good fortune to M. de Marbeuf who was reputedly captivated by the beauty of Madame Bonaparte. Letizia Ramolino was born in Ajaccio in 1749 or 1750. Her father had been an official—inspector of civil engineering—and after his death her mother had married a Genoese naval captain, François Fesch, by whom she had a son Joseph who was to become a cardinal under the Consulate.

There appears to be little doubt about the easy circumstances of the Bonapartes immediately before the French occupation. They owned three houses, the Milelli estate, vineyards, lands and a mill. Nevertheless their income should not be exaggeratd.

Even if the Bonapartes and their relations by marriage were to be numbered, along with the Pozzo di Borgos, lords of the Ajaccio hinterland, among the richest people of Ajaccio (they must have married into the richer families of the interior), their fortune remains negligible in comparison to those of the mainland. They seem, however, to have built up their fortune to the detriment of small-scale farming, thus attracting hostility towards themselves, hostility which was manifested by the ransacking of their house and devastation of their properties in 1793.

In fact, after the annexation, Charles Bonaparte was obliged to solicit for position and favours in order to maintain his rank and support his ever-growing family: after Joseph and Napoleon (named after an uncle who died in 1767) came Lucien (1775), Elisa (1777), Louis (1778), Paoletta, who was to become Pauline (1780), Marie-Annonciade, the future Caroline (1782), and Jérome (1784).

EDUCATION

Accounts of Napoleon's childhood are rare and of doubtful authenticity. But it is certain that at the end of 1778 Charles Bonaparte went to Versailles with his two sons, Joseph and Napoleon and his brother-in-law, Fesch. The latter had been awarded a scholarship to the seminary at Aix and in January the two boys entered the college at Autun. From there Napoleon went to Brienne in May 1779. The Royal Military College at Brienne-le-Château was one of the colleges which had been designated in 1776 by the Minister for War, the Comte de Saint-Germain, for the children of the nobility wishing to take up a military career. M. de Marbeuf had produced a certificate to say that the Bonapartes had no money, besides which Charles Bonaparte was obliged to present his credentials to the royal herald, M. d'Hozier de Serigny, in order to prove his nobility. Napoleon stayed at Brienne from 15 May 1779 until 30 October 1784. Did he display military genius in a snowball fight immortalized by his fellow-student Bourienne, an incident which in fact the editor of the *Mémoires* took from an English brochure translated in Year VI? Did his mother visit him at Brienne in 1784? He is said to have confided later to Montholon: 'So horrified was she by my thinness and by my sunken features that she claimed she had difficulty in recognizing me.'

In September, after being examined by Reynaud des Mont, under-inspector of schools, Napoleon was deemed suitable to enter the Military Academy in Paris. He arrived in the capital in about the middle of October. 'He is a small, dark young man, sad, gloomy, severe, but an arguer and a great speaker.' There are endless anecdotes concerning his stay in Paris; they are probably apocryphal. On 28 September 1785 Napoleon was posted to Valence to the Artillery Regiment of La Fère. He had passed out forty-second out of fifty-eight. The result was hardly brilliant. But his origins must be taken into account: his loneliness, the shortness of his stay at the Military School and the death of his father on 24 February 1785.

LIFE IN THE GARRISON

And so began Napoleon's monotonous life as a peacetime soldier: paperwork, manoeuvres, banquets, balls and the occasional trifling love affair. He found immense relief from boredom in reading. At a time when the pen was mightier than the sword he tried his hand at writing. In 1786 he made an outline of a history of Corsica, which is less good than others, but the conclusion of which throws light on his state of mind.

> If, by virtue of the social contract, it is proved that without any reason whatsoever, the body of the nation can depose the Prince, what is the position of a private [sic] who by violating all natural laws and by committing crimes and atrocities goes against the institution of government? Does this reasoning not come to the aid of the Corsicans in particular, since the sovereignty or rather the principality of Genoa was only by treaty. Thus the Corsicans have, by following all the laws of justice, been able to shake off the Genoese yoke and are able to do likewise with the French one. Amen.

This indictment of the French occupation precluded all hope of publication. But was Napoleon writing to be read? Rather he was expressing, in writing, his moments of depression. On 3 May 1786 he noted: 'Always alone among other men, I come home to dream by myself and to give myself over to all the force of my melancholy. In what direction is it bent today? Towards death? If I must die, would it not be as well to kill myself?' It reads like a suicide note. But there is also a literary affectation which strangely heralds the Romantic hero.

In him, hatred of France grew in proportion to his anguish for his country: 'Frenchmen, not content with having carried off all that we cherish, have also corrupted our morals. The present picture of my country and the powerlessness to change it is then a new reason to flee a land where duty dictates that I praise men whom honour dictates I should hate.'

Eventually he was given leave. His stay in Corsica was to last from 15 September 1786 until 12 September 1787. Since the death of his father and in the absence of his older brother, Joseph, should he not have been concerning himself with the family fortunes, and more particularly, with a complicated affair concerning a plantation? With the death of the father and with four children under ten still at home, the financial embarrassment of the family increased despite the fact that the

Bonapartes continued to occupy a high social position in Corsica. The retirement of Napoleon's uncle, the Archdeacon Lucien, who had cleverly known how to manage the family affairs, was cruelly felt. The matter of the plantation obliged Napoleon to go to Paris to defend the interests of his family against the state. There, if he is to be believed, he was 'taught the ways of the world' at the Palais-Royal, by a young lady of easy virtue. A six-month extension of leave, dating from 1 December was granted him, 'in order to attend discussions of the States of Corsica, his homeland, and to protect the essential rights of his modest fortune'. So on 1 January he was once again in Corsica. In May he left for Auxonne where his regiment had been stationed since December 1787. Monotonous garrison life began again, fortunately interrupted by classes at the Artillery school commanded by the Baron du Teil. He read increasingly. History, geography, political theory and economics interested him, but he neglected the sciences. He made abundant notes, always, however, picking out the essential ('St Helena, small island,' he marked in his notebook after having read the Abbé de Lacroix's *Géographie*.) He would often jot down a résumé to help his memory which was in any case excellent. Pen in hand, he would dispute the assertions of an author and he displayed a fairly lively critical faculty. Occasionally his reading inspired semi-fantastic short stories: *Le Masque Prophète* comes from Marigny's *History of the Arabs,* and *Le Comte d'Essex,* a ghost story, was inspired by John Barrow's *History of England*.

But Napoleon's culture must not be exaggerated. He was ignorant of part of the works of Rousseau, of most of Voltaire—he had only read the plays and the *Essai sur les Moeurs*. He had only read the first three volumes of *L'Histoire philosophique et politique des établissements et du commerce des Européens dans les deux Indes,* by the abbé Raynal; Montesquieu and Diderot were little known to him; he appears to have known nothing of *Les Liaisons Dangeureuses* by Laclos, an artillery-man like himself who found in literature a relief from his need for action. All his reading seems to have been to one end, in order to justify a thesis formed *a priori* in the burning imagination of the young islander straying beneath the inclement skies of France. Under Paoli and the Constitution of 1755 which the *philosophes* had so admired, Corsica had attained an ideal of government comparable to Lycurgus' laws for Ancient Sparta. In Napoleon's mind Paoli took on the proportions of a Plutarchan hero; he exalted him without ever having known him, and it seems, without his father having really spoken about him. He could only have formed an idea of Paoli's activities through Boswell's account of his travels which presented a very flattering picture of Paoli. Because Rousseau and Raynal had supported Corsican independence, they, for their part, became Napoleon's intellectual mentors; and the French monarchy had to be wiped out because it had destroyed Paoli's regime in order to rule, itself in Corsica. Before the fall of the Bastille, before Robespierre and Danton, Bonaparte was already a republican. At Auxonne, on 23 October 1788, he undertook a monumental work designed to expose 'the usurped authority which is enjoyed by kings in twelve European kingdoms'. Not that he espoused the claims of the 'mob', but he saw in the weaknesses of monarchy an opportunity for the revenge of Ponte Novo.

2

PAOLI'S MAN

On 15 July 1789 Napoleon wrote to his uncle, the Archdeacon Lucien, to inform him of his plan to go to the capital and settle his personal affairs, but, he added,

> I am at the moment receiving news from Paris. The news is astonishing and of a singularly alarming nature. The unrest has reached its peak. It is impossible to see where it will all end. M. Necker is on his way to Picardy—probably with the intention of going to Holland. Perhaps this evening, or perhaps tonight, we will be called to arms and sent either to Dijon or to Lyons. It would be most disagreeable and highly ruinous for me.

In fact at Auxonne the garrison was immediately alerted. It was not long before rioting broke out. He wrote to his brother, Joseph:

> I am writing this amidst the din of drums, arms and bloodshed. 'On Sunday evening the villagers, reinforced by numbers of foreign brigands who have come to pillage, began to ransack the main buildings where the farm workers lived, they have looted the customs—and several houses. The general is seventy-five years old. He felt very tired. He called the leader of the bourgeoisie and told them [sic] to take orders from me. After a number of manoeuvres we arrested 33 of them and we put them in the cells. Two or three of them are to be hanged summarily.

Napoleon seemed to nurture no great sympathy for the 'mob', but he had even less sympathy for the privileged, a class, however, to which he belonged. 'Throughout France blood has been shed but almost everywhere it has been the impure blood of the enemies of liberty and of the Nation, who for a long time have been growing fat at their expense.' In this letter to his brother Joseph, dated 9 August 1789, expounding on the results of the famous night of the 4th, he summed up thus: 'It is a great step forward.' In his hatred he confused the privileged classes with the monarchy which had exploited his native Corsica.

On 12 June he wrote a letter to Paoli where he made no secret of his feelings towards France:

> As the nation was perishing I was born. Thirty thousand Frenchmen were vomited onto our shores, drowning the throne of liberty in waves of blood. Such was the odious sight which was the first to strike me. From my birth, my cradle was surrounded by the cries of the dying, the groans of the oppressed and tears of despair. You left our island and with you went all hope of happiness. Slavery was the price of our submission. Crushed by the triple yoke of the soldier, the law-maker and the tax-inspector, our compatriots live despised.

Equally, Corsica inspired Bonaparte to write in an identical tone in his *Lettres à M. Necker*. 'It is impossible to have any doubt,' writes Frédéric Masson, 'about the opinions professed by Napoleon concerning the hatred which he feels towards the conquerors of his country and about the contempt which he feels for anyone who does not follow Paoli; he is Corsican, completely Corsican, nothing but Corsican.'

THE REVOLUTION IN CORSICA

The French Revolution which unfolded itself under the rather indifferent eye of the young officer had been welcomed with enthusiasm in Corsica. Like the other provinces of the kingdom, the island sent deputies to the States-General: the Comte de Buttafuoco, the same who had asked Rousseau for a Constitution, represented the nobility, Peretti Della Rocca the clergy, Salicetti and Colonna Cesari the Third Estate.

In August 1789, Bonaparte asked for leave during the winter semester. A normal request, but one which, all events considered, was surprisingly granted. Presumably he left Auxonne during the first few days of September, went down the Rhône and probably met in Marseille, one of his favourite thinkers, the Ábbé Raynal.

For fifteen months, until February 1791, it was only by the repercussions in Corsica that Napoleon was to know of the confusion which shook France. The island asked only to be integrated into the kingdom, instead of being treated as a conquered country. Such a claim seemed legitimate to the commander-in-chief of the French troops, the Vicomte de Sarrin. But this moderate had to contend with fanatic Royalists like his deputy, the Maréchal de Camp Gaffori, appointed on 20 August. The change of local council, however, took place calmly, a National Guard was formed in Ajaccio and Napoleon became lieutenant-colonel, second-in-command. Towards the end of summer trouble began. There were incidents over the institution of the National Guard, notably at Bastia on 5 November 1789. Bonaparte was implicated but it remains hard to determine the precise nature of his role. After the patriots had presented their complaints to the Constitutent Assembly, the Assembly, on 30 November, declared Corsica 'an integral part of the French Empire', and promised that Corsicans would be ruled by the same constitution as all other Frenchmen.

Did this decree satisfy the deepest aspirations of the population? It would appear that it did from Napoleon's letter to the Abbé Raynal: 'Henceforth, we have the same interests, the same concerns, we are no longer separated by any sea.' But the idea of a 'Corsican nation' was deeply rooted. The departure of numerous French people bore witness to the fears and doubts that shook the island. As early as 12 October, when it was suggested that the King should retain the title of King of France and Navarre, Salicetti, begging leave to speak, had exclaimed: 'The title of King of the French is sufficient, if that of King of Navarre is added, I am authorized and even obliged by my office to demand the addition of "King of Corsica".'

In February 1790 the same Salicetti was in favour of an assembly convened under the presidency of Colonel Petriconi at Bastia. General Paoli was to be granted an amnesty by the Constituent Assembly and asked to return. New administrative authorities were designated under a higher committee in which most of the responsibility for the island would be placed. The difficulties came mainly from the islanders 'beyond the hills' who considered themselves wronged by the distribution of employment and by the taxation system and who demanded that the island be partitioned. Joseph Bonaparte was opposed to this: 'Not long ago we were still slaves; we are barely reborn and they want to divide us and to multiply the mistakes of an absurd administration. Instead of the blame being put on all the different tyrants who have oppressed us, there is an attempt to sow discord among us and to make our compatriots responsible when, like us, they were victims.' Unity won the day.

Geographical but not political unity. The Corsicans remained divided into two camps: the Paolists or Patriots had had the upper hand from 1729 to 1769 until they were crushed by the French cannon at Ponte Novo; the Royalists or Gafforists had held sway since the French occupation and had sent respected orators like Buttafuoco and Peretti to the States General. The Revolution aggravated the division. The Royalists were still partisans of the Ancien Régime, they leant for support on the army and the administration; the Patriots rallied to the principles of 1789 and profited from strong popular support. It was manifested in the delirious welcome given to General Paoli on his return to the island on 17 July 1790.

The elections for departmental administrators took place without incident. At the Assembly held at Orezza with these elections in view, Paoli, once again the hero of the new movement, praised the generosity of the French nation: 'You have been her companions in servitude, she wants you to be her brothers under the same emblems of liberty.' So autonomy was excluded. The General invited the Corsicans 'spontaneously to swear perpetual loyalty and complete adherence to the auspicious constitution which unites us with this nation under the same laws and under a citizen king'. For him, the protection of revolutionary France seemed indispensable to the safety of the island, but apparently he was not in favour of total assimilation. He probably hoped for a federal union. In his speeches 'the motherland' remained Corsica, the French were not his 'compatriots' but his 'brothers'. And this was a sentiment which seems to have been shared by Napoleon, who, with his older brother, was deeply involved in the elections which agitated the island.

Elections which assured the triumph of the Paolists. Thus Joseph became President of the Directory of Ajaccio. The problem of unity having been settled, with the island becoming one department, and the nomination of administrators completed, there remained the capital city to be chosen. Bastia, Ajaccio or Corte? For the time being at least, Bastia won the day. Buttafuoco, the Royalist leader, had contended with the decisions taken at the gathering at Orezza. He accused Paoli of wanting definitive ties with England. What followed must prove him to have been right. But the Paolists would not suffer any criticism aimed at their idol. They replied by recalling Buttafuoco's treachery when on the occasion of a diplomatic mission entrusted to him by Paoli, he had suggested to Choiseul, of his own party, the annexation of Corsica to France.

While Buttafuoco's effigy was burnt in the streets of Ajaccio on 2 August 1790, some electors from Orizza decided to send Gentile and Pozzo di Borgo as deputies extraordinary to the Constituent Assembly in order to set forth the position of the Patriots.

Buttafuoco went ahead. On 29 October 1790 he took the platform at the National Assembly: 'Two audacious men, under the cloak of the public good, have continuously been spreading throughout Corsica odious calumnies concerning my behaviour and that of the Abbé Peretti. The people have been stirred up against us. M. Paoli has believed in these lies.' Confronted by Mirabeau (Napoleon's enduring admiration for whom led to his making the executor of the tribune, Frochot, Prefect of the Seine) and Salicetti, Buttafuoco and Peretti were unable to prevent the Corsican delegates from being admitted to the full honours of the session. The Corsican Royalists had suffered a grave setback.

Napoleon, who had obtained an extension of his leave, was in no hurry to return to the mainland. As a fervent Paolist, he took sides violently against Buttafuoco. On 23 January 1791, in the study of the Milelli family home, he was drafting his *Lettre à Buttafuoco,* the printing of which was voted for with enthusiasm by the Patriots' club of Ajaccio. This first piece of published writing by Napoleon deserves attention only by virtue of the author's personality. Stendhal exaggerates somewhat in claiming it as 'a satirical work, absolutely in the style of Plutarch. The fundamental idea is ingenious and powerful. It might have been a pamphlet written in Holland in 1630.' Paoli did not agree. He wrote to Joseph: 'I have received your brother's pamphlet. It would have been more impressive had it said less and been less partisan.' Only the closing peroration holds the attention. Having denounced Buttafuoco's activities, the author exclaims: 'O Lameth! O Robespierre! O Pétion! O Volney! O Mirabeau! O Barnave! O Bailly! O La Fayette! This is the man who dares to sit beside you! Drenched in the blood of his brothers, tainted with every sort of crime, he dares to call himself the representative of the nation—he who sold it.' This naming together of politicians, all of whom sat—though not without shades of difference—on the 'left wing' of the Assembly, indicates the side towards which Bonaparte's sympathies were drawn. Doubtless the reason for such a choice lay in the support which these deputies gave to the Corsican delegates. It was his attachment to Paoli which attracted Napoleon towards the Constitutent Assembly's most advanced revolutionaries. But credit can be given to a profounder feeling. One text enlightens us. It is thought to date from 1791, and must have been inspired by the King's flight. It is probably the draft for a pamphlet, which Bonaparte planned to publish, in favour of the republican argument which was beginning to develop.

> I have read all the speeches of the monarchist orators. I have seen in them great efforts to support a bad cause. They digress with assertions that they cannot prove. Truthfully, if I had had any doubts, they would have been dissipated by reading these speeches. To say that 25,000,000 citizens cannot live in a republic is an ill-advised adage.

TOWARDS THE BREAK

Once victorious, the Corsican patriots split over the civil constitution of the clergy, to which Paoli had rallied not without hesitation. The old leader had preached prudence. Perhaps he felt himself to be a little outmoded. On 9 May 1791, the election of Guasco as a constitutional bishop did little to help. A violent insurrection broke out in Bastia in June. It was put down with a certain amount of severity, and, worst of all, Bastia lost the rank of capital. Another victim of the insurrection was Paoli, who lost some of his prestige in the affair. As a result of this an anti-Paolist opposition manifested itself at the time of the election of deputies to a legislative Assembly called to replace the constituent. A crime of lèse-majesté: Arena presented himself against Leonetti—the great man's nephew.

Napoleon's faith in Paoli remained unshakeable. It was definitely a transformed France which Bonaparte found on his return to the mainland in February 1791. He had taken his twelve-year-old brother, Louis, with him to Auxonne, but neither the education of the boy, nor the revolutionary troubles, nor his posting to Valence on 1 June 1791, diverted his attention from his true country. Having dealt with the printing of his *Lettre à Buttafuoco*, he undertook a *History of Corsica* for which he requested 'the necessary documents' from Paoli. 'History is not written in youth,' his hero drily replied on 2 April 1791. Paoli decidedly displayed considerable coldness towards Napoleon. Perhaps this was due to irritation caused by a slightly overwhelming and somewhat exclusive admiration, the annoyance of an old conservative (which is what Paoli had finally become), towards a young Jacobin, or to bitterness towards Charles Bonaparte who had once rallied too swiftly to the French cause. Napoleon did not allow himself to be discouraged. Whilst working on a dissertation for the Academy of Lyons, of which we will treat later, and which included more praise for Paoli's Corsican reforms, he requested further leave.

In October he was once again in Corsica. This time he was hoping for an important rank in the batallion of volunteers; to this end he intrigued remorselessly and decided not the rejoin his unit on the mainland. On 1 April 1792 he was finally made lieutenant-colonel, second-in-command of the second battalion of volunteers. Unfortunately for him, he also had to take part in the confrontation between city dwellers and peasants which weakened Paoli's authority. Bloody brawls broke out in Ajaccio. Religious problems were always the root cause. Napoleon was not in any way personally responsible but the counter-revolutionaries won the day. Deemed to be rather troublesome, the second battalion of volunteers was sent to Corte. Napoleon, who was compromised in the situation, had to draw up a justificatory statement. Thus he put himself in opposition to the counter-revolutionary clan of the Peraldis and the Pozzo di Borgos.

This constituted the defeat of his Corsican ambitions, but it was a defeat which he still considered only temporary.

His primary objective now was to be reinstated in the army of the mainland. After all, due to his extended absence, he had just been struck off the cadre of his regiment. He was in Paris on 28 May; war had broken out in April; there were insufficient officers but his reinstatement was not immediate. For once, Bourriene's *Mémoires* can perhaps be trustd:

> In April 1792 I arrived in Paris where I found Bonaparte; our friendship dating back to childhood and college was completely revived. I was not very happy; adversity weighed him down. He was often short of money. We spent our time like two young people of twenty-three who have nothing to do and not much money; he was even harder up than I was. Each day we thought up new plans. We were trying to make some fruitful speculation. Once he wanted us to rent several houses which were being built in the rue Montholon in order to sub-let them immediately. We found the demands of the landlords exorbitant. Everything failed.

At last Bonaparte was reinstated, with the rank of captain. Strangely it was under one of Louis XVI's last signatures.

Was he present on 20 June when the people invaded the Tuileries?
And are witnesses to be believed, who claimed that Napoleon, in-
censed against the 'mob', declared that 'were he King, things would
not happen this way'? Yet on 3 July he was writing to his brother,
Lucien: 'To live peacefully, to enjoy the affections of one's family and
self respect—these things, my dear brother, are what one must aim
for.' Napoleon's statements from St Helena are to be mistrusted,
nevertheless he left an account of 10 August which shows the effect the
popular uprising had on him.

'At this hideous time', he was to tell Las Cases,

> I found myself lodging in Paris, at the Mail in the Place des Victoires.
> At the sound of the tocsin and on learning that the Tuileries were
> under attack, I ran to the Carrousel to find Bourrienne's brother,
> Fauvelet, who kept a furniture shop there. It was from this house
> that I was able to witness at my ease all the activities of that day.
> Before reaching the Carrousel I had been met in the rue des Petits
> Champs, by a group of hideous men bearing a head at the end of a
> pike. Seeing that I was presentably dressed and had the appearance
> of a gentleman, they approached me and asked me to shout 'Long
> live the Nation!' which, as one might imagine, I did without
> difficulty.

The excesses which accompanied the fall of the Tuileries showed
Napoleon that the 'dethronement of kings' was not as simple in
practice as it appeared on paper.

> With the palace broken into, and the King there, in the heart of the
> assembly, I ventured to go into the garden. The sight of the dead
> Swiss Guards gave me an impression of heaps of corpses such as I
> have never had since, on any of my battlefields. Perhaps it was
> caused by the smallness of the area or perhaps it resulted from the
> fact that this was the first impression of the kind which I had
> experienced. I saw well dressed women committing acts of the
> grossest indecency on the corpses of the Swiss Guards.

Louis XIV had been left with a horrifying memory of the Fronde
and a lively hatred for Paris. In the same way Napoleon was always to
mistrust the capital and to refuse to arm the suburbs. The 10th of
August must have shown him to what excesses the 'vilest rabble' will
go. Revolution advocated by the *philosophes,* yes; but no to popular

sion to a violent denunciation of social injustice which would not have
been disclaimed several years later by Gracchus Babeuf, had he read it.

'At birth', Napoleon asserts, 'man bears rights over the fruits of the
earth which are necessary to his existence.' Inequality among men had
to be abolished, but it could not be so long as religion and the law took
the side of those who profited from inequality. One page deserves to be
quoted in full:

> After the thoughtlessness of childhood comes the awakening of the
> passions; she who is to become the companion of a man's destiny
> must be chosen from amongst the companions of his leisure. His
> vigorous arm, together with his needs, demands work: he looks
> around him and sees the earth divided among a few, serving only to
> nourish luxury and superfluity; he asks himself what then are the
> rights of those people? Why does the idle man have everything, the
> working man almost nothing? Finally, why have I been left nothing,
> I, who have a wife and a senile father and mother to feed? He hurries
> to the minister of the church who is his spiritual mentor and
> expounds his doubts. 'Man,' replies the priest, 'never think about
> the existence of society. . . . God controls everything, trust in His
> providence. This life is but a journey. Everything is decreed by a
> justice which we must not seek to understand. Believe, obey, never
> reason, and work: that is your duty.' A proud soul, a sensitive heart
> and a natural intelligence cannot be satisfied with this answer. He
> takes his doubts and his worries elsewhere. He comes to the wisest
> man in the country—a lawyer. 'Wise man', he says to him, 'the fruits
> of the earth have been divided and I have been given nothing.' The
> wise man laughs at his simplicity, takes him into his study and there
> with deed after deed, contract after contract and will after will,
> proves to him the legitimacy of the divisions of which he is com-
> plaining. 'What! Are those the rights of these gentlemen?' he
> exclaims indignantly. Mine are more sacred, more incontestable,
> more universal. They are born with my sweat, they circulate with
> my blood, they are written on my nerves and in my heart. They are
> the necessity of my existence and above all of my happiness!' On
> finishing these words he snatches up the papers and throws them on
> the fire.

Who would have recognized in the author of these pages the future
inspirer of the Civil Code?

The work opens with, as an epigraph, a quotation from Raynal:

'There will be morality when governments are free,' and it contains a eulogy of Rousseau: 'O Rousseau, why did you have to live for only sixty years! In the interests of virtue you should have been immortal!'

Raynal and Rousseau—these were Bonaparte's intellectual preceptors in 1791. Nevertheless the writer's enthusiasm should not be exaggerated. Napoleon had made a list in a notebook of a certain number of rare and erudite words with a view to using them in his dissertation and, besides, the somewhat conventional revolutionary ideas cast doubt on the sincerity of the dissertation. It was above all a question of flattering the Académie de Lyon. Furthermore there was to be yet another setback: the manuscript was declared worse than mediocre. Thinking to please the Emperor, Talleyrand was to unearth it one day and present it to Napoleon. Bonaparte threw it on the fire. The ideas contained in the *Discours sur le bonheur* were outmoded.

'LE SOUPER DE BEAUCAIRE'

At all events the factors which determined Napoleon's rallying to the Revolution were material rather than ideological. In order to support his family, now in Marseilles, he was obliged to resume his army service. He rejoined the 4th Artillery Regiment at Nice. The Federalist revolt was shaking the South of France. Even if the chronology of events in Napoleon's life remains uncertain between the beginning of July and the end of August 1793 (did he for instance participate in the taking of Avignon?), one element seems certain: the *Souper de Beaucaire* proves his complete allegiance to Montagnard arguments.

Dated 29 July 1793, this pamphlet relates a conversation in which, it has been said, Napoleon really took part. This seems highly improbable. In fact it was a pamphlet designed for purposes of revolutionary propaganda and neither the place nor the date, 29 July, have any precise significance in Napoleon's life. The decision to publish this occasional piece of work with its cast of a Nîmois, a Marseillais, a mill-owner from Montpellier and a soldier, was backed by the authority of Salicetti who was on a mission in the South of France at the time with Augustin de Robespierre, Ricord, Escudier, Albitte and Gasparin. The Marseillais propounds the federalist point of view; the soldier contends with him bitterly.

You were told that you would cross France, that you would lend tone to the Republic, yet your first steps have failed. You were told that the South had risen up but you found yourself alone; you were told that four thousand Lyonnais were marching to support you, but the Lyonnais were negotiating a compromise.

In fact, the officer continues, the future of Marseilles is at stake in the insurrection. And, to use a curious argument,

Let the poor countries fight to the bitter end. The inhabitant of the Vivarais, the Cévennes, *or Corsica* exposes himself fearlessly to the bitter end: if he wins he has achieved his aim; if he loses, he finds himself, as before, having to make peace and in the same situation. But you! You lose a battle, and the fruits of a thousand years of blood, sweat and tears, of economy and of happiness become prey to the soldier.

Bonaparte distinguished very cleverly between federalism and the Royalist cause in order to underline the fact that the differences between the Girondins and the Montagnards were unimportant and that the real danger lay elsewhere.

'The Vendée wants a King, the Vendée wants a publicly declared counter-revolution,' states the Marseillais. 'The Vendée war is a war of fanaticism, despotism; ours, on the other hand, (that is the federalist insurrection) is the war of the true republicans—friends of law and order, enemies of anarchy and villainy. Do we not carry the Tricolor?'

Paoli's case is the same and one must therefore be prudent, replies the officer who then levels a veritable indictment at the one-time idol:

Paoli, too, hoisted the Tricolor in Corsica, in order to give himself time to deceive the people, to crush the true friends of liberty, and in order to drag his compatriots with him in his ambitious and criminal plots; he hoisted the Tricolor, and had the ships of the Republic fired at, he had our troops expelled from the fortresses and he disarmed those who remained . . . he ravaged and confiscated the property of the richer families because they were allied to the unity of the Republic, and all those who remained in our armies he declared 'enemies of the nation'. He had already caused the failure of the Sardinian expedition, yet he had the impudence to call himself the friend of France and a good republican.

The federalist troops should guard against playing into the hands of the common enemy: the Royalist, the Spaniard and the Austrian. Neither should they put their trust in the military talents of their leaders. The Napoleonic strategy was already in evidence.

What will our army do if it is centred at Aix? It is lost; it is a theory of military tactics that he who stays in the entrenchments is beaten; experience and theory agree on this point.

After having taken a somewhat lively turn with regard to an eventual Spanish intervention, the discussions close with the promise of a negotiation and a general reconciliation—a theme which Napoleon was to take up again after Brumaire. All of Napoleon is to be found in the *Souper de Beaucaire*, and it is not without reason that Panckoucke republished the pamphlet in 1821 and that Bourrienne also published it as an appendix to his *Mémoires*. In it Napoleon discovered the importance of propaganda, a field in which he proved himself master as early as 1793, with an easy style and a lively naturalness of debate. Despite some minor inaccuracies, the work shows the writer to be very well informed on the political and military situation in France. Naturally, *Le Souper de Beaucaire* made no mark at the time. Nevertheless, it far outclasses pamphlets which were being distributed by the other side or by the Jacobins.

TOULON

Bonaparte won notoriety at the Siege of Toulon. In September, Salicetti gave him the command of Carteaux's artillery, where he replaced Dammartin who had been wounded at Ollioules. On reaching Toulon Bonaparte mustered his artillery: there were two 24-pound cannon, two 16-pound cannon and two mortars. It was not very much. There was a shortage of munitions, but the efficiency of the gunnery made up for the lack of men and materials. General Doppet who replaced Carteaux was to write in his *Mémoires:*

> In addition to many talents this young officer brought with him a rare fearlessness and the most indefatigable energy. Every time I visited the posts of this army, he was at his; if he needed a moment's rest he would take it lying on the ground, wrapped in his overcoat; he never left his batteries.

He also made friends with the young officers whose careers he was to shape: Duroc, Marmont, Victor, Suchet, Leclerc, Desaix. Later, as Emperor, Napoleon was to confide in Las Cases:

> At the time of the formation of one of the first batteries, I there and then asked for a sergeant or a corporal who could write. A man came

forward from the ranks and wrote under dictation, leaning on the gunbank. The letter was hardly finished when a cannon ball covered the writing with earth. 'That's good,' said the writer, 'I shan't need any sand.' This joke and the calm with which it was delivered attracted my attention and changed the fortunes of the sergeant; it was Junot.

The government representatives *en mission* produced Captain Bonaparte for the rank of Battalion Commander. Faced with the incompetence of the military command, he presented a plan of attack—a plan which revealed the soundness of his judgement. He had, in fact, understood that the occupation of the Éguillette point could make it impossible for the English to hold the roadstead. It was necessary to take the fort of Mulgrave, known as Little Gibraltar, which defended the point. Dugommier adopted this plan on 25 November. On 11 December 1793 the offensive was decided upon. Five days later during the preliminary bombardment, the wind of a cannon-ball threw Bonaparte to the ground. He suffered a close brush with death. The attack was under way; on the 17th, at one o'clock in the morning, Fort Mulgrave fell.

At the time of the assault Bonaparte received a bayonet wound in the thigh. On the 18th, the English evacuated Toulon; meanwhile Bonaparte was nominated brigadier-general on the 22nd by the representatives *en mission*. The nomination was confirmed on 6 February 1794.

The protection of Augustin de Robespierre cost him the command of the artillery. Salicetti sent him to Nice to prepare an expedition against Corsica. Bonaparte multiplied his plans of attack against Italy. A plan was worked out which consisted in outflanking the Alps, held by the armies of the King of Sardinia, and taking possession of Oneglia. Oneglia fell on 9 April 1794, a success which confirmed the opinions of General Bonaparte. But in spite of the support of the Younger Robespierre, the Committee of Public Safety seemed to remain cold. Carnot would have advocated the offensive to the bitter end—to the Spanish frontier. Bonaparte sent back a memorandum entitled *Notes sur la position de nos armées de Piémont et D'Espagne* to underline the advantages of an attack against Piedmont. In it he asserted that a war with Spain would be long and expensive and would require consider-able forces by reason of the Spanish national spirit. A consideration which he was to forget in 1808. In addition, since the enemy to be beaten was Austria, the war should 'carry direct or indirect blows against this power'. Whereas the Emperor would be completely untouched by war in Spain. On the other hand:

> If the armies on the Piedmontese frontier were to adopt an offensive policy, they would oblige the house of Austria to guard the Italian States, and from then onwards this policy would conform to the general spirit of our war . . . if we achieve great successes, we will, in succeeding campaigns, be able to attack Germany through Lombardy, the Ticino and the Tyrol whilst our armies on the Rhine attack her in the centre.

The offensive had to be concentrated on Italy, the enemy's most vulnerable point. A general offensive, on all fronts, such as had been advocated at the Committee of Public Safety would achieve nothing.

> The Republic cannot support the offensive with her fourteen armies; she would not have enough officers, nor enough artillery or cavalry. Besides, it would be a military error to attack on all sides: the attacks must absolutely not be spread out, but rather, concentrated. The same can be said of military tactics as of sieges of fortresses: concentrate the firing on one place alone; once the breach is made, the balance is disturbed, all else becomes useless and the position is taken.

It goes without saying that Italy should not obscure the final objective, Austria. Bonaparte, a realist, remembered past disasters: 'Knock Germany, never Spain or Italy. One must never be put off the scent by pushing further into Italy (to Rome or Naples) while Germany presents a dangerous front and is in no way weakened.'

Carnot refused all withdrawal from the Spanish frontier in favour of the offensive in Italy. He found himself up against Augustin de Robespierre who had come to Paris to defend the ideas of his protégé. Can one go the whole way with Captain Colin who wrote that 'the Robespierres' interference in military matters alienated them irrevocably from Carnot, the Organizer of Victory, and sealed their fate'? Did intimations of a *coup* lead the Younger Robespierre to suggest that Bonaparte come to Paris to replace Hanriot? The fact remains that in the eyes of the Convention, Bonaparte was always 'The Robespierres' man', 'their maker of plans', in the words of one representative *en mission*. How could these biographers have forgotten that in July 1794 Bonaparte became a general elect, a confirmed patriot who had sworn himself to the Revolution! That he may have felt a real sympathy for Maximilien de Robespierre, the *Incorruptible*, cannot be discounted. The two men never knew each other, but there are certain affinities between them: they had both had a difficult childhood and they were both introverted and proud, with a great admiration for Rousseau. And, after all, they both dreamed of a state 'where no privilege exists, where equality would be complete and poverty unknown, where morals would be pure and where laws would be expressions of the will of the people, obeyed and respected by one and all.' In fact the young officer never openly declared himself to be in favour of Maximilien de Robespierre. Perhaps this was from prudence, or from a lack of interest in internal politics. The letter which he wrote on 20 Thermidor to Tilly, and which is reproduced by Coston, is curious: 'I have been somewhat moved by the catastrophe of the Younger Robespierre whom I loved and whom I believed to be pure, but were he my brother, I would have stabbed him with my own hand had he aspired to tyranny.' There is some doubt about the authenticity of the letter, but there is a temptation to say that this Bonaparte, pure and harsh, like St Just, is perfectly credible.

DISGRACE

The fall of Robespierre left Carnot free to direct operations as he pleased. The order was given to stop the offensive on the Italian frontier. This put an end to the plans elaborated by Bonaparte. But there was worse to come. Ricord, one of the representatives *en mission*, had, on 13 July, sent Bonaparte to Genoa to reply to an intimidating manoeuvre at the beginning of the month by the Austrians. Salicetti believed, or pretended to believe, in a secret plan set up by Robespierre and Bonaparte in liaison with the enemy. On 9 August 1794 the General was arrested.

He managed to clear himself and was freed on 20 August. In fact the representatives *en mission* needed Bonaparte because of the Piedmontese counter-attack. Dumerbion, who had been given the command of the army in the Alps and in Italy, sought his advice. By adopting Napoleon's plan of attack on Cairo he managed to ensure for the Army of Italy an excellent operational base for a future invasion of Piedmont. 'It is to General Bonaparte's talent that I owe the wise schemes which have assured our victory,' acknowledged Dumerbion. He held himself ready for a new offensive, aiming, on Bonaparte's advice, at separating the Sards from the Austrians. Carnot had the plan thrown out.

There remained one hope: the Corsican expedition which was still in preparation. It occupied Bonaparte's thoughts, but alas, he was not to take part in it. A consolation seemed to present itself. It was at Marseilles, through his brother, Joseph, that he met Désirée Clary, who belonged to a rich family whose fortune was based on the soap and textile trades with the East. Whilst Joseph married the eldest daughter of the house, Napoleon won the consent of the youngest, Désirée.

But fate was relentless. Bonaparte learnt that he had been struck off the cadre of the artillery and posted to the command of an infantry brigade in the Vendée. He made up his mind to go to Paris to explain his situation and to request a command in Provence. Aubry, a one-time captain in the artillery, had become the strong man of the Committee of Public Safety for military affairs. He was the man to approach, but Aubry suspected Bonaparte of Jacobinism and was ill-disposed towards his requests. Won over to the idea of the restoration of the monarchy, he became, under the Directory, a victim of Fructidor and later died in exile.

In order not to go to the Vendée, Napoleon managed to obtain leave. Besides which, he was probably ill. His morale was undermined by a cooling of his relations with Désirée Clary and by an undeniable financial embarrassment.

The living image of despair and a symbol of disillusion, Bonaparte cut a curious figure in the streets of Paris. The future Duchesse D'Abrantès, who knew him at the time, leaves us with a picturesque description:

> At this time Napoleon was so ugly, he cared so little for his appearance, that his un-combed and unpowdered hair gave him a disagreeable look. I can still picture him, entering the courtyard of the Hôtel de la Tranquillité, and crossing it with an awkward, uncertain step. He wore a nasty round hat pulled down over his eyes, from under which his hair, like a spaniel's ears, flopped over his frock-coat; his long, thin black hands were gloveless, because, he said, gloves were a useless expense; he wore badly-made dirty boots; an overall sickly effect was created by his thinness and his yellow complexion.

It was probably at this time that he wrote an outline for a novel, *Clisson et Eugénie*. Clisson was Bonaparte.

Clisson was born for war. While still a child he knew the lives of all the great captains. He meditated on military tactics at a time when other boys of his age were at school or chasing girls. As soon as he was old enough to shoulder arms, brilliant actions marked his every step. One victory succeeded another and his name was as renowned among the people as those of their dearest defenders.

Eugénie was Désirée.

She was sixteen years old. She was gentle, good and vivacious, with pretty eyes and of medium size. Without being ugly, she was not a beauty, but goodness, sweetness and a lively tenderness were essential parts of her nature.

Wounded in battle, Clisson sends his aide-de-camp, Berville, to reassure Eugénie. The two young people fall in love with one another. Clisson realizes his misfortune and decides to die in a battle which he has to fight:

Adieu to the one I had chosen for my life's arbitrator, adieu, companion of my happy days! I have tasted in your arms the supreme happiness. I had exhausted life and its fruits. What remained for me in the future but satiety and boredom? I have, at the age of twenty-six, exhausted the ephemeral pleasures of fame, but in your love I had tasted of the sweetest sensation of man's life. The memory rends my heart. May you live happily thinking no more of the unhappy Clisson! Embrace my sons! May they not have the burning soul of their father, for they would be like him, victims of men, of glory and of love.

This farewell of Clisson, about to die 'pierced by a thousand wounds', was also Bonaparte's farewell to life. The temptation to suicide reappeared. Despite his genius, fate was cruel to him. He had failed at everything.

4

BARRAS'S MAN

Paris became gay again. It is true there was a famine, but the Perron shone and the Palais-Royal was full—theatres overflowed. Then began the balls of the victims, where impudent luxury drowned its false mourning in orgies. A few days after Thermidor, a man who is still alive and who was then ten years old, was taken by his parents to the theatre. On leaving he admired the long line of shining carriages which he then saw for the first time. Men in jackets with low hats were saying to the spectators as they left: 'Do you need a carriage, sir?' The child did not easily understand these new expressions. He asked for an explanation but they only told him that the death of Robespierre had brought about great changes.

Thus Michelet closes his *Histoire de la Révolution*. Very soon, in fact, the intentions of those who had overcome Robespierre were revealed. These men then came to be known as the 'Thermidorians'. They were a mixture of surviving Girondins, prudent Dantonists and repentant Montagnards, all dominated by the 'silent majority' of the Plaine. The programme of these Thermidorians is contained in a formula launched by Boissy d'Anglas: 'a country governed by the landowners conforms to the social order, one where the non-landowners rule conforms to a state of nature'. This implied that the Revolution should cease forthwith, without the claims of the sans-culottes having been satisfied. The bitter proof of this was to be seen in the outskirts of the capital where penury caused by a bad harvest and the suppression of requisitions, fantastic price rises and the increase in unemployment, once again put the 'patriots' on the streets. They stormed the Convention on 12 Germinal Year III (1 April 1795), but, for want of leaders, were dispersed by the National Guard. There was another uprising on 1 Prairial (20 May). 'Bread and the constitution of 1793' were the keynotes of the policy. The lack of leaders once again made itself felt. The troops who had remained loyal to the Convention and the battalions of the National Guard from the western sectors easily dispersed the demonstrators. The last uprisings of the Revolution now appear to have been hunger riots rather than genuine political insurrections. The repression of them was none the less ruthless. The divisional leaders were decimated, the sans-culottes disarmed; once crushed, Paris was not to rise again for thirty years.

The Thermidorians reiterated: 'Cultivation of the soil, all production, all means of labour and all social order depend on the maintenance of property.' Defence of property, yes, but it must be remembered that it was property according to the distribution of 1795. The Thermidorians were the profiteers of the Revolution, those who had bought property confiscated from the Church or from the exiled aristocrats, or who had speculated in military supplies or over the loss in value of *assignats,* or who had cornered large public monopolies. An essential postulate of the programme was that the sale of national property should not be reconsidered. This programme gave the Thermidorians the support of the well-to-do peasantry who had been among the great buyers. On the other hand it rejected all ideas of restoring the Ancien Régime. The Thermidorian faction numbered far too many regicides for it to be able to envisage the return of Louis XVIII, the royal martyr's brother, even were he brought to power by the well-established, more moderate partisans in the west, the centre and the south.

After having voted the constitution of 1795 which conferred executive power on five directors and legislative power on two councils, the Ancients and the Five Hundred, the Convention had to break up. New elections were planned. Now the conservative intentions of the Thermidorians remained as yet little known to the provincial notables who associated them with the excesses of the Terror. Was there not a risk of a Royalist landslide which would again endanger, if not the collective power of the bourgeoisie, at least that of the Thermidorians? The decrees of 22 and 30 August 1795, which stipulated that two-thirds of the new Assembly should be chosen from among members of the Convention, were aiming above all at separating partisans of a constitutional royalty from 'Monarchical' and '*Feuillant*' assemblies. They were to cause another Parisian riot.

THE VENDÉMIAIRE GENERAL

Revolutionary Paris in arms was by now familiar, but a new aspect of the capital was to be revealed in 1795—the Paris of Royalist uprisings. Public opinion had not welcomed the Decree of the Two-Thirds; in it was seen, above all, the determination of the members of Convention to remain in power: in Paris all the sections but one had turned it down. It was a good opportunity for the moderate Royalists to try to take control of a power which they could no longer hope to win legally through elections.

On hearing of the disturbances which had occurred at Dreux, and at the instigation of Le Peletier who represented the Bourse section of Paris, seven Parisian sections declared themselves to be in a state of rebellion on 11 Vendémiaire (3 October 1795). The movement soon carried with it all the discontented. The commander of the armed forces, Menou, a nobleman, found it hard to disguise his sympathy for the rioters. The Convention put the responsibility for its operations in the hands of a commission of five, one of whom was Barras, the real victor of 9 Thermidor.

'It was no longer a question of fighting misguided patriots,' read the memoirs published in his name, 'but a very large number of battalions of the National Guard. These decent bourgeois who called themselves, and perhaps believed themselves to be, Republicans, did not realize that they had chosen cowardly and privileged conspirators. There was nothing better, when fighting serious adversaries, than to confront them with their natural enemies—the patriots who had been imprisoned as a result of Thermidor.'

Quite naturally Barras thought to officer them with Jacobin generals who had been unemployed since Thermidor. Meanwhile Bonaparte, whom he had known at the Siege of Toulon, was ceaselessly pestering for a command. He was sent for. The editor of the *Mémoires de Barras* is totally perfidious in his assertion that Bonaparte had already been unsuccessfully in contact with members of Le Peletier's faction. On the other hand Bonaparte greatly distorted the facts in his account of 13 Vendémiaire. According to the *Mémorial* he was approached by the Convention with a view to replacing Menou. He hesitated at length:

Was it wise to declare oneself, to speak in the name of France? Victory itself would be somehow odious, whilst defeat would ensure the eternal loathing of future generations. On the other hand, if the Convention falls, what will become of the great truths of our

Revolution? The defeat of the Convention would be he glory of the
foreigner and would set the seal of shame and slavery on our nation.

Therefore he made his decision. He accepted the command, but not
without making conditions. Let us turn to the *Mémorial*:

> He described vividly the impossibility of directing such an im-
> portant operation with three representatives who, in point of fact,
> exercised all the power and hindered all the operations of the
> general; he added that he had been a witness to the incident in the rue
> de Vivienne; that the government commissioners had been mostly to
> blame, but had, however, become the triumphant accusers in the
> heart of the Assembly. Struck by his reasoning, but unable to
> dismiss the commissioners without a long discussion in the
> Assembly, the Committee, in order to reconcile everyone, for there
> was no time to lose, decided to allow the general into the Assembly
> itself. With this in view, Barras was proposed as general-in-chief and
> the command was given to Napoleon, who in this way was rid of
> three commissioners without having had to complain.

This account is entirely false. The Convention never designated
Napoleon commander-in-chief. Neither the minutes of the proceedings, nor *Le Moniteur* mention his name, a name which was still
obscure, contrary to that of Barras, who had already saved the Convention in Thermidor. Was he even second-in-command on 13
Vendémiaire? He was probably called to serve again with other unemployed officers. The documents are explicit: 'The Committees for
Public and General Safety engage General Bonaparte to be employed
in the Army of the Interior under the orders of the people's representative, Barras, Commander-in-Chief of this Army.'
Barras, for his part, twists the truth when he attests, 'All day
Bonaparte did not leave the Carrousel, my headquarters, he only left it
to carry out a mission at the Pont-Neuf which had just been abandoned
by Carteaux.' The disposition of the army seems to have been the work
of Napoleon. The forces available to the Convention were mediocre;
there were five to six thousand men, no artillery and no munitions. It
was Bonaparte who gave the order to Murat, squadron leader of the
21st Chasseurs to fetch the cannon on the camp des Sablons and bring
them back to the Tuileries. It was again he who took the steps necessary to ensure the defence of the Convention by using the artillery to

cut off the avenues leading to the Tuileries, thus preventing the insurgents from concentrating their forces under the palace windows, as
they had done on 10 August. It was not without profit that he had
witnessed the downfall of the monarchy in 1792. On the other hand, he
did not bombard the Royalists who were installed on the steps of
Saint-Roch. Taking the topography into account, such a volley was
impossible, and it was Barras who, betook himself to the principal
battle areas and galvanized the troops of the Convention. Victory was
made easy by the lack of combativeness on the part of the National
Guard, their lack of artillery and the incompetence of Danican, the
insurgents' leader.

For the first time since Toulon, Bonaparte found himself on the
winning side. The officers who had saved the Convention were presented at the Assembly on 17 Vendémiaire. Fréron recalled that they
had, for the most part, been dismissed as patriots by Aubry. 'Don't
forget,' exclaimed Fréron, 'that the General of Artillery, Bonaparte,
named on the night of the 12th to replace Menou, with only the
morning of the 13th to plan the skilful dispositions whose fortuitous
results you have seen, had been withdrawn from his arm and seconded
to the infantry.' With the complicity of Barras, Fréron, who was
aspiring to the hand of the beautiful Pauline, was pushing the cause of
his future brother-in-law, General Bonaparte. Bonaparte then
officially received the title of general, second-in-command of the
Army of the Interior. On 24 Vendémiaire he became divisional
general; his rank confirmed, he took command of the Army of the
Interior after the resignation of Barras, on 3 Brumaire Year IV. In this
capacity he was given responsibility for the maintenance of order in the
capital, a position of trust, even if it had lost some of its importance
since the crushing of the left- and right-wing oppositions. He dis-
banded the National Guard, reorganized the Police Legion destined to
replace it, and purged it of the Royalist elements formerly appointed
by Aubry. But he also had to take the famine into account, the new rise
in the cost of bread, the shortage of wood for heating, and the unemployment which had been aggravated again by the prolongation of
the crisis. In order to forestall the exploitation of discontent at the
bakers' doors or in the markets, he dealt a blow to the Jacobins by
closing the Panthéon Club where they met. At his command he had a
total strength of about forty thousand men—a considerable figure for
the times—and he manoeuvred his troops in the streets of Paris to
discourage agitators. An anecdote, which may be apocryphal is

reproduced in the *Mémorial*.

Napoleon had, above all, to fight against a great dearth which was the cause of several popular incidents. One day—one among many others—when there was no bread and large crowds had gathered outside the bakers' shops, Napoleon was passing with a group of his officers to supervise public order. A crowd of people, mostly women, surrounded him, crushing him and crying out for bread. The crowd grew larger and more threatening until the situation became critical. A monstrously large fat woman drew particular attention to herself by her gestures and her words: 'All this gold braid does,' she cried, addressing the group of officers, 'is to mock us; so long as they eat well and grow fat they don't mind at all that the poor are dying of hunger.' Napoleon challenged her: 'My good woman, look carefully at me. Which of us is the fatter?' Now Napoleon was at that time extremely thin. 'I was as thin as a reed,' he used to say. General laughter disarmed the rabble and the officers continued on their way.

The liaison with Josephine Tascher de la Pagerie dated from this period. She was the widow of a general who had been guillotined and the mother of two children. Napoleon had met her at Barras's house before Vendémiaire. Forgotten were Désirée and the few light-hearted affairs which were rightly or wrongly attributed to him by the Duchesse D'Abrantès. If her contemporaries are to be believed, Josephine, who was thirty-three, looked somewhat faded. She was 'more than past her prime', wrote Lucien. According to one, her mouth was filled with 'decaying, stinking, yellow teeth'; another said, 'the line of her bust lacked grace and her feet were on the large side'; Josephine could never be tempting so long as she did not know how to please. But she did know how to charm Barras who made her one of his mistresses. Therein lies, perhaps, the reason for the fascination which she held for Bonaparte. Bonaparte counted on her to obtain an important command from Barras, who had become all-powerful since Vendémiaire. But personal interest was allied to pleasure. Besides, in order to inflame a novice like Bonaparte, Josephine had no need to display the talents attributed to her in a pamphlet of the day, *Zoloé*.

'I awake full of you,' he wrote to her.

Your portrait and the heady evening last night have deprived my senses of rest. Sweet and incomparable Josephine, what peculiar effect do you have on my heart? Are you angry? Are you sad? Are you anxious? My soul is broken with pain and there is no rest for your friend. But is there any more for me, when, giving myself up to the deep feeling which dominates me, I draw from your lips and from your heart a flame which burns me. Oh, how I noticed this night that your portrait is not you. You are leaving at midday. I will see you in three hours. Meanwhile, *mio dolce amor*, receive a million kisses, but give me none for they burn my blood.

Obviously Bonaparte is not Laclos. The crippling foolishness of this letter—and others which followed—might plead in favour of a sincere passion. The finest proof of this sincerity must be seen in the marriage which took place on 9 March 1796 between Napoleon Bonaparte and Josephine de Beauharnais. Without a doubt the general hoped, through this marriage, to ally himself more closely to the faction which governed France and of which Josephine had become an eminence grise. But it is most unlikely that Barras imposed this marriage on him in return for the command of the Army of Italy. For once sentiment played an important part in the life of the realist, Bonaparte. It must be acknowledged that even blasé contemporaries were considerably surprised by this union.

THE ARMY OF ITALY

War continued. Spain, Holland and Prussia had indeed just withdrawn from the coalition which had been designed to crush the French Revolution. But the main enemy, England, was still inaccessible. It was therefore necessary to strike at her Continental ally, Austria. The most vulnerable point was surely Italy. It was Bonaparte's idea which had already been expressed in Robespierre's time, and which he developed in front of the Directory, where he was brought daily to give an account of the situation in the capital. In fact Carnot remained hostile to all offensives of the kind and it was not possible to count, for an advance on Piedmont, on the sceptic, disillusioned Scherer, the commander-in-chief of the Army of Italy. He had written to Masséna:

I need the report of Aubernon (a commissioner) to silence schemers who claim from Paris that we could do better than we have done. You can imagine that I am referring to Bonaparte who besieges the Directory and the Minister with plans which are one more unreasonable than the other, and to whom they sometimes appear to listen.

Masséna called Bonaparte an intriguer whilst Augereau considered him an imbecile. Nevertheless, Scherer, tired of the criticism levelled at the Army of Italy, proferred his resignation on 4 February. On receipt of the letter, Bonaparte must have been summoned by the Directors and must have expounded his ideas to them once again. According to the *Mémoires* of La Revellière-Lépeaux, these ideas were partly accepted and at the suggestion of Carnot, Scherer's succession was granted to Bonaparte. Barras was content to approve this decision.

The overall plan drawn up by Carnot consisted in attacking Vienna with three armies. Commanded by Jourdan, Moreau and Bonaparte, they were to march on the Austrian capital, the first (eighty thousand men) through the valley of the Main, the second (also eighty thousand men) through the Danube valley—classic routes which had already been used in the seventeenth century. Finally, the third army was to attack through the plain of the Po and the valleys of the Austrian Alps. Inititally the Army of Italy should play no more than a static role, that of ensuring a diversion. It was through Bonaparte's interference that it was allowed to participate in the offensive.

On 26 March he was at Nice. The following day he received his subordinates, Masséna, Sérurier, Laharpe, Augereau. Even if legend has to some degree embellished this first meeting, his authority inspired their respect. On the 28th, Bonaparte wrote to the Directory that he had been very well received, but he announced the destitution of the troops in his charge. This should not be exaggerated, however. The Directory's commissioner, Salicetti, who was to be found once more at Baonaparte's side, was already at work mobilizing all resources. The famous proclamation: 'Soldiers, you are naked, you are under-nourished,' is legendary. It dates from St Helena, but it might be considered to summarize fairly well the longer and somewhat incoherent pronouncements made to demi-brigades reviewed hastily before battle.

We will not deal here with the details of a campaign which has been the admiration of all strategists.

An Austrian army and a Sardinian army, seventy thousand strong, held the interior slopes of the Alps and the Apennines from Coni to Genoa, thus safeguarding Piedmont. Bonaparte had thirty-six thousand men at his disposal. His plan consisted in separating the two opposing armies. Passing by the Col de Cadibone and the Bormida valley, he slipped between the two armies and struck the Austrians on his right at Montenotte on 12 April, and at Dego on 14 April, whilst

crushing the Sards on his left at Millesimo on 13 April. Cut off from
their Austrian allies, the King of Sardinia's troops were beaten again at
Mondovi on 21 April and requested an armistice six days later at
Cherasco. The gateway to Piedmont had been forced.

With the Sards disposed of, Bonaparte turned back against the
Austrians who awaited him on the left bank of the Po, near Pavia.
Having crossed the river at Piacenza he appeared to the south. The
Austrians, afraid of being outflanked, retreated, without fighting, to
the Adda where Napoleon advanced and forced on them, on 10 May,
the bloody battle of Lodi. Without striking a blow, Lombardy found
herself freed from Austrian domination. Milan welcomed Bonaparte as
a liberator. The General placed moderate patriots in charge of his
municipality—bourgeois and aristocratic liberals. Milan became a
centre of attraction for patriots throughout the peninsula. Terrified,
the Dukes of Parma and Modena hurriedly requested the peace which
Bonaparte granted them in exchange for heavy war taxes of which only
a part reached Paris. On 13 May Bonaparte had received directives
from Carnot instructing him to give up, for the time being, the invasion
of the Tyrol—an order which the General easily accepted. Moreau and
Jourdan seemed totally opposed to progress. Carnot was also inform-
ing him that Kellerman would be put in charge of the defence of
Piedmont, which Bonaparte refused in the name of the absolute necessity for unity of command in Italy. The energetic tone of the letter from
the victor of Lodi, followed by his resignation, surprised the Directory, who gave way. Bonaparte himself was surprised by the rapidity
of his military successes. It confirmed him in his opinion of his own
merit and whetted his ambition. 'After Lodi,' Napoleon was to say
later, 'I no longer saw myself as a mere general, but as a man called
upon to influence the destiny of a people. The idea occurred to me that
I could well become a decisive actor on our political scene.'

But it was advisable to remain prudent, and he obeyed the entreaties
of the Directory, who, influenced by La Revellière-Lépeaux, asked
him to 'cause the tiara of the self-styled head of the Universal Church
to totter'. The French army occupied Bologna, Ferrara and Longo; the
Pope finally consented to participate in negotiations in which
Bonaparte played an ambiguous role, by formulating accusations
against the '*prêtraille*' in his letters to the Directory, whilst secretly
bearing witness, in his correspondence with Cardinal Mattei, to a great
deference for the Holy Father. It was really a matter of providing for
the future—he had estimated the strength of religious feeling in Italy—

rather than of genuine conviction.

Meanwhile the situation in Germany was quite the reverse. The Archduke Charles beat Jourdan on 24 August; Marceau had been killed at Altenkirchen; Moreau was commanding, under doubtful conditions, a withdrawal described as 'strategic'. When the Austrians, free from worry in the west, turned southwards, Bonaparte found himself in a precarious position. The confrontation took place at Mantua, a fortified town which dominates the valleys of the Mincio and the Adige, valleys which formed the Austrian army's routes into Italy. The struggle lasted for six months, from 1 August 1796 to 2 February 1797. An army of seventy thousand men commanded by Würmser attempted to liberate the town which was under siege by Bonaparte, and was defeated at Lonato and Castiglione on 3 and 5 August 1796. In the space of five days Würmser lost twenty thousand prisoners and fifty cannon. A month later, with a second army of fifty thousand men, Würmser launched another attack by way of the Adige valley. Bonaparte went on ahead and annihilated the advanced guard at Roverdo on 4 September, then overthrew Würmser himself at Bassano four days later. The survivors threw themselves at Mantua which was now definitively blockaded since a final attack by Würmser on 15 September. The campaign lasted twelve days.

In November Alvinzi was given command of a third army, comparable in total strength to Würmser's. This time Bonaparte, lacking reinforcements, seemed to be in difficulty and evacuated Verona; in fact this was a ploy. By a daring manoeuvre, he wheeled round and took the army from behind in the Arcole marshes and after three days of fighting Alvinzi was obliged to retreat.

Alvinzi made one last attempt in January 1797. He had at his disposal seventy-five thousand men whom he made the great mistake of dividing in order to surround Bonaparte. The brunt of the attack took place on the plateau of Rivoli at the mouth of the Adige on 14 January 1797. Bonaparte had the advantage of knowing the ground and of having some excellent officers in Joubert, Masséna and above all Berthier who was a perfect Chief of Headquarters. Masséna attacked the enemy to the left, the charge of Lasalle's light cavalry redressed the balance in the centre and to the right, where Quasdanovitch had had the advantage in numbers. Finally Bonaparte was victorious. On 2 February Mantua fell. Master of Northern Italy, with freedom of action in the centre where the Pope had signed the treaty of Tolentino with the French on 17 February, and assured of the prudent neutrality of Naples, Bonaparte began to march in the direction of Vienna. From now on the principal role was reserved for the Army of Italy whilst the armies of Germany were quartered elsewhere on diversionary tactics. Vienna confronted Bonaparte with her finest general, the Archduke Charles, but in vain. The French troops broke across the Piave and the Tagliamento, and through the Col de Tarvis and found themselves at Semmering, a hundred kilometres from Vienna, when, on 7 April a five-day armistice interrupted operations. It was time. 'Alone the Army of Italy is exposed to the strength of one of the greatest European powers,' complained Bonaparte. Hoche and Moreau finally moved; the armistice which was renewed on 13 April, was turned by the Austrians into preliminaries to peace at Léoben on the 18th.

Thus, counter to the plans of the Directory, it was Bonaparte who had struck the decisive blow at the Austrians. His victories were achieved thanks to two types of strategic combination which surprised the enemy: the outflanking manoeuvre, which made it possible for him to take Milan without a real battle, just by marching, and the manoeuvre of the inside lines. This manoeuvre took place from behind the advance guard who were deployed in front of an enemy convinced that it was dealing with the entire army, thereby making it possible to surprise the enemy at one of their weaker points. All depended on the endurance of the troops. Masséna's division is a case in point: it fought at Verona on 18 January 1797. On the following night it covered thirty-two kilometres of snowy roads and arrived in the morning of the 14th on the Plateau of Rivoli, where it fought for the whole day of the 15th; it advanced another seventy kilometres in thirty hours, and on the 16th, reached La Favorite in front of Mantua—there to decide the victory for the French. 'The division had covered more than a hundred kilometres and taken part in three battles within four days.'

POLITICAL EXPLOITATION OF VICTORY

What was the main reason for these exploits? Loyalty to the leader. Napoleon knew instantly how to bind his soldiers to him, not only by material advantages (half their wages in cash, for instance), but by creating a state of mind peculiar to the Army of Italy. This became evident in 1797 when reinforcements arrived from Germany, and the merger was not easy.

Bonaparte used the press to create this state of mind. It was not a new idea, but it had never been put so systematically into practice. On 1 Thermidor Year V *Le Courrier de l'Armée d'Italie ou le patriote français à Milan* was founded and the editorship given to Jullien, a former Jacobin who had been implicated in the Babeuf conspiracy before serving under Bonaparte. The success of this journal brought another one in its wake, *La France vue de l'Armée d'Italie* which was edited by Regnault de Saint-Jean-d'Angély who had been part of the Constituent Assembly and who, compared with Jullien, represented the moderate wing of the Revolution. Distributed free, *Le Courrier de l'Armée d'Italie* brought the soldiers news from France, which naturally aimed at guiding them politically in the direction desired by Bonaparte. It also had the task of strengthening the attachment of the men to their leader who was described thus in the edition of 23 October: 'He flies like lightning and strikes like a thunderbolt. He is everywhere and he sees everything.' In another way *La France vue de l'Armée d'Italie* exalted the austere habits of this demi-god.

> Should one penetrate his private life one would find a simple man easily casting aside his grandeur among his family, his mind habitually occupied by some great idea which often interrupts his meals or his sleep, and saying with dignified simplicity to those who respect him: 'I have seen kings at my feet, I could have had fifty millions in my coffers, I could have laid claim to a variety of things, but I am a French citizen, I am the chief general of the Great Nation; I know that posterity will do me justice.'

The newspapers founded in Milan were aimed not only at the soldiers in the Army of Italy, but at French opinion which had already been conditioned by the publicity surrounding Napoleon's reports to the Directory, by the dispatch of flags and by the military successes. *Le Courrier* was widely distributed in France; there was a subscription charge but it is likely that the journal was handed out freely. Owing to plunder, Bonaparte was not short of money. 'It can be said of him,' noted Tocqueville, 'that he surprised the world before his name was known, for at the time of the first campaign in Italy it was written and pronounced in different ways.'

In this manner the success of the army in the peninsula was blown up or even distorted—in the case of the battle of Arcole for instance—because of cunning propaganda the importance of which no general, with the exception of Hoche, had estimated. We do not wish to undermine Bonaparte's victories, but, rather, to bear in mind the manner in which they were presented to his contemporaries. The Napoleonic legend was not born in St Helena, but in the plains of Italy.

From the time of Lodi, Bonaparte's eyes were turned towards Paris, he was aware of the unpopularity of the Directory; he also knew that the power was there to be taken provided that all those who had profited in some way from the Revolution could be carefully handled.

The Directory felt uneasy. Bonaparte was taking on unimagined political dimensions—he had at his disposal an army, a vast booty and several newspapers including one which appeared in Paris in February 1797 under the evocative title *Journal de Bonaparte et des hommes vertueux*. Here the purity of the General was opposed to the corruption of the members of the Directory. In the peace negotiations with Austria, Bonaparte paid no attention whatsoever to the instructions of the Directory which were transmitted by Clarke. He claimed Lombardy whilst Reubell of the Directory advised sacrificing everything for the Rhineland. Taking advantage of the massacre of the French at Verona on 17 April, he declared war on Venice on 2 May, and, without striking a blow, he took possession of the city on the 15th. This was a prelude to the carving up of the republic which made it possible to give Austria the necessary compensation for Lombardy and Belgium. Losing no time, on 29 June Bonaparte made Lombardy into a Cisalpine republic whose institutions were closely modelled on those of France. The republic was lacking a sea port: an ultimatum by Bonaparte to Genoa assured him of this outlet and the port was handed over to the French.

These personal politics of Bonaparte's irritated Paris. The attacks came from the monarchist right which had registered a great upsurge at the elections, and which forgave him neither the important role he had played on 13 Vendémiaire, nor his support of the Jacobins in Italy. Mallet du Pan made 'The wild-haired little runt' his favourite target. Then Dumolard, from the tribune of the Five Hundred, denounced the Commander-in-Chief of the Army of Italy as guilty of intervening in Venice and Genoa without having consulted the Directory and the assemblies. Disabled or wounded men from this army were maltreated and insulted on their return to France. They were asked to shout: 'Long live the King!'.

Bonaparte was well enough armed to defend himself. He had just captured one of the most important Royalist agents, the Comte d'Antraigues, and had his hands on the count's papers which included a report from Montgaillard—a soldier of fortune—recounting the negotiations with the Republic's military leaders to rally them to the cause of Louse XVIII. Pichegru, who had become President of the

Council of Five Hundred was found to be implicated.

In Paris the Directory was divided. Carnot and Barthélemy had rallied to the majority on the right to which Reubell, La Révellière-Lépeaux and Barras were hostile. Barras counted on Hoche whom he had been instrumental in making Minister of War, and envisaged a military *coup d'état,* but, by reason of his age, Hoche was not able to act. He was no longer thirty years old, and was not young enough. He suffered from seeing his reputation diminished by the attacks which came to be levelled at him and he died shortly afterwards from illness, despair or poison. However Barras was not lacking in encouragement from Bonaparte, who would have provided him with the proof of Pichegru's treachery; in any case he sent Augereau to Paris, bearing incendiary addresses from the Army of Italy: 'If you fear the Royalists, call for the Army of Italy who will swiftly wipe out the Chouans, the Royalists and the English.'

During the night of 17–18 Fructidor (3–4 September), Barras, Reubell and La Revellière put Augereau in charge of quickly capturing the Royalists. Pichegru and Barthélemy were arrested, Carnot managed to escape. Posters reproducing the papers seized by Bonaparte from d'Antraigues were stuck all over the walls in Paris. Once again Napoleon had frustrated the plans for a restoration of the monarchy.

But had he gained much from the *coup d'état*? Reubell, the enemy of the negotiations with Austria was still there; Augereau, drunk with success was criticizing his leader; Barras was keeping his distance.

'I beg you,' Bonaparte wrote to the Directory,

to replace me and to accept my resignation. No power on earth would be capable of making me continue to serve after this horrible sign of ingratitude from the government, which I was so far from expecting. My health, which has been considerably affected, imperiously demands rest and quiet. My soul also requires steeping once again in the crowd of citizens. For some time great power has been entrusted to me, I have used it on all occasions for the good of the country—never mind those who do not believe in honour and who might have suspected mine. My conscience and the opinion of posterity are my reward.

In fact the Thermidorians, after the test of Fructidor, could not do without Bonaparte. Jourdan was discredited, Moreau under suspicion, Augereau talked too much and Bernadotte expressed ultra-Republican opinions. The Commander-in-Chief of the Army in Italy was aware of this. He could therefore conduct negotiations with the Austrian representative, Cobenzl, as he pleased. It was he who, without consulting the Directory, inspired the articles of peace signed at Campo-Formio on 18 October 1797. Austria ceded Belgium to France and recognized the Cisalpine Republic. In return she was given Venice, but not the Ionian islands. As for the left bank of the Rhine, it was to be discussed at the projected Diet of Rastadt. Bonaparte confessed: 'The Parisian lawyers who have been put in the Directory understand nothing of government. They are mean-minded men . . . I very much doubt that we can remain in agreement much longer. They are jealous of me. I can no longer obey. I have tasted command and I would not know how to give it up.' Decidedly Lodi was an imporant turning point in his life.

On 26 October 'the Parisian lawyers' studied the text of the Treaty of Campo-Formio which was brought to them by Berthier and Monge. According to La Revellière-Lépeaux, the Directory had difficulty in accepting that Venice had been ceded to the Habsburgs. But French opinion had to be taken into consideration: there were many accounts of war-weariness; a reaction was feared from Bonaparte's soldiers. The Directory was already highly unpopular, therefore Barras saw to it that the treaty was ratified. But what was to be done with Bonaparte? In order to be rid of him he was given the command of the Army of England; he was supposed to prepare, in the north, an expedition against the British Isles. In the meantime, in order to keep him away from the capital, he was put in charge of completing at Rastadt the peace negotiations which had been begun at Campo-Formio. Bonaparte was becoming a highly embarrassing general for the Thermidorians. In the eyes of his contemporaries, he had conquered Austria and imposed peace on the Continent. When this was announced, 'all hats were thrown in the air', wrote a journalist from the *Rédacteur*, 'the enthusiasm was indescribable, the felicitous name of the peacemaker was on every tongue.'

5

THE EGYPTIAN EXPEDITION— ORIENTAL DREAM OR A POLITICAL MANOEUVRE?

'Twenty victorious battles become youth so well, they become a noble look, pallor and a kind of exhaustion.' The Directory was trembling before Bonaparte whose power suddenly seemed threatening. As commander of the Army of England, able to count on the blind devotion of the Army of Italy and having obtained at Rastadt the favour of some of the troops in Germany, the general had enough strength at his disposal to sweep away the executive power. The excuse was there: he only had to use the documents seized from the Comte d'Antraigues's portfolio to expose the intrigues of certain members of the Directory.

Bonaparte, with very sound political judgement, estimated that the moment was not yet ripe for another *coup d'état*. The Royalists had just been put down at Fructidor; the Jacobins would not have followed him and public opinion would not have consented to military rule since mistrust of the political generals remained so great. Bonaparte's prestige was founded not only on his victories, but also on his loyalty to the Republic. He presented an image of a hero totally free from compromise, of the only general who had not been beaten in the recent campaign. Popular engravings, songs and poems made him their own, and relayed the active propaganda which had been launched in Italy. At the theatre *Le Pont de Lodi* was staged and the victor's name cheered at every performance. The street where he lived, rue Chantereine, was even renamed rue de la Victoire. But one act of impudence, and the particularly versatile public opinion would have deserted him, as it did Hoche. Back in Paris, Bonaparte saw fit to display a modest, slightly bored attitude at the banquets and feasts given in his honour. He only abandoned this reserve in order to take the seat left vacant by Carnot in the Institut on 25 December 1797. He entered the Institut in the first class, that of the sciences. This was a clever move which ensured the support of the ideologues who represented the true 'conscience' of the Revolution on the wane. What is more, the prestige of the Institut further enhanced Bonaparte's glory. Due to this election the public sitting of 4 January 1798 had a panache all its own.

WHY EGYPT?

In fact, during a journey from 8–20 February 1798, Bonaparte had taken into account the difficulties which the plan to invade England presented. He risked losing all his prestige in an expedition where Hoche had already failed. In the report which he addressed to the Directory on 23 February he observed:

> Whatever our efforts, we will not acquire naval supremacy in a few years. To undertake an invasion of England without being lords of the sea would be the boldest and most difficult operation ever carried out. It would require the long nights of winter. After the month of April it would be impossible to undertake anything.

He suggested two other solutions: to attack Hanover, or to conquer Egypt—a plan which had been developed by Talleyrand, the Foreign Minister. The first solution was reasonable—too much so for Bonaparte's thirst for glory, equally too much so for the Directory, which was eager to be rid, as soon as possible, of an embarrassing general. The conquest of Egypt seemed madness. It meant depriving France of an army, and of an experienced general, at a time when war threatened to break out at any moment on the Continent; it meant attempting to escape the British fleet in the Mediterranean, and attacking a country which was as yet little known despite the insistence of Magallon, the French Consul in Cairo, on the simplicity of such a conquest. But the East caught Bonaparte's imagination; furthermore, the whole operation allowed him to leave the political situation in France to rot in his absence. Public opinion, on learning of the plan, was very enthusiastic for an expedition to a mysterious land made fashionable by Volney in *Les Ruines*. Finally the Directory saw, without displeasure, the removal of a formidable menace.

Egypt presented a triple interest; it made it possible in the immediate future, by occupying the isthmus of Suez, to cut off one of the trade routes from India to England; destined to become a colony, 'she would alone,' said Talleyrand, 'be worth all those that France had lost'; she would then provide a useful base for the future conquest of Britain's principal source of wealth—India, where Tipu Sahib was leading the fight against the British invasion.

The Eastern expedition combined scientific interest with military and economic objectives. It followed a long line of eighteenth-century voyages of discovery. A committee for the sciences and the arts was to accompany the army and to found an Egyptian Institute. Chosen by Monge, Berthollet and Arnault, twenty-one mathematicians, three astronomers, seventeen civil engineers, thirteen naturalists and mining engineers, as many geographers, three gunpowder and saltpetre experts, four architects, eight draftsmen, ten mechanical draftsmen, one sculptor, fifteen interpreters, ten writers and twenty-two printers bearing Roman, Greek and Arabic characters, made the journey. The list of these people's names is impressive: Monge, Berthollet, Costaz, the geometrician Fourier, the mineralogist Dolomieu, the astronomer Mechain, the naturalist Geoffroy-Saint-Hilaire, the doctor Desgenettes, the chemist Conté, famous for his lead pencils, the archaeologist Jomard, the orientalist Jaubert, the engraver Vivan Denon . . . not to forget the poet, Parseval-Grandmaison whose muse remained uninspired by this epic; a painter of flowers, Redouté, and a pianist, Rigel.

By giving a scientific character to his expedition, Bonaparte confirmed his alliance with the ideologues. In the final analysis the conquest of Egypt seemed to be, above all, an exercise of internal politics: Bonaparte was too much of a realist, despite the declarations attributed to him, to consider, like Alexander, carving out an Eastern empire. Starting with religion and language, there were too many obstacles in his path. It is undeniable that afterwards he envisaged dividing the Ottoman possessions with the Tsar, and that he later dreamed of an Egypt reborn under the French administration, and even of a Universal Empire. But in 1798 he was thinking, above all, of going away in order to avoid compromising the prestige he had acquired. Once the Mediterranean was crossed, Egypt seemed an easy prey. Bonaparte hoped by his victory to increase his glory whilst the government in Paris continued to disintegrate. He admitted it: he was aiming at France whilst awaiting Europe. When and how? He did not know as yet. But one can be sure that he did not think of shutting himself away in Egypt.

THE CONQUEST

On 19 May two hundred ships under the command of Admiral Brueys and carrying thirty-five thousand men, left Toulon.

Everything had been prepared within a month: soldiers, materials and ships—which is evidence of Bonaparte's impatience to leave Paris, temporarily of course; it also explains the inevitable gaps which soon appeared in the material preparations for the expedition. These preparations had not escaped the notice of the British Admiralty, but Nelson missed the French fleet twice and thought there must have been an intervention in Turkey. Meanwhile, in passing, Bonaparte took Malta without firing a shot. On 1 July he landed without resistance in the Bay of Alexandria. The town soon fell into French hands. But the army's enthusiasm disappeared at an early stage when confronted by the desert, the filth, the poverty and the heat. (Bonaparte had chosen the season very badly and appears never to have taken meteorological considerations into account when planning his campaigns.) According to an eye-witness, Bricard, 'Our soldiers were dying in the sand from lack of water and food; an excessive heat had forced them to jettison their spoils, and some, weary of suffering, had blown out their brains.' Many, despite the reading of a proclamation, were querying the reason for having come to such a hostile land. François Bernoyer, chief of supplies to the Army of the Orient, wrote to his wife:

> I have made inquiries into what our government anticipated when it sent an army to occupy the Sultan's States without any declaration of war and with no motive for declaring it. A little sagacity is all that is needed, I have been told. Bonaparte, by virtue of his genius and victories won with an army which had become invincible, had too great an influence in France. He was an embarrassment not to say an obstacle to those who hold the reins of power. I was able to discover no other causes.

That says all that need be said about the morale of the Army of the Orient.

As a province of the Ottoman Empire, Egypt was in fact subject to the military feudal system of the Mamelukes, originally slaves bought from among the populations of the Caucasus. This warlike caste ruled over a people consisting of small artisans, tradespeople and fellahin, all of whom were increasingly dissatisfied with their rulers, particularly since Egypt at the end of the eighteenth century was suffering from a marked economic slump. The warnings of the Consul Magallon were confirmed by the rapid collapse of the Mamelukes. One battle was enough: it took place at Giza, opposite Cairo, near the great pyramids, on 21 July. The Mameluke cavalry charges dashed themselves against the French infantry squares. The victory, which has become legendary, has been grossly exaggerated. It did at least ensure Bonaparte's possession of Cairo.

But on 1 August the French fleet which had escaped the British ships during the crossing was surprised by Nelson in Aboukir Bay and entirely destroyed. Bonaparte was a prisoner of his own victory.

The situation worsened with Turkey's declaration of war in September and the threat of an intervention by Ottoman forces. Sickness due to the climate also had to be taken into account. The hostility of the inhabitants was made apparent in the revolt of Cairo on 21 October which cost the lives of General Dupuy and of Bonaparte's favourite aide-de-camp, Sulkowski. this terrible insurrection revealed the extent of the Muslim leaders' forces.

Nevertheless everything was done to win the sympathy of the population. Religious beliefs were respected, the old feudal system was destroyed, the canals were rehabilitated, the economy was boosted. The levelling of the Suez isthmus and the works preparatory to the joining of the Red Sea and the Mediterranean were started under the direction of the chief engineer, Le Père. An Egyptian Institute, modelled on the Institut de France was founded. Its objective was 'progress and the spreading of enlightenment in Egypt'. Two newspapers were published in French: *Le Courrier de L'Égypte* and *La Décade égyptienne*. There was a re-launching of an Egypt freed from the economic and social, if not religious, restraints imposed by the Mameluke rule. The past was not forgotten: excavations at Thebes, Luxor and Karnak; the discovery of the Rosetta Stone as well as numerous sketches by Vivant Denon and his team of artists comprised the main elements of a fruitful harvest which was to lead to the publication, from 1809, of the great volumes of the *Description d'Égypte*.

War continued. The Turks were in fact marking on Egypt: Bonaparte went to meet them in Syria in February 1799. This expedition was carefully prepared. Gaza (where two thousand Turks were massacred), and then Jaffa, fell without difficulty. But the French were to fail at Saint-Jean-d'Acre which was defended by Pasha Djezzar and a former fellow-student of Bonaparte's, Phélippeaux. The town had been supplied with fresh provisions by Commander Sidney Smith's

British fleet, while, on the other hand, the French troops were short of siege artillery. In his letters, Bernoyer asserts that some generals, like Dammartin, worried by plans attributed to Bonaparte—such as that of having himself crowned King of Persia—'did everything to prevent the taking of Saint-Jean-d'Acre'. Sickness played its part. Besides, a Turkish army advancing from Damas had to be stopped near Nazareth on 16 April with the Battle of Mount Tabor. Another army which had landed at Aboukir on 25 July was crushed by Bonaparte who had hurried back to Egypt. Before that, Lanusse had crushed an uprising stirred up by El Modhy.

The oriental dream was becoming a nightmare—more especially as the news from Paris was bad. A lack of precise information led to the spreading of the most fantastic rumours. The naval disaster at Aboukir and the Cairo revolt were blown up by Bonaparte's adversaries; Bonaparte, cut off from France, lacking communications, had difficulty in reacting. The English were interfering and exposing Bonaparte's atrocities. They complacently described the massacre of French soldiers, overtaken by the plague, or of defenceless Turks. Bonapartist propaganda was spineless and found it hard to make a 'deportation of the general and the élite of the Army of Italy' sound credible. With the renewal of war on the Continent, public attention was turned to other battlefields. There was rumour of a *coup d'état* prepared by Sieyès with the agreement of a brilliant general, Joubert. Bonaparte's absence was turning against him. On 26 August, Kléber, who had been made Commander-in-Chief of the Army of Egypt, informed the troops of the departure of their general on the 23rd. The message left by the General himself explained this desertion as follows: 'Extraordinary circumstances alone have persuaded me, in the interests of my country, its glory, and of obedience, to pass through enemy lines and to return to Europe.' Bonaparte took with him Berthier, Lannes, Murat, Monge and Berthollet. He was taking a double risk: the British surveillance of the Mediterranean had to be avoided; and even though Bonaparte was ordered back officially on 26 May, he would still have to justify his departure. There were two miracles: the ship was not intercepted; and the report of the victory at Aboukir on 24 July arrived in Paris several days before Bonaparte. It gave the lie to the pessimistic rumours about the Army of Egypt, which had been rife up till then and it impressed the public with an account of Bonaparte's brilliant victory. It was forgotten that the Army of the Orient had reached an impasse and that its absence had weighed heavily in the first setbacks of the new Continental war. So Bonaparte had been right to distance himself from the Directory. In spite of the failures of the Egyptian expedition he returned to France in an aura of prestige won by far-off victories which had been exaggerated by the propaganda of his partisans. Joubert had been bribed, Moreau was too compromised, Bernadotte too prudent. The way was open. So the 'saviour in boots', called upon to end the Revolution and heralded by Robespierre in 1792 when he denounced the belligerent politics of the Girondins, was to be Bonaparte.

PART II

THE REVOLUTION
REDEEMED

'The Revolution is over,' Bonaparte repeated at intervals. It was obvious. For many historians the Revolution ended with the fall of Robespierre, but it would be more accurate to say that the *coup de grâce* dates back to the elimination of the *enragés*. By 1794 the Revolutionary movement had reached a point beyond which it could not go. Had it not, then, satisfied the principle demands of the peasants and the bourgeoisie? From that time the former were rid of the feudal yoke. By conspiracy or threat they progressively kept away any competition at the auction of clergy property. More than a third of the villagers in certain parts of the north or the east managed to acquire property—enough to satisfy the hunger for land which country people had manifested throughout the whole of the eighteenth century. Besides, with the nobility crushed, the fetters of the guilds shattered, the bourgeoisie—at least those who had managed to avoid loss—could look to the future with confidence. Even war, which had become victorious, made an economic boom possible. A boom, however, which did not on the whole include the ports.

Only the urban proletariat, the spearhead of the Revolution, had gained nothing apart from the temporary disappearance, after 1802, of famine and unemployment. In fact they had very quickly lost their leaders, the guillotine having greedily claimed even more of their heads than of the aristocrats'; also Babeuf's failure revealed objectives which were too vague and too utopian. The property problem had made impossible an alliance, once contemplated, between the bourgeoisie and the workers. The 'fourth estate' was still searching for a class identity which it was to discover through the industrial changes hastened by the Empire. For the moment it had run out of energy. 'This section of the population, so animated during the first days of the Revolution, had suffered so many appalling disappointments that it had long been subdued,' wrote Barras in his *Mémoires*.

The Revolution was over. Doubtless, but the pendulum must one day swing back. Vendémiaire and Fructidor had plotted against the Royalist threat, but had not removed it definitively. The Thermidorians needed a prop. Why not Bonaparte? The Revolution was over. But a revolution which stops is destined to failure. A pause was necessary, better to remove the passive element and to consolidate the gains of the bourgeoisie and of the well-to-do peasantry. Once again a task worthy of Bonaparte. The alliance was established between the General and the Thermidorians who had become Brumairians—a tacit alliance and one which was not free from the occasional inevitable abuse.

A re-making of the Constitution would not have been enough to establish a strong government capable of holding the respect of the opposition from within or without. Sieyès was soon to discover the virtues of a title—he was made a count—but it was not without ill will that he agreed to stand aside. In a space of four years Bonaparte rose from Provision Consul to Emperor. In seven years he had rid France of her Continental enemies—a still profoundly barbarous Russia ruled over by an autocratic Tsar, himself at the mercy of palace plots; Prussia whose military reputation acquired under Frederick II no longer had any bearing on reality, and an Austrian Empire which was a tangled and colourful web of separate nations with even the Chancellery of Vienna in great confusion. The northern courts, the decadent Bourbons in Naples and Spain, the Swiss cantons, and Portugal, despite its empire, were not worth considering. Great Britain alone, with her fleet, her credit and her identity could rival France whose presence she refuted at Antwerp; but, protected by the sea, England herself could ill support a blockade—her favourite weapon, which Napoleon turned against her. At Tilsit, in 1807, the French Revolution triumphed. Consolidated internally, the Revolution of France was recognized by Europe. Goethe could sing of the Revolution 'consummated in all which is reasonable, legitimate and European'.

1

THE DEBIT ACCOUNT

Traditionally, the history of the Consulate begins with a picture of France under the Directory, a country devastated by war, overrun in the west and the south by bands of brigands who ransacked public coffers and robbed travellers. Industry was in ruins, trade paralysed and finance in distress; soldiers lacking in food and money deserted the army in their thousands, in the hospitals people were dying of hunger; the nation was demoralized, indifferent to news from the frontiers, wanting only to profit from the pleasures offered by the capital. Such was France in 1799. Then a young general appeared who rectified the military situation, purged the political circles, relaunched the economy and founded new institutions. After anarchy came order, after defeat, victory. Does this contrast seem too simple to be true? Was the break between the Directory and the Consulate complete?

THE GREAT SURVEY OF YEAR IX
The source used, since Thiers, by all historians writing of France under the Directory, is known. The reports addressed by councillors of state to the Consular Government following investigations ordered by it at the beginning of Year IX, gave in fact a particularly gloomy picture of the situation only a few months after 18 Brumaire. Because these reports were not intended to be published and because they were signed by honourable men, Champagny, Thibaudeau, Fourcroy or Lacuée, they have seemed to guarantee truth.

The first thing which appears to have struck these travelling Councillors of State was the bad state of the roads. Fourcroy notes during his mission to the 16th military division that 'all the roads in the Department of the North, except the one from Lille to Dunkerque which is least used for trade, are in the worst possible condition. There are,' he adds, 'great muddy craters; a lot of paving stones have been torn up and on the whole the roads resemble a ploughed field.' In the Pas-de-Calais, uneven ground constantly caused light carriages to snap. The situation was no better in the south where Français de Nantes observed that two-thirds of the roads were impassable or especially bad.

Brigandage added further to the dangers. Very widespread in the west, it had recently shown a marked decline in the south—but Fourcroy reported that several months earlier it was impossible to cross the Ventoux without fear. 'Travellers in those parts were obliged to collect passports from the leader of the brigands, and to pay for the return of stolen goods. Posters warned carters that if they carried less than four louis they would be shot, and several were.' Calm, remarked the Councillor of State, Najac, had not yet returned to the Rhône which was being terrorized by the Companions of Jehu. Groups were organized in Paris to defraud the tolls which the Directory had re-established. 'They depend,' wrote Lacuée, on self-styled merchants and men of affairs, and even on organizations which pay them.'

At the frontiers the country bore the marks of invasion. At Valenciennes one house out of three was in ruins; along the Rhine the forests bore witness to repeated devastations; in Provence villages had been wiped out in their tens. The ravages of civil war were even more widespread: massacres, fire and looting had, in parts, reduced the Vendée to a desert.

But the councillors of state mostly blamed the previous regime for the administrative anarchy. The application of the law varied from one department to another. Barbé-Marbois, in charge of inspecting the 13th military division, wrote that 'the same objects were governed by opposing principles', and held the lack of agreement behind ministerial orders reponsible. The government envoys were especially interested in finance. Utter disorder seems to have reigned in the account books of the tax collectors, most of whom Fourcroy accused of being guilty of extortion. Even the army did not restrain itself from taking money from the State coffers, and Barbé-Marbois quotes the following from an officer: 'Riches belong to the brave; let's help ourselves; we will settle our accounts at the mouth of a cannon.'

The Directory also fell down over the religious problem which arose from the civil constitution of the Clergy.

'When knowledge of the human heart,' wrote Fourcroy, 'could not teach that the great mass of mankind needs religion, worship and priests, time spent with the inhabitants of the countryside—above all those who are furthest from Paris—and visits to all the departments I have known would, alone, have persuaded me.'

The failure of theophilanthropic worship and the *culte décadaire* underlined by these reports was, in the final analysis, the failure of the Directory which had attempted to impose them.

And material failure echoed spiritual failure. Najac writes of the ruin of the silk industry in Lyons, where there were four thousand three hundred and thirty-five fewer looms than in 1788. The answers of Frochot, the Prefect of the Seine, to Lacuée's questionnaire are pessimistic:

> The condition of the Parisian manufacturers has greatly deteriorated during the Revolution. On the one hand, the insubordination of the workers, the war, commercial stagnation, the difficulties of collecting debts and bankruptcy have forced contractors to restrain their speculations; on the other, payments which they have received in the form of assignats have swallowed up their advances, and ruined their resources, and most of them have then been obliged to borrow capital at a very high rate of interest which has sapped them daily whilst absorbing the greater part of their profits.

The canals in the north were in a bad way, around Rochefort marshes were spreading to the point of making the port uninhabitable; the deterioration of public works was marked. Speaking of trade in Marseilles, Français de Nantes wrote: 'Imports and exports in the last months of Year IX do not equal the trading activities of fifteen days of peace in past times.' Destitution was sometimes so widespread that it did not affect the working classes alone. Français de Nantes points out the case of two civil engineers who died of hunger, the state having failed to pay them. And what about the *rentiers*?

The Directory's record, then, is very poor, if these reports are to be believed. But has the negative element not been exaggerated? Was it fair to blame the Directory for mistakes made before it came to power?

THE ACHIEVEMENTS OF THE DIRECTORY
On reading the results of the investigations of the Year IX, the hostility of certain councillors of state towards the Revolution must be borne in mind. What is more, Alexandre d'Hauterive's *L'État de la France à la fin de l'an VIII* and many other pamphlets of the time show that, long

before the birth of the 'legend', Bonaparte's partisans were interested in blackening the Directory in order to justify the *coup d'état*.

The period immediately preceding the Consulate was not one of the most glorious in the history of France. But some successes have been deliberately left in the shadows, such as the triumph of Masséna over the Russians at Zurich, and Brune's rebuttal of an Anglo-Russian invasion at Bergen in Holland. As from 1799 these victories eliminated all danger from outside. Ramel's work of creating a system of tax administration which relieved the elected body of the duties of assessing and collecting taxes, has been forgotten. The education policy of the Minister of the Interior, later a member of the Directory, François de Neufchâteau, has been ignored. He had increased the number of central schools and had thought up the system of scholarships. His economic policies were no less worthy of attention. 'The people,' he observed, 'will become attached to a regime through prosperity alone." Well before Napoleon's Blockade, François de Neufchâteau had attempted to ensure French hegemony on the Continent by imposing trade agreements which benefited industry, by opening roads through the Alps and by closing Europe to British produce by an enforced customs system. The twelve initial shareholders had increased to a hundred by the end of 1798.

In order to carry out such policies successfully, the Minister of the Interior resumed the Ancien Régime's tradition of administrative investigations; hence the industrial investigations of Year V which dealt not only with production, but with the number of workers per factory, the development of mechanization, comparison with foreign products and the problems of trading prospects. A circular of 27 Fructidor Year VI launched the scheme for a statistical description of all departments. A district census 'of the population and of all livestock' was undertaken. François de Neufchâteau also envisaged setting up a roll of the whole population by district with remarks on the reasons for its increase or decrease.

In many ways the Directory's policies heralded those of the Consulate. Tradition has only remembered the political instability of a regime under pressure from two oppositions: on the left the Jacobins, and on the right the Royalists. The *coups d'état* and the insecurity arising from a disguised civil war overshadowed internal and external successes from which the Consulate was able to profit.

Recent historical researchers have shown that it was the Directory's misfortune to have coincided with a long period of economic depression stretching from 1796 to 1801. It had the onerous duty of liquidating the financial administration of the Revolution. Excessive issuing of *assignats* had by 1796 reached a point where the cost of printing was greater than the value of the paper money itself. Depreciation was accelerated by the creation of territorial money orders; the only result of their suppression was the decrease in bartering: if supplies had become abundant again, money was still not in evidence. Speculation rose from one to three per cent each month. Abolition of credit and the cutting down on the quantity of coins in circulation finally resulted in deflation. The rise in agricultural prices which had enriched the peasant was followed by a general drop which was further aggravated by a succession of good harvests. The price of a hectolitre of corn fell from 19.48 francs to 16.20 francs. The logical outcome of this slump was under-consumption in rural areas which in its turn caused trade and industry to suffer at a time when there were fewer commercial outlets in Europe and when a break with Turkey was being caused by the Egyptian expedition. The deflationary movement had repercussions on salaries and encouraged unemployment, preventing the urban workers from profiting sufficiently from the lowering of the price of bread.

There was stagnation in the large textile centres of the north and the west, a disastrous situation in the Lyons silk industry, and a commercial crisis in Paris. The ports did not present a more glowing picture. Marseilles had seen a decline in trade with the East for the reasons set out above; Bordeaux was in a state of collapse, having resisted so far due to the arrival of American ships which took on board wines and spirits despite the interdiction of the Directory, on 29 Nivôse Year VI; Nantes presented a picture of desolation; even Toulon was not spared despite her arsenal. The Bordeaux *Journal du Commerce* enumerated the ills which assailed 'the principal maritime cities'. These were extreme shortage of currency, bankruptcy and disruption caused to communications by the British Navy.

In the last years of the Directory, the depression which touched all social classes entirely destroyed François de Neufchâteau's efforts at rehabilitation.

It was the ending of economic stagnation (which became evident from 1801), combined with the spectacular way in which the short crisis of 1802 was overcome, which contributed to the belief in a miraculous resurgence of France for which the First Consul was held responsible. The fact remains that Bonaparte knew how to create the climate of confidence indispensable to a renewal of economic activity by winning the popularity of the bourgeoisie, without whom, in 1799, nothing would have been possible, in so far as the money and the talents lay with them. At the basis of the authority which the new Head of State had gained over the bourgeoisie lay several successes in the space of two years: a balanced budget, cash payment of *rente*, the pacification of the Vendée, the re-establishment of order, reconciliation with Rome, the end not only of the war on the Continent, but of war at sea. Molé confided in Tocqueville: 'I admit to having been dazzled on seeing so rapid a reconstruction of government. Everything seemed to me to be in pieces—irretrievably ruined. I was unable to imagine how anything could be reconstructed.' And he added, 'My youth prevented me from seeing the resources offered by the society of the time for such a work; that was my great mistake, I confess it.' The 'consular miracle' would not have been possible without the support of the notables and of the middle class. Again Tocqueville observed, 'On coming to power Bonaparte imposed an additional 25 centimes of tax and nothing is said. The people do not turn against him; on the whole what he did was popular. The Provisional Government was to take the same measures in 1848 and was to be cursed immediately. The former was making a much desired revolution, the second was making an unwanted one.'

2

THE NEW INSTITUTIONS

In December 1799 a saying was circulating in Paris: 'What is there in the Constitution?—There is Bonaparte.' But it was only by stages that Napoleon achieved full power. He was not the only one to triumph at Brumaire and he had first to separate from Sieyès; until the victory at Marengo, his power remained in doubt. The Thermidorians were wondering about his intentions.

As a stranger to the assemblies and having been absent from Paris under the Directory, Bonaparte hardly knew the politicians of his time; he had, therefore, to rely on his brother, Lucien, Cambacérès or Talleyrand for the appointment of his personnel; his experience of jurisdiction and of finance was limited and his interventions at the Council of State bore witness to areas of abysmal ignorance.

Therefore one must be careful not to see Bonaparte as the only architect of the great reforms under the Consulate. An important part of the rehabilitation of Year VIII should be attributed to those highly placed civil servants of the Ancien Régime, Lebrun and Gaudin. The work on the institutions carried out at the time bears their mark, it reflects the political determination of the new notables; it is a compromise between the victories of the Revolution and the institutions of the old monarchy minus the king and the nobility.

SIEYÈS'S HOUR
After the *coup d'état* of Brumaire, the victors set themselves to work. Executive power had been put in the hands of three Consuls, Sieyès, Roger Ducos and Bonaparte. They immediately chose their ministers. Cambacérès and Fouché were reserved for justice and the police, Gaudin was put in charge of finance and Berthier of war; Talleyrand

replaced Reinhardt in charge of external affairs on 22 November. Four ministers and two Consuls were survivors of the Directory. The *coup d'état* had favoured not new men but a new regime.

In fact, on the same evening commissions were set up for the preparation of a political reform. But the commissioners were quite without ideas; they turned to Sieyès who was renowned for his profound knowledge of constitutional law. The time had at last come for the former abbé whose passion was the drawing up of constitutions. After ten days of meditation, the oracle replied. Executive power should belong to a Grand Elector assisted by two Consuls, one in charge of war and one of peace, each one independent of the other and both chosen by the Grand Elector; legislative power should be in the hands of three assemblies consisting of men chosen from a list of notables. It was craven, for France would belong to the notables, that is to say the landowners. One of these assemblies, the Senate, could engulf the Grand Elector and the Consuls were they to become too powerful. Sieyès summarized his scheme with a formula which exactly defined its Caesarian quality: 'Authority comes from above and trust from below.'

It must be observed, however, that by his plan the people did not hand their prerogatives over to a man, but to an assembly, the Senate, which Sieyès himself intended to recruit from among the Thermidorians—those members of the Convention who had kept themselves constantly in power since the fall of Robespierre. As a man of the Revolution, Sieyès believed only in government by assembly and denied all individual power. How, under these conditions, could Bonaparte have come to terms with Sieyès's ideas? When the former abbé came to offer him the position of Grand Elector, an honorary post with an enormous salary, the General abruptly refused this role of 'fattening pig'. A keen tension was established between the two victors of Brumaire. According to Bonaparte: 'Sieyès believes himself to be alone in possessing the truth; when he is faced with an objection, he replies like one who claims to have been inspired and there is no more to be said.' For his part, Sieyès was publicly denouncing Bonaparte's intention of 'becoming king'—a dreadful accusation at a time when the Republican convictions of many Brumairians were still firmly anchored. Talleyrand employed his diplomatic talents in vain to bring the adversaries together. All at once the future of the new regime seemed compromised by dissension, and Barras, the one-time master of the Directory, was already envisaging an eventual return to power.

But it was Bonaparte who was seen as the true republican when it was learnt that he was refusing the post of Elector for life, destined for him by Sieyès. And, if police reports are to be believed, he gained, in this way, the good will of the public. Assured of popular support, the Consul summoned a meeting of the commissioners charged with drawing up a constitution. Meetings then took place, eleven evenings in succession, in a drawing-room of the Luxembourg Palace. Considerable amendments were made to Sieyès's plans. How was Bonaparte, so inexperienced in constitutional law, able to impose them? He was to explain later, on St Helena. 'These men who wrote so well and were so eloquent, were, however, devoid of any soundness of judgement, were quite illogical and argued pitifully badly.' This was a severe but accurate assessment. Bonaparte knew how to command the ideologues by his common sense, and more so, by his physical resistance. 'For public affairs, both administrative and military, strong intentions are needed, profound analysis and the capacity to concentrate at length without tiring.' Knowingly Bonaparte prolonged the discussions on the constitution late into the night with the intention of weakening his adversaries through exhaustion.

THE CONSTITUTION OF YEAR VIII

To one of his advisers, Roederer, Bonaparte declared, 'A constitution must be short and ——' Roederer interrupted, about to add, 'clear', when Bonaparte cut across him —— 'short and obscure.' In this respect the new constitution, which was reforming itself along Sieyès's major lines, but in Bonaparte's favour, was a masterpiece of ambiguity. Nevertheless, it soon became clear that power was concentrated in the hands of the First Consul although he was flanked by two other Consuls and by four assemblies, one of which was the conservative Senate, so dear to Sieyès. The people had played no part in the *coup d'état* and having played no part in the forming of a new regime, they were excluded from participating in it.

To all outward appearances universal suffrage had been reestablished. All citizens of twenty-one, who had been domiciled for a year in their commune, had the vote, but there were no elections, only presentations. The electors gathered together in the chief town of their region and designated a tenth of their number to draw up a list of notables in the communes. In their turn, these notables designated the same proportion of departmental notables, who, following an identical procedure, drew up lists of national notables. From these lists the government chose the communal and departmental officials and the members of the National Assembly.

Legislative power was divided between four assemblies. The government alone was responsible for initiating the laws, plans for which were prepared by a council of state comprising thirty to forty members, all nominated and presided over by the First Consul. These plans were then submitted to a Tribunate—an assembly of a hundred members, one fifth of whom were renewed yearly—which discussed them and then gave their opinion by means of a resolution of acceptance or refusal. The plans then went before a legislative body or *corps legislatif* (three hundred members, of which one fifth was to be renewed yearly). This assembly, having listened to three government commissioners explaining the intentions of the First Consul, and three tribunes expounding on their assembly's resolution, would then proceed to vote without a debate. The Senate consisted of sixty members all of whom were ineligible for any other public employment, who were aged at least forty, and who were recruited by co-option. They nominated the numbers of the Tribunate and of the Legislative Body by choosing them from the lists of national notables. As guardian of the Constitution, the Senate could declare unconstitutional and annual acts which were presented to it by the Tribunate. No publicity was given to its sittings, which was enough to isolate it from the nation.

This complicated mechanism which led to a paralysis of parliamentary power was fundamentally Sieyès's scheme and Bonaparte had carefully kept it. But he acted differently with regard to executive power. The Grand Elector disappeared to be replaced by three Consuls nominated for a period of ten years by the Senate. The first three, Bonaparte, Cambacérès and Lebrun were designated by the Constitution. The First Consul, Bonaparte, alone held the real power: he initiated laws which he promulgated; he nominated councillors of state, ministers and officials; he controlled war and peace. The two other Consuls merely had advisory powers.

The ministers were responsible to the Consuls. Properly speaking there was no ministry. Besides, encouraged by Bonaparte, personal antagonism divided these ministers. Lucien, Minister of the Interior, was in rivalry with the Minister of Police, Fouché, who was equally detested by Talleyrand. Some ministries were split by, for instance, the creation of a director-general, and then a Treasury Minister as well as a Finance Minister, and by a Director of War Administration as well as a Minister of War. Principally it was the Minister of the Interior who was being aimed at. Lucien protested when it was suggested that he should be flanked by two director-generals recruited from among the councillors of state. He could not, however, prevent the institution of a general directorship of civil engineering which was given to Cretet. 'It is useful,' declared his brother, 'for a Councillor of State to be called upon to manage affairs in order that the laws, which are the concern of his department, conform to needs and to the possibility of their being carried out.'

THE PLEBISCITE

An article of the constitution provided that 'the present constitution be at once offered for approval to the French people'. This rule, which had already been laid down under the Revolution with regard to the constitutions of 1793 and 1795, in fact served Bonaparte's ends. In place of elections, a plebiscite on the plans for the constitution was held which developed into a plebiscite on one man, thanks to Bonaparte's personality.

The plebiscite took place in a manner which cannot, in these days, fail to amaze us, but which did not surprise contemporaries. It was decided to open a register in every commune, where electors would write their names followed by a Yes or a No, which they could also justify. Such a method may have allowed everyone to explain his position, but it was not a secret ballot; furthermore, it did not take place everywhere at the same time. It began at once in Paris, but was held up in the provinces. Many people hesitated to come and vote, fearing that, in times of trouble, the lists of people who had expressed their opinions might become proscription lists. In order to reassure them, the government had to promise that the lists would be burned after the votes had been counted. Nothing of the sort occurred and most of those registers which were opened in administrative offices, town halls, and lawyers' and magistrates' rooms have been preserved to this day. These registers bear witness to the confusion in which the voting was carried out. Examination reveals the names of a large number of scholars and artists. A significant fact is that the former members of the Convention gave their vote to Bonaparte.

There were very few Noes. According to *Le Moniteur,* 12,440 Yeses were registered in Paris and ten Noes. The proportion of Noes was markedly higher in Corsica: no man is a prophet in his own country. The constitution was finally approved by 3,011,007 votes to 1,562. This was hardly surprising. It is exceptional for a government to lose a

referendum unless it is set on a path of self-destruction. But the danger
can come from abstentions. There were inevitably a large number of
them in Year VIII owing to the hasty conditions in whch the plebiscite
was arranged; to the administrators who, in some places, had not yet
taken up their posts; to the Jacobin influence which was still con
siderable in the provinces, and to the fact that the Royalists also had to
be taken into account. Whereas abstention could be explained in the
troubled times of the Revolution, was there not a risk, in more peaceful
times, of it being interpreted as a denial of the government, or at least as
a mark of defiance towards it?

Now Bonaparte needed a large popular support expressing itself in a
much higher proportion of the electorate. Lucien had understood this
necessity. On examining the results, a researcher, M. Langlois, has
brought to light the fiddles carried out by the Minister of the Interior.
The figure of three million Yes votes out of an electorate of nine million
seemed to represent a very clear majority. In fact there can only really
have been a million and a half Yes votes. It did not matter—Lucien saw
to it that the figures in the departments were all rounded off; in this
way, nearly 900,000 votes were recuperated. There were added
500,000 Yeses representing the vote of the army which had not been
consulted, but which it was claimed, somewhat hastily, manifested
Bonapartist leanings. The trick was successful. But in any case
Bonaparte had not waited for definite results before putting the
constitution into practice.

It is, then, impossible to draw serious conclusions from this vote,
since it was not a secret ballot and the results were fixed. But contemporaries are not to be believed who assert that 'every individual of
whatever age, sex, condition or region was not only given a vote, but
invited to sign'. Examination of the registers does not confirm such
assertions in any way. The results reflected public opinion but the
plebiscite as such, far from being a free vote by the people, was merely
the ratification of a *fait accompli*. 'In this way,' wrote A. Aulard in
1926, 'the plebiscitary republic was founded in France.'

In place of numerous representatives who had until then been
charged with legislation and government, the French people gave
themselves a single representative, Napoleon Bonaparte.

Even before it had been adopted, the consitution had come into
force. Political staff were recruited from among the moderates, former
Feuillants or Thermidorians with whom an effort was made to mix a
few notables who had previously stood aside. Some repentant

monarchists were added. The members of the Senate were principally chosen by Sieyès. They included generals (Kellerman, Hatry, Lespinasse, Sérurier), admirals (Bougainville and Morard des Galles), magistrates, scientists and scholars (Berthollet, Monge, Laplace, Daubenton, Lagrange), writers (Volney, Destutt de Tracy), bankers (Perrégaux), one painter (Vien). Thirty-seven out of sixty were career politicians (Cornudet). The Ancients and the Five Hundred produced Dubois-Dubais, Garat, Lenoir-Laroche, Vimar and Cornet to name but the best known; earlier assemblies produced Garan-Coulon, Dailly and François de Neufchâteau. The Tribunate was dominated by ideologues: Daunou, Benjamin Constant (pushed by Madame de Staël), Dupuis, Jean-Baptiste Say, Laromiguière, Andrieux, Marie-Joseph Chénier, Desrenaudes, Ginguené. There was a tendency to choose young men known for their critical powers. Thus Sieyès hoped to create an official and constructive opposition. He remained, unlike Bonaparte, a parliamentarian without a soul. With Sieyès master of France, the Tribunate would have played an important role.

Of the three hundred members of the Legislative Body, two hundred and seventy-seven came from former assemblies: Grégoire, Dalphonse, Bréard, for instance.

And so, as one regime succeeded another, the politicians inherited from the Revolution were to perpetuate themselves.

ADMINISTRATIVE REFORMS

Bonaparte had played a leading role in the working out of the constitution; the same cannot be said of the administrative reforms which were determined by the intervention of Chaptal and Cambacérès.

The liberal principles of the Revolution—collegiate power, the election and autonomy of local administrations—were abandoned by the law of 28 Pluviôse Year VIII (17 February 1800). Thus, efficiency being all important, politics became once again centralized. The division of the land into departments with subdivisions (*arrondissements*) and communes remained, but their administration was entrusted to a prefect in a department, a sub-prefect in an *arrondissement*, and to the mayor in a commune, all of whom were nominated by the First Consul but chosen by the notables. The prefect's role was reminiscent of that of the *intendant* of the Ancien Régime whose powers had, however, been limited by the existence of the privileged bodies, the *parlements* and Provincial Estates. Swept away by the Revolution, such obstacles no longer stood in the way of a prefect. The local councils (municipal and general councils, and those of the *arrondisse-ments*) nominated by the government had financial powers only. The councils in the Prefecture devoted themselves to contentious admini-strative matters.

Paris and the department of the Seine were special cases. In reaction against the collegiate institutions set up under the Revolution which had turned out to be inefficient, Bonaparte and his advisers established an administration inspired by that which preceded 1789. The depart-ment of the Seine was divided into three communal *arrondissements*. The first (Pantin, Belleville, Clichy, Passy) and the second (Vincennes, Montreuil, Sceaux) had a sub-prefect. The third *arrondissement*, which consisted of Paris, had none. The capital which had once again become a single commune, remained, nevertheless, divided into twelve municipal *arrondissements* each of which had a mayor who was responsible for registration of births and deaths. But the real Mayor of Paris was the Prefect of the Seine who was installed in the Hôtel de Ville and who inherited the powers of the Provost of Merchants. Paris had no municipal council, the General Council of the Seine took its place. It was thus hoped not only to avoid the presence in the city of an elected mayor who would have been more powerful than the Prefect, but also to prevent the institution of an assembly similar to the insurrectional commune of 1792 which was responsible for the September massacres. The capital, organized in the same way from the fiscal point of view as for conscription, was subject to careful super-vision. Since the task of the Prefect promised to be a weighty one, and since it was feared that he might neglect the security of the capital, he had a second magistrate attached to him who was especially responsi-ble for the maintenance of order. This was the Prefect of Police—successor to the Lieutenant-General of the Ancien Régime. On Fouché's recommendation, Bonaparte chose Louis-Nicholas Dubois, formerly a procurator at the Châtelet.

The prefects, like the Senate and the Legislative Body, were recruited above all, from members of the revolutionary assemblies. Frochot, Prefect of the Seine, Mounier who replaced a former legislator, Borie, in Ille-et-Vilaine, Dauchy (Aisne), Lameth (in the Basses-Alpes 1802), Marquis (Meurthe), Huguet (Allier), Giraud (Morbihan), Méchin (Landes), Eymar (Léman), Harmand (Mayenne), Joubert (Nord), Ricard (Isère), and Pougeard (Haute-Vienne) were all former members of the Constituent Assembly. Beugnot (Seine-Inférieure), Rabusson-Lamothe (Haute-Loire), Rougier de la Bergerie

(Yonne), Montaut-Desilles (Maine et Loire), Verneilh-Puiraseau (Corrèze), Boullé (Côtes-du-Nord), Richard (Haute-Garonne), Nogaret (Hérault), Lamarque (Tarn), Imbert (Loire), and Roujoux (Saône-et-Loire) came from the Legislative Assembly: Letourneur (Loire-Inférieure), Jean de Bry (Doubs, where he replaced Marsson in 1801), Thibaudeau (Gironde), Colchen (Moselle), Quinette (Somme), Jean Bon Saint-André (Mayence), Pelet de la Lozère (Vaucluse), Cochon de Lapparent (Vienne), Bailly (Lot), Musset (Creuse), Lacoste (Forêts), Delacroix (Bouches-du-Rhône), Guillemardet (Charente-Inférieure) and Brun (Ariège) had been part of the Convention; Texier-Olivier (Basses-Alpes) and Riou (Cantal) formerly sat in the assemblies of the Directory. Several generals were included as a reminder of the authoritative nature of the gathering. On the other hand there were few diplomats and writers (Ramon de Carbonnières refused).

The choice was made by the First Consul from lists presented by Cambacérès, Lebrun, Talleyrand and Lucien Bonaparte who often had the last word. Clarke also played his part, he imposed Shée, his uncle, on the Bas-Rhin; Lezay-Marnesia, a relation of Josephine's was to succeed him. Even when they had been ministers (like Bourdon, Delacroix and Faypoult), members of the Committee of Public Safety (Jean Bon Saint-André) or of the Directory (Letourneur), the prefects were no more than cyphers. The leading lights of the Revolution were dead or exiled. But these people, although of secondary importance, symbolized no less the spirit of 1789.

What was expected of these prefects? That they should represent the government in the departments; and that in cooperation with the department of Civil Engineering, which was enlivened by an exceptional team of great engineers (Prony, Becquey-Beaupré, Dumoustier, Brémontier), they should develop a programme of public works which had failed under the Directory, owing to lack of money. To improve the state of the roads seemed to be the very first priority, but they were also to turn their attention to the bridges, internal navigation, ports and fortifications.

The time was not yet ripe for assessment, but even though their first results were often brilliant, the prefects soon found themselves inundated with red tape. In his *Mémoires,* Vaublanc was to complain of the difficulties which he encountered as Prefect of the Moselle—but that was in 1810. Material problems were the first which the prefects had to overcome. Texier-Olivier reported on his installation to the Minister

of the Interior: 'After eleven days on the road and not without trouble
and exhaustion, I arrived yesterday at the post to which I have been
appointed. I was held up greatly by the bad condition of the roads and
the difficulty of travelling through the mountains.' The building
designated for the Prefecture was uncomfortable; on occasion it even
happened that the Prefect had to share it with the Bishop. At least the
distance from Paris ensured a greater degree of independence and
therefore greater power. It took news six days to reach the Prefect of
the Lot. At the time of the conspiracy of Year XII, this Prefect
complained of having known nothing of the plot except through the
papers and from information gathered by other officials. The prefects
were supposed to take the initiative. Their independence was, however, limited by the supervision more or less exerted over them within
the department by the bishop and by the commander of the military
division.

The law of 27 Ventôse Year VIII (18 March 1880) completed the
administrative reorganization of France by adapting the judicial
hierarchy to the new structure. Each district had a justice of the peace;
each *arrondissement* had a civil magistrates' court and a court of
summary jurisdiction, each department had a criminal court. Above
that, there were twenty-nine courts of appeal whose competences
corresponded roughly to the boundaries of the old provinces, and in
Paris there was a supreme court of appeal. There the Procurator-
General was Merlin de Douai, whom Molé described as having the 'gait
of a hyena', but whose knowledge of jurisprudence was exceptional.
The permanence of judges may have been re-established, but they had
become officials nominated by the First Consul, and at each tribunal a
government commissioner played the part of public prosecutor whilst,
at the same time, supervising his colleagues.

ECONOMIC REVIVAL

Of primary importance and more essential even than administrative
reorganization was a successful redressment of finances. The condition
was indispensable to any consolidation of the new regime. It is said that
in Brumaire only 167,000 francs remained in the state coffers.

Gaudin, a former collaborator of Necker, was posted to the
Ministry of Finance where he continued reforms which had been
undertaken by the Directory. In November 1799 an organization for
direct taxation was created. For the collection and assessment of taxes,
state agents were appointed to the elected bodies: directors and inspec-

tors drew up a register of taxes; there were receivers and tax-collectors—who were themselves obliged to pay a deposit. Like Ramel, who had attempted the same thing under the Directory, the government depended less on land tax than on indirect taxation (registration, tobacco, drink). The collection of taxes became regular and the state budget was finally balanced in 1802.

All that remained was the restoration of prestige. On 29 November 1799 Gaudin created a sinking fund, financed by the tax collectors' deposits, the direction of which was entrusted to Mollien who had, under the Ancien Régime, belonged to the Society of Farmers General. It was his job to diminish the public debt by buying back stock. In order to restore confidence in trade, the current account fund created by Perrégaux in 1796 made way for the Bank of France founded on 13 February 1800. It was a private bank controlled by directors (Perier, Perrégaux, Mallet, Lecouteulx, Récamier, Barillon) which had to ease and regularize the monetary market and to lessen crises by offering generous credit to financially embarrassed companies. Its main operations were the discounting of bills of exchange and promissory notes, advances on debt collections, the opening of current accounts and the issuing of promissory notes to stockholders. Its success was favoured by its association with the government. A law passed on 14 April 1803 gave it the exclusive right for fifteen years of issuing bank notes. The memory of *assignats* was apparently wiped out.

But the most spectacular psychological effect of the financial redressment was caused by the revival of the payment in cash of government rents. This measure contributed to increasing the popularity of the regime in bourgeois circles, and the renewed confidence made the establishment of a new coinage possible. In March 1803 a law brought in a franc of five grammes of silver—the famous 'Germinal franc' which was to remain stable until 1914.

The redressment of the first years of the Consulate was indeed spectacular, even taking into account the reforms already set in motion by the Directory. Must it be seen as 'the preface to a new Ancien Régime' or as the stabilization of the Revolution? Undoubtedly the prefects continued the work of the intendants, the Council of State replaced the King's Council, and the Prefect of Police of Paris replaced the Lieutenant-General. Bonaparte had belonged to the poor nobility of the Ancien Régime, and his entourage to the administration of the old monarchy. How could this have been forgotten when the moment came to reorganize France? But France had been transformed by ten years of revolution: that also had to be taken into account. From this compromise was born, according to Hippolyte Taine, 'contemporary France' whose institutions have lasted to this day. In fact they ensured the dominance of the new bourgeoisie, and not as has been wrongly suggested of a military dictatorship, for Bonaparte in order to lean on the notables, had specifically removed from the scene of political power the generals who had gravitated around the Directory. Regimes will pass, the institutions of the Consulate will remain unchanged. Empires, monarchies, and republics will be but symptoms of something else. Over and above the political instability, it is the permanence of the administration established under the Consulate which must be considered.

3

PEACE

The precise results of the plebiscite would be enough to confirm the absence of enthusiasm engendered by the *coup d'état* and by the new constitution. At the time of voting, the south was rather cool, Paris reserved and the Belgian departments icy. The approval of the army itself was not unanimous. As yet nothing differentiated the consular regime from the Directory. Great as Bonaparte's prestige may have been, it was hardly discernible among the clan of Thermidorians turned Brumairians. Many people thought they were witnessing a repetition of the Two-Thirds destined to perpetuate the power of the former members of the Convention, after the removal of those who were most compromised, like Barras.

Within two years Bonaparte's successes had changed public opinion, reassuring not only those who had benefited from the Revolution, bourgeois and peasants who had acquired national property, but also aristocrats who had remained in France, or who had returned. The *rentiers,* living off unearned income, were grateful finally to be paid in cash, and, according to police reports, the workers' confidence was also gained.

THE VENDÉE PACIFIED
The first success was the pacification of the Vendée. It had failed in 1795. Agreements signed in May had not been honoured as a result of excesses committed by both sides. Hoche, then at the peak of his glory, had worn himself out in sterile negotiations. In comparison with Bonaparte's, his was a strange career, doomed to failure. The execution of Stofflet, on 25 February 1796, had hardened positions on both sides, but had finally favoured the rise of Bernier the parish priest, of Saint-

Laud, to lead the Vendée. Bernier had been won over to the idea of an agreement with the Republic. Where Hoche had failed, Bonaparte was going to succeed, thanks to Bernier. After the *coup* of Brumaire, the latter, although without any illusions about the intentions of the First Consul, recommended the opening of new discussions. Confident of his authority, he ceaselessly demanded an end to hostilities. Despite calls to resistance from Frotté and then Cadoudal, a first armistice was signed on 24 November 1799 between Hédouville for the Consular government, and Châtillon, Autichamp and Bourmont for the rebels. The truce lasted until 22 February 1800.

In the Royalist camp certain illusions were being nursed with regard to Bonaparte's intentions, illusions which were unexpected after Vendémiaire and Fructidor, but then Barras and Augereau had played the principal roles. On the pretext of discussing some points of agreement, the Chouan chief, d'Andigné, was sent to Paris. Hyde de Neuville who, in the name of the Comte D'Artois, directed the 'English Agency' in the capital, prepared the interview through the intermediary of Talleyrand. On 26 December 1799 Hyde was ushered into the Luxembourg Palace in order to settle the details: 'A small man entered, dressed in a nasty greenish frock-coat. He hung his head, his appearance was almost shabby.' It was Bonaparte whom the conspirator mistook for a servant. But when the General approached the fireplace and lifted his head, 'he seemed to grow taller at once and the flaming, darting glance denoted Bonaparte'. The decisive interview took place the following day. There is no reason to doubt Hyde de Neuville's account. General d'andigné's is no less interesting. There is the same feeling of surprise at Bonaparte's physical appearance:

> We were shown into a ground-floor room. A small man with a bad complexion entered a few moments later. He wore an olive-green frock-coat, his hair was flattened and he had about him an air of extreme negligence, nothing led me to suppose that this could be an important man. I was therefore somewhat surprised when Hyde told me that this was the First Consul.

During the discussion, Bonaparte recognized, if not the legitimacy of the revolt in the west, at least the right of rebellion against an 'oppressor'. The treaty was discussed. The main clauses were agreed on: exemption from conscription in the rebellious departments, remission of overdue taxes, restitution of unsold property to the émigrés. The question of the king was mooted. 'I am not a Royalist,' affirmed

Bonaparte. Nevertheless all ambiguity was removed. . . . How could it have been otherwise? At the beginning of 1800 the First Consul was too closely linked with the old Thermidorians to make any sign of a reconciliation with the Royalists. This was confirmed to d'Andigné shortly afterwards:

> I absolutely did not want to leave Paris without letting Bonaparte know the real object of my mission. I wrote to him, therefore, to the effect that the purpose of my voyage had been to offer him, in the name of the Royalist leaders, all the means at their disposal if he would employ them to restore the monarchy. In this letter, which was extremely flattering to him, I spoke of the perpetual glory which he would bring to his name, of the eternal debt of gratitude which the French people would owe him. On the one hand, I indicated to him that there would be no reward above the service itself; on the other, I pointed out how little security he would find among men who, out of self-interest, had served different successive governments one after the other. Were he to suffer great setbacks, these men would turn against him with the same ease with which they had overturned the Directory as soon as they had seen that it was insecure.

This was a prophetic view which was to be confirmed in the immediate future by the June announcement of the outcome, at first uncertain, of Bonaparte's battle at Marengo. Bonaparte answered d'Andigné with a veiled refusal on 30 December 1799: 'Enough French blood has flowed in the last ten years . . .' However, for fear of his allies, he seemed not to wish to make this letter public. When, through the imprudence of the abbé Godard, all Hyde de Neuville's papers were seized, a copy of the First Consul's letter was among them. It was not published in the collection of Royalist documents presented to the public.

On 10 January 1800 Bonaparte sent out a proclamation in which he stated that there would be peace only with the submission of the rebels. 'Armed against France, there can only be men of no faith as of no nation, the perfidious instruments of a foreign enemy.' A concentration of troops under the command of Brune—called to the head of the Army of the West—gave added weight to these threats. First the aristocrats, Bourmont, Châtillon, d'Autichamp and Suzannet, gave up the struggle in January. Cadoudal only gave in in February after the uncertain battle of Grandchamp. As for Frotté, he fell into an ambush which was wrongly attributed to the First Consul. 'I did not give the order,' the latter in fact said, 'but I cannot claim to be angered by its execution.'

The Chouan rising was, for the time being, quelled. In his *Mémoires*, d'Andigné gave the reason for this set-back: 'The raising of arms by the Royalist party had initially had the consent of all right-thinking people in France. The good wishes of respectable people were behind us, but that was all. No individual outside our departments had rallied to us. England wished to supply us with some means of resistance; she refused to allow us to triumph.' If the Royalist cause had encountered some sympathy in the country as a whole, even d'Andigné admitted there would have been a change of opinion in favour of Bonaparte: 'On the whole the inhabitants of the Western Provinces saw with pleasure a treaty which gave them breathing space.'

In the south, reports were still alarming. On 4 February 1800 the police denounced the activities of the Abbé de Cyran, known as Desbaumes, and of the Marquis de Villard; 'The plan which has been worked out by foreign agents, the former heads of the Jalès faction and the life guards, is to destroy commerce, to intimidate traders, to cut communications, to oppose supplies to the army and to force the people to revolt.' 'Chouannerie'—the term was also used by the police in the southern regions—was hardly distinguishable from brigandage. After some rowdy debates in the Tribunate, the Legislative Body had to pass a resolution—the so-called Law of 18 Pluviôse Year IX (7 February 1801)—to establish certain courts without juries which would put a stop to brigandage. A decree of 4 Ventôse created special jurisdictions in thirteen western departments and fourteen southern departments. The effect was above all psychological: brigandage did not disappear entirely, but in the Vaucluse and the Var, everything points to the fact that the inhabitants experienced a great sense of relief, more especially as Bonaparte had been clever enough to temper firmness with indulgence. On 3 March 1800 he declared the émigré list closed as from 25 December. This made explicit his desire for national reconciliation whilst respecting the new rights of those who had acquired national property. Other measures were to follow' an estimated forty per cent of émigrés had returned by the beginning of 1802.

THE LAST TERRORISTS
The hesitation of the Jacobin generals on the left and the purging of provincial administrations had removed the danger of a civil war. The

former 'extremists' still had two alternatives at their disposal. They could provoke popular uprisings and exploit the discontent of the army or they could assassinate Bonaparte.

There was an outburst due to famine, otherwise the idea of a revolt in Paris was dismissed.

'The situation of the Faubourg Antoine,' explained a report of 16 May 1800, 'is such as to give no cause for concern. In fact trouble-makers try to make difficulties every day, but although most inhabitants are dissatisfied with the lack of work and the stagnation of commerce, they refuse to join any kind of movement and are firmly decided to play no part.'

Besides talking in cafés, the Jacobins in the capital only tried bribing the soldiers who had been there in large numbers since Brumaire. The Royalists had in fact done as much. The police reports of the first three months of 1800 bear witness to an undeniable disquiet. There was encouragement to insubordination; there were attempts to put some corps against the Consular Guard which was said to be better equipped and better paid; violence was unleashed in the streets in order to create a climate of uncertainty. Elsewhere, on the pretext of lack of supplies, riots broke out in certain provincial towns. In March rebels at Toulouse managed to get prices controlled, according to a bulletin of Fouché's dated 30 April, whose tone is anyway not alarmist. Disorders were noted in Marseilles as in other southern towns.

It is true that Jacobin propaganda was made difficult by the suppression of the liberty of the press. Jacobins were the main victims of this censorship. Newspapers had appeared free from any censorship until 17 January 1800. On this date a decree forbade all political journals published in Paris except thirteen (*Le Moniteur, Le Journal des Débats, Le Journal de Paris, Le Bien informé, Le Publiciste, L'Ami des Lois, La Clef du Cabinet, Le Citoyen français, La Gazette de France, Le Journal des Hommes libres, Le Journal du Soir, Le Journal des Défenseurs de la Patrie, La Décade philosophique*) which were allowed with the reservation that in the case of any opposition to the government, they would be immediately closed down. 'Newspapers' wrote Fouché, 'have always been the tocsin of revolutions; they announce and prepare revolutions and in the end make them indispensable. With a smaller number of newspapers, it will be easier to supervise them and to direct them more firmly towards the strengthening of the constitutional regime.' The spreading of news was controlled. There remained the clandestine circulation of pamphlets. These were soon crying out for 'tyrannicide'. Metge's *Le Turc et le Militaire français* invited the French to transform themselves into 'thousands of Brutuses'. An invitation which was heard. There were many attempts on the First Consul's life from Chevalier's infernal machine to a plan of one of General Hanriot's former aides to assassinate Bonaparte on the road to Malmaison. The police intervened: 'the Dagger Conspiracy', which aimed at stabbing the First Consul with a stiletto on 10 October 1800 in his box at the Opéra, probably resulted from 'café talk' blown up by the police. It ended with the arrest of the painter, Topino-Lebrun, of one of Barère's secretaries, of the Roman sculptor Ceracchi and the adjutant-general Arena, brother of the same Barthélemy Arena who was to have stabbed Bonaparte at the Council of the Five Hundred on 19 Brumaire. It is not suprising that, when on 24 December 1800, in rue Nicaise, an infernal machine exploded as the First Consul's carriage passed on its way to the Opéra, the 'exclusivists' were held responsible for the attempt. In vain did Fouché observe that the Jacobin circles were too well supervised for such an important *coup*. Bonaparte would hear nothing of it. A pretext had been found for ridding the capital of the last terrorists, although there was no reason to suspect the sincerity of the First Consul who was convinced of the Jacobin origins of the plot. On 14 Nivôse Year IX an act of the Senate decreed a hundred and thirty 'exclusives' be 'specially escorted outside the European territory of the Republic'. Some of them had been labelled '*Septembriseurs*' in order to make them all unpopular. Chevalier was shot; Arena, Ceracchi and Topino-Lebrun were sent to the scaffold. Lemare had for his part vainly tried to assassinate Bonaparte as he crossed the Alps at the time of the second Italian campaign.

The opposition on the left was crushed. There was absolutely no movement in its favour even when Fouché proved that the real instigators of the attempt in the rue Nicaise were Chouans—Saint-Rejeant, Carbon and Limoelan. The first two were caught and sent to the guillotine dressed in the red shirts of parricides. Hyde de Neuville denied any responsibility for the incident and fled. He could not, however, deny that the explosion had beent he Royalists' answer to the letter sent on 7 September by Bonaparte to Louis XVIII, who had again tried to return on 4 June. 'You must not hope to come back to France; you would have to walk over a hundred thousand bodies.' The carelessness of Saint-Rejeant and Carbon brought about the breaking up by the police of the Comte d'Artois's network which had remained active in the capital. Hyde de Neuville's rivals, Précy, Imbert-Colomès and Dandré who had founded the Augsburg agency in liaison with Louis XVIII, and who worked above all in the south, were no better off. Bereft of Wickham's English money, they left Augsburg for Bayreuth and were arrested by the Prussian authorities at the request of the French government, and their papers were sent to Paris where they were published by order of the First Consul in 1802.

The opposition seemed to have no success. The Brumairians who were themselves concerned over the hazardous affairs of the Italian campaign, had, after Bonaparte's departure for the peninsula on 6 May 1800, thought of preparing for a successor in case of death or defeat. Moreau, La Fayette, Bernadotte and a triumvirate including Talleyrand, Fouché and the senator, Clément de Ris, had been considered to replace the First Consul. The premature announcement of a French disaster at Marengo encouraged imprudence in certain quarters which allowed Bonaparte to stand apart on his return. The 'crisis' served his interests by impressing on the public that the First Consul was not a prisoner of the Brumairians' political faction—these ex-Thermidorians were by now hardly popular in the country. Bonaparte could place himself above factions and appear as the reconciler of the French.

THE RELIGIOUS PACIFICATION

Political peace would have been impossible without the suppression of the religious conflict. Because the Church and the throne had been linked under the Ancien Régime, the constituents had thought to reform the Church at the same time as the State through the Civil Constitution of the clergy. Because the Church's cause had seemed to be confused with that of the monarchy, the revolutionaries were carried away by a policy of dechristianization which many had not wanted. The Thermidorians decided, but too late, on a regime of separation which was above all inauspicious for the constitutional clergy who lost all official support, as well as losing the salary paid to them by the state. With a decimated clergy divided into constitutionals and non-constitutionals, buildings which had been confiscated and sold (Michelet tells in his memoirs how he was born in 1798 in the Church of the ladies of St Chaumont, rue St Denis, where his father had installed his printing press), and with faith on the decline in Paris and the provinces, the situation of the Church in France might have seemed desperate, besides which the unfortunate Pius VI was dying as a prisoner of the Directory. Many felt that the Apocalypse had come, that the end of the world was at hand. However, an élite had survived the persecutions and the masses remained attached to the outward forms of religion (bells, hymns and Latin) which theophilanthropy and the decadary cult had been unable to replace. Although fairly effective in urban circles, dechristianization had barely touched the country-side. The peasants had taken from it only that which served their ends—the removal of certain sexual taboos, and the general disappearance of tithes. So the new regime could not ignore the existence of a religious problem, a solution to which was essential to its future.

Catholics, in Paris at least, were reserved about a *coup* which appeared to bring no change since the government was still made up of Conventionals and ideologues. The First Consul's intentions were unknown and it is probable that Bonaparte himself had no very clear ideas about the religious problem, except that it was important to solve it as soon as possible.

Two solutions presented themselves to him. He had either to allow the movement for the restoration of religion to develop without interference, thereby setting the seal on the separation of Church and state, or he had to reach an agreement with the Pope in order to end the conflict and in this way to take credit for a rediscovered peace. Whereas some ideologues leant towards the first solution, Bonaparte was by temperament and by calculation drawn more towards the second. The difficulties which arose on the question of the Pope's authority over the French Church, the restitution of national property and the reconstitution of religious orders could not be resolved by liberty. It was more advantageous for the First Consul to negotiate with the Pope, not only in order to turn the Catholics away from the Bourbons, but in order to establish the authority of the new regime. In his report on the Concordat, Portalis perfectly summed up the state of mind of the First Consul: 'Order and public safety do not allow the institutions of the Church to be left to themselves.' Religion could turn out to be an efficient social restraint. Over and above pacification, Bonaparte wished for the restoration of a Gallican church devoted to himself. Calculated *raison d'état* and not personal faith dictated the behaviour of the First Consul. It is pointless to return to the old problem of Bonaparte's religious ideas.

The first measures taken by the Consuls were indicative of the government's desire to put an end to persecution. By the decrees of 18 December 1799 the non-alienated churches were again put at the disposition 'of the citizens of the communes in whose possession they had been on the first day of Year II', they were allowed to be open other than on the *decadi*. The decision coincided with New Year's Day. A police report noted that 'in the last few days there have been great crowds at the church doors. A large number of churches which were closed have been reopened to the satisfaction of crowds of both sexes. Many were shaking hands and kissing each other.' But it was still justifiable to query the real intentions of the First Consul. Before leaving for the Second Italian campaign, Bonaparte had explained to Talleyrand that he intended 'to make a channel for communications with the new Pope', Pius VII, who had just been elected with difficulty on 14 March 1800.

NEGOTIATIONS WITH ROME

The victory at Marengo, whilst securing Bonaparte's power, also allowed him to reveal his intentions. After having had a *Te Deum* celebrated on 18 June in the Cathedral at Milan—more to enlighten French opinion than 'to impress the people of Italy', as the *Bulletin de l'armée de réserve* claimed—he revealed to Cardinal Martiniana, at Verceil on the 25th, his plan to negotiate with the Pope. The news was immediately sent to Rome. Pius VII accepted the negotiations in principle without deluding himself as to the difficulties which would attend them.

Monsignor Spina, Archibishop of Corinth, was invited to Paris by Bonaparte. Having obtained the Curia's permission, he reached the capital on 5 November. It was only then that he discovered the name of the man who was to question him—the former Commissioner General of the Vendean armies, Bernier, to whom Bonaparte had entrusted the negotiations, under Talleyrand's authority. The latter, because of his past as a defrocked priest and because of his concubinage, could not in fact intervene directly. Neither could Grégoire, the 'constitutionals'' front-rank man, who endlessly preached mistrust of the diplomatic ruses of the Court of Rome. On the other hand, Bernier's career was more reassuring and he had proven diplomatic qualities. He needed them. Bernier knew how to be patient. He had secured the political pacification in the Vendée, and he put an end to the religious conflict— more than the generals, he was the principal architect of Bonaparte's glory. Very soon the discussions came up against the problem of the resignation of bishops. That of the constitutional bishops presented no problem, but it was not the same for former bishops whose resignation the Pope had requested. Could Pius VII insist on this final sacrifice from those who, despite the persecutions had wanted to remain loyal to the Holy See? There was a further problem: Rome wanted Catholicism to be declared the state religion of France, or at least the 'dominating religion', but the French negotiators had to contend with public opinion which would not have tolerated too obvious a return to the Ancien Régime. The last problem concerned Church property sold under the Revolution as belonging to the state. The Pope agreed not to demand restitution of these properties, but methods of compensation still had to be agreed. Rather than hand over a lump sum, Bonaparte preferred to undertake the maintenance of the clergy with a salary. This was a clever manoeuvre which favoured the treating of bishops and parish priests as state officials.

THE CONCORDAT

As a result of an intrigue by Talleyrand, a first scheme failed. Talleyrand had seen it as being too much to the disadvantage of married bishops, that is to say of himself. A new scheme was questioned after the explosion of the infernal machine. The discovery of the real instigators of the incident, Royalist agents, caused a hardening of the First Consul's attitude in the final discussions. Bonaparte was growing impatient. He needed the Concordat in order to secure his popularity and to separate the Catholics from the Royalist cause which still had many partisans. Rome's dawdling exasperated him. Threatened with a military occupation of the Eternal City, Pius VII's Secretary of State, Consalvi, had to leave for Paris. He was of quite a different calibre to Spina and was able to avoid the traps laid by Talleyrand. The final negotiations were dramatic. After three days of discussions over a text which had been endlessly corrected and re-corrected, 13 July was chosen for the official signing. At the very moment in which he was about to sign the deed with a flourish, Consalvi (expressly warned by Bernier) discovered that the text in front of him was not the one which had been agreed. There were protestations, threats to break off all negotiations and then the working out of a new Concordat. In fury, Bonaparte threw the document on the fire and dictated a ninth one which he planned to force on the negotiators without modifications. But Consalvi remained firm. At this point there was evidence of a certain characteristic of Bonaparte's. He did not press on in a path which could only lead to a deadlock. A conciliatory solution was reached. 'The convention between His Holiness Pius VII and the French government' was finally signed at midnight on 15 July. In the preamble, the government recognized the Roman Catholic religion as the religion of the great majority of French people. The reorganization of the Church of France was dealt with in the articles which followed. The principal points were that the Holy See together with the French government should examine a new division of dioceses; that the First Consul should nominate the bishops who would then be invested by the Pope; that bishops and priests should make an oath of loyalty to the government; in return they were to receive a salary and churches would be allowed to benefit from endowments.

Amongst believers there was a general feeling of relief. Without delay, Pius VII signed the treaty on 15 August 1801. By the papal brief *Tam Multa* he requested the legitimate bishops to hand in their resignation. Most of them obeyed; in the west a few of them formed a small anti-Concordat Church, royalist and schismatic, but they had over-estimated their public.

Shortly afterwards, Rome sent a legate to the capital and for his part Bonaparte replaced Cacault, his ambassador to the Eternal City, with a far more prestigious person, Cardinal Fesch, his uncle, the Archbishop of Lyons.

The new dioceses were soon decided upon and the new bishops ready to be designated: there were twelve former constitutionals (including Le Coz), sixteen non-juror bishops (for instance Champion de Cicé) and thirty-two new ones (among them Bernier who had hoped for the archbishopric of Paris, but was only made coadjutor and had to be content with the diocese of Orleans).

There were, however, reservations. They came less from the Roman Curia than from the French assemblies. The Council of State welcomed the Concordat with a reproachful silence; at the Tribunate the text of the agreement was openly mocked; the Legislative Body elected an atheist as president and the Senate co-opted Grégoire, the former constitutional bishop who had been a lively critic of the agreement. Finally, the army did not conceal its hostility.

Bonaparte made use of this easily dominated opposition in order, without the Pope's knowledge, to have drawn up by Portalis, the new Minister for Religion, organic articles which profoundly altered the spirit of the Concordat. From that time Rome could publish no Bull and could send no legate without the authorization of the government. It was forbidden for synods to meet without permission; the Gallican declaration of 1682 had to be taught in all seminaries. In future all ecclesiastics were to dress in the French way and every Church was to have the same catechism. In order to underline the fact that Catholicism had ceased to be the state religion, Chaptal, the Minister of the Interior, drew up the organic articles of the Protestant religions, providing for a state salary for Protestant ministers as for Catholic priests.

THE CONSEQUENCES OF THE CONCORDAT

On Easter Day, 18 April 1802, in Notre Dame de Paris, once again open for worship, there was a great religious ceremony to celebrate the return of 'peace to the conscience'. On coming away from the service, General Delmas, a fierce Republican, reputedly grumbled: 'What balderdash! The hundred thousand men who died to put an end to all this should have been there.' An unfair reproach. Except during the Terror, when Catholicism was confused with the monarchist cause, the Revolution had never, from its earliest days, been hostile to the Church. The Civil Constitution of the Clergy was more of an accident than a deliberate plot against Christianity. Popular enthusiasm, which was dominated by relief at the ending of the civil war, swept reservations aside and made an enormous bestseller of *Le Génie du Christianisme*, opportunely published by Chateaubriand.

And so the First Consul had achieved both his ends. He had established religious peace and he had submitted the Church to the authority of the state. With regard to the first point, Louis XVIII immediately appreciated the danger to his cause which the loss of the Catholic support represented. As soon as he learnt of the opening of the negotiations he directed credentials to Maury whom he charged with representing him at the Holy See and with causing the failure of all conciliation between the papacy and 'the monstrous government which has been devastating France for ten years'. But Pius VII sent Maury back to his diocese of Montefiascone. After the signing of the Concordat the Royalist fury manifested itself in violent pronouncements. Joseph de Maistre wrote: 'With all my heart I wish death to the Pope in the same way and for the same reason as I would wish it to my father were he to dishonour me tomorrow.' The weakness of Royalist opposition from 1803 to 1809 is partly to be explained by the settling of the religious conflict.

On the other hand Bonaparte's victory over Rome was more precarious. He had wished for a clergy dependent on the state but independent of the Holy See. But did Gallicanism, which found its justification at the time in a Christian monarchy, have any chance of a revival under a republic devoid of religious beliefs? The Holy See had to be preferable to a Head of State who admitted cynically that all he could see in the centre of Christianity was a political and social force. The Bishop of Nantes, Duvoisin, Fouché's friend and one of the most loyal partisans of the imperial regime, was to illustrate the anguish of bishops at the time of the conflict between the priesthood and the Empire: 'I beg the Emperor,' he dictated a few hours before his death, in 1813, 'to give the Holy Father back his freedom; the remaining moments of my life are still troubled by his captivity.'

TOWARDS A CONTINENTAL PEACE

With its coming to power, the Consulate found France to be in the grip of the second coalition formed by Austria, Russia and England. The re-establishment of peace was no less urgent for the fact that an invasion had been avoided in 1799. War with Europe had, after all, lasted for seven years. Bonaparte had been able to gauge the popularity he had acquired at the time of the peace of Campo-Formio.

As a first move he addressed himself to England and Austria in order to make them offers of peace, but neither the Prime Minister, Pitt, nor the Chancellor, Thugut, wished for negotiations. England's reply was even insolent: Pitt asked if the Jacobinism of Robespierre, of the Triumvirate and of the five members of the Directory had disappeared because of its concentration in one man who had been brought up in its heart. To tell the truth, Bonaparte did not expect a favourable reaction; but the cunning of his move assured him of support in France. In reply to attacks from the English press, *Le Moniteur* published anonymous articles which were, in fact, dictated by the First Consul: 'It is a very old practice to insult one's enemies. We cannot deny that in this field the English have the advantage over us.'

In order to bring down his nearest adversary, Austria, two solutions presented themselves to Bonaparte—a Turkish alliance in the manner of François I, or Louis XV's Prussian alliance. Descorches de Saint-Croix who was sent to Constantinople to negotiate over the problem of the occupation of Egypt with the Sultan saw his mission as made pointless by the capitulation of the French forces at El-Arish. The First Consul entrusted his faithful Duroc with a diplomatic mission to the King of Prussia. His welcome was favourable. Berlin was not hostile to a rapprochement which could bring Prussia a larger share of Germany. But in the end, the minister, Haugwitz, was only to offer mediation.

Bonaparte's feelings changed completely when Kléber—the English had not recognized the capitulation of El-Arish for which he was responsible—was victorious at Heliopolis. With his oriental dream re-awakened, Bonaparte decided in order to safeguard his conquest of Egypt not to discuss but to dictate the terms of peace.

THE SECOND ITALIAN CAMPAIGN

In Italy Masséna, besieged in Genoa, was heroically resisting Austrian pressure; Suchet was controlling the enemy on the Var. In order to put an end to Austrian attacks, Bonaparte conceived of a double offensive. Moreau was given the command of an army of a hundred thousand men who were to be sent on operations in Bavaria where, far from the Italian peninsula, they were to engage the forces commanded by General Kray. The First Consul was keeping Italy for himself. An audacious manoeuvre—the crossing of the St Bernard Pass—which the French press compared to the exploits of Hannibal, allowed him to surround the Austrians, but not without appalling suffering due to lack of equipment and of the experience necessary to manoeuvre such large numbers in the mountains. At the exit from the pass, Fort Bard, held by Captain Bernkopf, nearly proved fatal to the expedition. Narrow paths led round it, and these could only be followed by a small section of the already sorely tried artillery. Bonaparte entered Italy almost as ill-equipped as in 1796.

The purpose of this operation was to take the Austrians at Genoa and Nice from behind and to cut off the routes which led back to their bases. Now Bonaparte, instead of going to the aid of Masséna at Genoa, took the road to Milan which he entered on 2 June 1800. The reinforcements from Germany arrived by the St Gotthard pass. The Austrians were tricked and Mélas reacted as Bonaparte had expected by marching towards Milan to re-establish contact with his logistic support. But this scheme which had been so well worked out, was compromised by the premature fall of Genoa. Thereafter Mélas's army was in possession of a stronghold where provisions could be supplied to them by the British fleet. There was no longer any question of waiting for the enemy to attempt a breakthrough on Bonaparte's chosen territory; instead it was necessary to hurry towards Mélas in order to prevent his turning back towards Genoa. It was hard to make contact. Lannes was sent ahead with an advance guard. He waylaid the enemy at Montebello on 9 June, after which all trace of the Austrians was lost. In order to find them, Bonaparte was obliged to disperse his troops by sending off large detachments—one commanded by Desaix

—towards Genoa and the Northern Po. This was an act of imprudence which Napoleon was to repeat at Waterloo where at the decisive moment Grouchy's unit did not have time to return to the battlefield. On 14 June, Mélas, who had concentrated the whole of his forces on the Bormida, attacked Bonaparte whose total strength had been considerably depleted by the loss of the detachments which had been sent ahead. If these detachments had not returned in time, the battle which took place at Marengo could only have been won by the Austrians whose superiority in numbers was overwhelming.

At three o'clock in the afternoon, despite desperate resistance, Bonaparte's army decided on retreat and Mélas could have considered the Austrian victory as certain. But then, at about five o'clock, General Desaix, guided by the sound of the cannon, burst into sight with Boudet's division. The Austrians were taken totally by surprise; they had thought the battle over. By ten o'clock Mélas's troops had recrossed the Bormida—the French defeat was transformed into victory. A victory due to the return of Desaix who was killed shortly afterwards, and not to Bonaparte's military genius. With regard to this, Napoleon's accounts of the battle—from the bulletin of the Army of Italy to his dictations on St Helena—present very different pictures. The part played by Desaix has been minimized to the advantage of the First Consul.

THE TREATY OF LUNÉVILLE

The victory at Marengo was blown up by Bonapartist propaganda and strengthened the First Consul's authority at home. But the agreement signed by Mélas at Alexandria which provided for the Austrian evacuation of Piedmont, Lombardy and Liguria, did not put an end to the war. Vienna could still hope for a victory in Germany. Kray's defeats by Moreau in Bavaria gave this hope an illusory quality. Austria decided to negotiate. The new Chancellor, Cobenzl came to Lunéville for discussions with Joseph Bonaparte, but the arguments dragged lengthily on under the pretext that Austria's subsidy treaty with England forbade their making a separate peace before February 1801.

'It is easy to see,' wrote Joseph, 'that at each step towards a reasonable pacification, the Court of Vienna has been influenced by a realization of danger alone, and we must count above all on the attitude of our armies.'

Exasperated, the First Consul reopened hostilities. Whilst the Army of Italy under Brune's command started to march towards Lombardy,

Moreau, on the German side, surrounded the Archduke John on 3 December 1800 in the Forest of Hohenlinden and wiped out the major part of the Austrian forces, thereby opening the road to Vienna for the French. This was a dazzling victory for which Bonaparte was not to forgive his rival. With the success of Dupont at Pezzolo, Macdonald in the Alps and of Murat in the Kingdom of Naples, Italy was gradually passing into French hands.

The Austrians were therefore obliged to accept Bonaparte's conditions. Signed on 9 February 1801, the Treaty of Lunéville confirmed the Campo-Formio assignment of territories in Italy, Belgium and on the Rhine. In Italy, Austria kept only Venice. It recognized the Batavian, Helvetic and Cisalpine Republics—the latter had been increased by the addition of Modena and the Legations. Bonaparte's two objectives could be read between the lines of the clauses of this treaty: Italy and the Rhine. The Viennese recognition of the Cisalpine Republic consolidated French influence in Northern Italy. The ceding of Tuscany by the Archduke Ferdinand to the Infanta of Spain, wife of the Duke of Parma, confirmed that this influence had penetrated beyond the Cisalpine Republic. On the German side, Austria had to agree to the Rhine as the frontier between France and the Empire, but she found herself incapable of preventing French intervention in the problems concerning the compensating of the dispossessed princes of the Empire on the left bank of the river.

THE PEACE OF AMIENS

With Austria eliminated, there remained England and Russia. Bonaparte could expect great things from Russia. Paul I was in fact lost in admiration for him, and a francophile party had formed itself in a court wearied by the demands of the émigrés. To encourage this tendency, Bonaparte freed the seven thousand soldiers captured in Switzerland and wrote to the Tsar on 21 December 1800 in order to propose the alliance 'of the two most powerful nations in the world'. It was more especially a matter of dividing the Turkish Empire which would have given Constantinople to the Tsar and Egypt to France—a division to which England was hostile since she protected the Sultan in order to give herself cover in India. When the Tsar was strangled in his bedroom in March 1801 by officers bribed by the anglophile party, he was already moving away from London. He had, in December 1800, set up a League of Neutral Nations (Sweden, Denmark and Prussia) which closed the essential outlets of British trade. The bombardment of Copenhagen by the British Fleet, on 2 April, precipitated the dissolution of ,the League. The new Tsar, Alexander I, immediately initiated a rapprochement with England.

The news of Paul I's death was greeted with consternation in Paris: 'Paul I died during the night of 24–25 March,' *Le Moniteur* read. 'The English squadron crossed the Sound on the 31st. History will teach us how the two events are connected.' Meanwhile Bonaparte continued his overtures to Russia by sending Duroc to St Petersburg in April 1801.

He was aware that without maritime supremacy he could not conquer England, and therefore worked with this end in view. A secret pact had been concluded with Spain at San Ildefonso on 1 October. On condition that he promised an Italian kingdom to the Duke of Parma— a promise honoured at Lunéville—Bonaparte was to receive six warships and Louisiana which could serve as a point of purchase in the struggle against England. The Treaty of Aranjuez confirmed the stipulations of San Ildefonso on 21 March. By the Treaty of Florence on 29 March, the King of Naples ceded the island of Elba to France and closed her ports to the English. Agreements were reached with Algiers, Tunis and Tripoli. The Treaty of Mortefontaine, on 3 October 1800, re-established between France and the United States, 'a firm, inviolable and universal peace', based on the respect of the fundamental principles of maritime law.

The situation could be dangerous for England. Certainly war had brought her all the profits she could expect—the conquest of the French and Dutch colonies, the capture of Malta in September 1800, fruitful smuggling with Spain's American colonies, the growth of her influence in India, the imminent fall of Egypt after the assassination, on 14 June 1800, of Kléber. Kléber was replaced by the pale Menou who signed the capitulation of the French troops in August 1801.

But England was disturbed by the new prestige of France which spread to her own élite and gave rise to the development of a francophile party. Furthermore, the island's economy was threatened by a crisis arising from inflation and the bad harvests of 1799 and 1800. Increased prices provoked insurrections which had to be put down by the army. The Irish question and the King's madness further aggravated the situation. At the beginning of February, Pitt stood down in favour of Addington. Lord Hawkesbury, the new Foreign Secretary, made proposals for peace talks with Paris. In reply, Bonaparte sent Louis Otto of Baden to London. Negotiations nearly came to a halt over the Egyptian problem. Finally, at the preliminaries in London (1 October 1801) it was decided to return Egypt to Turkey, and Malta to her former owners, the Knights of Saint John, but the evacuation by the English was to be subordinate to the evacuation of the Neapolitan ports by the French. England was to return all her colonial conquests except for Trinidad and Ceylon.

Tired of war and desperately worried by the increase of poverty in the nation (fifteen per cent of English people had to be helped because of indigence), British public opinion welcomed the peace preliminaries with enthusiasm. There were, however, a few who deplored the lack of a trade agreement. France was grateful to the First Consul for having kept the promises of Brumaire by putting an end to conflict.

Finally a definitive treaty was drawn up at Amiens, where peace was signed on 27 March 1802 by Joseph Bonaparte and Cornwallis. An agreement had already been made with Russia on 8 October 1801 and on the following day with Turkey.

After ten years of being ravaged by war, Europe at last found peace again. In fact it was more in the nature of a truce. Napoleon had no intention of giving up his oriental dream and England had not been persuaded to recognize French hegemony on the Continent. With reference to Burke who, in 1790, saw in Europe a great void in the place of France, Sheridan exclaimed to the House of Commons, 'Now look at this map, France is everywhere.'

Nevertheless the Peace of Amiens had great repercussions.

The workers continue to speak of peace and of the First Consul with an enthusiasm which it is difficult to convey. Confidence in the government is boundless. It is not the same in high society where little attention is paid to this happy event and where, on the contrary, people seem appalled by it. They are content to say, with some kind of irony, that nowadays the people believe that larks will fall from heaven already roasted, and there is amazement at the constant good fortune which attends all the First Consul's activities.

In the provinces the news was greeted more warmly than in Paris, especially in the ports ruined by maritime operations. It is said that in Bordeaux houses were illuminated. If the prefects' reports are to be believed, the south, with the exception of the Mediterranean coast, was more reserved than the north. Whatever the case, Bonaparte's prestige was considerably increased by the ending of hostilities. After Campo-Formio and Lunéville, Amiens. Bonaparte seemed to be the man of peace. We are still a long way from the Corsican Ogre.

THE ECONOMIC CRISIS OVERCOME

In 1801 the stability of the regime was still in question. Undeniably the Jacobins and the Royalists had suffered serious set-backs. The announcement of the victory at Marengo had just strangled at birth plots which certain Brumairians, uncertain of the morrow, were hatching. The army said nothing despite the intrigues of some generals. Fouché made sure that the Parisian suburbs remained calm. But at any moment an uprising in the streets could carry with it all the forces of the opposition and sweep away the consular government. Above all, Bonaparte dreaded hunger riots. Neither Louis XVI nor the Montagnards had known how to deal with them. Perhaps the answer was force. 'Soldiers,' Napoleon confided to Gourgaud, 'do not like to fire on women, who with children on their backs have come to shout outside the bakeries.' The harvest of 1799 had been mediocre and the price of a bag of flour had risen suddenly. But in June order was restored. The news of the success at Marengo coincided with a fall in the price of bread – repercussions were all the greater.

Suddenly, in the spring of 1801, the cost of bread rose throughout France. In the capital, towards the end of summer, four pounds cost 18 *sous*. The tolerable limit for a worker's budget had been exceeded. The inhabitants of the outskirts of Paris, where the price was highest, came into the town for supplies and in this way the dearth was increased. Queues began to form outside the bakeries at four o'clock in the morning; a convoy was attacked in the rue Saint-Honoré. Pillaging became common in the provinces. In Marseilles, Lille and Amiens, the shops were protected by the army. Already orators who blamed the government for the penury were making speeches at street corners or on the market places. The atmosphere became dramatic when the economic situation grew worse simultaneously with the famine. There was unemployment in Lyons, Rouen and Sedan. The prefects' reports reflected a marked dampening of the public spirit. The bad days of the Terror seemed to have come again. The negotiations between France and England were eclipsed in the public mind by the economic deterioration and the fear of hunger. It was important to act quickly.

After some hesitation, on 27 November, Bonaparte convened his ministers for the Police and for the Interior, four councillors of state, Cretet, Defermon, Roederer and Réal, and the Prefect of Police, Dubois. Silence concerning the situation was imposed on the press:

'Famine is a subject that cannot be discussed with the people with impunity,' warned Chaptal. Five bankers were commissioned by a decree of 30 November to see that forty-five to fifty thousand hundredweight of grain per month reached Paris. Soon they were to be replaced by a company formed by the financiers Ouvrard and Vander-berghe.

'Bonaparte,' says Ouvrard in his *Mémoires*,

knew that all famines can bring unrest and commotion; worrying as they may be for an old government, they are even more so for a new one; he felt that his popularity was deserting him; he saw his authority debased if he were to tolerate rebellion, and compromised if he were to resort to force. He had at all costs to extricate himself, and so, with what eagerness did he accept our ideas!

Against a commission of two per cent, Ouvrard and Vanlerberghe planned to buy all the loads of grain which had already arrived in Dutch and English ports and to transfer them to Le Havre. 'The success was so immediate and so complete and the consignments which reached Le Havre and Rouen were so considerable, that in less than three weeks all fears were dissipated. It was all that was needed to put an end to the famine which afflicted France!' The psychological importance of the action is well illustrated by the Prefect of Police: 'These consignments have a good effect, they can prevent the rise in the cost of grain and flour and they do much to calm small worries.' The price of bread was now below the fatal level of 18 *sous* and the bakeries were settled once again. Paris had avoided a famine.

Shelters were opened in the capital and 'economical' soups were distributed to the poor in order to help the working-class population through the winter. Loans without interest were granted to some manufacturers in difficulty in Paris, Lyons and Amiens. 'In the circumstances in which we find ourselves, the Bank is too cautious,' Bonaparte wrote to Perrégaux, one of the regents, 'it could be more helpful.' The First Consul stimulated the Discount Bank whilst supervising the other establishments (the Commercial Bank, the Land Bank, the Caisse Lafarge and the *Société du Numéraire*) the conditions of which were reported to him by secret committees.

By the end of 1802, the crisis was over. Bonaparte had apparently succeeded where Louis XVI and the Revolution had failed. No attention was paid to the infinitely less serious nature of the depression, it was a question of panic rather than of hunger. Only the First Consul's triumph over famine and unemployment was noticed. This success was more decisive in the eyes of the public than Marengo, and the resulting psychological effect was as great as that caused by the Peace of Amiens.

4

A WASHINGTON CROWNED

After Marengo, 'the talk was all of heredity and dynasties,' wrote Thibaudeau, 'of strengthening the government and of weakening the influence of other state institutions, especially the Tribunate, and of finally organizing the nation. Lucien, the Minister of the Interior was one of the most ardent propagators of these ideas; Roederer supported them with all the power of his metaphysics and Talleyrand with the approbation of all departments.' Public opinion wanted a transformation of the First Consul's powers. Because of scruples or opportunism, Bonaparte kept quiet. Everything was almost jeopardized by Lucien who in October 1800 prematurely distributed a *Parallèle entre César, Cromwell, Monk et Bonaparte*. His brother sent him in disgrace to the French Embassy in Madrid and replaced him by Chaptal at the Ministry of the Interior. Nevertheless, encouraged by Bonaparte's entourage and the promises made to the Brumairians, the idea of a consolidation of consular power developed; it finally resulted in the Consulate for life in 1802, and two years later in the Empire.

'It is essential,' said Bonaparte to Thibaudeau, 'that either the governments which surround us should have a form which resembles our own, or that our political institutions should be rather more in harmony with theirs. A spirit of war always exists between the old monarchies and an entirely new republic. This is the reason for the strife in Europe.'

Thus the need to establish monarchical power in France for the sake of permanent peace was put forward. The word 'form' was essential. The spirit of the Revolution would be respected but the outward appearances of executive power would need changing; it required a title which would fit in with those of other European countries. The change was initiated with the excuse of expressing the nation's gratitude to the First Consul after the successes both at home and abroad of the two preceding years. But it was necessary to by-pass the 'political olass' who hesitated to go to the country yet again. The ballot of Year VIII had its origins in revolutionary procedure, those of Year X and Year XII were genuine plebiscites.

POLITICAL OPPOSITION

The Brumarians, and more especially the ideologues, were growing anxious. Bonaparte's importance was becoming greater and greater. The idea of a dictatorship other than collective horrified them all the more since Sieyès was removed from power. In conformity with Benjamin Constant's suggestions, he had filled the assemblies with his partisans in order to oppose the First Consul's ambitions with the legislative block, and the tribunes had manifested their suspicion at an early date. At the opening of the first session they had elected as their president, Daunou, a member of the Institut. Speaking of the Palais-Royal, where the assembly sat, Duveyrier had exclaimed: 'If one dared to mention here an idol of fifteen days, we would remember that in this place an idol of fifteen centuries' standing was overthrown.' Murmurings had greeted a speech by Riouffe comparing Bonaparte to Hannibal. The opposition won over the Legislative Body at which Grégoire presided. We must not exaggerate, however. The tax law of Year X, the law concerning prefectures and the legal reorganization were passed without difficulty.

The second session opened in November 1800. Inspired by Ganilh, Mallarmé, Andrieux and Constant (prompted in his turn by Madame de Staël), the Tribunate's opposition was resumed with increased violence. A scheme concerning national archives was turned down, as was the plan dealing with procedure for criminal verdicts. Bonaparte was annoyed. On 5 December, in the Council of State, he attacked 'these crusaders of 1793 whose self-respect seems offended by ill-extinguished memories.' He continued: 'the result of all this will be that they will see that we make as few laws as possible, we will be limited to those which are indispensable, like the budget law, and we will have to remain quiet about the rest.' The warning passed unnoticed. The battle continued over emergency measures, state debts and justices of the peace. Bonaparte grew angrier: 'There they are, two dozen metaphysicians who should be thrown overboard. They are vermin on my clothing; but do they think I can be outwitted, like

Louis XVI?' The threat to the ideologues was explicit.

A new session began in October 1801. Dupuis, the author of *L'Origine de tous les cultes* was elected to the Tribunate. This atheist, and former member of the Convention, was hostile to Bonaparte's negotiations with Rome—a further affront to the First Consul. The word 'subject' used in one of the peace treaties signed with Russia, Bavaria, the United States, the Two Sicilies and Portugal angered Ginguené, Costaz and Jard-Panvilliers. But the major battle was to be fought around the first schemes for the civil code. Bonaparte had to withdraw his text on the enjoyment of civil rights. This was a set-back. A set-back which was underlined by the intervention of Chazal who was insolent enough to remind Bonaparte, at the moment in which he was leaving to receive the title of President of the Italian Republic, that no French citizen could accept employment from a foreign government.

The renewal of a fifth of the tribunes and legislators gave Bonaparte the opportunity to rid himself of the partisans of ideology. Cambacérès, the Second Consul was behind the operation. Instead of having a draw which was normal procedure, the Senate named the three hundred who were to keep their seats and nominated the twenty-four new members, although this was not allowed by the Constitution. And so Benjamin Constant, Laromiguière, Ginguené, Daunou, Jean-Baptiste Say, Andrieux, Isnard, Ganilh and Bailleul all disappeared discreetly. In the Legislative Body, where resistance had been dulled because of the silence of its members and the anonymity of the votes, those who fell were either close to Sieyès or the friends of Madame de Staël: Bréard, Lacretelle . . . There were no protests. In fact the ideologues who were designated rather than elected had no popular support. They believed in the power of their own intellectual prestige with which to impress Bonaparte and public opinion. Deserted by half the Brumarians and abandoned by the public, who were quite indifferent to their fate, they were easily overcome. Self-interest took precedence over principle. Bonaparte's victories weighed more heavily than the complete works of the ideologues. Madame de Condorcet's and Madame de Staël's salons were not France.

Another area of resistance was the army. Its cadres were profoundly Republican which was hardly surprising. All the generals owed their rapid advancement to the Revolution. 'That which they took to be love of the Republic was above all love of the Revolution,' wrote Tocqueville. 'In fact, among the French, it was only the army whose every member without exception had profited from the Revolution and had a personal interest in it.' Idleness caused by peace on the Continent and jealousy of a more fortunate leader inspired resentment equally. Moreau was surrounded by agitation; Augereau, Lecourbe and Delmas held inflammatory discussions. At Rennes, in the entourage of Bernadotte and his deputy, General Simon, the plot known as the 'pots of butter' was hatched—these pots were used to convey anti-Bonaparte pamphlets. Bonaparte, however, without difficulty, called the ringleaders to order and Decaen left for Mauritius whilst Richepanse went to Guadeloupe. Lecourbe was dismissed and then implicated in a moral scandal; Brune became ambassador in Constantinople.

In addition to the Republican generals' lack of character (particularly Bernadotte who, as the brother-in-law of Joseph Bonaparte, was spared), was the attitude of the troops. Military plots remained the prerogative of the officers; the men played no part. The end of hostilities did not displease them. Suspected of dealing with the opposition and of being against the plan for a life Consulate, Fouché was removed from the police. With circumspection, it is true; the Ministry was abolished and the Minister nominated to the Senate.

Official exploitation through propaganda of Bonaparte's successes was facilitated by the fact that the Royalists were living in hope, the Jacobins were decimated and the idealogues were now out of action. Bonaparte appeared as a hero: he was the man who had re-established not only internal but external peace, he was the bulwark of the revolutionary victories, the national reconciler who allowed the return of the émigrés whilst safeguarding confiscated property. He had re-established the clergy but denied feudal rights. Popular enthusiasm inspired by Napoleon can be seen reflected in Lamartine's *Mémoires:*

The first display I can remember of political enthusiasm struck me in a village courtyard beside the yard of our house. It was the enthusiasm of a young man, named Janin, slightly more educated than his neighbours, who taught the children of the parish to read. One day, to the sound of a clarinet and a drum, he came out of the tumbledown building which served as a school. He gathered the boys and girls of Milly around him and showed them some pictures of great men which were being sold by a hawker. 'There,' he told them, 'you can see the Battle of the Pyramids, in Egypt, won by General Bonaparte. He is the small, thin, dark man, who with a long sabre in his hand is cutting capers in front of these heaps of hewn stones known as the pyramids.' The hawker spent his morning selling these echoes of national glory while Janin explained them to the wine growers. His enthusiasm communicated itself to the entire village. These were my first intimations of glory. A horse, a plume and a long sabre were always symbolic. For some time these people thought they were soldiers, perhaps for ever. On winter nights in the stables the hawker's goods were discussed and Janin was continually being invited to their houses to decipher the texts of these beautiful and truthful images.

Verse played its part—from that of the official poet to the modest pupil of a central school:

> Toi qui ne connus pas l'enfance dans la vie
> Qui suivant les élans de ton puissant génie
> Par la gradation craignant d'être arrêté,
> Arriva d'un seul pas, à la maturité.[1]

Or again:

> Il est l'espérance
> Et l'appui de la France,
> Il lui rendra toute sa splendeur,
> V'la ce que c'est d'avoir du coeur.[2]

The *Journal de Paris* represented Bonaparte as follows:

The prodigious strength of the First Consul's senses allows him to work for eighteen hours a day, to concentrate for eighteen hours on the same problem, or on twenty different ones without the difficulties and tiresomenesses of the one hindering the other.

A vast conditioning of the mind which began at the first Italian campaign, rapidly bore fruit. Both the notables and people were won over to Bonaparte.

There was a shift among the politicians who supported the First Consul and who were divided into clans: Fouché against Lucien; Talleyrand and Roederer, the eminence grise of the early days of the

---

[1] 'Thou, who in thy lifetime knew no childhood, who followed the impulse of thy powerful genius, fearing to be stopped by degrees, reached maturity in one single step.'
[2] 'He is the hope and the support of France, he will give her back all her splendour, that's what it is to have a heart.'

Napoleon's birthplace at Ajaccio in Corsica.

Napoleon's mother. Laetizia Bonaparte was renowned for her beauty. She was even accused of having been unfaithful to her husband, Charles Bonaparte, with M. de Marbeuf. Concerning her son's destiny, a now famous saying has been attributed to her: 'Long may it last!'

Bonaparte aged sixteen. At the time he was as yet undecided between military glory and a literary career. Four years later the revolution was to break out.

Bonaparte's first love. Josephine de Beauharnais, a general's widow who had become Barrass's mistress under the Directory, married Bonaparte with little enthusiasm. She grew gradually fonder of him, whereas he, having no children, was considering repudiating her.

After the defeat of Austria in 1809, Napoleon married Marie-Louise, the Emperor's daughter. She was no beauty.

The Army of Italy in the state in which it was found by Bonaparte. It was undeniably destitute but the quality of the soldiers was unarguable. It was with them that Bonaparte won his first victories.

Bonaparte embarked for Egypt from Toulon in the greatest secrecy. Soldiers had been joined by scholars which lent a certain tone to the expedition. Note that the uniforms were absolutely unsuited to the Egyptian climate.

The Egyptian Campaign was the point of departure, not only for the fashion in things Egyptian (sphinxes, pyramids, etc.) but for Egyptology as a science. Champollion was the first to decipher the hieroglyphics under the Restoration.

This picture shows the plans for the invasion of England provoked by the breaking of the Peace of Amiens: a Channel tunnel (already!), an attack by balloon, and the landing of an army carried across by a fleet from Boulogne.

Napoleon's coronation on 2 December 1804 was met with derision throughout Europe. Here the Emperor crowns himself. Pope Pius VII is depicted as obese though he was in fact thin, and Josephine was not so stout, either. An interesting comparison can be made with David's *Sacre*, which is tied to Napoleonic propaganda.

The Battle of Eylau was one of the most indecisive and bloody of Napoleon's battles. Gros's contemporary painting can be seen today in the Louvre.

Paris at the beginning of the nineteenth century. In the forefront is one of the mills which provided the capital with flour.

The development of the port at Cherbourg was one of the most important works undertaken during the Empire. This statue is post-Empire.

Four portraits of Napoleon in 1795, 1796, 1802, 1810, showing the man's prodigious rise and the physical fattening of the face. The Emperor's stoutness can be attributed to treatment by his doctor, Corvisart, which is supposed to have cured the scabies caught at the Siege of Toulon.

Propagandist picture in which the Emperor's four brothers feature: Joseph, Lucien, Louis and Jerome; his three sisters, Caroline, Pauline and Elisa; his brother-in-law, Murat, and his son, the Aiglon.

Four of Napoleon's best generals: although Kléber was killed in Egypt, Murat became King of Naples, Massena Prince of Essling, and Ney Prince of Moscova.

Consulate, also against Fouché. The most flexible Brumarrians, or those most convinced of the necessity of strengthening executive power, Talleyrand, Cambacérès and Roederer, leaned towards the moderates, Barbé-Marbois, Muraire, Dumas, Portalis, victims of Fructidor and partisans of a constitutional monarchy. Siméon summarizes as follows the attitude of these heirs to the 1789 'monarchists' who replaced the ideologues.

> The people, who are the owners and dispensers of sovereignty can change their government. The return of a dethroned dynasty, overthrown more because of its faults than by virtue of any misfortune, could not suit a self-respecting nation. If the Revolution has tired us, are there not other alternatives, now that it has run its term, than the replacement of this yoke which was broken twelve years ago? Let us not mistake for a revolution that which is but the consequence of the Revolution. We will bring it to an end.

In this way an element of 'neo-monarchism' developed which favoured the permanent consolidation of Bonaparte's power.

THE CONSULATE OF LIFE

Bonaparte's success justified a measure of national recognition which the Tribunate demanded on 6 May 1802. But the Senate, whipped up by Fouché, the leader of partisans of the Republic, only offered the premature re-election of Bonaparte for a period of ten years. With a mixture of political cunning and legal guile, Cambacérès advised the First Consul to accept only 'if the will of the people commanded it', which was tantamount to demanding another plebiscite. The wording of the question completely changed the decision of the Senate. The nation was asked, not about a premature re-election for ten years, but about a renewal for life of Bonaparte's power.

'Should Napoleon Bonaparte be Consul for life?' That was the question.

It is worth noting, in passing, the new designation. Until now it had been 'Citizen Bonaparte' or 'General Bonaparte'. For the first time since Bonaparte left Brienne, where he had been subjected to so much sarcasm, his unusual Christian name was brought out from the shadows: 'Napoleon', until then often spelt 'Napoleone', and it was to appear in an official text. There had been a move from General Bonaparte to Napoleon Bonaparte, the time was near when he would be called 'Napoleon', 'Bonaparte' being relegated to obscurity.

The plebiscite on the question of whether Napoleon Bonaparte should be Consul for life was conducted in exactly the same way as the referendum on the Constitution of Year VIII. There were 3,600,000 Yeses to 8,374 Noes. On 2 August 1802 the Senate, for good or for ill, proclaimed Napoleon Bonaparte, 'Consul for Life'.

The number of Yeses had increased by 500,000, which was to be expected even if there had been some fiddling. They reflected public opinion. The peace of Amiens, religious pacification and the amnesty for the émigrés had earned for Bonaparte a great many Royalist votes, as well as the votes of moderates who had formerly abstained. On the other hand he was abandoned by the Republicans. The registers no longer showed the names of conventionals who had stood aside since Brumaire, and the ideologues of the Institut avoided the poll. And so the divorce between Bonaparte and the advance wing of the Brumairians was confirmed. As for the eight thousand Noes, many of them came from the army. Certain measures, however, had to be taken. Stanislas de Girardin wrote:

> One of our generals summoned the soldiers in his command and said to them, 'Comrades, it is a matter of nominating General Bonaparte Consul for life. You are free to hold your own opinion; nevertheless, I must warn you that the first man not to vote for the Consulate for life will be shot in front of the regiment.'

Among the opposition the reappearance of a distinguished face from the past is worthy of note: La Fayette. 'I cannot vote for such authority until the freedom of the public has been adequately guaranteed, and so I shall give my vote to Napoleon Bonaparte.' In a letter to the First Consul he justified his vote at length.

> General, as the first among men who see themselves in the context of all centuries, you cannot have wanted a revolution with so many victories, so much blood, pain and wonder, to end for yourself and the world in an arbitrary regime.

In a register of the Department of the Seine, under the obscure name of Sieur Duchesne, the following vigorous sentence is to be found: 'As every friend of liberty should do, I answer no, because this perpetuation of power in the same hands can, under no circumstances, be allied with the principles of a wisely constituted government.' Duchesne was not harassed.

THE THERMIDOR REFORM OF YEAR X

The *senatus consultum* passed on 4 August 1802 after the plebiscite modified the regime instituted in Year VIII. It considerably increased the powers of the First Consul to whom the right of presenting his successor to the senate was granted. This was an important step towards heredity. The First Consul was also empowered to decide all peace treaties and alliances and to designate the other Consuls; he was also given the *droit de grâce*, or right of reprieve.

The changes favoured the Senate too. Although it no longer played any part in the designation of Consuls, it gained the power to control, by means of a *senatus consultum* (voted by two-thirds of those present), 'everything which has not been provided for by the Constitution and which is necessary to its working'; it had the duty of explaining 'those articles which give rise to different interpretations'; and finally, with a relative majority and by a *senatus consultum* it could adopt various exceptional measures. It could reduce individual liberty, suspend juries and dissolve the Legislative Body or the Tribunate. Whilst having its powers increased, the Senate was at the same time tamed: its members were still recruited by co-option, but the First Consul had the right to bring their number up to a hundred and twenty by appointing 'without preliminary presentation by the departmental electoral colleges, citizens distinguished by their talents or their services'. Besides, the First Consul had important means of enticement at his disposal, not only because of the suppression of the inconsistency which had in Frimaire Year VIII denied the senators all other public office, but by the distribution of *sénatoreries,* endowments of land for life with a house and an income of 20–25,000 francs (one per appeal-court competence). So the Senate became the most important of all the state assemblies. But in fact, as Bonaparte confided to his brother, Joseph, 'the Senate derived all its importance from its agreement with the government; it was destined to be a body of old and tired men, incapable of struggling against an energetic consul.'

Equally, the other assemblies lost an important part of their powers. The Legislative Body no longer sat regularly; the Tribunate was reduced to fifty members and the Council of State gradually became merely an administrative jurisdiction.

The system of confidential lists was replaced by electoral colleges in cantons, *arrondissements* and departments. The regional assemblies, made up of all the citizens domiciled there, presented candidates to the municipal councils and to the justices of the peace, from the list of the hundred most highly taxed drawn up by the prefect. It designated the members of the electoral college of the *arrondissement* and the electoral college of the department. The latter were chosen from the list of the six hundred most highly taxed. The colleges of the *arrondissements* presented two candidates for every vacant seat in the Tribunate and in the Legislative Body, the departmental colleges presented two candidates for every vacant seat in the Legislative Body and in the Senate. It was a return to national representation by locally elected members, and was apparently an advancement of the representative principle although the system was one based on tax-paying electors. In fact, the First Consul indirectly controlled these appointments since he nominated the presidents of the electoral colleges and could, by his own authority, add ten members to each *arrondissement* college and twenty to the departmental colleges.

It was during the summer of Year X that the, as yet republican, regime of Brumaire was transformed into a despotism which lacked only the name 'monarchic' or 'imperial'.

A RETURN TO THE MONARCHIC FORMS OF POWER
Here is Thibaudeau's account of Bonaparte's arrival at the Senate on 9 Fructidor Year XI.

> It was the first time that he really displayed in public the whole magnificence of his supreme power. From the morning, the bridges and the streets where he was to pass were guarded. A double row of troops lined the streets from the Tuileries to the Luxembourg Palace! The First Consul was in a coach drawn by eight horses. He was followed by six government carriages for the Second and Third Consuls, the ministers and speakers from the Council of State, and accompanied by a escort of many magnificent aides-de-camp, generals of the guard and inspectors-general from all the different regiments. A deputation of ten senators greeted him at the foot of the steps.

What a far cry from the Consul of Brumaire. This was already a sovereign making his way to the Luxembourg Palace.

Liveries reappeared, people no longer addressed each other in the second person singular, there were ceremonies, masses at Saint-Cloud and there was hunting. A Consular Guard was introduced. A predominantly military court was created, but there crept into the entourage of Josephine (who in 1802 was given an official rank) ladies with aristocratic names—Mesdames de Rémusat, de Lauriston, de Talhouet and de Luçay. Etiquette became more and more particular and court dress was worn. Everything presaged the revival of monarchical forms and the great laws of Year X foreshadowed the social politics of the Empire. Whilst the return of the émigrés was being accelerated, the re-establishment of a nobility seems to have been hinted at in the creation of the Légion d'honneur which met with a lively resistance. It required three sittings of the Council of State and then it was passed by a narrow margin (14 votes to 10); it was also violently resisted by the Tribunate and the Legislative Body where the scheme was approved with difficulty.

No doubt it was designed to reward soldiers—or civilians—who had rendered great services to the Republic. For the arms which had previously been given them, was substituted a hierarchical order, consisting of sixteen cohorts, an administrative councillor and a Grand Chancellor. Its riches came from unsold national property. Although its members were under an obligation to pay lip service to the ideal of combating any re-establishment of the feudal regime and the titles appertaining to it, some Brumairians saw this vanguard of a new patriciate as a betrayal of the Republic by Bonaparte.

On 28 Floréal Year X (18 May 1802) Savoye-Rollin attacked the scheme in the Tribunate: 'The institution [of the Légion d'honneur] literally wounds the constitution;' he went on to specify, 'By consenting to it among you, you accept a patricite which will have a growing tendency to give you back an hereditary and a military nobility.' In his turn, Chauvelin denounced it as a body established and spread throughout France thanks to the chief towns of the cohorts, whose hierarchy together with its dependent and collateral branches competed to form a large and powerful organization which threatened a return to that 'esprit de corps which distorts the finest thoughts and corrupts the most generous intentions'. Finally the Tribunate only approved the plan by 56 votes to 36. The following day the Legislative Body declared itself by a vote which, when the conditions of the times are taken into account, was hardly more convincing—116 in favour and 110 against.

Despite all the reservations expressed, the Légion d'honneur, instituted on 19 May 1802, met with tremendous success. Nearly 9,000 decorations were conferred in two years. Intellectuals, like Stendhal, were disdainful. The army was enthusiastic as can be seen from Coignet's description of the great distribution of 14 July 1804. The date was chosen deliberately by Bonaparte. By 1808 there were 20,275 members of the Légion d'honneur.

Even if he sometimes came up directly against the left, Bonaparte knew how to preserve the acquisitions of the bourgeois revolution. The law of 11 Floréal Year X left secondary education based on Latin and mathematics to the notables. The Civil Code, which was the work of Portalis, Tronchet and Maleville, was only promulgated on 21 March 1804. It sanctioned the disappearance of the feudal aristocracy and the maintenance of the principles of 1789: individual liberty, equality under the law, freedom of work. Codification in itself was contrary to the spirit of the Ancien Régime. But on the subject of divorce (the banning of divorce for reasons of incompatability, the continuance, with restrictions, of divorce by mutual consent and the re-establishment of the *séparation de corps* which had been annulled by the Revolution), on women as minors and on the exclusion of illegitimate children from inheritance, the code marked a definite turning back in comparison with revolutionary legislation. The will of the father became, once again, the basis of the family, and the division between legitimate and illegitimate families was re-established. Free enterprise and competiton, dear to bourgeois hearts, were proclaimed. It was a code made for a conservative society whose main interest lay in the owning of land—stocks and shares were ignored—it could be called 'the victory of the legal mind over the philosophical mind'. It was a welcome victory for the departmental notables according to the prefects' reports. Thereby, a social hierarchy was established in favour of the notables, the liberal professions were reconstituted and given rules, chambers of commerce were established in large towns. So the bourgeoisie became the main support of a regime which also guaranteed the peasants against a return to feudalism. Only the workers were sacrificed. The law of 22 Germinal Year XI (12 April 1803) renewed the interdiction against their forming themselves into groups and compelled them to carry *livrets*. But the First Consul kept the price of bread down (it fell from 12 *sous* a pound in 1803 to 9 *sous* the following year), and guaranteed employment thanks to a revival of trade, which furthermore encouraged a rise in salaries.

So the evolution towards a monarchic regime could continue. It was in fact precipitated by the renewal of conflict with England. Since the English had initiated the hostilities without declaring war, France could not blame her leader for the conflict. Rather, there was a tendency to increase his power in order to ensure the defence of the land. A dictatorship of public safety was needed. How could it be entrusted to anyone other than Bonaparte? At this moment the Royalists inopportunely chose to renew their plotting against the First Consul. This resulted in a strengthening of his popularity and in his fate being tied to the fate of revolutionary victories.

THE CONSPIRACY OF YEAR XII

In October 1803, several Chouans, taken by surprise in Paris, were arrested, taken before a military commission and condemned to death. One of them, Querelle, asked to be allowed to speak before being shot. He revealed that he had arrived in the capital at the same time as Cadoudal who planned to assassinate the First Consul. The revelations sowed terror among the police who were already disorganized because of Fouché's dismissal on 15 September 1802. The *grand juge*, Régnier, who was in charge of the Police, assisted by the Councillor of State, Réal, did not have his predecessor's breadth of vision. Now the affair began to take on considerable proportions as the result of the confession of a certain Bouvet de Lozier, who following a failed suicide attempt, named the instigators of the plot as Moreau, the hero of Hohenlinden, whose prestige in the army was comparable to Bonaparte's, and Pichegru who had been deported at the time of the Fructidor *coup d'état* and who had secretly returned to France. Interrogation of Bouvet revealed the main aims of the plot as 'the re-establishment of the Bourbons, the reorganization of assemblies by Pichegru; a movement in Paris supported by the presence of a prince; an attack directed against the First Consul by main force; the presentation of the Prince to the armies by Moreau who would have already prepared the way.'

After an extraordinary meeting of the Council, Bonaparte decided to arrest Moreau. But public opinion was against him. Bonaparte's rival was seen as the victim of political machinations, more especially as Cadoudal and Pichegru could not be found. All the police reports indicate the emotionalism of the Parisians and the discontent of the army. However, events soon turned in Bonaparte's favour. Pichegru and then the Comte d'Artois's representatives, Polignac and Rivière, fell into the hands of the police. In his turn, Cadoudal was arrested, which proved the reality of the plot. The crowd assisted the police in apprehending the Chouan. It was a sign that political opinion had made an about-turn.

During the interrogation of Cadoudal, mention was made of a

prince whose arrival in France wa expected. Now Louis de Bourbon
Condé, Duc d'Enghien, happened to be at Ettenheim near the French
frontier. On the advice of Talleyrand (who later denied it), Bonaparte
had him removed from German territory on 15 March 1804. The Duke
arrived in Paris on 20 March, and during the night of 20th–21st he was
brought before a rapidly formed military commision. He denied all
participation in a plot but admitted having taken arms against revolutionary France. Organized by Savary, his execution took place at 3
o'clock in the morning in the moat of the Château de Vincennes.

Whatever Chateaubriand may have claimed, his death caused not a
stir in public opinion. Joseph reports that during a dinner at
Mortefontaine, in March 1804, he pitied the Duc d'Enghien his fate,
while a most eminent member of the former aristocracy, who had not
emigrated, approved of the execution: "Should the Bourbons, then, be
allowed to plot with impunity? The First Consul is deceived if he
supposes that the nobility who did not emigrate, above all the historic
nobility, have a great feeling of interest for the Bourbons. How did
they treat Biron, and my ancestor, and a great many others?" It was
not until the Restoration that the principal actors in the drama—
Talleyrand, Savary and Napoleon himself in the *Mémorial*—attempted
to justify themselves.

At the time, the investigation into the conspiracy continued. The
case against Moreau and Cadoudal (Pichegru had been found strangled
in his cell), opened on 25 May 1804. On 25 June twelve Chouans
including Cadoudal went to the scaffold. The aristocratic conspirators
(Polignac and Rivière) were pardoned. Moreau, initially condemned to
two years in prison, was finally banished.

Badly planned, the great conspiracy of Year XII was, furthermore,
the victim of economic circumstances; the low price of bread, and the
lack of unemployment removed the main causes for popular discontent. The protagonists of the plot seemed to be the allies of a country at
war with France. Finally, Moreau's ambiguous attitude discouraged
the army. The failure of the plot did not put an end to Royalist
agitation—other plots were to follow—but it was a decisive blow. In
future anti-Napoleonic action was to be concentrated in secret
societies, military and masonic lodges, or mystical and charitable
associations. In 1812 their united action helped by an economic depression resulted in General Malet's *coup d'état*.

For the time being the conspiracy of Year XII involuntarily served
Bonaparte's ends. The revolutionaries saw in the consolidation of the

First Consul's power, which since the execution of the Duc d'Enghien had become associated with 'the horrors of the Revolution', the only bulwark against attempts to restore the monarchy. It was not without cause that the regicide conventional, Alquier, declared, 'The im pending elevation of the First Consul to the imperial and hereditary dignity completely satisfies my wishes.' Bonaparte was more than ever 'the saviour'.

THE CONSTITUTION OF YEAR XII

The conspiracy made a large section of public opinion indignant. Cleverly, Bonapartist propaganda took a hold of public emotion. Well directed, the press made its readers understand the necessity of stabilizing the First Consul's power on solid foundations. 'The great number of plots which are woven against my life inspire no fear in me,' affirmed Bonaparte. 'But I cannot deny a deep feeling of distress when I consider the situation in which this great people would have found itself today had the recent attempt succeeded' (it is to be understood that the advantages resulting from the Revolution would immediately have been threatened). The Senate replied by an address on 27 March which envisaged constitutional reform. Heredity was the key problem. Consulted as to whether the government of France should have an hereditary basis, the Council of State showed hesitation. The expected proposition came from the Tribunate. A former revolution-ary, Curée, presented a motion 'which tended towards the idea that Napoleon Bonaparte, at present First Consul, should be declared Emperor of the French and that the imperial dignity be declared hereditary in his family.' Only Carnot opposed this proposition publicly. On 4 May the vote of the Senate approved it. Ideas for formulas began to flow. The new constitution was rapidly drawn up and was promulgated by a *senatus consultum* on 18 May 1804 (28 Floréal Year XII).

This text of 142 articles founded a new regime, the Empire, and adapted old institutions to this regime.

'The government of the Republic is entrusted to an emperor who takes the title of Emperor of the French.' The title had been chosen in preference to that of 'King' in order to take care of revolutionary sensibilities. Napoleon had been beguiled by its reference to Charlemagne and by its 'unlimited' nature.

'His numerous enemies in Europe,' observed Thiers, 'by every day attributing to him plans which were either not his or not yet his, by repeating in a multitude of papers that he was dreaming of rebuilding the Eastern Empire, or at least that of the Gauls, had prepared all minds, even his, for the title of Emperor.'

The second article designated the holder, Napoleon Bonaparte, without specifying the precise nature of his power. The Empire was a reality established by force of circumstances. The imperial dignity was to be handed on to the Emperor's direct descendants—excluding women or their issue (echoes of the old monarchy), but as he had no son, Napoleon could choose his successor by adoption from among the children and grandchildren of his brothers. These adopted children would have to make way for any children born to Napoleon after their adoption. The novelty lay in adoption: because he had made the Empire, Napoleon assumed the right to dispose of it as he pleased. Public opinion agreed to heredity largely because Napoleon had no children. It seemed, above all, to be the surest means of maintaining a stable government and of putting an end to intrigue and plotting. This in no way represented the acceptance of a Bourbon-style dynasty. The Empire was first and foremost a dictatorship of public safety, designed to preserve the achievements of the Revolution.

A new stage was reached in the reconstitution of the nobility by the creation of six important dignitaries (Grand Elector, Arch-Chancellor, Arch-Treasurer, Arch-Chancellor of State, Grand High Constable and Grand Admiral) and of important officers of the Empire (among them sixteen marshals). The dignitaries presided over the electoral colleges.

The self-evident other side to this new absolutism was that, from the Emperor to the humblest official, all holders of authority were called on to swear an oath of allegiance. In this way the Empire established a difference between itself and royalty, it retained an element of the 'public safety' outlined above.

In addition, two commissions were instituted in the Senate—the commission for individual liberty, whose duty it was to examine arbitrary arrests, and the commission for the liberty of the press, designed to restrain the abuses of censorship. In fact these commissions merely gave advice to ministers and could apply no sanctions.

A third plebiscite was organized. The people were asked to accept 'the heredity of the imperial dignity through the direct, natural, legitimate and adoptive descent of Napoleon, and the direct, natural and legitimate descent of Joseph Bonaparte and of Louis Bonaparte'. There was no mention of the imperial title.

The results were announced on 6 November 1804: 3,572,329 Yeses to 2,569 Noes. In some communes the registers merely bear the words 'Unanimous vote of Yes'. Many Parisian votes were qualified.

Aspiring poets expressed themselves wholeheartedly:

> Regnez nouveau César sur la nouvelle Rome,
> Et n'oubliez jamais qu'un empereur est homme.[1]

Or again:

> Je ne suis rien et, je fais plus qu'un roi
> Eux si puissants que feront-ils de moi?[2]

The results occasioned great rejoicing. A general, commanding the Department of the Charente, refused any form of celebration. His name? General Malet.

THE CORONATION

An unexpected conclusion to the plebiscite was the coronation. The architect of the Concordat had, like Louis XVI, the last King of France, to call upon the divine right. The idea seemed shocking to the Brumairians who were still too steeped in the spirit of the Revolution. There was a lively resistance to it in the Council of State. The ceremony was to take place in Paris rather than Rheims or Aix-la-Chapelle, and Napoleon took it into his head that in order to revive the imperial tradition he should make the Pope come to the capital. Pius VII accepted in the hope of gaining some concessions over the organic articles. A small difficulty nearly upset everything. The religious marriage of Napoleon and Josephine was hastily arranged for the night of 1–2 December.

On 2 December 1804 in Notre-Dame and in the presence of the diplomatic corps, the court, the assemblies and the representatives of the 'loyal towns' a sumptuous ceremony took place which has been immortalized by David and Isabey. The ceremony had been carefully scrutinized and revised by Portalis and Bernier. It was essential to avoid anything which might give rise to laughter from the unbelieving public and anything which would have indicated the superiority of the spiritual over the temporal. Napoloen, as is well known, crowned

---

[1] 'Reign, new Caesar, over a new Rome, and don't forget that an emperor is a man.'
[2] 'I am nothing and I do more than a king; they who are so powerful, what will they do with me?'

himself—an action not of independence, nor of personal improvisation as is often said, but one which resulted from protocol and which had been discussed at length as had public communion. Then the Emperor himself crowned Josephine. Was this a capricious act, did he do it for love, or was it a political manoeuvre?

After the withdrawal of the Pope came the oath. The solemn oath was to counter-balance the religious ceremony and was essential to satisfy the scruples of the former revolutionaries. At this moment the alliance between Napoleon and the notables was solemnly sealed. 'I swear,' declared the Emperor, 'to uphold the integrity of the Republic's territory, to respect and to impose the respect of the laws of the Concordat and religious freedom, to respect and impose the respect of equal rights, political and civil liberties, the irrevocability of the sales of national property, to raise no duty and to establish no tax except through the law, to uphold the institution of the Legion of Honour, to rule only in the interests of the happiness and glory of the French people.' By this oath, Napoleon asserted himself as the 'crowned representative of the Revolution triumphant'. He announced that he would serve the interests of the post-1789 propertied class, hoping in turn to be served by them and, perhaps, thinking already of merging these new notables with the old families. He presented himself, wrote Balzac in *Les Paysans* as 'the man who vouched for the possession of national property'. His coronation was steeped in this idea.

5

VICTORIES ON THE CONTINENT

The Treaty of Amiens had put an end to the conflict which since 1792 had opposed revolutionary France to the Kingdoms of Europe. The old monarchies were yielding; they recognized, at least in France, the legitimacy of the new ideas of liberty and equality which they had not been able to stifle by military intervention. Not only was Bonaparte the man who had made peace, but he appeared to have redeemed the Revolution.

Did the formation of a new coalition in 1805, which was the predictable outcome of the breaking off of diplomatic relations with England two years earlier, favour the continuation of revolutionary wars or was there a question of new wars for which Napoleon would be responsible? Contemporaries were in no doubt. England was renewing a struggle which she had only interrupted in order to allow herself a breathing space. French opinion unhesitatingly laid the blame for the break on England.

The English, according to the news bulletins from London,

> say that war at present seems almost a certainty, that the press and preparations for war are so active that there can be no doubt that their government really has hostile intentions. They add that, besides, there can be no more favourable moment, that it is the only way to distract the First Consul from the improvements which he is preparing in the interests of France and which, were they carried out to their fullest extent, would leave no hope for England.

In their turn, despite some hesitation, historians have accepted the terms 'third coalition' and 'fourth coalition' thus admitting to a continuity. The campaigns of 1805 and 1806 are still those of the 'Great Nation'.

THE BREAK

'The English speak of nothing but war. They claim to have received letters from London, both yesterday and the day before, announcing that following the King's message, Parliament voted considerable sums, the levying of large numbers of troops and the immediate arming of forty ships of the line,' says a police report of 14 March 1803. Another report of 16 March from the same source reads: 'Macdonald, the Duke of York's doctor, who is living at present in the rue du Bac, says that all the English officers in Paris with whom he is in close contact think that war is a certainty.' On 21 March, 'Some English people announce that new letters from London say that war preparations are increasingly active, that the press has never been so strong, that nothing is being overlooked in the preparations, that no one in the whole of England doubts the inevitability of war.' So, through information gathered on behalf of the First Consul, the collapse of Anglo-French relations can be followed. The break became final on 17 May 1803. As it was possible to see from the police reports, the English took the initiative in the hostilities. Their grievances were numerous. Whitworth, their ambassador in Paris, had enumerated them in a private conversation which was immediately reported to Bonaparte by his police:

1. It was agreed at Amiens not to interfere with Switzerland, and armed forces had interfered in Switzerland. 2. In stipulating the evacuation of Malta, Russia's guarantee had been promised and the Court of St Petersburg was only prepared to grant her guarantee by means of a garrison on the island which would suit neither England nor France; 3. A trade agreement had been promised and no one would heard of it now; 4. Finally the real motive for arming was not admitted.

England was bitterly disappointed by Bonaparte's refusal, under pressure from the manufacturers and because of mercantilist conviction, to start trade negotiations. The memory of the treaty of 1786 which had ruined the textile industry by opening France freely to English products was still fresh. Barely out of a civil war, France would have been incapable of standing up to British competition. But there was something more serious: Bonaparte intended to reserve the Continent for French trade. London was worried by the transformation of Germany. On 23 February 1803 the diet of the Empire had altered the map in favour of the large states, Prussia, Bavaria and

Württemberg. The Arch-Chancellor of the Empire, Dalberg, who had presided over this reshaping, had thrown his hand in with the French. Austria, allied to England, found herself increasingly ousted. In Italy, the French occupation reached Genoa and Tuscany. Since 19 February, Bonaparte had been Mediator of Switzerland. The French hold in Belgium was already very strong and it was tightened in the Batavian Republic. As many markets were lost to England. Even more tiresome was the fact that Bonaparte was establishing bases for a great colonial empire. Perhaps a reappearance of the Oriental dream? Peace was signed with La Porte on 26 June 1801 and Brune was sent as ambassador to Constantinople. Sebastiani went to the Mediterranean during September 1802 and his report on the state of Egyptian defence, which was published in *Le Moniteur* on 30 January 1803, called for a new French intervention. On 7 August a naval demonstration against Algiers had been carried out, and on 18 June Decaen had been nominated head of the banks of India and Mauritius where he was sent to live. Cavaignac became commissioner for commercial relations in Muscat on 20 June. On 24 September 1802 Victor was nominated Captain-General of Louisiana which had just been conceded to France by Spain. Was this, perhaps, the birth of an American dream? With Victor Hugues, Frances regained its influence in Guiana. With a base in North America, New Orleans, and Cayenne in South America, the First Consul's schemes were becoming clear. Bonaparte sent his brother-in-law, General Leclerc, with twenty-five thousand men to re-establish order in Saint-Domingue (Santo Domingo), a former French possession which had been taken over by a Negro, Toussaint-Louverture. But the American dream was to crumble rapidly; it was badly prepared and no attention had been paid to the climate—the expedition to Saint-Domingue, decimated by yellow fever and by the revolt of former slaves, finally failed in December 1803. In May, the First Consul had sold Louisiana to the United States. Finally, with the exception of Sebastiani's, the missions to the East resulted in nothing. Decaen had to withdraw to the Mascareignes islands. The Imam of Muscut refused Cavaignac's proposals. Under the pretext of science, Baudin's expedition to the southern hemisphere, between 1800 and 1804, had tried to establish French influence on the southern coast of Australia which, at the end of the voyage, was renamed, notably in the atlas published by Poron and Lesueur, 'Napoleon's Land', but there again lay failure. The attempts at colonial imperialism had not succeeded for lack of continuity of vision and because of the disproportionate difference between the means and the end in view; but they did indicate an awakening of French ambitions overseas which was reason enough, in itself, to disturb the British cabinet.

It was the problem of the evacuation of Malta which caused the break. Confronted by France's encroachment in Europe, England had no intention of abandoning such an important pawn which had been taken back from France after only a brief occupation. Bonaparte retorted that he had withdrawn his troops from the Neapolitan ports in keeping with the agreement and that he would be intransigent over Mediterranean affairs, particularly where Malta was concerned.

Talleyrand made himself the spokesman for the head of the government. 'The First Consul is thirty-three years old and, as yet, he has only destroyed states of the second order; who knows how much time would be needed, if it were necessary, to change the face of Europe again and to revive the Western Empire?' The tempo increased rapidly. On 13 March 1803 Bonaparte had a calculated altercation with the British ambassador. London replied with an ultimatum which demanded the evacuation of Holland and of Switzerland, then of Holland only, on condition that the British forces retreated from Malta, but not from the base at Lampedusa, within ten years.

In May, Bonaparte proposed arbitration by neutral powers. Malta would be provisionally occupied by the Russians. But the English had no intention of letting go of a bastion in the Mediterranean which commanded the route to Egypt on which the French had openly set their sights. On 16 May came the break. All French ships at anchor in British ports were seized. For his part, Bonaparte immediately arrested all the English residents in France while his troops occupied Hanover and several ports in southern Italy. War began again.

The initiative came from England, but war served Bonaparte's ends. With the task of redressment in hand, the Republic consolidated and danger from outside averted, there might have been a risk of the revolutionary bourgeoisie ousting the First Consul whose personal power grew ceaselessly and threatened their freedom. At all costs the image of a saviour had to be maintained: 'The First Consul does not resemble those kings, by the grace of God, who consider their states as a heritage. He needs brilliant actions, and therefore war,' Bonaparte is said to have admitted. But neither was war unpleasing to a bourgeoisie which although anglophile in its tastes, was anglophobe in its interests. The economic power of Great Britain had to be overthrown; war seemed to be the only way of ruining perfidious Albion at a time when

French theorists were asserting that all prosperity depended on vigorous profiteering and financial orthodoxy based on hard currency to the exclusion of credit.

THE FRANCO-ENGLISH WAR

In order to conquer England, Napoleon considered an old scheme of the Directory's: invasion. Formerly Hoche had proposed as the first objective, Catholic and oppressed Ireland, which, since the War of Independence, had been in a state of complete turmoil. The severe repression which had followed General Hoche's attempt had made this solution quite impossible. England herself had to be confronted—a landing at Dover and then a march on London. England had recently proved her naval superiority by blocking the French ports and by taking back Santa Lucia and Tobago. Now the crossing of the Channel necessitated the mastery of the seas for ten hours, after which resistance on land from the English army would be utterly mediocre. The occupation of London should take place without a shot being fired. This was an optimistic hypothesis which failed to take into account the English capacity for resistance and the difficulties of an army cut off from its base by the sea. In any case the problem of crossing the Channel remained overwhelming. But here again optimism seemed to be the key-note.

> Only a few leagues separate us from England and whatever the presumed surveillance of the ships, they cannot be sure of a continuity of action and the co-operation of the elements necessary to the interception of a flotilla which will have the advantage of a superior position, multiple means at its disposal and speed under way.

This text is essential to an understanding of the strategy initially chosen by Napoleon and his advisers, a strategy of attack by surprise, dependent on a fleet laden with soldiers. The fleet was to comprise three thousand ships. On 28 July 1805 there were only two thousand, one hundred and forty. The position was settled. Napoleon made Boulogne his headquarters. He had two hundred thousand men at his disposal, who were thus kept out of Paris and out of the way of political intrigue. Although Boulogne was near enough to Paris for Bonaparte to have controlled internal politics and military affairs at the same time, it was in fact 'the worst port on the Channel', the one in which it was easiest for the English to observe the preparations. The 'multiple means' left much to be desired. What good were lighters or gunboat launches? An incident on 20 July 1804, in which a terrible storm destroyed a dozen ships, demonstrated the fragility of the fleet. It had to be admitted as quickly as possible that recourse to the squadrons was indispensable. As for the 'speed under way', two tides have to be ridden in leaving the port of Boulogne. So the fundamental problem of the mastery of the Channel reappeared. The various plans contemplated, based on a surprise attack by the fleet on the English coast, under cover of night during the bad season, were put aside.

When Spain entered the war, however, the initial strategy was changed—her fleet was an important contribution and from then onwards the essential role of the navy was to be revealed. The instructions of February–March 1805 provided for the squadrons from Brest (under Ganteaume) and Toulon (under Villeneuve), avoiding the British blockade, to make their way to the West Indies, where they would be joined by the squadrons from Rochefort (under Missiessy), from Cadiz and from El Ferrol. This would oblige the English to send their fleets to the West Indies and the Mediterranean and would in turn liberate the Channel.

On 30 March 1805, Villeneuve left Toulon; Missiessy had already left Rochefort on 11 January, and Gravina, in his turn, left Cadiz. But the meeting in the West Indies never took place. This was due to an absence of co-ordination between the French and Spanish fleets and an alteration to the original plan, as Napoleon asked Ganteaume to remain in Brest. Other alterations followed which came up against the problem of communications; furthermore the time allowed by the Emperor was too short. The fleets missed their rendezvous and returned to their home ports. At the same time the British admiralty had been able to avoid the dispersal of their fleets. Lord Barham's instructions were peremptory: in the event of uncertainty as to the movements of the enemy, everyone was to rally to Ouessant (Ushant) in order to guard the entrance to the Channel. That is where decisive superiority was essential, for if the enemy controlled the Channel, England was lost. Back in Europe, Villeneuve found himself charged with a new mission—to come together with Allemand, out from Rochefort, and to extricate the squadron from Brest. It was an impossible mission. Villeneuve preferred to look to the future and lie low in Cadiz. Meanwhile Napoleon was growing impatient. The situation on the Continent was deteriorating, the operation had to succeed with the minimum delay. Hence the pressing orders which reached Villeneuve at a time when Napoleon had already given up the idea of a landing. On

26 August the Emperor made his decision. On the 29th, the first detachments left for Germany. Napoleon deemed Villeneuve responsible for the failure of an undertaking in which no one in Boulogne had had any faith. Beset by contradictory orders, Villeneuve finally put to sea and, off Cape Trafalgar, he encountered Nelson and Collingwood on 21 October. The Franco–Spanish line was broken through, one vessel was blown up and seventeen were capture. Villeneuve sur rendered. Dumanoir, who had managed to flee, was crushed at the battle of Ortegal. It was a decisive victory for the English fleet, thanks mainly to the high technical standards of their crew and the precision of their gunners, but it was a victory heavily paid for by the death of Nelson, killed on board the *Victory* by a bullet fired by an able-seaman from the *Redoutable*. It was decisive victory in that Napoleon no longer had a fleet capable of confronting England. Discouraged, he left the mastery of the seas to the English—that is the final victory. But no one knew yet, not even the Prime Minister, Pitt, that the English had won the war.

AUSTERLITZ

English gold had not remained idle on the Continent. It brought about a coalition, the third against France. Russia was easily persuaded: Alexander I envied Napoleon, anglomania was in the ascendant in St Petersburg where the execution of the Duc d'Enghien had made a great impression. The Tsar's chief adviser, the Pole, Czartoryski, urged his master to go to war with France. England promised £1,250,000 a year for every hundred thousand men engaged in the war by the Russians. Aggravated by the territorial modifications decided by the French in Germany and in Italy, Austria joined the coalition, as did the Bourbons of Naples.

The formation of this coalition recalled those which England had set up against the Revolution. It was, therefore, unlikely to surprise the French. Napoloen himself, in his proclamation of 30 September 1805, spoke of the 'third coalition': 'Soldiers, your Emperor is in your midst, you are but the vanguard of a great people. If it is necessary the people will rise up to a man at the sound of my voice, in order to confound and dissolve this new league which has been woven out of the hatred and the gold of the English.'

A certain unrest, however, resulted from the renewal of operations on the Continent. There were rumours concerning the coffers of the Bank of France—Napoleon was said to have emptied them when he left for his campaign. Unrest turned to panic. It was an unnecessary panic, but one which increased the embarrassment of the Bank which was already compromised by the incompetence of the Minister for the Treasury over an immense speculation in Mexican piastres mounted by Ouvrard. The depression of 1806 (to which we will return) was, above all, a crisis of confidence resulting from the renewal of hostilities on the Continent. Through the bulletins of the Grande Armée which explained and justified military operations, Napoleon was able to reestablish the 'morale of the nation'. From 1806, these bulletins were widely distributed. Actors read them aloud in the theatres, teachers read them to their pupils, parish priests commented on them from the pulpit; they reached even the most out of the way villages, where their arrival was heralded by a ringing of bells or a sounding of drums. The effect of them was increased by the press and by poetry. *Le Bulletin impérial* was the title given to some 'heroic stanzas' written in 1806 by Colson. In this way a link was established between the military forces and the country, and the fiction of a national army was maintained, when, in fact, the Grande Armée was no more than an instrument for the purposes of the Emperor.

But more than the bulletins, Napoleon's electrifying victories reestablished confidence. From Boulogne, on 13 August 1805, he had dictated a plan of campaign which foresaw the Grande Armée moving from the north coast towards Germany. Far from catching the Emperor off his guard, the surprise attack by the Austrians on Bavaria, France's ally, gave him an opportunity to withdraw from the hornet's nest of Boulogne. Whilst command of the camp was entrusted to Brune, the Grande Armée divided into seven corps (under Bernadotte, Marmont, Davout, Soult, Lannes, Ney and Augereau, with the cavalry reserve under Murat) marched towards the Rhine, in accordance with the itineraries which had been planned in advance. Within twenty days, the Grande Armée was concentrated at Mayence. Through the valley of the Main, and Donauwörth on the Danube, Napoleon had managed to cut off the line of retreat of the Austrian aggressor, General Mack. Beaten at Elchingen, where Ney distinguished himself, on 14 October, the Austrians retreated to Ulm. Mack capitulated on 20 October 1815, the eve of Trafalgar. The first part of the campaign had lasted two weeks.

Despite what has been written about the campaign, it did come up against some material difficulties. Although every soldier on the Rhine received the necessary pairs of shoes and his pay until 23 October, and supply lines, as the army penetrated deeper into Germany, were well organized, by 22 November there were already eight thousand sick. Many horses had perished as a result of the swift march and theft was so rife in the rear that Napoleon, by an order of the day on 25 November, was obliged to institute military commissions.

From Ulm, Napoleon advanced on Vienna which fell without resistance on 15 November. Francis II had evacuated his capital in order to combine forces with Tsar Alexander. The 'battle of the three emperors' took place on 2 December, the anniversary of the coronation, on a battlefield chosen by Napoleon himself—Austerlitz.

Napoleon's finest victory was also the clearest in conception. The Emperor's plan was simple. The plateau of Pratzen was to be abandoned to the Austro-Russians and the divisions deployed in front of the plateau (Soult in the centre, Davout on the right, Lannes and Murat to the left), the enemy should then plan to turn the French army by attacking the intentionally weakened right wing, in the hope of cutting off their line of retreat towards Vienna. For this scheme to succeed the enemy would have to weaken its centre at Pratzen in order to strengthen its left wing. As soon as this mistake had been made, Napoleon would scale the plateau and break through the weakened centre of the Austro-Russian lines, cutting the enemy army in two and destroying the weaker wing. Everything went according to plan. The battle began at seven o'clock with sunrise and ended at dusk, four o'clock in the afternoon, with the Russians in full flight. 'I had already seen several battles lost,' remarked one of the main participants, the émigré, Langeron; 'I could not imagine such a defeat.' The enemy lost 27,000 men, 40 colours and 180 cannon. While the Russians were retreating by stages, the Austrians were starting negotiations which resulted in the signing of the Treaty of Pressburg on 26 December 1805. Despite Talleyrand's recommendations for moderation to Napoleon, Austria ceded Venice, Istria and Dalmatia to the Kingdom of Italy (formerly the Cisalpine Republic which became a kingdom by the will of the Emperor who had himself crowned in Milan on 26 May 1805). Swabia and the Tyrol were given to the Electors of Württemberg and Bavaria. Austria also undertook to pay an indemnity of thirty-two million in bills of exchange and eight million in cash. The accounts of the commissariat reveal the fruitful nature of the 1805 campaign.

The consequences of the defeat of Austria were immense for Europe. Already master of northern Italy, Napoleon surrounded

Rome, installed himself in the south, and by a simple decree, dated 27 September 1805, 'as though he were merely dismissing a prefect', he took the Kingdom of Naples from the Bourbons who had imprudently joined the third coalition. 'Soldiers! The dynasty of Naples has ceased to reign. Its existence is incompatible with the peace of Europe and the honour of *my Crown* [it was no longer a question of the 'Great People' or the 'Great Nation'] 'March, hurl the weak battalions of the tyrants of the sea into the waves—if indeed they are awaiting you—lose no time in telling me that the whole of Italy is subjected to my laws and to those of my allies.' Joseph, who had refused the Kingdom of Italy, received without any opportunity for discussion, the throne of Naples. 'Tell him that I am making him King of Naples, but that the slightest hesitation, the slightest uncertainty will ruin him. I recognize as relations only those who serve me. Those who will not rise high with me, will not be of my family. I will make a family of kings, or rather of viceroys.' Joseph and Masséna marched on Naples with forty thousand men. Ferdinand IV followed by his terrible wife, Maria-Carolina, had to flee to Sicily. There was no resistance among the people, rather, indifference. On 15 February the new monarch made his entry into Naples. Nothing seemed to resist Napoleon.

Austria was chased not only from Italy, but from Germany too. The victories of the Revolution had pushed the French frontier back to the Rhine. The respite of 1803 had led to a first simplification of the map of Germany. Austerlitz opened the door to new possibilities: the Grand Duchy of Berg was given to Murat, Neuchatel to Berthier, the Electors of Bavaria and Württemberg were granted royal crowns by the decision of the Emperor who thus substituted himself for the old institutions. The new kingdoms with all the principalities of south and west Germany became part of a Confederation of the Rhine placed under the leadership of France. The Confederated States of the Rhine, whose capital was Frankfurt, the seat of a diet consisting of two colleges, recognized Napoleon and left foreign politics to him, the right of war and peace, and the command of the armed forces. This secession brought with it the ruin of the Holy Roman Empire which was reduced to Austria, Prussia and a few states in the north. On 6 August 1806 Francis II renounced his title of Emperor of Germany and as Francis I (a rare example of retrogradation), called himself hereditary Emperor of Austria.

The Batavian Republic became the Kingdom of Holland and was entrusted to Louis. An active matrimonial policy completed the diplomatic successes. Adopted by Napoleon—and his successor to the throne of Milan—His Imperial and Royal Highness, Eugène de Beauharnais married Augusta of Bavaria. At the Peace of Pressburg and under the guise of a concession to Austria, the future separation in perpetuity of the throne of Milan and the Imperial French throne was agreed. Napoleon was also considering making a marriage for Jerome as soon as his union with the American, Elizabeth Patterson, could be ended. Jerome was to marry in 1807, the daughter of the King of Württemberg, whilst Stéphanie de Beauharnais, adopted for the occasion by Bonaparte (she was Josephine's cousin), was to marry the heir to Baden.

French public opinion welcomed the victory of Austerlitz with enthusiasm. It anticipated peace which was so ardently desired. The *Journal de Paris* of 4 December reported:

> Yesterday morning, at break of day, three artillery volleys announced to the Parisians the opening of peace negotiations, and from the strongly felt joyous reaction which this news excited in all classes we can be sure that the lustre of our victories carried away all hearts, for people were considering, together with the glory of the victor, the hope of an imminent peace which has always been their great and main concern.

This gave a good impression of public feeling, which was confirmed by the prefects' reports.

The Peace of Pressburg seemed to herald a general peace. The ceding of Hanover to Prussia seemed to herald the birth of a Franco–Prussian axis which would guarantee a balance of power on the Continent. The fickle Tsar had begun to negotiate. In England, Pitt, finished or so they said, by Austerlitz, had disappeared to be replaced by a Whig, Fox, who was better disposed towards France and who was above all convinced of the inadequacy of his European partners. In June, Lord Yarmouth arrived in Paris. The Tsar's representative, Oubril, had been there since May. From the English point of view the stumbling block was Sicily which Napoleon wished to take from the Bourbons; on the Russian side, Czartoryski who was pushing Alexander towards the East, was removed in favour of the francophobe, Budberg. All hope of peace vanished. A fine occasion for the re-establishment of a balance in Europe was missed.

The French were bitterly disappointed, added to which Napoleon's strange politics gave rise to veiled concern. What was the significance of the creation of new royalties, the dynastic orientation of French diplomacy? What part did matrimonial bargaining and the distribution of crowns play in the interests of the Great Nation which had been evoked at the start of the campaign?

One of the main beneficiaries, Murat, is said to have criticized his brother-in-law in the following terms: in elevating you to the throne, the French believed they had found a leader adorned with a title which would place you above all the sovereigns of Europe. Today you pay homage to powerful titles which are not yours, which are in opposition to ours and you will only show Europe how much you value that which we do not have—the distinction of birth.'

'Monsieur, le Prince Murat,' the Emperor is reputed to have replied, 'I am always confident of you at the head of my cavalry. But we are not concerned here with military manoeuvres, it is a question of politics, and I have carefully considered the matter. This marriage (between Eugène and the daughter of Max Joseph of Bavaria) displeases you. It suits me and I regard it as a great success, a success which equals the victory at Austerlitz.' Perhaps Murat was, after Lucien, the most clear-sighted of Bonaparte's relations. He warned Napoleon when Napoleon was in the process of betraying the Revolution. Were certain ministers aware of the warning? Since the crisis of Marengo, Murat had been drawn into the orbit of Talleyrand and Fouché. His name was to be heard again at the secret meetings of the revolutionary notables when, in 1808, the Spanish war took an awkward turn, and in 1814 Italy was to look towards this brilliant 'cavalryman and king' whom history has rather hurriedly dismissed as a ruffian. Should this political clear-sightedness be attributed to his wife, Caroline?

JENA

But in 1806 there was no time to waste in discussing Napoleon's intentions, his loyalty to the principles of the Revolution or the transformation of the 'Great Nation' into the 'Great Empire' and of this 'mounted Robespierre' into a new Charlemagne. Military operations were already beginning again. For the second time since 1792, France and Prussia crossed swords.

Berlin was unarguably responsible for this new war; the conflict undoubtedly prolonged the revolutionary wars. This was the 'fourth coalition' in action against the ideas of 1789. After a moment's disarray the country closed ranks around its saviour. Never was the danger greater. Since Frederick II, Prussia had been regarded as the first power in Europe.

Her intervention in 1806 could have changed the course of the war. Napoleon had offered her Hanover in permanence in the event of an alliance, and provisionally were she to maintain a friendly neutrality. For their part, Russia and Austria had begged Frederick William III to join the coalition. The King of Prussia's advisers recommended ostensibly arming whilst deferring all intervention. The victory of Austerlitz and the question of Hanover were reason enough for their prudence, but Berlin was concerned by the formation of the Confederation of the Rhine: Would 'German unity' have to go through Paris? In fact on 22 July 1806, the year in which general peace seemed so near, Talleyrand had held out bright prospects to the Prussian minister: 'His Prussian Majesty can unite, under a new federal law, the states which still belong to the Germanic Empire, and claim the imperial crown for the House of Brandenburg.' What would have been the outcome of a division of Germany into two confederations? Was Napoleon sincere? His offer of restoring Hanover to England was interpreted by Berlin as a betrayal and brought about a Russo–Prussian rapprochement on 12 July. Finally Prussia allowed herself to be dragged into the war: from 9 August she was mobilizing her forces; on the 26th she gave an ultimatum to France: Napoleon was to take his troops back across the Rhine before 8 October. The ultimatum reached Napoleon at Bamberg. In a moment of economy he had left the Grande Armée living off the country in Germany. The proclamation of 6 October left no doubt as to Napoleon's intentions. When he had dealt with the bitterness of his soldiers ('The order for your return to France had been given; triumphal festivities awaited you, and the preparations for your return had begun in Paris'), Napoleon blamed Berlin for the new hostilities and recalled the incident of the plains of Champagne where, in 1792, the Prussians had already met with 'defeat, death and shame'. This was a subtle way of underlining that the same struggle continued fourteen years later. In the first bulletin of the Grande Armée he spoke of the 'frenzy' of Queen Louise of Prussia who had been the most violent in the unleashing of hatred against France. 'Frenzy' was indeed the word: with her finances in a state of collapse and with the support of the upper classes only, Prussia threw herself into the war without awaiting the arrival of her ally, Russia. On the whole public opinion was indifferent. The Prussians planned to invade Bavaria with three armies: sixty thousand men under the command of the King and the Duke of Brunswick, fifty thousand Saxons and

Prussians under the Prince of Hohenlohe, and thirty thousand under Ruchel. Before they were able to come together, Napoleon intercepted them. On 14 October, at Jena, he surprised Hohenlohe. The French superiority of numbers transformed the Prussian defeat into a total rout. The official account of the battle given in the fifth bulletin records:

For two hours both armies were shrouded in a fog which was eventually dissipated by a fine autumn sun. The two armies saw each other within a cannon's range. The left wing of the French army backed by a village and some woods was commanded by Marshal Augereau. The Imperial Guard separated it from the centre which was occupied by Marshal Lannes and his corps. The right wing was formed by Marshal Soult's corps. The enemy army was large and displayed a fine cavalry: its manoeuvres were carried out with precision and speed. The Emperor would have liked to delay fighting for two hours in order to await, in the position he had just taken up after the morning's attack, the troops who were to join him, and above all his cavalry. But the enthusiasm of the French won the day. Several battalions were engaged at the village of Holhstädt and he saw the enemy displace itself in an attempt to dislodge them. Marshal Lannes received the order to march in echelons without delay, to support the village. Marshal Soult attacked a wood to the right. The enemy's right wing having made a move towards our left, Marshal Augereau was ordered to repulse it. In less than an hour the action had become general. Two hundred and fifty thousand or three hundred thousand men with seven or eight hundred cannon disseminated death and presented one of history's rarer sights. On all sides there were constant manoeuvres as on a parade ground. Among our troops there was never the slightest disorder, victory was not in doubt for one moment . . . Marshal Soult advanced, having captured the wood which he had been attacking for two hours. At this instant the Emperor was informed that the reserve divisions of the French cavalry were beginning to be positioned, and two new divisions from Marshal Ney's corps were positioning themselves on the battlefield in the rear. All the reserve troops were then made to advance on the front line which, finding itself pressed in this way, overthrew the enemy in the blinking of an eye and put them to full flight. For the first hour their flight was ordered, but it became horribly disorganized as soon as our divisions of dragoons and our cuirassiers, led by the Grand-Duke Berg were able to participate in the affair.

Three leagues to the north, at Auerstädt, Brunswick's main force confronted Napoleon's vanguard commanded by Davout who was assisted by three remarkable divisonals, Friant, Gudin and Morand. Davout withstood the blow and even overthrew Brunswick who was fatally wounded in the action. Deserters from the two Prussian armies became intermingled and caused a general panic. Had Davout flinched, the outcome of the battle would have been different. It is to be noted that the official account is very discreet with regard to the fighting at Auerstädt. Neither is there anything about Bernadotte who, situated between the two battlefields, did not intervene.

At one go, the Prussians had lost thirty-seven thousand dead and wounded, twenty thousand prisoners and their entire artillery. The fortresses fell without resistance with the exception of Kolberg, Danzig and Graudentz. On 27 October Napoleon entered Berlin while Frederick William was taking refuge with the Tsar.

Without delay, Napoleon dictated the fate of conquered Germany. He ordered the taking possession of all the Prussian states between the Rhine and the Elbe, those of the Duke of Brunswick, the Prince of Orange and the Elector of Hesse-Cassel. Prussia had to pay a vast indemnity: 159,425,000 francs. By the decree of 3 November 1806 her former possessions were divided into four departments, Berlin, Custrin, Stettin and Magdeburg, all under the authority of a governor-general, Clarke who was assisted by the Intendant-General, Daru, the Treasurer-General, Estève and the Collector-General of Taxes, La Bouillerie. On the other hand the Emperor pardoned Saxony, and the day after Jena he liberated her prisoners, six thousand soldiers and three hundred officers, and then made her Elector King. Saxony then joined the Confederation of the Rhine with its six dukes of Saxe-Weimar, Gotha, Meiningen, Hildburghausen and Coburg. The Saxon contingent for the remainder of the war was fixed at twenty thousand men. So Northern Germany in her turn came under French domination.

THE FRANCO-RUSSIAN WAR

There remained Russia. Napoleon reinforced his army. (The *senatus consultum* of 15 December authorized the levying of eighty thousand men, sixty thousand of whom were to be dressed, shod and equipped

immediately in the three centres of Boulogne, Mayence and Potsdam.)
Next he went to meet the Russians in eastern Prussia. But the field of
operations was adapted neither to his genius, nor to the living conditions and manoeuvres of the Grande Armée. Furthermore, as they
withdrew the Russians burnt everything, which made supplies difficult. On the other hand, the Russian army, which was both large and
tenacious, was operating on terrain and under climatic conditions
which suited it to perfection. A lightning war was soon succeeded by
the problem of sinking in quicksand, difficulties of supplies, cold, rain
and, in the rear, isolated attacks by Prussian partisans. On 6 February
Napoleon wrote to Daru, 'You should not hide from yourself the fact
that nothing which you sent the army arrived because the army was
marching all the time; whereas, if everything could have left with the
army, it would have been amply fed.' The confrontation of the two
forces took place at Eylau, on 8 February 1807 in the middle of a
blinding snowstorm. The battle was drawn. Napoleon thought that he
had surprised the Russians, but it was he who was surprised in an
inferior position. Bennigsen brought seventy thousand men to meet
the fifty thousand French. Augereau's corps lost its way in the blizzard
and was annihilated; the Russian offensive very nearly broke through
the centre of the French formations. Napoleon only rectified the
situation by mounting an enormous cavalry charge of eighty
squadrons under Murat's command. Night fell and the Russians were
still holding their ground when Ney arrived on their right and forced
them to withdraw. There were strewn on the snow some twenty-five
thousand Russians and perhaps eighteen thousand Frenchmen. Gros's
famous painting is traditionally used to evoke this battle. Another
aspect of the battle was described by Percy, the surgeon to the Grande
Armée.

Never was so small a space covered with so many corpses. Everywhere the snow was stained with blood. The snow which had fallen
and which was still falling began to hide the bodies from the grieving
glances of passers by. The bodies were heaped up wherever there
were small groups of firs behind which the Russians had fought.
Thousands of guns, helmets and breastplates were scattered on the
road or in the fields. On the slope of a hill, which the enemy had
obviously chosen to protect themselves, there were groups of a
hundred bloody bodies; horses, maimed but still alive, waited to fall
in their turn, from hunger, on the heaps of bodies. We had hardly

crossed one battlefield when we found another, all of them strewn with bodies.

The 64th bulletin was not able to disguise the horrifying facts: 'After the battle of Eylau, the Emperor spent several hours every day on the battlefield which was a horrible sight. It was his duty. Burying all the dead was a tremendous job.'

Napoleon, nervously exhausted, suspended operations. He settled in the castle at Finkenstein, where he prepared a new plan of campaign against the Tsar: Sebastiani at Constantinople, Marmont in Dalmatia, and Gardanne, who had been sent to the Shah of Persia in Teheran, were to turn part of the Russian forces back towards the East. In March 1807, Danzig, besieged by Lefebvre and some excellent artillery officers of genius like Lariboisière and Chasseloup-Laubat, fell, opening up the road to Poland. At the same time Napoleon increased his total strength. Supplies were, however, still difficult. Transport was paralysed by the lack of horses and by the inadequacy of the waterways network. This resulted in a problem of provisions which caused a vast increase in numbers of deserters and in pillaging. 'If I had six thousand hundredweight of flour at Osterode, I would be master of my movements,' sighed Napoleon on 8th March 1807.

Operations began again in the spring. Napoleon marched on Königsberg where the main stores of the Russian army were to be found. Bennigsen attempted an attack on the flank in order to free the citadel. The confrontation took place at Friedland on 14 June, with the Russians in a disadvantageous position, their backs to the River Alle. Lannes, who had been confronting the enemy since three o'clock in the morning, prolonged the operation in order to give Napoleon time to hasten from Eylau with the greater part of his troops. The real battle began at five o'clock in the afternoon. It lasted six hours. On the left and in the centre, Mortier and Lannes had the task of containing Gortchakov. To the right, Ney, without counting his losses, was to break through the enemy's left wing which was commanded by Bagration, capture Friedland which dominated the terrain behind the Russian army and cut off the bridges over the Alle, which the Russians had used to cross the river. Lannes and Mortier would then take the offensive. By eight o'clock Friedland was in French hands; at ten o'clock Lannes and Mortier were pushing Gortchakov into the Alle, since without the bridges he was unable to retreat. Hundreds of Russians were drowned. The day cost the Tsar twenty-five thousand men and eighty cannon. His army beat a retreat across the Niemen.

Despite the mediocrity of the English subsidies, the war with Turkey and the threat of a Polish uprising, all was not lost. Nevertheless, Alexander, whose moods vacillated between enthusiasm and deep depression, decided to negotiate with Napoleon. The meeting of the two emperors took place at Tilsit, on 25 June 1807, on a raft in the middle of the River Niemen. 'Sire, I hate the English as much as you do!' 'In that case peace is established.' This exchange explains the agreement between the two emperors. There was not, as has been offensively suggested, a division of the world, but an alliance against England.

As Albert Vandal rightly observes,

> Napoleon's aim was to conquer England and to bring about a general peace. Of all the powers, Russia seemed the best situated to help him to this end. She could help him by her geographical position, which was both joined to the mainland and on the sea, by her strength and by the vastness of the means at her disposal. In her present state of disarray she offered him what he proposed to her, to struggle together against England.

The Prussians immediately, and later the Turks, bore the cost of the agreement signed on 7 July. The states between the Elbe and the Rhine which were confiscated from Prussia and part of Hanover, formed the Kingdom of Westphalia which Napoleon gave to Jerome. The Polish parts of Prussia made up the Grand Duchy of Warsaw which was entrusted to the King of Saxony and with Westphalia joined the Confederation of the Rhine. The Confederation was swallowing up the whole of Germany with the exception of Prussia and Austria. Napoleon offered to mediate in the Russo-Turkish conflict; in the event of the Sultan's refusal the Ottoman provinces in Europe were to be carved up, leaving the Turks with only Constantinople and Rumelia. Alexander, who recognized all the changes in Europe, for his part offered to mediate in the Franco-English war; in the event of a refusal Alexander undertook to join Napoleon in bringing pressure on the courts of Copenhagen, Stockholm and Lisbon with a view to closing their ports to British merchandise. In the new strategy defined by Napoleon since the setback of Trafalgar and known as the 'Continental Blockade', Russia became the all-important trump card. The English were to experience it bitterly from the beginning of 1808. Never was Napoleon so close to victory nor the Continent to a general peace.

TO WHAT END AUSTERLITZ AND JENA?

Contemporaries were fascinated by Napoleon's overwhelming victories at Austerlitz and Jena. Clausewitz and Jomini have analysed at length Napoleon's military genius and opened the way for nine-teenth- and twentieth-century theorists and strategists. Napoleon, however, made many errors of judgement. Take, for example, his rejection of technical innovations—Fulton's 'water waggon driven by fire', or Congreve's rockets, Jean Alexandre's telegraph and Major Coutelle's observation balloons. All his campaigns were carried out with arms from the Ancien Régime—the 1777 gun (barely modified in 1803) and Gribeauval's cannon. He remained indifferent to the researches of Berthollet who proposed to replace the saltpetre (potassium nitrate) in gunpowder with potassium chlorate; he ignored Forsythe's replacement of the flint-lock by a percussion cap aligned with the powder. He knew that the Prussian gun had a sharp blade with which the troops could open the cartridges without having to bite them. This inexpensive innovation made it possible for Frederick William III's infantry to fire more quickly than the French. Napoleon attached no importance to it. He even decided to give twelve cavalry regiments back the helmet and breastplate which had gone out with Louis XIV. His amazing ignorance of climate and geography, which were illustrated by the terrible losses in Egypt and Saint-Domingue due to natural conditions, have been stressed less frequently. The imprudence which caused him to cross the Oder in 1806 without taking into account from the start the snow, the mud and the cold, is often forgotten. Ignorance of the terrain and the absence of scouts put him in very awkward positions at Marengo and Eylau.

A bad chess player, Napoleon was nonetheless convinced, as were all the generals produced by the Revolution, of the merits of the offensive. Clausewitz was to demonstrate, on the contrary that 'every offensive is weakened by the very fact of its advancing'. The Russian campaign was to prove him right: 'Half a million men crossed the Niemen, a hundred and twenty thousand fought at Borodino, and even fewer reached Moscow.' Clausewitz concluded that 'the defen-sive form of battle is stronger than the offensive'.

Napoleon's ideas of strategy were not new. They came straight from Guibert and the divisional principle, the army being made up of autonomous corps, each with two or three infantry divisions, a cavalry division, some artillery and administration. The main reason for his successes was his capacity to alternate between the spread-out formation when marching and a concentrated formation in battle. By dispersing his troops on the march, he was able to live, without difficulty, off the country, and could create a net into which the enemy who continued to manoeuvre in a group could be caught. Mack, remaining stationary at Ulm, was surrounded; the Prussians on the move in 1806 were also surrounded by Napoleon and found themselves obliged to fight with their front line reversed which resulted in the rout at Jena. War became a matter of lightning speed. When the enemy marched in separate columns, Napoleon could manoeuvre in 'inside lines', slowing down one column or the other by detachments whose duty it was to delay their progress. Meanwhile, he would attack one of the columns with his main force, crush it, and then turn against the other. The whole manoeuvre depended on the net-like formation of his march which allowed him, at any given moment, to draw the strings and enclose all or part of the enemy. During battle he knew how to exploit the enemy's mistakes or even how to provoke the error which would bring about their downfall, as at Austerlitz. At worst, the unexpected intervention of a separate corps on the flank or from the rear of his enemy created the 'incident' which decided the victory. But Europe was soon to learn the rules of this new game and to scent the traps which the Emperor laid. Napoleonic tactics were no longer to come up against armies in the open country, but the entrenched forces of Portugal, Borodino and Waterloo. More and more, the weight of numbers, difficulties of communication, and language problems in an increasingly international army prevented the mobility of the first Italian campaign. Napoleon manoeuvred less and less, instead seeking the advantage of strength in gigantic batteries or in massive cavalry charges, as at Eylau. So battles became butchery. From the time of the campaign in eastern Prussia at the end of 1806, the decline was in evidence. The surprise effect which had favoured the lightning war had ceased to play a part.

In 1806 and 1807 Napoleon still found a favourable political climate in Poland. The Poles were expecting him to restore their kingdom. Vienna and Berlin had not resisted the entrance within their walls of the victor of Austerlitz and Jena. With guerrillas, Napoleon was to come up against a new form of warfare against which he could find no answer. The strength of the Revolutionary armies and, initially, of the Grande Armée, lay in the fact that a national army was confronting bands of mercenaries. When, as a result of heterogeneous recruitment, the Grande Armée lost its national character, its era of victory was over.

Napoleon's generals and marshals were hardly strategists, but rather chargers, (Ney, Murat, Delort, Lasalle, Saint-Hilaire, Pacthod, Pajol, Compans, Curely, Claparède). Some were honest diplomats (Lauriston, Caulaincourt, Andréossy). There were some 'cowards' (Monnet, but not Baraguey d'Hilliers or Dupont, despite their problems), some crooks (Dutertre), some corrupt (Chabran), some deserters (Sarrazin, Bourmont), some succeeded their fathers (Abbatucci and Aboville). Some died in captivity in atrocious conditions (Lefranc), others were dismissed for republicanism (Ambert, Delmas, Monnier) or suspected sympathy for Moreau (Durutte). The greatest number, however, were mown down by grape-shot before they could prove themselves (Desaix, Valhubert). Napoleon was always to remember his aide-de-camp, Muiron.

In the end the reservoir of men was to begin running dry. Conscription was no longer able to supply the 'Ogre' with enough soldiers. With the superiority in numbers finally lost against a united Europe, Napoleon was to be condemned, more especially as the proportion of losses, until then favourable to the French, was to level out. From Eylau, the army seemed badly equipped, badly officered, and often undisciplined. Few men remained from the Boulogne forces and they were all non-commissioned or in the Guard. The ill-instructed recruits of 1806 and 1807 constituted four-fifths of the whole strength. National spirits had fallen. War was taking place far from France and the vital interests of the country did not appear to be threatened. The bourgeoisie were concerned by the disregard of natural frontiers and were only reassured by the prospects of new outlets for their trade. The Chamber of Commerce in Paris, 'taking into account the state of war in which the bad faith of the enemy had placed the Republic', had, on 5 Prairial Year XI, given the First Consul, as a token of respect, a vessel with a hundred and twenty cannon to be named *Commerce de Paris*. But the nation's heart was not in the war. Apart from human losses the war cost the country nothing; it took place in foriegn countries. It cost nothing, but was, on the contrary, a source of income. From Daru's accounts it has been possible to draw up a balance sheet for the campaign from 1 October 1806 to 15 October 1808. Extraordinary taxes produced 311,662,000 francs, property rates produced 79,667,000 francs and foreclosure of coffers produced 16,172,000 francs. To the various taxes levied on the enemy could be added the remounting of the cavalry which meant 40,000 horses, and other supplies, making a total of 600 millions in all officially taken from

Prussia, not to mention spoils. According to Daru, the expenditure of the Grande Armée was 212,879,335 francs, of which the Paymaster-General would have taken 248,479,691 francs. So the campaigns in Prussia and Poland cost the French taxpayer nothing. Public opinion, already conditioned by the bulletins, could but approve, and more so, as the victories of 1805 and 1806 had shocked the whole of Europe and, coming after the two Italian campaigns, had assured Napoleon's reputation for invincibility. The Revolution had chosen its redeemer wisely.

6

THE CONTINENTAL BLOCKADE

After Tilsit only England remained for Napoleon to fight. He may have been victor on the Continent, but he could not expect to rule the seas. The disaster of Trafalgar and the tardy rebuilding of the French fleet prevented him from attacking the British Isles immediately. Therefore he envisaged a new form of struggle—economic warfare.

Wishing to knock British industry and the trade on which her power depended, Napoleon asked, or obliged, the whole continent of Europe to close its ports to vessels and merchandise coming from England. Since the breaching of the Peace of Amiens, Bonaparte had been trying, by the coast system, to forbid British ships access to the Continental coasts in his power. He was still motivated by the defensive worry of protecting French industry from British competition. By the decrees of Berlin and Milan, the extension of the Blockade to the whole of Europe became the corner-stone of his foreign policy. Henceforth, anyone who did not participate in the Continental System was against him. There was no longer any possibility of neutrality in the conflict between Napoleon and the lords of the ocean.

THE ORIGINS OF THE BLOCKADE
Their history had taught the French to see financial credit as an unstable and fragile foundation, whose collapse brought with it the fall of the government which depended on it. England's most vulnerable point was, without doubt, its monetary system. From Thomas Payne to Lassalle, whose treaty, *Des Finances de l'Angleterre* appeared in 1803, numerous writers had drawn attention to the English national debt which had increased beyond measure, to a paper money which was beginning to be discredited and to thousands of men threatened by

unemployment. British prosperity appeared so imposing, economists like Saladin or Monbrion asserted, but was it not in reality quite artificial? To close the Continent to Great Britain was to bankrupt her and to force her to beg for peace. The Directory, in conflict with proud Albion, had thought of applying such a policy, but had not had the means.

After the breaking of the Peace of Amiens, Napoleon revived the plan. The expression *Blocus continental*, Continental Blockade, is used for the first time in the Grande Armée's 15th bulletin published in *Le Moniteur* on 30 October 1806.

But, borrowed from the Directory, the idea already featured in an extempore speech of Bonaparte's at the Council of State on 1 May 1803, the eve of the breaking of the peace. Miot de Melito has preserved it in his *Mémoires*:

> Our losses at sea will be regretted, perhaps even the loss of our colonies, but we will assert ourselves on the Continent. We have already acquired a large enough expanse of coastline to render ourselves formidable. We will add yet more to this expanse. We will form a more complete coastal system and England will weep for the war she will have undertaken, with tears of blood.

In fact it was a question of turning against England a weapon which she had used first—from the Hundred Years War until the struggle against Louis XVI—and which she had just decided to use again on 16 May 1806 when an order in council had declared the coasts of France blockaded. An unreal blockade, but one which justified the inspection by British cruisers of ships, mostly American, which were trafficking with the Empire.

After Jena, Napoleon thought himself powerful enough to react and signed, on 21 November 1806, the Decree of Berlin which instituted the Continental Blockade—perhaps the description 'English blockade' would be preferable since 'Continental Blockade' might seem to describe British naval action. The Emperor's decision was unexpected and somewhat brutal. Napoleon does not appear to have consulted the chambers of commerce, but they had let their wishes be known. On 23 Nivôse Year XII, Delessert in Paris had demanded prohibition in favour of taxation as a means of protecting burgeoning industry. In 1806 the Continental Blockade seemed to be the only way to boost the economy which had been shaken by the united merchants' crash in which the Treasury had been unwisely involved. The idea was therefore welcomed by traders and to a certain extent by the merchants immediately concerned. The exchange rate improved noticeably during the last days of 1806; 'The interest on money in commercial transactions has improved in Paris', noted a report from the Chamber of Commerce.

THE CONTINENTAL BLOCKADE

As his grounds for the Berlin Decree, the Emperor stated that, contrary to 'the right of individuals acknowledged universally by all civilized countries', England, deeming all the citizens of an enemy state to be her enemies, captured the crews of merchant ships and even the passengers, whom she held as prisoners of war. She extended the right of seizure, which should only have been applied to the property of the enemy state, to private property. She declared in a state of blockade, 'places which all her united forces would be incapable of blocking, entire coastlines and a whole Empire'.

The Emperor added:

As the monstrous abuse of the blockade has, as its only aim, the prevention of communication between nations and the promotion of England's commerce and industry whilst ruining commerce and the industry on the Continent, and as it is a natural right to fight the enemy with the same arms which it uses, we have determined to apply to England the methods which she has used in her maritime legislation, and have as a result decreed: Article I, the British Isles are in a state of blockade.

So in the actual text of the Berlin Decree it was a question of blockading England and not the Continent. Since Napoleon did not have the necessary fleet he was obliged to close the Continental ports to English merchandise and vessels. Henceforth,

all trade and all communication with the British Isles are forbidden. Any British subject found in countries occupied by French troops or their allies will be held as a prisoner of war; all stock, all merchandise and all property belonging to England, whatsoever its nature, will be declared lawful prize. The trading of English merchandise is forbidden and all merchandise belonging to England or originating from her factories or her colonies is declared lawful prize.

The decree was communicated to 'the Kings of Spain, Naples, Holland and Etruria, whose subjects, like ours, are victims of the injustice and barbaric English maritime legislation'.

So Napoleon replied to a maritime blockade with a territorial blockade. 'I wish,' he said in a well-known phrase, 'to conquer the sea through the power of the land.' There was nothing new in the prohibition of English products, but this time neutral states were also implicitly affected since the Blockade abandoned its protectionist nature to become an instrument of war.

THE DECREES OF MILAN

London replied to the Berlin Decree by the Orders in Council of November 1807. The British cabinet declared all French ports and the ports of countries at war with England to be strictly blockaded. It meant to forbid all trade that was not with Great Britain and to facilitate on the other hand trade between Britain and Napoleonic Europe. Therefore freedom of the seas was only allowed to ships which had put into a British port and paid a transit tax which averaged twenty-five per cent.

Returning blow for blow, Napoleon ordered by the first Decree of Milan (23 November 1807) the seizure of any ship which had put into an English port, and by the second decree (17 December 1807) the seizure of all ships which had obeyed the Orders in Council.

The first Decree of Milan ended with a direct invitation to America to topple British maritime power.

Circumstances were ideal. After the incident of the frigate *Chesapeake,* which the English Admiral Berkeley had bombarded on 22 June 1807, President Jefferson had on 2 July excluded British warships from the United States' territorial waters. Napoleon was counting on an alliance with America. But a sequence of unforeseen circumstances compromised this alliance which was, however, indispensable to the realization of these plans. By a decision made on 18 September 1807, the Emperor had authorized his corsairs to seize from neutral ships on the high seas any merchandise coming from England. Under the circumstances Jefferson preferred, by an act of embargo voted on 22 December 1807, to keep all ships on the American run in his ports. As a result, on 17 April 1808, Napoleon signed the Decree of Bayonne declaring all American ships entering European ports to be lawful prize. 'The United States', he told Gaudin, 'have placed an embargo on the vessels. It is therefore obvious that the ones which claim to come from America in fact come from England and their papers are falsified.' This was, after all, to risk friction with the new power which was the United States, and to compromise the chances of a rapprochement which would have favoured the success of the Blockade.

THE APPLICATION OF THE BLOCKADE

After Tilsit, the Russian alliance made it possible for Napoleon to envisage closing the Continent entirely. A document of 1807 speaks of 'the great and powerful effect of the alliance between the two foremost world powers. At their command the whole Continent arises and obeys their desire to join together against the enemy. This state of war by many powers against the islanders will annihilate their trade, paralyse their industry and make the sea, their most fruitful domain, useless; it is a beautiful idea and a plan of such magnitude that it is extremely difficult to carry out. But it has been carried out.'

Between July and November 1807 the Continent in fact closed itself almost entirely to British trade.

Denmark allied itself to France on 31 October 1807 by the Treaty of Fontainebleau. So the Tönningen route was also closed to British traffic. Austria and Prussia, conquered, were equally obliged to accept the Blockade, but it was above all the loss of the Russian market after the Treaty of Tilsit which dealt the most telling blow to English trade. The effect was not immediately felt because of the late closing of the Ruissian ports, but in the long term England risked losing materials of primary importance to her fleet, like hemp, flax and timber.

Holland which since 1806 had been entrusted to Louis Bonaparte, had welcomed the Blockade with reservations. The new sovereign realized that the system, were it to ruin England, could not fail to ruin Holland first. He attempted to dodge the severest clauses, but, called to order by his brother, he was obliged to give in and to publish a decree on 15 December 1806 which established the Blockade in his kingdom. Nevertheless, he allowed the development of considerable contraband as a kind of safety valve for the Dutch economy. Threatened by Napoleon with military intervention in his kingdom, he decided to publish, on 28 August 1807, a more robust decree, and subsequently seized about forty British ships in Dutch ports. By the end of 1807 Holland was almost entirely closed to British merchandise.

Napoleon had to close first the northern coast of France and then the southern coast to the English. Severe measures were taken in Italy. On 29 August 1807 General Miollis ordered the requisitioning of British merchandise in bond at Leghorn. Pisa was also occupied and garrisons were established in the ports of the Papal States, at Ancona, Pesaro and Civita Vecchia.

In Spain a decree of 19 February 1807 proclaimed the rigorous application of the Blockade. Communication with Gibraltar was cut off. In her turn, after much beating about the bush, Portugal was forced to participate in the Continental System at the end of 1807. Giving way to a French ultimatum, the Portuguese ministers agreed on 6 November to put an embargo on British ships. On 8 November they gave the order to arrest British subjects and to seize their goods. The decision came too late for the invasion of their territory by French troops to be avoided. On 21 November it was learnt that Junot had crossed the Portuguese frontier. The blow was particularly harsh for British trade. Already exports to Lisbon in 1807 had dropped by forty per cent since 1806.

THE BRITISH CRISIS OF 1808
By the end of 1807, the Blockade had been adopted by all the European powers except for Sweden which had remained loyal to the British alliance. The consequences of the closure of the Continent were felt in London almost immediately. The first six months of 1808 were especially difficult for the British economy. During the first three months the value of exports fell from £9,000 to £7,244. The second three months showed a marked drop in comparison to 1807—£7,688 as against £10,754. These difficulties were only aggravated by the breaking off of relations with the United States who had been supplying the British with their cereals and cotton. The stagnation of colonial produce on the market was accompanied by a crisis in the exportation of British manufactured goods. Industrialists in Manchester were unable to liquidate their stocks of cotton, and the situation was no better in Scotland or elsewhere in Lancashire. There was a serious crisis in the wool industry, and a rise in the price of flax followed the breaking off of relations with the Baltic.

As a result of rising prices, social disturbances broke out in Lancashire in May and June of 1808. In August 1808 the first symptoms of the devaluation of the pound became apparent. Napoleon could henceforth envisage a victory which he announced to the Legislative Body in 1807:

England, punished by the very cause which had inspired her own cruel policies, sees her merchandise refused by the whole of Europe and her vessels laden with useless riches, roaming the vast seas which they claim to rule, and searching in vain from the Sound to the Hellespont for a port which will receive them.

PART III

THE BALANCE

Napoleon reached his apogee, not at the time of the birth of the King of Rome in 1811, but in 1807, after Tilsit. From that time the whole Continent was either allied to France, or her vassal. Totally isolated, England found herself threatened by a financial collapse as a result of the closure of European ports to her merchandise. France's natural frontiers, the Rhine, the Alps and the Pyrenees were assured; the old dream of the monarchy and of the Committee of Public Safety had become a reality. At home, the depression of 1808 had finally been overcome, like that of 1801, which showed the ruling power to be perfectly in control of the economic mechanism of the times. After two centuries of absolutism, the suppression of liberty was felt only by the bourgeoisie, but, above all, the bourgeoisie feared disorder. Inter-party struggles seemed to have burnt themselves out despite a few acts of brigandage whose political significance was not always evident. A new social balance was in the making. The notables were the principal beneficiaries, but the people's trust was in the man who guaranteed the gains of the Revolution: the sale of national property, the division of common land and civil equality. Salaries had been raised and unemployment had greatly diminished, at least in Paris. In comparison with the hard conditions which were to follow, the workers kept a, no doubt exaggerated, memory of a 'golden age', which was not to be destroyed by the increased burden of conscription and the horrors of the 1814 and 1815 invasions. Never was France so powerful, so united nor so respected. It was a brief moment before the first cracks appeared. A privileged moment in which to describe Napoleon's France. An exceptional moment for which the country was to remain nostalgic throughout the nineteenth century. As much as in official propaganda and military victories, the origin of the success of the imperial legend lies in this passing moment of territorial, political and social equilibrium.

1

THE NAPOLEONIC EMPIRE

The diversity of Imperial France was astonishing. In an *Itinéraire* published in 1806 and re-published in 1811, and which compares favourably with Reichard's *Guide des Voyageurs*, Langlois gives some valuable advice. The traveller is advised not to enter France with a sealed parcel or even with simple sealed letters on pain 'not only of being thrown into prison, but also of a 500-pound fine for each letter'. On the other hand, he is advised to carry about his person double-barrelled pistols and, above all, never to trust postillions. A traveller with his own carriage must be satisfied with one chest, a cowhide trunk and one casket for jewels, money and bills, supplied with screws which make it possible to secure it strongly to the carriage or to the bedroom in the inn: 'A franc should be allowed for every league travelled by stage-coach including tips for the postillions and the driver, and five francs at each staging post for two horses, a master and one servant.' Stendhal was not of the same opinion when he calculated the expenses of his journey from Grenoble to Paris in Year XII.

But the author of the *Itinéraire complet de l'Empire français* stresses the differences most particularly between northern and southern France, between the western departments and those on the left bank of the Rhine, he speaks of contrasting mentalities and countrysides, activities and wealth, all of which the traveller should take into account. The same observation was made by Nemnich of Hamburg in the precious account of his journey published by the great Cotta of Tübingen in 1810.

NORTHERN FRANCE
To the north, Imperial France was no longer limited by the frontiers of

the Ancien Régime, but extended to Belgium and, after the annexation of the Kingdom of Holland, it included the United Provinces. Only the coastline and the mouth of the Rhine lent a unity to northern France which countryside and language belied.

To the north, then, lay Holland, the former Batavian republic which became a kingdom in 1806 under Louis Bonaparte, only to be brutally annexed to France in 1810 when Napoleon could no longer tolerate his brother's manifestations of independence. Louis had already been severely reprimanded by the Emperor when he wished to adapt the Civil Code to local law: 'A nation of 1,800,000 inhabitants cannot have a separate legislation. Rome gave her laws to her allies; why should the laws of France not be adopted in Holland?' Afterwards, the application of the Continental Blockade precipitated the conflict between Napoleon and his brother. In order to avoid ruining his kingdom, whose economy depended on maritime trade, Louis was after all obliged to tolerate English contraband, thus making Holland the weak point of the Continental System. And so, from 1808, Napoleon decided on annexation. The unsuccessful invasion of Walcheren by the English in July 1809 confirmed him in his intentions. Louis was asked, from March 1810, to hand over, without compensation, all lands to the south of the Rhine. Henceforth, seven thousand Frenchmen were supposed to supervise the Dutch coastline. In fact there were twenty thousand. Louis anticipated the Emperor by abdicating on 1 July 1810.

The nine Belgian departments encompassed the former Austrian Low Countries and the principality of Liège and were generally less agitated. The development of Belgium dates from this union with France. The political transformation may have been profound since even the memory of the former principalities was wiped out by the administrative and judicial standardization undertaken by the French, but the economic and social upheavals were even greater. Admittedly the nobility, despite the loss of privileges, retained property and influence in the countryside. But the sale of national property which affected the Church took place, not to the advantage of the peasants who were prevented by religious scruples from acquiring the estates of the clergy, but to the advantage of a bourgeoisie which up till then had carried no weight outside the principality of Liège. Thanks to the capital which they made from speculation over national property and thanks to the possibility offered to them by the opening of a vast market, these bourgeois took an interest in the development of industry. At Gand a mechanized cotton industry appeared, which was founded on the introduction of English machinery. In 1808 there were 500 looms, whereas just two years later there were 2,900. The Continental Blockade and the mining legislation favoured coal mining. In 1795 Belgium was producing 800,000 tons of coal, but in 1811 she produced 1,300,000 tons. War stimulated the Hainaut metallurgy. Antwerp, which Napoleon visited in 1803 and again in 1810, was the centre of a large ship building industry—four ships (two with 74 guns) were launched in 1807.

Belgium played a more and more important part in the industrial life of the Empire. She supplied half the coal and a quarter of the blast furnace material. The German traveller, Nemnich, noted that, after Paris, Gand was the most important city 'distinguished for the diversity of her manufactures'.

Unlike Holland, which depended too much on outside trade, Belgium, then, profited greatly from the French occupation. This explains the absence of opposition to the imperial regime. The bourgeoisie was content with a political system which favoured its economic interests; the nobility having long looked towards Vienna, rallied to Napoleon after his marriage to Marie-Louise and agreed to sit in French assemblies. The Duc d'Arenberg and the Comte de Mérode sat in the Senate. In spite of conscription which had provoked an uprising in 1798, and in spite of the conflict with the Pope, the Belgian peasantry maintained their attachment to Napoleon until the very end. The proof lies in the small percentage of deserters and in the outburst of patriotism which accompanied the reconstruction of the French army after the Russian disaster in 1813.

There remained Northern France proper, with her industrial cities such as Lille, Valenciennes and Amiens.

Lille was both the industrial centre and the agricultural market centre of a region which produced, in particular, oil seeds from which several hundred mills made oil which was exported to Holland, Aix-la-Chapelle or Düsseldorf. Hops, tobacco, flax and tulips were also produced. The town itself harboured not only lace-making and sugar refineries but English-style cotton mills. Nankeen, satins and stuffs known as 'napoleons' were woven at Tourcoing.

Valenciennes had suffered more from the Revolution. The rich families who led a worldly life there had been decimated, but despite exorbitant prices, cambric, woven in cellars, and lace maintained their reputation.

The cotton industry was thriving in Saint-Quentin—where the

number of workers rose from 502 in 1806 to 1,500 in 1810—and at Amiens where Morgan and Delaye were the first to instal spinning jennies. By 1806 there were 15,348 spindles.

There was a boom in mining at Anzin, which, in the long run, established the northern region of France as one of the most industrialized parts of the Empire. This boom was due to the installation of machines powered by steam, and the weight of coal mined rose from 242,277 hundredweight in 1807 to 420,706 in 1809.

The morale of the northern departments was excellent. There was a marked decline in brigandage which had been rife around 1800, when brigands known as *chauffeurs* were burning the feet of their victims. There was also a definite drop in the numbers of deserters and in military absenteeism. In 1803 there were about 300 deserters in the Pas-de-Calais, only 134 in 1804 and twelve in 1812.

EASTERN FRANCE

To the east, the Rhine was no longer a frontier. Alsace had rediscovered a prosperity which she might well have considered lost. There, the Empire encouraged the production of tobacco and sugar beet, and was in favour of afforestation. Plantations multiplied, as did official pasture-land. The Continental Blockade made the development of industry in the Haut-Rhin possible. There were two large spinning companies, Gros, Roman et Cie with 5,038 spindles and 185 workers at Wesserling in 1806, and Dolfuss et Cie who had 1,404 spindles and 72 workers that same year. Industrial advance caused the population of the great cotton centre, Mulhouse, to rise from 6,000 to 8,000 inhabitants. Alsace was assimilated without difficulty.

Assimilation progressed equally in the four departments of the left bank of the Rhine which had replaced some ninety-seven states. The population there alone was around a million and a half. Economic development was undeniable there also. There were two new factors— one, the suppression of tithes and of seigniorial rights which stimulated agriculture (bringing about the boom in sugar beet, extensive afforestation and an increase in vineyards), and, two, the elimination of British competition which benefited metallurgy and the textile industry. At Crefeld the number of silk mills doubled; at Aix-la-Chapelle, where the population rose from 10,000 to 30,000 inhabitants, the number of factories multiplied tenfold; in 1811, the Roër was the most industrialized department of the Empire with 2,550 firms and 65,000 workers.

Measures, like the suppression of tolls, were taken to improve navigation on the Rhine. The Rhine itself in fact began to alter in character. Henceforth, the upstream traffic of raw materials from the Rhine basin became far greater than the downstream traffic of colonial merchandise from Holland which had become scarce since the Blockade.

The growth of industry and trade caused the development of a commercial bourgeoisie who were to become the main supporters of the Napoleonic regime. But the local nobility, despite the loss of its rights and privileges, was wary of complaining about the new system; it found its way into the Sub-Prefectures, the General Council and without much difficulty the Senate. As for the peasants, they welcomed enthusiastically the end of brigandage (the renowned Schinderhannes was disabled) and the Civil Code. (In no other annexed country was the Code so frequently translated or commented on). Opinion in the Rhineland seems to have been won over to France by the wise administration of prefects like Lezay-Marnesia at Coblenz and Jean Bon Saint-André at Mayence. They knew how to avoid too extreme a policy of gallicization especially where language was concerned. Without becoming French, the Rhinelanders were aware of the differences between themselves and other Germans. The francophobe declarations of Görres, the founder of the *Mercure rhénan* met with only a feeble reaction before 1813.

French influence penetrated to the heart of Germany with the Kingdom of Westphalia being created in 1807 from the lands of the Duke of Brunswick, the Elector of Hesse, and the Göttingen, Osnabrück and Grubenhafen lands which had been confiscated from the Elector of Hanover. And so there was a French Germany as opposed to a German France on the left bank of the Rhine. 'This kingdom,' the Emperor announced on 24 August 1807, 'will bring into existence a people which was formerly divided under so many sovereigns that it did not even have a name. The inhabitants of so many different states will finally have a country, they will be ruled by a French prince.' The prince was Jerome, Napoleon's youngest brother, whom the Emperor invited to fulfil the hopes of the German people in a letter of 7 July 1807:

May individuals who are not of noble birth and who are talented have an equal right to your consideration and to employment; may all sorts of bondage and intermediary ties between the sovereign and the lowest class of the people be entirely abolished. The benefits of the Code Napoleon, public legal proceedings and the establishment of juries will be so many distinctive characteristics of your monarchy.

With the assistance of Siméon from the Council of State, Jerome divided his kingdom into eight departments each under a prefect. The judicial hierarchy was modelled on the French one. The body politic was elected by electoral colleges. The staff consisted of a mixture of German aristocrats and intellectuals (Jean de Muller, Leist, a professor of law at Göttingen, Jacob Grimm) and Frenchmen (Norvins, Pichon, Duviquet, Lecamus). Feudalism was abolished by a decree of 23 January 1808; but even if statute labour came to an end, certain taxes (quit-rents, and feudal dues) were simply declared redeemable. So the peasants were short of money. In fact the prefects, by causing the division and abolition of common land, in order to hasten the disappearance of compulsory rotation of crops, had shaken the rural communities. Nevertheless, it must be admitted that the ideas of the Revolution were, despite a limited application, widely diffused in Germany.

WESTERN FRANCE
One of the weaker points of the Empire was the west of France: the Vendée. The pacification of the Year VIII followed by the failure of Cadoudal in Year XII had not entirely put an end to Royalist agitation. The Comte de Puisaye was still working for the English. In his *Mémoires* he defined the direction in which he intended his action to go:

> In the long run, all civil war is but a sequence of fights between those who have nohting or who do not have as much as they would like, whether of riches, distinctions, privileges, or authority, and those who, according to the former, have too much of these things. The introduction of an element of fanaticism may bring some diversity of form or detail, but brings no diversity of principle.

Puisaye was in fact paralysed by émigré intrigues. There were further blows to the conspirators in 1808. After the arrest of Prigent, Puisaye's principal agent, and of Chateaubriand, the writer's cousin, the Jersey agency was left without leaders. Besides, Puisaye quarrelled with d'Avaray, Louis XVIII's favourite.

In the Sarthe, the Mayenne, the Maine-et-Loire and the Loire-Inférieure brigandage was still rife. The police bulletin of 11 March

1809 analysed the causes of such persistence: it was hard for measures to be concerted in the four departments, there was inertia among the inhabitants, there was the influence of the *Petite Église* (the part of the Church opposed to the Concordat), there were fewer *gendarmes* and magistrates were indulgent. But where did the brigands come from? Fouché saw three classes of them; the first, and smallest, consisted of 'the criminals of the area who have taken the opportunity to thieve and to lend political tone to their brigandage'. The second class, 'which formed the main basis of the movement, is made up of deserters and rebellious conscripts'; the third group consisted of 'former Chouans some of whose names turn up again, but above all, whose spirit and behaviour recur'. As for the Anglo-Royalist scheming: 'Brittany is too repressed and too well supervised, Normandy believes too strongly in inactivity, and hopes for a first uprising are centred on the Maine.'

The western ports were, to all intents and purposes, blocked and in every bay and cove fishing or coasting vessels were brought to a standstill. Discontent was therefore rife and the public mood uncertain.

In order to disarm the opposition, Napoleon spared the Vendée: conscription there was lower than in any other part of the Empire: with a view to supervising it, he decided to found a town right in the heart of the Vendée and in 1804 chose the site at La Roche-sur-Yon on the edge of the woodland. The new city, which was the department's principal city, took Napoleon's name. But by 1812 it had only 1,900 inhabitants. Finally, in order to win over the Vendée, Napoleon granted, in 1808, a fifteen-year exemption from taxes to all whose dwellings were destroyed during the civil war on condition they were rebuilt by 1 January 1812. 'Do they still speak of the Bourbons?' the Emperor asked the solicitor Torlat at the of his journey to the west in 1808. 'Sire,' replied the lawyer, 'for a time now your glory and your bounty have caused them to be forgotten.' Torlat was a flatterer and Napoleon was not fooled. It is nevertheless true that, between 1808 and 1812, the west was still scarred by the civil war and profoundly yearned for peace. There was proof of appeasement in the decree of 6 November 1810 which reduced the brigades of *gendarmerie* in the western departments to a hundred and fifty.

CENTRAL FRANCE

Auvergne was not remarkable for her riches, she even seemed to have been somewhat overlooked by imperial politics. The south-west was able to supplement its, at times meagre, resources with the production of wood and tobacco (after 1806 factories which only used an eighth part of local produce and imported tobacco from Virginia showed a deficit). But Central France could only present a picture of desolation according to the prefects' reports. In the Year IX, the Prefect of the Haute-Loire wrote:

> The division of common land has been a real bane to agriculture. The region whose principal sources of riches were the extensive pasture-lands spread among the mountains, had, through reclamation of land, entirely lost it resources. Grassy mounds away from the hilly areas have been transformed into cornfields. The first rains wash away the little soil that there is and after one or two harvests of grain, there remains an arid and denuded rock in place of great pasture-lands which richly supplied thousands of livestock.

The devastation of nationally owned and private woodlands was a further disaster, as were the abuses of grazing, the proliferation of goats against which the intendants' former prohibition no longer held good.

And so there was a high rate of emigration from Auvergne, at least temporarily. The Revolution had slowed it down, but it was increased as a result of conscription during the first years of the Empire. The capital was seen as a refuge from whence it would be possible to avoid military service. With the perpetual levies and the shortage of local labour, emigration to Paris declined. But another form of emigration took its place, the emigration of children. According to the Prefect of the Cantal, 'There is some sort of black band which, every year, travels through the poorest and most isolated communes recruiting a small army of children who are taken to Paris where they are made to become chimney sweeps or beggars.' But morale remained good, and even though life was rough, the peasants did not complain.

SOUTHERN FRANCE

If contemporaries are to be believed the two main coastal districts of southern France—the Mediterranean, and the Atlantic—presented a picture of desolation. The German, Nemnich, described La Rochelle in 1809:

> Before these inauspicious times, La Rochelle was a hive of great activity. Now the silence of death reigns there; there is not a soul to

be met in the streets; there is as much grass here as in a field; the population which has been reduced by half for the most part remains indoors because there is nothing to do outside.

The export of spirits to England was in fact at the mercy of the vicissitudes of the Blockade. The situation was the same in Bordeaux. Nemnich wrote:

Instead of progress, there is a permanent fear of an even greater recession. The population has been reduced to 60 or 70,000; some people estimate that it has fallen even lower. Hundreds of houses are uninhabited and the old plans for expansion are laughable. A few ships are to be seen dotted sparsely on the wide surface of the sea, and the endless view is no longer cut off by a forest of masts.

The consequences of this commercial stagnation, which was not, as we shall see, completely straightforward, were that with a lack of maritime speculation, merchants tended to invest in land industries. The sugar refineries produced some of the finest sugar in France, which was sold mostly in the south-east. Bordeaux also harboured some fifty tobacco factories and paper mills. But other industries, like glassworks and cooperage, were in a bad way. Although in the Landes, Duplantier had continued Bremontier's work of planting pines, and although the countryside around Bordeaux was experiencing an exceptional boom, particularly in vineyards, the problem of outlets was becoming increasingly acute. And therefore the public mood in Bordeaux was bad.

Things were no better on the Mediterranean coast. The English Blockade was becoming increasingly strict, and the imperial regime was falling into discredit for its incapacity to maintain coastal security. Every evening in 1813 the British fleet dropped anchor in the roadstead at Hyères. 'Her presence cannot cause alarm since she has no troops to disembark and therefore can undertake nothing on our islands or along our coast. Only her audacity and the confidence with which her boats go up and down the roadstead are wounding.' Already in 1808, Maurice de Tascher wrote in his diary: 'The English squadron, consisting of twelve vessels and four frigates, is exactly blocking the Port of Toulon.' The great prosperity of Marseilles was no longer; the suppression, in 1794, of the free ports followed by the Continental Blockade, caused the total stagnation of trade.

The industrial situation was no less catastrophic. Limoux cloth still found a market in Italy, but the manufacturers in Carcassonne had lost their outlets in the East. Even before the crisis of 1810, the Nîmes silk industry was in trouble. Hopes that the United States would replace the Spanish market soon came to nothing. The Marseilles soap-works which had also been exporting large quantities of red woollen bonnets from the Hérault to the Orient, were also victims of the war. The slowing down of commerce led many dealers to invest their capital in the soap-works. Hence a boom in production coincided with the crisis of outlets. Finally the Mediterranean departments suffered from the inadequacy of their cereal production. Each year they had to import a large quantity of corn and could only compensate for this by the sale of other products which often proved difficult and which mainly depended on the vineyards and arboriculture. Under the circum stances, it is hardly surprising that reports on the public mood were so pessimistic. The Sub-Prefect at Aix wrote, 'Men dedicated to govern ment are rare. They are only to be found among public officials and magistrates. Partisans of the Emperor can be counted, but the worried and discontented abound.'

The Royalists were not alone in agitating; anarchy was equally rife around Marseilles, in the Var and the Alps. Alliances were sworn. In 1811 the police uncovered a plot whose leader was apparently Guidal, Malet's future accomplice. It was a plot to hand the Toulon seaboard over to the English. The Prefect of the Bouches-du-Rhône accused Barras of being at the centre of this intrigue. Barras was at the time living in the South of France for health reasons and was obliged to go into exile in Rome.

Higher up the Rhône, Nemnich affirmed that the economy in the region of Lyons was, on the other hand, in excellent shape. After the destruction by the Terror and the troubles of the Directory, there was an astonishing boom in manufacturing due to the activity of the Chamber of Commerce, Jacquard's technical innovations in mechanics and Raymond's in dyeing. But Lyons owed this boom above all to the new routes through the Alps, more especially to the Mont-Cenis Pass. So the town had no difficulty in obtaining Illyrian and Levantine cotton and Piedmontese rice; by the same route i was able to export books and cloth. After 1801, traffic from Lyons repre sented seven-eighths of local trade. After the turmoil, society was rediscovering its equilibrium little by little. Intellectual life returned to its former brilliance and in no way deserved Benjamin Constant's severe judgement of 1804: 'This town seems to me to unite the bore dom of small German market towns with all the insipidity of small

French towns.' In fact Lyons was the centre of the religious revival so closely linked to Ballanche's philosophy.

Geneva was united with Bonneville and Thonon in the department of Léman which was created on 25 April 1798, and, as Benjamin Constant recalled in his memoirs of 1799, it symbolized the Protestant republican spirit as opposed to the Catholic monarchist spirit of the Savoyards. The union was a bad one. A few factories were established in the town but the remainder of the department devoted itself entirely to agriculture. In fact, Geneva became considerably poorer. Incorporated within a rigid system, the town had lost its traditional role of depository and intermediary. The return of internal peace was counter-balanced by commercial and financial stagnation with which certain elements of the bourgeoisie were very impatient.

The *Confédération helvétique,* of which Napoleon was mediator, shared this security. Swiss opinion welcomed in Napoleon the man who, as he had done in France, had put an end to inter-party struggles and above all who had swept away the unpopular Helvetian republic. The 1803 act of mediation maintained a regime of equality among the citizens whilst preserving the autonomy of the cantons. It also preserved the social advantages of the Helvetian regime established by the Directory, and kept the former confederation's federal tradition. In fact there was, in addition to the act of mediation, a treaty of alliance which gave the Confederation the standing of a satellite state. This caused protestations among the aristocrats who had taken the Austrian side, and discontent among the tradesmen and industrialists who were affected by the Continental Blockade; also a certain irritation on the part of the Swiss at the time of the French annexation of the Valais in 1810 or the occupation of the Tessin.

FRENCH ITALY

The Alpine barrier no longer existed during the First Empire. Milan was attached to the upper valley of the Rhône by the Simplon Pass. As early as 1802, Bonaparte had understood the economic and strategic importance of this route, but until 1810, the Simplon did not play the part expected of it. It was criticized for enabling the Milanese to carry on a fruitful contraband with Switzerland to the detriment of France. The Mont-Cenis Pass was favoured on the whole. The Savoyards had begged for this route which connected the Maurienne to Chambéry. The Lyons silk industry had also supported a route which made it possible to procure with ease its raw materials from Piedmont, and even from the Levant via Ancona and the Adriatic. Piedmont also favoured the development of the Mont-Cenis route which would be advantageous to her trade. After 1805 Mont-Cenis therefore became the obligatory pass for the great axis of Paris–Turin–Genoa. The decrees of 1807 and 1808 confirmed this choice. At the time, the traffic through the Mont-Cenis Pass was four times that of the Simplon. In 1810 the situation changed. The annexation of the Valais made the Simplon more important again by simplifying the work of the customs officers. Because, since the annexation of Illyria, a congestion of Levantine cotton was feared on the Mont-Cenis route, a decree of 12 April 1811 granted the same customs rights to the Simplon as those enjoyed by the Mont-Cenis. Traffic was then divided between the two routes.

Under Napoleon's rule the map of Italy was considerably simplified.

The fifteen departments of French Italy stretched from Turin to Rome, which was to be taken from the Pope in 1809 and to become the second city of the Empire. The Kingdom of Italy, consisting of twenty-four departments, was administered from Milan by a viceroy, Eugène de Beauharnais. Finally, the Kingdom of Naples, removed from the Bourbons who were pushed back into Sicily, profited from a relative independence under, first, Joseph Bonaparte and, then, Murat. Italy therefore found itself setting out on a path to unification, and Napoleon on St Helena was to take a certain pride in it—though not without exaggerating:

> As for the fifteen million Italians, their unification was well under way; only time was needed and each day the unity of principles of legislation, of thought and of feeling, ripened among them, and with this unity assured, human integration could not fail. The union of Piedmont to France and that of Parma, Tuscany and Rome were to my mind only temporary. The only aim was that they should be supervised and that the national education of the Italians should be guaranteed and furthered.

So to the wish for political unity, grossly exaggerated by Napoleon on St Helena, was added a wish for judicial unity. The introduction of French laws was aimed, in Rome as in Turin, at establishing the annexation. In Milan it aimed at preparing for the annexation, whereas in Naples the intention was to crush the opposition of the old feudalism. Supported by a force of forty thousand men, whose job involved the control of brigandage which was particularly active,

Joseph undertook an important work of reorganization. He instituted a Minister of the Interior and provincial intendants modelled on the French prefects. He reorganized the fiscal system and established a property tax and the sale of Church property. Joseph was fortunate in being surrounded by excellent ministers, Miot, Roederer and Salicetti. With Murat, who succeeded Joseph in 1808, the Neapolitan bourgeoisie became associated with government, particularly thanks to the two great ministers, Zurlo for the Interior and Ricciardi for Justice, who dominated the government. At the same time a middle class developed, consisting of officials and the militia, and it was from this class that the *carbonari* were to develop. Naples was coming to life again despite the constrictions of the Continental Blockade. All former jurisdiction was abolished.

In the north (Lombardy, Tuscany and Piedmont), where legislation was already more advanced as a result of the enlightened despotism of Vienna and also the Italian Enlightenment, Napoleon's innovations caused no sensation. This was not the case in the south. In Rome the Pontifical Tribunals disappeared; this profoundly upset the Roman bourgeoisie which mostly consisted of lawyers. An even greater change was brought about with the introduction of divorce, which upset the Italian clergy. With the arrival in Italy of the French troops under the Revolution, seigniorial rights had been abolished; Napoleon's occupation ratified this abolition with certain variations in the south at least. But the Italian peasantry did not profit from the French domination by acquiring property; rather, property was transferred from the aristocracy to the bourgeoisie which allowed for the continued maintenance of large estates on which the new landlords were able to develop up-to-date production. In Piedmont the rice fields, under the management of wealthy farmers turned landowners, spread considerably. The effects were disastrous to public health. 'The rice-fields continue to reap men,' the Prefect of Sesia wrote in 1803. But otherwise the French administration encouraged agriculture, different forms of afforestation, irrigation in the regions of Mincio and the Adige, the draining of the marshes around Verona and the introduction of model sheep-folds. Corn and mulberry trees were grown in the north, whilst in the south, cotton, woad and sugar cane were on the increase.

Napoleon intended using Italy to supply France with agricultural produce. But as far as industry was concerned he merely saw Italy as a market for goods manufactured in France. Conditions were, however, favourable for industrialization in the north where corporations had been abolished long before the arrival of the French. In fact the Piedmontese silk works were in danger; raw or spun silk was finding its way straight to Lyons. So trade between France and Italy adopted the form of relations between a parent state and a colony.

National resistance was weak in northern Italy. Large landowners as well as former Jacobins accepted posts in the new administration. In Rome the situation was quite different. There, the bourgeoisie had depended too much on the noble families and the Holy See to be able to break away from them. As for the great families, with few exceptions (one Borghese, one Spada, and one Chigi), they kept their distance. Rome was not to forgive the French for the removal of Pius VII nor for plans to establish the Vatican in Paris. Conscription on the whole aroused public feeling more than the national humiliations did. When the new Prefects of Trasimeno and Rome announced the first levy on 30 April 1810, a third of those called up went underground. Tournon's great works which involved draining the Pontine marshes in three years, the construction of terraces and gardens stretching from the Villa Medici to the Villa Borghese, the excavation of ancient Rome and the transformation of the Roman countryside into an immense cotton field, did not compensate for the absence of Pius VII. Not for long would Rome be the second city of the Empire, despite Napoleon's vast plans for her. The precarious balance achieved in Italy in 1807 was upset only two years later by the removal of the Pope.

PARIS

Paris remained the capital of the Empire in spite of the intention expressed by Napoleon in 1804 to establish the seat of his government at Lyons, close to the Italian frontier. The city harboured the governmental seat at the Tuileries, the assemblies (the Legislative Body at the Bourbon Palace and the Senate at the Luxembourg Palace) as well as ministries and director-generals' offices.

The picture presented by the capital whose population had risen in fifteen years from 500,000 inhabitants to 700,000, had not changed much under the Empire. Napoleon's Paris was still Louis XVI's Paris, with a few extra monuments such as the Vendôme Column finished by Gondoin in 1810 with Chaudet's statue of the Emperor on top, the triumphal arch on the Place du Carrousel which Percier and Fontaine finished at the end of 1808, the foundations of the Étoile conceived by Chalgrin, the rue de Rivoli with its arcades, the church of the

Madeleine which had been begun before the Revolution and which Napoleon hoped to make into a temple of glory, and a few quays and bridges. The list is not negligible but the appearance of Paris was not changed as drastically as Napoleon would have liked. He would have liked a grandiose city made up of palaces and public monuments.

Under the Empire the great exodus from the provinces towards Paris began. But emigration was still seasonal. Forty thousand workers came to Paris every year in the working season. Many of these workers remained in the town during the dead season and congregated in slums in the centre where they were to form the kernel of the dangerous classes later to be discovered by Eugène Sue and Victor Hugo in the time of Louis-Philippe.

Paris's new industrial boom which had started during the Revolution, continued in fact, during the Empire. The disappearance of English competition favoured the cotton industry. Scientific dis coveries and the necessities of war explain the advances made by the chemical industry and mechanical construction. The influx of foreigners stimulated the manufacture of luxury goods (goldsmiths, clock-makers and cabinet-makers experienced a boom). But this boom was not based on solid foundations because of the hostility of the administration which feared too great a concentration of workers in the capital. Neither was this concentration wanted by the industrial Parisians. Of the ten thousand workers employed by Richard-Lenoir barely a thousand were in Paris. This was in order to satisfy an administration who feared overcrowding in the capital of the Empire. The authorities' constant concern was the avoidance of famine, unemployment and epidemics.

The superiority of Paris really expressed itself in artistic and intellectual spheres. Having tasted the delights of the capital, Stendhal could only despise the provinces. This attitude was unjustified, for after all the provinces had their newspapers, their academies and theatres. But they could not compare with those in the capital. Hence the fascination which Paris held for the rest of the Empire.

UNIFICATION

How stable then was France, with the manufacturers' prosperity in the north and the east, the cornfields of the Île-de-France and the Norman *Bocage,* but with ruination in the ports and an accentuated economic backwardness in the Massif Central? Furthermore there were forty-two million inhabitants speaking at least six languages, not including patois. The balance achieved in 1807 was perhaps a very precarious one.

In order to maintain unity, Napoleon took his inspiration from Roman principles. He gave primary importance to communication routes. As early as 1805, he wrote, 'Of all paths and roads, those which unite France and Italy are the most politic.' And in 1811 he wrote, 'The road from Amsterdam to Antwerp will bring Amsterdam twenty-four hours closer to Paris, and the road from Hamburg to Wesel will bring Hamburg four days closer to Paris; this assures and strengthens the union of these countries to the Empire.' The decree of 16 December 1811 established a grading of the fourteen first-class roads stretching out from Paris towards the distant parts of the Empire. The most important were Road 2, which went from Paris to Amsterdam via Brussels and Antwerp, Road 3 from Paris to Hamburg via Liège and Bremen, Road 4 towards Mayence and Prussia, Road 6 from Paris to Rome through the Simplon and Milan, Road 7 from Paris to Turin via Mont-Cenis and Road 11 from Paris to Bayonne.

The quality of the roads should not be exaggerated. The ruts found by Poumiès de la Siboutie on his way from the Dordogne, where he lived, to Paris were quite deplorable. Maurice de Tascher for his part, preferred the waterways and, in his *Journal*, he gave a picturesque description of his journey along the Saône. Letter post was organized in the service of the state from 16 December 1799 and afterwards entrusted to La Valette who established for the Emperor a dispatch system whose merits he praised highly in his *Mémoires*. The state extended its control to public transport for travellers and goods, particularly by the decree of 20 May 1805. Only haulage remained free. In French society the postmaster became a notable, but travel remained an adventure. Poumiès de la Siboutie tells us that it took a hundred and twenty hours to go from Bordeaux to Paris by stagecoach. 'One left at six or seven o'clock in the morning and stopped around midday for lunch. One travelled all day and in the evening stopped to dine and slept till morning.' Many people only travelled on foot. At that time a great deal of walking was done, which explains the endurance of Napoleon's soldiers.

Napoleon, inspired by the Romans, imposed a common legislation on his Empire. The Civil Code was introduced in all annexed countries and in all dependent kingdoms. A new society was to be born in which the peasant would be liberated from seigniorial rights, and in which the bourgeoisie would be the economically powerful class. Napoleon saw in the Civil Code an instrument of war against feudalism which he knew how to handle when the moment was ripe. 'Establish the Civil Code in Naples,' he wrote to Joseph in 1806, 'then everything which is against you will be destroyed within a few years and that which you want to preserve will be strengthened. This is the great advantage of the Civil Code.' Except for annexed territories, he was careful not absolutely to impose the code everywhere. He was a reformer who knew how to advance by stages. It can be seen from the language used. The administration was naturally operated bi-lingually, and responsible posts were given in preference to Frenchmen, but Italians, Belgians and Dutchmen had seats in the Senate. Some prefects, mostly of Belgian origin, held office in French departments. In annexed countries teaching was allowed to keep its own identity; French did not become an obligatory second language, there was no attempt to destroy the soul of conquered provinces. Besides, the mixing of nationalities brought about by conscription was an important factor in the integration of peoples with a different language. In 1806 the Sub-Prefect of Montélimar noted that in the 'afore-mentioned Provence, the Languedoc and in the southern part of the Dauphiné, the patois idiom is used rather less generally; troop movements, travellers and the soldiers returning to their homes must have taught the French language to a certain number of individuals.'

Finally, unification was also economic. All departments were surrounded by the protectionist cordon of the imperial customs which forbade all foreign competition. This Empire which stretched from Danzig to Bayonne represented a market of eighty million consumers. The key to the Napoleonic economic system lay in the fact that this market was reserved for French industry to which other parts of the Empire were obliged to supply raw materials. 'My principle,' Napoleon wrote to Eugène de Beauharnais, 'is France before everything!' Marcel Dunan, the historian of the Continental System has written:

Politically Napoleon wished to surround himself with vassals and not with allies; economically he did not want friends but dependants. He did not consider offering his states the advantages which he demanded of other countries for French trade and industry. Our products had to circulate everywhere, entering freely, they had even to be favoured by a series of concessions negotiated in a cavalier fashion, but the frontiers remained inexorably closed to all foreign competition, and articles to which the multiple prohibitions did not apply were taxed more or less heavily and brought millions to the coffers of the imperial customs.

Until 1810 this at least served the interests of the new French bourgeoisie. Very soon the image of the Revolution was to be confused in annexed countries with an economic imperialism which was often brutal and quite out of proportion with the possibilities of production in France proper, a France which had as yet barely recovered from the civil war from which she had just suffered.

2

THE RULE OF THE NOTABLES

If Bertin l'Aîné, painted in about 1832 by Ingres, symbolizes the France of Louis-Philippe, then Français de Nantes, as seen by David, with his flushed face, his corpulence and the braided uniform of an important personage must best exemplify the aspirations of the French under the Empire. They wanted riches, positions and honours. The reign of the new notables had begun. To quote Barante,

> Public authority in every field and in all its degrees had for several years passed into the hands of officials who had been chosen neither for their capabilities, for their experience nor for the respect which they enjoyed. The opinions which they professed, the successive opportunities of the Revolution, accidents of election, and the trust or favour of government representatives were their only passports to promotion. It was to this new aristocracy that the Convention had bequeathed France. The upper class which consisted of men distinguished for their talents, their social position, their independence or the exercise of public duties had been decimated by the scaffold, exile and persecution . . . riches had been destroyed by confiscation, bankruptcy and the over-production of paper money.

Bankruptcy and paper money, in combination with national property, were the origins of the new notables' fortunes. A. Malraux found an unexpected formula with which to explain this new moneyed aristocracy: 'It is because of Napoleon that Madame Récamier on her chaise-longue succeeds the *Maja desnuda*.'

THE FOUNDATIONS OF THE NEW SOCIETY
In 1808 land was still the essential basis for wealth, even if others were

beginning to appear. To the prestige which still attached itself to the possession of land had been added a feeling of security in land, which had developed since the disastrous inflation of *assignats*. The land had been freed from feudalism and the Civil Code had sealed the abolition of the Ancien Régime. The inviolable and sacred right of property was limited only by the rights of the state. The Code was designed for the property owner—above all the landowner. More attention was paid to real estate than to chattels. In 1807 the cadastral survey was begun which was to decide the distribution of land and to ratify the sale of national property.

The liquidation of this property followed, but at a very reduced pace. The decree of 9 Floréal Year IX which anyway excluded the resale by bond-holders and the granting of property designated by the redemption of the two-thirds bonds, suspended sales which began again with the passing of the laws of 15 and 16 Floréal Year X and of 15 Ventôse Year XII. The number of sales under the Revolution had reached 1,100,674 but after Year X there were only 40,000. This is to say that stocks were low due to the quantity of sales during the Revolution and the restitution of property to aristocrats and 'manufacturers.' Furthermore the decree of 15 Brumaire Year IX gave four millions worth of national property to hospices, and more went to the Légion d'honneur and to the *sénatoreries*. In the north, sales were still considerable, but in the west and south they were in perpetual decline. In the Haut-Rhin and Lorraine they had stagnated. Who were the buyers? On average, ten per cent were dealers and merchants, about as many again were lawyers, seven or eight per cent were former noblemen, a few were officials or ecclesiastics, the rest were peasants, groups of whom had often formed themselves into companies. Because the land in question was of poor quality, producing little income and often made up of isolated pieces which could not be regrouped, the era of the speculator seemed to come to an end, except around Paris (particularly in the Seine-et-Marne) where the Prefect under the Consulate had to annul adjudications following certain coalitions 'of a handful of greedy men'. Small landowners profited from these last sales, although not so much in the east as in the north and south.

The transfer of communal property decided on as a result of Treasury difficulties, by the law of 20 March 1813, was to relaunch speculation, although only briefly and in limited areas (there is no trace of sales in the Haute-Loire or in the Dombes).

Interest was then directed towards uncultivated private property which the owners, who were old aristocrats or bourgeois, were obliged to sell because of difficulties resulting from the Revolution, and which Rémusat summarized very well in his *Mémoires*: 'Sequestration, revolutionary measures and bad harvests had ruined estates, deprived them of an income and aggravated debts'; and it was only at the cost of long and difficult legal proceedings that rights of succession were won back, only to be sold again immediately. The payment of farm rents in devalued *assignats* had struck the former rich landowners a hard blow. Often a repatriated émigré would have to concentrate his entire resources on the recuperation of a particular estate. Because of this he would have to sell some of his lands.

Financiers, merchants and manufacturers enriched by speculation in colonial commodities, or as a result of the boom given to industry by the Continental outlets, immediately became buyers and invested their money in land. It would seem significant that out of 1,056 of the largest landowners in France, 130 were manufacturers and merchants. The fortune of a Richard-Lenoir, a Ternaux or a Récamier came partly from urban or rural landed property. These fortunes were built up above all during the Revolution from national property. When Bidermann went bankrupt in January 1811, he owned assets which exceeded his liabilities by 1,800,000 francs, but the assets were in land and it was impossible for him to realize them.

Capital invested in land was safe. But land was also a source of social prestige. In December 1802, Fiévée noted that the members of the electoral colleges being recruited from among the most highly taxed citizens caused 'an increase in the value of large landed properties'. At the beginning of the nineteenth century it was impossible to conceive of an élite which was not landed. The hierarchy was still decided by the ownership of land.

THE NOTABLES

The whole Napoleonic system depended on the notables who dominated the economic, administrative and legal life of the country. The notion, if not the word, appeared at the time of the Constitution of Year VIII which entrusted them with departmental and national public offices. But it is through the lists established as a result of the law of 13 Ventôse Year IX that the notables' social context can best be understood. What should the dominating criteria be—birth, age, merit, or fortune? Former revolutionaries were hostile to 'birth', Bonaparte was opposed to fortune: 'A title cannot be created from wealth. Who are the rich? The buyers of national property, the suppliers, the thieves. How can a *notabilité* be founded on fortunes acquired in these ways?' Even if a man's good name played a part, the prefects' reports indicate that money, in fact, became the essential criterion of a regime appointed by colleges of tax payers, but in which the First Consul reserved the right to nominate officials, and the Senate nominated the assemblies. With the reform of Year X, the members of departmental colleges had been elected for life from among the six hundred most highly taxed citizens in the department. These lists give us the first picture of the notables who were to dominate the political life of France at the beginning of the nineteenth century.

In the case of Paris, a marked predominance of landowners and *rentiers* (more than 240) has been established. There were seventy-two tradesmen (although the *patente*, or tradesman's tax, was sometimes excluded from assessment of tax payable). There were fifty-four highly placed officials. Some of the professions were well represented, with twenty-two lawyers and fifteen bankers; but there was only a limited group of, for instance, doctors. The average income varied according to the section of Paris. It was 40,000 francs in La Fontaine de Grenelle, 35,000 in the Roule section, 12,000 in la Réunion, and 15,000 francs in Arcis. Incomes were never below 5,000 francs. This average annual income of 5,000 francs, or 100,000 francs of capital is the figure most frequently found in the provinces although in less privileged areas it might be as low as 3,000 francs.

So what was a notable under the Empire? He was a landowner, (very often a former nobleman), a *rentier*, an important tradesman, a lawyer, usually a notary or a solicitor, whose income from real estate was generally above 5,000 francs. If he was among the six hundred most highly taxed persons in his department he would have had a chance of entering the electoral college in the main town, even of becoming president, and of being appointed a senator or a deputy in the Legislative Body. Undoubtedly it was possible to exercise enormous influence in a department without possessing a large fortune, and also to enter the college of the *arrondissement*, the recruitment for which was not based on tax. But this small landowner who might be the 'conscience' of a little town could not enter the departmental college which was reserved for the six hundred mostly highly taxed. In tax assessment, the amount of land-tax payed was a determining factor since, with a few exceptions, there were no fortunes in stocks and shares. A mentality which was to be perpetuated was born. Although the possession of an investment portfolio was, with the development of capitalism, to acquire an importance which it could not have in 1808, it was never going to be able to withstand competition from landed property (houses, farms, woodlands) which seemed after successive devaluations to be the safest investment.

The fact remained that the government stockholder was, of all the notables, the one most interested in the survival of the regime. Napoleon made no mistake about it. He insisted on knowing every day the rate for the five per cent government stock, and in order to reorganize the money market which had been compromised by agiotage, he laid down rules for the stockbroking profession and for the activities of the Stock Exchange. The effect of the consular decisions was slow in making itself felt, despite payments in cash, because of the war and the financial crash of the united merchants. But the *rentiers'* mistrust disappeared after the victory of Friedland: the five per cent stock which was at 17.37 on 8 February 1800 rose to 93 by 27 August 1807. Over three years it was to become stablilized at around 84.

The notable was often an official. Balzac was one of the first to underline the growing importance under the Empire of a population of employees who depended on the government for honours and for their means of existence. On 21 April 1809, Cretet, the Minister of the Interior, established the first statute of officials. A scale of salaries was then worked out. Salaries were at last paid regularly and they played a decisive role in the prestige of public office. There were two thousand candidates for twenty-four posts at the time of the creation of the Audit Office. In Paris a prefect earned 30,000 francs whereas a provincial prefect earned between 8,000 and 24,000 francs. A sub-prefect was paid between 3,000 and 4,000 francs, and an inspector-general of civil engineering earned 12,000 francs. The head of an administrative division received 12,000 francs, a departmental head, graded first class, received 6,000 francs, a second head 4,500 francs, a drafter of deeds received 3,400 francs and a clerk from 2,000 to 3,000 francs. At the top of the hierarchy, a councillor of state's salary was 25,000 francs to which were added considerable perks. On the other hand the 'talents', as they were called at the time—that is members of the Institut, doctors, writers and teachers—occupied a very small place on the list of notables. Proof enough that the regime was based on the tax. The notable was a man who held authority, albeit the authority of an employer over his workmen, of a highly placed official over his clerks, or of a landowner over his farmhands and tenants. At the basis of this authority lay money. The age of a fortune was not taken into consideration. More often than not the riches of the notables dated from before the Revolution and had increased as a result of the Revolution. The Dietrichs, the Rambourgs and the Wendels continued to dominate the ironworks; more than fifty per cent of the firms founded before 1789 were in textiles. Nearly all the big business people of the Ancien Régime were to be found again in industry under the Empire. The same goes for the banks where the Mallets, the Hottinguers, the Lecouteulx and Perrégaux had begun to build themselves a fortune before 1789. It must be significant that in the inquiry which the Consulate ordered to find the twelve people who paid the highest land-tax, a nobleman often headed the list—Luynes in the Seine-et-Oise, the Duc de Luxembourg in the Seine-et-Marne. The old bourgeoisie whose income came from the land profited greatly from the sale of government property and withstood the changes better than the administrative bourgeoisie. And rich merchants specializing in a three-sided trade in Nantes or Bordeaux turn out to have performed some skilful reconversions. The new notables came from administration, from politics and above all from speculation in national property, colonial commodities, *assignats* and military supplies.

THE OTHER FRANCE: THE WORKING CLASSES

Although France was growing more middle class, it remained profoundly rural. In any case the peasant world offered a wide diversity, from the large landowner who speculated over the sale of his produce to the small tenant farmer whose situation was often difficult. The hold of the notables (whether the old nobility or the new landowners) over the countryside was hardly debatable. All the prefects confirmed their influence and the government did not underestimate it.

Two categories profited from the advance of agricultural production and from the circumstances resulting from war. They were the landowner and the journeyman. The large landowner, thanks to his capital and to the productivity of his lands, grew richer in times of famine, particularly in 1801; at other times he benefited from the increase in trade outlets of which Napoleon's conquests assured him. 'The victories of our armies, by extending the limits of the Empire, considerably benefit the sale of our agricultural produce,' Caillot wrote in his *Mémoires*, 'so immense quantities of grain passed into nations whose poor land could not produce an ear of corn.' This accurately describes the position in the north and the east, although not the position on the Atlantic coast.

The journeymen, who made up the rural proletariat (about sixty or seventy per cent of country dwellers were journeymen), profited from the shortage of farm hands due to a more and more demanding conscription. The resultant rise in salaries between 1798 and 1815 reached nearly twenty per cent. With improved conditions, they could sometimes even buy property—only a small amount, it is true—in the last sales of national property. Fauchet, the Prefect of the Var indicates several people in his department who acquired, 'by dint of economy and deals which did not overburden them' a little field which they cultivated outside their working hours. In the *arrondissement* of Provins, the 6,271 recorded labourers cultivated 34,680 hectares out of a possible 84,000. It is perhaps not so strange as it might appear that journeymen even had servants—a kind of sub-proletariat of cowherds, shepherds and carters. This improvement in their position gave rise to some irritation: 'Journeymen,' noted the author of the departmental statistics for the Nord, 'have shown themselves to be insolent and daring since army conscription has put them in greater demand.' In order to avoid excessive rises, servants and seasonal labourers such as harvesters, were forbidden to form groups.

Circumstances were less favourable for the farmer and tenant farmer. Whereas the big farmer, like the landowner, profited from the rise in prices and the increase in trade outlets, the small farmer was confronted by serious difficulties. After a moment of euphoria the rise in the price of corn was barely eighteen per cent between 1809 and 1812, whilst the rise in farm rent for the same period reached thirty-seven per cent. Let us take the case, described by the Prefect of the Meurthe, of a farmer from the *arrondissement* of Lunéville who cultivated a property of twelve hectares. His rent was 1,200 francs; he had to pay a ploughboy and a herdsman, both of whom were employed throughout the year, he had also to be sure of the services of casual labourers in certain seasons. To all this was added maintenance of farm implements, food and clothing. The farmer's entire expenditure exceeded 3,488 francs whereas his income reached 3,646 francs. Profits came from the sale of corn either in the market or to itinerant merchants who came to fetch it from the farms. The length of leases—from three to nine years—was far too limited and represented a serious handicap. The situation of the share-cropper or tenant farmer who paid part of his crop in rent was even worse. According to Sismondi, nine-tenths of those who cultivated land were share-croppers. They worked land which was not highly productive and their marketable surplus was not enough to enable them to benefit from the advantages made available by the new state of affairs. Nevertheless their condition was considerably improved: their share was no longer subjected to tithes and was often exempt from tax. In his *Mémoires sur le Métayage*, Gasparin notes that share-croppers were the class in France least burdened with taxes.

Wine growers, usually smallholders, were, however, a particular case. According to sub-prefects' reports, a moderate year producing good-quality wine was preferable to a year of great abundance by reason of the decrease in costs and the increase, on the other hand, of the price per hectolitre. Costs were in fact greater—manure, vine-props, cultivation, casks. Even for the Bordelais confronted with the problem of exports to England the income was low.

Nevertheless, as late as 1809 properties were being bought from the imperial regime who guaranteed a return to security due to the decrease in brigandage, a fairer distribution of taxation and the maintenance of revolutionary gains (the abolition of feudal rights, and to a certain extent the sale of national property). Unquestionably living conditions in the countryside improved. As early as 1805, Peuchet remarked in his *Statistiques élémentaires de la France*:

> More bread and more meat are eaten in France today than formerly. The country-dweller who knew nothing better than rough food and unhealthy drink, today eats meat and bread and drinks good cider and beer. Colonial commodities (like sugar and coffee) have also spread around the countryside with the increased wealth of cultivators.

And Chaptal himself recognized:

> The ruinous system for the countryside combined with requisitions and conscription should have made the Emperor odious to the peasants, but that is not the case. They were among the warmest partisans, because he reassured them about the return of tithes, feudal rights, the restitution of property to émigrés and the oppression of the lords.

The Emperor found this popularity equally among the ranks of the urban proletariat. These town dwellers, artisans, craftsmen, low-paid workers who had been in the forefront during the great revolutionary days of Paris, and who at Lyons had supplied the greater part of the

Chaliers' strength, and at Marseilles that of the terrorists, had without much difficulty, rallied to the Empire. The idea of the sans-culottes was no more than a memory at which only a few police veterans would still tremble. How can such an infatuation for Napoleon—the word is not too strong—be explained?

The legal position of the worker in fact grew worse under the Empire. The law of 22 Germinal Year XI instituted the *livret*, a document which he was obliged to hand to his employer when he was engaged and which was returned to him on leaving. This document made the worker dependent on his master and made it possible for the police to supervise migrations of workers. But it is sometimes forgotten that the Minister of the Interior used the poverty of workers to justify the introduction of the *livret* which was no more than a return to a practice of the Ancien Régime. Firms attempted to entice workers away from rival organizations; the workers therefore, with no regard for previous agreements, tended to profit from the advantages which this overbidding brought them. The aim of the *livret* was to safeguard for manufacturers a more or less stable workforce. But the employers, especially in the building trade, were subject to no sanctions and themselves encouraged workers to get around the law by engaging them without the *livret*. Furthermore, attempts made by the police to control the movement of workers through employment bureaux, ended in failure.

Any coalition or union was forbidden by articles 414, 415 and 416 of the penal code. All the same, there were a large number of strikes, especially in Paris. No doubt they were limited to one site or at least to a few elements of one trade, and they lasted no longer than eight days. They never took on a political character. They were caused, above all, by the introduction of machinery (at Lille in 1805, at Sedan in 1803) or by the length of the working day. In 1801 the workmen employed to erect scaffolding for the fête of 14 July in Paris demanded a ten per cent increase; the ring-leaders, among them a wine merchant, were arrested by the police; in August 1802 building works were interrupted on the Pont d'Austerlitz. The approach of the coronation provided a pretext for the workmen employed in Notre-Dame in 1804. The following year the men working in the Louvre refused to have their working day lengthened. The strike of 1805 was more serious and was extended to a large number of public works. There was another strike in August 1807 when the stone-cutters at the Louvre came out. A very serious incident occurred on the site of the Arc de Triomphe at the Étoile in March 1810 as the result of an accident, which necessitated the intervention of the armed forces. There, it was a matter of spectacular demonstrations—a number of coalitions which ended in a compromise. In October 1806, a police regulation determined a new timetable for public works in Paris: only one hour's break was laid down, between ten and eleven o'clock. Workers refused to return to these old rules, they demanded a tea-break for what they called their 'meal on stone' in the afternoon. A significant detail: 'They claimed that if the Emperor had been in Paris, His Majesty would not have allowed the passing of the regulation.' The movement began on 6 October and only ended on the 13th with the agreement that the workers would lunch between ten and eleven o'clock and would have tea on site between half past two and three o'clock. It was an exceptional case. Repression was often severe, with imprisonment or the dismissal of ringleaders in the provinces. But the bosses were not spared. When they combined to lower wages, the police immediately obstructed their plans, no doubt more for reasons of law and order than because of any concern for fairness. But such an attitude impressed the workers in the capital favourably and explains the popularity of the Emperor in the suburbs. So the Parisian paper-manufacturers, to put a stop to the claims of their workers, requested a fixed maximum salary and were shown the door by Dubois, the Prefect of Police. In 1801 and 1810 the rates laid down by the hatters' employers were also nullified.

The conciliation boards instituted, by a law of 18 March 1806 for the purpose of arbitration between employers and workers, were far from being as fair as Napoleon had foreseen. But the worker had sufficient means at his disposal. *Compagnonnages*—workers' associations—although illegal, reappeared. Should they be forbidden? Réal, one of the chiefs of police recommended tolerance: '*Compagnonnage,* which is a kind of masonry, exists since time immemorial. I despair of fruitfully attacking its essence, and limit myself to the prevention of its excesses in so far as that depends on me.' Could he have done otherwise? Particularly as the various *compagnonnages* wasted their time in brawls among themselves and took no political action. Hence a certain accommodating attitude on the part of the Imperial Police in the provinces, if not in Paris.

The drain caused by the Napoleonic wars emptied the towns, as well as the countryside, of younger men and caused a grave crisis of manpower. No doubt the proportion was low in comparison to the population which was of a working age, but the most active element and those most in demand were removed. Seasonal immigration, which consisted of some forty thousand workers who came to the capital in search of work in the summer months, began to decline around 1812. On visiting some work sites in Paris in December 1813, Napoleon was surprised to see only old men. 'You can find as many old men as you need,' replied the contractor, 'but they have neither the courage nor the strength for the work. As for the young, you don't see them any more. Conscription has swept them away.' There was no certainty of relief because of the length of the wars.

The worker did not complain so long as he avoided military service. Such a shortage naturally favours the rise of wages. The rise varied according to the profession: it was particularly marked in the building trade but much less so in the textile trade. The rise was greater in Paris than in the provinces, which was the cause of so great a seasonal emigration to the capital. The rise was irregular and was interrupted by the crisis of 1810. It can be estimated at more than twenty-five per cent since 1789 (but the cost of living had risen equally, except for the price of bread which, at Napoleon's will had remained in Paris at less than 18 *sous* for four pounds). A worker in the capital earned between 3 and 4 francs, that is to say, taking Sundays and holidays into account, less than 900 francs a year which was not very much in comparison to a councillor of state's 25,000 francs. In the provinces, the average wage of a labourer was 1 franc-20 in 1801; a more specialized worker would earn between 1 franc-60 and 2 francs, but the cost of living was lower than in the capital except for bread.

However, the disappearance of unemployment and a relative rise in wages brought about an improvement in material conditions. Undoubtedly there were many accidents at work and sickness took its toll. In the overwhelming report established by the Prefecture of Police in 1807, it is to be seen that life expectancy rarely exceeded fifty in certain professions (shoemakers, bakers, carders), and suicides occurred frequently. Alexis de Ferrière remarks in Year IX: 'The workman has marginally improved his diet; he eats meat more often and drinks fermented liquor, his clothes are cleaner and of better quality.' Other sources confirm this. The Englishman, Birkbeck, remarked in 1814 that the working class in France was much higher up the social ladder than in England. Besides, Napoleon favoured the establishment of societies for mutual help—for example, the society for the miners of Liège which was decreed on 26 May 1813. The society was financed by a two-per-cent deduction from wages and participation of the

employer based on five per cent of these wages. The experiment
heralded the present-day social security system in France.

This comparative well-being and the absence of class consciousness
(with the exception of arms manufacturers there were very few large
enterprises, the national average being around four men to a workshop) explain, as much as any niggling police supervision, the calm of
the suburbs. A calm which was to last until 1830.

A CLOSED SOCIETY

The rise of Murat, the innkeeper's son who became King of Naples, or
that of Marshal Lefebvre's wife—a former laundress, popularized as
Madame Sans-Gêne (Mrs Free-and-Easy) in the play, *Madame Sans-
Gêne,* by Sardan and Moreau—might lead to the belief that there was
considerable social mobility under the Empire. In fact, the large landed
properties were, more often than not, of long standing; they survived
the Revolution without harm, or else were reconstituted after 1800; the
most recent dated from the Revolution. Woe betide those who were
unable to profit from the sale of national property. Despite some
remarkable examples, such opportunities became rarer under the
Empire, where only speculation in colonial commodities and looting
from conquered countries continued to thrive. In the long run only the
privileged profited from the conquest of Europe with gratuities from
special estates for generals, highly placed officials and members of the
old nobility, and commercial profits for manufacturers and traders.

Beyond this, social advancement was difficult. In certain regions
peasants continued to acquire small properties, but they had no opportunity to escape from their condition except through military service.
Herein lay the inconvenience of a return to stability.

Furthermore, social promotion through the army was not as simple
as it might be thought. It became difficult for a simple soldier to rise
from the ranks under the Empire despite the increase in numbers of
battalions and the formation of them into six companies. Examination
of military registers show that before Year XII, the proportion of
officers passing out from a military academy was not more than two
per cent; between 1807 and 1809 it rose to fifteen per cent. The
well-known Coignet who entered the service in 1799 was only a
corporal in 1807 and sergeant in 1809; he finally became a lieutenant in
1812. No simple soldier in Napoleon's Old Guard had found a
marshal's baton in his pouch. (Lefebvre was already a general in
command of the military division of Paris at 18 Brumaire, and he owed

his rise to the Revolution.) At best, apart from the Légion d'honneur which brought a salary with it, a soldier could only hope to reach the rank of lieutenant, and the pay which he would earn, not without difficulty, would put him in a superior position to his fellows who had remained peasants.

The caste mentality began to develop at the top of the hierarchy. A solidarity forged in the wars of the Revolution established itself; dynasties were born. Take the case of Berthier: two of the Marshal's brothers became generals, one sister married an old officer, d'Haugéranville, their son, also, was to find rapid advancement. César Berthier's son-in-law, Bruyères, became the Marshal's aide-de-camp. The cases of the Dejeans, the Neys and the Leclercs connected to the Davouts are similar.

Can Ymbert's *Moeurs administratives* be believed, in which he wrote in 1826:

> When a divisional chief replied to Napoleon's questioning satis-factorily, fluently and without hesitation, he returned from the Tuileries with the ribbon of the Légion d'honneur, or with the dignity of a councillor of state. This was one of the compensations for an iron rule: when a man was talented, be he chief, second-in-command or a clerk, in however humble a position fortune had placed him, Napoleon with his Herculean arm, would seize him by the hair and place him on a pedestal, saying: 'Behold my creature'.

Public office was not, contrary to what has been written, a way to social advancement: clerks did not become divisional chiefs, neither did heads of department become councillors of state. When in 1807, the Audit Office was established, twenty per cent of the new members came from national accountancy, seventeen per cent from the Tribunate, five per cent from the magistrature and five per cent from the Farmers-General. There were no new men, but there were honour-able ends to careers. Following the sudden promotions which came after 1789, a strict hierarchy, which lessened chances of promotion, established itself in administration as well as in the army. The objection can be made that a period of fourteen years is too short to allow for social rises. But a guess can be made as to how Napoleon saw the future. The new élite was to come from the auditors of the Council of State. 'I was arranging the happiest of circumstances for my son,' the Emperor confided in Las Cases. 'For his sake I was raising, in the new school, the large class of auditors to the Council of State. Their education completed and their time come, they would, one fine day, have filled every position in the Empire.' Instigated by a consular decree of 19 Germinal Year XI, the Audit Office developed quickly. In fact recruitment took place instantly among the sons, sons-in-law or nephews of ministers, senators, councillors of state, generals and prefects. These circles provided the auditors until the end of the Empire. Hence the birth of dynasties which if not bourgeois, were at least administrative. Regnier, Abrial, Treilhard, Roederer, Mounier, these were the names of those first auditors. Equally there can be found members of the former bourgeoisie; Anisson-Duperron or Vincent-Marnolia—bankers' sons—Perrgaux and Lecouteulx, who, like d'Arberg, were members of the Belgian nobility. From 1809 onwards, candidates were obliged to be in possession of an annual income, either in the form of an annuity or provided by their family, of 6,000 francs.

Charles Durand observed that

> The insistence on an income or an allowance of 6,000 francs officially removes from the ranks of the auditors all less well-off young men however well educated, however gifted, hard-working and well-bred they may be, and coming as they may from well-to-do and respected families. An official, however high ranking, the president of a tribunal, a *maître des requêtes* or a general, cannot, if he has no means beyond his salary, make his son, even his only son, an auditor. Even less, forom now onwards, may the son of a general killed on the battlefield or of an administrator who died in harness leaving no fortune, aspire to such office.

'The principal obstacle is fortune,' Stendhal quite rightly wrote to his sister at the time of his joining this body. He had to have proof of an income of 7,000 *livres* to become an auditor. Equally, a security had to be paid in order to become a district collector of taxes. Voluntarily badly paid, judges also could only be recruited from among the well-off citizens.

The élitist nature of the regime was further strengthened by the creation, on 17 March 1808, of the Imperial University, which aimed at forming to the same mould the young bourgeoisie whose secondary schooling had been sanctioned by a diploma, the *baccalauréat*. With the introduction of the *Grandes Écoles* (like the Polytechnic), further education may have regained an importance which it had lost under the Ancien Régime, but primary education was neglected, to all intents and purposes abandoned to the friars of the Christian schools.

Opportunities of becoming a member of the administrative élite were henceforth reserved for a plutocracy grown rich through the Revolution, or perhaps for the former aristocracy. Napoleonic society represented a return to order in favour of the notables.

3

A WARTIME ECONOMY

France's economic boom was tied to the coming to power of the notables. The fabulous destinies of the 'bourgeois dynasties' can also be dated from that time. Likewise one is tempted to see the triumph of capitalism in France as rooted in the Empire. This theory is encouraged by Napoleon's having confided to Caulaincourt in 1812, 'It is I who have created French industry.' In fact legislation developed which perhaps favoured large firms, although probably unintentionally. Mechanical progress was encouraged by a government which paid more attention than any of its predecessors had to economic problems, but whose control must not be exaggerated. Finally, statistics played an important part in the writings of the time, even though they were not invented by the Empire. In any case this new economy was subject to a circumstance of war, the Blockade. Victory apparently opened up fabulous markets to French industry—the European markets which had hitherto belonged to England; but production in Napoleonic France was not sufficient to supply these markets because of late and slow mechanization. The Atlantic ports, former eighteenth-century pathways to expansion, were ruined by war at sea, and the future coal-mining centres of the interior had not yet really established themselves. Certainly new crops were being cultivated as a result of the shortage due to colonial produce being no longer imported, but there was difficulty in the export of wines and spirits to the main client, Great Britain. Confronted by the crises which were shaking the economy, the notables of the First Empire seemed as yet not to have assimilated the economic mechanism which made England's fortune. To be sure, the industrial revolution and capitalism were in their early stages. But the hour had struck.

THE AGRICULTURAL SYSTEM

'What is agriculture? It is the basis of the wealth of the state, the principal workshop to which all others come for provisions,' wrote Pradt in Year X. This was echoed by Napoleon, who called it 'the soul, the first basis of the Empire'. Which is to say that since landed property remained the essential source of wealth, so agriculture remained the principal economic activity.

Pradt, in his book *De l'État de la Culture en France,* under the patronage of Arthur Young and of English agronomy, invited agriculturalists to improve their methods. He outlined a vast programme to which neither the consular nor the imperial government was indifferent—the creation of experimental farms, acclimatization of foreign plants, 'particular care to be taken of useful animals', a greater interest to be taken in vineyards.

Agricultural societies had been suppressed by the Revolution, but were reintroduced in Year VI. There were fifty-two in 1808. They played an important part in the improvement of farm implements and in the extension of artificial pastures. The impetus came especially from Paris where the society published a memorandum, of which it printed a thousand copies at the expense of the department. To theoretical discussion were added the reports of consultations given to landowners who had asked for advice on their difficulties. In the provinces there were competitions for the abolition of fallow land and the introduction of lucerne. But private initiative often exerted more influence than agricultural pamphlets, a case in point being the La Roche estate in the Doubs where the Comte de Scey, in agreement with the Prefect Jean Debry, undertook the cultivation of sugar beet.

In fact, progress was slow during the Empire. Out of fifty-two million hectares which then made up France's surface, Chaptal writes that there were twenty-three million hectares of cultivatable land, three and a half million hectares of pasturage, the same of meadowland and about four million hectares of undefined terrain such as heath and wasteland; there were seven million hectares of woodland. Fallow land decreased only in the rich regions like Normandy, Alsace or the north of France. The great problem remained the lack of manure. There was inadequate stock, added to which the manure was of poor quality, having been badly prepared from a basis of rotten straw. Improvement in implements was very limited (the Brie plough was used, for economic reasons preference was given to the sickle over the scythe, threshing was done with a flail).

As for new crops, the potato was only really to come into its own under Louis-Philippe. Tobacco was subject to price fluctuations in the south; during the winter of Year XIII the price per pound rose to 16 *sols,* but from 1806 onwards the profits decreased. This decrease was caused by the ending of imports of tobacco from Virginia and the proliferation of clandestine manufacturers. The government reacted by decreeing, on 29 December 1810, that all tobacco should be bought by the Régie des Droits, collected and sold by licensed retailers. Tobacco factories then began to make their appearance, like Tonneins in the Lot.

Napoleon welcomed with enthusiasm Delessert's invention for extracting sugar from beet. In a report of 23 March 1811 the Minister of the Interior stated that 'beet is one of the best plants which can be used to feed livestock, it is one of the most productive and it has a most fortunate effect on the improvement of land, making it suitable for the production of cereals'.

'The increase of this crop,' added Montalivet, 'must be ensured by its tremendous advantages, and besides, the land necessary to produce enough beet to provide all our own sugar does not exceed 35,000 hectares. Each department of the Empire need only supply a quota of between 100 and 400 hectares.'

Import duty and duty on consumption of sugar from the colonies had already been fixed by decree on 5 August 1810. They were maintained, and subsidies were paid to manufacturers. But returns on sugar remained mediocre despite the proliferation of refineries: Passy, Château-Thierry, Bourges, Pau, Castelnaudary, Douai, Mons, Namur, Parme.

Cotton was even less successful; factories founded in the Bouches-du-Rhône and the Pyrénées produced nothing. On the other hand woad was very successful in the south; the experimental school at Albi perfected the technique. But industrial plants disturbed the ways of the countryside, and the rural notables, who might have been able to impose them, were frequently unable to see their point. At best a sure rent and a quick profit was sought.

Habit triumphed equally in stock-farming. Several centres for rams (Sabres, Loriol, Adge or Cambrai) or stallions (Pau, Tarbes, Perpignan, Grandpré in the Ardennes or Le Bec in Normandy), the crossing of Ovins with Spanish merinos, or the appearance of buffaloes in the Landes did not suffice to reconstitute former herds. In the Alps, transhumance was still the rule. From October until May more than fifty thousand animals came down to graze in Provence, in summer they went up to the mountains in columns of two thousand. The locals collected some manure as they passed whilst complaining of the increase in the number of wolves. Prefects' reports stress that the main obstacle to progress in stock-farming lay in the way land was parcelled out, just as the mediocre production of cereals could be explained by the poor-quality manure. It was a vicious circle in which French agriculture found itself caught so long as it refused artificial pastures.

Devastation of the forests continued. Goats were the forests' main enemy; 'They are the ruin of the forests whose perpetuation they prevent,' wrote the Prefect of the Basses-Alpes, Alexandre de Lameth. On 6 January 1801 and again on 26 January 1805, the administration of the forests was reorganized. A director-general presided over a council of five members. Inspectors travelled over the thirty-one wooded *arrondissements* of the Empire which were entrusted to wardens assisted by general keepers. All in vain—forest crimes remained numerous. There were eight million hectares of forest, 1,800,000 of which were in private hands, the rest belonged to the state and to the communes.

There remains the vine which was particularly prosperous under the Empire. Around 1808, according to Chaptal's estimations, vineyards covered 1,613,939 hectares and produced thirty-five million hectolitres of wine. 'What a frenzy of vines, France is covered with them,' wrote a contemporary. The diversity of the produce was enormous, from Burgundy where Chambertin passed for the Emperor's favourite wine, to Champagne where Moët and Chandon imposed their sparkling wines. Despite the Blockade, exports of Bordeaux wines, always in great demand, continued to the Continent by road, but also by sea towards England, by means of the licence system—2,593 gallons in 1805, 13,105 in 1809. On the other hand, around Paris only 'thin' and 'sour' wines were to be found which served to supply the capital. Under the circumstances it is easy to understand the interest attached to the cultivation of the vine: the arts of planting it, pruning it and fertilizing it were the subject of much writing. Cadet de Vaux, for his part, insisted on the use of chemicals in the preparation of wine.

La Feuille du Cultivateur reported that apart from vineyards which were well looked after, other aspects of agriculture were non-existent or defective. An exaggeration which underlines the backwardness of the French agronomy compared with the English. Prefects often blamed this backwardness on the apportionment of common land. The

sale of national property, on the other hand, made possible the cultivation of large estates which had until then been left to lie fallow by the
Church. This depended, however, on the estates having been bought
by large farmers or agriculturalist landlords; social prestige was often
more important than profitability in the buying of land by new
notables who, in their turn, sacrificed arable land to parks and pleasure
gardens and to game forests. This annoyed Napoleon. 'I will not suffer
an individual to make twenty hectares of land barren in a grain-
growing department, in order to make himself a park.' His anger was
short-lived.

PROGRESS IN INDUSTRY

In a space of four years the French were able to measure progress in the
realm of industry. The exhibition of Year IX had brought 220 exhibitors to the Louvre, the following year there were 540. War interrupted
this tradition which was reinstituted in 1806 when the new exhibition
was attended by 1,422 exhibitors from every department. To judge
from the reports of the jury whose duty it was to examine the exhibits,
every industrial activity of the day was represented: cloths, cashmere,
serge and bunting, fancy materials, velvet and silk, hats and ribbons,
lace and blonde lace, hemp, flax, cotton, dimity and piqués, muslins
and nankeen came from the textile industry; irons and steels from
metallurgists; spinning machines represented mechanics; alum, soda,
iron and colour sulphate from the chemical industry; there were crystal
and china, gold and silver objects from Biennais, and clocks from
Breguet . . . A special place was reserved for state manufacturers:
porcelain from Sèvres, Gobelin tapestries and more from Beauvais,
Savonnerie carpets. Detained by the Prussian campaign, Napoleon
was not able to visit the exhibition. Champagny wrote to him on 4
October 1806: 'Everyone is in agreement that the earlier exhibitions
were far from exciting such crowds. It is a proof that our manufacturers
have made progress.'

Three industries were in the forefront: the cotton industry,
chemicals and armaments.

The first was not favoured by the Emperor who reproached it for
importing raw materials and preferred to encourage the production of
silk, flax or wool. Since attempts at acclimatization in the South of
France and Italy had failed, the industry had to resign itself to the use of
fibre from the Middle East or Brazil. But the disappearance of competition from England, as well as the fashion for nankeens, dimity and

printed calico, proved to be a powerful stimulus in keeping with the development of luxury. Technical progress was important especially in spinning where finer and finer threads were spun. Mule-jennies and flying shuttles were introduced everywhere. 'It is in cotton-spinning machines that our industry appears to have made the greatest progress,' Champagny pointed out to the Emperor in his letter of 4 October. Philippe de Girard's machine for spinning flax should have been mentioned and Jacquard's loom, but production from English machinery was still four or five times greater than from French machinery.

There was also a great boom in chemicals. For a long time France had been dependent on foreign supplies for soda, which was extracted from barilla imported from Spain and Sicily to supply the country's glass-works, laundries and dyers. The renewal of war with England, followed by difficulties with Spain, caused a spectacular rise in the price per hundredweight from 45 francs in 1807 to 350 francs in 1808. One solution was to grow barilla in Provence, but it was not enough. A decree of 13 October 1809 relieved the soda industry of its taxation burden, for example the tax on salt used in the factories, of which there were thirty-three. The price per hundredweight of Spanish soda fell from 120 to 55 francs. In another area, bleach—chlorine extracted from salt and diluted with water—had a great success. In his factory, Chaptal produced all acids, sodium chlorate and lead salts.

The high figures for production in the armaments industry are hardly surprising. To the former manufactories at Maubeuge, Charleroi, Saint-Étienne, Tulle and Klingenthal were now added those at Mutzig, Liège, Turin and Culembourg. Total production reached 265,800 weapons in 1806. The workers, whilst being subjected to an army regime, were spared the battlefield—hence, perhaps, their large number. The manufacture of arms was subject to the supervision of inspectors-general whose reports ended up at the sixth bureau of the Ministry of War directed by Gassendi. Napoleon has often been held responsible for the absence of technical progress in armaments. But in reality, it was often bureaucracy which hindered improvements. When the armourers pointed out that 'the frequent renewal of the dog screw on an infantryman's gun comes from the ease with which it breaks when a soldier carelessly pulls the trigger with the battery reversed', and that it would be desirable to make this screw out of steel, not iron, the plan was hidden away in the War Ministry portfolios without having been shown to the Emperor.

Mechanization, without which the industrial revolution would have been impossible, was welcomed enthusiastically by Chaptal. In fact, the steam-engine was barely used under the Empire. Except at Le Creusot with its coke blast-furnaces, metallurgy marked time.

In the long run, however, two factors prepared the way for the boom of capitalism. Napoleonic legislation sanctioned the triumph of free enterprise thanks to the continued suppression of guilds, in spite of some inclination for their re-establishment on the part of the Imperial Police. If the government intervened, as in the case of mining concessions, it was on the side of private interests. Contrary to the law of 28 July 1791 which gave every liberty to the 'surface landowners', the new mining law of 21 April 1810 separated the soil from the sub-soil and made the state responsible for granting the right to mine the latter. Mining concessions were granted for the payment of a fee which was moderate compared to the profits; they were, all things considered, not very numerous and made a first concentration of mining possible. Relics of the Ancien Régime were abolished. On the left bank of the Rhine, collective use of blast-furnaces and forges disappeared, French law having transformed the former hereditary leases into free hereditary property. Finally, the commercial law of 1807, by creating anonymous companies, favoured new contributions of capital.

As well as the legislation a second factor must be taken into account —investment in land, which was the basis for the development of metal-casting in the eighteenth century, tended to fade out during the Empire in favour of banking which appeared to have more success. For instance, in the Dauphiné, in the case of the Périers, Augustin looked after both his bank and his printed calico factory at Vizille.

In the Napoleonic legend the great heads of industry stand next to the marshals and councillors of state. Richard (1765–1839) was a cotton king. This peasant's son had practised every trade by the time, in association with Lenoir-Dufresne, and thanks to fortunate speculation in national property, he opened a drapers' shop, the profits of which were soon considerable. Richard and Lenoir 'invented' fixed-price sale. Moving on from commerce to manufacture they installed work-shops for weaving and spinning in the former convent of Bon-Secours, in rue de Charonne. From Paris they spread to the provinces: Alençon in 1800, Sées in 1802, Laigle in 1806. . . . In 1810, at the death of Lenoir, the business employed 12,800 workmen. Another great figure of the textile industry was Oberkampf who, before the Revolution, had established a cloth-painting workshop at Jouy. In 1805 it had 1,322 employees and made an annual profit of 1,650,000 francs. François de Wendel (1778–1825) rebuilt in iron and steel a fortune of which he had been dispossessed as an émigré: the buying back of Hayange and then of Creutzwald in 1809, and finally the acquisition of Moyeuvre in 1811 marked a new stage in the destiny of this family. Mention should also be made of Ternaux who revolutionized the cloth industry, of Douglas and his wool-teaseling machines, and of Koechlin.

Despite the dearth of certain raw materials and the shortage of sources of energy, French industry was overflowing with optimism between 1806 and 1810. The return of order and security, the re-emergence of luxury and the increase of trade outlets as Napoleon's conquests spread (Napoleon did not hestitate to put pressure on his allies to make them open their frontiers to French produce) are at the basis of a euphoria which was to lead to acts of imprudence.

But this industrial development worried the more conservative notables. Chaptal summarized their fears, although always in favour of progress himself:

When war or prohibitions close outlets for industrial products, it is painful to see groups of inactive men who suffer. They became excited and often disturb the peace of the public. Doubtless it would have been desirable if, instead of forming these agglomerations in order to exploit some kind of industry, they had remained scattered around the countryside where manufacturing would have been a useful addition to work on the land.

For fear of a social explosion, the Parisian authorities put a break on the capital's manufacturing boom which was already hindered by the lack of raw materials and sources of energy.

ADVANCES AND RECESSIONS IN COMMERCE

Although the Continental Blockade may have ensured to industry an effective barrier of protection, it did, on the other hand, precipitate the decline of the great ports, at least of those (like Calais, Boulogne and Dunkerque) where privateering and coastal trade were not sufficient to make up the economic difference, or whose rivers and canals did not stretch far enough back into the interior. This was the case with La Rochelle. 'The ruin of the colonies and the continuation of war enormously prejudiced maritime towns. Never has every commercial undertaking been so discouraged. Many people are ruined,' the

General Council of the Charente-Inférieure pointed out at their session of Year XII. Between 1804 and 1810, barely sixty ships flying a Northern European flag, and about twenty American ships come to fetch wine, salts and liqueurs, were to drop anchor in the harbour of La Rochelle, according to the *Annuaire statistique du département* of 1813. The most important commercial business of the locality, belonging to the brothers Garesché was unable to survive and left liabilities of 900,000 francs.

Nantes and Bordeaux were better able to support the Blockade. With the Peace of Amiens the arming of the colonies had regained some of its lost glory. In 1802 Bordeaux armed nearly two hundred and eight ships for the colonies, 'A figure fairly comparable to those of the end of the Ancien Régime', according to historians' estimates. That year, the port received two hundred and twenty cargo-loads from the colonies.

Where armaments were concerned, the French and Bourbon islands took over from the West Indies. Finally exports of important growths from Bordeaux to England reached their former tonnage. The Atlantic ports were more favourably situated than the Channel ports which were under the constant surveillance of the British fleet, so Bordeaux, after 1803 until 1807, was able to preserve part of its trade thanks to neutral countries like the United States and Denmark. The tightening of the Blockade, however, affected the trade of neutral states and from 1808 nearly all commerce ceased. It was the licence system, and to a lesser degree the armaments business which saved the port from asphyxia. Meanwhile, inland from Bordeaux, a phenomenon of 'de-industrialization' was taking place which finally affected the greater part of the Atlantic region.

A similar respite was experienced in Marseilles between 1801 and 1807 before Trieste, Leghorn and Malta finally took over from her.

'The Emperor had acquired Genoa in Year XIII, Leghorn in 1808, the Treaty of Vienna gave him Trieste. That which flattered national pride, increasingly troubled the Marseillais merchants,' wrote Thibaudeau in his *Mémoires*, and as Prefect of the Bouches-du-Rhône, he was well placed to hear the complaints of the Marseillais. 'They regarded these three foreign ports as intruders in the French family, rivals whom the Emperor favoured as newcomers.'

This is a significant indication of the disquiet which the Emperor's ceaseless policy of annexation was beginning to cause among the notables.

The trade fair at Beaucaire saw its decline as being tied to that of

Marseilles. It has been frequently underlined, however, that internal commerce profited vastly from the circumstances. The shift towards the aast favoured the great navigable rivers; the Rhine turned Strasbourg into a depository on a European scale. It is hardly surprising that Napoleon took up the canal policy begun by the monarchy (canal de Saint-Quentin, canal de l'Ourcq, etc.). As for the attention paid to the roads, this was inspired by the example of Ancient Rome. The decree of 16 December 1811 established a differentiation between imperial and departmental roads. Such roads naturally improved the circulation of merchandise and made it possible for couriers and messengers to travel faster. In fact it still took fifteen hours to travel from Paris to Orléans and the survey of road traffic in 1811 brought to light delays caused by the habits of messengers and carters. But, for Napoleon, the highways had, above all, a strategic value. The Simplon road, begun on 9 October 1805 and completed in 1809 ensured French domination of Italy. The same can be said of the Mont-Cenis pass. Lyons profited from its opening to increase its commercial importance.

Other factors stimulated internal trade: monetary stability; the adoption of the metric system, although this did not take place, it is true, without lively resistance; the promulgation of a commercial law in 1807; and the establishment of chambers of commerce whose role was simply advisory, but whose opinions might be able to enlighten the government. This commercial transformation took place more rapidly in Paris than in the provinces.

THE CRISIS OF 1805

Several crises bore witness to the vulnerability of the French economy. The last of these crises, to which we will return, was to prove fatal to the regime. The vulnerability resulted from the weakness of the government's credit: the least crisis of confidence was enough to shake it and it was even possible during times of stability. It was clearly evident in the affair of the united merchants which took on unexpected proportions in 1808.

In a note of February 1806, Fiévée made a penetrating analysis of the situation; he saw abuses of speculation in a capital whose financial resistance was not as stong as London's. As from September 1805, Barbé-Marbois, the Minister of the Treasury had reduced the crisis to its right proportions—a lack of confidence produced at a delicate moment.

He had, initially, allowed hsimself to become involved with the clever speculators, Ouvrard, Desprez and Vanlerberghe in a plan to import Mexican piastres into France. When the affair went sour, rumours spread about the possible instability of the Bank of France; considerable withdrawals resulted, so much so that it was whispered that the Emperor, on leaving for a new campaign, had completely emptied the coffers. There were near riots among the crowds at the pay desks. The victory of Austerlitz re-established confidence after a fashion. But as a result of the sudden scarcity of currency, a series of bankruptcies followed, the most well known of which was the Récamier one. Stagnation in the textile industry further aggravated the situation. Unemployment took a hold of the great manufacturing centres—the winter of 1806 to 1807 was another rough one for workers in Paris and Lyons. The industrial depression which began in the early part of 1806 became general from Normandy to Alsace and from the north to the south. Napoleon reacted energetically; from February 1806 he reinforced protectionism which was a veritable prelude to the Blockade decreed in Berlin on 21 November of the same year; he made large loans to industry and he gave orders for luxury goods. By the spring of 1807 the crisis had been overcome. As in 1802, the regime gained new popularity and developed too great a feeling of security which was to blind it in 1810. The 1805 depression was merely a crisis of confidence in the Bank of France, complicated by the over-production of textiles which may or may not have been tied to the deflation of credit. The opinion of economists is divided. Agriculture was not touched; the harvests of 1805, 1806 and 1807 were satisfactory. This aspect of the problem was overlooked: the exhibition of 1806 with Ternaux's fine cloths, Bellanger's cashmeres, Richard-Lenoir's dimity, Nast and Dilh's porcelain, Seghers's oilcloths, Salleron's leathers, Thomire's bronzes, Jacquemard and Bernard's wallpapers, proved the vitality of industry. Napoleon was praised. Already, like a good courtier, the Minister of the Treasury, Barbé-Marbois, who was, however, about to lose his job, wrote to Napoleon at the beginning of January 1806 to say that the clouds were lifting. And why? 'The news of Your Majesty's imminent return suffices to improve all business considerably. Bankruptcy has immediately ended in Paris.'

4

THE EMPIRE STYLE:
BOURGEOIS OR NAPOLEONIC ART?

The style is never called 'Napoleonic', but 'Empire'. Doubtless this is not so much to emphasize the role played in official art by what would be called today 'the ideology of the dominant class', that is the bourgeoisie, as to underline the great man's alleged philistinism.

In fact, this sovereign who threw the books which he disliked out of the window of his berlin, was indeed an unusual reader. How wretched was the education of this Emperor who knew nothing of the most elementary rules of spelling and who confused the River Elbe with the River Ebro, and Smolensk with Salamanca. And what smiles would be provoked by the historian who spoke of 'the age of Napoleon' in the same tone as he spoke of the age of Pericles or of Louis XIV. Napoleon's military dictatorship does not have a good reputation. No French regime has ever been accused of stifling the intellectual and artistic life of the time to such an extent. And yet, no government has perhaps been more closely concerned with these matters than the government of the general who asserted: 'There are only two powers in the world, the sword and the mind. In the long run the sword is always conquered by the mind.'

Bourgeois taste triumphed, despite the emphasis on war and the failure of a culture said to be orientated by the direction given to literature, art and the sciences by Napoleon. If, on the contrary, an assessment were made of art at the height of the Empire, there might be some surprises.

A DECLINE IN LITERATURE?
Much has been said of a decline in literature for which Napoleon has been held responsible. Only Chateaubriand and Madame de Staël

deserve attention—and they belonged to the opposition. The imperial regime is said to have dried up all inspiration, stifled all independence and cast eighteenth-century styles into an official mould. The main cause for complaint was censorship, a niggling censorship even though it was in the hands of men of letters. It is true that Sade was imprisoned at Charenton, but he was allowed a certain degree of liberty and was able to put on theatrical performances—albeit not sadistic ones—for certain privileged persons chosen at the discretion of Coulmier, the director of the asylum. His diary, which has since been found, reveals facilities 'of all kinds' from which he benefited. Desorgue's fate was similar, but shorter-lived; Brifaut was obliged to alter the subject matter of *Don Sancho* because of the Spanish War. But once he had turned Barcelona into Babylon (which in French have the same metre and rhyme) he encountered no further obstacles. Raynouard's *Les États de Blois* were forbidden in 1810, the author had made too many political allusions, but he was not harassed.

Why disguise the fact that this literary decline caused by censorship had its roots in the Revolution? Repression under the Revolution was far more pitiless than under the Empire: Chénier and Roucher were guillotined, whereas no writer was ever executed under the Empire. François de Neufchâteau for his *Pamela*, Destutt de Tracy and Garat were all imprisoned as well as Sade and Laclos. Marie-Joseph Chénier was obliged to give up his *Timoléon* which presented too accurate a picture of Robespierre. Several plays were completely outlawed (Racine's *Athalie* or Voltaire's *Mahomet*), others had all allusions to the monarchy or Christianity removed. By contrast the Empire appears infinitely mild. Which does not mean that supervision became any less strict under Napoleon. The decree of 29 July 1807 reduced the number of theatres in Paris to eight: the Comédie-Française, the Théâtre de l'Impératrice (the Odéon), the Opéra, The Opéra-Comique, the Variétés, the Gaîté, the Ambigu-Comique and the Vaudeville. As a result, 'no play could be put on in any other theatre, neither could the public be admitted to one, even freely; no posters could be made, no printed or hand-written notices distributed.' Each theatre had a chosen repertoire assigned to it. But the decree has not always been fully understood. It was designed to replace anarchy with order and to avoid the failures which obliged theatres to close.

Later, in 1810, the same control was applied to bookselling and printing. Preoccupation with policing was much in evidence. The number of Parisian bookshops was reduced to sixty, a licence was introduced as well as an oath 'to print nothing contrary to the duty owed to the sovereign or to the interests of state', all of which amounted to putting the bookshops in government hands. But the printing trade was in need of reforms. A report on printers established in the capital around 1808 recorded one hundred and fifty-seven, most of whom, notably Michelet's father, were 'miserable and without licences'. According to the author of the report, they vegetated without any real professional qualifications many of them having merely become extempore printers since the Revolution. Only a few businesses flourished, Firmin-Didot or Agasse, Panckoucke's son-in-law. Complaints were numerous: 'Sooner or later publishers will take steps to use presses in the provinces where they will find cheaper paper and where the printer is paid less by the day.' This solution was adopted furthermore by Mame. Booksellers themselves were not blameless. Barba had acquired a distressing reputation in the trade for the illegal selling of books. According to Werdet—Balzac's publisher and the author of *De la Librairie*, published in 1860—some booksellers, for example Bossange, acquired licences for importing colonial products, the market for which was controlled by England. The only condition imposed by the imperial government was that goods to an equivalent value should be exported to Great Britain. So they loaded several ships with books which they dumped in the Channel, the resale of the colonial commodities being supposed easily to cover the price of the works sacrificed. But Bossange's speculation was not successful and he had to restrict his activities.

Another advantage of the general control of printing was the publication of a *Journal général de la Librairie* which listed all published books.

This policing, then, had its positive sides and cannot, alone, be responsible for the alleged decline of literature.

OFFICIAL AND FRINGE LITERATURE

A frequently quoted saying has been attributed to Napoleon, 'The minor works of literature are for me and the great are against me.'

Did the Institut, in particular the French language and literature side of it, deserve the criticisms levelled at it?

The French language and literature section was a descendant of the Académie, reconstituted in 1803. In it were seated, alongside politicians like Sieyès, Maret or Cambacérès, poets like Parny (known, above all, for his *Guerre des Dieux* (1799) which was to be persecuted by censorship after the Concordat), Legouvé who had an enormous success with his *Le Mérite des Femmes* in 1801, and Lebrun-Pindare who had finally rallied to Bonaparte after having defended Robespierre in an *Ode à l'Être Suprême*. His caustic wit was dreaded. The following quatrain referred to one of his colleagues:

> On vient de me voler . . .
> —Que je plains ton malheur.
> —Tous mes vers manuscrits.
> —Que je plains le voleur.[1]

The poetry may have been somewhat flat, but it appealed, especially in Legouvé's case, to a bourgeois public fond of moralizing.

The greatest poet of the day was Delille, professor at the Collège de France and a hardworking translator of Virgil. He died in 1813 and was given an official funeral. A rival began to emerge: Baour-Lormian, the clever adapter of Macpherson ('Ossian') who had made Celtic poets so fashionable.

The theatre was represented in strength at the Académie with Collin d'Harleville, the charming creator of the Baron de Crac; Picard, who heralded Labiche with *La Petite Ville* and *Monsieur Musard ou le Vieux Fat*; Alexandre Duval; Andrieux; and, above all, Étienne, whose *Les Deux Gendres* (1810) was one of the greatest successes of the time. Once again it was the bourgeois public who acclaimed plays which flattered whilst mocking it.

In the field of tragedy and historical drama, mention should be made of Ducis, translator and adaptor of Shakespeare in France; Marie-Joseph Chénier; Népomucène Lemercier (*Pinto*, 1800; *Christophe Colomb*, 1809), and, in particular, Raynouard, whose *Les Templiers* was triumphantly successful in 1805 due to a certain Cornelian ring:

> Qui désire échapper déjà se déshonore. . . .[2]

And again:

> L'homme a créé l'honneur, Dieu créa la vertu.[3]

[1] "'I have just been robbed . . .'
—"How I regret your misfortune."
—"All my lines in manuscript."
—"How I pity the thief."'

[2] 'He who wishes to escape is already disgraced.'
[3] 'Man has created honour, God created virtue.'

There were also some historians in the French language and literature section, Lemontey, Lacretelle and Michaud, and a survivor from the eighteenth century, Bernardin de Saint-Pierre. The obscurity into which most of the authors mentioned here have fallen sometimes seems undeserved. Some, like Delille, doubtless merit oblivion; but others, like Raynouard were not totally uninspired.

Ideology, however, was dominant, that is to say as it was reflected by the last champions of the philosophers of 'enlightenment': Volney, Garat, Destutt de Tracy, Cabanis, Naigeon, Roederer. At the Académie's elections they were opposed to the neo-Christian-monarchist current (Fontanes, Chateaubriand) whose influence was to be felt in the *Journal de l'Empire* thanks to an article by the critic, Geoffroy, which Stendhal himself read with consuming interest.

But the Académie was divided into rival schools—those of Maret and of Régnault de Saint-Jean-d'Angély. Étienne's candidature gave rise to a furious battle between the two schools.

A flood of hagiographical works was connected with official literature, from Lesur's *L'Épopée des Francs* to *Austerlitz* by Millevoye who with Chênedollé was one of the best poets of the period.

In contrast was fringe literature. The free-thinking element which had already been persecuted during the Revolution, in the name of Robespierrian virtue, was stifled under the Empire as being contrary to the principles of the bourgeois society which Napoleon had substituted for the old world of the artistocracy. Laclos may have been reinstated, but only as a general; besides he died in 1803. Restif de la Bretonne was allowed to vegetate as an employee of the Ministry of Police. His last works, for he continued to write until his death in 1806, did nothing to improve his material conditions. Despite the support of Mercier, he was dismissed from the Institut. Sade ended his days in the asylum at Charenton in 1814. Louvet disappeared in 1797, Nerciat in 1800; Mirabeau predeceased them at the beginning of the Revolution. Casanova died in 1798.

Another fringe current was 'enlightenment' which was equally foreign to the preoccupations of the new bourgeoisie. Saint-Martin, 'the unknown philosopher', died in 1803 and the movement seemed to have run out of steam. A few publications, however, relaunched it—Fabré-Pélaprat's work on the Knights Templar, the *Recherches sur l'origine et la destination des Pyramides* by Dewismes in 1812 and *Les Vers dorés de Pythagore* by Fabre d'Olivet, published the following year. Ballanche and the Lyons mystical school occupy a place apart.

A few writers are hard to classify, such as Senancour with his *Obermann* (1804) which heralded Romanticism, Charles Nodier whose satirical pamphlet, *La Napoléone* caused him some trouble with the consular police; and particularly Joseph Fiévée whose *La Dot de Suzette*, republished in 1803, paints one of the most ferocious pictures of Thermidorian society. The last of a long line of moralists (Chamfort's *Pensées* were published in 1803) was Joubert, whose work remained unpublished until after his death. Azaïs and his theory of compensation should also be mentioned.

Gastronomic literature, whose exponents before Brillat-Savarin were Berchoux and Grimod de la Reynière, is in a category of its own. It expresses the hedonistic appetites of the parvenus.

There remains the political fringe: Madame de Staël and Chateaubriand. Their fates were different, however. The former was ordered into exile at Coppet, the latter was called to the Académie. Nevertheless, it was Chateaubriand who complained the most.

Bonaparte was irritated by Madame de Staël's provocative and unfeminine character. Her books precipitated the break. *De la littérature considérée dans ses rapports avec les institutions sociales* (1800) defended ideas which were fairly alien to the preoccupations of the First Consul. Her theories concerning climate, emancipation from old customs and the exaltation of a 'republican' literature found no echo in Bonaparte. Her novels with feminist leanings, *Delphine*, and then *Corinne*, ran counter to the principles of the bourgeois society in which women were subordinate to their husbands. Imprudently, Germaine compromised herself with Bernadotte and Moreau. She had to leave Paris. Coppet became a centre of opposition whilst, at the same time, its mistress took endless steps to regain favour, but succeeded only in pestering. At Coppet she meditated on her great book *De l'Allemagne*, and drew up a parallel between philosophy and German literature on the one hand, and French writers and thinkers on the other. A parallel which showed the Germans to advantage, which is hardly surprising since Hegel had finished writing his *Phänomenologie des Geistes* and Kant had just died in 1804. But it went too far. The book was seized and destroyed: Madame de Staël fled abroad.

Le Génie du Christianisme which was preceded in 1801 by *Atala* and by *René* in 1802 made Chateaubriand, unlike Madame de Staël, into an official writer. The work responded to the government's views in favour of a religious restoration. The author was rewarded with the position of Secretary in the embassy in Rome, then of Plenipotentiary in the Valais. The reward was insufficient in the eyes of the author of *René*. The execution of the Duc d'Enghien supplied him with a pretext for absenting himself. While contemplating a Christian epic, he undertook, in 1806–1807, a great journey 'from Paris to Jerusalem'. The outcome of these travels was *Les Martyrs* (1809) which was published just when the quarrel between the Pope and the Emperor was taking a tragic turn. Failure. Elected to the Académie in 1811, he was not allowed to deliver his maiden speech, which condemned instead of praising his predecessor, Marie-Joseph Chénier, the conventional regicide.

'I was determined,' he wrote in the *Mémoires d'outre-tombe*, 'to make my demands for liberty heard, and to raise my voice against tyranny.' But he showed no excess of courage until 1814.

Two thinkers heralded the future. In 1808 Fourier launched his *Théorie des quatre mouvements*, Saint-Simon meanwhile speculated in national property.

POPULAR LITERATURE

Popular literature cannot be neglected. Song soon developed a seditious element (*Le Conscrit du Languedoc, Le Roi d'Yvetot* by Béranger in 1813); whereas vaudeville remained harmless in its portrayal of society.

Some entertainment may be derived from the frivolous poetry of Piis and the *Almanach des Muses,* but it must be admitted that the novels of Madame Cottin and Madame de Genlis are unreadable.

Two styles were the rage. Firstly, the black novel inspired by the Gothic works of Walpole, Anne Radcliffe or Lewis. Ducray-Duminil's works (*Victor ou l'Enfant de la Forêt*, 1796, *Coelina ou l'Enfant du Mystère*, 1798, *Lolotte et Fanfan*, 1807) and Pigault-Lebrun (*Monsieur Botte*, 1802, *L'Homme à projets*, 1807) sold in unbelievable numbers. Secret passages, haunted castles, masked men and seduced maidens, fathers' curses and filial recognition delighted not only the coachmen and *concierges* who could read, but also a bourgeois readership.

The same themes were adapted to the stage by Loaisel-Tréogate, Caigniez, 'The Racine of the Boulevards', and above all, Pixérécourt who compared himself without false modesty to Sophocles. Melodrama was, as its name indicated, a drama with songs and dance. Neither Boïeldieu nor Kreutzer scorned it. It was, however, the subject of violent polemics between La Harpe, who supported an

élitist theatre, and Mercier, who exclaimed: 'Why do you close your
theatre to the people, proud or avaricious nation? The poor man has a
greater need than others to weep and to be moved. What writer will
consider the good people and give them healthy and agreeable sus-
tenance? Who will preside at their honest pleasures and teach them
how to partake of them?' Crowds flocked to see the melodramas.
Pixérécourt's *La Femme à deux maris* was performed 451 times in Paris
and more than a thousand times in the provinces.

The First Empire was a period in which there was a vast increase in
reading. Napoleon himself gave the example and his librarian kept him
informed of new works. 'The number of subscription libraries increased daily,' the Paris printers' and booksellers' report pointed out
on 21 October 1809; 'barbers are taking a hand in them.' What was
being read? Ducray-Duminil and Pigault-Lebrun, translations of Mrs
Radcliffe and Walpole. 'Academic' literature, with the exception of
Chateaubriand, was absent from the library lists. On the other hand
there was a marked taste for learned societies: Mangourit founded the
Société des Antiquaires de France in 1813 and Malte-Brun brought
geography back into esteem.

THE FASHION IN FINE ARTS

The taste for painting and sculpture became an infatuation. Artistic
publications increased greatly, the theories of Winckelmann or of
Quatremère de Quincy were discussed; Legrand translated Piranese's
work on architecture; Amaury Duval stressed the influence of painting
on industrial skills; conversely Reveroni Saint-Cyr showed how the
arts were perfected by the exact sciences. In 1801, Ballanche published
Du sentiment dans ses rapports avec la littérature et les arts, but his
work was eclipsed by Chateaubriand's *Le Génie du Christianisme.*
Landon produced the *Annales du Musée et de l'École moderne des
Beaux-Arts.* Private collections proliferated (Fesch, Lucien Bonaparte,
Vivant Denon, Soult); Europe, thanks to the conquests, lay open to
men's curiosity. The price of paintings, despite an abundant supply,
rose ceaselessly. In the Salon, where admittedly entry was free, crowds
jostled for space. 'What an abominable crowd,' remarked a contemporary. 'Porters! Fishwives! And valets!' The Musée Napoléon also
attracted the public. Thirty thousand visitors came to the exhibition of
paintings from Italy. No doubt pride in military victory was even more
responsible for the crowds than artistic curiosity. Napoleon very well
understood what a marvellous instrument art was for propaganda. 'His

Majesty's intention,' wrote Montalivet to Denon in 1810, 'is that the opening of the Salon should take place during the festivities which will be held in honour of the Grande Armée and that the Muséum should also be in full glory at this time.' A certain ostentation could be discerned in the Emperor's relationship with artists. In 1808 he went to the Salon determined to honour Gros. He distributed decorations, chatted with the artists and pretended not to know who had painted *La Bataille d'Eylau;* but when he had finished presenting medals, he turned and, removing his own cross of the Légion d'honneur, he pinned it to the artist's chest. On going to see the painting of the coronation which David had just finished, he looked at it in silence for a long time and, according to Delécluze, he 'then took two steps towards David, raised his hat and, bowing slightly, said in a loud voice: "David, I salute you."'

David reigned unrivalled over the world of painting which, thanks to official and private orders, was extremely active. Principal painter to the Emperor, Senator, Officer of the Légion d'honneur, member of the Institut, David reached his zenith. He it was who painted all the great moments of the epic: *Bonaparte au Saint-Bernard, La Distribution des Aigles, Le Sacre.* He did not, however, neglect antiquity. Under the Consulate he painted *Léonidas aux Thermopyles,* which he completed in 1814; in 1809 he painted *L'Amour et Phaéton;* in 1812 *Homère et Calliope.* With him triumphed the neo-classical aesthetic with which his name is connected.

He had numerous pupils. His son counted four hundred and thirty-three. The main ones can be seen in a painting entitled *L'Atelier de David.* There is Gros, the infant prodigy of David's family—classical in 1801 with *Sappho à Leucade,* he too bore witness to the Napoleonic legend with his historical paintings, *Aboukir, Eylau* (1807) and *Les Pestiférés de Jaffa* (1804); there is Gérard (1770–1837), who joined David's studio in 1786 and who abandoned *Bélisaire* or *Psyché* to specialize in portraits of the imperial family and of great dignitaries. Girodet-Trioson (1767–1824) made his mark with *Le Sommeil d'Endymion* as early as 1793; his *Ossian ou l'apothéose des héros français morts pour la patrie,* ordered in 1800 for the gilt drawing-room at Malmaison, *Les Funerailles d'Atala* and above all *Le Déluge* (1806) which was to be preferred to David's *Sabines* in the decennial competition of 1810, make him one of the greatest masters of the day. More could be said of Hennequin who left some interesting work, Fabre (1766–1837), David's second pupil to win the Grand Prix de Rome,

Alexandre-Évariste Fragonard, son of the great Fragonard, who died
in 1806 and was a faithless disciple of David whom he abandoned for
the Gothic style, Franque, Mulard, Wicar, Drolling or Revoil. Ingres
(1780–1867) occupies a place apart. His portraits of Napoleon arrest
the attention with their majestic almost Byzantine quality. But he also
painted the series of *Odalisques* which presents a more voluptuous
image than David's of the female form.

Not all artistic activity was devoted to neo-Chassicism. Painting also
had its fringe—for instance Prud'hon (1758–1823), a stone-cutter's son
from Cluny who was influenced by the Germans, had mixed in revolutionary circles and who had been introduced into official society by
Frochot, the Prefect of the Seine, also from Cluny. *Le Triomphe de
Bonaparte* in 1801 established his reputation; he became the decorator
for the great festivities given in the Emperor's honour in Paris. Jean
Broc (1771—1850) rebelled against David's influence and rejoined the
Primitives, insisting, under the influence of Maurice Quay and Charles
Nodier, that art should have absolute originality and purity, a theory
of which Ingres was also aware. Broc was the long unrecognized
painter of an extraordinary *Mort d'Hyacinthe* (1801). The school
condemned Weenix's gamebirds and Panini's ruins, which were in turn
defended by Suvée.

Every style was respected. Valenciennes (1754–1819) published a
treatise on painting in which he defended the historic landscape as
background to scenes from antiquity or mythology. Landscape itself
was still in fashion with Hubert Robert, who did not die until 1808,
Bidault (1758—1846), or Moreau l'Aîné (1739–1805). Boilly (1761–
1845) distinguished himself in the painting of family scenes: *L'Arivée
de la Diligence* (1804), *Le Départ des Conscrits de 1807* or *La Lecture
du 7ᵉ Bulletin de la Grande Armée* (1808); he was rivalled by Taunay
(1755–1830). Duplessis-Bertaux's field was the military anecdote;
Danloux compared favourably with the masters of portrait painting.
The animal painter, Huet, died in 1811, but Carle Vernet (1758–1836)
specialized in horses. Neither should Meynier (1768–1832) be overlooked.

Géricault (1791–1824) heralded Romanticism with the dramatic
movement in his *Portrait équestre d'un officier de chasseur à cheval* in
1812, and his *Le Cuirassier blessé* in 1814. Like Delacroix, Géricault's
artistic formation took place less in studios than in the Musée
Napoléon where he discovered, pell-mell, the paintings of Titian and
Velasquez, Caravaggio and Ribera, Rubens and Rembrandt. Like

Vigny and Lamartine, Géricault was tempted by military life and was to engage in the King's Red Musketeers and to follow the sovereign to Gand during the Hundred Days, before returning to civilian life.

The purpose of this dry enumeration of painters is to show the extraordinary abundance of talent which flourished under the Empire. Napoleonic painting is too easily summed up as a few reconstructions in the antique style, battle scenes, and portraits of dignitaries: *L'Enlèvement des Sabines* by David, Gros's *Eylau* and Gérard's *Madame Récamier*. These are three masterpieces no doubt, but which give no idea of the breadth of production during the first fifteen years of the nineteenth century. The libertine and the sentimental styles disappeared, but the Empire, influenced by Chateaubriand and by Lenoir's Musée des Monuments français invented the Troubadour or neo-Gothic style, reminiscent of imaginary Middle Ages; it took its inspiration for the resuscitation of old myths from 'Ossian', and, by decentralization (the boom in provincial museums dates from the decree of 14 Fructidor Year IX which provided them with 846 paintings) favoured the development of regional centres. Grobon in Lyons, Claudot in Lorraine and Constantin in Provence. France may appear to have trailed behind in the development of the grotesque in Europe (Fuseli in Germany, Blake in England). This is not so. Vafflard (1774—1837), unjustly forgotten, among others, illustrates this mode in his arresting *Young et sa Fille* (1804).

Unquestionably, neo-classicism triumphed, but there was a tendency for diversity which sprang above all from the conquest of Europe. Isabey was to spend a certain amount of time in Vienna; in 1812 David was employed to paint for Prince Youssoupof. On the other hand, Piranese settled in Paris. And can it be forgotten that Goya became official painter to Joseph Bonaparte?

SCULPTORS AND ARCHITECTS

Classicism also triumphed in sculpture. But there are fewer master-pieces than in painting. It is not surprising. Pajou, Clodion and Houdon faded out. Chinard (1756–1813), Roland (1746–1816), Cartellier (1757–1831) and Moitte (1746–1810) replaced them. Trapped by the rules of classicism, they often lacked inspiration; their virtuosity is, however, undeniable, particularly in Chinard's bust of Madame Récamier or in Cartellier's bas-relief for the colonnade of the Louvre. Thanks to the freshness of his inspiration, Chaudet, a more personal artist, established himself with mythological themes which he revived from 1791. He is best known for his statue of the Emperor in Roman costume which was placed on the top of the column in Place Vendôme. But he cannot be compared to Bosio (1768–1845) who sculpted the bas-reliefs on the same column, nor to the Italian, Canova (1757–1822) whose influence was considerable. His *Napoléon nu*, inspired by the Belvedere Apollo, was not shown by order of the Emperor who was offended by the Academy of Athletes which had given him the statue. Nevertheless Canova specialized in the imperial family. Pauline as Venus and Madame Mère as Agrippina caused a sensation. But despite the attentions of Napoleon, the artist preferred Rome to Paris.

Architecture, too, was dominated by neo-classicism. Gondoin (the School of Medicine), Peyre, Chalgrin (the Odeon and the Arc de Triomphe), Poyet (works for the Legislative Body), Vaudoyer, Célerier (Variety theatre), Vignon (the Madeleine) and Brongniart represented official architecture. But although French architecture may appear to have been turned towards the past, new ideas were appearing. On the technical level the use of iron was introduced, especially in the building of bridges (the Pont d'Austerlitz and the Passerelle des Arts) and in domes. (The corn-market had an iron and copper dome built for it by Bélanger in 1806 following a fire.) On the theoretical level both Durant (1760–1834), a former pupil of Boulé and a professor at the Polytechnic, and Rondelet (1743–1829), one in his *Recueil et parallèle des édifices de tout genre anciens et modernes*, the other in his *Traité théorique et pratique de l'art de bâtir*, defended a conception of architecture based on utility rather than beauty in which the role of the engineer would henceforth predominate. Ledoux died in 1806; his ideal city did not influence the Napoleonic creations of Pontivy and La Roche-sur-Yon.

Napoleon's favourite architects were Fontaine (1762–1853) and Percier (1764–1838), the true inspirers, with David, of the Empire style. Napoleon's hesitations in dealing with vast plans have often been described—the transformation of the Invalides into a temple of Mars; the joining of the Louvre to the Tuileries; triumphant arches, the reconstruction of Versailles, the creation at Chaillot of a royal palace for the King of Rome, and of an administrative town on the Champ de Mars. When confronted with the plans, the Emperor was incapable of making a decision. Only the triumphal arch by Fontaine on the Place du Carrousel, was completed. Today it may appear somewhat cramped, but it should be seen in the former context of the Tuileries

Palace. The Temple of Glory planned for La Madeleine was the subject of several plans and caused Napoleon many regrets. He is said even to have envisaged a matching one on the hill at Montmartre, 'a kind of temple of Janus' where peace treaties would be proclaimed. The joining of the Louvre and the Tuileries was frequently discussed and constantly postponed. Fontaine's diary reveals an unexpected side to Napoleon's character, full of uncertainty and paralysed by the fear of making a mistake. The same hesitation occurred over Versailles. Gondoin presented a plan for fifty million francs. Percier and Fontaine were more restrained. Finally Napoleon concluded: 'Nothing must be done if one cannot build something which rivals in beauty the part built by Louis XIV.' As far as Chaillot was concerned, Percier and Fontaine had conceived a very grandiose plan which was revealed in *Résidences de Souverains*. Compulsory purchasing began but, owing to war, not a single new monument was erected. 'Too great ambition,' Napoleon declared, 'leaves palaces unfinished.' Can a reflection of this attitude be seen among the new dignitaries who built little and were content to rearrange the old houses of the aristocracy? Apartment buildings were prescribed by the bourgeoisie, who also substituted shop windows for the signboards of the old shops. The triumph of the Egyptian and Doric styles can be seen in the private architecture of the early days of the Consulate. This was followed by vast derivations from the Italian Renaissance which was often admirably adapted as in the Palladian rue de Rivoli.

DECORATIVE ARTS: THE EMPIRE STYLE

An Empire style can best be discussed in the context of interior decoration. Percier and Fontaine dictated their ideas to cabinet makers. Mahogany reigned supreme, either solid or as a veneer for 'second-class furniture'. Frequently it was inlaid with thin strips of light wood in order to avoid too great an expanse of darkness. Pieces of furniture were often supported by carved stands or pedestals or by claw feet. The uprights on a commode or chest of drawers were decorated with caryatids which supported the top; straight lines in furniture became fashionable. Decoration took its inspiration from the Egyptian, Greco-Roman or Etruscan styles. Mythology (goddesses and swans) went side by side with symbols of the warrior (swords, arrows and helmets), bees were juxtaposed with eagles. Metalwork in silver, gold and bronze played an important part in the dressing-table given by the City of Paris to Marie-Louise in 1810 and in the King of

Rome's cradle—masterpieces by Prud'hon, Odiot and Thomire. Biennais was another great goldsmith who was established under the sign of the 'Violet Monkey'. It was he who engraved the gold and silver for the Coronation.

Whilst sofa tables and tripod tables were everywhere, new pieces of furniture were appearing, like cheval glasses, pin trays and curule-chairs. Reichardt described Madame Récamier's bedroom as follows:

> It is very high and almost entirely surrounded by tall looking-glasses in one piece. Between the sheets of looking-glass and above the large marquetry doors can be seen some white panelling with threads of brown. The end wall, facing the windows, consists of one enormous looking-glass. It is there, with its head against the wall, that the ethereal couch of the goddess of the place can be seen.

This bed, so little used, except by its owner, has elsewhere been described: 'The bed is said to be the most beautiful one in Paris; it is made of mahogany decorated with brass and raised on two steps made of the same wood. At the foot of the bed, on a pedestal, is a beautiful lamp made of brass.' Only the beds made for Josephine at Fontaine-bleau were comparable with this prestigious couch. They were made by Jacob-Desmalter (1771–1841), a master of the new style, whose production was vast: 217 beds, 58 consoles, 87 secretaire writing-desks, 106 writing tables and 577 seats for the Palace of Fontainebleau alone. Equally precious are the Sèvres vases, illustrated with battle scenes or scenes from mythology. Isabey designed the famous Marshals' table which was admired by Stendhal.

As woodwork and metalwork played a part in the new decor, so did textiles. Printed calico, at which Oberkampf excelled, became popular, as did silks (in keeping with the boom in the Lyons work-shops due to Jacquard's loom), damasks and brocaded satins. As Madame de Genlis noted, 'For reasons of ostentation materials were pleated on the walls, instead of being stretched.'

DRESS

The attitude to clothing was no different from the attitude to interior decoration. Antiquity ruled supreme, with, however, an element of the East (the success of cashmere). Colours remained dark and materials were heavy in order to please the Emperor who wanted them to be sumptuous, at the back of his mind there being the idea of supplying more work to the textile industry. Men's clothing was still influenced by the Revolution, but trousers, which were an essential part of the sans-culottes' dress had long been proscribed by the bourgeoisie. The frock-coat, the tail-coat and the straight waistcoat, lent a false impression of uniform. This preoccupation could even be seen in an unexpected way in women's fashion: hair was piled up in the form of a shako, skirts were straight and cut like a scabbard, boots and epaulettes or cross-belts were worn. The prestige of public office derived partly from the uniform in which the Emperor dressed his officials. There was an Empire style in dress. Napoleon alone avoided it with his more or less battered little hat, his grey frock-coat and the green suit of the *Chasseurs de la Garde*. And so the figure he cut was as unusual as his name which was already becoming legendary.

MUSIC

A harp or piano, preferably an Erard, was usually to be found among the furniture of a good bourgeois family. The pianoforte had, in fact, ousted the harpsichord. 'You cannot enter a drawing-room,' wrote a contemporary in 1803, 'without finding a pianoforte. You will hear young persons who at ten years old are prodigies on this instrument.' This says everything about the importance of music.

Doubtless Napoleon was as unmusical as it is possible to be. He sang out of tune, according to all reports. Without doubt concerts were designed to flatter the tastes of a public which came above all to hear arrangements of their favourite tunes at the opera. Certainly religious music was in eclipse as it had been under the Revolution; and finally the proximity of Weber, Beethoven and Schubert without doubt completely overwhelmed the French and Italian masters who were fashionable in France. Can the Empire be blamed? There remained the *Marche consulaire* or the *Rigaudon des Manchots*.

The Opéra, established in the rue de la Loi, now Square Louvois, was prospering despite financial difficulties due to abuse of free seats and to the temperaments of the singers. Opera was the genre preferred by Napoleon and his contemporaries, including Stendhal, who kept a detailed account in his diary of the performances he had seen. The Emperor particularly appreciated Italian opera. His favourite composer was the Neapolitan, Giovanni Paisiello, Rossini's rival. But Napoleon was equally enthusiastic about Spontini's *Vestale* in 1807 with its processions of Roman legionnaires. In 1808 the Emperor ordered him to write *Fernand Cortez ou la Conquête du Mexique* with a libretto by Esmenard and Jouy. The libretto, it is true, counted for more than the music in the admiration provoked by the work which was first performed on 28 November 1809. The *Journal de l'Empire* gave an account of it in an article which stressed how perfectly well the illusions had been understood.

> This subject exactly suits the age in which we live. The people who can see, under their very eyes, miracles of intrepidity and of heroic endurance, contemplate the pale reflection of these virtues on the stage with all the more pleasure and interest. Does not Cortez, conquering a vast empire with seven hundred infantrymen, naturally remind everyone of the hero who, at the head of legions more to be recommended for their courage than their numbers, has embarrassed the most formidable enemy lines, dispersed innumerable armies and overcome Europe's efforts at conspiracy?

The turn taken by events in Spain finally condemned *Fernand Cortez* which involuntarily exalted Spanish patriotism after having sung the praises of the Saviour.

Dealings with Cherubini were difficult. 'The Emperor,' the Florentine was to say later, 'requested from me an unreasonable type of music.' Napoleon finally made Paër master of music in his household.

The French were not forgotten. Méhul triumphed in 1807 with *Joseph,* but popular taste was, above all, for Lesueur, Berlioz's master. Inspired by the poems of 'Ossian', *Les Bardes* provoked great enthusiasm which was not shared by Stendhal. It was eclipsed in 1807 by *Le Triomphe de Trajan,* an apologia for the Empire which indulged in the most shameless flattery. The march composed by Lesueur for Napoleon's entry into Notre-Dame at his coronation was played for Trajan's triumphant arrival at the Capitol. The sumptuous nature of the production (with Franconi's circus horses and a hundred and thirty-two costumes) in combination with the singers, Madame Branchu and Lainez, supposedly the best of the day, and the Emperor's approval were all determining factors in its success.

Equally, the ballets at the Opéra drew large crowds which were divided into admirers of Vestris, of Duport and of Gardel, the star dancers of the day. Concerts were also performed at the Opéra. It was on his way to hear Haydn's *Creation* that Bonapare narrowly escaped the explosion of the infernal machine on 24 December 1800.

Grétry, Dalayrac, Boïeldieu, Trial and Monsigny were all popular and provided the repertoire for the Opéra-Comique. It is to be wished that the tunes of these small masters might be heard at concerts once again. Sentimental music in which the composer and performer Garat specilized, was very successful, as was military music with the *Bataille de Marengo,* a sonorous rendering of the battle whose principal phases were faithfully recalled by Viguerie. Martini must also be mentioned as the author of *Plaisir d'amour ne dure qu'un moment.*

Musical life, then, was not dormant, as has sometimes been suggested. Only symphonic music in the style of Stamitz, Haydn and Mozart was temporarily stilled in France as was the development of religious music. But the Revolution was as responsible as theThe Empire at least founded the Prix de Rome for music and, under the direction of Sarrette, developed the Conservatory.

SCIENTIFIC PROGRESS

Parmentier's case is exemplary and is worthy of note. He is supposed to have popularized the potato in France (it was not, in fact, until the July Monarchy that this plant became widespread), he advocated the use of grape sugar instead of cane sugar from 1793, and he was one of the most fervent supporters of the Napoleonic regime. With no illusions about the efficiency of medicine which was still very basic, he believed in the virtues of hygiene and nutrition as means of preventing epidemics. The part he played in the Council of Health in Paris is as yet little known, but something can be divined of the obscure battle he fought against contagious diseases. Parmentier was convinced that 'enlightenment' could only be advanced through authoritarian means.

This was also Napoleon's opinion, based for authority on the Academy of Sciences. Napoleon's indifference to scientific discoveries has been too rapidly surmised because of the failure of Fulton's plans. Unlike the preceding regime (it is a great point of difference with the Revolution), Napoleon did not consider using scientific discoveries in the framework of war. The most singular case concerns observation balloons which were built at Meudon under the direction of Major Coutelle and which had been used by Republican generals at Charleroi and at Fleurus. The Emperor dissolved the balloonist corps, refusing to appreciate its importance in lighting the ground. From 1804 onwards French troops were bombarded by Congreve's rocket, but Napoleon did not take up the challenge. He was uninterested in science. This was to be seen in Egypt. But how can he be blamed? No sovereign was ever more attentive to the scientific movement or encouraged it so much. Lacépède was made Grand Chancellor of the Légion d'Honneur.

Lagrange, Monge and Berthollet became senators, Fourcroy a councillor of state. Fourier was Prefect of Grenoble where he encouraged the first efforts of the young Champollion.

A few names should be remembered. In the field of mathematics, Monge (1746–1818) founded descriptive geometry; Lagrange (1736–1813) published his treatise *De la Résolution des équations numériques* in 1808, and *La Mécanique analytique* in 1811, Laplace (1749–1827) undertook his *Traité de Mécanique céleste* and his *Théorie analytique des Probabilités*. Chemistry was dominated by the names of Berthollet (1748—1822), author of the *Statique chimique* who instigated the work of the Arcueil society; Fourcroy (1755–1809), who developed Lavoisier's principles of chemistry; Gay-Lussac (1778–1850), in collaboration with Thénard, studied alkaline metals and discovered the concept of electrical resistance. Natural sciences branched out thanks to Lamarck (1744–1829) who interested himself in invertebrates, to Cuvier (1769–1832) who invented palaeontology and comparative anatomy, and to Geoffroy Saint-Hilaire (1772–1844) who was to oppose Cuvier on the subject of the unity of organic composition in nature. Medicine is equally rich in great names: Bichat died in 1803; Corvisart was the Emperor's doctor; Pinel, the head doctor in La Salpêtrière[1] who alleviated the condition of the mentally sick; Dupuytren, the surgeon; Laënnec, who in 1815 applied the principles of acoustics to ausculation of chest diseases. Pharmacy owes much to Vauquelin (1763–1829), and to Cadet de Gassicourt, the Emperor's pharmacist. On the technical level, Lebon's discovery of lighting gas was not applied practically, but Leblanc perfected artificial soda.

Some new names made their appearance, the youngest came from the École Polytechnique—Arago and Sadi Carnot. Others perfected discoveries which were to revolutionize modern science: Fresnel, Ampère, Cauchy.

What other regime can pride itself on having presided over the birth or rise of such a galaxy of scientists?

ALL IN THE SERVICE OF ONE MAN

'That which I seek above all,' Napoleon said to Vivant Denon, 'is grandeur; the large is always beautiful.' A taste for the monumentl and the sumptuous replaced the 'sweetness' of the last years of the Ancien Régime. The Louis XVI style was judged to be too light and made way, in literature as in furniture, in architecture as in music, for a heavy, not

[1] A home for old and mentally sick women in Paris.

to say ponderous, style—massive mahogany, engraved bronze, thick materials, oratorical sentences, stately music, Roman triumphal arches. Although Sainte-Beuve was not afraid to write that 'military triumphs have more than once been rivalled by the splendours of the contemporary arts, such as a page of the *Martyrs,* a battle by Gros or Spontini's *La Vestale,* sarcasm was not lacking. Somewhat unjustly, Napoleon has been compared to Louis XIV; but the one had barely fifteen years of power, the other, a particularly long reign; the balance is unequal.

Far from being disastrous, the imperial record is positive: an original style was born, there was intense artistic activity stimulated by official orders, Paris became the intellectual capital of Europe.

There is doubtless another side—the way in which art was made to serve one man. From 1805 onwards there were no limits to adulation. One painting showed all the peoples of the earth come to salute the bust of the Emperor; there were a Chinaman, a Negro, and even a Red Indian with multi-coloured feathers on his head. Admiration soon bordered on the ridiculous. 'What an honour for God that such homage should be rendered to him by so great a genius!' a preacher welcoming Napoleon to church declared from the pulpit. Napoleon himself was obliged to put a stop to this excessive cult: 'I dispense you from comparing me to God,' he wrote to Decrès. But he sighed, 'I came too late, there is nothing great left to do. Yes, I admit, I have a fine career, I have gone far, but how different from Alexander. When he described himself to the people as the son of Jupiter, the whole of the East believed him. As for myself, if I were to announce I was the Son of the Eternal Father, there is not a single fishwife who would not hiss as I passed. People are too enlightened today.' But by using art for his propaganda, Napoleon undoubtedly continued the Revolution without going back to Louis XIV.

After all, there seems to be a tendency to forget that Balzac, Hugo, Musset, Vigny, Berlioz and Delacroix were formed under the Empire. It should be remembered that their imaginations were fired by reading the bulletins of the Grande Armée. 'In the lycées,' said Vigny, 'schoolmasters never ceased reading the bulletins of the Grande Armée to us, and our shouts of 'Long live the Emperor!' interrupted Tacitus and Plato.' It was in considering these bulletins that Thiers and Sainte-Beuve declared Napoleon to be the greatest writer of his time.

Through the rediscovery of the meaning of the epic and by deciding on a programme of glorification of the hero, Romanticism responded to the ideal which Napoleon had attempted to impose on the writers and the artists of his time. Where the authoritarian way had failed, the legend succeeded. The epoch of Napoleon was, when all things are considered, the Romantic era.

PART IV

THE NOTABLES
BETRAYED

At the time of the meeting between Alexander and Napoleon at Erfurt in 1808, Talleyrand went to the Tsar: 'Sire, why have you come here? It is up to you to save Europe and you can do it only by standing up to Napoleon. The French people are civilized, their sovereign is not. Therefore the Tsar of Russia must be the ally of the French people.' On another occasion he was even more precise: 'The Rhine, the Alps and the Pyrenees are the conquests of France; the remainder is the Emperor's, France does not approve.' By France we understand the new bourgeoisie for whom Talleyrand was speaking.

The first bone of contention between the notables and Napoleon was the creation of the *noblesse de l'Empire*. Despite the care which was taken, it seemed contrary to the principle of equality, it favoured the reappearance of the old aristocrats; it might even have been a prelude to the re-establishment of detested feudalism. The Austrian marriage again underlined the monarchical tendencies of Napoleon's power—in 1806 the word 'Republic' had disappeared. Was the Emperor betraying the oath of 1804? It finally became hard to forgive his authoritarianism. The lack of freedom became as unbearable as the lack of sugar and coffee. From 1808 people were glad to denounce the despotism of the Emperor in private.

The Spanish affair accelerated the breaking up of the Brumairians. In 1808, Napoleon had consolidated the Revolution. The only fly in the ointment was the war with England. Some revolutionaries, among them Fouché, were to try to renew negotiations at the price of concessions which Napoleon was determined not to allow. He hoped for the support of part of the bourgeoisie, for, despite the ruin of the French ports, there was a boom in the industries protected by the Continental System. Hence the encouragement to industry and the many declarations in its favour promulgated by the Emperor.

But in fact the Spanish affair was met with reserve by the majority of notables, especially once its real nature was revealed. There was nothing to be gained from the Franco-English conflict: no economic advantage could come from it (except in the field of military supplies), especially after the uprising of the American colonies against French domination. It was all a question of Napoleon's dynastic madness. For the first time war was not the result of a European coalition formed against Revolutionary France, but of the desire of the leader, which this Revolution had given itself, to seize another crown. The fact that it was a Bourbon crown was of little importance. The manner in which Napoleon proceeded shocked not only Europe, but French opinion.

'He took,' wrote Chateaubriand, 'the crown of Naples from Joseph's head and placed it on the head of Murat; the latter handed the former the Spanish crown. Bonaparte with a single stroke forced the crowns down over the brows of the two new kings, and they went off, each in his own direction, like two conscripts who had exchanged shakos on the quarter master's instructions.'

The spectacular reconciliation of Talleyrand and Fouché arose from concern about the excessive development of Napoleon's Empire and about a policy which no longer conformed to the logic of the Revolution.

Lively nationalistic reactions in Germany as well as Austria's resistance to the 1809 campaign could but strengthen the fears which war in Spain had aroused. A doubt was cast on the stability of Napoleon's conquests. Carnot, as it has been seen, had already rejected Robespierre's plans for expansion in 1794. The policy of 'sister republics' so dear to the Directory was outmoded. Napoleon wanted the whole of Europe. But one lucid section of the bourgeoisie was asking if France could afford it.

The economic depression of 1810 caused the final break between the notables and the imperial regime. Speculation reached its limits, banking, trade and finally industry were shaken; it was the turn of agriculture in 1811; then in 1813 production was slowed down by the loss of trade outlets. Three black years jolted the optimism of the business world whilst increasing the discontent in rural areas.

Defeat came and the break was complete. The breadth of the Russian disaster turned Napoleon's chief supporters against the regime. On the one hand there was the new bourgeoisie who no longer wished to invest in an enterprise which had ceased to bear fruit. The determination to double the stake and the love of risk which characterized Napoleon were completely alien to the cunning and careful provincial merchants. On the other hand there was the peasantry who had grown tired of the burden of supplying, more or less alone, men for a war which no longer defended the conquests of '89, but which served the dynastic interests of an individual.

1808 was the turning point in the Napoleonic adventure; it was the real beginning of the end.

1

FROM SAVIOUR TO DESPOT

'The need for a temporary absolute dictatorship which is sometimes essential to save a state, put out of mind all ideas of what might result from such a power, and nobody thought that glory was incompatible with public liberty,' wrote Bourrienne in his *Mémoires*. Were these liberties not guaranteed by 'the institutions which the spirit and the enlightenment of the times had called for?' Benjamin Constant himself admitted that an 'exception' was justified by a state of war. But the dictatorship of public safety inspired by Ancient Rome and by enlightened dictatorship (in the eighteenth-century sense) had been succeeded by a hereditary monarchy. It was, of course, a matter of making the new regime acceptable to the sovereigns of Europe, who would have balked at too much republicanism, and thereby consolidating the social victories of the Revolution. By leaning on the bourgeoisie, Napoleon could have secured the future of his dynasty and established a solidarity between the Empire and the notables. On the contrary he began to separate himself from them in 1808: the personalization of power put an end to the proper functioning of regular political institutions, and liberties disappeared. Napoleon did not believe in 'constitutions'; he believed that vanity and not the desire for liberty had caused the Revolution. 'Such badly elected, level-headed governments can only be the shortest path to anarchy,' he declard to Molé. To which Molé was later able to reply: 'France had never believed that a state of affairs could last, based on force, preserved by constraint and justified by glory.'

NAPOLEON

The frail General of the Army whose thin sallow face was framed by long hair had made way for a small, rather stout man with a full face, a waxy complexion and short hair. There remained no physical re semblance between Bonaparte and Napoleon. But there remained the look, sometimes imperious and sometimes charming, the smile, described by Chateaubriand as 'affectionate and beautiful' and the lilting Ajaccio accent.

Much has been written about Napoleon's extraordinary capacity for work, his prodigious memory, his admirably ordered mind, and no doubt there are those who have been equally impressed by his genius for dramatic presentation. His contempt for men has been mentioned, his immeasurable pride, his extreme nervousness which threw him into fits not unlike epilepsy; but too much faith cannot be put in the *Mémoires* of Bourrienne and Chaptal, his unfortunate collaborators. Napoleon was bad-tempered but loyal in his friendships, and his prejudices were almost a habit (he was never supposed to have liked Gouvion Saint-Cyr or Jourdan). He was an anxious man who hesitated when confronted by Fontaine's plans for the joining of the Louvre and the Tuileries, or over the end of the Empire, and unable, if Rogniat is to be believed, to make certain military decisions. Legend and counter-legend have clouded the truth about Napoleon by exaggerating at times his qualities, and at times his faults. His correspondence reveals his lack of moderation, but also his good sense, his harshness, but also his softer side. Fondly he wrote to Eugène de Beauharnais on 14 April 1806: 'You must have more gaiety in your house, it is necessary to the happiness of your wife and for your health. A young woman needs to be amused, particularly in her situation.' Two dry lines written to his brother Louis were enough to acknowledge the birth of his nephew: 'I compliment you on the birth of your son. I wish this prince to be called Charles-Napoleon.' It was the future Napoleon III.

And what about women? Napoleon was to tell Gourgaud, 'I have never really been in love, except perhaps, a little, with Josephine. And, furthermore, that was because I was twenty-seven years old.' He soon grew tired of her infidelities, her spending and her capricious ways (the little dog Fortuné who used to bite Bonaparte's calves in the intimate warmth of the conjugal bed). The Emperor had at least two children outside wedlock: Léon in 1806, with Éléonore Denuelle de la Plaigne, a reader of Caroline's; and Alexandre in 1810 with Marie Walewska. He may also have had a daughter, Émilie, the future Comtesse de Brigode, with Françoise-Marie Leroy. No liaison—and there were many—had the slightest effect on Napoleon's life. A warrior's rest.

Woken at seven o'clock, the Emperor had the newspapers and the police reports collected by Duroc, the palace marshal, read to him; he examined bills from suppliers and talked with members of his household. By eight o'clock he was in his office dictating his correspondence to his secretaries, Bourrienne, then Méneval and Fain, and looking through police bulletins. The *petit lever* at nine o'clock was followed at ten by breakfast which took ten minutes and was washed down by the habitual Chambertin diluted with water, following a tradition in herited from the Ancien Régime. Then he returned to his office where the study of documents, statements and reports awaited him, and he consulted the maps prepared for him by Bacler d'Albe. At one o'clock in the afternoon he attended the sittings of the Council of Ministers, the Council of State or the administrative councils. He dined at five o'clock, but, in fact, often did not sit down until seven. After dinner, he lingered in the drawing-room with the Empress, glanced through the most recent books indicated to him by his librarian, Barbier, then returned to his office to finish the day's work. He went to bed at midnight and awoke at three o'clock to consider the more delicate affairs of state; he would then take a hot bath, and went to bed again at five.

Only journeys and military campaigns altered this way of life. Then the Emperor had at his disposal a special berlin fitted out with drawers and compartments for his papers. An escort of chamberlains and aides-de-camp either preceded or followed him. In order not to waste time he dictated while in his carriage; the mail was despatched at stopping places by Berthier, his chief of staff or by his secretaries.

However, by the end of the Empire, the strain of overwork had become apparent. All witnesses confirm the partial loss of his intellectual energy. The sense of propaganda remained. Rarely can an historic personage have taken so much care over the figure he cut: a little hat and a grey frock-coat, his hand in his waistcoat—the caricaturists and picture makers in Épinal can have had little difficulty in capturing the likeness of the Emperor.

NAPOLEON'S POLITICAL IDEAS

Napoleon's political ideas had evolved considerably. A few scribblings and sketches, the *Lettre à Buttafuoco* and *Le Souper de Beaucaire* had revealed a young officer searching, on the eve of the Revolution with sincere idealism, and after his failure in Corsica with realism, for an ideal government. He was later to find it—the Empire. The wielding of power did not, however, discourage political thought. At the Council of State, with his family and in his correspondence he took pleasure in expressing his ideas. Starting from concrete cases he devolved a political philosophy. A philosophy which was closer to Machiavelli than to Rousseau who had in any case been repudiated since the Consulate. On 7 June 1805 he sent advice to Eugène who had become Viceroy of Italy: 'Show for the nation which you rule an esteem which must be increasingly manifested as you discover reasons for esteeming it less. There will come a time when you will realize that there is very little difference between one people and another.' Another *Prince* could be written on the basis of the advice contained in his letter. Secrecy should be the mainspring of the art of governing, the prince should speak as little as possible and listen as much as possible. 'The strength of a silent prince cannot be measured,' wrote Napoleon. 'When he speaks he must have an awareness of great superiority. The prince should give no credit to spies and should mistrust foreign ambassadors for,' the Emperor observed, 'an ambassador will not speak well of you because it is his job to speak ill.' Finally, the prince must show himself to be unyielding with regard to scoundrels: 'The discovery of a disloyal clerk is a victory for administration.' Strength, Napoleon wrote elsewhere, is the essential principle of all government. 'Weakness produces civil war; energy maintains the peace and prosperity of states.' Only an authoritarian regime could be established to overcome the crisis inherited from the Revolution—the Brumairian regime. An authoritarian regime which was absolutely not responsible to an English-style parliament. 'The Government,' he declared in 1804, 'is no longer, as it was, an emanation of the Legislative Body; it is only very distantly connected to it.' One idea recurs forcibly, that of an appeal to the nation, or in Bonapartist language, 'an appeal to the people.'

> The Legislative Body is the guardian of the public property; its job is to assess taxes; if it were to oppose laws of purely local interest, I would allow it to have its way; but if an opposition capable of interfering with the workings of government were to be formed, I would resort to the Senate to have it adjourned, to change it, or to break it, and I would, if necessary, appeal to the nation which is behind all that.

But he wrote to Lebrun who was in charge of administering Holland: 'I have not taken over the government of Holland in order to consult the rabble of Amsterdam or to do what others want.'

The influence of absolute power accentuated one of Napoleon's characteristics: in a government where one man is responsible for everything, self-confidence soon destroys any critical faculty. 'My people of Italy know me well enough never to have to forget that I have more knowledge in my little finger than they have in all their heads put together.' From self-importance it is an easy step to cynicism: 'I have always noticed that honest people are good for nothing.'

The dictatorship of public safety, of popular origin ('Recourse to the people has the double advantage of legalizing the prorogation and of purifying the origins of my power which would otherwise have always remained questionable'), became the fourth dynasty which the Emperor hoped would be acceptable to the old monarchies ('I have shown that I wish to close the door on revolutions. The sovereigns owe it to me that I have arrested the revolutionary torrent which threatened their thrones. Every throne would topple if my son's fell,' he confided to Caulaincourt). He became more and more convinced that the aristocracy should be the principal support of the hereditary monarchy which he intended to found: 'It is the true, the only support of a monarchy, its moderator, its lever, its rudder, a real balloon in the air.' Rousseau made way for Montesquieu, and the support of the notables was rejected in favour of the old nobility.

THE IMPERIAL FAMILY

Family surroundings can rarely have played so important a part in the life of a statesman. The story of Napoleon's relations with his family, told with success by Frédéric Masson, is no more than a long succession of quarrels and reconciliations. The Emperor's brothers and sisters, however, had no cause for complaint. From the beginning of the Empire the Bonaparte family formed a dynasty of French princes whose descendants were to inherit the crown. Joseph (1768–1844), the eldest, to whom Napoleon for a long time gave tokens of a certain respect, received the Kingdom of Naples confiscated from the Bourbons in 1806, then replaced Charles IV on the throne of Spain. Louis (1778–1846), who had married Josephine's daughter, Hortense de Beauharnais, obtained the Kingdom of Holland in 1806. An excellent sovereign, he took to heart the interests of his state, stricken as it was by the Continental Blockade; from then onwards a conflict with his brother was inevitable. Jerome (1784–1860), whose escapades at the time of his marriage to the rich American, Miss Patterson, had provoked Bonaparte's anger, was reconciled to the Emperor in 1805 and married on 12 August 1807 to the King of Württemberg's daughter. Six days later he became King of Westphalia. Only Lucien (1775–1840) who was, however, the most intelligent, did not receive a kingdom, although he became Minister of the Interior, ambassador to Spain and a tribune. He had married Madame Jouberthon against his brother's will and was obliged to retire to Rome to his estate at Canino which the Pope raised to the status of a principality. Elisa (1777–1820), the wife of an obscure Corsican officer, Felix Bacciochi, whom Napoleon made a senator, became Princess of Lucca and Piombino and later Grand Duchess of Tuscany. Pauline (1780–1825) whose beauty was immortalized by Canova, married, after Leclerc, the Prince Borghese; finally Caroline (1782–1839), married to Murat, became Grand Duchess of Berg and Queen of Naples.

As kings, Napoleon's brothers were, in the Emperor's mind, the mere instruments of his politics. He wrote to Louis on 6 May 1808: 'I read in the Paris newspapers that you are making princes. I beg you earnestly not to do so. Kings do not have the right to nominate princes: this right is inherent to the imperial dignity.' To Elisa he wrote from Schönbrunn on 27 August 1809: 'You are a subject, and like all French people you are obliged to obey the orders of ministers.' As consequences of imperial politics developed which were often contrary to the interests of their states, Napoleon's brothers and sisters tended to espouse the aspirations of their peoples, thus threatening the unity of the Empire. From 1810 Napoleon began to regret the thrones which he had distributed. The birth of the King of Rome, on 20 March 1811, was to alter his vision of the Empire. He wanted to take back, for his son, lands which he had imprudently given away. In Holland, Louis was the first victim of this change of policy which finally threatened Murat too. Furthermore such politics annoyed public opinion in France; the interest of the nation took second place, now only dynastic motives counted. Finally, Napoleon's family did him a disservice, less through intrigue than because of the picture it presented of a clan exploiting France and then Europe in order to build up enormous fortunes and to satisfy its dubious appetites.

THE GOVERNMENT MACHINE

Although the Republican calendar lasted until 1 January 1806, and although the description 'République française' remained on the coins until the end of 1808, from 1804 the imperial government comported itself as a personal dictatorship without the Consulate's trappings and appearances of legality. Gradually the influence which the notables had thought to have preserved despite the foundation of the Empire disappeared. The will of one man predominated and this will corresponded not to the interests of the bourgeoisie, but to the whims of an individual.

Ministers were reduced to the role of simple executives and henceforth all their correspondence passed through the hands of the Emperor. In 1804 Chaptal had left the Ministry of the Interior; in 1807 Talleyrand was replaced in foreign affairs by the conscientious Champagny; dismissed in 1810, Fouché handed the police over to the 'policeman' Savary. It was a matter of replacing strong personalities, who might have altered imperial decisions, with devoted servants of no talent. The Minister of the Interior (Cretet and then Montalivet) was thought to have too much power and lost some of it to the Ministry of Manufacturing and Commerce created in 1811 on behalf of Collin de Sussy. The general directorships which limited the powers of ministers were increased.

On the other hand, the counter-balance provided by the assemblies, which were already weakened under the Consulate, vanished. Although the Tribunate had been divided into three sections by the Constitution of Year XII, and therefore no longer produced a systematic opposition, it was abolished in 1807. The Legislative Body whose members were recruited from among officials and former officials, saw its sessions reduced to a few weeks. Napoleon is said to have envisaged its disappearance. At the time of the re-election of deputies in 1807, the percentage of abstentions was very high in most of the electoral colleges responsible for presenting candidates. The electors were, obviously, sulking over elections which had no real value. The government itself seemed to be uninterested: in 1812 there were 399 members to be nominated in the colleges of the *arrondissements* of the Seine and 139 in the departmental college. The Senate was wary of any impulse for independence despite the relative power of the commissions for the freedom of the press and for individual liberty. The Senate even quashed the decision of the Court of Assizes in Brussels which had acquitted Werbrouck, the Mayor of Antwerp, who was accused by Bellemare, the Commissioner-General of Police with whom he had quarrelled, of fraud and extortion. Interned in Charenton, Sade appealed in vain to the senatorial commission which made no pronouncement on his fate.

For its part, the Council of State, which had been so important under the Consulate, lost part of its influence. Napoleon attended it less frequently and imposed his decisions without listening to the councillors, if Thibaudeau is to be believed. This loss of power was, however, relative, since a record held by the Secretary to the Council, Locré, which has recently come to light, shows Treilhard on 6 June 1810 contradicting the Emperor's suggestions on the Courts of Appeal at least six times: the Emperor was in the minority and bowed to the vote of 11 November 1813. On the other hand the class of auditors—to which Stendhal belonged—became increasingly a nursery for future administrators. Thus the role of the Council as a melting pot was recognized. Since the important laws had been passed, it was, after all, normal that this assembly should devote itself essentially to administrative jurisdiction.

The magistrature did not maintain its fixity of tenure for very long. The *senatus consultum* of 12 October 1807 entrusted the job of weeding it out to a senatorial commission appointed by the Emperor. The law of 20 April 1810 reorganized the administration of justice and replaced the courts of criminal justice by assize courts which sat in the department's main town. The jury was chosen from a list of sixty persons prepared by the Prefect. Pursuit of the criminal was the procurator's business, the examining magistrate issued arrest warrants. The Courts of Appeal changed their name to Imperial Courts.

In the prefectures there appeared a new generation of men who were often members of the old nobility and who were more amenable to injunctions from above: Molé was appointed Prefect of the Côte d'Or in 1807; Montalivet, Prefect of the Manche and then of the Seine-et-Oise before becoming Minister of the Interior in 1809; Pasquier replaced Dubois at the Prefecture of Police in 1811. The Austrian marriage precipitated the invasion of the prefectures by the old aristocracy (Cossé-Brissac, La Tour du Pin, Breteuil). But favouritism also played a part—Abrial, son of the former minister, or Régnier, son of the *grand-juge*. The recruitment of prefects depended more and more on the goodwill of the Emperor; those who had believed in a certain security of employment must have been biting their fingernails. Administrative memoranda became more and more arbitrary. They were issued by the Minister of the Interior, the Minister of Police and the Director-General of Conscription. Little by little, these memoranda were to absorb the energies of the prefects who, according to Savary in a note to the Emperor, should also be appreciated by virtue of their birth, their fortune and of 'Your Majesty's particular favours'. They were also judged by the authority they exercised over the general councils which during 'lightning sessions' had been reduced to making decisions destined to remain dead-letters. The absence of any real mayoral power added to the low regard in which municipal offices were held.

Whilst legislative machinery was simplified by the disappearance of, or the decrease in the power of, the assemblies, administration was being divided up into more and more compartments in the form of general-directorships or of *arrondissements*. The Prefect of the Moselle, Vaublanc, noted that this dividing up was carried to such extremes in the last years of the Empire that it became impossible to untangle the confusion. The beautiful administrative machinery was finally jammed as a result of imperial mistrust and of centralization carried to extremes. On the eve of the battle of Leipzig, Napoleon was asked to agree to the Commissioner of Saint-Malo's expenses, thus his attention was distracted from a confrontation which was to be decisive for the future of Germany.

Henceforth, Napoleon alone made decisions, even over matters of secondary importance. If he summoned private councils, it was strictly with a view to modifying the draft of a *senatus consultum,* never to ratify a peace treaty or an alliance in the way provided for by the Constitution. The councils of Ministers on Wednesdays were by now mere formalities, according to Baron Fain:

> The Emperor never subjected himself to signing in Council. As soon as the plan for a decree was presented, it was placed on the desk with the report and the necessary documents. A work-sheet containing a summary of the different plans put forward by the minister served as a folder for the dossier which was left to be signed. The ministers then left the meeting with no more than an impression of what had been said and done in their presence.

The Emperor preferred administrative councils, to which Mondays, Thursdays and Saturdays were given over, and which could last from nine o'clock in the morning to seven o'clock at night.

'The object of the administrative councils was to examine in depth one matter alone or one kind of matter. As often as not,' Fain observed, 'it was a question of drawing up certain budgets, like the civil engineering budget, or the budget for military or maritime engineering.'

The Emperor summoned councillors of state, technicians and chiefs of departments. The minutes of these meetings have been preserved. Everyone gave his opinion but in the event of an opinion being considered, it was the Emperor alone who made the decision. By calling this kind of council, Napoleon was merely aiming at keeping himself informed, particularly as he often hesitated over technical problems—a side of his character which is usually little known.

A paradoxical situation was to be reached in which the budgets for the city of Paris were approved by administrative councils before even having been examined by the general council which had become the municipal council for the capital, and were applied with no regard for the opinion of Parisian notables.

IMPERIAL FINANCES

The machinery of government was expensive. To control expenditure, an Audit Office was instituted in 1807, presided over by the former Minister of the Treasury, Barbé-Marbois who had been dismissed after the United Merchants' crash. Napoleon hoped to draw the necessary funds from indirect taxation. From 1804 to 1810 tax on drinks was reintroduced; in 1806 the unpopular salt-tax was renewed; from 1810 the state monopoly of tobacco was instituted.

The general direction of taxes fell into the hands of the 'Anacreon of the Fiscal system', Français de Nantes. This time popular discontent coincided with that of the notables. Taxes from the Ancien Régime as well as the unpopular salt-tax were reappearing. The spirit of revolt could almost be felt in the countryside. War was no longer financing war. In 1805 Napoleon had instituted a special fund called the Extraordinary Fund, administered by La Bouillerie under the authority of Daru, the Intendant-General of the occupied countries.

The Extraordinary Fund is said to have received 734 millions between 1805 and 1809. A *senatus consultum* of 30 January 1810 set up the Extraordinary Domain entrusted to Defermon and which the Emperor used only by decree for subsidizing the army's expenses, as a reward for great military or civil services rendered, for public works and to encourage the arts. The Extraordinary Domain was financed by war levies, and by investments carried out by the administration. But with the Spanish affair, loot was no longer the result of victory. The defeat of Austria in 1809 allowed for a last refloating in conditions which are little known. Then came the catastrophe foretold by the economist, Francis d'Ivernois.

THE IMPERIAL UNIVERSITY

Napoleon's aim for the University was the formation of a framework for the Empire. 'There can be no fixed politics,' he said, 'without a teaching body with fixed principles.' The law of 11 Floréal Year X, which instituted the *lycées,* resulted in failure: different kinds of mediocre staff were recruited, there was excessive militarization of pupils as well as bad administration of finances. *Lycées* were unable to compete with private establishments. On 10 May 1806 a law was voted which created, 'under the name of Imperial University a body entrusted exclusively with public teaching and education throughout the Empire'. The members of the teaching body had to agree to 'special, temporary civil obligations'. Fourcroy set to work on the details of the law. Twenty plans were examined before the signing, on 17 March 1808, of a decree containing 144 articles which laid down 'the basis of teaching in the University's schools'. The University had the monopoly of teaching, and was placed under the authority of a Grand-Master assisted by a University council and a body of general inspectors. It was divided into academies or educational districts administered by rectors who themselves had councils and inspectors under the. Every teacher had to have the Grand-Master's authority to teach and every school had to have his authority before it could open. Every institution was obliged to pay the University an annual sum. Education was divided into three categories: primary education, which Napoleon left to the Christian friars; secondary education which was entrusted to the *lycées* and communal colleges, and higher education which was in the hands of the faculties of Arts, Sciences, Law, Medicine and Theology. The prestige of success in the *baccalauréat* developed, under the Empire, into a passport to success. The training of teachers continued to be ensured by the *École normale* which was reorganized in 1810. So Napoleon affirmed his desire to cast the new élite in a mould of his liking. The notables were not mistaken. The Imperial University was not welcomed with pleasure; in fact it did not answer the purpose which Napoleon had assigned to it.

The poet, Louis de Fontanes, was appointed Grand-Master of the University instead of Fourcroy who had drawn up the plans and subsequently died of sadness. The scholar had been discarded because of this revolutionary past. Fontanes perhaps saw a lucrative retirement in his post, or, more probably, a means of safeguarding his future by accommodating the Church which was threatened with a total loss of control in education. He made ultramontane Catholics members of the

University council—people like Bonald or the Abbé Émery, and he appointed numerous ecclesiastics as headmasters and vice-principals of the *lycées*, or as teachers. Thus he betrayed the Emperor's intentions in favour of neo-Catholicism.

The monopoly was not in the end quite as absolute as might be supposed. Besides the Catholic secondary schools, there remained private schools and boarding schools run by individuals, which were subject to the supervision of the inspectors, and incorporated in the University. Far from coming to an end, the *lycées'* competition from private schools, particularly Church ones, grew increasingly.

An affair in which a state secondary school was staffed by priests blew up in 1810 in Saint-Pol-de-Léon and annoyed Napoleon, 'Tell the Grand-Master that he should deal with the prefects, not with bishops, and he is not to make public education a party political or religious matter.' On 17 July 1810 the Minister of Police sent a circular to the prefects inquiring into the *lycées* and into the nature of the education they provided. The investigation confirmed the success of religious establishments and of the Church's hold over the young. The future élite was not being marked by the Napoleonic stamp. The decree of 15 November 1811 finalized and modified the one of 17 March 1808. Henceforth the Catholic schools were placed under the authority of the University. There could only be one Church school per department and its pupils were obliged to wear a religious habit. In all schools education was restricted to simple classes and learning by heart. Even the pupils in Church schools were obliged to follow the same courses as those in the *lycées*. In 1813 Montalivet pointed out in the *Situation de l'Empire* that there were 68,000 pupils in *lycées* and state schools and 47,000 in private schools. Nevertheless, the 1811 decree was frequently by-passed by bishops with the collusion of Fontanes and the inspectors. Guizot recorded in about 1816 that the administration of the University under the Empire had not 'ceased to propagate religious principles, pious practices and good moral doctrines'. This did not displease the notables.

THE BREAKING AWAY OF THE NOTABLES
Faced with the encroachment of a power which was becoming more and more absolute, the notables finally grew uneasy. The Caesarian image developed into a vast deception masking a government which no longer cared for the interests of the notables and which followed the path to its own destruction.

But the opportunities to express this discontent and to destroy the popularity of the regime had become fewer and fewer. The Paris Chamber of Commerce denounced the fateful consequences of the war on trade. 'Uncertainty as to the duration of war,' it reported, 'adds to the awkwardness of the situation by preventing speculation which would be ruinous in the event of peace.' A circular of 31 March 1806 forbade the publication or divulgence of this opinion without the authorization of the Ministry of the Interior. Neither could the Parisian bourgeoisie express itself through the General Council of Manufacturers, as all publicity concerning their proceedings was forbidden.

The establishment of a general directorship of printing and book-selling on 5 February 1810, and the consequent limiting of printers had heralded new press control. This soon came into being—the decree of 3 August 1810 authorized the publication of only one paper per depart-ment. Provisionally, only a few literary or scientific papers were allowed and papers carrying announcements concerning sales of property or merchandise. From October 1811 the papers in Paris were reduced to four—*Le Moniteur*, *La Gazette de France*, *Le Journal de Paris* and, confiscated from the Bertin brothers on 18 February 1811, *Le Journal des Débats* which became *Le Journal de l'Empire*.

Police control of newspapers was absolute. Besides, on 17 Septem-ber 1811, the decree of Compiègne confiscated all the Paris papers for the benefit of the state. Profits were divided among the police, courtiers and men of letters. No more draconian regime was ever instituted. Newspapers, now entirely in government hands, became dull and insipid and were totally devoid of interest. By the end of the Empire the Parisian bourgeois was deprived of coffee, sugar and his newspaper. It was a lot to ask of him.

The bourgeoisie had suffered the Terror, it bore with impatience police control under the Empire. Back in the Ministry of Police, Fouché had made the general force extremely efficient. He had divided the business of the Ministry into four sections entrusted to the Councillors of State, Réal, Pelet de la Lozère and the Prefect of Police, Dubois. Desmarest was particularly in charge of the department which dealt with conspiracy. Except for the fiasco over General Malet's conspiracy in 1808, when rivalry instigated by Napoleon between the Ministry of Police and the Prefecture completely confused the issue, the Imperial Police foiled intrigues and conspiracies. All Puisaye's attempts from London to set up a network in the west were destined to failure. The conspirator, Le Chevalier, was executed on 9 January 1808; Prigent who was planning an uprising in the west was captured on 5 June of the same year.

But Fouché knew equally well how to gain the confidence of the aristocrats, for instance by alleviating Polignac's conditions of detention. His leaving the Ministry caused tremendous fear. Savary, who replaced him, did not have the same finesse as the 'machine gunner of Lyons'. His brutality had been shown in Spain. As head of the police, his blunders were endless. So he conceived the idea of providing servants with a special police document or *livret*. This was interpreted as a new means of supervising well-to-do households. The measure caused a general outcry and to all intents and purposes was not applied by employers. Under cover of 'moral and personal statistics' he undertook the card-indexing of the whole of France and interfered with the marriages of rich heiresses and the daughters of the old nobility. This intrusion into people's private lives finally discredited the services of the police department. It was not Fouché who created the myth of the Imperial Police. On the contrary, under him it was as discreet as possible. It was Savary's clumsiness which revealed the degree to which the regime had gradually become a police state.

The absolute monarchy may have been, as in Saint-Simon's famous formula, a 'long reign of vile bourgeoisie' (an opinion which the bourgeoisie did not share), but in 1807 the bourgeoisie again ceased to reign under the imperial government which had become the instrument of the whims of an individual. The evolution was contrary to what had been hoped for: it had been hoped that the public safety dictatorship would gradually develop into a liberal constitutional government. In fact, as Molé pointed out,

Napoleon's genius, his nature, made him eschew any sharing of authority. Unity was, in his eyes, an indispensable condition of a strong government; all contested, limited or restricted power was, in his view, condemned to hesitation and deprived of those sudden inspirations to which he himself owed the performance of certain miracles . . . At the moment in which his sun was setting, do you know where he thought of seeking a remedy and the conditions of stability which he wanted for the future? He reproached himself with having given too much freedom to the Legislative Body, with having allowed them meddle too much in affairs, and with having granted too great an importance to the Senate.

How could the notables, who had, without regret, seen the disappearance of the Ancien Régime, allow order to give way to daring and authority to tyranny?

2

A MISTAKE:
THE NOBLESSE DE L'EMPIRE

'The absurd dogma of equality is always the favourite one of shop-keepers,' the Jacobin Fouché had warned. Napoleon did not hear him. Even before the war in Spain he had made his first mistake—the creation of a nobility. He had said that at the origin of the Revolution lay vanity—liberty was merely a pretext. By making it possible for the notables to aspire to the new nobility, Napoleon hoped to make them accept the suppression of liberties. He also intended to integrate the revolutionary bourgeoisie and the old aristocracy who would thus be lured away from the Bourbons. This calculation was doubly mistaken. The old aristocracy only paid lip-service to the usurper and the shop-keepers mourned for their lost equality, at least if Fouché is to be believed. Dismay spread to the rural world—would feudalism be revived, despite the 1804 oath? In short, the new nobility was greeted far from enthusiastically.

STAGES IN THE NEW CREATION
The idea of equality was so deeply embedded in the country that it took Napoleon eight years to found a new nobility, although, since 1804, no one could foster any illusions as to the nature of his regime.

'There are two things for which the nation is not ready,' the First Consul admitted to Roederer, 'they are hereditary office and the nobility. An hereditary nobility whose origins lay in noble actions and in great services rendered to the state could not last. However, it was considerably preferable to a newly instituted nobility which would suddenly raise noblemen above their peers.'

The lists of notabilities which had barely been drawn up and which might have formed a basis for a new aristocracy, disappeared under the

Constitution of Year X in favour of electoral colleges in which the Empire was not interested. According to Roederer, Bonaparte was against the lists of notables for fear that a new nobility born of the Revolution might form behind his back. Hence the indifference which he subsequently showed towards the electoral colleges.

Can the institution of the Légion d'honneur be seen as a step towards the re-establishment of a nobility, this time designed by Bonaparte? Like the lists of notabilities, did it not aim at choosing an élite on which the consular government could lean? An élite which, unlike the notables, distinguished itself not by wealth, but by services towards the state, and which was appointed by the First Consul.

The Constituent Assembly had forbidden, on 30 July 1791, 'all outward signs which imply distinctions of birth', but had refrained from legislating on the problem of a 'unique national decoration which might be awarded for virtue, talent and services rendered to the state'. The Convention had allowed that awards might be granted to 'citizens who had served the state exceptionally'. Finally, the Directory had increased military awards in the form of honorary arms. But these marks of distinction did not violate the principle of equality. They merely excluded the civil element. The creation of the Légion d'honneur by Bonaparte aimed at broadening the concept of reward; it solved the Constituent Assembly's problems. The word 'order' did not appear in the draft and the word 'legion', whose origins were entirely Roman, was aimed at reassuring public opinion. Resistance was none the less lively in the Council of State where Berlier is said to have exclaimed: 'The proposed order leads towards an aristocracy; crosses and ribbons are the playthings of the monarchy.' 'Why,' Napoleon is said to have replied, 'should the institution not be common to soldiers and civilians? Those men who first caused despotism to blanch and who proclaimed liberty, have they not equal rights with the soldiers who have defended the state against foreigners?' The debates in the Tribunate were no less rowdy. The Legislative Body produced 166 votes in favour and 110 against the Légion d'honneur, which being based on an oath and endowed with property contained the seeds of a new nobility.

The granting of *sénatoreries* (a life interest in landed property to Senators) was a further step towards a new aristocracy. The *senatus consultum* of 14 Nivôse Year XI provided for one *sénatorerie* within the jurisdiction of each court of appeal, an administrative division for which a senator had moral responsibility. Every *sénatorerie* brought with it a house and an income from state-owned property of about 20,000 to 25,000 francs which was supposed to cover the travelling and entertainment expenses of the senator who was obliged to spend part of the year in his *sénatorerie*. Nothing would have offended the egalitarian sentiments of the French if these *sénatoreries* had not been granted for life and if they had not seemed like the beginnings of a new feudalism.

Like the lists of notabilities, the Légion d'honneur and the *sénatoreries* in the long run represent attempts to re-establish the nobility. At the end of 1804 the Légion d'honneur suffered from a financial crisis from which it did not recover. The decree of 28 February 1809 took away the rural property administered by the cohorts of the Légion in exchange for 2,082,000 francs at five per cent. This was a decisive turning point: the Légion d'honneur had to relinquish any idea of forming an aristocracy which, thanks to its landed property, would have had great influence, and it became what

The holders of some *sénatoreries* were bitterly disappointed when they discovered that the income from these lands came from properties which were widely dispersed. For instance, the *sénatorerie* of Agen was supported by estates in the Gers, in the Lot-et-Garonne, the Seine-et-Oise and the Eure-et-Loir, which greatly complicated the collection of income intended for the senator. This was generally the case with very few exceptions. The holder of the *sénatorerie* of Riom complained, 'The administration is tiresome and costly, production almost nothing and the holder despairs of overcoming the obstacles which stand in the way of simply collecting his income.' At Bourges, Garnier-Laboissière deplored 'the existence of such small holdings which are so far from one another as to necessitate the employment of as many small farmers, whose solvability is always so questionable as to bring about frequent losses or litigation.' It was a far cry from the fief and his principality.

The failure was intentional. Bonaparte had set France on another path, that of an aristocracy which derived its riches and its influence from the imperial government. The Brumairians would have liked a nobility which merely set the seal on their conquest of power and the continuation of it. Napoleon could not adapt to that. His mistrust of the notables led him to restrict the power of the electoral colleges and to make the regional establishment of senators quite impossible in this he was helped by the scarcity of national property. Harder to explain is the lack of interest which soon became evident in the Légion d'honneur. The increase in decorations from 1805 shows that the Emperor intended its role to be limited to that of a simple reward, which is what it still is in republican France today.

The nobility with all the trappings of a court came into being at the Tuileries. Initially limited in number, the First Consul's household gradually expanded. The visit of the Etrurian rulers in June 1801 favoured protocol and the reintroduction of liveries. The ceremonial was ostentatious. Boots and trousers disappeared to be replaced by buckled shoes, silk stockings and breeches. A decree of 12 November 1801, which was not printed, appointed a Governor and four Palace Prefects. Not only did honours granted to Josephine continually increase, but aristocratic women began to play an important part in the entourage of the First Consul's wife: Mesdames de Luçay, de Lauriston, de Talhouet, etc. The establishment of the Consulate for life started an evolution which the proclamation of the Empire was to sanction. But precaution was meanwhile necessary. Endless justifications were produced for the reappearance of certain positions at court —'These travesties attracted ridicule at first, but people soon grew accustomed to them,' wrote Fouché in his *Mémoires*. Molé, for his part, observed, 'Bonaparte was embarrassed to appear before Republicans and the army with the pomp and trappings of supreme power.' There were many reservations, not only on the part of the army but among the bourgeoisie itself. Some had been disturbed to see the émigrés return. Who would profit from the re-establishment of the nobility, if not the old aristocrats? Fiévée was not mistaken; in a note of December 1802, he analysed public feeling: 'The great difficulty lies in understanding how to make or remake a nobility. Can these titles which originated with public office, and which by abuse had become made personal and transferable, begin again where they left off?'

The re-establishment of monarchical forms of power made the creation of a nobility inevitable. A decisive step was the decree of 30 March, 1806 which gave the title of 'prince' to the members of the Imperial family. It was the first stumbling block to the principle of equality. 'The condition of the princes called upon to reign over this vast Empire and to strengthen it by alliances cannot be exactly the same as that of other Frenchmen.' The distribution of crowns and the Emperor's matrimonial policies also served as justification. But what can be said of the other decrees promulgated on the same day? Princess Pauline and her husband Prince Borghese were given the principality of Guastalla, Prince Joachim Murat was given the Duchies of Cleves and

of Berg, and Berthier had Neufchâtel. In the states of Parma and
Piacenza three duchies known as grand-fiefs were set up: 'We reserve
the right,' the Emperor stated, 'to grant that the investiture of the said
fiefs be passed on hereditarily, through primogeniture, to the legitimate and natural male heirs of those in whose favour we shall grant
them.' Did this not constitute a re-establishment of the nobility, even if
the new fiefs were all situated abroad?

The definitive step was taken two years later. The decree of 1 March
1808 reintroduced the former ranks of the nobility, with the exception
of viscountcies and marquisates. The great dignitaries of the Empire
bore the title of 'prince' and 'serene highness', ministers, senators and
councillors of state for life, presidents of the Legislative Body and
archibishops became counts. Presidents of electoral colleges, the first
presidents of the Supreme Court of Appeal and of the Audit Office,
bishops of the Empire and the mayors of thirty-seven loyal towns
received the title of 'baron'. Knights were also accounted for. This
reintroduction of old titles was accompanied by the right to a coat of
arms. The Council of the Seal for titles was created by a second decree
on 1 March 1808. This Council consisted of an Arch-Chancellor, three
senators, two councillors of state, an attorney-general and a general
secretary, and dealt with problems arising from the granting of coats of
arms which were submitted to the Emperor for approval. Napoleon
had found a clever compromise between the French taste for honours
and the idea of equality proclaimed in 1789. A nobleman of the Empire
was not exonerated from tax, had no privilege and was not exempt
from general laws. Feudal rights remained abolished, and although
financial advantages were often granted to new dignitaries, these were
not tied to the titles. When a title was accompanied by a place name,
this place was always situated outside France.

Titles were rewards for services rendered to the state either in
military or in civil life. They were comparable to the distinctions of
Ancient Rome which granted only precedence. The letters patent of 10
September 1808 which confer the title of 'Duke of Danzig' on Marshal
Lefebvre, show the Emperor's intentions.

Wishing to give our cousin, the Marshal and Senator Lefebvre, a
testimonial of our goodwill, because of the attachment and loyalty
which he has always shown us, and in order to recognize the
distinguished services which he rendered us on the first day of our
reign [i.e. 19 Brumaire], and which he has not ceased to render

since, and to which has just been added the brilliant capture of the town of Danzig; and particularly desiring to hallow the memory of this glorious and memorable occurrence by a special title, we have decided to confer on him, and we hereby do confer on him, the title of Duke of Danzig with an endowment of land situated without our states.

We intend the said Duchy of Danzig to be possessed by our cousin the Marshal and Senator Lefebvre and transmitted through heredity to his male children, both legitimate and natural, by primogeniture, that the duties and conditions together with the rights, titles, honours and prerogatives attached to the duchies by the constitutions of the Empire be properly enjoyed.

It is to be noted that the Emperor gave the Marshal no property, income or building either in or near the town of Danzig. The title was merely the simple souvenir of a siege, a cognomen in the Roman style. The endowments would always be made up of income from lands situated outside France. Care to satisfy public opinion which was hostile to any re-establishment of feudalism was allied to a deliberate desire to link this nobility to the future of the Great Empire.

These titles were strictly personal and not hereditary. They re warded an individual and not, as formerly, a family. However the title became transferable with the establishment of a *majorat*. The *mojorat* was an asset which had to be indissolubly linked to the title and was transferable with it. It could be in real estate, unmortgaged, or in shares in the Bank of France and government stock; the size of the *majorat* varied according to the title. The Emperor's intentions can easily be divined. Memories of a difficult youth and of noblemen ruined on the eve of the Revolution led him to protect the titles which he was resuscitating from loss of privileges by assuring them, at least of the income from their *majorat*.

Open to all, this nobility was mainly recruited, by its very nature, from among soldiers, officials and notables, but very disproportionately, with fifty-nine per cent from the first, twenty-two per cent from the second (councillors of state, prefects, bishops, magistrates) and only seventeen per cent from the last (notables who after all held public office, senators, members of the electoral colleges and mayors). Commerce, industry, the arts and the liberal professions played an insignificant part.

It is hardly surprising that reservations were to be found in these circles. The banker, Hottinguer, wrote in his diary, 'Commerce sees, as one of its finest rights, the right of being judged by equals. Napoleon wanted hierarchies at all costs.' 'The financiers are discontented,' specified Fiévée, 'because social distinctions based on souvenirs and services relegate them to the third degree.'

It is harder to discover the feelings of the other notables, since elevation to the nobility was more usually automatic and resulted from public office: the Senate, the Council of State . . . it is only by the numbers of *majorats* established that interest in the institution of the nobility can really be judged. Perhaps with the notables it was not as great as might be supposed. Certainly the Council of the Seal for titles was soon inundated. Thus at its sitting on 28 October 1808 it examined the *majorats* of the Counts Laforest, Chauvelin, Mérode de Westerloo, Darjuzon, Contades (president of the electoral college of the Maine-et-Loire); Estève (Treasurer-General of the Crown), Perregaux (auditor in the Council of State), Wals-Serrant (president of the electoral college of Finistère), Mercy d'Argentau (Chamberlain), Duval de Beaulieu (Mayor of Mons), etc. Among the barons examined on the same day were nine prefects, about ten members of electoral colleges and several magistrates. But many absentees can also be pointed out—because of mislaid documents, perhaps, or indifference. Even the army was undecided. 'I have held in my hands,' wrote Pasquier, a member of the Council, 'a considerable number of requests for advancement in the nobility, as though it were a regiment.'

By attracting the former aristocracy Napoleon had hoped to bring about a fusion of the two élites—twenty-three per cent of ancient names and fifty-eight per cent of bourgeois. Although the latter were in the majority, it was not without dismay that they saw the old nobility playing an increasingly large part at court and in the prefectures. Susceptibilities were aroused and old hatreds reawakened. The creation of the *noblesse de l'Empire* seemed like a pretext for bringing the old privileged classes to the top of the social hierarchy. There was a very real fear, if the prefects' reports on public feelings are to be credited. However, Napoleon did not wholly succeed in his attempt to rally the old élite. To be sure, many great names are to be found among the *noblesse de l'Empire:* Noailles, Montmorency, Turenne, Montesquiou. The attractions of position and money played a decisive role. But how sincere was this rallying? Pasquier has explained how he only agreed to serve the Empire, in order better to prepare for the future.

The foundation of the *noblesse de l'Empire* was apparently a mistake and a failure. It was a mistake in so far as the Brumairians had no desire to see an aristocracy re-established—the resistance put up by the assemblies to the creation of the Légion d'honneur has been described. Usually, in France, egalitarian tendencies are allied to levelling down. It is preferable to destroy the upper classes than to equal them. Hence the scandal provoked by Guizot's albeit sensible reply to those who demanded a lowering of taxes under the July Monarchy: 'Make yourselves richer.' The notables accepted the honours conferred on them and ended up thinking of themselves as noblemen. Pasquier spoke amusingly of Garnier, whose ideas were opposed to the creation of a nobility but whose 'title of count teased his ears agreeably'. But the newly ennobled were not to remain grateful to the regime.

Hence failure. The *noblesse de l'Empire* did not constitute the dynastic support for which Napoleon had hoped. The Emperor admitted to Caulaincourt in 1812 that the new nobility had not come up to his expectations. Two years later, the old nobility were taking back their titles while the new ones were busy forgetting the Emperor.

3

A DEVIATION IN FOREIGN POLICY: THE SPANISH HORNETS' NEST

It was after Tilsit that Napoleon decided on direct intervention in Spain. Since 1788 the Iberian peninsula had been ruled over by Charles IV, a weak and easygoing prince who had abandoned all real power to his wife, Maria-Luisa of Parma, and to the Prime Minister, Godoy. The accession of Charles IV had coincided with the end of a great colonial era which had increased tenfold the profits of the parent state without having caused the luckless inflation of the sixteenth century. But not all Spain had shared equally in the development: unlike the bourgeois of Cadiz and Barcelona, the Galician and Andalusian aristocrats and peasants were untouched by the transformations brought about by the century of 'enlightenment'. Spain was deeply divided, one half having been won over to new ideas, and the other having remained traditionalist. Godoy, who had become Prime Minister at the age of twenty-five, was fully aware of this division, and, despite the unpopularity which resulted from his rapid rise to power, he managed to maintain an equal balance between 'black Spain' and 'enlightened Spain'; but he engaged in a complex diplomatic game which was to be his downfall and was to favour Napoleon's intervention.

It was an intervention born of Napoleon's own initiative, albeit somewhat encouraged by Talleyrand and Murat. The Emperor's first error was his vision of a sinking Spain which he took from travellers' accounts and diplomats' reports and which led him to believe that he could pose as a saviour come to regenerate the peninsula. A new Brumaire, in fact. Although Spain suffered from the Blockade, the crisis only touched commercial and industrial Catalonia, Valencia and Cadiz. It did nothing to interrupt the population boom in a country which had a million inhabitants in 1765 and twelve million in 1808. A vitality which should have given the lie to Napoleon's optimism as to the ease with which he could conquer the peninsula. The second mistake was to think that France was behind the Emperor in this war. The campaigns of 1805 and 1806 were imposed on her; they conformed to the logic of the revolutionary wars, and had therefore been accepted by public opinion. With Spain it was a different matter; for the first time a factor which had been unknown since 1789 played a part— dynastic interest. The Bourbons had been replaced by the Bonapartes and, in the long run, it was this which was at stake in the fight. Napoleon might think that such a replacement would be acceptable in France. More than the eventual seizure of Spanish loot, it was a matter of introducing the new ideas of 1789 to a country ruled by a backward regime, subjecting Spain to French influence and integrating it with the Continental System. In fact, even Bordeaux was anything but pleased. Except in some business circles—which were attracted by Spanish wool and American mines, but were soon disabused—public opinion, even in the south, according to prefects' reports, greeted the Spanish adventure coldly. The idea of natural frontiers was too deeply ingrained: the notables were disturbed by the idea of intervening beyond the Pyrenees. It was one of the first signs of a rift between Napoleon and the French bourgeoisie.

GODOY'S FOREIGN POLITICS

Having signed the Peace of Basle which in 1795 put an end to the war between France and Spain, Godoy, who had been dubbed 'the Prince of the Peace', directed his country towards a rapprochement with the Republic. By the Treaty of San Ildefonso in 1796, Spain became France's ally. An alliance which the Consulate was careful not to neglect. The ambassador in Spain, Lucien Bonaparte, did his best to detach Madrid from Portugal, England's economic bastion on the Continent. Godoy, appointed General of the Spanish troops, invaded the neighbouring territory and crushed the Portuguese army before the intervention of the English. Already the bourgeois of Cadiz were showing signs of weariness: they greeted the Peace of Amiens with joy. The long interruption of colonial trade had ruined Spanish finances, paper money had depreciated by seventy per cent. So when the conflict between France and England started up again, Godoy attempted to stay out of the war. On 19 September 1803 Bonaparte had to write a threatening letter to Charles IV, revealing to him 'the immense abyss opened by England beneath the throne which the Spanish dynasty had occupied for a hundred years', and exposing the intrigues of Godoy 'the real King of Spain'. The warning was heard and the Spanish fleet participated in French maritime operations until the disaster of Trafalgar. Thinking that luck had now deserted Napoleon, Godoy called the Spanish to arms against an enemy whom he did not name but which was easily identifiable. Was it not a suggestion that the coalition should attempt diversionary manoeuvres in the Pyrenees and did he not open negotiations with London after the capture of Buenos Aires by a British squadron? The defeat of the coalition revealed to the Prime Minister the extent of his mistake. A mistake which had formerly been made by the Bourbons of Naples who, violating their treaty of neutrality with France, welcomed an Anglo-Russian army. Portugal, for her part, continued, apparently rather than really, to submit to England's economic hold: 354 ships flying the British flag entered her ports in 1806. Portugal supplied colonial commodities to France and her 'neutrality' no longer seemed advantageous. All the more reason for Napoleon to tighten his hold on the Mediterranean states.

The first blow was to the Bourbons of Naples. With one stroke of the pen, Napoleon dethroned them by a proclamation dated 27 December 1805: 'The dynasty of Naples has ceased to reign: its existence is incompatible with the peace of Europe and with the honour of my crown.' Raised to the rank of sovereign, Joseph Bonaparte took possession, without difficulty, of the kingdom abandoned by Maria-Carolina and Ferdinand IV who took refuge in Sicily. It was, however, necessary to pacify Calabria, and the Straits of Messina could never be crossed.

Next, Napoleon turned back against Portugal which was refusing to apply the Blockade. In October 1806, Napoleon had declared to the Spanish ambassador: 'I count on Spain to reduce Portugal to my system.' In January 1807 he specified his intentions: 'to strike the English through their trade with Portugal'. Many Spaniards were against this intervention; they thought—and recent works by Portuguese historians have confirmed their opinion—that Great Britain's part in Portuguese trade should not be exaggerated, and that the occupation of Portugal would provoke the seizure of Brazil by the English, and, before long of Spain.

Godoy, on the other hand, was encouraging the Emperor to intervene against the Kingdom of Braganza in the hopes of acquiring a Lusitanian principality. The division of Portugal was decided by the

Treaty of Fontainebleau in October 1808. The south was given to Godoy, the north to the Queen of Etruria (whose Italian possessions Napoleon envisaged annexing). The centre with the capital was kept in reserve. Junot, at the head of twenty-five thousand men, marched on Lisbon and took it on 30 November 1807. The royal family fled to Brazil after having closed the ports to English trade, too late to appease Napoleon.

In Lisbon, despite the entreaties of the liberals and of the Franco-Portuguese like the industrialist Ratton, Junot did not attempt to introduce reforms. Although Napoleon had stipulated the application of the Civil Code in the country, Junot did nothing and contented himself with forming a Portuguese legion. It has been claimed, but without conclusive evidence, that Junot was hoping to become king of central Portugal. In any case his incompetence compromised French chances.

But by sacrificing the Kingdoms of Etruria and Portugal to his personal greed, Godoy had opened Spanish ports to Napoleon's armies.

THE BAYONNE AMBUSH

The ease with which he dethroned the Bourbons of Naples could only encourage Napoleon to start again in Madrid. Under the pretext of protecting Portugal from British military action, French troops infiltrated the peninsula with, in fact, little difficulty. Napoleon was even asked by the court to intervene in Spanish affairs. The Infante, Ferdinand, Prince of Asturias, influenced by his tutor, the Canon Escoigniz, was considering the overthrow of Godoy. Encouraged by the French ambassador, in a letter to Napoleon on 11 October 1807, he suggested marrying a princess of the imperial family in exchange for his support against the favourite. On discovering the 'Escurial con spiracy', Godoy persuaded Charles IV to have his son arrested. Ferdinand beseeched his father for clemency: 'Sire, my papa, I have done wrong . . .' he wrote to Charles IV who, for his part, denounced 'this dreadful attempt' to Napoleon, and begged him for his advice.

The revolt of Aranjuez provided the Emperor with the occasion for intervention. On 17 March 1808 an uprising, resulting from an aristocratic intrigue and the discontent of the people who were shocked by Godoy's immorality, provoked the favourite's fall and the King's abdication. According to Champagny's memoirs the Aranjuez uprising changed,

. . . not the views of the Emperor which were to use Spain to increase
the power of France, but the steps which he proposed to take in
order to achieve this. His first plan had been to overthrow the
'Prince of the Peace' which would have met with the approval of the
Spanish people, and to rule in his stead with men of his own
choosing. The revolt of a son against his father seemed to give him a
more plausible excuse and must lead to an even greater result.

After Charles IV had protested against the violent way in which he
had been treated, Napoleon summoned the royal family to Bayonne in
order to arbitrate in the conflict between father and son. The princes
offered no resistance, but the Spanish public was shocked to see a
foreign sovereign settling its internal affairs. On 2 May 1808, just as
Charles IV's youngest son was being put in a carriage to be sent to
Bayonne, a riot broke out which was severely suppressed by Murat—
the *Dos de Mayé* and the *Tres de Mayo* immortalized by Goya. There
were around three hundred dead. The news reached Bayonne; it
should have warned Napoleon and drawn his attention to the national
feeling of exasperation in the peninsula. Napoleon contented himself
with using it to terrorize the Bourbons. At the end of a violent scene,
Ferdinand returned his crown to his father and in his turn the old king
abdicated in favour of 'his friend, the great Napoleon'. The Emperor
did not want the crown for himself; he offered it to his brother, Louis,
who refused it. Joseph was obliged to accept it unwillingly on 6 June.
With a bad grace, Murat, who thought he had been being useful in
Madrid, made do with Naples. In order to regularize the proceedings,
a junta of notables gathered in Bayonne between 15 June and 7 July to
work out a 'constitution' modelled on the French one. They abolished
torture and *majorats,* but left the nobility and the Inquisition in place.
   Later, on St Helena, Napoleon was to admit: 'I badly mismanaged
the affair, I confess; the immorality must have been far too latent, the
injustice far too cynical, and the trick was a bad one since I
succumbed.'
   What can have encouraged Napoleon to involve himself in such a
hornets' nest? The contempt for the Bourbons who betrayed him at
Naples and Madrid has been blamed. 'They are my personal enemies,'
he told Metternich. Napoleon's fascination for Louis XIV has been
recalled: the Emperor confided,

   The crown of Spain has, since Louis XIV, belonged to the family
   which ruled France, and the cost, in treasures and in blood, of

setting up Philippe V cannot be regretted, for it alone established the French preponderance in Europe. It is, then, one of the most beautiful portions of the great King's legacy, the Emperor must collect it all; he must not, and cannot, abandon a single part.

This imperative dynastic policy (the putting of members of his family on the thrones of Europe) weighed as heavily with Napoleon as did the necessity of the struggle against England which obliged him to secure the loyalty of Spain, but not to conquer it.

Did an attraction for the supposed riches of Spain also play a part? Talleyrand is said to have produced an exaggerated description of them in order to distract Napoleon from Austria. Napoleon's aim was to obtain more money (the myth of Iberian opulence based on American piastres) and ships (memories of the Invincible Armada). The complicity which the Emperor anticipated on the part of the *afrancesados*, partisans of liberal reform, might have led him to think that the overthrowing of the dynasty would present no problems. 'This nation was ready for great changes and was forcefully crying out for them; I was very popular there,' Napoleon declared to Las Cases several years later.

Napoleon's reasoning was not entirely wrong. The uprising had not been the work of the Bourbons (Ferdinand several times offered his services to Napoleon), nor of the councils, nor of the enlightened classes who favoured the introduction of reforms. The resistance came, above all, from the working classes and the Church. It was less the result of patriotic feeling than of a social reaction to an economic crisis (the Continental Blockade, by hindering colonial traffic, seriously harmed the interests of Spain), and of the will of the Spanish clergy and the large landowners to oppose changes which partisans of France wanted to introduce. The fact remains, however, that national pride also played a determining role. The arrogance and the perfidy of the French, violently denounced by Cevallos in the *Exposé des moyens employés par l'Empereur Napoléon pour usurper la couronne d'Espagne,* aroused the masses. By its brutality and contempt for the Spanish nation, the Bayonne *coup d'état* offended many *afrancesados* themselves, who already saw in Napoleon a neo-despot betraying the ideals of the Revolution. Had the junta been at Madrid and not at Bayonne, had Charles IV been dismissed and Ferdinand kept, the revolution would have been popular and events would have taken a different turn, Las Cases remarked in front of Napoleon on St Helena.

Among the *Josefinos* were to be seen the political and intellectual élite of Spain: Azanza, O'Farril, Cabarrus, Urquijo, Moratin—the delicate author of *Oui des jeunes filles*—or Goya, who, having painted Charles IV, was, without a pang of conscience, to paint Joseph. On the other hand, others, although fewer, such as Jovellanos or Quintana, joined the patriots and refused reforms imposed from outside.

THE SPANISH RESISTANCE

Within a few weeks an insurrectionist army of a hundred thousand men, mostly peasants and artisans with a framework of professional soldiers, had formed itself in Spain. 'Everyone realizes that it is the people at their most unlettered who have decided on war,' an *afrancesado*, Reinoso, remarked with disdain. The great, the rich, civil authorities, all those who feared disorder, were ready to rally to Joseph. A few executions dispensed by popular justice put a break to their pro-French zeal, but they rarely had anything to do with the guerrilla war whose leaders were of modest origins with names like 'One Arm', 'The Sticky One', 'Three Hairs'. Oviedo revolted on 24 May, Saragossa on the 25th (where the resistance was to last many months under the command of Palafox), Galicia on the 30th, Catalonia on 7 June. Encouraged by the cabinet in London which was eager to avoid the resistance breaking up into local particularism, a national junta headed by the former minister, Jovellanos, gathered at Seville and then at Cadiz. It declared war on France in the name of Ferdinand VII. Joseph was only able to enter Madrid on 20 July 1808 after Bessières' victory at Medina del Rio Seco six days earlier. Although the Basque country, Castile and Catalonia had been taken back without serious difficulties, the new king sent pessimistic letters to Napoleon from his capital which had given him an icy reception. The Emperor, for his part, refused to countenance the possibility of serious resistance until the news reached him that General Dupont, in charge of operations in Andalusia, had been surrounded by the Spanish at the approaches to the Sierra Morena and that his men—mostly young conscripts dying of hunger and thirst—had had to surrender at Baylen on 22 July 1808. It was the first time that Napoleon's troops had been beaten in open country. 'We are French, we are still breathing, and we are not the victors,' wrote one of the survivors of Baylen, Maurice Tascher.

Distraught, Joseph left Madrid and took refuge near the frontier. The French were discovering a new kind of war. The explosion of hatred of which they were the object surprised them. About the brutal, undisciplined French soldiers, the Spanish said:

> Ils pissent devant les femmes
> Et après la digestion
> Font l'explosion
> Por el organo del culo.[1]

Lannes was disturbed: 'The siege of Saragossa bears no resemblance to war as we have fought it up till now.'

The resistance movement spread to Portugal, where at the request of a junta established at Oporto, an English contingent of sixteen thousand men commanded by Wellesley, the future Duke of Wellington, was landing, Junot decided to attack, but, the victim of his own numerical inferiority, he was beaten at Vimeiro. On 30 August he signed the Convention of Cintra which provided for the repatriation of the French and of the Portuguese who had compromised themselves with the French. Emboldened, the English marched into Galicia where they profited from the complicity of the population.

These disasters, especially Baylen, caused a sensation in Europe; they put an end to the legend of the invincibility of the Grande Armée. In fact the real Grande Armée had remained in Germany and the conquered troops mostly consisted of conscripts, seamen and foreign contingents. But English propaganda soon made use of the news, and packets of satirical pamphlets announcing Dupont's defeat were landed on the French coast by the British fleet. In Prussia, the patriotic party hastened reform; Austria, which had been quite overwhelmed by the dethroning of the Bourbons in Spain, began to arm again. Among Napoleon's allies, there was concern. Stadion wrote of the King of Bavaria, 'The difficulty with which he controls the feelings of indignation caused by the annihilation of this dynasty and by the reflections on himself and his own uncertain and dependent situation, is at all times apparent.'

ERFURT

It was becoming impossible for Napoleon to neglect the Iberian peninsula. But to transfer the Grande Armée from Germany to Spain was to risk playing into the hands of Austria who was hoping for revenge. The Russian ally had to be entrusted with the supervision of Vienna. The two sovereigns agreed to renew their encounter at Tilsit,

[1] 'They piss in front of women, and after digesting they explode from the arse.'

by meeting at Erfurt, a temporarily French enclave in Thüringen. There was considerable disagreement. Alexander's advisers wanted French troops to evacuate Prussia in order to deprive Napoleon of a military basis against their country. In principle this evacuation had been fixed for 1 October 1808, but Napoleon, needing money, strove to collect the greater part of the indemnity imposed on Prussia by means of military pressure, and therefore delayed the departure of his troops. In the East, the plan for dividing up the Turkish Empire met an obstacle in Constantinople, which Napoleon did not want to hand over to Alexander. Alexander accused the French of doing nothing to facilitate the occupation of Finland and he was beginning to find that his partner was getting all the advantages from the alliance, without conceding anything in exchange. The fact that Napoleon finally granted the evacuation of Prussia, conditional upon the payment of 140 millions and the undertaking that the Prussian army would not exceed forty-two thousand men, was not enough to improve relations between the allies.

Napoleon presented himself at Erfurt in a demanding mood; he needed all his charms. And so the court and the Comédie-Française were part of his entourage. Removed from foreign affairs since 9 August 1807, Talleyrand was surprised to be recalled from Valençay where he had become the gaoler of the Spanish princes. Napoleon revealed his plans to him:

> We are going to Erfurt and I wish to come back free to do what I want in Spain; I want to be sure that Austria will be disturbed but contained, and I do not wish to be engaged in any specific way in the East. Prepare an agreement for me which will satisfy the Emperor Alexander and which is, above all, directed against England and with which I can feel well at ease; for everything else I will help you, there will be no lack of prestige.

Talleyrand prepared the plan; Napoleon added two articles. The first provided that he should himself establish the causes which would determine Russia's going to war with Austria. The second determined the immediate sending of Russian troops to the Austrian frontier. In these two clauses lay all that was at stake at Erfurt.

Napoleon arrived first, on 27 September 1808. All the crowned heads of the Confederation of the Rhine were gathered in the town: 'a flower bed of kings', they said. Alexander was not in the least impressed by this array of ceremony. His attitude towards Napoleon was changing. If Metternich's *Mémoires* are to be believed, Talleyrand decided to heap coals on the fire. Clever at knowing which way the wind was blowing, the former Minister of External Affairs made himself the spokesman for a bourgeoisie who were disturbed by Napoleon's apparently unlimited imperialism which generated interminable war. Then, encouraged by Talleyrand who was thus consciously playing into Austria's hands, Alexander refused to accept the two clauses put forward by Napoleon. They did not feature in the agreement signed on 12 October whereupon Talleyrand immediately informed the Viennese cabinet. Assured of Russian neutrality, Austria decided to open hostilities in the spring.

On another point Napoleon also failed. He would have liked to win the hand of one of the Tsar's sisters, and he charged Talleyrand with sounding out Alexander. 'I admit,' the former minister revealed, 'that I was frightened for Europe by another alliance between France and Russia. To my mind it had to be arranged so that the idea of the marriage was sufficiently considered to satisfy Napoleon and so that there were enough reservations to make it difficult.' Prepared by Talleyrand, Alexander restricted himself, in front of Napoleon, to general matters with a view to gaining time. But a month later, Caulaincourt announced to the Emperor the engagement of the Grand-Duchess Catherine to the Prince of Oldenburg; the Tsar's other sister, Anna, was only fourteen.

In order to gain positive results from Erfurt, Napoleon should have offered the Tsar Constantinople. He could not bring hmself to do so. Hence the agreement signed on 12 October only dealt with matters of secondary importance: Finland was given to the Tsar along with the Romanian provinces of Moldavia and Walachia: in exchange, Article 10 provided that 'in the event of Austria declaring war on France, the Tsar undertook to declare war on Austria and to take the side of France'. But such an assurance remained vague since Alexander had refused Napoleon's more precise clauses. So a threatening letter which was sent to the Austrian Emperor was signed only by Napoleon, Alexander being content to advise the Austrian representative, Baron Vincent, against armed intervention.

On 14 October the two sovereigns separated. The meeting at Erfurt ended in diplomatic failure for Napoleon. However, nothing was yet lost for him if he managed to solve the Spanish problem quickly, and in such a way as to be able to bring the Grande Armée back to the Danube by the spring.

NAPOLEON IN SPAIN

On 29 October 1808 Napoleon left Paris at the head of a hundred and sixty thousand men divided into seven army corps under Lannes, Soult, Ney, Victor, Lefebvre, Mortier and Gouvion Saint-Cyr. The Guard was also part of the expedition. A few skirmishes were enough to open the road to Madrid to Napoleon. The Somosierra Pass was forced by the Polish Light Horse on 30 November, and Madrid fell on 4 December. Two days earlier, Napoleon had taken steps to ensure the support of the liberals; he had suppressed the Inquisition, feudal rights, interior customs duty, and a third of the convents.

But the first part of the campaign had revealed the weaknesses of the French marshals. So Lefebvre and Victor, who were rivals, managed, through lack of co-ordination, to let the Galacian army escape; equally Ney, deprived of Lanne's support was unable to crush the army of the centre. A new mood appeared in the ranks. On 22 December, in appalling weather, the men grumbled and refused to advance across the Sierra Guadarrama. Napoleon was obliged to get off his horse to give them an example. When the news of this insubordination reached Paris it caused a sensation. Fouché mentioned it, not without an ulterior motive, in his bulletin of 18 January 1809.

Meanwhile, the English general, Moore, had regrouped his forces and was marching on Burgos with the intention of cutting the French communications. In his turn, Napoleon attempted to take the English from the rear, but his manoeuvre was thwarted by bad weather and lack of information.

Napoleon was at Astorga on 1 January when a voluminous packet of dispatches reached him. When he had read them, he refrained from pursuing the English and announced that he would stay in Astorga for several days. On the 3rd he decided to return to Paris, leaving Soult in command. Despite the victories of Lugo on the 7th and Corunna on the 16th, Soult was not able to prevent the English from re-embarking.

What news had suddenly caused Napoleon to leave Spain at a time when he still had to reach Lisbon and Cadiz? According to the usually well-informed Pasquier,

Napoleon could not long remain ignorant of the fact that Austria was arming so actively as to indicate some very serious plans. Finally he had been informed that, giving way to pressure from England, she was preparing to take advantage of his absence in order to cross the frontiers, invade Bavaria, wage war up to the Rhine and thus bring about the deliverance of Germany. It was a fine occasion to attempt so considerable an undertaking. In fact everything in the Austrian states got under way when Napoleon hurried to confront this new peril. This was one of the moments in his life when his very soul must have been prey to the keenest agitations.

Pasquier mentions another reason for Napoleon's sudden return: 'the intrigues which were rife in the heart of his own government', and, more especially the rapprochement between Talleyrand and Fouché who had formerly quarrelled. 'The astonishing part of this agreement,' noted Pasquier, 'was the commotion which two people who should have been so prudent saw fit to make. Either they believed themselves to be very strong because of their union, or they were extremely sure of the Emperor's ruin.' As on the eve of Marengo, the two accomplices may have envisaged the disappearance of the Emperor and they may have considered putting Murat in his place. Such intrigue betrayed the weariness of the imperial regime and the concern of the notables over incessant war.

THE NATURE OF THE WAR IN SPAIN

The situation in Spain was better when Napoleon left than on his arrival. The capital had been taken back and the English contingent expelled, and Saragossa, after a three-month siege in which forty thousand people perished, fell on 20 February 1809. But these successes did not put an end to the war in Spain. It was a confused war, the cruelties of which may have been exaggerated by popular imagination. The war was made difficult for the French troops by natural conditions, difficulties of supplies in a poor country which even in normal times could not feed its population, and by the guerrillas who attacked columns and convoys with people who, as a result of religious propaganda and xenophobia, were fanatics. Individual revenge, social and regional antagonism and the passionate nature of the Spanish people made the conflict totally irrational.

Napoleon's mistake was to consider Spain as though it bore any similarity to France in 1789. The reforms which he or his brother, Joseph, introduced in Spain could only guarantee the sympathy of the most enlightened section of the bourgeoisie, of the young officers and of a few ecclesiastics who were hostile to the Inquisition. And among the *afrancesados*, how many officials were keen to keep their jobs and how many army suppliers were interested in the vast profits which war would bring them.

Another mistake was the attempt to awaken local differences in order to divide the enemy. In vain Augereau had newspapers printed in Catalan which dealt with old themes of autonomy. In fact, the dispersed centres of resistance confused Napoleon's marshals who were accustomed to fighting in open country against a single enemy.

For the first time, the Napoleonic concept of a lightning war based on operations to force the enemy rapidly to negotiate, failed. The French army became bogged down in the peninsula without being able to carry off any decisive victories. So the Empire found itself short of soldiers. More men had to be conscripted. In 1809, the class of 1810 were levied in advance, not without resistance. Fouché's reports indicate several demonstrations against war from 1808 onwards, in Bordeaux and in Paris. And on 4 December 1808, Metternich wrote: 'The military strength of France has been reduced by half since the rising in Spain.'

War had long continued and had ceased to pay. In his pamphlet published in 1812, *Napoléon administrateur et financier*, the Genevan economist, Francis d'Ivernois stressed the financial consequences of the operations in Spain:

> Until 1809, Napoleon had followed his triumphant career using only the spoils from the conquered enemy with which to attack another enemy and to plunder it in its turn. With the exception of the incursion into the Spanish peninsula, all the others were so short and so productive, that having reimbursed the expenses of the campaign by victory, he always came home with treasure that helped him to equip conscripts the following year, and to support them in France until they arrived on foreign territory. But by sending them beyond the Pyrenees, he has launched himself on such a costly undertaking that instead of gaining 250 million francs from each campaign, he finds himself condemned to spend equally large sums, which, all of a sudden, make the difference between gaining and losing, receiving and spending.

Finally, the war in Spain saved England from her economic crisis by breaching the Continental Blockade. The uprising not only weakened the coastal system imposed by Napoleon in Europe, by attracting French armies to the peninsula, and thus leaving the way open for a contraband which could only be encouraged by penury and the increased cost of colonial commodities on the Continent. Equally the Spanish ports were reopened to British exporters, making available to them the vast market of the American colonies which they had long coveted. From July 1808 trade had started again between England and the insurgent provinces. It was interrupted during Napoleon's campaign, but developed considerably in 1809 making possible the quick sale of large stocks of manufactured goods. The opening up of the American Spanish colonies which had rallied to Ferdinand VII, was slower, but no less important to English exports. D'Ivernois observed in a pamphlet of 1809, entitled *Les effets du Blocus continental sur le commerce, les finances, le crédit et la prospérité des Iles britanniques,* that the Blockade could have been effective if 'at the same time as the French government was taking such violent steps to close European markets to the British Isles, it had not taken even more violent ones to open Southern American ones to them'.

The consequences of the war in Spain were, therefore, disastrous for Napoleon. On St Helena, he recognized that, 'This unfortunate Spanish war has been a real sore, the prime cause of the misfortunes of France.' Above all, it contributed to the turning of the bourgeoisie against the Emperor, and even more so, of the working classes, who had been hit by more and more demanding conscription. The legend of the 'Ogre' was born in 1809 from the levies necessitated by operations in the Iberian peninsula. It is impossible not to see Napoleon himself as the colossus who threatens a crowd of human beings and animals in one of Goya's most famous paintings executed between 1808 and 1809.

4

THE AWAKENING OF NATIONALISM

With the campaign of 1809 Napoleon had lost the initiative: war was forced on him by Austria who judged that the moment had come in which to avenge Austerlitz. 'If war is not part of Napoleon's calculations, it is essential that it should be part of ours,' wrote the Austrian leader, Stadion, who was negotiating an alliance with Prussia, now free from French occupation. He was anticipating an uprising of northern Germany and even some rebellion among the sovereigns of the Confederation of the Rhine. A fervour of patriotism had overcome Vienna, where Joseph Hormayr the poet of 'the national idea' was launching his *Austrian Plutarch* and Castelli his soldiers' songs, *Kriegesliedes für die österreichische Armee*.

This campaign was greeted favourably by public opinion which had changed since the execution of the bookseller, Palm, who had been shot for distributing anti-French satire, *L'Allemagne dans sa profonde humiliation*. The Emperor of France was held responsible for disrupting the precarious balance of Europe. 'There are circumstances which are incompatible with each other,' noted Metternich, 'France's actual power is incompatible with the preservation of all the other thrones of Europe.' Anti-Napoleonic propaganda in Austria drew its main inspiration from the pamphlets circulating in the Iberian peninsula.

Napoleon, on the other hand, would have liked to avoid conflict at a moment in which he was engaged in Spain and when he could discern signs of weariness in France, a weariness resulting from the uninterrupted sequence of wars. Alexander could have prevented the hostilities with Austria. Napoleon dispatched an aide-de-camp from Valladolid who was to suggest to the Tsar that identical communiqués be sent to Vienna, followed by the breaking off of diplomatic relations should the Austrian cabinet not reply satisfactorily. The Tsar refused and Napoleon had to renounce his plan. Already, his near-failure in Spain had dealt a terrible blow to his prestige. The cleverly handled rapprochment between Talleyrand and Fouché who had fallen out, echoed like a warning shot. The notables were keeping their distance. So the new conflict occurred under inauspicious conditions. In front of Napoleon lay an armed Austria and an excited Germany, behind him insurgent Spain with the English in Portugal and treachery in Paris. He had not had a more difficult hand to play since Marengo.

THE BAVARIAN CAMPAIGN

On 8 February 1809 the partisans of war in Vienna prevailed by impressing on Francis I that the financial crisis would shortly affect the English subsidies promised for the start of the campaign. The initial plan provided for a surprise attack on the Rhine which was to carry Prussia along with it and provoke national uprisings against the French occupying troops. In the end, the Archduke Charles decided to attack Bavaria where he hoped to rouse the population against France. Meanwhile the Archduke John was preparing to invade the Italian peninsula and the Archduke Ferdinand had been sent to occupy Warsaw.

On 10 April 1809 the Kingdom of Max Joseph of Bavaria was invaded. A call by the Archduke to the 'German nation', drawn up by Schlegel, announced, 'We are fighting to give her independence and national honour back to Germany.' Napoleon seems to have been surprised by Austria's going to war which he had not expected before April. The Army of Germany, the command of which he had reserved for himself (the Grande Armée was still engaged in Spain) was forestalled by the Austrians. 'Never,' wrote Savary in his *Mémoires*, 'had Napoleon been so taken off his guard.' Thanks to the order for 'action and speed' which he gave his generals, he was able to right the situation rapidly.

After having crossed the Inn and driven off the Bavarian troops, the Archduke Charles's one hundred and twenty-six thousand men were delayed by rain and difficulties of supplies. Napoleon arrived at Donauwörth on the morning of 17 April. In five days, from the 19th to the 23rd, by the battles of Thann, Abensberg, Landshut, Eckmühl and Ratisbon where Napoleon was slightly wounded in the foot, the Archduke Charles was repulsed. 'Soldiers you have justified my expectations,' announced Napoleon in his proclamation of the 24th.

'Within a month we will be in Vienna.' The Archduke Charles's calculations had been frustrated, as the Bavarians had not responded to his advances. Max Joseph's Minister, Montgelas, wrote to his sovereign, 'Graf von Stadion has come to understand the enormous mistake he made in changing the plan of operations. He would have found a large number of partisans in northern Germany, whereas in Bavaria he found not one. Instead of beginning by attacking the weakest point of the Confederation, he chose the strongest.'

Beaten at Eckmühl, the Archduke Charles was able to escape by Ratisbon and the left bank of the Danube. With his flanks threatened by the Austrian forces from Bohemia and the Tyrol, Napoleon travelled down the river more slowly than he had in 1805.

The campaign was continued outside Vienna which Napoleon entered for the second time on 13 May. His icy welcome was a contrast to the curiosity mixed with a certain sympathy which had been manifested in 1805. The Austrians, situated on the heights, had destroyed the bridges across the Danube. The Emperor decided to cross the river downstream of Vienna by means of the island of Lobau. Between 17 and 20 May he had a bridge of boats constructed, and during the night of the 20th–21st Masséna and Lannes occupied Aspern and Essling with their corps. The following day they were attacked by the Archduke Charles's forces which were numerically superior, and were soon isolated by the breaking of the bridge which joined the bank and the island of Lobau. The bridge was rebuilt that night and during the morning of the 22nd, and the offensive began again towards Wagram. Then the current carried away the great bridge. Lannes, having run out of munitions, was obliged to return to Essling where he was mortally wounded. With the bridge repaired, Masséna was able to take the survivors, under cover of night to the island of Lobau. The setback at Essling, greatly exaggerated by Austrian propaganda, caused a sensation in Europe. After all, the *Allgemeine Zeitung* announced the capture of twenty-five generals and the death of the Emperor. The resistance of the Austrian troops was unusual. They were no longer the soldiers of 1805. The desire to win, which had been lacking in the 'disillusioned mercenaries' at Austerlitz, now inspired the soldiers of the Austrian Empire. Napoleon was discovering German patriotism.

THE CRISIS OF THE GREAT EMPIRE
Whilst Napoleon was entrenched on the island of Lobau, where he had to stay for a month waiting for reinforcements from Italy, the Empire

was threatened at several points.

In Germany, as a result of Austria's appeal, several insurrections broke out. The most important was in the Tyrol—Austrian lands given by Napoleon to Bavaria. There, in April, the innkeeper, Andreas Hofer, stirred up the inhabitants in the name of 'God, the Emperor and the country.' As in Spain, conditions in a mountainous, backward country under the influence of monks and hostile to foreigners, were favourable to guerrilla warfare. The Tyrolean uprising was only definitely suppressed in January 1810 and Andreas Hofer was shot. In 1809 in Westphalia, Lieutenant Katt attempted a sudden attack on Magdeburg; and Major Schill, who left Berlin at the head of his regiment tried in vain to invade the Kingdom. In May he was thrown back on Stralsund where he died. Equally, Colonel Dornberg failed in an operation against Kassel.

Schill's adventurous march on Westphalia was echoed in Saxony by the Duke of Brunswick's son and his hussars of death. His proclamation to the Germans read: 'My brothers, ring the tocsin, may this signal of fire light in your hearts the pure flame of love for your country.' His black legion crossed Dresden, Leipzig, Brunswick, Hanover and Bremen with impunity.

All attempts stemmed from the same plan, a plan which had long been premeditated but which failed because of the conspirators' impatience. Nevertheless these attempts did reveal the fermentation in Germany which until that time had remained dormant under Napoleon's domination. From the Tyrol to the Baltic a new force was awaking for which the philosopher, Fichte, became spokesman in the fourteen speeches he made to the German nation in the Berlin Academy, between 13 December and 20 March 1808.

In Spain, where Napoleon had left his best troops, Joseph's authority was flouted by the marshals, who between them committed endless errors. Under the leadership of energetic and cruel men like the brothers Mina, or the *Empecinado,* guerrilla warfare increased. At the beginning of 1809, Soult had launched a victorious attack on Portugal, but, after the fall of Oporto in March, he restricted himself to secondary operations. Can Soult's sudden passivity be interpreted as a desire to have himself proclaimed King of Portugal under the title of Nicholas I, as was insinuated by Ney who had difficulty in agreeing to serve under him, and by General Thiébault whose *Mémoires* tend to be malicious where the great military leaders of the day are concerned? No doubt these were slanderous rumours, but rivalry between

Napoleon's marshals made it possible for the English to land considerable reinforcements under Wellesley's command in April 1809. Thanks to the tactics adopted by the future Duke of Wellington, who made his soldiers shelter behind natural crests in the land and take aim, the French troops, who were advancing in the open suffered heavy losses, and on 12 May the English took back Oporto and obliged Soult to evacuate Galicia.

Taking advantage of Napoleon's difficulties in Austria, the British cabinet decided to land in the Low Countries. On 29 July 1809 forty thousand English settled in Walcheren at the mouth of the River Escaut and on 13 August took Flushing whilst the French forces were withdrawing to Antwerp.

In Paris, concern grew. Fouché, the interim Minister of the Interior while Cretet was ill, took it upon himself to mobilize the National Guard in the northern departments and entrusted the defence of Antwerp to Bernadotte whom Napoleon had just dismissed. In Paris the National Guard was reconstituted; and the Provençal coasts were alerted as an attack by the British fleet was expected. Fouché's energetic action was at first approved by Napoleon, but finally alarmed the Emperor who suspected the Duke of Otranto of ulterior motives. Worse still, Napoleon felt himself replaced. He was no longer the only bulwark of the revolutionary bourgeoisie. Shortly afterwards the too-powerful Minister of Police was dismissed.

Finally, in Rome, the situation had worsened. Plus VII had refused to apply the Continental Blockade in his states. To Napoleon's declaration, 'Your Holiness is the sovereign of Rome, but I am its Emperor'; the Pope replied that the spiritual mission of the Church forbade him to take sides in a temporal dispute between his children. The departure of Consalvi, one of the few moderate elements in the Vatican, only made matters worse by leaving the field clear for the intransigent Cardinal Pacca. On 21 January 1808 Napoleon had to order General Miollis to occupy the Papal States. Still intoxicated by the success of his entry into Vienna, he decided to annexe them on 16 May 1809.

The arrest of the Pope on 6 July dramatized the quarrel between Napoleon and Pius VII, and thereby alienated Italian opinion from the Emperor and encouraged the Spanish revolt. With Gentz, who denounced 'the enslavement of Germany', Cevallos who revealed the 'darker side' of Bayonne, Gillray's caricatures and Kotzebue's imprecations, an intellectual élite was whipping itself up against Napoleon.

In 1804 Beethoven had torn up the dedication to the *Eroica,* and Goya was meditating on the *Dos de Mayo.* The Emperor had arms on his side, but spiritually Europe was turning against him.

WAGRAM

On 14 June the Army of Italy, commanded by Prince Eugène and Macdonald, beat the Archduke John at Raab and joined up with Napoleon's army. It was time indeed.

During the night of 4–5 July, under cover of a storm, the Emperor decided to cross the Danube to the south of Enzersdorf. The following day, French troops were deploying themselves in the Marchfeld whilst part of the Archduke Charles's strength had withdrawn to Wagram.

On the evening of the 5th, Napoleon had the Army of Italy, supported by the corps from Saxony, attack the Austrian forces, but as a result of a mistake by the Army of Italy who had mistaken the Saxons for the enemy, the operation had to be called off.

The battle began again at dawn on the 6th. The Archduke Charles had disposed his strength—a hundred and forty thousand men and four hundred cannon—in a T shape in order to squeeze the French between the two wings of his army, the right being supposed to advance to Aspern and cut Napoleon off from the Danube, the left being supposed to throw the French back towards the river. The angle of his formation was situated at the village of Wagram.

For his part, Napoleon confronted the Austrian left wing with Davout and Oudinot's corps, the right with Bernadotte's and Masséna's whilst holding in reserve the Guard and the Army of Italy in order to bring them rapidly into the most vulnerable points.

At about eleven o'clock, the Archduke Charles could have believed that victory was within his reach; his right wing was forcing the French to retreat as it approached Aspern; in the centre the Saxons were losing ground. But Napoleon immediately launched Macdonald and the Army of Italy on the fray, after a colossal hundred-gun battery positioned by Drouot had stopped the Austrian advance. Elsewhere Davout was out-flanking the enemy at Veusiedel and Oudinot was capturing Wagram. After twelve hours of battle, the Archduke Charles, who had lost more than fifty thousand men, was withdrawing towards Moravia. Lacking sufficient cavalry, Napoleon could not disrupt the Austrian forces and carry a decisive victory. He had to recognize that the Army of Germany, made up partly of foreigners and partly of conscripts was not equal to the Grande Armée at Austerlitz and Jena.

Fighting began again at Znaïm on 11 July, but the Archduke asked for an armistice on 12th.

THE PEACE OF VIENNA

Immediately after the armistice, parleys began between the Foreign Minister, Champagny, and Metternich. They were concluded at Schönbrunn on 14 October 1809. Aware of the difficulties which confronted Napoleon and Alexander with regard to the Grand Duchy of Warsaw, the Austrians tried to drag the negotiations out. But on 1 September the Russian ambassador warned them that, as yet, the Tsar would not break off relations with France.

Napoleon, anxious to boost his prestige, imposed harsh peace conditions on Austria. By the Treaty of Vienna, Francis I ceded to France Carinthia, Carniola, a large part of Croatia including Fiume, and Istria with Trieste. As compensation for being invaded, Bavaria was given Salzburg and Engadin, the Upper Valley of the Inn. Northern Galicia with Cracow and Lublin went to the Grand Duchy of Warsaw. As for the Tsar, despite his ambiguous attitude he found himself with Eastern Galicia and Tarnopol. Austria's losses were heavy, added to which she had to pay an indemnity of 75 millions.

German national feeling was not appeased by the defeat of Austria. During the military parade at Schönbrunn, two days before the signing of the Treaty of Vienna, a young Saxon student, Frederick Staps, attempted to stab the Emperor. When Napoleon asked him, 'Is a crime nothing to you, then?' Staps replied: 'To kill you is not a crime, it is a duty.' The Emperor's reaction is known from Champagny's memoirs: 'The dagger raised against him did not frighten him, but it revealed to him the mood of the German people, their need for peace and the fact that they were prepared to sacrifice everything for it.'

Finally, the break with Russia appeared inevitable. Alexander had been cruelly disappointed by the Treaty of Vienna. He had, after all, hoped to be given the Grand Duchy of Warsaw. For his part, Napoleon, who had decided to separate from Josephine (the divorce was announced on 16 December 1809 and the annulment by the metropolitan tribunal on 12 January 1810), had considered obtaining the hand of the Tsar's youngest sister. Alexander delayed his reply and as a refusal seemed probable, the Emperor turned towards Austria. Metternich immediately realized the advantage to be gained from a marriage which would disrupt, once and for all, the Franco-Russian alliance. Doubtless such a union would be a stain on the Habsburg family but it would be enough to present the Emperor's request as an ultimatum by the conqueror. The hand of Marie-Louise, daughter of Francis I, was officially asked for on 6 January 1810 and was granted to Napoleon the following day. At the same time a refusal arrived from the Tsar who had thus been fooled. Metternich's calculations turned out to be correct—the Franco-Russian alliance was over.

Berthier, forgetting for the occasion his title of Prince of Wagram, went to Vienna to fetch Marie-Louise. She arrived in Strasburg on 22 March 1810. In his impatience to see her, Napoleon rode ahead of the procession. The meeting took place at Compiègne on 28 March. The civil marriage was celebrated at Saint-Cloud on 1 April, and the religious ceremony the next day in the square drawing-room of the Louvre. Napoleon, at last, became part of 'the family of kings' and could believe that he was accepted by them.

This alliance disturbed not only the regicides who had to face the fact that the Emperor, by his marriage, became the late King's nephew, but also the notables who, on the whole, disapproved of the ceremonies. On St Helena, Napoleon, 'brutally awakened from his dream of monarchic legitimacy', confided that he should have married a French woman and, above all, not a princess. He saw clearly, but too late. 'An Austrian woman brings bad luck,' the saying went. In fact, concern was spreading. Was Napoleon not betraying the Revolution? Would he not, now, re-establish the old nobility and their privileges? Foreign and internal conquests seemed equally threatened. A wave of nationalism aroused Europe against France. The most clear-sighted were not mistaken. Fearful cracks appeared in the fabric of the Empire despite the Pyrrhic victories on the Danube. It was becoming harder and harder to contain Europe. Since the war in Spain, hatred of conscription was increasing. Fouché warned the Emperor on 11 September 1808: 'The working class evinces a strong dissatisfaction with conscription. In areas where they live, sealed papers have been distributed which contain provocative manuscripts against the government, addressed to girls, women, everyone.' In 1809 there were many more of these incidents. And more serious still was the fact that the soldiers had begun to behave like mercenaries. The 17th Dragoons stated in Bordeaux: 'The Emperor should not go to war if he has not enough money to pay the soldiers. We do not want to get ourselves killed for nothing.' Whereas in Europe war was becoming national, in France it was losing this characteristic. Is this an explanation for Napoleon's future defeats?

5

RELIGIOUS DISCONTENT

What were the results in France of the conflict between the Pope and the Emperor? This old problem which dated back to the darkest Middle Ages recurred in 1809 and once again set the spiritual against the temporal. Public opinion seemed to be indifferent. So indifferent that even the old Voltairian or Gallican reactions, which would have served the imperial cause, played no decisive role. The fact remains that the notables did not forgive Napoleon for the collapse of the Concordat. The two questions which distressed them can be deduced from prefects' reports on the public mood—would the end of religious peace bring back civil war, and could the Pope now question the 1809 recognition of the sale of Church property? It seems likely, although this is not mentioned by the prefects, that these same notables held Napoleon's megalomania responsible for the conflict. Little was known about the occupation of Rome and it was little understood. It happened at a time when the Grande Armée was trampling on Austria, when the war in Spain was becoming bogged down—was a new front opening up in Italy which had since the sixteenth century been the tomb of French imperialism? These unnecessarily pessimistic questions appeared in a pamphlet which was immediately seized by the police. The spiritual aspect developed later; with the Pope in captivity old apocalyptic phantoms were roused and the taste for conspiracy revived. On the whole, faith was absent from the debate.

THE IMPERIAL CHURCH
There was no better proof of the decrease of religious influence on the new society, than the laicization of services which had traditionally been rendered by the Church: public assistance, teaching, registration

of births and deaths. Undoubtedly the pessimism of the ecclesiastical authorities often seemed excessive. The work of practical reconstruction was encouraged by the government. But the new distribution of dioceses presented many problems, among them parish boundaries (in Paris, they were severely criticized for their unequal sizes), the restitution of Church buildings which was compromised by the ill-will of the preceding occupants, and, above all, vacant livings which resulted from a crisis in vocations. The crisis was one of quantity despite a marked increase between 1806 and 1810 in the number of ordinations. It was also a crisis of quality, and in this way even more significant of the discredit into which the Church had fallen. 'We no longer find young men from the higher classes of society intending to become ecclesiastics,' wrote the Bishop of Quimper to the minister in charge of religion in March 1811. 'Our resources have been reduced to the class of poor farmers.' The same claim, full of bitterness, came from the Bishop of Besançon who deplored 'the disappearance of those priests whose fine education, profound studies, broad and varied knowledge, combined with the other advantages of birth, delighted the Church, enlightened all classes of citizens and seemed to add to the powerful influence of religion.' Le Coz gave the reason for such a disaffection: 'The Church property has disappeared.'

The situation was particularly difficult for the religious orders who were confronted by Napoleon's hostility. The decree of 3 Messidor Year XII (22 June 1802) declared the dissolution of all unauthorized congregations. Encouragement was only given to some missionary orders whom Napoleon wished to use to prevent the penetration of British influence in the East, and to orders of women who were indispensable in hospitals and in teaching. By a decree of 23 March 1805 Madame Mère was given the title reserved by the Ancien Régime for dowager queens. She became protectress of the hospital associations. The 1808 inquiry gives the figures for all the dioceses as a total of 10,257 nuns, of whom 4,792 were teachers and 5,465 worked in hospitals. Some dioceses had fewer than fifty nuns: Digne, Chambéry; others had more than five hundred: Nancy, Rouen and Lyons. Besides these nuns, the friars of the Christian schools opened establishments in fifty-seven towns.

As a result of the official government take-over, the Church became an agent of despotism which weakened it and antagonized the élite. One catechism was taught throughout France which included among duties towards God, 'love, respect, obedience and loyalty towards the

Emperor, military service and contributions for the defence of the Empire'. Pastoral letters and episcopal ordinances played a part in the evolution of the imperial cult: Napoleon's armies were ranked with the divine armies, the nation became a chosen people, and the war became a holy war ordained by God against the impious. Rarely has the pulpit been so supervised. An imprudent sermon by the Abbé Fournier resulted in his being sent to the mental home at Bicêtre and then to penal servitude in Turin. Cardinal Fesch managed to have him freed, but not without some difficulty. In his turn, Frayssinous was silenced in 1809. More bulletins of the Grande Armée than lives of the saints were to be found in the *Journal des Curés*. On a more subtle level, the higher reaches of the clergy whom the Concordat had made into officials became part of the world of the notables. In degrees which varied from diocese to diocese, ecclesiastics were to be found in the *arrondissement* colleges, in the municipal council and even in the *mairie*. So the Church became an instrument of government in the same way as the army and the police. 'My prefects, my bishops, my police', this list of Napoleon's perfectly describes the Church's position. Its docility was the counterpart to the end of the schism. A docility which Bonaparte was able to appreciate as soon as the organic articles were applied. The Pope's objections found no echo among the French clergy. But the Emperor expected to meet with the same docility from the Pope. When war with Austria broke out, Napoleon occupied Ancona. He was surprised by the violence of Pius VII's protest against this violation of papal sovereignty. Napoleon's crushing if belated reply was, 'I have considered myself, like my predecessors of the second and third generation, as the eldest son of the Church, and have only the sword with which to protect and shelter her from being defiled by the Greeks and the Muslims.' With the establishment of the Continental System, Napoleon insisted on the closing of the ports in the Papal States to British merchandise. England was, after all, an heretical state. Could the Pope remain neutral in a conflict which Napoleon quickly turned, for his own purposes, into a confrontation between Roman Catholicism and Anglicanism? 'Your Holiness is sovereign of Rome, but I am its Emperor. All my enemies must be hers.' Pius VII remained as unmoved by religious arguments as by military threats. Napoleon discovered little by little that he had underestimated his adversary's resistance.

THE CAPTIVE POPE

On 21 January 1808 General Miollis received the order to invade the Papal States and occupy Rome. It was accomplished on 2 February. Alquier, the French ambassador warned the Emperor that Pius VII's determination seemed unshakeable. Napoleon was resolute about the annexation of Rome. But first he had to solve the Spanish affair and then confront Austrian aggression against Bavaria. An imperial decree signed at Schönbrunn on 16 May 1809 united the Papal States to France. Miollis hoisted the French flag on the Castel Sant' Angelo on 10 June. Pius VII immediately replied with a Bull excommunicating 'the usurpers, abetters, advisers, supporters and executors of this sacrilegious violation'. 'I hear that the Pope has excommunicated me. He is a raving lunatic who must be shut up,' wrote the Emperor on 20 June. Was this an angry reaction, or a carefully considered decision? Radet, who commanded the police in the Eternal City, did not hesitate. The Quirinal Palace was invaded, Pius VII was asked to renounce his temporal power and, when he refused, taken by force out of Rome with his chief adviser, Cardinal Pacca. The latter has left an account in his memoirs of the illustrious prisoner's pitiful journey from Florence to Grenoble, and to Savona via Avignon and Nice. Orders and counter-orders revealed the hesitations of Napoleon who had been taken by surprise by the excessive zeal of his subordinates, and who was attracted by the idea of establishing the Pope in Paris where he had already brought the Sacred College. On 6 July 1809 Pius VII arrived in Savona. He stayed there until 9 June 1811. Despite the reverence with which he was surrounded, he behaved as a prisoner, refusing any allowance, washing his soutane himself and spending his days in prayer. It was a misleading passivity. Pius VII used the power at his disposal, a power with which Napoleon had imprudently left him when the Concordat was signed. Without having fully realized the consequences of the concession, Napoleon had granted the Pope the right of consecrating bishops. As a prisoner of the Emperor, the Pope refused to consecrate the bishops nominated by Napoleon to the vacant sees.

Napoleon had to result to an expedient; he therefore had the Chapter confer the title and authority of capitular vicar on the bishops. This was not accepted without some hesitation, notably in Paris after the death of Cardinal Belloy in June 1808. In his conflict with the Pope, Napoleon needed the backing of a united Gallican church. There were rifts in the ecclesiastical committee which met in 1809. It simply proposed a national synod which would play a purely advisory part; but Napoleon did not accept it. At the time of his divorce, he was again to find himself in an embarrassing situation. Was it a matter for the Holy See? M. Émery, confronted with the differences between the Gallican and the Roman law, favoured the former, which suited the Emperor. But the Roman Cardinals in Paris argued differently. Thirteen of them refrained from attending the religious marriage of Napoleon and Marie-Louise. Furious, the Emperor forbade them to wear the insignias of their office and exiled them to the provinces. But, confronted by the reservations of a second ecclesiastical committee and the failure of a conciliatory mission to Savona, he was finally obliged to convoke a council. Presided over by Cardinal Fesch, the council opened on 17 June 1811. But Napoleon did not find the servility he expected in this gathering of French and Italian bishops. The French clergy was annoyed by the intrusion of the state into spiritual matters; the Emperor had forgotten how sensitive the Church was in this respect and, in vain, grew angrier and increased his threats. Fesch himself, the Emperor's uncle, pronounced the opening oath: 'I recognize the Holy Catholic and Roman Church, apostolic and Roman, mother and mistress of all churches. I promise and swear to a true obedience to the Supreme Roman Pontiff, the successor of St Peter, Prince of the apostles and Vicar of Jesus Christ.' Belmas demanded the Pope's freedom before the debate began. The commission, entrusted with studying the question of consecrating bishops, against the Emperor's wishes declared the council unqualified for the task. In his turn, the Emperor decided to dissolve the council and had the main opposition leaders arrested—Hirn, Bishop of Tournai, de Broglie, Bishop of Gand, and Boulogne, Bishop of Troyes. Napoleon had hoped that the council would give the metropolitans the power to invest bishops in the instance of the Pope's refusal. This did not happen. On 2 August having obtained by threats each bishop's individual agreement to the plan, the Emperor decided to reopen the council. A delegation from the council was sent to Savona to ask for the Pope's approval. He gave it, but in a form which did not please the Emperor. Napoleon really wanted a sycophantic Pope installed in the Île de la Cité in Paris. He was convinced that after a victorious outcome of the Russian campaign, the Pope would give in. In order to force him, Napoleon ordered him to be moved to Fontainebleau. But Napoleon was a beaten man when he next saw Pius VII. This time, after the disaster of the retreat from Moscow, the Emperor had a pressing need for the Pope's agreement. He obtained, by intimidation, the Fontainebleau Concordat, signed on 25 January. The problem of canonical investitures in the event of the Pope's absence from Paris was solved. But Napoleon, breaking his promise, hastily publicized the text widely by having it published in *Le Moniteur*. Pius VII repudiated the Concordat. 'We wish it to be altered in order that it should not damage the Church nor injure our soul.' On 21 January 1814 Napoleon ordered Pius VII to be sent back to Savona and, on 10 March, to Rome. The Pope had won.

THE CONSEQUENCES OF THE CONFLICT

Public opinion seems to have been more surprised than really moved by the occupation of Rome and the Pope's captivity, at least according to police bulletins and prefects' reports. Only an élite of young people with a profound faith and deeply rooted Royalist convictions reacted by broadcasting the Bull in which the Emperor was excommunicated. Networks were built up and secret associations founded, modelled on the free-masonry which was held responsible for the Revolution; charitable organizations acted as screens to political activities: Ferdinand de Bertier's Chevaliers de la Foi, the Society of the Heart of Jesus; Aa, whose influence on public opinion must not be exaggerated.

Public opinion began to be aroused in 1811. Little information was given out about the national council. But the public learnt about the bishops' resistance to the Emperor from various sources. From Belgium to Italy the excitement took a disturbing turn. Although the west, which was well supervised, remained calm, the south-east and the centre became agitated. 'On every side,' states a police bulletin of the first days of January, 'the devout are proclaiming that if the Emperor lives another ten years, there will be no more religion.' Dioceses had no bishops, parishes no priests, ecclesiastics were imprisoned or deported—had the days of persecution returned? Civil and military officials, even Catholics, carried out orders without protests. But the depths of men's consciences were unknown. Satire denouncing imperial despotism was on the increase. Discontent was established and turned the notables away from the regime for which they had prayed.

The Empire's record is, however, not altogether bad—bishops became closer to the people, huge benefices were suppressed, parish priests had a reasonable standard of living and were sure of a salary which was considerably better than the former 'adequate emolument'.

The Church gained in esteem, an esteem which it owed to Napoleon but which was to be a weapon to turn against him. From 1812 onwards an increasing number of preachers denounced the absurdity of war and agreed to hide deserters. Under the influence of the clergy, the divorce between the Emperor and the nation established itself little by little.

6

THE ECONOMIC CRISIS

From 1809 to 1812 the war was fought in the ports and along the Continental coastline, not on the battlefields. Once again it seemed that the coasts and ports would have to close themselves to British trade in order to bring about the fall of the 'oceanocrats'. All the English pamphlets did less to turn public opinion against the Blockade than did the violations brought about by the implacable logic of the Blockade itself—the barely tolerated lack of coffee, tea, sugar, cocoa and spices, rises in the cost of leather and cotton, spectacular investigations of merchandise and the corruption of customs officers. In December 1811 Jerome, the King of Westphalia, warned his brother: 'Unrest is at its peak, the maddest of hopes are entertained and cherished with enthusiasm, the example of Spain is put forward, and, if war breaks out, all the lands situated between the Rhine and the Oder will be the centre of a vast and active uprising.' Worse still, the economic weapon of the Blockade was turning against France, causing, in 1810, a financial crisis which, as a result of a bad harvest, developed into a general economic crisis. For the first time the government seemed unable to control the crisis. In it Napoleon lost some of his popularity.

SMUGGLING
The optimistic views which Champagny was developing concerning the ruin of the perfidious Albion were belied by the recovery of the English economy in 1809. How can this recovery be explained other than by the development of a contraband on the Continent despite customs cordons and summary justice?

In the Mediterranean, Malta, which harboured some thirty to forty

British firms, Gibraltar and Salonika were the principal centres of an active contraband. In the Adriatic, British cargoes were unloaded without difficulty in Trieste. At the entrance to the Baltic, Gothenburg ensured trade with northern Europe.

A report stated,

> English trade is carried on under a Swedish flag. The ships disguise their cargoes and on the pretext of carrying Swedish goods, they bring colonial commodities. Many ships enter the port of Copenhagen flying a Danish flag and bearing colonial commodities; and, although they come straight from England, they are supposed to come from Iceland or Norway with Icelandic or Norwegian produce.

In the North Sea, Heligoland supplied the German ports. From September 1807 the island was occupied by the British. From April 1808 trade developed there with the complicity of the British government. An English agent pointed out that trade in Heligoland was increasing every day, and that regular shipments were sent there from England, which caused prices to fall to an equitable level. He had no doubt that this trade would increase and that all the enemy's vigilance would not be able to prevent it. He pointed out that in the preceding ten days seven little boats had left, some with cargoes worth two to three thousand pounds. It was, he said, a matter of swopping colonial produce and manufactured goods for foodstuffs and grain.

Once these goods had landed on the Continent they circulated on a wide axis. From Amsterdam they travelled up the Rhine by barge to Arnhem where they were transferred to carts; the Grand Duchy of Baden they were distributed throughout Germany. Besides, Hamburg competed with Amsterdam by supplying Frankfurt through land routes. Often the goods continued their journey up the Rhine to Switzerland. From Trieste, American cottons and colonial produce reached Vienna, then Strasburg and Basle, Munich and Leipzig. Only the French frontier was sufficiently supervised to discourage smugglers. In the Doubs, in May and August 1808, there were genuine pitched pattles between customs officers and bands of armed smugglers. Scandals frequently broke which involved people in high places. The seizure in Strasburg in 1808 of cloth from Berne by two customs officials from La Wantzenau revealed that the civil engineer, Robin, was taking part in a smuggling enterprise which collected merchandise coming from Frankfurt in Hanau. Shortly afterwards a new affair was discovered in which doctors and big businessmen from Strasburg were implicated. Contraband developed even more in 1809, especially around Mulhouse. There were some hundred thousand smugglers and even some insurance agents were known to cover their tracks.

So smuggling played into the hands of England. But the revival of the British export trade to the Continent was stimulated above all by the Spanish uprising. François Crouzet, the Blockade's most recent historian justly remarks:

> If six months of depression and stagnation were followed by a further six months in which a revival in exports and industrial activity heralded the boom of 1809–10, it was primarily because of the Spanish uprising. In fact, this uprising opened, or reopened, to British exporters the important markets in the Iberian peninsula and in Latin America. Furthermore, by drawing the attention of the Emperor and a large part of the Grand Armée to the peninsula, it left the way open to smuggling in Northern Europe and the Mediterranean.

As we have seen, the war in Spain was the Emperor's first diplomatic error, and by it he allowed England to overcome an economic crisis which could have been fatal to her.

THE CONTINENTAL SYSTEM

While the English were, with no difficulty, finally mopping up the colonies belonging to France and her allies; while they were taking Cape Town and then Java from the Dutch, Guadeloupe and Mauritius from the French; while they were settling in America where, in 1810, the Spanish colonies of Mexico, Peru, Chile and Columbia, followed by Paraguay in 1811, were revolting against the 'Usurper Joseph', Napoleon was demonstrating his incapacity to control smuggling on the Continental coasts. In order to strengthen his system he had to adopt a policy of annexation—Ancona, the Legations, Parma, Piacenza and Tuscany, the Papal States and the Illyrian provinces (including Trieste), which had been taken from Austria at the Peace of Vienna, all passed into French hands. Furious with his brother, Louis, for having tried in vain to negotiate, through the bankers, Baring and Ouvrard, a peace with England which would have protected the economic interests of his kingdom, Napoleon confiscated the left bank of the Waal in March 1810, and, after the abdication of the King, he annexed Holland on 9 July 1810. This annexation, explained Champagny, 'completes your Majesty's empire and the execution of your system of war, politics and commerce; it is a first step, but a necessary step towards the rebuilding of the navy; finally, it is the most effective blow which Your Majesty could strike against England.' The *senatus consultum* which united Holland to France also incorporated into the Empire part of the Grand Duchy of Berg, the lands of the two Salm principalities, the Duchy of Oldenburg, a considerable part of the Kingdom of Westphalia and the three Hanseatic towns of Hamburg, Lübeck and Bremen which formed three new departments: the Ems-Supérieure (Osnabrück), the Bouches-du-Weser (Bremen) and the Bouches-de-l'Elbe (Hamburg). 'The immense stocks in Heligoland would risk being sold on the Continent if a single spot along the coasts of the North Sea remained open to English trade,' explained Champagny. In order to put a stop to Swiss smuggling, Napoleon occupied the Tessin and the Valais in November 1810.

This frenzied annexation which was the logical consequence of the Continental Blockade caused a sensation. It further accentuated the imbalance in Europe and interfered with the stability of Napoleon's Germany by flouting the authority of the kings whom the Emperor had created there. It irritated the whole of Europe, including the Tsar whose brother-in-law was the Duke of Oldenburg. Even in France there was considerable dismay at the dangerous development of departments which destroyed the harmony and compromised the future of a country limited by its natural frontiers. These politics justified themselves by the Blockade; but when Napoleon stretched the rules by introducing a system of licences, the Continental Blockade became unpopular.

THE LICENCES

The new steps taken by the Emperor did not put an end to smuggling; quite simply, smuggling moved eastwards. 'The roads from Russia to Prussia, from Poland and Moravia to Vienna and from the Provinces of the Ottoman Empire into the Austrian Empire, were crowded with merchandise,' the consuls' correspondence observes. The Danube took the place of the Rhine. The whole of Europe made extraordinary journeys to Vienna for supplies of cotton. These voyages were described several years later by Jean-Baptiste Say in his condemnation of protectionism:

Ships were sent from London laden with sugar, coffee, tobacco, and yarn for Salonika. From there these goods were taken by horse or by mule across Serbia and Hungary to the whole of Germany and even to France, so that produce being used in Calais came from England, which is only seven leagues away, after a detour, the expense of which was equal to the cost of travelling twice round the world.

On the other hand, the Blockade revealed itself to Napoleon as a double-edged weapon. England was crammed with stocks of commodities and threatened by unemployment and inflation, the Continent, which did not yet have enough alternative produce (sugar beet, for example, was in its early days), was suffering from a dearth of raw materials and colonial commodities. Jefferson's embargo had deprived French industry of American cotton. Manufacturers were only receiving cotton from Naples and the Levant and these supplies were insufficient. To the complaints of the industrialists were added those of consumers who found that wools and linens were too expensive. Imports of unrefined sugar fell from twenty-five million kilos in 1807 to two million in 1808, The price of coffee rose ceaselessly.

The Minister of the Interior, Cretet, admitted on 1 June 1808,

Colonial commodities are rapidly growing so much more expensive that one could not explain how buyers can be found for cotton from Pernambuco at 11 to 12 francs the pound, for sugar at 5 to 6 francs and coffee at 8 francs, if it were not obvious that the enormous profits made on these commodities are gambled on the stock exchange. In the whole affair people of all classes are concerned.

Finally, European exports were also affected. The complaints of agriculturalists and ship owners were added to those of the industrialists and consumers. After all, the Continent sold corn, fruit, wool, wood and, above all, wine to England. The Bordeaux Chamber of Commerce indicated a glut of spirits in 1809. Besides, there had been a bumper corn harvest in 1808 and peasants complained of not being allowed to export their surplus.

One last argument forced Napoleon to weaken his Blockade: it was the fall in income from customs dues which deprived him of an important source of tax at a moment when he found himself engaged in a war in Spain which brought no income.

England had set the example by authorizing a licensing system for the import of French wines and spirits and other articles of which a list was drawn up on 19 July 1808. Napoleon was won over to this idea and

Cretet informed the prefects by a circular of 14 April 1809: 'His Majesty, with the intention of encouraging the permitted export of grain and of wines and spirits, liqueurs and dried or crystallized fruits and vegetables, has decided to grant special licences to ships wishing to carry such cargoes.'

So Napoleon, confronted by the failure of a Blockade which was merely enriching smugglers, himself became a smuggler. He established a direct trade with England whilst forbidding the same to his allies, whether vassals or neutral states. France abounded in colonial produce whereas the rest of Europe was deprived, French traders instead of English smugglers therefore distributed it throughout Europe. To the monopoly of European markets which Napoleon intended to reserve for French industry was added, then, the monopoly of colonial commodities.

This mercantile nationalism is expressed through the decrees of 1810 which mark a turning point in the conception of the Blockade.

The first step was the decree of 3 July which decided that licences would in future only be given to French ships, and that the only authorized exports were 'all goods manufactured in France and commodities from French land whose export [is] not forbidden', which meant cereals and spirits.

Soon afterwards came the Decree of Saint-Cloud of 25 July which put all the Empire's maritime trade under Napoleon's authority: 'From 1 August,' the Emperor decided, 'no ship may leave our ports for a foreign destination unless she is supplied with a licence signed by our hand.' These licences were supposed to allow for the importing into France of all the produce the country needed; French traders would then redistribute it on the Continent for a fee.

Finally, on 5 August the Trianon Decree stipulated the duty to be paid on importing colonial commodities: 800 francs per hundredweight for cottons from Georgia, 400 francs for Levantine cottons, and the same price for coffee. The duty was enormous, and was calculated so that the commodities would cost the consumers no more than they did as contraband, but henceforth the profits went into the state coffers and not into the smugglers' pockets.

All that remained was to apply the decree. The states under French influence presented no problems, to be sure. However, the King of Bavaria, speaking on behalf of the discontented, did not hesitate to write to Napoleon to the effect that these measures were harder on France's allies than on her enemies. Napoleon wished to make an example in order to put an end to the protests, and to sell colonial stocks immediately at the new rate. He chose Frankfurt, since the town was 'filled with English and colonial merchandise,' which he ordered to be seized at once. Two infantry regiments commanded by Friant and the Mayence customs officers took part in the operation which brought the Treasury some ten millions.

The Decree of Fontainebleau was the last stage of this turning point. It was dated 19 October and accentuated the severity of the new customs policies. All trading of colonial commodities in Europe must be definitively stopped in order to prevent competition with France. A considerable impression was made in Frankfurt by the autos-da-fé of 17, 20, 23 and 27 November. The result was that all trade in the town was ruined. Discontent spread throughout Germany. More seriously still, stability in business circles was affected, panic infected the banks and French commerce.

THE FRENCH CRISIS 1810–1811

The new system produced the crisis of 1810 which reached its peak at the time of the birth of the King of Rome.

Speculation in *assignats* had been replaced by dealing in colonial commodities which had increased tremendously since the Berlin Decree and which was ruined by the 1810 decrees. The British exporter could no longer be paid by the German, Swiss or Dutch trader whose merchandise had been seized, and the French importers who had given advances to firms in Amsterdam, Basle and Hamburg could not recuperate their money. Warnings of the crisis became evident in May 1810. In correspondence with Napoleon, Mollien, the Minister of the Treasury, denounced the effects of gambling on colonial commodities, particularly the rising trend in speculation in Holland and the Hanseatic towns. In September Rodde, the large firm in Lübeck, went bankrupt, bringing in its wake the collapse of Parisian banks: Laffitte, Fould, Tourton. Further bankruptcies followed in November and December. A report stated, 'Every market in France, Germany and Italy is shaken.' The year 1810 ended in a flood of bankruptcies in Paris and Lyons.

The first months of 1811 augured difficulties. The silk industry suffered particularly: in Lyons, the number of working looms was reduced by half. Tours, Nîmes and Italy were equally affected. The crisis spread to cotton—in Rouen workshops were soon using no more than a third of the raw materials they had been using in 1810; in the north, the slump was even more marked. Wool, in its turn, was affected. A quarter of the drapers stopped payment. Although the depression was less serious in metallurgy, neither the Haut-Rhin, the Moselle nor the Pyrenees were spared.

In August and September discounts did not reach a twelfth of the figure for the preceding year. Twenty thousand of the fifty thousand workers in Paris were unemployed by the end of May. Napoleon resorted to his usual expedients, he gave loans to industry (Richard-Lenoir, Gros-Davilliers), large orders for the court (a decree of 6 January 1811 made it compulsory to wear a silk suit at the Tuileries), and great earthworks were undertaken. Towards the end of the summer the crisis seemed to have reached its end, but a bad harvest prolonged it. Whilst the south was suffering from a drought, a series of storms wiped out part of the crops in the Parisian basin. The situation was not disastrous, but fear of hunger awoke old reactions. The Minister of the Interior wrote: 'Disappointed expectations exaggerated the problem and public opinion which always tends towards extremes has favoured rising trends in speculation and the increase in the price of corn.'

Suddenly the price of bread rose in Paris from 14 to 16 and then to 18 *sous* in March 1812. And even at this price round loaves were impossible to find after the early hours of the morning. Finally the reintroduction of the *maximum* was envisaged. Because of revolutionary overtones it was renamed *taxe*. The result of the decree of 8 May 1812, which fixed a maximum price per hectolitre of corn in the Seine and adjacent departments, was that all corn disappeared from the markets. On the other hand, in the Bouches-du-Rhône, where the Prefect, Thibaudeau, was careful not to apply the *maximum*, the town of Marseilles was more or less adequately supplied.

If there was no sign of mutiny in Paris, it was because the price of bread never rose above 20 *sous* at which point the working classes would have been in dire need, also Rumfort soup was widely distributed and, above all, there was no connection between unemployment and hunger. However, a demonstration of women from the faubourg Saint-Antoine was only just avoided as the Emperor passed through the Charenton gate on 19 January 1813. Napoleon had systematically dealt with the capital. Let us recall one of his most famous sayings: 'It is unfair that bread should be maintained at a low price in Paris when it costs more elsewhere, but then the government is there, and soldiers do not like to shoot at women with babies on their backs who come screaming to the bakeries.' His attitude had not changed since the crisis of Year X.

Things were different in the provinces. In the Manche, a hectolitre of wheat rose from 20 francs in the second fortnight of August 1811 to 30 francs in the first half of March 1812. The situation at Cherbourg, for instance, became dramatic: 'The poverty of men working in the port becomes more and more horrifying and even with money, bread is unavailable; for three days many workmen have been living off vegetables which are insufficient for hard-working labourers,' a report pointed out. Corn was disappearing from the markets. At Caen, on 2 March 1812, riots broke out in the market. 'Send me the Prefect and I'll flay him like an old horse,' yelled one demonstrator, a knacker by trade. The rioters were joined by conscripts from Calvados. Thieving and pillaging accompanied the violence, but by 3 March order was restored. Still, there remained poverty aggravated by the difficulties of the textile industry.

'On approaching Lisieux,' wrote the Commissioner of Police for Caen, 'ghastly pale faces are to be seen, and failing bodies, miserable people are everywhere, sitting on the side of the roads, awaiting the results of the travellers' sympathy. Milk, cooked herbs, cheese and coarse bran are the food of the peasant who cannot even afford oat bread.'

The Alpes-Maritimes, a department at the opposite end of France, suffered from the same dearth. The Prefect remarked, 'Last spring the poor classes from the country communes lived only off wild herbs and roots which they eat with no seasoning and no salt; in some places salt was replaced by the use of sea-water. Individuals presented a dreadful sight as they succumbed to poverty and died of hunger.'

Where the harvest was satisfactory, famine was caused by unemployment due to the collapse of the textile industry. This was the case in the Aisne, whose Prefect observed,

> In no circumstances did the hardships result from a complete absence of grain, but from the difficulty of being able to afford it, for, although controlled, the price was too high for the people. Quite a large number of people ate oat bread; others were even reduced to mixing bran with milk. But these sad examples are rather the result of great poverty, a complete lack of work and pecuniary resources, than of a dearth whose effects we have never experienced, for we have, on the contrary, been able to give help to neighbouring departments.

EUROPE
IN 1812

UNITED KINGDOM
OF GREAT BRITAIN
AND
IRELAND

North Sea

Dublin

London

Calais
Boulogne
Cherbourg
Le Havre
Brest
Rouen
R. Seine
Paris

Amsterdam
Antwerp
Brussels
Liège
Cologne
DUCHY
OF DASSA

A t l a n t i c

O c e a n

F R E N C H

E M P I R E

R. Loire

Nantes

R. Meuse

Basle
Province of
Neuchâtel
Berne

Geneva

Bordeaux

Lyons

R. Garonne

R. Rhône

Turin

Toulouse

Nice

Marseilles

KINGDOM OF PORTUGAL

Saragossa

Madrid

Barcelona

KINGDOM OF SPAIN

Lisbon

Valencia

Balearic Isles

Minorca

Majorca

Seville

Granada

Cadiz

Gibraltar

Tangier

Mediterranean Sea

Legend	
Empire of Napoleon (Direct rule)	
Empire of Napoleon (Dependent States)	
Independent States, theoretically allies of Napoleon	

Copenhagen

Baltic Sea

Republic of Danzig

Tilsit

Koenigsberg

RUSSIAN

EMPIRE

Lübeck

Hamburg

Bremen

DUCHY OF MECKLENBURG

R. Elbe

Stettin

KINGDOM OF PRUSSIA

R. Vistula

Warsaw

Kiev

R. Dnieper

Hanover

Berlin

KINGDOM OF WESTPHALIA

KINGDOM OF SAXE

Dresden

GRAND DUCHY OF WARSAW

GRAND DUCHY OF HESSE

DUCHY OF SAXONY

Breslau

Cracow

Galicia

GRAND DUCHY OF FRANKFORT

GRAND DUCHY OF WÜRZBURG

Prague

Bohemia

Austria

R. Dniester

Stuttgart

KINGDOM OF WÜRTEMBERG

KINGDOM OF BAVARIA

Munich

Salzburg

AUSTRIAN EMPIRE

Vienna

R. Danube

Budapest

Hungary

Moldavia

Gotthard Pass

Brenner Pass

Carinthia

Transylvania

KINGDOM OF ITALY

Milan

Venice

Trieste

Illyrian Provinces

Slavonia

Belgrade

Wallachia

Bucharest

Black Sea

R. Po

Genoa

Bosnia

Serbia

OTTOMAN

Province of Lucca

Florence

Province of Montenegro

Adriatic Sea

Adrianople

Constantinople

I. of Elba

Rome

Corsica

KINGDOM OF NAPLES

Naples

Albania

EMPIRE

KINGDOM OF SARDINIA

Corfu (Fr.)

Aegean Sea

Palermo

Ionian Isles (Eng.)

Athens

KINGDOM OF SICILY

Morea

So unemployment and dearth either combined or took turns in aggravating the poverty.

Troubles broke out almost everywhere: mills and bakers' shops were stormed, carts and boats carrying corn were attacked and pillaged, farms were burnt by bands of beggars who grew increasingly numerous and more threatening. Posters appeared:

> Suffering people
> Without bread or work
> You are sleeping!

Or again:

> Notice to the people,
> Bread, work or death.

Some notables were threatened, like Barbier, the big trader from Rennes and brother-in-law of the Minister:

> You great rascal, Barbier, usurer, hoarder of grain, open up your granary, or die!

A few threats frightened those towards whom they were directed—a lighted torch above the doorway of a landowner or rich farmer. The bourgeoisie, threatened in person and through its property, took fright. Although Napoleon was absorbed by the preparations for the Russian campaign, he had to intervene. To be sure there had not been very many riots; besides Caen, Rennes and Charleville had been the most important. Nevertheless, authority was flouted, property threatened and disorder was everywhere. An example had to be made. Caen was chosen. Napoleon sent General Durosnel there with a large number of troops. A council of war met on 14 March. Eight people were condemned to death, two in their absence. The six present, of whom two were women lace-makers, were executed on the 15th. On the 17th the troops left the town. 'The guilty suburbs are dismayed and begin to tremble, and already, within two days, stolen objects have been replaced,' wrote the Prefect. Elsewhere the police were reinforced. But although the troubles spread to some forty departments, they never endangered the government, and so a return to order took place swiftly. By the end of the year the agitation had quietened down.

In most departments the harvest of 1812 was satisfactory. That of 1813 was particularly abundant and favoured a return to a normal situation.

It was at this moment that agriculture was affected by a series of collapses due to the loss of outlets in the north and the east; Contemporaries had the impression of one long depression lasting for three years, whereas, in fact, there were three different crises in succession—over-production resulting from speculation, a relatively bad harvest, further over-production caused by the loss of the German outlets.

What should be noted, however, is that the Emperor's prestige was diminished by the crisis. The rural world and the Parisian workers no doubt still remained attached to the Emperor in spite of everything. After all, he had maintained the price of bread at a reasonable level in the capital and had avoided too serious disorders in the countryside. On the other hand, the bourgeoisie was definitely detaching itself from the regime, whilst in Europe, the harshness of the Trianon and Fontainebleau decrees had alienated German and Dutch sympathy and prepared the way for the revolts of 1813.

THE ENGLISH SLUMP

Yet, Napoleon was never closer to victory than in 1811. Initiated by the weakening of the pound sterling and by the bad harvest of 1809, an economic crisis was in fact breaking out across the Channel.

The strengthening of the Continental System and the energetic steps taken with regard to English contraband, combined with the saturation of Continental markets following the enormous exports of colonial goods in 1809, dealt a serious blow to British trade. On the other hand, in order to win new clients in South America, English businessmen had allowed payment to be deferred for too long and had swamped their markets with goods which had to be sold at a loss.

A monetary crisis, the rise in the cost of cereals, a loss of exports, and disappointments in the Spanish colonies were, in 1810, the first elements of a depression which was to worsen the following year. In 1811, the loss of foreign trade in some sectors resulted in a complete collapse. The total value of exports dropped enormously. Industry was affected, at first cotton, then metallurgy and finally ship-building. Unemployment spread and workmen's wages dropped at a moment when the bad harvest of 1811 caused a marked rise in the cost of living. Riots involving the breaking of machinery shook Nottingham in 1811. From the Midlands the movement spread to Lancashire and Yorkshire. Contemporaries were convinced that the breakers of machines were preparing a general uprising against the government and a massacre of the rich. In fact Luddism was, above all, an explosion of popular discontent resulting from unemployment and the rise in the cost of bread. From the outside point of view the English crisis took a new turn with the breaking off of Anglo-American relations which resulted on 18 June 1812 in a new war between Great Britain and the United States.

At the end of 1812, England's position was disturbing, while matters on the Continent appeared to be improving. For the second time, the application of the Continental Blockade caused the island a serious economic crisis complicated by social troubles. For the second time, too, at the moment in which Napoleon was perhaps going to be able to break England, he launched a new military venture. Napoleon had expected his licensing system to finance the war which he was preparing against Russia; but by facilitating the export of cereals to the British Isles, he saved the English from famine. No doubt he had never considered starving England; but no one can say what turn the Luddite movement might have taken if England had been cruelly struck by famine. The objective was always her economic ruin. If he had returned victorious from Moscow, Napoleon would probably have entirely closed the Continent to British merchandise. The Russian winter was to save the English economy from catastrophe as the war in Spain had done in 1808.

7

THE DEFEATS

Did one of Napoleon's ministers really say to Marmont in 1809, 'Do you want me to tell you the truth and to reveal the future? The Emperor is mad, completely mad, and he will turn us all, such as we are, arse over heels, and the whole thing will end in an appalling catastrophe'? This well-to-do bourgeois was displaying a certain lucidity; he was expressing the growing concern of the notables confronted by an incessant sequence of wars. The natural frontiers, geographical limits which had been the objectives of foreign policy from Richelieu to Talleyrand, had long since been surpassed. Who could have denied that the simple machinery of conquest must inevitably lead to disaster, a disaster which threatened in addition the principles of the Revolution? The catastrophe occurred in 1812; it was gigantic in proportion to the events which preceded it. It brought about the formation of the greatest European coalition that France had ever had to confront.

THE ORIGINS OF THE
FRANCO-RUSSIAN CONFLICT

The rupture which the Tsar desired with France fitted in with the political and economic situation. On the diplomatic level, Alexander had not gained the advantage he hoped for from Tilsit. The division of Turkey was constantly postponed by Napoleon who, as master of Rome, had now turned his thoughts to Constantinople. The formation of the Grand-Duchy of Warsaw heralded the revival of a Polish kingdom, a kingdom which Russia did not want at any cost, if it was to be subjected to French influence. Already, by the annexation of the Duchy of Oldenburg and the Hanseatic towns, France was establishing her control over the Baltic. French imperialism had just touched Russia at her sorest points. Her economic interests were threatened. The application of the Blockade had put a stop to exports of corn, hemp and wood destined for England. Napoleon had given them no alternative outlet, hence the keenly felt discontent of the Russian landowners. Sources reveal that the value of Russian exports destined for France reached 257,000 roubles, whereas France was importing into Russia 1,511 roubles' worth of goods. Faithful to his mercantilist ideas, Napoleon easily accommodated himself to this imbalance of Russian trade. But could the Tsar accept such a drain? Lesseps, the General Commissioner for trade relations in St Petersburg, drew his minister's attention to this disastrous situation in a letter dated 22 April 1809: 'The present rate of exchange proves incontestably the degree to which Russia is ruffled by political events.' And to be more specific:

> Last year the only ships to avoid the enemy fleets blockading the Baltic had managed not to be sighted or had protected themselves illegally from the rapacity of these fleets. It is a fact that without exports, the balance of trade is entirely against Russia. The glut of her hemp, her wood, her tallow, her pitch, her potassium, her leather, her iron and a thousand other articles which take up considerable space but are of little value, must bring about her total ruin if this situation goes on for many more years.

Of three hundred and thirty-eight ships recorded in 1809, only one left for Bordeaux which indicates the inadequacy of the outlet offered by France. And French ships were not bringing Russia the produce which she needed. A report by Lesseps on 22 March 1810 points out that ships coming from Bordeaux and Marennes during the year 1809 were admitted without serious formalities 'because the needs of Livonia and Courland were such that an insurrection was to be feared in the event of the ships being prevented from unloading'.

In fact, far from exporting produce of primary importance, France sent Russia spirits, scents, porcelain and jewellery.

From 1809, the attitude of the Russian authorities to the Blockade had to be considerably modified: they closed their eyes to the arrival of supposedly neutral ships. At Riga, trade with England is said to have remained the same as in normal years. The ukase of 31 December 1810 struck French luxury products. It was an inevitable reaction designed to put an end to the imbalance of Russian trade. In a letter of 25 March 1811 the Tsar justified the new charges by 'the extreme embarrassment in which maritime trade finds itself and the horrifying fall in our exchange'.

But political pressure on the Tsar was as strong as pressure from business circles. The Tilsit agreement had been badly received at the court of St Petersburg. The French intercepted and informed the Tsar of a letter which revealed the existence of a plot to overthrow Alexander in favour of his sister, Catherine. Mindful of the fate of his father, Paul I, who had been betrayed by his entourage, the Tsar began to back-track immediately after Tilsit—hence his passivity at Erfurt, the refusal of a matrimonial alliance with Napoleon and attempts to side-step the Blockade. In addition to the court and trade there was the army which had refused to fraternize with the French at Tilsit. According to Davydov in his war memoirs,

> Only curiosity to see Napoleon and the fact of witnessing a few details of a meeting between the two greatest emperors in the world distracted us a little. But there was an end to our amusement. We wanted nothing to do with the French company. Not one of us tried to make friends with, or even to get to know, a single Frenchman, despite their efforts, in obedience to a secret order from Napoleon, to charm us with all kinds of politeness and amiability. 1812 was already with us, its bayonet steeped in blood right up to the muzzle, its knife embedded to the hilt.

Napoleon, too, had been disappointed by the agreement at Tilsit. Neither had he appreciated Russian reticence at Erfurt and at the time of the Franco-Austrian war. He could not tolerate the slightest breach in the Continental System at a moment in which, once again, England seemed on the brink of bankruptcy.

The chambers of commerce (led by that of Lyons) had, from 1806, pressed for a renewal of commercial relations. Champagny wrote to Caulaincourt on 7 December 1807: 'His Majesty commands me to speak to you about French trade. It stands alone in St Petersburg. There can never be a finer occasion in which to revive it.' But very soon the tone was lowered. The distance, the cost of transport, the uncertainty of credit and the existence of more accessible outlets in Germany and Italy finally dissuaded French traders from considering Russia. The definitive loss of this market, then, was only moderately harmful and in the eyes of French traders did not justify the possibility of a war.

Despite the reservations of the notables, Napoleon wanted this war. To his mind it fitted into the framework of the Anglo-French conflict.

It was the logical outcome of the Continental System. How much credence can be put in Napoleon's confidences to Narbonne which were later relayed to Villemain?

> This long road is the road to India. Alexander left from as far away as Moscow to reach the Ganges. You know about General Gardanne's and Jaubert's missions to Persia; nothing much came of them, but I have the map and the condition of the populations to be passed through in order to go from Erivan and Tiflis as far as the English possessions in India . . . Imagine Moscow taken, Russia overthrown, the Tsar reconciled or murdered by a palace plot, a new or dependent throne perhaps; and tell me if it is not possible for a large army of Frenchmen and auxiliaries to leave Tiflis and gain access to the Ganges, and that the touch of a French sword is all that is needed for the framework of mercantile grandeur to collapse?

If these declarations are authentic were they not aimed at deluding Narbonne? Was Napoleon sincere, or was he intoxicated by the size of his army in 1812?

From 1811 the ordnance department, more especially the topography department under Bacler d'Albe, was entrusted with the drawing up of maps for the coming campaign. Equipment was collected at La Fère, Metz, Mayence, Wesel and Maestricht to be dispatched to Danzig. The Emperor believed in a rapid war. He is supposed to have asserted to Narbonne, 'Barbarous peoples are superstitious and have simple ideas. A terrible blow at the heart of the Empire, at Moscow the Great, Moscow the Holy, will deliver this blind unresilient mass into my hands in a moment.' He counted on the Lithuanian serfs rising against their overlords at the approach of the Grande Armée and on the collapse of the rouble (to be on the safe side Napoleon had some false coins made). He was, however, given several warnings. Captain Leclerc, who had collected some of the documents concerning Russian statistics, remarked in January 1812, that 'if the Emperor Napoleon sent his army into the Russian interior, it would be annihilated like Charles XII's at Poltava, or forced to a hasty retreat.' And, he added, 'I think that only a Russian can fight a war in Russia.' At the beginning of 1812, other voices were raised against the danger of opening a front to the East while the Spanish affair was not yet settled. The Brumairians' spokesman, Talleyrand, did not disguise his scepticism, even before 'the beginning of the end'.

War broke out in June 1812. The Tsar, supported by England, had formed the sixth coalition which consisted only of Russia. For the first time, France's numerical superiority was overwhelming. In principle, Napoleon could count on Prussia and Austria. In fact, Metternich had done everything to reassure the Tsar. 'What guarantee do you give me?' the Russian ambassador asked. 'The interests of the Austrian monarchy itself,' Metternich replied. The King of Prussia wrote to Alexander to confirm: 'If war breaks out, we will do no harm that is not strictly necessary; we will always remember that we are united and that one day we must be allies again.' Meanwhile Austria and Prussia eagerly supplied a contingent for Napoleon's formidable army of six hundred and seventy-five thousand men. An army which included Swiss, Poles, Italians, Belgians and Dutchmen . . . in short the whole of the Emperor's Europe.

On 17 May Napoleon was at Dresden. 'A garden of kings' was gathered there and the sumptuous ceremonies which took place have often been described. Has it been pointed out that for the first time before embarking on a campaign, Napoleon did not present himself as head of the Revolution, but as a monarch welcoming his neighbours, the Emperor of Austria and the King of Prussia? It was then that he allowed himself to say that events in France would have taken a different turn if his 'poor uncle' had been firmer. The poor uncle was Louis XVI whose nephew-in-law Napoleon had become through his marriage to Marie-Louise. The revolutionary bourgeoisie must have shuddered.

Everything intoxicated him and convinced him that he would have an easy victory in Russia. He wrote to Marie-Louise from Posen on 1 June that he would be back with her in three months. Echoes of the Revolution. The service officers heard him with surprise at Torun singing, at the top of his voice, *Le Chant du départ*: 'From North to South the warrior's trumpet has sounded the battle hour, tremble, enemies of France . . .'

On the banks of the Niemen he was to be heard humming *Marlbrough s'en va-t'en guerre*. Rarely did he embark on a campaign in such a good humour. In fact Russia had only a hundred and fifty thousand men divided into two armies with which to oppose him. But an important event cast a dark shadow over the horizon: peace was signed at Bucharest between the Russians and the Turks. 'The ignorant disciples of Mahomet made peace at the moment when they could make amends for the consequences of a hundred years of unfortunate wars,' wrote Jomini.

THE DISASTER

The French troops crossed the Niemen at Kovno on 24 June. Napoleon swooped on Vilna to separate the Russian forces; he hoped to annihilate them one after the other and then dictate the terms of peace. But he found nothing. The Russian soldiers were withdrawing from the invader, leaving a desert behind them. Napoleon thought he would catch them at Smolensk on 17 August, but they avoided him again.

In two months no serious battle had been fought, meanwhile the strength of the Grande Armée was continually being sapped. A hundred and fifty thousand soldiers were already out of action. Sickness, desertion and lack of supplies caused the loss of some five to six thousand men a day. According to the evidence of the future Bishop of Butkevic who was in Lithuania at the time, the French seemed badly prepared. The dragoons who had become lancers had had to exchange their guns for lances which they did not know how to use; 'horses reared, cavalrymen grew impatient'; equally 'the lack of experience in shoeing the artillery horses in order to cross the frozen Steppes in the north, necessitated the abandoning of many cannon.' To satisfy French opinion, Napoleon had counted on Prussian and Polish resources only. The hostility of the Prussians, reservations in Poland, bad roads and insufficient harvests all played their part. Furthermore Napoleon failed to catch the enemy while his army disintegrated little by little, his men worn out by forced marches in too lengthy stretches.

The ideas advocated by Count Lieven and Clausewitz triumphed. After all, Clausewitz, who was now in the service of the Tsar, had asserted in the Russian military headquarters that Napoleon would perish, conquered by the gigantic dimensions of the Empire, if only Russia knew how to play her hand—this meant sparing her strength until the last moment and making peace under no circumstances. He recommended 'the evacuation of the whole countryside up to Smolensk and that they only start to fight properly in this region'.

This was to be the version circulated by the Russians after the campaign. In fact, Clausewitz, in his account of the campaign, has clearly shown that the scorched-earth tactics were only applied accidentally by headquarters. If the generals withdrew, it was, above all, through fear of confronting Napoleon and of being beaten by him, and not through calculation.

But would the holy city of Moscow allow itself to be taken without a battle? The old general, Kutusov, was ordered to block the invader's path. He installed himself on the Moskva, to the south of Borodino.

After a relentless and appallingly bloody battle, Napoleon broke through on 7 September. Tolstoy was later to sing of the 'Russian victory at Borodino'. It is fairer to speak of the 'French success on the Moskva' since, on the 14th, the Grande Armée entered Moscow. But the losses were considerable and, furthermore, an immense fire destroyed three-quarters of the city making it uninhabitable. Finally, Alexander firmly refused to negotiate.

Once again, Napoleon discovered national war, one which combines patriotism with religious fanaticism, and puts a whole people against the invader. War seen as a game of chess between decent people gave way to a conflict in which no holds were barred, where the rules were no longer respected.

Napoleon was cut off from his Empire by distance—a courier took fifteen days to liaise between Moscow and Paris. So, tired of waiting on Alexander's goodwill, and despite supplies which would have lasted through the winter, Napoleon gave the order to retreat in mid-October. On the 19th, the army evacuated the city. Nothing would have been lost, despite the heavy casualties already suffered, if Napoleon had not returned by the same route as he had come. Unfortunately for him, Kutusov forced him, by the Battle of Maloyaroslavets on 24 October, to take the Smolensk route across countryside which had been devastated first by the Russians and then by the French army marching on Moscow. What is more, the soldiers were as heavily laden with booty as they were with supplies. Cold was added to hunger. After Smolensk the temperature fell to −20°C and even to −30°C. Interminable nights without fire or light. Daybreak revealed a long line of men wrapped in rags from head to foot (their shoes had long ago worn out), dragging themselves through the snow and leaving corpses, waggons and cannon in their wake. Anything was better than to fall into the hands of the Cossacks who harried the column. In his memoirs, a Russian officer, Boris Uxkull, tells how moujiks bought French prisoners in order to throw them into cauldrons of boiling water or to impale them. They cost two roubles a man. Russian historiographers have dwelt insistently on the part played by partisans which seems to them to have been more decisive then the climate.

Even if the extent of the disaster has been exaggerated in the imaginations of many, the scenes of horror recounted by the survivors were not invented. The crossing of the Beresina by two bridges made of planks, which were set up in the icy water by Eblé's pontoneers, took a dramatic turn. Ségur described it:

this deep, wide, confused mass of men, horses and chariots besieging the narrow entrance to the bridges which it overflowed. The leaders, pushed by those who followed, pushed back by the guards or the pontoneers, or impeded by the river, were crushed, trampled under foot or hurled into the drifting ice of the Beresina. There arose from this immense and horrible throng, sometimes a deafening hum, sometimes a great clamour mixed with wailing and dreadful curses.

On 16 December, only eighteen thousand men apparently recrossed the Niemen; during the days that followed others arrived in small groups. The total losses in deaths, prisoners and deserters are estimated at three hundred and eighty thousand soldiers. It was one of the greatest disasters in history and its very magnitude has enhanced the Napoleonic legend.

THE LOSS OF GERMANY

Napoleon left his army on 5 December at around ten o'clock in the evening in order to return hastily to Paris where he arrived during the night of the 18th–19th. It was a long journey about which we have been fully informed by Caulaincourt. The news of General Malet's failed *coup d'état* which will be dealt with in the following chapter had deeply impressed the Emperor. He admitted to being irritated by the disregard in which high officials, like Frochot, had held the King of Rome: 'The continual changes of government have accustomed men to them.' He envisaged the future defection of the Senate and planned to replace it with a House of Peers, 'but in a truly national spirit'. All the notabilities would be admitted. Sensible to the criticisms which he felt were aimed at him by the bourgeoisie whom he hoped to disarm with his peerage, he applied himself to justifying his government to Caulaincourt: 'I love power, they say. Well then, are those in the departments entitled to complain? Never have the prisons been emptier. Does one complain of a prefect without getting justice? First Consul, Emperor, I have been king of the people; I have ruled for them in their interest, without allowing myself to be deflected by the shouting and self-interest of certain people.' The people? Napoleon immediately specified: 'I say the people, that is the nation, for I have never favoured what is often understood by the word "people"—the rabble. Neither have I favoured the great lords, for if the lack of intelligence and the misery of the one predisposes them to disorder, the pretensions of the others make them at least as dangerous to authority.'

Which is tantamount to saying that Napoleon's government looked to the bourgeoisie for its social foundations. He had, then, to restore the confidence of the bourgeoisie, which had been shaken by the announcement of the retreat in the 29th bulletin. 'Our disasters,' the Emperor confided to Caulaincourt, 'will cause a great sensation, but my arrival will counter-balance the distressing effects.'

On 19 December he declared to Decrès and Lacuée de Cessac, 'Fortune has overlooked me. I was in Moscow, I thought to sign a peace treaty. I stayed there a long time. I made a great mistake, but I will have the means of putting it right.'

Napoleon was already at work. Bad news arrived ceaselessly. The Prussian general, York, whose corps was part of the French army, went over to the Russians when the Convention of Tauroggen was signed on 31 December. Eastern Prussia rose against French domination and the movement spread to Silesia and Brandenburg. On 28 February 1813, under pressure from his advisers and from the student world which was leaving the universities empty in order to enlist, Frederick William signed an alliance with the Tsar and launched 'the war of deliverance'—'the holy war' sung by Arndt, Körner and Rückert. However, with characteristic speed, Napoleon managed to draw from a France, presumed to be exhausted, three hundred thousand conscripts of eighteen and nineteen who were to be trained as they took the road for Germany. In fact, he refused to abandon Spain where two hundred and fifty thousand seasoned soldiers were immobilized as well as a well-trained cavalry whom he was to miss in decisive moments. To Caulaincourt he already insisted, 'The Spanish war only exists in the guerrillas.' And he added: 'Since the opposition to the new order comes from the lower classes, only time and the action of the upper classes directed by a strong, wise government, supported in its turn by a national police force and by the body of the French people, can calm this excitement. The hatred will disappear when it is seen that we are merely bringing the country wiser and more liberal laws better adapted to the times in which we live than are the old customs of the Inquisition which governed the country.'

Perhaps he was merely seeking to reassure himself. The mistake had been to enter Russia before the Spanish affair had been settled. By 1813 it was too late. The English were in the peninsula and the Emperor could no longer withdraw from his southern front. To leave Spain, as some critics suggested he should, would be folly. The whole structure of the Empire would crumble. Meanwhile the German courts hesitated to join Prussia and Russia. The Confederation of the Rhine sent the contingents which the Emperor demanded.

Attack alone could still save everything and Napoleon knew it. The finalized plan, as it was revealed on 11 March 1813 in a memorandum to Eugène who had succeeded Murat as Commander-in-Chief of the Grande Armée at Leipzig, is no less striking than the famous dictation from the Boulogne camp:

> Having made every attempt to give the impression that I plan to advance on Dresden and into Silesia, my intention will probably be to advance on Havelberg (under cover of the Thuringer mountains and the Elbe), to arrive by forced march at Stettin with three hundred thousand men and to continue the army's march to Danzig which can be reached in fifteen days; and on the twentieth day of the movement when the army has crossed the Elbe, that town will have been taken and we will control Marienburg and all the bridges cross the Lower Vistula. This is the order for the offensive. For the defence, the principal aim is to cover the 32nd military division, Hamburg and the Kingdom of Westphalia, the Havelberg point constitutes that.

Napoleon planned to engage in these operations in May. The Saxony campaign was swift and enabled Napoleon to taste victory again. He beat Blücher and Wittgenstein who commanded the Prusso-Russian forces at Weissenfeld and Lützen (on 1 and 2 May). After having forced them back beyond the Elbe, he pursued them and beat them again at Bautzen and at Wurschen (on 20 and 21 May). How much the cavalry's absence handicapped Napoleon has often been stressed: he was unable to destroy the enemy. But a new element came into play. It was the relentless quality of the Prussian forces in the fray which turned the battles to butchery. 'The animals have learnt something,' Napoleon admitted. On 4 June a two-month armistice was signed at Pleschwitz.

In fact Napoleon could not hope for a decisive victory, but Prussia and Russia, even united, were not capable of conquering France: thus Austria found herself in the position of arbitrator. Were matrimonial alliances to prove stronger than the old solidarity of the European coalitions? Would the hatred of Prussia prevail over contempt for the aristocracy? Without letting his opinion be known, Metternich offered himself as mediator. But from the start of negotiations he let his conditions for a return to peace on the Continent be known: the restitution of Prussia and the eventual disappearance of the Con federation of the Rhine. Conditions which, it can be seen, did not question France's natural frontiers and which might have been accepted by the notables. But what about Napoleon? The meeting between the Emperor and Metternich at Dresden on 26 June, even if the Austrian diplomat gave a slanted account, clearly shows how weak the victor of Bautzen's position was. 'What then, do you expect of me?' Napoleon asked brusquely. 'That I should dishonour myself? Never! I would die before I ceded one inch of territory. Your sovereigns, born on the throne can be beaten twenty times and still return to their capitals. I cannot do that because I am an upstart soldier. My domination will not be able to survive from the day I cease to be strong and consequently to be feared.' This was a psychological error in so far as France, tired of war, would have agreed to the restitution of the Illyrian provinces and the renunciation of the Polish cause. It was also a mistake on Napoleon's part to think, as he confided to Metternich, that Vienna would remain neutral. He was failing to take into consideration pressure from England: English subsidies alone could help the Austrian cabinet to resolve the financial crisis with which it was struggling. News from Spain confirmed the collapse of French domination on the peninsula and tolled the knell of Napoleon's power. On 27 June, Metternich, under England's leadership, signed the agreement of Reichenbach, which remained a secret at the time, with Russia and Prussia. Vienna was to declare war on France if France refused the principles of peace put forward by Metternich. The congress opened at Prague in the middle of July, the armistice having been prolonged until 10 August. It only lasted for a few sittings. Austria had already decided on her position. On the 11th she declared war. The allies mobilized three armies, the Northern Army under Bernadotte who brought Sweden into the coalition, the Silesian army with Blücher and the army of Bohemia commanded by Schwarzenberg.

Napoleon had planned a triple offensive—to the north, Davout against Berlin, in the centre Ney was to attack Blücher, finally he would, himself, advance on Bohemia. Thus the Emperor dispersed his forces and depended too greatly on the initiative of marshals accustomed to passively obeying his orders. Although Napoleon halted the Bohemian army at the battle of Dresden (26–28 August) where Moreau was killed, bad news was accumulating for the French. Vandamme was defeated at Kulm, Macdonald at Katzbach, Oudinot at Grossbeeren to the south of Berlin and finally, Ney at Dennewitz.

On the 31st, Peyrusse heard Napoleon reciting the following lines by Voltaire:

> J'ai servi, commandé, vaincu quarante années
> Du monde entre mes mains, j'ai vu les destinées
> Et j'ai toujours connu qu'en chaque évènement
> Les destins des États depend d'un seul moment.[1]

The Emperor had fallen back on Leipzig and on 16–19 October he fought the 'Battle of the Nations'—three hundred and twenty thousand allies against a hundred and sixty thousand French. The first confrontations at Wachau, Partha and at Lindenau were either victories or the outcome was uncertain. On the 17th Napoleon remained strangely inactive. On the 18th, the third day of the battle, a decisive event took place. The defection of the Saxons under the command of Reynier was soon followed by that of the Württemberg cavalry. 'Up until this moment,' noted Major Odeleben who was close to the Emperor, 'he had displayed the greatest calm, the same as ever; this set-back caused no change in his manner although signs of discouragement could be seen on his face.' On the 19th, the allies laid siege to Leipzig, the retreat of the French was understood from the premature explosion of the bridge over the Elster. More than eighty cannon and hundreds of waggons, as well as Macdonald's, Lauriston's and Reynier's troops were still in the town; Paniatowski drowned trying to cross the river. The Grande Armée bulletin dated at Erfurt, 14 October 1813, noted:

> The losses occasioned by this unfortunate event cannot yet be evaluated, but they are estimated to be around twelve thousand men and several hundreds of waggons. Circumstances have been changed by the disorder in the army: the victorious French army is arriving at Erfurt like a beaten army.

As he retreated to Frankfurt and then Mayence, Napoleon had, in passing, to sweep aside the Bavarians at Hanau on 30 October. They were commanded by Wrede who had also defected.

Soon the ravages of typhus were added to the losses due to war and to an appalling retreat in the rain.

[1] I have served, commanded, conquered forty years
Of the world in my hands I have seen the fortunes
And I have always known that on every occasion
The destiny of States depends on a single moment.

On 9 November, Napoleon was at Saint-Cloud. The situation was disastrous: Napoleonic Germany was crumbling. The Kingdom of Westphalia no longer existed. All the members of the Confederation of the Rhine were hastily disengaging themselves in order to reach agreements with Austria. Montgelas, Bavaria's chief minister, had made the first movement on 8 October. Even the Rhine was threatened. Görres made it the symbol of German unity in his *Rheinische Merkur,* and included in the *Volkstum,* Switzerland, who repudiated her mediator and declared her neutrality. On 29 December a diet of fourteen cantons which met in Zurich had reneged the 1803 act and agreed on a provisional constitution. In Geneva, France's enemies, the Lullin de Chateauvieux, the Pictet de Rochemonts and the Saladins, re-established the Republic and demanded to join the Confederation.

THE LOSS OF HOLLAND

No resistance had been aroused by the transformation of Holland from a kingdom into French departments. 'A certain feeling reigned among the population,' Dumonceau wrote in his *Mémoires,* 'there was a lot of talk but nevertheless people remained calm and resigned.' A revival of commerce was expected with the disappearance of the customs, a reduction in taxation was counted on since French taxation was considerably lower than Dutch, and it was thought that political domination would be lenient under Lebrun, the Duke of Piacenza, who was entrusted with the reorganization of Dutch administration. Disappointment was keen. Lebrun's arrival in Amsterdam was accompanied by a reinforcing of the Dutch customs system which was placed under the authority of a Frenchman. Special tribunals were set up to fight smuggling. Finally, the burning of vast quantities of merchandise annoyed the population. Riots, which were severely repressed by Réal, broke out in April 1811. Provincial particularism and religious hatred had divided Holland; hatred of France encouraged unity. The retreat from Moscow, followed by the explosion of nationalism in Germany, stimulated the opposition. At the announcement of the defeat of Leipzig, the Director of Police, Devilliers du Terrage admitted that 'the country's inhabitants are becoming convinced that soon they will have ceased to belong to France'. On 15 November General Molitor had to leave Amsterdam for the left bank of the Yssel as the allied troops approached. His departure was the signal for a national uprising. On the 16th, Lebrun had to flee; on the 17th, while the French troops were evacuating Holland, a provisional government was set up. Hamburg had long since been lost for identical reasons as Puymaigre points out in his *Mémoires*:

> The union of the Hanseatic provinces to France was a cruel mockery. The inhabitants were said to be French and, as such, were subjected to our taxation. On the other hand, they remained foreigners in so far as we could worsen their lot with new annoyances. Less than that was needed to cause a nation to despair. However, such was the force of the illusions with which Bonaparte charmed us that we were surprised that the Hambourgeois were not zealous subjects of the Emperor.'

THE END OF THE KINGDOM OF ITALY

The consequences of Napoleon's defeats naturally reached the Kingdom of Italy. Italian losses had been heavy during the Empire's last campaigns. Officially only a hundred and two soldiers and a hundred and twenty-one officers returned out of twenty-seven thousand men engaged by the Viceroy Eugène in Russia. Twenty-five thousand men disappeared in the German campaign. As many troops as would be needed to ensure the defence of a profoundly demoralized kingdom. Leopardi wrote:

> O misero colui che in guerra è spento,
> Non per li patrii lidi . . .
> Ma da nemici altrui
> Per altra gente . . .[1]

To the threat of an Austrian invasion was added a new danger from the south. Murat was infuriated by the incessant, and often unjust, public reproaches of his brother-in-law, and he wanted to keep his Neapolitan throne whilst contemplating an Italian unity which would be to his own advantage. He therefore engaged in some imprudent negotiations with the Austrians. For his part, Metternich, who was obliged to concentrate the majority of his troops in Germany, needed an ally in Italy. It was, in any case, not until after the disaster at Leipzig that the King of Naples made up his mind: he would contribute towards chasing the French out of the peninsula. Meanwhile English merchandise was allowed into the Kingdom again.

---

[1] Wretched is he who is killed in battle not in defence of his native land, but by another's enemies and for another people. Leopardi: *All' Italia*

LEVANTAMIENTO SIMULTANEO DE LAS PROVINCIAS DE ESPAÑA CONTRA NAPOLEON AÑO 1808.

The first cracks appeared in the Empire with the uprising of Spain against Napoleon in 1808. This Spanish engraving illustrates the popular insurrection against Joseph Bonaparte who had been put on the throne of Spain by his brother.

The *Dos de Mayo*, Goya's representation of the massacre on 2 May 1808 when the people of Madrid rose up against a Mameluke detachment of Napoleon's Imperial Guard.

The King of Rome rejoicing at the satellite states of the Empire created by his father—in fact ephemeral soap bubbles.

The struggle between the Pope and the Emperor which resulted from the annexation of Rome in 1809 and which culminated in Napoleon's attempting to impose the Fontainebleau Concordat on Pius VII. The poet Alfred de Vigny evoked this famous scene in his *Servitude et Grandeur Militaires*.

The Prince de Talleyrand-Périgord of the old nobility, who was Napoleon's Foreign Minister for several years. He betrayed Napoleon after Erfurt and participated in the collapse of the Empire by having the Senate proclaim the fall of the Emperor in 1814.

The Imperial Army in retreat from Moscow negotiating the Beresina, 26–8 November 1812.

English caricature showing Marshal Ney forcing Napoleon to abdicate in 1814. The defection of the marshals precipitated the fall of the Empire.

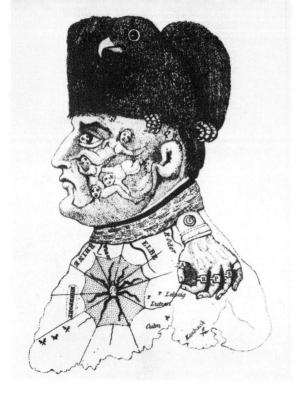

In 1814, immediately after the fall of the Empire, the black legend took over. Napoleon's imperialism was denounced, as was the vast death rate caused by his warmongering madness.

'The flight of the Eagle' was the name given to Napoleon's return from Elba. At Laffrey the army was swayed and, for the most part, joined the Emperor.

In 1815, on his return from Elba, Napoleon tried to rouse the people at the Field of May ceremony. The historian, Michelet, has left an account of this. It was a failure.

Fouché, the former member of the Convention who became Minister of Police under the Directory, favoured the coming to power of Bonaparte at Brumaire. He was three times Minister of Police under Napoleon, was made Duke of Otranto, and betrayed the Emperor in 1815 by allowing the second Bourbon Restoration.

Sergeant Ewart of the 2nd Royal North British Dragoons capturing the standard of Napoleon's 45th Regiment of the Line, known as 'Bonaparte's Invincibles'. Waterloo, 18 June 1815.

The English coming to see Napoleon in the Plymouth roadstead.

An illustration by the well-known Charlet from the *Mémorial de Sainte-Hélène* showing Napoleon indulging in gardening.

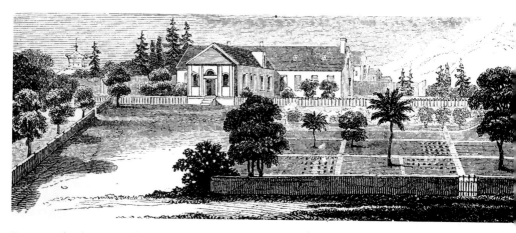

Longwood, where Napoleon lived on St Helena. Here the fallen Emperor spent his last years.

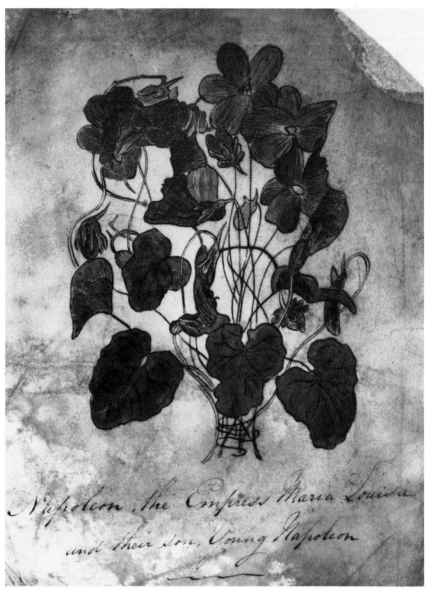

Napoleon, the Empress Maria Louisa and their Son, Young Napoleon

A fine example of Bonapartist propaganda from after the fall of the Empire. The violet became the Napoleonic emblem and Napoleon was given the nickname 'Père la Violette'.

At the beginning of October, Eugène lost Illyria. The Austrians, helped by the Tyrolean uprising and the Bavarian alliance, were crossing the Alps. The French had to withdraw to Tagliamento and then to the Piave. Meanwhile, the Neapolitan troops were marching northwards. The situation was hopeless for Eugène. On 17 April 1814 he was obliged to give up the struggle. On 3 February the Austrian commander-in-chief, Bellegarde, had announced, the re-establishment of former governments. Napoleon himself, in order to embarrass Murat who had his eye on the Papal States, freed the Pope on 1 January, and ordered him to be sent to Rome. Murat, in his turn, was no longer sure of keeping his throne. French domination of Italy was over.

THE SPANISH DEFEATS

For a long time Joseph's fate in Spain had been sealed. England had felt the necessity for an event on the Continent which would determine the course of affairs. Should it be Belgium or Spain? The failure of Walcheren in 1809 persuaded the British cabinet to concentrate on the peninsula. Arthur Wellesley, the future Duke of Wellington, was ordered, not without some reservations by Parliament, to settle in Portugal with his back to the sea where the fleet would ensure supplies, and to launch yearly raids on Madrid in order to wear the French out. Rivalry among the marshals, and their incapacity—with the exception of Suchet in Catalonia—to win local sympathy, the lack of manpower left at their disposal by Napoleon, and increasing losses (Lapisse was killed at Talavera in 1809, Senarmont before Cadiz in 1810, Lagrange was seriously wounded at Tudela in 1808, Colbert died in 1809) all favoured Wellesley's plans, which resulted in the defeat at Talavera on 27 July 1809 of Victor and Jourdan who were quarrelling. He was rewarded for this success with the title of Viscount Wellington.

In Madrid Joseph soon became a mere phantom king receiving orders from Paris and subjected to a mentor in the person of Soult. Besides which, Masséna had been asked to dislodge Wellington. He laid a trap for him by having Ney surround Ciudad Rodrigo where the last regular Spanish army was enclosed. Wellington did not move. Ciudad Rodrigo fell and Masséna marched on Lisbon, but first he came up against the Portuguese scorched-earth tactics and then the fortified lines of Torres Vedras. 'The darling Child of Victory' marked time until March 1811. Napoleon had ordered Soult to leave Seville and help Masséna. But Soult dawdled in Badajoz and then returned to

Andalusia. Masséna had to beat a retreat, a retreat which would have been successful if Wellington had not surprised the French at Fuentes de Oñoro on 4 May.

Napoleon recalled the Young Guard from Spain, thus weakening the southern front in favour of the Army in Russia. He limited the essentials of his strategy in the peninsula to the protection of the Madrid-Bayonne axis and even offered the English to evacuate Spain whose integrity would be guaranteed by a dynasty, the origins of which he did not specify. The offer was rejected. Wellington again took the offensive and broke through Marmont's lines near Salamanca; he entered Madrid which Joseph had abandoned but, threatened by a combination of Clausel's forces (Clausel had succeeded Marmont) in the north, Soult from the south and Suchet who was established at Valencia, he was obliged to leave the capital in haste and, due to disagreement among the marshals, narrowly missed being surrounded. There was a further great offensive in 1813, against the French troops who had withdrawn behind the Ebro in indescribable disorder. Civil officials, generals' mistresses and waggons laden with loot were all confused with soldiers. On 21 June 1813 at Vitoria, Wellington attacked the centre and the left flank of the French formations. Joseph was nearly taken prisoner whilst soldiers surged back towards the frontier, abandoning cannons, arms and baggage. Only Suchet held fast for some time in Catalonia. Napoleon relieved his brother of all command and appointed Soult lieutenant-general in Spain. The Duke of Dalmatia then rediscovered an energy which seemed to have abandoned him as a subordinate, and launched an offensive, but he was stopped at Pamplona. On 8 October Wellington was crossing the Bidassoa. In the middle of November, taking a somewhat belated lesson from these defeats, Napoleon sent Laforest to Valencay where Ferdinand VII was being held, with a letter which read: 'The present political circumstances of my Empire bring me to desire the end of the Spanish affair. There England is encouraging anarchy, Jacobinism, and the abolition of the monarchy and the nobility with a view to establishing a republic.' The dynastic order existing in Spain before 1808 was to be reinstituted, the French armies were to evacuate the peninsula, prisoners of war were to be exchanged. The treaty once signed would be applied as soon as the English evacuated Spain. Once he had overcome his initial surprise Ferdinand VII could only accept. The Bourbon restoration had taken place.

THE RUIN OF THE COLONIES

Even before Napoleon's first Continental defeats, England, as mistress of the seas, had captured France's colonies and those of all her allies. Santa Lucia, Tobago and Saint-Pierre fell immediately hostilities were reopened. In Martinique, Villaret-Joyeuse capitulated in February 1809; Guadeloupe succumbed the following year. Guiana was attacked by an English squadron and occupied. Senegal suffered the same fate. From 1810 France no longer had any colonial possessions in America or Africa. In the Indian Ocean Rodriguez Island was taken in 1809; Mauritius, where Surcouf, aboard the *Revenant,* had mounted a last expedition in 1807, fell in its turn. The Seychelles succumbed in 1811. Java which, as a result of the annexation of Holland, had become a French colony in July 1810, was immediately subjected to British attacks, and capitulated on 13 September 1811, after six weeks of fighting.

An article in *Le Moniteur* pointed to the unexpected consequences of the loss of French possessions overseas: 'The occupation of our small colonies was fatal, but the sentimental ties which link them to the parent state will tighten and their pride will swell under the domination of an enemy who knows only how to humiliate those who fall into its power.'

As for the Spanish colonies (such as Peru, Mexico, Argentina), by dethroning the Bourbons, Napoleon had opened the way to them for the English. In 1806 when Admiral Popham, who had taken the Dutch territory of the Cape of Good Hope in January, wanted to attack Buenos Aires, the English had been repulsed by a Frenchman, Jacques de Liniers with the support of the population. But after the French intervention in Spain, the colonials organized themselves into *cabildos,* refused to recognize Joseph, called on London for help and shot Liniers. The English were already practically masters of Brazil where in 1808 a squadron had taken the Portuguese royal family who were fleeing Junot. In return British traders had been granted very advantageous customs rights. With Napoleon's involuntary complicity, Spanish America presented an equally extensive market. But the uprising which had been so imprudently instigated spread, between April and July 1810, to Caracas, Buenos Aires, Santa Fé da Bogota and Santiago in Chile. The impetus came from its energetic leaders: the Mexican, Hidalgo; the Venezuelan, Miranda, who had been a French Republican general in 1792; Bolivar, who was supposed to have attended Napoleon's coronation; San Martin, and many others.

So all Napoleon's Continental allies had lost their colonies. It is often forgotten that the consequences of the imperial adventure were world-wide, stretching from Java to Caracas; they even reached Australia with Baudin's expedition under the Consulate. The destiny of the world beyond Europe was changed as much as the destiny of old Europe.

8

THE FALL

It is with sorrow that I perceive the attitudes of mind of my compatriots in the great circumstances through which we are passing. A marked determination would be needed to re-establish the former dynasty, or at least a common interest to which all minds would be bent; but there is not a feeling nor an idea which might serve as a rallying point. The hatred inspired by a tyrannical and usurping government is felt more or less strongly by everyone, but still it gives way, with most people, to the self-interest necessary to preserve the tranquillity of the individual and his present existence under a regime which favours such conditions. Men are tired, new revolutions are feared, there is no enthusiasm for the preservation of rights nor for the return of Henry IV's descendants. There is such a lack of action that foreigners are blamed for not imposing, with their armed forces, the restoration in whose favour Frenchmen are prevented from speaking out by fear or other petty passions.

Rarely can the contradictory feelings of the notables at the time of the 1814 crisis have been so well expressed as by Maine de Biran in his *Journal Intime*.

Since 1808, the bourgeoisie had wanted to be rid of a saviour who had become not a little embarrassing, whilst withdrawing from the prospects of a change which might threaten their interests. Ingraditude was tempered with cowardice. Napoleon's defeats by the allies supplied the opportunity which had been awaited for six years. The notables themselves were not capable of overthrowing the Emperor. They needed outside help. Was the lost legitimacy of 1789 to be recovered with the King? Alas, it soon became apparent to the clear-sighted, such as Fiévée, that by accepting to tie the restoration to the invasion of France, Lous XVIII had perhaps made a mistake and compromised, in the long run, the chances of the Bourbons, whilst preparing for the short return in the near future of the man who had been able, in the eyes of the people, to oppose a united Europe.

THE MALET AFFAIR

General Malet's plot had revealed the fragility of the imperial government. During the night of 22-23 October 1812 the former general, who since his 1808 attempt had been interned at Vincennes and then in the clinic at Dubuisson, had gone with two accomplices, Boutreux and Rateau, to the Popincourt barracks. There, he had announced to the barely awakened Major Soulier that the Emperor was dead and a provisional government had been formed. He next went to the La Force prison to free two generals, Lahorie, Moreau's former chief of staff, and Guidal who had been compromised in a plot involving both Royalists and Republicans. On his orders, Lahorie proceeded to arrest Savary, the Minister of Police, and the Prefect of Police, Pasquier. Already the Prefect of the Seine, Frochot, was preparing a room in the Hôtel de Ville in which to welcome the new government. It would have all succeeded if Hullin, the commander of the Paris garrison, had not put up some resistance to Malet. The three generals and their main accomplices were tried on 28 October and shot on the 29th. In keeping with the official line, the extravagant nature of the plot was dwelt on for a long time. The fact remains that the famous Imperial Police had proved its incompetence by allowing its chiefs to be arrested so easily, and that the soldiers who had obeyed General Malet's orders in good faith did so with more enthusiasm than sorrow. Who was behind Malet? Talleyrand and Fouché. It is unlikely. The notables? Surely not. It seems that it concerned a reconciliation which had already been initiated in the south, in fact, between some Royalists (who at least were prudent), and a handful of unrepentant Republicans. Villèle explained this clearly in his *Mémoires*: 'The Royalists and the Republicans must have agreed to combine their efforts until the convocation of the first assemblies which, with Bonaparte toppled, would make a sovereign decision between the re-establishment of the Republic and the restoration of Louis XVIII.' Without the support of the notables the plan seemed somewhat unrealistic, but, as Fiévée remarked, 'If this movement had lasted a little longer, some wise men would have been found to direct those madmen.' Napoleon reacted to the disregard in which high-up officials and simple soldiers held the King of Rome by cancelling the orders by which Cambacérès presided over various councils in the master's absence, and, by a *senatus consultum* of February 1813 he made Marie-Louise regent and established an advisory council consisting of princes of the blood and grand dignitaries. The Legislative Body's session from 14 Febrary to 25 March 1813 was even less well attended than previous ones had been. When Napoleon left for Germany the internal situation was serious, from both an economic and a social point of view. Discontent was growing, riots against the *droits réunis* (taxes on alcohol, tobacco and salt) were breaking out in Cosnes and various other towns, but no serious political manifestation was noted. The bourgeoisie did not yet dare to speak out.

THE BREAK

On 14 November 1813 Napoleon returned to the Tuileries. For the second time he returned defeated. He planned to galvanize all energy and to stimulate public opinion by giving special lustre to the Legislative Body's session. The manoeuvre was obvious. It was essential to reconcile the notables. By the *senatus consultum* of 15 November 1813 the Emperor ordained that the Senate and the Council of State should, in a body, attend the sittings in the Chamber. But he spoiled this plan of enticement by intervening in the designation of the President of the Legislative Body. He nominated Régnier, who was not a deputy but a jaded Minister of Justice who was to be replaced by Molé; Caulaincourt was to replace Maret as Foreign Minister, and Daru was to supplant Lacuée in charge of war administration. In 1810 Lacuée had succeeded Dejean in this essential area of government.

For their part, the allies, who were preparing to invade French territory, were also launching a plan of enticement. On 4 December they published a manifesto: 'The allied powers do not make war on France but against the domination which, unfortunately for Europe and for France, the Emperor Napoleon has too long exercised beyond the limits of his Empire.' France's natural frontiers, the Rhine, the Alps and the Pyrenees were guaranteed. It was unhoped for, if not sincere. The notables were not deaf to the call.

It was, then, in an atmosphere of tension that the Legislative Body's session opened on 19 December 1813.

As evidence of his good faith with regard to the allied propositions, Napoleon offered to keep the senators and deputies informed of all documents concerning the current negotiations. The assemblies elected two commissions, one of five senators and one of five deputies, to study the negotiations. In the Senate everything went according to plan. The same could not be said of the Legislative Body. The chosen deputies came from departments which had suffered from the Blockade: Lainé was deputy for Bordeaux, Gallois for the Bouches-du-Rhône, Raynouard for the Var; the two others were also southerners: Flaugergues came from l'Aveyron and Maine de Biran from the Dordogne. They took the opportunity which presented itself of making known the discontent of the electorate. In his report, Lainé concluded that the enemy did not wish to destroy France, but 'to enclose us within the confines of our territory and to curb the impulse and the ambitious activities which for twenty years have been fatal to all the peoples of Europe.' The Emperor should not continue 'war except to defend the independence of the French people and their territorial integrity.' In order to stimulate national feeling he was asked to 'maintain the constant and total application of the laws which guarantee the liberty, safety and property of Frenchmen, and the free exercise of the nation's political rights.' This charter of the notables was adopted by 229 to 31 votes. The warning was clear, but Napoleon refused to listen. Despite Cambacérès' counsel of moderation, he forbade the printing of the report and adjourned the Legislative Body. Even Savary admitted that this caused a sensation throughout the country. The Emperor keenly reprimanded the deputies present at the sitting of 1 January 1814. He threatened to change sides on the social level, to ally himself to the 'fourth estate' and to awaken old revolutionary demons in France: 'What is the throne? Four pieces of gilded wood covered in a piece of velvet. The throne is in the nation and I cannot be separated from it without harming it, for the nation needs me more than I need the nation. What would she do without a guide and without a leader . . . Do you, then, wish to emulate the Constituent Assembly and start a revolution? But I will not be like the king who existed then . . . I would rather be part of the sovereign people than be an enslaved king . . . Go back to your departments!'

Did Napoleon mean to take up the cudgels of the Revolution? Did he want to revive the spirit of '93? He sent twenty-three senators or Councillors of State to precipitate conscription and to organize the National Guard who had been reconstituted by the decree of 26 December. In his diary Stendhal explains how he helped Saint-Vallier at Grenoble. In fact the operation had no heart. The twenty-three deputies and councillors were old, the youngest, Montesquiou and Pontécoulant were fifty, and the oldest was seventy-four. Some of them were even Royalists (Sémonville). Except for near the frontiers, the country was tired of war.

Conscription had been moderate until 1808. Between 1798 and 1807, 985,000 men had been levied, which meant a thirty-sixth part of the population. Exemptions and replacements had been numerous. But from September 1808 the demand for men had become more and more pressing. A 'lucky number' or the buying of a replacement was no safeguard for the future. In April 1809 the Emperor asked the Senate for 30,000 more men from the 1810 intake and for further levies on the classes of 1806, 1807, 1808 and 1809. A further intake of 36,000 men was then requested. Agricole Perdiguier in his *Mémoires d'un compagnon* recounted how his older brother, having been replaced by a porter from Avignon, still had to leave for Spain. After the lull of 1810 and 1811, the call-up, scheduled for 1 January 1813, was advanced to 1812. In 1813 after the levy, 350,000 more men were called up, 100,000 of whom were conscripts of 1809, 1810, 1811 and 1812. There was a new call during the month of April, 180,000 men were put at the disposition of the War Ministry. On 24 August, because of the turn of events in Spain, the Emperor levied 30,000 men in the southern departments from the classes of 1814, 1813, 1812 and previous years. In October 1813, 160,000 men were raised from the 1815 class, but married men were exempted. There was a further demand in November, since Napoleon wanted no more levies among allies. 'We have reached a time when we must not count on foreigners.'

So the legend of the 'Ogre' was born. Resistance to conscription became organized. According to Stanislas de Girardin, Prefect of the Seine-Inférieure, in recruitment centres young men were to be found,

who have had their teeth pulled out in order to avoid serving. Others have managed to make them almost all decay by the use of acids, or by chewing incense. Some have produced sores on their arms and legs by blistering themselves, and to make these sores, so to speak, incurable, they dressed them with water and arsenic. Many have given themselves hernias and some apply violent acids to their genitals.

Groups of deserters scoured the countryside, creating a climate of insecurity. This resistance even took a political turn in the north, under the direction of Fruchard. The deserters profited from the encouragement of priests and the complicity of the inhabitants, who hid them and fed them.

The time was past when Agricole Perdiguier's father admonished his elder son for deserting and sent him back to the army. The prefects themselves, a La Tour du Pin in the Somme and a Barante in the Loire, kept deserters informed of the movements of search parties. In February 1814, 1,028 deserters were counted out of 1,600 men called up.

The burden of taxation, which had long been bearable, was growing heavier all the time; on the other hand officials' salaries were decreased by twenty-five per cent. Confronted by the financial collapse which accompanied his defeats, Napoleon had had to resort to expedients. The hatred aroused by the reintroduction of the *droits réunis* was only increased by requisitions and an additional thirty *centimes* on general taxation. In 1814 the *patente* was doubled as were other duties, but already no one was paying them.

Finally, French territory was invaded for the first time since 1792 and, all at once, France discovered the horrors of war; she had only known of its glories from the Grande Armée bulletins.

Everyone was affected: the economy appeared to be profoundly shaken by the loss of foreign markets and of the manufactories situated on the frontiers—at Liège, for example. The collapse of stock bore witness to a total crisis of confidence. 'Opinion is formed by trade movements,' the Prefect of the Rhin-et-Moselle admitted. The bourgeoisie's dreams of economic hegemony collapsed. England's technical and commercial superiority could no longer be contested. The Continental victories had served no purpose, and so the continuation of war seemed useless. Furthermore its continuation brought with it a state control which, however mild, still seemed unbearable. The notables were badly hit by the *senatus consultum*, of 3 April 1813, ordering the raising of 100,000 guards of honour chosen from among the sons of the rich and noble families of the Empire, who were to arm and equip themselves at their own expense. Those with good reasons for avoiding service were compelled to pay a heavy tax. Some fought courageously under Pully, Lepic or Defrance; but others, in Tours, for instance, went so far as to envisage an uprising. The unrest spread to the cadres of the army who were annoyed by the sudden promotion of newly rallied noblemen. An old Republican, General Michaud, unburdened himself in a family letter in 1813: 'Services rendered count for so little that I believe one dares unwillingly to claim they should be valued. I would be less distressed if I only thought I were forgotten.'

Could the few measures taken by the government help it to regain its popularity? The putting up for sale of some common land aimed not only at providing the state with some income but also at satisfying the peasants' hunger for land. It was a failure since the disastrous economic situation left the peasants with no money to spend. Commercial licences were multiplied, but too late to avoid several echoing bankruptcies.

Except in the north of France, and, apart from a few personalities like Carnot at Antwerp, Davout at Hamburg and Lecomb at Belfort, the invading armies encountered nothing but inertia, and even acquiescence.

Once again, and in a situation comparable to that of Louis XIV at the end of his reign, the Emperor was aware of his lack of legitimacy. The nobility, who had formerly rallied to him, abandoned him for the true sovereign. Little by little, the notables who looked back to the 1791 Constitution went over to this camp. Despite a few patriotic reactions in invaded areas, the people demonstrated their apathy, if not their hostility towards the Emperor. Napoleon had to conquer or perish. It is in this context that the campaign of France has a moving aspect.

THE CAMPAIGN OF FRANCE

Three allied armies crossed the Rhine at the end of 1813. Bernadotte immediately marched on Belgium; Blücher and Schwarzenberg (this last army with the Tsar of Russia, the Emperor of Austria and the King of Prussia) marched on Paris after having come together on the Aube. Napoleon could barely oppose two hundred and fifty thousand men with eighty thousand conscripts. He left Soult to check Wellington's advance in the south, in order to deal with more urgent matters. How good was Napoleon's army? The clothing workshops in Bordeaux, Toulouse, Nîmes and Montpellier had supplied an insufficient quantity of greatcoats; there were only nine hundred saddles where five thousand were needed; rations of bread, meat and spirits were mediocre, military hospitals were soon overcrowded. Napoleon confided to Mollien on 7 January, 'I am rather worried about the soldiers' pay.' Finally, armaments left a lot to be desired despite the production of two hundred and forty thousand guns in 1813.

Luckily for Napoleon, Blücher and Schwarzenberg made the mistake of separating in order better to live off the country. Blücher took the Marne and Petit Morin route, Schwarzenberg went by the Aube and the Seine. This presented Napoleon with an easier prey. He went from one to the other and managed to stop Blücher at Champaubert on 10 February and then to strike him some heavy blows at Montmirail, Château-Thierry and Vauchamps. He then turned back on Schwarzenberg who was threatening Fontainebleau, beat him at Montereau on 18 February and pushed him back beyond the Aube. With seven victorious battles in eight days, and the thoroughly demoralized, even divided, allies withdrawn, was victory about to smile on Napoleon? The Tsar with the help of Bonaparte's old Corsican rival, Pozzo di Borgo, then inspired the allies with a new spirit, and strengthened their ties by the Treaty of Chaumont on 1 March. Prussia, Austria, England and Russia undertook not to conclude an independent peace and to keep a hundred and fifty thousand men armed until Napoleon was finally defeated.

The offensive began again. Beaten at Craonne on 7 March, Blücher entrenched himself on the Laon plateau from where Napoleon could not dislodge him. Furthermore the Emperor had to prove himself equal to Schwarzenberg who had started to advance again. But with inferior numbers, Napoleon could not contain the Austrian at Arcis-sur-Aube on 20 March. He then conceived the plan of cutting off the allies' supply lines by marching on Saint-Dizier instead of continuing to defend Paris. The allies were about to fall into the trap and began to retreat towards Metz, when some letters sent to Napoleon from Paris were intercepted. They mentioned a strong Royalist party in the capital. Alexander, on the advice of Pozzo di Borgo, commanded the continuation of the march on Paris. Napoleon's plan, which was too daring, had failed.

On 29 March, the allies reached the outside of the city. On the 30th the battle began. From the 28th the former King of Spain, Joseph, had advised the regency council to leave the capital in accordance with some instructions which the Emperor had sent him from Nogent at the beginning of February. The following day, the Empress and the King of Rome left Paris. Only the Prefect of the Seine, Chabrol, remained, with Pasquier, the Prefect of Police—and Talleyrand who, by trickery, had avoided joining the regency at Blois and found himself thus with a clear field.

Paris did not resist. It was demoralized, lacking in fortifications, and, with the exception of the working-class suburbs, it had become very hostile to Napoleon and feared it might suffer the same fate as Moscow. The National Guard with Marmont's and Mortier's two corps went into some action, for honour's sake, on the Belleville and Charonne heights and at the Clichy gate where Moncey was in command. But the enemy's numerical superiority was too great. The city capitulated on the evening of the 30th. The allied troops, preceded by the Tsar and the King of Prussia, entered Paris on the 31st. Lyons had fallen without much resistance on 21 March. Since 12 March Bordeaux, by the instigation of the Mayor, Lynch, was flying the white flag and the Comte d'Artois was at Nancy. Rochechouart had tried to swing Troyes over to the Royalist cause. Soult was retreating on Toulouse, unsure of the feelings of the inhabitants who were being worked upon by the Chevaliers de la Foi. Royalist agents, especially Semallé, Vitrolles and Gain-Montagnac became increasingly active. This was somewhat dangerous as there was nothing to prove that the allies would not finally reach an agreement with the 'Tyrant'. The decisive hand would be played in Paris. Gain-Montagnac confirmed it: 'If Paris declares itself for the King, the provinces will follow suit. They are well enough prepared to follow the impulse of the capital, although not sufficiently to give the impulse.' And Schwarzenberg: 'In the present circumstances it is for the city of Paris to hasten the peace of the world . . . Let her declare herself, and from that moment the army which is outside her walls will support her decisions. Parisians, you know the situation of your country, the conduct of Bordeaux . . . in that example you will find an end to war.'

THE ABDICATION

Talleyrand had clearly understood that the hand would be played out in Paris. He could count on Pasquier, the Prefect of Police, and on a majority of the senators.

As soon as the allies entered Paris, Royalist demonstrations took place. Canler claims that the police was not against them, but his evidence is suspect. Talleyrand was counting on the Senate. In reality the fatal blow to the imperial regime came from the General Council of the Seine, an assembly despised by Napoleon who drew up the budgets for Paris without heeding its advice. The Council had its revenge. On 1 April one of its members, the lawyer Bellart, had a proclamation voted by thirteen out of fourteen voters and out of a real strength of twenty-one councillors. This proclamation was widely broadcast on the 2nd, and read;

Citizens of Paris! Your magistrates would be traitors to you and to the country, if, for vile personal reasons, they continued to stifle the voice of their conscience. Their conscience cries out that you owe all the ills which overwhelm you to one man alone. He it is who, each year, by conscription, decimates our families. He it is who has overburdened us with more than fifteen hundred millions of taxes in place of the four hundred million which France paid for freedom, happiness and tranquillity under our good former kings; and he threatens to increase this taxation. He it is who has closed the seas of the two worlds to us, who has dried up all the sources of our national industry, snatched labourers from the fields and workers from the factories . . . Fearing the truth above all else, has he not, outrageously and in the face of Europe, dismissed our legislators because for once they were tempted to tell him with as much tact as dignity . . .

As a result of these considerations the Council declared that it 'formally renounced all obedience to Napoleon Bonaparte; and expressed most ardently the wish that the monarchical government be re-established in the person of Louis XVIII and of his legitimate heirs'. M. Fleury has quite rightly remarked that it was the bourgeois in the Council (Lebeau, Bellart, Barthélemy, Delaitre) who led the fight and not the former aristocracy. Talleyrand judged the attempt to be premature and forbade all publicity in *Le Moniteur*. He hoped for the fall but wanted it to happen with solemnity. On 1 April he had had the Senate vote the formation of a provisional government by two agents of Louis XVIII, Dalberg and the Abbé de Montesquiou and by two of his own partisans, Jaucourt and Beurnonville. Talleyrand assumed the presidency. On 3 April the Senate took the decisive step and announced the fall of Napoleon, who was guilty 'of having violated his oath and threatened the rights of the people by levying men and taxes contrary to the constitutions'. So the bourgeoisie intimated its dismissal to the 'saviour'.

And what about Napoleon? He had hastened back after the failure of his manoeuvre and had reached the inn, La Cour-de-France, at Juvisy, two hours away from Paris, when he learnt of the fall of the capital. He withdrew to Fontainebleau. Nothing was yet lost. After all he had sixty thousand men at his disposal, some of whom cried: 'To Paris!' when he reviewed them on the 3rd. He could hope that, in the last resort, Austria might intervene on his side out of regard for Marie-Louise. By refusing to continue fighting, Marshals Ney, Berthier and Lefebvre were responsible for his giving in. Pressure from them, particularly Ney, persuaded the Emperor to abdicate in favour of the King of Rome on 4 April. This abdication has been too often called a 'Brumaire the wrong way round'. Caulaincourt, Ney and Macdonald left for Paris to negotiate with the Tsar. Alexander hesitated, he feared a renewal of fighting. Perhaps he would have accepted a regency in the King of Rome's favour, if the announcement of the retreat of General Souham's corps, for which Marmont has been blamed, had not led him to think, quite rightly where the leaders were concerned, that the army was far from being unanimously behind Napoleon. He insisted on an outright abdication and guaranteed the conquered man the sovereignty of the island of Elba. On the 6th Napoleon resigned himself to this abdication. But on the 7th, when the soldiers acclaimed him on parade, he was tempted to go back on his decision; again, on the 11th, he wrote to Caulaincourt telling him not to use the signed act. Suicidal tendencies were then re-awakened in him. According to Caulaincourt he made one attempt on the 8th and another during the night of the 12th–13th. The Treaty of Fontainebleau was signed assuring him of the possession of the island of Elba and of a pension of two million francs per year from the French government, so on 20 April Napoleon resigned himself to leaving after the famous good-bye scene in the courtyard of the Château de Fontainebleau.

LOUIS XVIII

On 6 April the Senate had summoned Louis XVIII. No one wanted a new 'saviour' in the person of Bernadotte; a regency by Marie-Louise would have allowed Napoleon, indirectly to settle accounts with those who had abandoned him; the Duc d'Orleans was not the real pretender and only Louis XVIII had legitimacy on his side. But the senators intended to go back only as far as 1791, and not to 1789. Certainly the monarchy would be re-established, but it would be a constitutional monarchy. A commission of senators was entrusted with the drawing up of a plan. Barbé-Marbois, Destutt de Tracy, Emmery and Lambrechts were part of it with the former Consul, Lebrun. Reference to 1791 was explicit in the new constitution which was presented to the provisional government. Louis XVIII was 'freely called to the throne' and the text of the constitution was submitted to the 'approval of the people'; ministers would be responsible to the chambers and liberties were guaranteed. This constitution, which was not altogether devoid of merit, founded an English-style parliament. But could Louis XVIII accept these conditions in the name of legitimacy, especially since the senators—Thermidorians who had supported themselves in 1795 by the Decree of the Two Thirds and then after Brumaire by filling the Consulate assemblies—announced that they would all be part of the new Senate provided for in their plan. Those who had profited from the Revolution and the imperial regime refused to stand back. They were already discredited by the proclamation of Napoleon's fall in which they had heaped the Emperor with accusations of abuses of power, all of which abuses they had approved in the days of absolute imperial power, and now they finally destroyed their credit and that of the constitution in the eyes of the public. It was easier for the supporters of legitimacy, the Barruels, the Maistres and the Bonalds, to attack the constitutional plan with violence. Barruel even saw it as 'an invention of hell'.

What would Louis XVIII do? He reached Compiègne on 29 April and announced his plans on 2 May by the declaration of Saint-Cloud, which was drawn up by his principal advisers, among them Blacas. The declaration announced the sovereignty of the King and not of the people, a new constitution would be drawn up in which fundamental liberties and national representation would be guaranteed, as well as the voting of taxes and equality under the law. It was a refusal of all forms of absolutism but it denied the sovereignty of the people which was incompatible with the idea of legitimacy. This resulted in the Charter of 4 June, which was the work of fervent Royalists like Dambray, Ferrand and Montesquiou, and of Thermidorians modelled on Boissy d'Anglas who, with Lanjuinais, was one of the architects of the 1795 Constitution.

It was a charter and not a constitution, dated in the nineteenth year of Louis XVIII's reign (starting from the death of Louis XVII in the Temple) and granted by the King. These causes of irritation to the liberals weighed little compared with the concessions. The Charter guaranteed that everybody should be freely admitted to all employment, freedom of the conscience was guaranteed, equality in taxation, and the sale of national property—in short all the victories of the Constituent Assembly. In order to reassure the *rentiers,* it recognized all the financial agreements of preceding governments. Executive power was given to the King, and legislative power to two chambers—the Chamber of Deputies, elected for five years by a suffrage based on property qualifications, and which the King had the right to dissolve; and a chamber of peers of whom the sovereign could nominate an unlimited number.

All the specialists have drawn attention to the fact that the 1814 Charter was 'far more liberal' than the constitutions of Years VIII, X and XII, 'and more reasonably practical' than that of 1791. Would France regain the political equilibrium which she had lost in 1789? She could then have economized on several revolutions and new saviours. Unfortunately, with Napoleon overthrown, conditions for peace with Europe were being discussed. By the Treaty of Paris on 30 May, the 1792 French frontiers were restored; only Savoy, Avignon and Montbéliard remained of the revolutionary conquests. Belgium was annexed to Holland, Venetia and Lombardy were returned to Austria; as for the rest, their fate was to be decided at the Congress called to take place at Vienna. Numerous fortified towns in Germany, Italy and Belgium, notably Antwerp and Hamburg, were restored and considerably re-fortified. French pride was wounded. This surrender, consented to in fact by Talleyrand, represented 'the Bourbons' hand-out to the Allies', the loss of the conquests being the condition of the restoration of the monarchy. A parallel was established between Napoleon, the defender of an invaded France, and Louis XVIII, the sovereign 'brought back in the foreigners' wagon'. As a result the legitimacy suffered. The émigrés' blunders did the rest until finally Napoleon was missed. France had lost the chance to recover her political stability.

9

1815: THE LAST CHOICE

On the road to exile, behind the carriage taking Louis XVIII to Gand on 20 March 1815, rode Vigny and Lamartine; Géricault was not far away; Chateaubriand himself was somewhat delayed. The Royalists were unable to oppose the return of Napoleon. Legitimacy was leaving, followed by the Romantics of the morrow; the past and the future were thus united in an inglorious defeat, but one which would be of endless fascination to writers, from Chateaubriand to Louis Aragon or Anouilh.

The movement which was carrying Napoleon towards Paris was primarily a peasant and working-class one; the army was to rally to the Emperor later, and, in the case of the higher cadres, only partially. It was the awakening of the 'Fourth Estate' in Provence which facilitated Napoleon's march on the capital. Fear of the re-establishment of feudal rights in the countryside and fear of increased unemployment in the towns, more than all political intrigue, pushed the urban and rural proletariat towards the man who had already saved the Revolution and guaranteed its social conquests. The notables remained silent, they were relieved to see the disappearance of a monarchy which favoured too greatly the old aristocracy, but they were disturbed by the re-appearance of a man who symbolized a renewal of war with Europe.

Once again, as on his return from Egypt, Napoleon was confronted by a choice. If he excluded negotiations with Louis XVIII he could, still, ally himself with the bourgeoisie by making political concessions, and by putting himself forward as the protector of their interests in the face of foreign intervention. But, strengthened by popular support, he could also lead the Revolution along the path which had been inter-rupted by the fall of the *enragés* in 1794. Despite the country's lassitude and the break with the bourgeoisie in 1814, salvation must, after all, have lain in this last solution.

ELBA

The Treaty of Fontainebleau had granted Napoleon the sovereignty of the island of Elba which had formerly been united to France by the *senatus consultum* of 26 August 1802 and which, in 1809 had come under the general government of the Tuscan departments. In 1802, Lachevardière had published an interesting study of the economy of the island in the *Annales de Statistique;* in it he especially stressed the mineral riches (lead and iron) and the importance of the island's ports.

> The island's situation, between the south coast of the French Republic and the states of Naples and Sicily, makes the occupation of at least one of its ports very interesting from the point of view of French trade. Such an occupation could provide either a port of call or a depository for goods from the Two Sicilies and the East. Commerce has given a primitive and unconsidered people a very high degree of prosperity; under the auspices of a powerful government it could lend the island a hitherto unknown brilliance.

Such was the new domain of which Napoleon took possession on 4 May 1814. He immediately reorganized the administration which was under the authority of an Intendant (Balbi), a Governor (Drouot) and a Treasurer (Peyrusse). The customs, registration of births and deaths, and hospitals were reformed, fortifications were raised and vineyards planted. Napoleon undertook the building of a theatre. Considerable activity for a man in his full prime. Napoleon was not yet the failing and obese man of St Helena. It is true that he was the sovereign of Elba whereas on St Helena he was to be a mere prisoner.

Installed in the Mulini palace where he had summoned Madame Mère and Pauline to join him, he received numerous visitors, mostly English, whom he invited to his table. Apparently he had made up his mind to end his days on the island. In fact this attitude disguised a secret activity: after all he was constantly in touch with the mainland, thanks to the clandestine correspondence of his agents. He was fully aware of the state of France and of the discontent which resulted from Bourbon politics. The army was grumbling about redundancy, which a return to peace made inevitable, and was further aggravated by the rehabilitation and promotion reserved for Condé's officers. Peasants who had acquired national property were in some areas exposed to the hostility of the former landowners. There was a reawakening of the old Voltarian spirit among the bourgeoisie which resulted from an increasing number of public processions and religious ceremonies. Désiré Monnier recounted that 'One sees courtiers taking communion three times in a morning at different altars in the hope of being spotted by Madame la Dauphine.' English manufactured goods which, with the suppression of the Blockade, entered the country freely, finally reduced the workers to unemployment. Despite the efforts of Louis XVIII, the France of the white flag and that of the Tricolor were deeply opposed to each other. In his *Mémoire au Roi,* which met with great success, Carnot who had become popular as a result of his heroic defence of Antwerp, castigated Louis XVIII's entourage:

> If you wish to appear distinguished at court, be careful not to say that you are one of the twenty-five million citizens who defended their country courageously against the enemy invasion, for you will receive the reply that these would-be citizens were so many rebels and that the alleged enemies were always friends.

The Bonapartists took advantage of the discontent. Some generals (Exelmans, Lefebvre-Desnoettes) plotted with Fouché's support. A particularly violent satirical paper, *Le Nain Jaune,* dared to praise the fallen Emperor and relayed policies from the drawing-rooms of the Duke of Bassano and Queen Hortense. How then could Napoleon not be tempted to return to the mainland?

Other reasons also encouraged him. Marie-Louise and the King of Rome had not come to join him. The Empress was indulging a perfect love affair with Neipperg whom Metternich had pushed into her arms while Francis I kept his grandson near him. Money began to be short; Article 3 of the Treaty of Fontainebleau had provided Napoleon with an annual income of two million francs, but the Tuileries cabinet was turning a deaf ear. Disturbing rumours came from Vienna where Talleyrand and Castlereagh were planning the deportation of Napoleon to a more distant island—Santa Lucia was suggested. Failing that, the assassination of the Emperor was envisaged; a former Chouan was said to have been given command of Corsica with that in mind.

Around 12 February the former Sub-Prefect of Reims, Fleury de Chaboulon, managed to reach the island and revealed the Bonapartist intrigues and the feelings of the army towards Napoleon. This information determined the Emperor to hasten his departure.

On 26 February, after ten months of exile, Napoleon left Elba on board the *Inconstant*. He had only a handful of men at his disposal—seven hundred soldiers—with which to reconquer his Empire. Jomini has denounced the foolhardiness of such an undertaking and it is reasonable to wonder about the existence of an ambush laid by Austria and England to destroy Bonaparte and to rid Europe of him forever. The inactivity of the English, who were certainly informed of the Emperor's departure, was, in fact, disturbing, and Napoleon himself claimed at the time to have benefited from Austrian complicity. His adversaries really had no need of the Emperor's return to France as a pretext for sending him to another island. After all, it would have been a dreadful risk to take with a man like Napoleon. It is more logical to point to the gambling streak which Napoleon constantly revealed. It is clear that the fable of Austrian assistance was entirely invented by the Emperor in order to reassure public opinion. He was to confide in Davout in the secrecy of the Tuileries: 'I am going to open my heart to you and tell you everything. I have allowed people to think, and I must allow them to think that I am acting in collusion with my father-in-law, the Emperor of Austria. Everywhere it is announced that the Empress is on her way with the King of Rome, that she will arrive at any minute. That is not the truth, but I am alone against Europe. That is my situation.'

THE FLIGHT OF THE EAGLE

Throughout Napoleon's astounding career perhaps nothing was more prodigious than the march which led him in twenty days from Golf-Juan to Paris. He landed on 1 March, avoided the Rhône valley where he feared resistance from Royalists, marched into the Alps and, by mountainous paths, headed for Grenoble where the public had been prepared by the surgeon, Émery, and the glover, Dumoulin. From the boundaries of the Dauphiné the peasants' welcome was, on the whole, favourable. There remained the army's attitude. The meeting at Laffrey reassured Napoleon; the soldiers refused to fire on him. The rallying of La Bédoyère and the entry into Grenoble, where the inhabitants had broken down the gates to make way for the Emperor, transformed the march on Paris into a triumphal journey. In Grenoble two thousand peasants armed with burning torches shouted, 'Long live the Emperor!' On 10 March Napoleon entered Lyons where the silk-workers gave him an enthusiastic welcome.

Paris only learnt of Napoleon's landing on 5 March. Resistance measures by Soult who was Minister of War, provided for the regrouping of the forces from the Lyonnais, the Dauphiné and the Franche-Comté under the command of the Comte d'Artois assisted by his two sons and three marshals. An enactment outlawed Napoleon and called upon all soldiers to rush at him. The situation for Louis XVIII was not in any way desperate. he could count on the support of the national Guard, of the constituent bodies and of the Chambers. Seen from Paris, the feelings of the army seemed to favour the Bourbons. After all, Ney promised 'to bring back the usurper in an iron cage'. Masséna in Marseilles and Oudinot in Metz were announcing their Royalist sympathies and the stronghold of Antibes had resisted Napoleon's advance. Paris remained surprisingly clam. A police report of 7 March 1815 pointed out:

> One could judge how far we had come from Revolutionary days for, in the past, thousands of groups would have been formed, proposals and violent propositions would have been made on one side or the other. Today people met and questioned each other nervously; Bonaparte was accused of wanting to disturb our peace and to bring civil war and war abroad as a means of sacrificing France yet again, if he could, to his devouring ambition. But no one anticipated measures which the government judged useful.

Government stock fell, however, from 81 to 75 francs.

But the Comte d'Artois's plans for resistance collapsed with the defection of the troops. On 17 March Ney rejoined Napoleon at Auxerre. On the night of the 19th–20th, the King had to leave the Tuileries in order to take refuge in Gand. 'Louis XVIII claimed he would die in the middle of France. Had he kept his word, the legitimacy could last another century,' exclaimed Chateaubriand in the *Mémoires d'outre-tombe*. On 20 March, at nine o'clock in the evening, Napoleon entered the Tuileries over which flew the Tricolor.

THE LIBERAL EMPIRE

Henri Houssaye has successfully proved that the triumphal march of 1815 owed nothing to the plot prepared by a few muddle-headed Bonapartists (Exelmans, Drouet d'Erlon) who appear, rather, to have been disconcerted by the Emperor's sudden return.

The movement which brought Napoleon back to the Tuileries was the combined work of peasants, workers and the army, who were all discontented with the Bourbons. Fear of a return to the Ancien Régime, the workers' concern at the spreading of unemployment and the soldiers' cult for the Emperor served Napoleon better than the intrigues of, for instance, Maret or Lefebvre-Desnoëttes.

The misunderstanding was becoming evident. Napoleon thought that he would be brought back by notables disturbed by the infringement of the émigrés. Popular enthusiasm had been expected (the decrees of 21 March which abolished the nobility and feudal titles, expelled the émigrés from the land and ordered the sequestration of their property aimed at fostering this enthusiasm), but the Emperor was not counting on this alone. From Grenoble, the coldness of the authorities showed Napoleon he was mistaken: the bourgeoisie would have nothing to do with him. Apparently he nominated the same ministers (although they occasionally showed reticence): Decrès to the Admiralty, Gaudin to Finance, Mollien to the Treasury, Maret to the Secretariat of State, and even Fouché to the Police (the Duke of Otranto would have preferred Foreign Affairs), but Napoleon knew that France could no longer be governed as before. It was like a return to 1793. 'A backsliding of the Revolution,' a contemporary remarked with some exaggeration. 'Nothing has surprised me more on returning to France,' Napoleon confided in Molé, 'than this hatred of priests and the nobility which I find as universal and as violent as it was at the beginning of the Revolution. The Bourbons have restored their lost force to the ideas of the Revolution.

No doubt this blaze of revolutionary feeling was confined to certain regions, especially to the south-east of France, but it impressed Napoleon. It disgusted him. 'I do not want to be King of the *Jacquerie*," he said. Which was tantamount to refusing the Jacobin solution in 1799. However, the popular movement forced him into the arms of the liberals, his old adversaries, who had now become the lesser evil. Carnot was given the portfolio of the Interior in homage to the 'organizer of victory', and Benjamin Constant, after an interview at the Tuileries with the man whom he had compared only a few days earlier to Ghengis Khan and Attila, became a political adviser.

Designed to rally the liberal bourgeoisie, one of the decrees passed at Lyons had ordered that 'The electoral colleges meet at an extraordinary assembly at the Champ de Mai in order to modify our constitutions in the interest of the Nation.' Benjamin Constant may not have played so large a part in outlining the new constitutional plan as the *Mémoires sur les Cent Jours* claim. However he was probably responsible for the progress offered by the Additional Act in comparison with the Charter: the lowering of tax quotas, responsibility of ministers to the chambers (jurists from Joseph Barthélemy to Radiguet have discussed at length whether or not the Additional Act established a parliamentary regime), public debates, suppression of censorship, abolition of *juridictions d'exception,* and religious freedom. There were, however, two mistakes, one of which, the heredity of peers (which meant the preservation of the nobility) was due to Napoleon. In the eyes of the public this and the fact that the act was called 'Additional' to the constitutions of the Empire (which implied no change in the regime) compromised the liberal nature of the text. Numerous pamphlets hostile to the Act then appeared and the plebiscite was a failure; out of five million electors there were only 1,532,527 Yeses and 4,802 Noes. The mass of abstentions was particularly marked in the west and the south; only the north, the east and the south-east voted strongly Yes and, on the whole, the countryside was more favourable to the plan than the towns were.

The Parisians were disappointed in the Champ de Mai ceremony where the results were announced. Michelet, who was seventeen in 1815, later wrote:

> At the time I was full of *Athalie.* I cannot explain my amazement when I saw Bonaparte appear in a Roman emperor's robe, a white one. The innocent robe of the young Eliacin. It suited neither his age nor his dark skin, nor the circumstances, for he had not returned to give us peace.

By the middle of April popular enthusiasm had waned and the notables who were sceptical about the new regime were still sulking. Their spokesman, Fouché, summarized their feelings to Pasquier:

> This man—I mean Napoleon—has been cured of nothing and returns as much a despot, as eager for conquests, in fact as mad as ever . . . The whole of Europe will fall on him, it is impossible for him to hold out and all will be finished for him within four months. I ask nothing better than the return of the Bourbons, but things must be arranged rather less foolishly than they were by Talleyrand last year. Nobody must be at their mercy. There must be well determined conditions, and good and solid guarantees.

Despite the Duc de Bourbon's failure, the Royalist resistance was organized in the Vendée. The decision to reintroduce conscription there had had a disastrous effect. On 15 May rebellion broke out in the Vendée, under pressure from the old leaders, Suzannet, d'Autichamp and Louis de La Rochejaquelein. On the 22nd Napoleon was obliged to form the Army of the Loire under General Lamarque. The eight thousand men thus immobilized were to be severely missed at Waterloo. Some generals and marshals, Maison, for instance, had followed Louis XVIII.

The opposition of the liberals was added to that of the Royalists. The liberals filled the new Chamber of Representatives after the elections in which the number of abstentions was often over fifty per cent. Raynouard, the author of *Templiers,* was elected to the college of Brignoles by twenty-six votes to his opponent's ten. La Fayette reappeared as did many members of the Convention (Barère, Cambon, Drouet, Lanjuinais—although others, like Rochegude, had declined). Some familiar names featured (Defermon, Mouton-Duvernet, Arnault, Chaptal, Bonet de Treich, Bouvier-Dumolard), but many were unfamiliar. Manuel, who was to become the spokesman for the liberals, was one of the new faces. Although it had only been chosen by a handful of electors the Chamber envisaged for itself a more active role than Napoleon wished to allow it. The first skirmish occurred when the adversaries of the regime made Lanjuinais president. On 6 June they refused to swear an oath of obedience to the constitutions of the Empire. Fouché was discreetly manipulating the strings of the parliamentary opposition.

TOWARDS WAR

Napoleon's return was doomed to failure. Two dangers in fact threatened the regime. Despite the purge undertaken by Carnot, the administration was not totally reliable. (The purge was mainly of the prefectoral corps and successive governments were to make a habit of this practice.) In his diary, the famous architect, Fontaine, summarized the attitude of mind of many officials: 'It was impossible for us to reawaken the illusions of the dream which had just ended. Nothing could make us believe in a change of fortune, unheard-of in history. We were certain that it was all over, and yet we had to carry out the orders we were given.' Bondy who had succeeded Chabrol in Paris was uncertain, and what of Lameth in the Somme or d'Angoisse in the Haut-Rhin?

The passivity of the administration contrasted with the workers' eagerness. The idea of a federal association had developed spontaneously in the West, with a view to combatting the 'malevolence', which meant Royalism. 'Why shouldn't we do in 1815 what we did in

1792? Our position is the same,' the retired Lieutenant-Colonel Beaufort wrote to Napoleon. 'Let us, true Frenchmen, friends of the *patrie* unite.' 'Generally a federal spirit had arisen,' observed Thibaudeau, 'like at the beginning of our great Revolution.' It first became manifest at Nantes which being situated between the Vendée and Chouannerie had reason to fear civil war. Some young citizens of Nantes planned to make a pact uniting them to neighbouring towns. These Breton towns welcomed the idea with enthusiasm and sent deputies to Rennes. There, they drew up the federative pact. At first the Emperor's name was not mentioned; action was being taken for the defence of the country and for the maintenance of order. After a change of mind, the Emperor's name was added. The pact was signed by fifteen hundred deputies. It was denounced to the Emperor as a revolutionary attempt. When he had read it, he said: 'It is not good for me, but it is good for France.' Other provinces followed suit by forming a federation and putting themselves in contact with Brittany. But far from encouraging these federations, the government, with the exception of Carnot, seemed to fear them. Their zeal was allayed. *Le Moniteur* announced that the men in question were, by their birth and the standing of their families, eminently respectable, and although the government dared not forbid the federations, they were never used, but left to their own devices. They served, in fact, very little purpose. The movement reached Paris where the inhabitants of the suburbs of Saint-Antoine and Saint-Marcel, who had suffered from being unable to defend the capital in 1814, formed a federation. A great patriotic demonstration took place in front of the Emperor on 14 May. Twelve thousand workers and former soldiers filed past Napoleon. An orator evoked the threat of war. This would not be merely a war of national defence, its aim would be the liberation of all peoples from the yoke of oppression. 'It stank of the Republic,' noted a witness.

Careful to satisfy the bourgeoisie and the National Guard, Napoleon did not use the force which offered itself. He intended to remain the saviour of the only bourgeois revolution. The notables had abandoned him in 1814; he dared not, however, draw conclusions in 1815.

War seemed inevitable. As soon as the news of the Emperor's landing reached Vienna, in a Congress divided between France, Austria and England on the one hand and Russia and Prussia on the other, the coalition against Napoleon was re-formed. On 13 March the allies by a solemn declaration banned Napoleon from Europe. On the

25th they renewed the Treaty of Chaumont.

Napoleon attempted in vain to appease their anger, by affirming that he recognized the Treaty of Paris and by sending emissaries to the Tsar and the Emperor of Austria. The allied powers were determined to overthrow him once and for all. Napoleon had no illusions and by a decree of 22 March he ordered from the manufacturers two hundred and fifty thousand arms; another decree, on the 28th, recalled the non-commissioned officers who had left the army. By 30 April four armies and three observation corps were formed.

WATERLOO

Wellington was in Brussels with ninety thousand English, Hanoverians, Dutch and Belgians; Blücher was at Namur with a hundred and twenty thousand Prussians. Considerable strengths of Austrians and Russians were marching towards France. Napoleon's plan was to compensate for his inferior numbers by crushing Wellington and Blücher before the arrival of the allied reinforcements.

He entered Belgium with a hundred and twenty-five thousand men divided among the Guard, the cavalry and the five army corps under Drouet d'Erlon, Reille, Vandamme, Gérard and Lobau. Soult's position had been held in former campaigns by Berthier who had fallen or been pushed from a window of the Bamberg Palace in Bavaria on 1 June. Grouchy commanded the right wing, Ney the left wing; Napoleon in the centre had to provide the reinforcement for his lieutenants to strike the decisive blows.

The other troops had to be dispersed in the Vendée (Lamarque), on the Var (Brune), in the Alps (Suchet) and the Jura (Lecourbe) and at the frontiers of the Rhine (Rapp).

Napoleon crossed the Sambre at Charleroi on 15 June, as he moved into an angle formed by Wellington and Blücher. At Quatre-Bras, Ney, with the left wing and after some bitter attacks, forced the English to beat a retreat. At ligny, Napoleon, with Grouchy, forced Blücher back towards Liège but because Drouet d'Erlon, who had worn himself out with marches and countermarches between the two battlefields, failed to intervene at the right moment, the victory was not a decisive one. Napoleon then turned on Wellington. While Grouchy, with Vandamme's and Gérard's crops, was sent to pursue Blücher, the Emperor rejoined Ney and together the centre and left flank of the French army repaired to meet the English. They found Wellington on the evening of the 17th entrenched to the south of the village of

Waterloo, in front of the forest of Soignes on the Mont-Saint-Jean plateau, where the English were formed into squares and had occupied the farms of Papelotte, Hougoumont and la Haie-Sainte below. The French established themselves on the neighbouring plateau of la Belle-Alliance. The front was only four kilometres wide compared with the ten at Austerlitz. The exhaustion of the men, worn out by bad weather, mud and lack of supplies, prevented Napoleon from manoeuvring; this and the muddy ground forced him to put off the attack until midday on 18 June. It was this delay which destroyed Napoleon by allowing the Prussians who had escaped from Grouchy to appear on the battlefield and cause the French to be routed.

The first cannon shot exploded at around eleven-thirty. Napoleon's tactics consisted in destroying the English left flank in order to prevent a combination with the Prussians. But Drouet d'Erlon and Reille's attacks were strongly repelled. Napoleon then decided to attack the centre. Several times Kellermann's and Milhaud's charges nearly broke through the English squares, but the appearance of Bulow on the right at about two o'clock obliged Napoleon to send most of his reserve to that side, under the command of Lobau.

At all costs the English centre had to be forced. The Emperor launched his entire cavalry at the enemy, 'a sea of steel' with Ney at its head. But the cavalry were so densely massed on a front of only fifteen hundred metres that the English firing precision was faced with a target comparable to Drouet d'Erlon's corps earlier. 'With no decisive success they swirled among the English infantry squares.' Victory would have been ensured by the presence of the infantry but they were containing the Prussians and immobilized near Plancenoit. At about seven o'clock on the front which the cavalry had just charged, Napoleon attempted a last attack with five battalions of grenadiers and Chasseurs de la Garde. 'The Guard, supreme hope and supreme idea', was mown down in its turn by English fire, and obliged to retreat. At the same moment, a new Prussian corps under Zielten appeared to the extreme right towards Papelotte. The retreat of the Guard, combined with the sudden arrival of a new enemy just where Grouchy was expected, gave rise to a general panic from which the English profited to launch an offensive in their turn. The retreat was transformed into a rout which did not stop until it reached the frontier. Only the Old Guard remained unshaken, and covered the disordered surge back towards Charleroi. Grouchy, who had allowed Blücher to escape, managed, however, to bring his troops back across the frontier unharmed.

THE SECOND ABDICATION

When Napoleon reached Paris at dawn on the 21st he was fully aware that the Chamber of Deputies, which was mostly liberal, was preparing to remove him from power once again. The notables wanted to rid themselves of an embarrassing saviour. His brother Lucien, Davout and La Bédoyère urged him to adjourn the Chamber, to proclaim the country in danger and with the support of the population to try to hold out in front of Paris which was better fortified than in 1814. The people acclaimed him in front of the Elysée where he had taken refuge. He had only to make a gesture, but once again he refused to become 'Emperor of the rabble', and explained himself in a way which was unexpected from him. 'You see,' he is supposed to have declared to Benjamin Constant, whilst indicating the demonstrators who chanted his name, 'I have not heaped honour on them and gorged them with money. What do they owe me? I found them and I have left them poor. But they are enlightened by the instinct of need, the voice of the people speaks through them. If I want, within an hour, the actual Chamber will no longer exist. But a man's life is not worth that price. I did not come back from the Island of Elba for Paris to become a blood-bath.'

By spreading the most alarmist of rumours about an eventual dictatorship, Fouché pressed the deputies to summon Napoleon to abdicate. Aghast, the Chamber declared itself to be assembled in permanence. In this show of strength, it was the Emperor who gave way. Utterly depressed, Napoleon ended by abdicating in favour of his son in the early afternoon of the 22nd. A provisional commission of five members was nominated; it consisted of General Grenier, Carnot, Caulaincourt, Quinette and Fouché, who presided.

On 24 June Davout, who had been won round to Fouché's game, urged Napoleon to leave Paris. In fact the Duke of Otranto feared that a popular movement or a military *coup* would upset his plans. The Emperor gave in once more and left for Malmaison on the 25th. But Fouché, who was secretly working for the return of Louis XVIII, considered that Malmaison was too close to Paris. Napoleon should distance himself from the capital. On 3 July the city capitulated. On the 6th, the former regicide accompanied Talleyrand to Saint-Denis to see the King who had resigned himself to leaving Fouché in charge of the police. The scene has been immortalized by Chateaubriand in one of the best known pages of the *Mémoires d'outre tombe*:

Suddenly the door opened; and silently there entered vice leaning on the arm of crime, M. de Talleyrand supported by Fouché; the infernal vision passed slowly in front of me, went into the King's study and disappeared. Fouché was coming to swear faith and homage to his lord; the trusty regicide, kneeling, put the hands which had made Louis XVI's head roll in the hands of the martyr king's brother; the apostate bishop stood surety for the oath.

Those who had acquired national property could rest at ease, as could all those who had profited from the Revolution; the brief meeting at Saint-Denis between the King and Napoleon's two former ministers took the place of a coronation for Louis XVIII. On 8 July the King re-entered Paris: deprived of the notables' support, and refusing to depend on the people, the Napoleonic adventure had lasted only a hundred days. The Prefect of the Seine, Chabrol, happily counted them from the King's departure until his return.

10

THE LEGEND

The last act was to determine the destiny of the saviour: St Helena. The Restoration thought that it could cast a veil over the years 1789–1815, but Napoleon from the top of his rock was to take it upon himself not only to record them, but to claim them for his glory. The saviour of the well-to-do was transformed by Balzac and many others into 'the Napoleon of the people'.

THE TRAP
On 3 July 1815 Napoleon was at Rochefort where he awaited the promised safe-conduct passes at the maritime prefecture. Several plans were then considered. Major Baudin suggested Napoleon should force his way out, whereas Joseph proposed he should rejoin the army in the Gironde under Clauzel. On the orders of the provisional government, General Beker, who was accompanying Napoleon, put him on the frigate *Saale*, which was to take him to the Île d'Aix. On the 9th, when Napoleon was again on the *Saale*, the government commission declared that any officer who attempted to bring him back onto French territory was a traitor to his country. Napoleon became an outlaw. He returned to the Île d'Aix where efforts were made for him to escape. To America? The temptation was great. Encouraged by Maitland who commanded the British ship *Bellerophon* as part of Admiral Hotham's squadron which was crossing the Bay of Biscay from Quiberon to the mouth of the Gironde, Napoleon was persuaded to hand himself over to the English in order to escape from the French Royalists and Blücher. According to Las lases,

The Emperor gathered us together in a sort of council. We discussed every possibility. The English blockade could not be broken through. There were only two alternatives, either to return to land and engage in civil war or to accept Captain Maitland's conditions. We decided on the latter; once on board the *Bellerophon*, we thought we would already be on British soil. The English would at once be bound by the laws of hospitality . . . we would be, from that instant, subject to the civil law of their country.

Hence the famous letter: 'I come, like Themistocles, to sit at the hearth of the British people; I put myself under the protection of her laws.' Had Maitland deluded Napoleon in an attempt to capture the Emperor without fuss? Probably. On 15 July Napoleon embarked on the *Bellerophon*. The snare closed around him. But British public opinion had to be taken into account. Tremendous curiosity was aroused when the ship dropped anchor in Torbay. Maitland reported that they were surrounded by boats and that people hurried from all sides to see this extraordinary man. Napoleon appeared frequently on the bridge and the gangway and at the windows in the stern. The same curiosity was evident at Plymouth, it was a curiosity to which Napoleon lent himself with a good grace. He was trying to arouse a feeling of sympathy on his own behalf. His partisans, who were more numerous among liberals than might be expected, had, it appears, conceived a two-point plan: to obtain a writ of habeas corpus and to make the Emperor land. His freedom on English soil would have already been provisionally guaranteed in writing. The former judge from the West Indies, MacKenrot, accused Rear-Admiral Cochrane of failing in his duty by not having attacked Willaumez's squadron off Tortola; he demanded Napoleon be called as a witness. Thus a writ of *habeas corpus ad testificandum* was obtained, requiring Napoleon to appear before the court on 10 November. But the *Bellerophon* weighed anchor before the writ could be delivered to Lord Keith who commanded the squadron at Plymouth. In fact, on 31 July, Lord Keith had gone to the *Bellerophon* to inform the Emperor that he was to be deported to St Helena. Napoleon's fate was finally sealed. Had he become a planter in the United States or sipped tea with old English ladies, the legend which was to surround him would have been quite shattered. He had to be a martyr.

ST HELENA

Napoleon and his companions in exile were transferred to the

Northumberland which left Plymouth on 9 August 1815 and landed at St Helena on 17 October. The crossing was uneventful. Samuel Decimus, a sailor on the *Northumberland*, whose account was found in 1976, claimed that Napoleon and his entourage were good humoured throughout. Barely larger than Belle-Isle, St Helena, a bastion of black basalt, and all that remained of an extinguished volcano, was used as a watering place by the ships of the East India Company. The inhabitants were a mixture of all the races on earth: Europeans, Negroes, Hindus, Malayans and Chinese. It was ruled by an aristocracy made up of high officials from the Company and large landowners whose estates were still cultivated by slaves. Napoleon lodged for two months with the Balcombes at The Briars. These two months were a time of relaxation for him after the nervous exhaustion produced by the collapse of his power and the tiring journey on the Northumberland. On 10 December he moved to Longwood House.

'A house made to measure to serve as a gaol,' the present French Consul at St Helena notes. 'All together, at the front of the buildings, the Emperor's rooms were exposed to the view of the English and the French; around a muddy courtyard poky little rooms could serve as offices; set back a little are the main buildings which would house 'the family', not including the invisible but ever present English officer in supervision.'

Napoleon's entourage, in fact his last court, included General Bertrand, aide-de-camp to the Emperor since 1807, who took Duroc's place as Grand-Marshal of the Palace; General Montholon who had carried out diplomatic missions; General Gourgaud, first orderly officer, and a civilian, Las Cases who as a nobleman had rallied to the Empire by necessity rather than conviction. He had become Chamberlain and then *maître des requêtes* at the Council of State. His son had accompanied him to St Helena. There were two women, constantly vying with each other: the wives of Bertrand and Montholon. The domestic side at Longwood was attended to by the first valet, Marchand; the Mameluke from Saint-Denis known as Ali; Cipriani, whose role as butler masked his activities as an agent; the Swiss, Noverraz, and Santini, the man of all work and keeper of the purse.

We are very well informed about everyday life at Longwood since all Napoleon's companions in exile, including Marchand and Ali, left their memoirs.

In the stifling atmosphere of the island, Napoleon divided his time between walking within the area authorized by the English, dictating to his companions, and reading. At Longwood there was a library of two thousand books, whose titles are known. It was a dreary life made even more tedious by the foggy, rainy climate and by the tense atmosphere caused by the rivalry and touchiness of the members of the entourage. In addition there was the pestering of Hudson Lowe. He was governor of the island, a subordinate of mediocre intelligence, a prisoner to regulations, and he was, furthermore, quite distracted by too heavy a responsibility.

Little by little the prisoner's health declined. In 1817 he was violently shaken by dysentry and rheumatic pains. Sickness took a hold of him despite the efforts of the Irish doctor, O'Meara, who was expelled by the governor for complicity with the French. In 1819 there were increased bouts of giddiness. The naval doctor, Stokoe, who diagnosed hepatitis due to the climate, was sent back to England. He was replaced by the somewhat disturbing Antommarchi. Around July 1820 nausea and stomach pains occurred. Soon Napoleon could eat only soups and meat jelly. On 5 May, 'at forty-nine minutes past five,' Bertrand noted in his diary, 'the Emperor drew his last breath. In the three last minutes, he heaved three sighs. At the moment of crisis, there was a slight flicker of the pupils; an irregular movement from the mouth and chin to the brow; the same regularity as of a clock. That night the Emperor had pronounced the name of his son and then: '*at the head of the army.*' The evening before he had asked twice, 'What is my son called?' Marchand had replied, "Napoleon."'

FROM LEGEND TO MYTH

Now that he had gone from the world's stage which he had occupied for nearly twenty years, was the fallen Emperor destined to oblivion? He was too clever a propagandist not to be aware of the effect of absence on men's memories, and so was to launch his last battle from the rock of St Helena and to shape the image he hoped to leave to posterity.

Undoubtedly, the legend was not born on St Helena. It was forged during the first Italian campaign in the newspapers which were destined to raise the morale of the troops, but which taught France about Lodi and Rivoli. the Napoleonic legend blossomed with the official cult of the Emperor which the imperial catechism established— the feast of St Napoleon and endless thanksgivings. But it was after 1815 that its real nature developed.

New social conditions were a determining factor. Popular loyalty to Napoleon was undeniable under the Empire. The workers from the Parisian suburbs, at least some of them, were still ready to fight the invader in 1815. All the police reports underline their attachment to the Emperor. Among the peasants, Napoleon's prestige was equally great, although it was somewhat clouded over in the last years by the *droits réunis* and conscription.

This prestige was to grow endlessly after the fall of the Eagle. The industrial revolution, which had been slowed down by war during the Revolution and the Empire, upset the former structures as old artisans were laid off in favour of machines, cheap labour in the shape of women and children was employed, and a slump in salaries occurred on a labour market which was already overcrowded with demobilized men. The Empire, a time of full employment, high salaries, plentiful and cheap bread, became for all these outcasts a veritable golden age. Napoleon became, without difficulty, 'the father of the people'. The same reaction took place in the countryside where, at least until the law on the émigré millions was passed, the peasants trembled for the national property they had acquired under the Revolution. Furthermore Napoleon's glory was also the glory of that army of peasants who had conquered Europe. These old soldiers, condemned by their wounds to idleness, justified their social uselessness through the tales of war which they told their neighbours of an evening—Balzac has shown this clearly. They were the best protectors of the cult, the true authors of the legend as they relayed their tales, for the newsmongers were now forbidden and the new mayors were destroying the municipal collections of the Grande Armée bulletins.

Concern spread to the bourgeoisie. With its new privileges forever threatened by a return to the past, the bourgeoisie discovered, on a political level, that the legitimacy had been going a long time and that a return to stability was precarious. Undoubtedly Charles X succeeded without difficulty to Louis XVIII in 1824, but the sneers which accompanied the coronation showed that the monarchy had lost its old charisma. Béranger wrote:

> Charles s'étend sur la poussière
> Roi! crie un soldat, levez-vous!
> Non, dit l'évêque; et par saint Pierre,
> Je te couronne; enrichis-nous.
> Ce qui vient de Dieu vient des prêtres,
> Vive la légitimité![1]

[1] "Charles lies down in the dust. "King!" shouts a soldier, "get up!" "No," says the bishop; "and by St Peter, I crown you; make us rich. What comes from God comes from the priests. Long live the legitimacy!"'

Seventeen eighty-nine marked a definite turning point. A Republican and liberal opposition endlessly made points to the detriment of the throne. Napoleon's stroke of genius lay in using this opposition to his advantage, in his taking a hold of the rising forces which were shaking old Europe.

Curiosity about the outlaw was unending. In 1817, the *Manuscrit venude Sainte-Hélène d'une main inconnue* had a tremendous success until it was forbidden. These apocryphal memoirs of Napoleon were probably by a Genevan friend of Madame de Staël, Lullin de Chateauvieux. But they were eclipsed by Las Cases's publication in 1823 of the *Mémorial de Sainte-Hélène*. The *Mémorial* was probably the greatest bestseller of the nineteenth century. Between the first edition in 1823 and Charlet's illustrated edition in 1842 four more editions appeared with additions and corrections. Between 1815 and 1816, Las Cases had collected Napoleon's confidences—and what confidences they were!

Royalist pamphlets had depicted Napoleon as the inheritor of the Terror, and as Robespierre's disciple. Far from rejecting such an heritage, Napoleon accepted it: 'The Emperor,' Las Cases noted, 'said that despite all its horrors, the Revolution had nevertheless been the real cause of our moral regeneration.' The same man who had broken with the ideologues affirmed 'the irresistible ascendant of liberal ideas'. 'Nothing could destroy or wipe out the great principles of our Revolution,' he added. 'These great and beautiful truths must last for ever, we have so interwoven them with lustre, with monuments and with wonder . . .' Liberator of people, Napoleon would also be their unifier: 'The impulse has been given and I do not think that after my fall and the disappearance of my system, any great balance will be possible in Europe other than that provided by conglomeration and the confederation of great peoples.' The defence of revolutionary conquests and the unification of the peoples of Europe are the two essential causes of the long wars for which Napoleon has been blamed, but which were in fact desired by the absolute monarchs.

In 1816 these remarks, if indeed they were made, were addressed to the Whigs, the English liberals whom the prisoner hoped would improve his lot. The choice of spokesman was judicious. Napoleon knew that his confidant was taking notes and that this former émigré who had lived in London would be able to find the right words to sway British opinion. But such affirmations, which were probably altered by Las Cases and adapted to the political circumstances of 1823, were also aimed at international opinion. By these declarations, Napoleon laid claim to the two rising forces of the nineteenth century—the nationalism and the liberalism against which he had fought. As a prisoner of the Holy Alliance, the fallen sovereign could bury the anti-liberal Caesar in favour of a democratic Napoleon, the soldier of a Revolution which belonged no longer to the bourgeoisie alone, but which had encompassed the Fourth Estate.

The operation would have been difficult without the emotion which arose from the Emperor's martyrdom on St Helena. This miserable and lonely end on a rock lashed by the sea struck the imagination of the Romantics. A whole generation, the 'children of the century', brought up on the bulletins of the Grande Armée, found in the *Mémorial* the noise of battle of which it was deprived by the restored monarchy. Victor Hugo's father had served in Italy and Spain, Alexandre Dumas's in Egypt. Initially Royalist, Romanticism swung towards a poetic Bonapartism which provided the Napoleonic legend with the literary support without which its success could not have been so brilliant. Hugo and Balzac, Musset and Vigny with more subtlety, Dumas and Eugène Sue with less genius, all became poets of the Empire. At the same time, the world of employees was mourning the golden age of bureaucracy over which Napoleon had reigned. And the people remained convinced that it was their cause which Napoleon had espoused at Brumaire. Louis Geoffroy wrote a *Napoléon apocryphe* in which the Emperor, having conquered Russia and the East, became Master of the world. Returning to the Cape from Sydney he passed by St Helena but ordered Admiral Duperré not to put in there! Nerval was fired with enthusiasm but Flaubert remained indifferent.

The legend reached its height in 1840 at the time of the return of the ashes; it ensured Napoleon III's success. 'It is quite something,' grumbled Guizot, 'to be all at once a national glory, a revolutionary guarantee and a principle of authority.' Napoleon III's defeat at Sedan occasioned an eclipse of the legend and put an end to dreams of a Napoleonic dynasty. But the idea of the plebiscite and of appealing to the people survived as the only way in which to reconcile democracy and the strong power of a saviour. France was awaiting this saviour in order to have her revenge on Prussia and to reconquer Alsace-Lorraine; her hope was inspired by Jena, she thought she had found another Bonaparte in Boulanger, and in 1900 Edmond Rostand wrote *L'Aiglon*, a prelude to the warlike assaults of 1914 whose authors had been nurtured on Daudet's *La dernière classe* and Marbot's *Mémoires*.

Napoleon was popular again. From Job to Detaille, from Sardou to Esparbès, he inspired soldiers, painters and writers. It was a new conquest. A literary and artistic Brumaire. Gone were the reservations of old republicans, readers of Quinet and Lanfrey; voiceless were the supporters of the old legitimacy who believed in Taine and his *Régime moderne* in which Napoleon was painted as a soldier of fortune. Never were more books, or more engravings derivative of Charlet and Raffet, devoted to the saviour, than between 1885 and 1914.

Napoleon had, in fact, like Tristan or Don Juan, taken on a new dimension. The legend had become a myth. Napoleon's universality meant that he could inspire Dostoevsky ('Yes, I wanted to become Napoleon. That is why I have killed,' declares Raskolnikov) and Tolstoy (*War and Peace* is dominated by Napoleon), Nietzsche in *Die fröhliche Wissenschaft* and Thomas Hardy in *The Dynasts*. Kipling composed *A Saint Helena Lullaby* and Emerson has Napoleon appear in *Representative Men*. Conan Doyle abandoned Sherlock Holmes for *The Great Shadow*. Nor did the world of music remain indifferent. Beethoven removed his dedication to Napoleon from his Third Symphony, but Berlioz composed a cantata in 1835 on *Le Cinq Mai*; in 1943 Schoenberg was to write an *Ode to Napoleon* in which Napoleon was to be likened to Hitler, but to Robert Schumann we owe *The Two Grenadiers* after Heine; Tchaikovsky branded 1812 with his *1812 Overture*, but Prokofiev is less definite in his opera *War and Peace*. More films have been made about Napoleon than about Joan of Arc, Abraham Lincoln and Lenin combined. He has been the subject or the target of each and every nationalism: Austrian (*The Young Médard* by Curtiz), German (Grune's *Waterloo* and Wenzler's *The Hundred Days* around 1930), English (*The Iron Duke* or *Lady Hamilton*), Nazi (*Kolberg* made in 1944 by Harlan on instructions from Goebbels), Stalinist (*Kutuzov* in 1943), Polish (Vajda's *Ashes* in 1968) and of course, French with Gance and Guitry. Neither has he been overlooked by Hollywood directors (Ford, Walsh, Vidor, Sidney and Mann). He has been used in the 'detente' (*Waterloo*, shot in Russia in 1970 by a Russian, Bondartchouk, for an Italian director with Orson Welles as Louis XVIII) and in pornography (*L'Auberge des plaisirs*, on the Emperor's alleged impotence).

Chaplin thought of interpreting Napoleon as a character who had become a myth of the cinema, like Arsène Lupin, Garbo (who played Marie Walewska), Mickey Mouse or Laurel and Hardy. Caran d'Ache used him in his comic strip at the *Pieds Nickelés*, and he even features in science fiction (*Le voyageur imprudent*). No art form, has remained indifferent to the man of whom Balzac wrote 'he could do everything because he wanted everything'.

The myth is inexhaustible, then, and open to every interpretation; (for Marx, the destroyer of feudalism; for Freud, the frustrated younger brother) it is one which other myths enhance: myths of women (the frivolous Josephine, the faithless Marie-Louise and the touching Marie Walewska); of Talleyrand, the prince of diplomats and Fouché the inventor of the modern police; of soldiers on half pay, of the Bugeauds, Bros, Fabviers, Pougets and others like Parquin, dedicated to boredom or to plotting; the King of Rome coughing up blood like Marguerite Gautier (*La Dame aux Camélias*); and finally the Revolution. Through the *Mémorial*, the fall of the Bastille and the victory at Austerlitz became part of the same historical movement.

CONCLUSION

Faced with internal or external threats to its interests, the French bourgeoisie has always been able to invent a saviour. Napoleon opened the way for Cavaignac, Louis-Napoleon Bonaparte, Thiers, Pétain and de Gaulle. And because the bourgeois's principal virtue is ingratitude and its major defect lack of courage, the separation of the saviour from his inventors has more often than not come about through a national catastrophe. Usually the saviour bears the responsibility for this catastrophe. After a few years a suicidal tendency can be discerned in him, a tendency which was present even in de Gaulle, according to Malraux. Is he weary of power or disgusted by his role? The saviour appears out of tragic circumstances (a *coup,* a revolution or a national defeat), he disappears in an apocalyptic atmosphere. Another saviour will take his place and the wheels will start rolling again. In all this can be seen the consequences of the disappearance of the principle of legitimacy on which the old monarchy was based before 1789.

Napoleon is the archetype for these saviours who are landmarks in the history of nineteenth- and twentieth-century France.

The middle bourgeoisie, the well-to-do peasants and a few businessmen were those who profited most from the Revolution. Thanks to the money at their disposal in 1789, many of them were able to buy national property and build up large landed fortunes at a time when stock was collapsing, and then, through loans, they had been able to gain the goodwill of the peasants whose land was divided up. The only way in which the Revolution could be brought to a close was through an alliance of the bourgeoisie and the peasantry around one man or one principle. The man was found: Bonaparte. The principle was already known: property. It behoved Bonaparte to maintain the advantages already acquired, by fixing a point of no return to the past and by restraining the forward march of the Revolution. For, as has often been pointed out, the effect of the Revolution on the bourgeoisie and the peasants was to make the poor poorer and the rich richer. The Fourth Estate, the rural and urban proletariat had to be contained. The *enragés,* more than Babeuf, who was too theoretical and too muddled in his actions, was already to question again the principle of property which had just been declared 'sacred'.

Bonaparte found the answer: a war taking place abroad absorbed energy and channelled it towards the battlefield. A shortage of soldiers favoured the raising of salaries: Paris was won over with little difficulty and the price of bread was held at a reasonable level. In short, those of the people who had avoided the horrors of Eylau or Beresina had the impression of a new golden age.

The bourgeoisie could consider itself satisfied: war spared its sons, thanks to the system of replacements, and it cost nothing because the victor levied enormous indemnities from conquered lands. In fact, war enabled the bourgeoisie to cultivate, at little cost, its chauvinism (the word came into being at that time) by reading the bulletins of the Grande Armée.

But war had its limits: the natural frontiers of France. By his endless conquests in Italy and Germany, Napoleon must have been building up resentment in Europe. France must finally succumb to a general coalition of her enemies. And would she not then lose the advantages acquired by the Revolution? After the victories, Talleyrand preached moderation. Napoleon replied by calling on the necessity for vast industrial outlets. The manufacturers, who were clearer-sighted, pointed out that production was not high enough to supply, single-handed, the whole of Europe: the Russian market, for instance, was too big for France to be able to supplant England completely. Furthermore, the Continental Blockade, the basis of Napoleon's foreign policy, was ruining the French ports.

The break between Napoleon and the Brumairians—those who had created Brumaire and those who had ratified it by the plebiscite which followed—can be dated precisely: 1808, with the Spanish affair. The Revolutionaries were somewhat shocked when the first crowns were distributed among the Bonaparte family in 1806. But was this not a continuation of the system of sister-republics which was so dear to the Directory? The more intelligent realized that the creation of a new nobility could not benefit them for long; the marriage of Napoleon and

Marie-Louise confirmed their fears of a return to the pst. Meanwhile the war in Spain ceased to be profitable for the first time; lightning war had seen its day. D'Ivernois showed that the army's entrenchment in the Iberian peninsula threatened to ruin France little by little. To what end? The notables never believed in the Napoleonic dynasty, the Malet affair was evidence of this. The coronation was no more than a ceremony designed to regularize the new regime in the eyes of Europe's monarchs. At its deepest level the founding of the Empire signified a dictatorship of public safety in favour of the well-to-do who had profited from the Revolution. For forgetting this and for imagining that he could establish a new dynasty destined to rule Europe, the saviour was condemned to writing his *Mémoires*. St Helena heralded Chislehurst, the Île d'Yeu and Colombey.

With the eclipse of Lesueur's *Les Bardes,* and Napoleon's favourite opera proscribed, Rossini thought he could revive the musical refinements of the eighteenth century and reawaken Mozart. Unfortunately monarchies were henceforth to be constitutional; dynasties had no future. In 1830 the composer of *William Tell* understood this and said no more. Meyerbeer and Offenbach were to hold sway. Other Sarastros appeared but the music of the *Flute* had lost its magic. The first saviour was also the greatest; those that followed were mere parodies.

NOTES

INTRODUCTION

Sources

The debates are in *Le Moniteur* and in Buchez and Roux, *Histoire Parlementaire de la Révolution française*, Vol. XXXVIII (1838). To be consulted with interest are the reports of the Central Bureau published by Aulard in *Paris sous la Convention thermidorienne et le Directoire*, Vol. V (1902; nothing would have suggested a *coup d'état* to anyone trusting these reports). The reports of the military headquarters, as yet unpublished, are disappointing. The newspapers of the time are interesting (*Gazette nationale, Le Journal de Paris*). The *Mémoires* are an important mine of information, though often unreliable, it is true. Written at the time of the event, *Dix-huit Brumaire* by Lombard de Langres, can be discounted, so can the works of Cornet (*Notice historique sur le 18 Brumaire*, 1819: 'this day was a day of dupes in so far as power passed into hands which had not been sufficiently feared'), Gallais (*Histoire du 18 Brumaire*, 1814; pamphlet) or the anonymous *Notice sur le 18 Brumaire par un témoin* (1824). On the other hand, the reminiscences of Bigonnet (1819), Gohier (1824), Bourrienne (1829), despite his prejudice, Barère (1844), Marmont (1857), Lucien Bonaparte (ed. Iung, 1822), Barras (1895), Jourdan (in *Carnet historique et littéraire*, 1901), Lavalette (1905), Thiébault (1908) supply some useful information. The memoires of Fouché and of Talleyrand are very suspect, Lecouteulx's reminiscences are too short.

Works

L'Avenèment de Bonaparte by A. Vandal has remained a classic (1902–1907). It should be complemented by the later studies of A. Espitalier, *Vers Brumaire* (1914); J. Bainville, *Le Dix-huit Brumaire* (1925; shows that 18 Brumaire was a revolutionary day like any other); A. Meynier, *Les Coups d'État du Directoire*, Vol. III (1928); G. Bord and L. Bigard, *La Maison du 18 Brumaire* (1930; amounts to a political history of the Directory); Bessand-Massenet, *Le 18 Brumaire* (1965; excellent iconography); Goodspeed, *Bayonets at Saint-Clond* (New York, 1965); J. Tulard, *Le 18 Brumaire*

(*Douze moments clés de l'histoire de France*, 1973, pp. 151–73). Points of detail, like the legend of the daggers, are dealt with by Aulard in *Études et leçons*, Vols. II, III and VII.

Open Questions

Did the situation in which the Directory found itself make a *coup* necessary? All the Brumaire historians think so. There was no other way out. The roles of the main personalities are, on the other hand, less well known. What caused Barras's inactivity? Was he tricked by the conspirators? (Garnier, *Barras*, 1970). Did he get the millions which Talleyrand was supposed to give him? A. Vandal, P. Taxotte (*La Révolution française*), L. Madelin thinks so; Garnier is more reserved. *Les Mémoires de Barras* deny such a theory. There is more information on Sieyès, thanks to two essential studies: Netton, *Sieyès* (1901); P. Bastid, *Sieyès et sa pensée* (new ed. 1970) which is complemented by R. Marquant *Les Archives Sieyès* (1970, which includes a word from Benjamin Constant warning Sieyès against Bonaparte on 19 Brumaire). L Madelin explains the role of the police, completely unobtrusive owing to Fouché's double dealing (*Fouché*, Vol. I, 1923). Other participants: Talleyrand (G. Lacour-Gayet, *Talleyrand*, 1928, Vol. I, ch. XX); Réal (Bigard, *Le Comte Réal, ancient Jacobin*, 1937) and above all Lucien (Pietri, in *Lucien Bonaparte*, 1939) who thinks that Lucien was not trying to work for his own ends as Masson claimed in *Napoléon et sa famille*, but that he was completely in the conspiracy with Sieyès.) Incontrovertibly, if the spineless Boulay de la Meurthe, or Danon, had presided over the Five Hundred, Bonaparte would have been outlawed. It was Lucien who assured the success of the plot and who saved the outward appearances of legality. F. Pietri has taken up this idea and pushed it rather too far in *Napoléon et le Parlement* (1955). According to him there was no '*coup d'état*'but 'a normal constitutional revision which Bonaparte had, for his part, uselessly disturbed'.

As to the neo-Jacobin element, it has been analysed by I. Woloch, *Jacobin Legacy: The Democratic Movement under the Directory* (Princeton, 1970), without however the questions on the nature and the social composition of the movement having been answered. How was 18 Brumaire financed? The bankers were reserved. Lecouteulx de Canteleu was aware of the preparations for the *coup* which he, as head of the departmental administration of the Seine, favoured. But there is no trace of his having seen to the financing of the operation. The young Michel offered two millions, but after the *coup d'état*. It must then have been the tradesmen who subsidized the operation, and more especially, Collot, the former supply officer to the Army of Italy, who must have advanced 500,000 francs (Payard, *Le Financier Ouvrard*, 1958). Another tradesman concerned in the plot was Simons, who obtained a large order for wood for the navy in return for this service (Stern, *Le Mari de Mlle Lange, Simons*, 1933). Tradespeople had been annoyed by the new policies of the Directory: on 4 October 1799 a law had obliged them to supply within a month an account of all their dealings since 1795, accompanied by the relevant papers. On 29 October it was forbidden for them to pay themselves out of the tax collections in the different public funds.

I. 1   THE FOREIGNER

Sources
Only printed sources are quoted. The earliest known letters of Napoleon (the first is dated 25 June 1784) have not been included in the *Correspondance Générale,* published under the Second Empire. Of interest are letters to a certain Emma published by Leidgendecker in the *Revue des études napoléoniennes* of 1933, p. 52. Napoleon's early writings have been published by Masson and Biagi, *Napoléon, manuscrits inédits* (1910) and by J. Tulard, *Napoléon, oeuvres littéraires* (Vol. I, 1968). The *Mémoires* are numerous but unreliable: those of Joseph (1853) occasionally inaccurate; Abrantès deserves her name of Abracadabrantes; Bourrienne's *Mémoires* are partly apocryphal and plagiarize an English pamphlet translated into French in Year VI (*Some Account of the early years of Bonaparte at the Military School of Brienne, by Mr. C. H.*); Romain's *Souvenirs d'un officier royaliste* (1824) is hostile; Des Mazis *Cahiers,* published by P. Bartel in *La Jeunesse inédite de Napoleon* (1954), are confused and full of mistakes. (cf. R. Laulan, 'Of what value are the notebooks of Alexandre des Mazis?', *Revue de l'Institut Napoléon,* 1956 pp. 54–60). Aimé Martin is superficial, (*Intermédiare,* 30 Jan. 1891, col. 127–8). Chaptal (*Souvenirs* pp. 181–3) is concise. Finally, the *Mémoires historiques et inédits sur la vie politique et privée de l'Empereur Napoléon par le Comte Charles d'Og . . . élève de l'école de Brienne* (1822), which is only a pamphlet, must be entirely rejected.

Works
Numerous works have been inspired by Napoleon's youth. It is as well to mistrust Coston, *Biographie des premières années de Napoléon Bonaparte* (1840); Beauterne, *L'Enfance de Napoléon* (1846); Nasica, *Mémoires sur l'enfance et la jeunesse de Napoléon* (1850), and Colonel Iung, *Bonaparte et son temps 1769–1799* (3 vols, 1880–81). Excellent, on the contrary, are Masson et Biagi, *Napoléon Inconnu* (2 vols, 1895) and A. Chuquet, *La Jeunesse de Napoléon* (Vol. I 1897, serious although without references). Useful complements are to be found in Marcaggi, *La Genèse de Napoléon* (1902), M. Mirtil, *Napoléon d'Ajaccio* (1947), P. Bartel, *La Jeunesse inédite de Napoléon* (1954). Agreeable without adding new elements are Lorenzo de Bradi, *La Vraie Figure de Napoléon en Corse* (1926); L. Madelin, *La Jeunesse de Napoléon* (Vol. I of his *Histoire du Consulat et de l'Empire*); H. d'Estre, *Napoléon, les années obscures* (Vol. I, 1942); Georges-Roux, *Monsieur de Buonaparte* (1964); J. Thiry, *Les Années de jeunesse de Napoléon* (1975). L. Garros *l'Itinéraire* (1947) is indispensable for chronology.

For the Corsican aspect it is essential to consult numerous histories of Corsica, by Ambrosi (1914), Albitreccia (1939), Arrighi (republishing), Grégori (1967), Sédillot (1969) and above all L. Villat, *La Corse de 1768 à 1789* (1925) and Chr. Ambrosi, 'Les Deux annexions de la Corse' in *Problèmes d'Histoire de la Corse* (1971, pp. 7–22; he recalls that Genoa had only conceded the exercise of her sovereignty in 1768 and that the Corsicans only really became French with the Revolution), Boudard, *Gênes et la France*

(1962). On everyday life: Arrighi (1970).

Open Questions

The origins of the Bonapartes have been the subject of lively debates. We will only mention two books here: L. de Brotonne, *Les Bonaparte et leurs alliances* (1901) and J. Valynseele, *Le Sang des Bonaparte* (1954, excellent, despite several misprints, making for instance, Charles Bonaparte die in 1788, p. 25). His conclusions are convincing: 'Provincial nobility, Noblesse de robe', claiming, without proof but not without an element of probability, to be descended from a Tuscan family of the same name.' On the genealogy of the Ramolinos, cf. F. Beaucour, 'La Famille maternelle de Napoleon I' in the *Bulletin de la Société de Pont-de-Briques*, 1974, pp. 263–336. There is a biography of Charles Bonaparte by X. Versini (1977), and on Madame Mère there is Larrey's *Madame Mère* (1892). There remains L. Peretti (1932) fundamental, and A. Decaux (1951) was been content to copy the former.

The fortune of the Bonapartes presents numerous problems. The study of P. Lamotte, 'Les Biens de la famille Bonaparte', *Etudes Corses* 1956, confirms that they were persons of standing. It would appear, however, that the Bonapartes were to suffer from the annexation without becoming the paupers that Masson depicts. Serious difficulties began with the death of the father.

A further point of disagreement: the date of Napoleon's birth (and the place of birth: it has been situated in Britanny!) Basing his opinion on a brochure by Eckard (*Napoléon est-il né français?*, 1826), Chateaubriand gives the date as 5 February 1768. Iung, in *Bonaparte et son temps* (Vol. I, hostile to Napoleon), affirms that Napoleon was born on 7 January 1768 and that his brother Joseph, who would not then be the eldest, was born on 15 August 1769. Charles Bonaparte would have had to substitute birth certificates for Napoleon to have been old enough to go to Brienne. Hypothesis which has been destroyed by F. Masson. Napoleon himself, in his private writings, gives 15 August 1769 as his own date of birth, and it is the date marked by Charles Bonaparte in his *Livre des dépenses*.

Endless legends have misrepresented Napoleon's education. On Brienne, besides Masson and Chuquet, are A. Assier, *Napoléon à l'école de Brienne* (1874), and above all Prevost, *Les Minimes de Brienne* (1915); and we might add the special edition of *Souvenir napoléonien* (1972). We are better informed on Napoleon's stay at the École Militaire in Paris, thanks to R. Laulan's research (particularly 'La chère à L'École militaire au temps de Bonaparte', *Revue de l'Institut Napoléon*, 1959 pp. 18–23) and that of General Gambiez, 'Napoléon Bonaparte à l'École royale militaire de Paris' (*ibid.*, 1971, pp. 48–56).

Question marks which hang over the garrison life in Valence and the journeys to Corsica are the subject of excellent restatements in Garros' *l'Itinéraire*. We hold that it is unlikely that Napoleon went to Strasburg in 1788 (Pariset, 'Le lieutenant Bonaparte étudiant à Strasbourg', *Revue historique*, 1917, p. 78). On Auxonne: M. Bois, *Napoléon Bonaparte lieutenant d'artillerie à Auxonne* (no date) is very reliable. Add to it: J. du Teil, *Napoléon Bonaparte et les generaux du Teil* (1897) and B. Simiot, *De quoi vivait Bonaparte?* (1952). Thanks to Napoleon's own plentiful notes we are well informed about his reading. But whence does his fanatical admiration for Paoli spring? Apparently from Boswell, according to A. Dupuy, 'Un inspirateur des juvenilia de Napoléon', *Bulletin Association Guillaume Budé*, 1966, pp. 331–9. Read also F. Ettori, 'Pascal Paoli, modèle du jeune Bonaparte', *Problèmes d'Histoire de la Corse*, 1971, pp. 89–99. Remember that at that time everyone wrote, from Robespierre to Carnot, from Hérault de Séchelles to Fabre d'Églantine.

A detail: the origin of Napoleon's Christian name. Le P. Delehaye has shown (*Mélanges Pirenne*, Vol. I) that Saint Neopolus or Neopolis never existed. A clerk may have thought that Naples was a saint's name. H. Grégoire (*Bulletin de l'Académie royale de Belgique*, 1936, pp. 351–7) believes the name to have German origins: Nibelung. Y. David in *Le musée national de la maison Bonaparte* (1968) takes stock of the problems arising from the fact that the house where Napoleon was born has been turned into a museum. Cf. also G. Hubert, 'La Maison Bonaparte', *Rev. Inst. Napoléon* (1968). In *Souvenir* devoted to Napoleon (September 1977), G. Godlewski clears Madame Mère of the charge of infidelity made by Montbas (*Revue des Deux Mondes*, 15 September 1952) and P. Bartel (*Figaro littéraire*, 1 May 1954).

I. 2   PAOLI'S MAN

Sources
In *La Revue des Deux Mondes*, 15 December 1931, Ernest d'Hauterive published some important letters: 'Lettres de jeunesse de Bonaparte'. Besides Joseph's *Mémoires*, those of Lucien and Bourrienne should be consulted with caution. Napoleon's writings are collected in *Napoléon. Oeuvres littéraires* (ed. Tulard), Vol. II (1968). With regard to Corsica, Volney's article, 'Précis sur l'état actuel de la Corse' (*Le Moniteur*, 20 March 1793), is a violent indictment of Paoli.

Works
F. Masson's *Napoléon inconnu* (1895); A Chuquet's *La Jeunesse de Napoléon* Vol. II, *La Révolution* (1898) and J. B. Marcaggi's *La Genèse de Napoléon* (1902) even if doubtful in detail, remain fundamental. The books by L. Madelin, J. Thiry, Estre and P. Bartel, referred to in the previous chapter, bring to light no new documents on Corsica at the time of the revolution. On the other hand, M. Mirtil's *Napoléon d'Ajaccio* (1947) contains unpublished material from the Corsican archives. Two important theses, which refresh the memory, unfortunately remain in typescript: J. Defranceschi's *La Corse française, 30 Novembre 1789, 25 Juin 1794* (1969) and F. Beaucour's *Un fidèle de l'Empereur, Jean-Mathieu Alexandre Sari* (Vol. I, 1972).

Open Questions
It is not easy to come to grips with the political struggles of the Corsicans in

1789. The union formed around Paoli against the francophile Royalists was soon shattered. To understand the matter clearly one might consult Casanova's *La Corse et Les États-Généraux de 1789* (Ajaccio, 1931); F. Pomponi, 'Sentiments révolutionnaires et esprit de parti en Corse', *Problèmes d'Histoire de la Corse* (1971, pp. 147–48), and F. Chailley-Pompei, 'Troubles de Pâques 1792' (*ibid*. pp. 179–89).

Paoli's politics remain obscure. Perhaps they resulted from the pressure of events rather than creating them. Defranceschi shows in his thesis that, initially, Paoli did not want to separate Corsica from France in order to give her to England. He maintains that such a legend was invented by Rossi in his *Osservazioni storiche sopra la Corsica,* and taken up again by the Bonapartists. He places all responsibility for the break on the Convention which accepted without verifying the calumnies against Paoli. D. Perelli, *Lettres de Pascal Paoli* (Bastia, 1884–89, 6 vols) should also be consulted, as well as Jollivet, *Paoli, Napoléon, Pozzo di Borgo* (1892), and, on a point of detail, C. Bordini, '*Nota sulla fortuna di Pasquale Paoli' Rassegna storica del Risorgimento* (1923).

If Pozzo di Borgo has been closely studied (P. Ordioni, *Pozzo di Borgo,* 1935; Albertini and Marinetti, *Pozzo di Borgo contre Napoléon,* 1966; J. M. P. McErlean, *The Formative Years of a Russian Diplomat,* 1967; D. Carrington, 'Pozzo di Borgo et les Bonaparte' *Problèmes d'Histoire de la Corse,* pp. 101–129), Salicetti, for the essential part he played in Corsican events, deserves a more detailed biography (Franceschini 'Salicetti et Napoléon', *Revue des Études Napoléoniennes,* Sept. 1930, pp. 131–55, and J. Godechot, 'Salicetti', in *Studia in onore di Nino Cortese,* 1976, pp. 257–72). Beaucour's *Sari,* Vol. I, p. 91, shows that it was Salicetti who, remembering that Paoli had been the King of England's protégé, was the first to arouse the suspicions of the Convention. As yet little light has been thrown on the origin of Napoleon's writings: besides N. Tomiche's *Napoléon écrivain* (1952) see E. Desprez, 'Les origines républicaines de Napoléon. Le mémoire sur la Corse en 1793', *Revue historique* (1908), which corrects the mistakes of Masson and Chuquet, and J. Feuvrier, 'Napoléon Bonaparte à Dole' in *Correspondance archéologique et historique* (1911) which explains the conditions under which the *Lettre à Buttafuoco* was printed.

The first military campaign in which Napoleon could have displayed his genius—the affair of La Maddalena—has attracted considerable attention. If Napoleon was in no way to blame for the failure of the enterprise, Paoli's liability is not proved: E. J. Peyrou, *L'Expédition de Sardaigne, Le Lieutenant Bonaparte à la Maddalena,* Paris 1912, blames Truguet; G. Godlewski, 'Bonaparte et l'affaire de la Maddalena', *Revue de l'Institut Napoléon,* 1964, pp. 1–12. Bonaparte's own testimony appears in *Oeuvres littéraires* Vol. II pp. 331–52.

Lucien's attitude, which precipitated the break between the Bonapartes and the Paolis, has been the subject of much controversy. In *Lucien Bonaparte* (1939), Pietri, who is very sympathetic towards him, shows him in opposition to Napoleon ('he seems to have had a tendency to become a tyrant'), and clears him of all treachery towards Paoli: 'The violent language attributed to

Lucien with regard to Paoli relates to a journey to Toulon which he was to make *after the break* between Paoli and the Bonapartes' (p. 45). Here Lucien's *Mémoires* would be accurate. On the other hand Defranceschi blames Lucien entirely in 'Paoli et les frères Bonaparte', *Problèmes d'Histoire de la Corse* p. 141). He sets himself to prove that there was no opposition between Paoli's reputed anglophilia and Napoleon's revolutionary francophilia. It was Lucien, acting without having consulted his brothers, who without doubt provoked the break and led Napoleon, in his turn, to accuse Paoli in his *Position politique et militaire de la Corse aux premiers jours de juin 1793*. There was a Bonapartist clique in Corsica (the Sari, Po, Costa, Barbieri and Lafranchi families) which Beaucour has brought to light (*Sari*, Vol. I, p. 100). Defranceschi defines their social context with the help of the list of 1,003 Corsican refugees to Marseilles, 'The good republicans', whose origins he compares to the whole of Corsican society: it was the well-to-do city dwellers who chose the path to exile, (*La Corse française 1784–1794*, p. 247). This clique was beaten in 1793 by the partisans of the Peraldis and Pozzo di Borgo. They were to have their revenge in 1796 at the time of the reconquest of Corsica after the resignation of Pozzo di Borgo who had rid himself of Paoli. The latter, once again exiled in England, was to illuminate his house as a sign of joy at the declaration of Consulate for life.

I. 3. ROBESPIERRE'S MAN

Sources
The big edition of Napoleon's correspondence, undertaken during the Second Empire, begins with the Siege of Toulon and becomes, thereafter, an essential source. Besides Volume I, Volume XXIX contains an account of Toulon (pp. 1–26) dictated on St Helena. Complement it with *Oeuvres littéraires* (ed. Tulard) Vol. II (1968). Besides the *Mémoires*, where Napoleon evokes Toulon, the *Mémoires* of Doppet, Marmont and Victor could be consulted. The evidence of the duchesse d'Abrantès is more reliable here than in other parts of her endless *Mémoires*. Documents concerning Napoleon figure in H. Wallon's *Les Représentants en mission*, Vol. III (1889).

Works
Two fundamental works are Chuquet's *La Jeunesse de Napoléon* (Vol. III, *Toulon*) and J. Colin's *L'Éducation militaire de Napoléon* (1901). Here again Garros's *Itinéraire* is a valuable guide. For the revolutionary context, P. Gaxotte and J. Tulard's *La Révolution française* (1975) which has a copious bibliography. Suggestive but debatable are Vol. II of *La Révolution française* by Furet and Richet (1966) and A. Soboul's *Précis* (1962).

Open Questions
The material difficulties of the Bonaparte family have been the subject of contradictory evidence; read Gaffarel's assessment, *Les Bonaparte à Marseille, 1793–1797* (Marseille, 1905), and P. Masson's *Marseille et*

Napoléon (Paris, 1920). O. Lemoine, in *Le Capitaine Bonaparte à Avignon* (1899), has dispelled the legends spread by local scholars concerning Napoleon's participation in the Avignon affair. The *Mémorial* gives a fairly embellished account of the Siege of Toulon which has gripped the imagination of Épinal. Useful particulars in Teil's *L'École d'artillerie d'Auxonne et le siège de Toulon* (1897); Cottin's *Toulon et les Anglais en 1793* (1898), Nel's *Bonaparte au siège de Toulon*. Recouly's *L'Aurore de Napoléon Bonaparte à Toulon* (1929) is mediocre. It was at Toulon that Napoleon caught scabies (Helmerich's *Le Secret de Napoléon*, p. 138) in conditions which are different to the heroic ones described in the *Mémorial*.

Was Napoleon a convinced Jacobin? Aulard thinks he was: 'Bonaparte republicain', *Études et leçons sur la Révolution*, 9th series, pp. 71–92. The problem of relations with Robespierre has been taken up by J. Tulard, 'Robespierre vu par Napoléon', *Actes du Colloque Robespierre* (1965). Bonaparte thought that the 'Incorruptible' was preparing to put an end to the Revolution once he had purged the Convention of the most corrupt representatives.

Carnot's opposition to Napoleon's Italian plans is incontestable. It should not be exaggerated: cf. Reinhard; *Le Grand Carnot*, Vol. II. The date of Napoleon's arrest and the place of incarceration have given rise to a number of imposing and often contradictory studies. What in particular was Salicetti's role? Mauquin has attempted to clarify it: 'Salicetti et l'arrestation de Bonaparte à Nice', *Revue des études napoléoniennes* (Nov.–Dec. 1934). Augustin-Thierry ('Un amour inconnu de Bonaparte', *La Revue des Deux Mondes*, 15 Nov. 1940) has drawn attention to the idyll of Napoleon and Émilie Laurenti in March 1794. Émilie's father is said to have saved Napoleon from a journey to Paris after his arrest, obtaining permission for the officer to remain, while under arrest, on bail in his hosts' house.

All Napoleon's plans for the operations in Italy have been preserved, and have been analysed by Camon in *La Première Manoeuvre de Napoléon* (1937) and more generally by Krebs and H. Moris in *Campagnes dans les Alpes pendant La Révolution 1792–1793* (1891).

The liaison with Desirée Clary is treated by Hochschild: *Desirée, reine de Suède et de Norvège* (1888), and is completed by Girod de l'Ain: *Desirée Clary d'après sa correspondance inédite avec Bonaparte, Bernadotte et sa famille* (1959). F. Verang's *La Famille Clary et Oscar II* (Marseilles, 1893) could also be read.

There has been much controversy over the authenticity of the date of *Clisson et Eugénie*. F. Masson (*Napoléon dans sa jeunesse*, p. 111) has argued that Bonaparte's unhappy love for Desirée was the inspiration for *Clisson et Eugénie* which, because of analogies with *La Nouvelle Corse*, he prefers to situate around 1789. He only wishes to see in it the influence of Rousseau. It is hard to accept Masson's point of view: Clisson is twenty-six years old, like Bonaparte in 1795; Eugénie is sixteen, Desirée's age when Bonaparte met her for the first time; she was called Desirée-Eugénie. Askenazy who was the first to publish *Clisson et Eugénie* (*Manuscrits de Napoléon en Pologne, 1793–1795*, Warsaw 1929) discovered a lacuna in the middle of the novel. These papers were part of the collection of André de Coppet (for their history see J. Gallini, 'L'étrange odyssée de *Clisson et Eugénie*', *Revue de l'Institut Napoléon*, July 1955, pp. 82–92) and have been resold in London. The complete text is to be found in Napoléon, *Oeuvres littéraires* (ed. Tulard), Vol. II, pp. 440–53. For the evolution of Napoleon's signature see Ciana, *Napoléon, autographes, manuscrits, signatures* (1939).

I. 4. BARRAS'S MAN

Sources
The minutes of the sittings of the Directory are in the National Archives (AF III); the directorial decrees have been published in part by Ant. Debidour: *Recueil des actes du Directoire executif*, 4 vols, 1910–17 (goes as far as Feb. 1797). For the Thermidorian Convention, the Councils of the Ancients and of the Five Hundred, besides the minutes which have been preserved (J. Chaumié, *Les papiers des assemblées du Directoire aux Archives nationales*, 1976), refer to *l'Histoire parlementaire* by Buchez and Roux, and to *Le Moniteur*. On the evolution of opinion read the police reports and extracts from the press published by Aulard, *Paris pendant la réaction thermidorienne et sous le Directoire* (5 vols 1898–1902).

Napoleon I's *Correspondance*, Vols I–III is fundamental. Complement it with Léonce de Brotonne, *Dernières Lettres inédites de Napoléon I* (Vol. I 1903), and the love letters to Josephine (the best editions are those by J. Bourgeat, 1941, J. Savant, 1955, and S. d'Huart, 1970). It seems that the most brilliant letters have not yet been published. Vol. XIX of the *Correspondance* contains the accounts of 13 Vendémiaire and of the Italian campaign dictated by Napoleon on St Helena. Add Arnna's *Pages de l'épopée impériale*, 1952.

The text of the treaties can be found in D. Clercq, *Recueil des traités de la France depuis 1713 jusqu'à nos jours*, Vol. I, 1864 (particularly the peace of Campo-Formio).

There are numerous *Mémoires*. Besides the *Mémorial de Sainte-Helene*, those of the members of the Directory should be mentioned: Barras (ed. Duruf 1895; very hostile to Napoleon; La Revellière-Lépeaux (1893, also hostile to Napoleon); Carnot (*Mémoires sur Carnot publiés par son fils*, 1861, not of great interest); Reubell (fragments in *La Nouvelle Revue rétrospective*, 1904); Barthélemy (ed. Dampierre 1914); The military ones, if suspect, are more interesting; Masséna (1848–50), Victor (1847), Marmont (1857), Gouvion-Saint-Cyr (1830), Jourdan (1818), Landrieux (1893), Savary (1900), Roguet (1862), Pelleport (1857), Thiébault (Vols I and II, 1893–4), etc. Further testimony: Thibaudeau (2 vols 1824), Abrantès (1831), Hortense de Beauharnais (ed. J. Hanoteau, 1927), Fain, *Le Manuscrit de l'an III* (1828), Hamelin (*Revue de Paris*, 1926).

For the other side, the following cannot be overlooked: Archduke Charles, *Grundsätze der Strategie*, (French translation by Jomini, 1818, and Mallet du Pan, *Correspondance inédite avec la cour de Vienne, 1794–1798* (1884). Joseph de Maistre, however, remains the great theoretician of the Counter-

Revolution and Napoleon's future adversary. In 1797, he published the third edition of his *Considérations sur la France* in Basle; the work was to be reprinted in 1802 and 1814. For the chronology of the other works: R. Triomphe, *Joseph de Maistre* (1968, hostile) and the edition of the complete works (1884–7). Roederer's thought can be juxtaposed to his in *Journal de Paris* or the Lycée lectures (Roels, *La notion de représentation chez Roederer*, 1968; Cabanis, 'Roederer', *Revue de l'Institut Napoléon*, 1977). On the émigré press: Maspéro-Clerc, *Peltier* (1973).

Works

The end of the Thermidorian Convention and the Directory have been the subject of several syntheses; A. Mathiez, *La Réaction thermidorienne* (1929), G. Lefebvre, *Les Thermidoriens* (1937) and *Le Directoire* (1946); M. Reinhard, *La France du Directoire* (1956); Mathiez et Godechot, *Le Directoire, an IV–an V* (1934); A. Soboul, *Le Directoire et le Consulat* (1967); D. Woronoff *La République bourgeoise* (1972). On 13 Vendémiaire there is only Henri Zivy, *Le 13 Vendémiaire An IV* (1898). On the other hand the Italian campaign has been the subject of endless works among which the following should be mentioned, beginning with Clausewitz's study published in 1833 (republished 1975), Bouvier, *Bonaparte en Italie* (1899); Fabry, *La Campagne d'Italie* (3 vols 1900–1901, fundamental); Driault, *Napoléon en Italie* (1906); Estre, *Les Années eblouissantes. Italie, 1796–1797* (1944); M. Reinhard, *Avec Bonaparte en Italie* (1946, from letters of his aide-de-camp, Sulkowski); A. Fugier, *Napoléon et l'Italie* (1947); J. Thiry, *Bonaparte en Italie* (1973, with copious bibliography). Biographies have been written about the main generals: Sérurier by Tuetey (1899); Masséna by Gachot (*La première Campagne d'Italie*, 1902), Laharpe by Sécrétant (1897), whilst Joubert has a special edition of *Visages de l'Ain* (1969) devoted to him. On the army itself: J. Godechot, 'L'Armée d'Italie de 1796 à 1799' (*Cahiers de la Révolution française*, 1936); also Godechot *Les Commissaires aux armées sous le Directoire* (2 vols, 1937).

Open Questions

Barras, who dominates the period, still awaits his biographer: H. d'Alméras, *Barras et son temps* (1930); J. Vivent, *Barras, le roi de la République* (1937); J. Savant, *Tel fut Barras* (1954); J.-P. Garnier, *Barras, roi du Directoire* (1970) are superficial. On the protection which he gave Bonaparte, cf. Monteagle, 'La première rencontre de Barras et de Bonaparte', *Revue de l'Institut Napoléon*, 1958, pp. 141–5.

There is a tendency today to play down Bonaparte's role in Vendémiaire. Zivy (*Le 13 Vendémiaire*, p. 74 onwards) has shown convincingly that he was nominated general, second-in-command of the Army of the Interior, only after the uprising had been crushed. On 14 Vendémiaire, in his report, Merlin de Douai mentions generals who distinguished themselves but quite overlooks Bonaparte. Nevertheless Napoleon must have played an important part from the point of view of strategy, compared to Barras at least, because he was rewarded with the command of the Army of the Interior. He took advantage of it to alter recruitment to the Police Legion in charge of maintaining order in Paris, favouring the entry of advanced elements who were to be compromised later by the Babouviste movement (J. Tulard, 'Le recrutement de la Légion de police sous la Convention thermidorienne et sous le Directoire', *Annales historiques de la Révolution française*, 1964, pp. 38–64). He had above all to confront the problems of provisions. (Cf. Reinhard, *La France du Directoire*, Vol. I, 1956.)

Many books have been written about Josephine: her infidelity is proved. (L. Hastier, *Le Grand Amour de Joséphine*, 1955; A. Gavoty, *Les Amoureux de l'impératrice Joséphine*, 1961; A Castelot, *Joséphine*, 1964); but little is known of her political role; perhaps it was non-existent.

The Italian campaign has found in G. Ferrero (*Aventure, Bonaparte en Italie, 1796–1797*, 1936) a critic in Bouvier's line; he shows how Bonaparte dissembled his defeats (*Bonaparte en Italie*, 1902), and in Fabry who destroys the myth of the 'destitution' of the Army of Italy (Fabry, *Histoire de l'armée d'Italie*, 1900). For Ferrero, Bonaparte was no more than the faithful executor of plans made by the Directory, in both military and diplomatic matters—an extreme point of view which has given rise to some observations by Louis Madelin (*L'Écho de Paris*, 17 and 24 February 1937) and by Lieutenant-Colonel Gallini (*Revue militaire générale* of April 1937).

One cannot, however, dispute the fact that as from 1796 Bonaparte did considerably rearrange to his advantage the account of operations in Italy. Interest has recently been directed towards the newspapers which he, concerned with propaganda, had published: Marc Martin, *Les Origines de la presse militaire en France à la fin de l'Ancien Régime et sous la Révolution* (1975). Unfortunately little is known about the financing and distribution of these papers. Jullien, the editor of the *Courrier de l'Armée d'Italie*, was a strange character; in spite of his very advanced ideas he lived through the political troubles without coming to much harm (H. Goetz, *M. A. Jullien*, 'l'évolution spirituelle d'un révolutionnaire' (weak) and M. V. Daline, 'Marc-Antoine Jullien après le 9 Thermidor', *Annales historiques de la Révolution Française*, 1964 to 1966).

Bonaparte's Italian politics are better known since P. Gaffarel's *Bonaparte et les Républiques italiennes 1796–1799* (1895) and *L'Italie et Napoléon* (1936) by G. Bourgin and J. Godechot. Did Bonaparte, in May 1796, promise the Milanese delegates, Resta and Melzi, that religious beliefs would be respected, and the right of self-determination for the population? It is probable. Did he speak of Italian unity? That, on the other hand, seems unlikely. See Jacques Godechot, 'Les Français et l'unité italienne sous le Directoire', *Revue politique et constitutionnelle*, 1952 pp. 96–110 and 193–204; chapter III of *L'Histoire de l'Italie moderne* by the same author; Renzo de Felice, *Italia Giacobina* (Naples, 1965); G. Voccarino, *Patrioti 'anarchistes' e l'idea dell' unità Italiana* (Turin 1956); A. Saitta, 'Struttura sociale e realtà politica nel progetto costituzionale dei giacobini piemontesi', *Società*, 1949, pp. 436–75. D. Woronoff has summarized it well (*La République bourgeoise*, pp. 93–5). Bonaparte's contradictory attitudes, whereby during the summer of 1796 he allowed unrest to develop in Lombardy in the name of independence and unity, and then, confronted with the anxiety of the Directory after the discovery of the Conspiracy of the Equals, he crushed the movement in favour of the formation by Modena, Reggio, Ferrara and Bologna of a Cispadane Republic in October.

These Italian politics were not in accordance with directives from the Directory, whose foreign policy has been brilliantly interpreted by Albert Sorel *L'Europe et la Révolution française*, Vol. V, 1903; and R. Guyot, *Le Directoire et la paix de l'Europe, 1795–1799* (1911). B. Nabonne, *La Diplomatie du Directoire et de Bonaparte* (1951) has more especially thrown light on the role of Ruebell in defining these politics and his opposition to Carnot. The Directory, with Ruebell, were committed to the 'system of the Rhine', with the Italian conquests serving as currency: Lombardy, taken by Bonaparte was to be exchanged for the left bank of the Rhine. But Bonaparte did not want to relinquish Lombardy. Did he see in it a point of departure for a grandiose eastern policy (Villat, *Napoléon*, p. 391)? This seems exaggerated. But perhaps he nurtured Italian ambitions encouraged by his origins. The opposition of Bonaparte's political system to that of the Directory, now well known, was affirmed at the time of Clarke's mission. It was Venice which made a compromise with Austria possible and added Belgium and Lombardy to the left bank of the Rhine. With regard to this it is normal to question the origin of the 'Veronese Easter' which produce an excellent excuse for an intervention against Venice (cf. the *Mémoires* of Landrieux).

Speed was essential. Suratteau ('Le Directoire d'après des travaux récents', *Annales historiques de la Révolution française*, 1976, p. 197), remarks that Bonaparte did not want a victory of Jourdan or Moreau in Germany to re-establish a balance that could be used by the government (cf. Bourdeau, *Les armées du Rhin au début du Directoire*, 1909). Rivalry with Hoche is discussed by A. Sorel, *Bonaparte et Hoche en 1797* (1897).

Influenced by Barras, Bonaparte would, above all, have served the politics of Carnot (Reinhard, *Le Grand Carnot*, Vol. II, 1952). All the more easily and with Carnot's agreement, he abandoned the Piedmontese patriots who were drawing their inspiration from Buonarotti who was compromised in the Conspiracy of the Equals.

What was Bonaparte's attitude on the eve of the Fructidor *coup d'état*? He went along with Carnot for a long time (he was still in contact with him through Lavalette, according to Suratteau, *op. cit.*). But he none the less told Barras of the comte d'Antraigues's documents proving the treachery of Pichegru (according to A. Ollivier, *Le Dix-Huit Brumaire* he had expurgated any mention of a 'probable entente' between General Bonaparte and the Royalists). On the comte d'Antraigues, Pingaud, *Le comte d'Antraigues* (1899) and, above all, J. Godechot, *La Contre-Révolution* (1961) may be consulted. There is little to be drawn from Montgaillard's *Mémoires Secrets*, published in 1804. Read also G. Caudrillier, *La Trahison de Pichegru et les Intrigues royalistes dans l'Est avant Fructidor* (1908).

According to a memorandum by the journalist, Barbet, the members of the Directory, of which Barras was one, knowingly allowed Bonaparte to develop his personal propaganda: 'Bonaparte's name was useful to ensure the success of 18 Fructidor' (Mathiez, *Le Directoire*, p. 375). In fact the General of the Army of Italy had no need of encouragement and, as Barbet realized, 'The influence of the general was already gaining its natural ascendancy over and above all civil elements.'

The *coup d'état* of 18 Fructidor has been the subject of a study, which has lasted well, by A. Meynier (*Les Coups d'État du Directoire*, Vol. I, *Le 18 Fructidor an V*, 1928) who does not really believe in the Royalist plot. Augereau who, in cooperation with Bonaparte, was the Directory's executor, deserves a biography.

On the looting by the Army: Saunier, *Les Conquêtes artistiques de la Révolution et de l'Empire* (1902), and F. Boyer, 'Les résponsabilités de Napoléon dans le transfert à Paris des oeuvres d'art de l'étranger', *Revue d'Histoire moderne et contemporaine*, Oct. 1964, pp. 241–62.

The Peace of Campo-Formio assured France of considerable territorial advantages: Belgium, the left bank of the Rhine, and a predominant influence over the Cisalpine Republic. But it was extremely dangerous. In *Napoléon et l'Empire*, Vol. I, p. 61, M. Reinhard rightly remarks that 'it involved France in an Italian venture the repercussions of which could not but endanger peace itself. The abandonment of the left bank of the Rhine in the context of a territorial reorganization by Germany at Rastadt heralded a long series of difficulties.'

In his memoirs, Hamelin enumerates the presents which he had to give to Josephine in order to Bonaparte. He tells how the confiscation of the Idrian mines brought the purveyor, Callot, a million francs, the same to Bonaparte, 100,000 francs to Berthier, 50,000 francs to Bernadotte and Murat. The other side of the epic is as yet little known.

I. 5   THE EGYPTIAN EXPEDITION—ORIENTAL DREAM OR POLITICAL MANOEUVRE?

Sources

Jean Thiry in *Bonaparte en Égypt* (1973) gives a good summary of source manuscripts many of which have not been published. Reference must be made to the *Correspondance de Napoléon* Volumes XXIX and XXX of which consist of the official account of the campaigns in Egypt and Syria. There was a useful new edition of *La Décade égyptienne* in 1971. There are many *Mémoires*: Berthier (*Relation des campagnes du général Bonaparte en Égypte et en Syrie*, 1801); Bernoyer (*Avec Bonaparte en Égypt et en Syrie, 19 lettres inédites*, ed. Tortel, 1976); Bourrienne; Bricard (1891); Denon (*Voyage dans la Basse et la Haute-Égypt*, 1802); Desaix (*Journal de Voyage*, ed. Chuquet, 1907; Desgenettes (*Souvenirs d'un médecin de l'armée d'Égypt*, 1892); Desvernois (1898); François (1903–1904, unreliable); Geoffroy-Saint-Hilaire (*Lettres écrites d'Égypte*, 1901); Gerbaud (1910); Jollois (*Journal d'un ingénieur attaché à l'expédition française, 1798–1802*, ed. Lefèvre-Pontalis, 1904, excellent); Kléber ('Carnets', *La Revue d'Égypte*, 1895); Krettly (1838, disappointing); Lacorre (1852); Lavalette (1910); Malus (1892); Marmont

(Vols. I & II, 1857); Millet (1803); Miot (*Mémoires pour servir à l'histoire des expéditions en Égypte et en Syrie*, 1804); Niello-Sargy (1825); Redouté (*Revue politique et littéraire*, 1894); Reynier (1827); Savary (Vol. I); Talleyrand; Thurman (1802); Vaxelaire (1900); Vertray (1883); Villiers du Terrage (1899; important). The admirable work *Description de l'Égypte* (20 vols., 1809–22) should also be consulted. The enemy's point of view is given by Nicolas Turc, *Croniques d'Égypte* (ed. Wiet, 1950), and Nelson, *Despatches and Letters* (London 7 vols; 1844–6). On Tipu-Sahib's India: Michaud, *Histoire de Mysore sous Hyder-Ali et Tippo-Sahib* (1801).

Works
Many works have been written about the expedition to Egypt. We note only the most important: Wilson, *History of the British Expedition to Egypt* (London, 1802, the origin of all denunciations of French atrocities; in 1815 Wilson was to alter his opinion); Reybaud, *Histoire scientifique et militaire de l'expédition française en Egypt* (10 vols., 1830–6), very out of date); Boulay de la Meurthe, *Le Directoire et l'expédition d'Égypte* (1885); R. Peyre, *L'Expédition d'Égypte* (1890); La Jonquière, *L'Expédition d'Égypte* (5 vols., 1900–1907; fundamental); Hanotaux, *Histoire de la Nation égyptienne* (Vol. V, 1934; description of Egypt before the French expedition); Bainville, *Bonaparte en Égypte* (1936); Charles-Roux, *Bonaparte, gouverneur d'Égypte* (1936); Estre, *Bonaparte, le mirage oriental, L'Égypte* (1946); Vendryès, *De la probabilité en histoire, l'exemple de l'expédition d'Égypte* (1952, more philosophical than historical); Benoist-Méchin, *Bonaparte en Égypte et le rêve inassouvi* (1966, brilliant); J. C. Herold, *Bonaparte et l'expédition d'Égypte* (Fr. trans. 1962; hostile to Bonaparte); J. Thiry, *Bonaparte en Égypte* (1973). *Revue des études napoléonniennes*, special number, January 1925. *Souvenir napoléonien*, special number, 1977.

Detailed bibliographies concerning particularly works published in Egypt are to be found in the articles of J. E. Goby, *Revue de l'Institut Napoléon*, 1955 (pp. 4–16) and 1976 (pp. 207–13). On Desaix: A. Sauzet, *Le Sultan juste* (1954). For Kléber: Lucas-Dubreton (1937).

Open Questions
Les Origines de l'Expédition d'Égypte were studied in 1910 by Charles-Roux. Magallon's memoir, which drew attention to the weakness of Mameluke rule, was published in *La Revue d'Égypte* of September 1896. Perhaps he over-emphasized a little the decline of Egypt. André Raymond, in *Artisans et commercants du Caire au XVIII siècle* (1975), gives a much less gloomy picture of it. What was Talleyrand's rôle? G. Lacour-Gayet (*Talleyrand*, Vol. I, pp. 317–8) accuses him of never having considered really supporting Bonaparte's military action with a diplomatic move in the form of a mission to Constantinople as had been agreed. Therefore Bonaparte was obliged to rebuke the Turkish attacks. On the other hand Guyot believes in Talleyrand's sincerity. Talleyrand did not leave for fear of being ousted as Foreign Minister in his absence. C. L. Lokke ('Pourquoi Talleyrand ne fut pas envoyé à Constantinople?' *An. his. Rev. Fr.*, 1933, pp. 153–9) in fact holds the

Directory responsible as they did not want to be without an experienced minister in their negotiations with the United States.

Benoist-Méchin may have exaggerated Bonaparte's 'Oriental dream', of which studies have been made particularly by G. Spillman, *Napoléon et l'Islam* (1969), and which is said to go back as far as Campo-Formio (after the fall of Robespierre, Bonaparte did consider hiring out his services to Constantinople). To be sure Bonaparte declared to Bourrienne in 1798, 'Europe is just a mole-hill. Everything is breaking down here. One must go to the East; all great glory comes from there!' But during the Egyptian expedition he was thinking, above all, of French politics. Besides, could the oriental *dream* ever have become *reality* ? A union with India was difficult and Tipu-Sahib's revolt remained limited (cf. Saint-Yves, 'La Chute de Tippo', *Revue des Questions historiques*, 1910, and Paul Morand's charming novel, *Montociel*).

Did Bonaparte consider the re-establishment of the former kingdom of Jerusalem on behalf of the Jews? *Le Moniteur* of 22 May 1799 attributes to him a proclamation inviting Jews from Asia and Africa to join him. J. Godechot has proved that it was false (*Les Juifs et la Révolution française*, 1976, pp. 68–9).

About the stop in Corsica on the way back to Paris, read Ch. Barbaud and L. Carbo, 'Le retour d'Égypte', *Revue des Études napoléonniennes*, Nov. 1922, pp. 161–98, which elucidates all the problems arising out of Napoleon's stay on the island.

The conditions of Bonaparte's election, by 305 votes out of 624 electors, to the Institut in the class of physical sciences and mathematics, have been described by Lacour-Gayet, *Bonaparte membre de l'Institut* (1921). The General's learning was not beyond the stage of Bezout's lectures.

II. 1   THE DEBIT ACCOUNT

Sources

On the state of France in Brumaire, besides the *Almanach National* of Year VII and Year VIII, the essential sources date from the Consulate, therefore their incomplete and partial nature must be borne in mind: F. Rocquain, *L'État de la France au 18 Brumaire* (1874; reports from councillors sent on missions to the departments); A. Aulard, *L'État de la France en l'an VIII et en l'an IX* (1897; reports by Fouché and the Minister of the Interior). The statistics of the Prefects in Year IX complete this documentation: The Aisne by Dauchy, the Allier by Huguet, the Aube by Bruslé (cf. Bourdon, *Révolution française*, 1912, pp. 102–103), the Bouches-du-Rhône by Michel, the Charente by Delaistre, the Doubs by Debry, the Drome by Colin, the Gers by Balguerie, the Ille-et-Vilaine by Borie (studied by H. Sée, *Annales historiques de la Révolution française*, 1925, p. 151–63), the Loire Inférieure by Huet, the Lozère by Jerphanion, the Lot-et-Garonne by Pieyre, the Meurthe by Marquis, the Mont-Blanc by Saussay, the Moselle by Colchen, the Basses-Pyrénées by Serviez, the Bas-Rhin by Laumond, the Rhône by

Verninac, the Haute-Saône by Vergnes the Sarthe by Auvray, the Seine-Inférieure by Beuguot (Dejean, *Révolution française,* 1906, pp. 512–37 and 50–52), the Deux-Sèvres by Dupin, the Tarn by Lamarque, the Vendée by Lebretonnière and the Vosges by Desgouttes were all the subject of publications between Year IX and Year XII. The best was provided for the North by Dieudonné, 3 vols., Year XII, recent reissue to be complemented by S. Botin's *Annuaire statistique.* These statistics have been the subject of a study by J. Bridenne in *La Revue du Nord,* 1964, pp. 371–83. Read G. Hottenger *l'État économique de la Lorraine au lendemain de la Révolution d'après les mémoires statistiques des préfets de l'an IX* (1964). Among the pamphlets: Hauterive, *De l'État de la France à la fin de l'an VIII* (renowned work of Year IX, pure Bonapartist propaganda); Ramel, *Les Finances de la République de l'an IX* (1801; defends the activities of the Directory); F. d'Ivernois, *Tableau historique et politique des pertes que la Révolution et la Guerre ont causées au Peuple français* (London, 1799).

Works

The historiography of the Directory is discussed in L. Sciout, *Le Directoire* (1895–7); M. Reinhard, *La France du Directoire* (1956); A. Soboul, *Le Directoire et le Consulat* (1967); D. Woronoff, *La République bourgeoise* (1972). Among local studies which show the Directory's attempts to take the administration in hand again: M. Reinhard, *Le Département de la Sarthe sous le régime directorial* (1935); Suratteau, *Le Département du Mont Terrible sous le régime du Directoire* (1965); Clemendot, *Le Département de la Meurthe à l'époque du Directoire* (1966); J. Merley, 'La Situation économique et politique de la Haute-Loire sous le Directoire . . .', *Cahiers d'Histoire,* 1971, pp. 393–402. The economic circumstances ruined the Directory's efforts at rehabilitation: Dejoint, *La Politique économique du Directoire* (1951), and, above all Charbert, *Essai sur le mouvement des revenus de l'activité économique en France de 1798 à 1820* (1949). On one of the architects of rehabilitation, François de Neufchâteau: the biographies of J. Lhomer (1913), Lacape (1960), Marot (1966, cf. report by J. Tulard, *Journal des Savants,* 1966, pp. 234–42). On everyday life: M. Lyons (1975) and Godechot (1977).

Open Questions

Long overwhelmed by right-wing (L. Madelin, *La France du Directoire,* 1922) or left-wing historiography (Mathiez, *Le Directoire,* 1933; ends at Fructidor), has the Directory been the victim of the Napoleonic legend? Nowadays there is some attempt to rehabilitate it, elements of which can be found in Gaxotte and Tulard, *La Révolution Française,* p. 404. A. Soboul sees no gap between the Directory and the Consulate; merely that, instead of a revolutionary dictatorship there was a military dictatorship. The financial reforms of the Consulate owe a lot to Ramel (M. Marion, *Histoire financière,* Vol. IV); brigandage continued under the Consulate (M. Marion, *Le Brigandage pendant la Révolution,* 1934; G. Sangnier, *Le Brigandage dans le Pas-de-Calais de 1789 à 1815,* 1962); it was the Directory which invented the Continental Blockade (G. Pariset, *Études d'Histoire révolutionnaire et contemporaine*, 1929, p. 113). 'The Consulate was to inherit undertakings which were already in execution, and to take the credit. In politics only the short term is effective.' (Woronoff, *La République bourgeoise*, p. 225).

II. 2   THE NEW INSTITUTIONS

Sources
The collection of the Secretariat of State at the national archives (AF IV) is essential. The whole of series F should be added for the Ministry of the Interior (the records of the prefects are to be found in the series FIBI), and BB for Justice. Add to them series K, L, M of the departmental archives. The debates of the assemblies can be seen in *Le Moniteur* and the *Archives parlementaires* (new series, Vols. I and II) and in Buchez and Roux's *L'Histoire parlementaire*. For the laws, besides the *Bulletin des Lois* consult Devergier's more convenient collection (Vols. XI, XII and XIII). The text of the constitution of Year VIII is given by J. Godechot, *Les Constitutions de la France* (1970). A good description of the administration can be found in the *Almanach national* (yearly). Aulard published in 1894 the *Registre des délibérations du Consulat provisoire*. Chaptal has supplied from 1801 the *Analyse des procès-verbaux des Conseils généraux des départements* (Years VIII and IX). *Recueil de lettres circulaires et instructions émanées du ministre de l'Interieur* (1820) can also be referred to. *Correspondance de Napoléon I* (Vols. VI–VIII), with the addition of L. Brotonne and Lecestre, is indispensable. Among the *Mémoires:* Baranti (Vol. I, 1890), Barère (Vol. III), Barthélemy (1914), Beugnot (1889), Billaud-Varenne (ed. Begis, 1893, on the Republican opposition), L. Bonaparte (ed. Madelin, 1945), Gaillard (*Un ami de Fouché d'après les Mémoires de Gaillard*, by Despatys, 1911), Gaudin (1826; essential for the financial history of the period), Mercier (*Bull. Soc. archéol. et hist. de l'Orne*, 1962, pp. 99–126; interesting concerning the Bank of France and the General Council of the Orne), Miot (1858), Mollien (ed. Gomel 1898; fundamental), Pelet (*Opinions de Napoléon*, 1833), Plancy (1904), Puymaigre (1884), Réal (ed. Musnier-Desclozeaux, 1835), Roederer (*Journal*, ed. Vitrac, 1909), Thibaudeau (*Mémoires sur le Consulat*, 1827; *Mémoires*, 1913); remarkable evidence on the Council of State and the prefectures), Vaublanc (1833). Also read Ramel, *Des Finances de la République* (Year X). Publication promised of Cambacérès' memoirs.

Works
A good description of the institutions is given in A. Edmond-Blanc, *Napoléon Ier. Ses institutions civiles et administratives* (1880; very clear); Poullet, *Les Institutions françaises de 1795 à 1814* (1907; old fashioned and confused); F. Ponteil, *Napoléon Ier et l'organisation autoritaire de la France* (1956; useful); J. Godechot, *Les Institutions de la France sous la Révolution et l'Empire* (ed. 1968, essential); F. de Dainville and J. Tulard, *Atlas administratif du Premier Empire* (1973).

The origins of the constitution of Year VIII are explored by M. Deslandres,

Histoire constitutionnelle de la France, Vol. I (1932), and above all J. Bourdon, *La Constitution de l'an VIII* (1942). The plebiscite of Year VIII is the subject of a very new study by C. Langlois who has exposed Lucien Bonaparte's falsifications, (*Annales historiques de la Révolution française*, 1972, pp. 42–65, 231–46, 390–415). The role played by Cambacérès in the establishment of the new institution is known thanks to his biographers Vialles (1908), Thiry (1934), Papillard (1961) and above all J. Bourdon (*Bulletin de la Société d'Histoire moderne*, 1928, pp. 67–74) and P. Metzg 'Cambacérès remplaçant de Bonaparte an VII–an XIII', *Révolution française*, 1902, pp. 528–51). Only a few superficial works have been inspired by the Assemblies: Dutruch: *Le Tribunat*, 1921; Welschinger, 'Tribuns, députés et sénateurs de 1804 à 1810' (*Revue hebdomadaire*, 1898, pp. 246–63); L. de Brotonne *Les Sénateurs du Consulat et de l'Empire* (1895), and J. Thiry's useful *Sénat de Napoléon* (1931). On the other hand the Council of State has been well documented despite the loss of its archives. To the large collective volume, *Le Conseil d'État 1799–1974* (1974), the following precise and detailed works by C. Durand should be added: *Études sur le Conseil d'État napoléonien* (1949); *Le Fonctionnement du Conseil d'État napoléonien* (1954); *L'Emploi des Conseillers d'État et des Maîtres des Requêtes en dehors du Conseil* (1952); *Les Auditeurs au Conseil d'État de 1803 à 1814* (1958); *La Procédure contentieuse devant le Conseil d'État de 1800 à 1814* (1953); 'Les intérêts commerciaux et le recrutement du Conseil d'État sous le Consulat et l'Empire' (Conseil d'État. *Études et Documents*, 1962, pp. 189–206); *La Fin du Conseil d'État napoléonien* (1954). Other works: Marquiset, *Napoléon stenographié au Conseil d'État* (1913; debates in the Council in 1804 and 1805); J. Bourdon, *Napoléon au Conseil d'État* (1963, unpublished minutes by Locré); T. Sauvel, 'L'Empereur et le Conseil d'État statuant au contentieux, 1806–1815' (*Revue de Droit public*; 1973, pp. 1389–403).

Much has been written about the prefects. Some general works can be useful. Aulard, 'La Centralisation napoléonienne' in *Études et Leçons*, Vol. VII (1913), pp. 113–95; Regnier, *Les Préfets du Consulat et de l'Empire* (1913); P. Henry, *Histoire des Préfets* (1950); J. Savant, *Les Préfets de Napoléon* (1958; a useful list of prefects with an appendix of their administrative notes; some inaccuracies); C. Durand, *Quelques aspects de l'administration préfectorale sous le Consulat et l'Empire* (1962; very new; criticizes Savant); J. Waquet, 'Note sur les origines des premiers préfets du Consulat', *Actes du 96ᵉ congrès nat. des Soc. Sav. 1971* (1976); relates places of birth and nomination of prefects; it underlines that more than a third of the prefects no longer held their positions after Year X; Whitcomb, 'Napoleon's prefects', *American Historical Review* (1974); J. Tulard, *Les Préfets Napoléoniens* in the symposium *Histoire des préfets* (1977). Biographical elements are to be found in H. Faure, *Galerie administrative ou Biographie des préfets* (1839) and at a stretch Lamothe-Langon, *Biographie des préfets* (1826). Regional studies include: Dejean, *Un Préfet du Consulat, Beugnot* (1897); Saint-Yves and Fournier, *Le Département des Bouches-du-Rhône de 1800–1810* (1899); Levy-Schneider, *Jean Bon Saint-André* (Vol. II, 1901); Chavanon et Saint-Yves, *Le Pas-de-Calais de 1800 à 1810* (1907); Pingaud,

Jean de Bry (1909); Benaerts, *Le Régime Consulaire en Bretagne* (1914); Viard, *L'Administration préfectorale dans le département de la Côte d'Or* (1914); Barada, 'Les préfets du Gers sous le Consulat et l'Empire', *Annuaire du Gers*, 1922, pp. 415–31; R. Durand, *L'Administration des Côtes-du-Nord sous le Consulat et l'Empire* (1925; model study which considers every aspect of the prefectorial office); E. Gauthier, 'Les préfets du Calvados sous le Consulat et l'Empire', *Mém. académie de Caen*, 1942, pp. 467–96; Rocal, *Du 18 brumaire à Waterloo en Perigord* (1943); L'Huillier, *Études sur l'Alsace napoléonienne* (1947); J. Godechot, 'Les premiers préfets de l'Aude', *Actes Congrès rég. Soc. Sav. de Carcassonne* (1953, pp. 17–33); L. Gros, *La Maurienne sous le Consulat et l'Empire* (1955); J.-L. Thiry, *Le département de la Meurthe sous le Consulat* (1957); Soulet *Les Premiers préfets des Hautes-Pyrénées, 1800–1814* (1965); P. Boucher, *Cochon de Lapparent* (1969); Derlange, 'L'administration préfectorale de Dubouchage dans les Alpes-Maritimes, 1803–1814' (*Nice historique*, 1969, pp. 119–24); G. Clause, 'Un préfet napoléonien, Bourgeois de Jessaint, préfet de la Marne', *Vie en Champagne* (1970, pp. 10–16: the résumé of a voluminous thesis for a doctorate as yet unpublished, and devoted to a case of exceptional prefectorial longevity); M. Rebouillat, 'L'administration préfectorale dans le département de Saône-et-Loire', *Revue d'Histoire moderne*, 1970, pp. 860–79; G. Thuillier, 'Le corps préfectoral de la Nièvre de 1800 à 1814' *Sociétés Savantes* 1970 (1974, pp. 413–32); Riouffol, 'Un type de mauvais préfet', *Revue de l'Institut Napoléon* (1976, pp. 21–9; Rabusson-Lamothe, Haute-Loire); Eckert; 'Lezay-Marnesia', *Saisons d'Alsace*, 1964, pp. 265–311.

The sub-prefects are less well known: G. Clause, 'J.-B. Drouet, sous-préfet de Sainte-Menehould, 1800–1914', *Revue de l'Institut de Napoléon* (1975, pp. 51–71); A. Antoine, *La Sous-Préfecture d'Auxerre, 1811–1816* (1908). There are only a few studies on the General Councils: J. Godechot, 'L'opposition au Premier Empire dans les conseils généraux et les conseils municipaux' (*Mélanges Jacquemyns*, Brussels, 1968, pp. 385–91, grants voted were less than had been demanded by the prefects on the occasion of the imperial celebrations; mainly concerning the south-west); Curie-Saimbres, 'De quelques Préoccupations des préfets et du conseil général tarnais sous le consulat' (*Congrès fed. Soc. Languedoc-Pyrénées; Roussillon-Gascogne,* 1971, pp. 407–26); A. Maureau, 'Le personnel du conseil général du Vaucluse an VII–1815', *Revue de l'Institut Napoléon* (1977). Nothing on the communes except for J. Bourdon's general remarks, 'L'administration communale sous le Consulat', *Revue des Études napoléoniennes*, 1914, pp. 289–304, and a point of detail concerning Lyons in Dutacq's study, 'Napoléon et l'autonomie communale' *ibid.*, Nov. 1922, pp. 199–204. The councils of the prefectures have also been neglected: J. Bienvenu, 'Recherches sur la pratique contentieuse des conseils de préfecture, an VIII–an XII', *Rev. hist. Droit*, 1975, pp. 12–37; Laporte on Puy-de-Dôme, *Rev. Auv.*, 1960.

Paris occupies a particular situation described by J. Tulard, *Paris et son administration, 1800–1830* (1976). On particular points: Passy, *Frochot* (1867; some documents were lost in a fire at the Hôtel de Ville in 1871); M. Roussier, *Le Conseil général de la Seine sous le Consulat* (1960); M. Fleury and B. Gille, *Dictionnaire biographique du Conseil municipal de Paris et du Conseil générale de la Seine, 1ᵉ partie (1800–1830)*, (in the process of being published; a fundamental work for a knowledge of Parisian notables); Felix's manual (ed. 1957 by Levy & Col).

The essential workings of government and the secretariat of state are studied by Ernouf, *Maret* (1878). There is little to be learned from J. Savant, *Les Ministres de Napoléon* (1959, anecdotal). On the Ministry of the Interior, Pigeire, *Chaptal* (1932); on justice, J. Bourdon, *La Réforme judiciaire de l'an VIII* (1942) and *La Formation de la magistrature sous le Consulate décennal, an VIII–an X* (1942). *Tribunal et Cour de Cassation. Notices sur le personnel 1791–1879* (1879); on finance, Stourm, *Les Finances du Consulat* (1902); M. Marion, *Histoire financière de la France depuis 1715*, Vol. IV (1925, essential works); R. Bigo, *La Caisse d'escompte et les débuts de la Banque de France* (1929, excellent); G. Ramon, *Histoire de la Banque de France* (1929; excellent); R. Lacour-Gayet 'Les Idées financières de Napoléon', *Revue de Paris* (1938 Vol. III, pp. 562–93; Fr. La Tour, *Le Grand argentier de Napoléon, Gaudin, duc de Gaëte* (1962); R. Szramkiewicz, *Les Régents et Censeurs de la Banque de France* (1974, important). The old studies by Braesch, *Finances et Monnaie révolutionnaire* (1937) and *l'Histoire du Franc* (1953) by R. Sedillot can be brought up to date with M.-O. Piquet-Marchal, 'Pourquoi la France a-t-elle choisi le bimétallisme en 1803?', *Revue Hist. Droit*, 1973, pp. 579–626.

Open Questions

Administrative history which has long been neglected is experiencing a boom. Now, the Consulate and the Empire were really golden ages of bureaucracy because of the centralization under the regime and because of its authoritarian character. Although life in offices begins to be better understood (J. Bourdon, 'Les conditions générales de nomination des fonctionnaires au début du Consulat', *Bull. Soc. Histoire Moderne*, 1931, pp. 31–3; G. Thullier, *La Vie des Bureaux sous le Premier Empire, Témoins de l'Administration*, 1967, ch. II; J. Tulard, 'Les directeurs de ministère sous l'Empire', *Actes du colloque sur les directeurs de ministère XIXᵉ–Iʳᵉ moitié XXᵉ siècle*, 1976), little is understood about the ministers' decision-making powers. How much weight did their entourage carry—the Gaillards, Jals or Beauchamps around Fouché, the Montronds, Le Chevalier, Roux–Laborie and others like Villemarest who made up Talleyrand's flock? Their control over services seems nil, they overlooked technical tasks. The ministerial department was only to develop with the parliamentary regime (J. Tulard, 'La notion de cabinet ministeriel sous le Consulat et l'Empire' in *Histoire des Cabinets des Ministres de France*, 1975). The creation of directors-general who rivalled the ministers in power could well be studied (Petot, *L'Administration des Ponts et Chaussées*, 1958). They came from the Council of State (Duchâtel from the Registration Department, etc.).

The financial redressment has been the subject of many works but not all the answers have been provided. G. Thillier, from a basis of various brochures (Basterreche, *Essai aur les Monnaies*, Year IX; Des Rotours, *Mémoires sur la* nécessité d'une refonte générale, Year XI, and Bérenger's reports) has thrown light on the monetary anarchy of the Consulate and the origins of the law of 7 Germinal Year XI concerning the manufacture and checking of currency. G. Thuillier is severe with the reform: 'By setting a real currency against ledger account, this law involved France for a half a century in a rigorous gold standard which partly restrained the industrial boom'. ('La réforme de l'an XI', *Revue de l'Institut Napoléon* 1975, pp. 83–102). The same author has underlined the persistence of the land banks ('Pour une histoire des banques de sols', *Revue de l'Institut Napoléon*, 1973, pp. 45–53). What then was the monetary reserve? According to G. Thuillier, taking into account emigration and liquidization caused by the melting down of religious plate, and cash imported from Belgium and the Rhineland, this reserve would be as high as 2.6 milliards ('Le stock monétaire de la France en l'an X', *Revue d'histoire économique et sociale,* 1974, pp. 247–57).

It has frequently been recalled that the institutions given to France by the Consulate took their inspiration from the Ancien Régime (Council of State, Prefects, and in 1807 the Audit Office). This 'reactionary' side of the Napoleonic legislation, which 'on a revolutionary basis re-established a structure of the old style', is confirmed also in the field of hospitals where 'on the foundations laid by the Directory, most of the institutions execrated by eighteenth-century philosophers and economists rose up again' (development of private charity, re-establishment of the *Filles de la Charité,* recall of almoners . . .). All this is shown by J. Imbert, *Le Droit hospitalier de la Révolution et de l'Empire* (1954).

What was the value of this administration? From Balzac to Vivien it seems to have caused great nostalgia. Bonin tried to found an administrative science; Herbouville and Stendhal dreamt of a school of administration (G. Thuillier, *Témoins de l'administration,* 1967; P. Legendre, *Histoire de l'administration,* 1968). But G. Ardant shows that it was of mediocre benefit ('Napoléon et le rendement des services publics', *Revue de défense nationale,* 1953). J. Favier, in a note on the papers of the Secretariat of State (*Inventaire général de la Seine AF,* Vol. I), exposes the strict subordination of ministers to Bonaparte from the beginning of the Consulate.

II. 3 PEACE

Sources
The sub-series F[7] at the national archives is essential for the plots. Add series Aa of the archives of the *Prefécture de Police.* For religious affairs sub-series F[18] (denominations) is fundamental. There is a lot to be found in the diocesan archives. The *Correspondance de Napoléon I* is very interesting on the subject. The development of public opinion can be found in Aulard, *Paris sous le Consulat,* Vol. II (1904). The cases against Demerville and others, and against Saint-Rejeant and Carbon, were published in Year IX. The negotiations for the Concordat are the subject of a vast publication by Boulay de la Meurthe, *Documents sur la négociation du Concordat* (6 vols. 1891–1905).

For what followed: Delacroix, *Documents sur la réorganisation de l'Église de France, 1801–1809* (1957). The feelings of the constitutional clergy are well brought out in the correspondence between Grégoire and Le Coz (ed. Pingaud, 1906). From the administrative point of view: Portalis, *Discours, rapports et travaux sur le Concordat* (1845). Among the *Mémoires,* for the plots, cf. Andigné (1901), Desmarest (ed. Grasilier, 1900), Fauche-Borel (suspect, 1829), Fauriel (1886, the author was Fouché's secretary), Fouché (ed. Madelin, 1945), Gaillard (ed. Despatys, 1911), Hyde de Neuville (1888; fundamental), Lavalette (1905), Nodier (1831; a great deal of invention, but fairly accurate portraits of police chiefs, among them the famous Bertrand), Peuchet (1838; archivist of the *Préfecture de Police*). On the Concordat, the evidence of Consalvi (ed. Crétineau-Joly, 1864) is fundamental despite the criticism which has been aimed at him. The campaign of 1800 in Italy was the subject of an official report by Berthier to which should be added the accounts of Coignet (ed. Mistler, 1968), Marbot (1891), Masséna (1849), Thiébault (*Journal du blocus de Gênes,* 1801), Victor (unfinished, 1847). On the German campaign: Decaen (Vol. II, 1911); on the end of Egypt: Bricard (1891), François (1903), Millet (1903), Reynier (1827), Thurman (1902).

Text of the Treaties of Lunéville and Amiens in the *Recueil des Traités de la France* by A. de Clercq (Vol. I, 1864).

Accounts of English and German travellers are useful (Yorke, Fr. trans. 1921; Heinzmann, 1800; Kotzebue, trans. Pixérecourt, 1805; Reichardt, ed. Laquiante, 1896). Read A. Babeau, *Les Anglais en France après la paix d'Amiens* (1898) and Holzhausen *Les Allemands à Paris sous le Consulat* (1914; Schopenhauer was one).

Works
There are numerous works on the pacification of the west: L. de la Sicotière, *L. de Frotté,* 1888; Chassin, *Les Pacifications de l'quest,* Vol. III, 1899; Lenotre, *Tournebut* (1910), E. Gabory, *Napoléon et la Vendée,* 1914; L. Dubreuil, *Histoire des Insurrections de l'Ouest,* Vol. II, 1930; Roussel, *De Cadoudal à Frotté* (1962). Many studies have been inspired by the myth of the power of the police under the regime, from Horace Raisson (1844), to L. Madelin, *Fouché,* and E. d'Hauterive, *Napoléon et sa police* (1943). Also by d'Hauterive: *Mouchards et Policiers* (1936, from the Inspector General Veyrat to the spy Schulmeister). Portraits of heads of the *Préfecture de Police* (Henry, Piis, Bertrand, Boucheseiche) in J. Tulard, *Paris et son administration 1800–1830* (1976). A portrait of a commissioner: M. Le Clère, 'Louis Beffara', *Revue de la Criminologie de la police technique,* 1951, pp. 1–8. Refer also to Guyon, *Biographie des Commissaires de Police* (1826), and to P. Montarlot, 'Un agent de la police secrète, Jean-Marie François', *Bul. Soc. His. cont.,* 1912. A general view of the plots in H. Gaubert, *Conspirateurs au temps de Napoléon I* (1962), and L. de Villefosse and J. Bouissounouse, *L'Opposition à Napoléon* (1969). The Jacobin attempts are described by Gaffard, 'L'opposition républicaine sous le Consulat' *Revue française,* 1887, pp. 530–50; Hue, *Un Complot de police sous le Consulat* (1909; thinks that the dagger conspiracy was a plot engineered by the police and Bourrienne); F. Masson,

'Les complots jacobins au lendemain de Brumaire', *Revue des Études napoléoniennes,* 1922, pp. 5–28. 'La machine infernale' (J. Lorédan, 1924; J. Thiry, 1952) served as a pretext for being rid of the Jacobins: J. Destrem, *Les Déportations du Consulat et de l'Empire* (1885); G. Lenotre, *Les Derniers Terroristes* (1932); R. Cobb, 'Note sur la repression contre le personnel sans-culotte' in *Terreur et subsistances* (1964). Le Clère has reconstructed the details of the inquiry which led to the Chouans (*Revue de criminologue,* 1951, pp. 33–6; cf. also E. Daudet, *La Police et les Chouans,* (1895). On the south: G. Lewis, *The Second Vendée* (1978).

On the military plots: Gaffarel, 'L'Opposition militaire sous le Consulat', *Revue française,* 1887, pp. 865–87, 982–97, 1,096–1,111; E. Guillon, *Les Complots militaires,* 1894; G. Augustin-Thierry, *La Mystérieuse affaire Donnadieu* (1909; an individual attempt on Bonaparte's life in which Fournier-Sarlovèse was concerned).

The crisis of Marengo, treated so masterfully by Balzac in *Une Ténébreuse Affaire,* inspired C. Rinn, *Un Mysterieux Enlèvement* (1910), and Hauterive, *L'Enlèvement du Sénateur Clément de Ris* (1926). Fouché's responsibility is evident if not proved. There have been several studies of the Royalist intrigues: L. Pinguad, *Le Comte d'Antraigues* (1894; one of the best spy networks); G. Lenotre, *L'Affaire Perlet* (1923; on the Royalist agent Fauche-Borel); Reiset, *Autour des Bourbons* (1927; an attempt at poisoning Louis XVIII; the roles of d'Avaray, of the Chevaliers de Cussy and de Puisaye). On the counter-police: F. Masson, 'La contre-police de Cadoudal', *Revue des Études napoléoniennes,* 1923, pp. 97–112; E. d'Hauterive, *Figaro policier* (1928; Dossonville was the sort of Royalist conspirator who infiltrated the official police); by the same, *La Contre-Police royalist en 1800* (1931; another infiltration by Dupérou). Also worth reading: R. Bailly, *Ange Pitou, conspirateur et chansonnier* (1944). The amnesty measures taken with regard to the émigrés are analysed in Forneron's old books (*Histoire générale des Émigrés,* Vol. III, 1907), Daudet (Vol. III) and above all J. Vidalenc, *Les Émigrés français* (1963) and Castries, *La Vie quotidienne des Émigrés* (1966).

So much has been written about the Concordat and the religious problems that it is impossible to quote it all. Excellent syntheses have been produced by V. Bindel, *Histoire religieuse de Napoléon,* Vol. I (1940); A. Latreille, *L'Église catholique et la Révolution française,* Vol. II (1950); Jean Leflon, *La Crise révolutionnaire* (1949, *Histoire de l'Église* by Fliche and Martin); A. Dansette, *Histoire religieuse de la France contemporaine,* Vol. I (1948), and above all S. Delacroix, *La Réorganisation de l'Église de France après la Révolution,* only Vol. I has been published (1962, a very detailed thesis). On the new way of thinking: B. Plongeron, *Théologie et politique au siècle des Lumières* (1973). The negotiations for the Concordat have been well summarized by Boulay de la Meurthe, *Histoire de la Négociation du Concordat* (1920); the outcome has been examined by A. Latrielle, *Napoléon et le Saint-Siège 1801–1808* (1935). For Pius VII refer to his biography by Mgr. Leflon (only Vol. I has appeared, 1958), the application of the Concordat is known thanks to a multitude of regional studies: Levy-Schneider, *L'Application du Concordat par un prélat d'Ancien Régime, Mgr*

Champion de Cicé (1921, on Aix); J. Leflon, *Bernier, évêque d'Orléans* (1938, fundamental); Roussel, *Le Coz, archevêque de Besançon* (1898); E. Gabory, *Mgr Duvoisin, évêque de Nantes*; A. Durand *Un Prélat constitutionnel*, Jean-François Perier (1900, on Avignon); C. Ledré, *Le Cardinal Cambacérès, archevêque de Rouen* (1943, exhaustive); Mazin, *Mgr Pidoll* (1932, on Le Mans); Preteseille, 'Un Prelat d'Empire, Barral, archevêque de Tours', *Bull. Soc. Arch. Touraine* (1969, pp. 507–27); Pinet, *Le Diocèse de Valence sous le régime du Concordat. L'épiscopat de Becherel* (1963); J. Dissard, *Mgr d'Aviau* (1953, on Bordeaux); Clause, 'La mise en application du Concordat dans la Marne', *82ᵉ Congrès des Soc. Sav.* (1957, pp. 293–306; on Rheims); Palluel, *L'Épiscopat de Savoie au début du XIXᵉ siècle* (1972, on Chambéry); Le Douarec, *Le Concordat dans un diocèse de l'ouest* (1958; Mgr Caffarelli at Saint-Brieuc); Guillaume, *Mgr d'Osmond* (1892, on Nancy); Tacel, 'Mgr de Villaret, évêque d'Amiens', *Revue de Rouergue* (1955, pp. 1–30); Lyonnet, *Le Cardinal Fesch, archêveque de Lyon* (1891); L. Mahieu, *Mgr Belmas* (1934, on Cambrai); G. Lacroix, *Un Cardinal de l'église d'Arras, Charles de la Tour d'Auvergne* (1960); Chapusot, *Mgr Colonna d'Istria* (1970, on Nice); A. Lorion, 'Mgr Leblanc-Beaulieu', *Revue de l'Institut Napoléon* (1960, pp. 263–74, on Soissons); Deriès, *Mgr Rousseau* (1930, on Avranches); Villepelet, 'Le diocèse de Bourges sous le Concordat', *Cahiers Hist. arch. Berry* (1972), and above all two exemplary monographs: Godel, *La Reconstruction Concordataire dans le diocèse de Grenoble* (1962), and C. Langlois, *Le Diocèse de Vannes, 1800–1830* (1974). On the abbé de Pradt, Dousset's rapid biography (1959) should be complemented by the special number of *Cahiers d'histoire*. Resistance to the Concordat gave rise to the schism of 'The Little Church': C. Latreille, *L'Opposition religieuse au Concordat* (1910), and Drochon, *La Petite Église* (1894), are very old-fashioned. The following are preferable: Billaud, *La Petite Église dans la Vendée et les Deux-Sèvres, 1800–1830* (1962); P. Flament, 'Recherches sur la Petite Église au diocèse de Sées' (*Revue de l'Institut Napoléon* 1975, pp. 21–50). The political implications are dealt with by A. Dechêne, *Le Blanchardisme* (1932). Among the heresies: C. Hau, *Le Messie de l'an XIII* (1955). On the everyday life of the clergy: *Cahiers du Berry* (Dec. 1968).

The 1805 inquiry made it possible to make a first assessment: Laspougeas, 'Une source de l'histoire du clergé dans le diocèse de Bayeux: le recensement départemental de 1805', *Annales de Normandie*, 1974, pp. 73–88.

For the progressive control of the press, besides Hatin: Cabanis, *La presse sous le Consulat et L'Empire* (1975, excellent); Vol. I of *L'Histoire générale de la presse* (1969); Albert, *Histoire de la presse* (1970); Périvier, *Napoléon journaliste* (1918, on *Le Moniteur*); Welschinger, *La censure sous le Premier Empire* (1887); Le Poittevin, *Le liberté de la presse, 1789–1815* (1901, on the *Journal des débats*); Perivier (1914, on the *Bulletin de Paris*); Riberette, *Rev. Inst. Nap.*, 1969.

The Italian campaign of 1800 has not aroused as much interest as the earlier Italian campaign, although Bulow made a study of it from 1810. Read Cugnac, *Campagne de l'armée de Réserve en 1800* (1900–1901). Driault, *Napoléon en Italie* (1906), Gachot, *La Deuxième Campagne d'Italie* (1899) and *Le Siège de Gênes* (1908), Fugier, *Napoléon et l'Italie* (1947). Some new aspects in Rodger, *The War of the Second Coalition, a Strategic Commentary* (1964). The decisive battle took place in Germany at Hohenlinden: Picard, *Hohenlinden* (1909). On the loss of Egypt: Rousseau, *Kléber et Menou en Égypte* (1900). For the Peace of Amiens, Sorel's famous pages in *L'Europe et la Révolution française* (Vol. VI, 1903) are enough.

Open Questions

Despite copious documentation, the role of the negotiators of the Concordat continues to fascinate some historians (C. P. Caselli, 'Il Cardinale Caselli', *Rivista storica svizzera*, 1976, pp. 33–86). The same can be said of the political problems tied to abiding by the Concordat: Lavaquery opened the way with *Le Cardinal de Boisgelin* (1921). Attention has also been drawn to the origins of the bishops, often strangers to their dioceses: E. Hout, 'Un Lyonnais évêque de Versailles', *89ᵉ Congrès des Soc. Sav.*, Lyons, 1964, pp. 915–29; Balmelle, 'Un Auxois évêque de Mende, archevêque d'Avignon, Mgr Morel de Mons', *83ᵉ Congrès des Soc. Sav.*, 1958, pp. 37–9. A comparison with the prefects would be useful based on Bernard's collection of biographies of bishops. Was the application of the Concordat in any way advantageous to the humbler clergy? The problem has been raised by J. Leflon, 'Le clergé du second ordre sous le Consulat et l'Empire', *Rev. Hist. Egl. Fr.*, 1945, pp. 97–135. Besides which it is a shame that S. Delacroix's thesis, *Les Congrégations religieuses sous le Consulat et l'Empire,* should have remained unpublished (EPHE, Vᵉ section, 1955). For the discussion of all the problems one cannot do better than to refer to Plongeron and Godel, 'Un quart de siècle d'histoire religieuse', *Annales hist. Rev. fr.*, 1972, pp. 181–203 and 352–89.

It is sometimes forgotten that Protestantism was also the victim of dechristianization: shortage of ministers, reduced funds and profound discord (Bordeaux against Sainte-Foye, the Norman Bocage against Caen). This is why Bonaparte, even if he had wanted to, could not have made Protestantism the national religion of the French (M. Guerrini does not think that he thought of it: *Napoléon devant Dieu*, 1960). Daniel Robert has shown in a masterly thesis, *Les Églises reformées en France, 1800–1830* (1961), that the organic articles gave a new impetus to Protestantism. This thesis replaces an old book by C. Durand, *Histoire du Protestantisme français pendant la Révolution et l'Empire* (1902), cf. also *l'Histoire du Protestantisme* by E. G. Léonard. But D. Robert also underlines the dangers caused to the reformed Churches by Napoleonic policies: the artificial regrouping into consistories of six thousand souls, the suppression of synods (in fact dependent on government authorization), the making of the ministers into officials and the forbidding of relations with foreign communities all went against Protestant tradition.

Was Napoleon an anti-semite as Boisandré claims in a pamphlet reissued in 1938, or in favour of Jews as is claimed, and deplored, by the abbé Lemann in the title of his study *Napoléon et les Israélites? La prépondérance juive* (1895) or again by F. Pietri, *Napoléon et les Israélites* (1965) who wanted to show that by the assimilation of Jews voted by the Constituent Assembly (but which remained a dead letter), Napoleon had hoped to complete his work of religious pacification. The Jewish Assembly of 1806, the 1807 Sanhedrin, the decrees of 1808—were they all so many steps towards the making of Judaism into the third official religion? The same point of view is to be found in an article by Sagnac, 'Les Juifs et Napoléon', *Revue d'histoire moderne, 1900–1901*. R. Anchel in *Napoléon et les Juifs* (1928) only wishes to stress the positive aspects: the official organization of the religion; for the rest he thinks that Napoleon, influenced by his entourage from the Ancien Régime, despised Jews and passed the law on usury of 1807 against them. This attitude imitated Mathiez who could not bear the image of the Revolution and the Empire as protectors of minorities to be altered (R. Anchel, 'Napoléon et les Juifs', *Annales Hist. Rev. fr.*, 1928 and symposium, *La Révolution française et les Juifs* (1976). See also S. Schwarzfuchs, *Napoleon, the Jews and the Sanhedrin* (1979).

Les Francs-Maçons fossoyeurs du Premier Empire: there is a great deal of exaggeration in the title of this pamphlet published by C. de Flahault in 1943. After its reorganization by Roettiers de Montaleau (cf. masonic calendars published at the time by the Grand Orient and G. Bourgin, 'La Franc-Maçonnerie sous l'Empire', *Revue française*, 1905), freemasonry limited itself to speeches in honour of official authorities and at large banquets (Bouton, *Les Francs-Maçons manceaux et la Révolution française, 1741–1815*, 1958; G. Gayot, 'Les Francs-Maçons ardennais à l'époque du Consulat et de l'Empire', *Revue du Nord*, 1970, pp. 339—66). The support among officials, despite the evidence of Arnault, was very limited. The lodges were strictly supervised and Napoleon had nothing to complain about, except where the military lodges were concerned, opposition to which gave rise to the famous myth of Colonel Oudet's *Philadelphes* which was put about by Nodier in particular. Was Napoleon himself a freemason? J. Palou (*La Franc-Maçonnerie*, 1964) thinks so and he reproduces masonic documents which refer to a participation by Napoleon in masonic proceedings. J. Boisson, *Napoléon était-il franc-maçon?* (1967) is sceptical. In his turn, and in a very convincing manner, J. Ligou, himself a freemason, destroys the hypothesis of Napoleon's freemasonry (that of Joseph is unquestionable): '*Les Bonaparte et la Franc-Maçonnerie*', *Problèmes d'Histoire de la Corse*, 1971, pp. 233–53.

Apart from Fareinisme, the contemporary profusion of religions has aroused no interest. People had been profoundly disturbed by the events of the Revolution—the execution of the King and the capture of the Pope seemed to presage the Apocalypse. Prophets and visionaries were sought by the police, not on religious grounds but for the sake of order and morality. This was not without reason, moreover. One can read in Fouché's bulletin of 16 August 1805: 'The object of the *state sect for reparation* is to *repair* by means of prostitution and the most abandoned debauchery, the crimes of impurity and lewdness of the corrupt world.' A strange way to combat sin!

II. 4   A WASHINGTON CROWNED

Sources

Le Moniteur and the *Archives Parlementaires* are essential to a knowledge of the assemblies. The main decrees can be found in Duvergier's collection (Vols. XIII–XV); the text of the constitutions is published, with commentaries, by J. Godechot, *Les Constitutions de France* (1970). For public opinion, there are two essential sources: Aulard, *Paris sous le Consulat*, Vols. III and IV (1906–9), Remacle, *Relation secrètes des agents de Louis XVIII, 1802–1803* (1899), the *Correspondance* of Napoleon (Vols. VII–X) and the *Lettres de Cambacérès à Napoléon* (ed. Tulard, Vol. I, 1973) clarify the intentions of the government.

There are numerous *Mémoires*: Bourrienne (1829), Carnot (by his son, Vol. II, 1893), Caulaincourt (1933), Chateaubriand, Cornet (1824), Desmarets, *Quinze ans de haute police* (ed. Grasilier, 1900), Fouché (1824), Fauche–Borel (1829), Fauriel (1886, interesting on the police), Hulin (1823), Miot (1858), Musnier-Desclozeaux on Réal (1835), Pasquier (1893), Roederer (*Journal*, ed. Vitrac, 1909), Savary (1828), Talleyrand (1891), Thibaudeau (*Mémoires sur le Consulat*, 1827). The essentials of the trial of Moreau and Cadoudal were the subject of a publication in Year XII and of the *Recueil des interrogatoires subis par le général Moreau*. Read also the correspondence of the duc d'Enghien by Boulay de la Meurthe (4 vols., 1904–13). Fiévée's evidence, *Correspondance avec Bonaparte* (Vols. I & II, 1836; cf. J. Caritey, *Rev. adm.* 1961. Read H. Tulard's *Note* in the archives of the Préf. de Police (1862), inventory series Ba.

Works

The Constitutions are analysed in M. Deslandres, *Histoire constitutionelle de la France* (Vol. I, 1932). On the political opposition read the essential works: L. Madelin, *La Contre Révolution sous la Révolution* (1935), J. Godechot, *La Contre-Révolution* (ch. XVIII, 1961), Gaubert, *Conspirateurs au temps de Napoléon I* (1962); J. Vidalenc, 'L'Opposition sous le Consulat et L'Empire,' *Annales Hist. de la Rév. française* (1968, pp. 472–88); L. de Villefosse and J. Bouissounouse, *L'Opposition à Napoléon* (1969, hostile to Napoleon and favourable to the ideologues). Ideology leads this opposition, turning itself against the one it pushed towards power, but who turns out to be a despot without 'understanding'. The role of the salons is well known thanks to A. Guillois, *Le Salon de Mme Helvetius, Cabinis et les Ideologues* (1894) and *La Marquise de Condorcet* (1887). Seen through the Tribunate and the Legislative Body: A. Gobert, *L'Opposition des assemblées pendant le Consulat, 1800–1804* (1925); F. Pietri, *Napoléon et le Parlement* (1955, maintains, somewhat excessively, that Napoleon always respected the decisions of the assemblies); C. Durand, *L'Exercise de la fonction legislative de 1800 à 1814* (1956; a lively critique and an addition to Pietri's book).

On the neo-monarchist element expressed through *Le Journal des debâts* and *Le Mercure de France*: A. Cabanis, 'Le courant contre-révolutionnaire sous le Consulat et l'Empire', *Revue des Sciences politiques*, 1971, pp. 9–87.

The army was a hotbed of ceaseless intrigue. Many generals had reservations about Bonaparte's victories and declared their Republican sympathies. Read, rather than the somewhat out-dated study published by Gaffarel in *La Révolution française* in 1887 ('L'Opposition militaire sous le Consulat' which is completed by two other articles in 1888 and 1889 on 'l'opposition républicaine' and 'l'opposition littéraire'), E. Guillon, *Les Complots militaires sous le Consulat et l'Empire* (1894, excellent) and G. Augustin-Thierry, *Conspirateurs et Gens de Police* (1903, a somewhat romanticized account of the 'pots of butter' conspiracy).

But most has been written about the great conspiracy of Year XII: H. Welschinger, *Le Duc d'Enghien* (1888, very old-fashioned); Huon de Penanster, *Une Conspiration en l'an XI et en l'an XII* (1896; lively critiques by Caudrillier, 'Le Complot de l'an XII', *Revue historique*, 1900, pp. 278–86; 1901, pp. 257–85; 1902, pp. 45–71); Picard, *Bonaparte et Moreau* (1905); F. Barbey, *La Mort de Pichegru* (1909; supports the suicide theory); J. Durieux, 'L'arrestation de Cadoudal et la Légion d'honneur', *Revue des Études napoléoniennes* (1919, pp. 237–43); M. Dupont, *Le Tragique Destin du duc d'Enghien* (1938; superficial); Lachouque, *Cadoudal et les Chouans* (1952); Garçot, *Le Duel Moreau–Napoléon* (1951); La Verende, *Cadoudal* (1951; more literary than historical); B. Melchior-Bonnet, *Le Duc d'Enghien* (1954); duc de Castries, *La Conspiration de Cadoudal* (1963); J.-F. Chiappe, *Cadoudal et la Liberté* (1971; the best synthesis on the subject); J.-P. Bertaud, *Bonaparte et le Duc d'Enghien* (1972; excellent, numerous documents quoted; Marco de Saint-Hilaire, *Cadoudal, Moreau et Pichegru* (ed. Poniatowski, 1977).

On the court: H. La Lachouque, *Bonaparte et la Cour Consulaire* (1958).

The Coronation is well known, not only thanks to Isabey's album which was re-published in 1969, but also through three studies: F. Masson, *Le Sacre et le Couronnement de Napoléon* (1925, fundamental), H. Gaubert, *Le Sacre de Napoléon I* (1964; anecdotal) and José Cabanis, *Le Sacre de Napoléon* (1970). On the other hand, G. d'Esparbès and H. Fleischmann, *L'Epopée du Sacre* (1908) is out of date. The evidence of simple soldiers on the ceremonies is interesting: Coignet, Lecoq (*Revue de Paris*, 1911), etc. On the symbolic element of the coronation, the Napoleonic coat-of-arms and the insignia of power: H. Pinoteau, 'Probleme napoleonischer Symbolik', *Der Tappert* 1970–1972–1974. The three colours were kept on the flags.

Open Questions

Certain stages in the passage from provisional Consulate to Empire have been well explained by P. Sagnac, 'L'avènement de Bonaparte à l'Empire', *Revue des Études napoléoniennes* (1925, pp. 133–54, 193–211). Lucien's role is well-known from Pietri's biography, as is Fouché's from Madelin's biography. Cambacérès's effective action can more easily be seen from his correspondence which was found by Jean Duhamel and published in 1973 by J. Tulard. On the plebiscite concerning the Consulate for life, the results of research by Langlois are to be eagerly awaited. Fiddling was not so necessary as in Year VIII because, if prefects' reports on public opinion in the departments (arch. nat. FI CIII) are to be believed, Bonaparte's successes had earned him great popularity. It was this popularity which made it possible for him to eliminate parliamentary opposition. There are differences of opinion between François Pietri, who believes in Bonaparte's respect for the deputies (why would the First Consul have respected representatives who were designated rather than elected?), and Charles Durand who has drawn attention to the inaccuracies and excesses of Pietri's thesis. Durand seems to have the upper hand. The fact remains that Bonaparte, despite the harshness of his remarks, manipulated the senators and maintained a parliamentary fiction, perhaps as a result of the alliance concluded in Brumaire.

When finally promulgated, the Civil Code established a society founded on property and equality, but this equality remained 'the equality of landowners' (Bertraud). There is a good analysis of the evolution of ideas concerning landed property and inheritance in P. Sagnac, *La Législation civile de la Révolution française* (1898): 'From the Constituent Assembly to the Convention, all revolutionaries have the right to property and subsequently the right to make a will, as a result of society'; around 1800 the doctrine was modified, the defenders of the natural origins of property and wills predominated. Boulay de la Meurthe and Duveyrier maintain that the right to property precedes society and that the right to dispose of it is also a natural right. The same change took place with regard to paternal authority; the Consulate reacted against absolute hereditary equality. Sagnac saw in it the mark of Roman law; in fact André-Jean Arnaud, *Les Origines doctrinaires du Code Civil* (1969), shows that article 544 (property rights) comes not from Roman law, but from modern Romanists and was taken up by Pothier. Other articles (notably 1134) were inspired by Pothier (1689–1772). R. Martinage-Baranger for his part has demonstrated the influence of Bourjon, an eighteenth-century jurist (*Bourjon et le Code civil,* 1971). Also useful are R. Savatier's *Bonaparte et le Code Civil* (1927) and Garaud, *La Révolution française et la famille* (1978).

The death of the duc d'Enghien is a turning point in the evolution towards the Empire; it reassured the regicide conventionals and other Brumarians who were highly compromised in the Revolution (Talleyrand, Roederer) and strengthened their alliance with Bonaparte. The Empire could adopt the character of a dictatorship of public safety. But did the First Consul want the death of the duc d'Enghien? Henri Welschinger makes him responsible for the execution. On the other hand J. Dontenville, in 'La Catastrophe du duc d'Enghien', *Revue des Études napoléoniennes* (1925, pp. 43–69), heaps abuse on the unfortunate Bourbon. Maricourt (*La Mort du duc d'Enghien,* 1931) stresses the mistake of Réal, who having received at 8 p.m. orders from Bonaparte to interrogate the prince, only reached Vincennes after midnight when all was over. Jean-Paul Bertaud thinks the executions of the duc d'Enghien and Cadoudal were wanted by Bonaparte as so many 'ceremonies' with which he intended to revive the Terror and to strike the popular imagination by underlining the differences of the two Frances— Revolutionary France and Royalist France. It is hard to determine the parts played by Talleyrand, Caulaincourt and Savary. In any case, Napoleon spoke plainly on St Helena: 'I had the duc d'Enghien arrested and sentenced because it was necessary to the safety, the interest and the honour of the French people, at a time when the comte d'Artois, by his own account, was maintaining sixty assassins in Paris. Under similar circumstances I would act in the same way.'

G. Mauguin's article, 'Le plébiscite pour l'hérédité impériale en l'an XII', *Revue de l'Institut Napoléon* (1939, pp. 5–16), speaks rather too quickly of a 'unanimous France'; the opposition no longer dared to show itself and the fact remains that public opinion seems to have welcomed the Empire. After all, the vicomte de Ségur said of Bonaparte: 'He is a man whom nobody likes, but whom everybody prefers.'

Note that the Coronation music was discovered by J. Mongrédien and has been recorded by Phillips. It was composed by Lesueur and Paisiello.

II. 5   VICTORIES ON THE CONTINENT

Sources
Consult E. Driault on the foreign policy, 'Les sources napoléoniennes aux archives des Affaires etrangères', *Revue des Études napoléoniennes*, 1913, pp. 161–86, and the 'Chroniques' of M. Dunan on the Commission of diplomatic archives in the *Revue de l'Institut Napoléon*. The war archives are essential for the military operations as is the *Correspondance* of Napoleon I which should be complemented by E. Picard and L. Tuetey, *Correspondance inédite de Napoléon conservée aux Archives de la Guerre 1804–1810* (Vol. I). Add to that *Lettres, décisions et actes de Napoléon à Pont-de-Briques et au Camp de Boulogne*, by F. Beaucour (1977). Useful pocket edition of the bulletins of the Grande Armée by J. Tulard (Col. 10–18, 1964). The essential texts concerning the campaigns have been collected with an excellent commentary by J. Delmas and P. Lesouef in *Napoléon Bonaparte, l'oeuvre et l'histoire: Napoléon chef de guerre* (1969). The operations can be followed in J. C. Quennevat's remarkable *Atlas de la Grande Armée* (1966). Berriat's *Législation Militaire* (1812) cannot be left out, neither can the numerous volumes devoted to uniform from Sauzey (1901) and Bucquoy (1907) to L. and F. Funcken, *L'Uniforme et les Armes des Soldats du Premier Empire* (1969) and Quennevat, *Les Vrais soldats de Napoléon* (1968; after Adam, Bagetti, Faber du Faur, Zix and le Bourgeois de Hambourg). Cf. also Vernet's plates published by J. and R. Brunon, and *Soldats et Uniformes du Premier Empire* under the direction of Dr Hourtoulle, without forgetting the studies in detail and the plates published regularly by the *Carnet de la Sabretache*. On general conditions of service, the *Dictionnaire des généraux et amiraux français de la Révolution et de l'Empire* by Six (1934–8); add Labarre de Raillicourt (1963 and 1966).

Mémoires are abundant. For Saint-Domingue, Malouet's *Mémoires* end in 1799; note especially Pamphile de Lacroix (1819) and Norvins (*Mémorial*, Vol. II, 1896). On Austerlitz: Barrès (1923), Bigarré (1893), Coignet (ed.

Mistler, 1968), Comeau (1900), Gervais (1939), Marbot (1891), Pils (1895), Pouget (1895), Rapp (1923), Thiébault (1893). On Jena, add to Marbot, Pils and Rapp, Lavaux (no date), Levavasseur (1914), Lorencez (1902). On Eylau: Choderlos de Laclos (1912), Puffeney (1891) and Putigny (1950, unreliable). On Naples: Desvernois. About the camp at Boulogne, Bellavoine's notes, published by F. Beaucour in *La Revue du Nord* (1968, pp. 435–48) are picturesque. Not to be neglected are Brun (1953), Tupinier (*La Revue de France,* 1924, pp. 709–40). The *Mémoires* and *Correspondance* of Joseph (1853, Vol III), Jerome (1861, Vols. II and III) and Eugène de Beauharnais (1858, Vols. II and III) are essential, as are the *Documents historiques et réflexions sur le gouvernement de la Hollande* by Louis Bonaparte (1820), and the *Mémoires* of Queen Hortense (1927). From the Russian point of view: Berrigsen, *Mémoires 1806–1813* (no date 3 vols.). On the mentality of the troops: Fairon and Heuse, *Lettres de Grognards* (1936). Read also Volume I of the *Correspondance generale* of Paul-Louis Courier (1976). On Saint-Domingue, *Correspondance* of Leclerc (ed Roussier, 1937) and Moreau's descriptions of Saint-Méry (1798).

For the treaties: De Clercq, *Recueil des traités de France,* Vol. II. Main diplomatic documents: *Select dispatches from the British Foreign Office Archives relating to the third coalition* (ed. Holland Rose, 1904, fundamental); *Mémoires et correspondance du Prince Czartoryski avec l'empereur Alexandre* (ed. Mazade, 1887); *Vnyechnaya politika Rossy* (documents from the Foreign Minister of the USSR, cf. account by M. Spivak, *Revue de l'Institut Napoléon,* 1976); P. Bailleu, *Briefwechsel König Friedrich-Wilhem's III und der Königin Luise mit Kaiser Alexander I* (1900); Montgaillard, *Mémoires diplomatiques* (published by C. de Lacroix, 1906); Talleyrand, *Lettres à Napoléon, 1800–1809* (ed. Bertrand, 1889); *Ambigu* by Peltier in London.

Works

The following out-dated diplomatic histories can be ignored: Bignon (1838), Capefigue (1840), Lefebvre (1847) and also Bourgeois (*Manuel d'Histoire diplomatique,* Vol. II, 1898). On the other hand, Sorel (*L'Europe et la Révolution française,* Vol. VI, 1903), Driault (*Napoléon et l'Europe,* Vol. II, 1912), Fugier (*La Révolution française et l'Empire napoléonien,* 1954), *Napoléon et l'Europe* (joint authorship, 1961), Connelly, *Napoleon's Satellite Kingdoms* (1965), Sieburg *Napoleon und Europa* (1971) are very useful.

The colonial politics of the Consulate were one of the main causes for the break: good exposés in G. Hardy, *Histoire de la Colonisation française* (1943), Saintoyant, *La Colonisation française pendant la periode napoléonienne* (1931, very detailed), C. A. Julien, *La Politique coloniale de la France sous la Révolution, le Premier Empire et la Restauration* (1955, roneotype). From among the extensive literature on Saint-Domingue, the following should be noted: the general histories by Metral (1825), Nemours (2 vols., 1925–8) and James (*Les Jacobins noirs: Toussaint-Louverture et la révolution de Saint-Domingue,* 1949), a debatable portrait of the 'black Napoleon' by A. Césaire (1960). On Louisiana: Krebs, 'Laussat préfet de la

Louisiane (August 1802–April 1804)', *Revue de l'Institut Napoléon*, 1953, pp. 65–72; Villiers du Terrage, *Les Dernières Années de la Louisiane française* (1904). E. Wilson-Lyon, *Louisiana in French Diplomacy* (1934), and I. Murat, *Napoléon et le Rêve americain* (1976) all believe in the reality of a Napoleonic American policy. The great voyage of Humboldt and Bonpland in South America should not be forgotten: useful extracts from Humboldt's account to be found in *L'Amérique espagnole en 1800* by J. Tulard (1965), and Bouvier and Maynial, *Bonpland* (1952). On Baudin: J.-P. Faivre, *L'Expansion française dans la Pacifique 1800–1842* (1953).

The French intervention in Switzerland which was a further cause of unrest for England has been studied by Guillon, *Napoléon et la Suisse* (1910); M. Dunan, 'Napoléon et les cantons suisses', *Revue des Études napoléoniennes*, 1912, pp. 190–218.

Napoleon's Italian politics have been described in detail by L. Pingaud, 'Bonaparte président de la République italienne' (1914) and 'Le royaume d'Italie' (articles in the *Revue d'Histoire diplomatique*, between 1926 and 1934). A clear résumé in Fugier, *Napoléon et l'Italie* (1947).

The plan for a landing in England has been analysed in Vol. III of *Projets et tentatives de débarquement aux Iles britanniques* (1901) by Desbrière. The English point of view is given by R. Glover, *Britain at Bay, Defence against Bonaparte 1803–1814* (1973). Consult the *Bulletin Historique de la Société de Sauvegarde de Pont-de-Briques* which contains several detailed articles on the camp at Boulogne. Also on the Boulogne camp Cf. Nicolay, *Napoléon aux camps de Boulogne* (1905), H. Rose and A. M. Broadley, *Dumouriez and the Defence of England against Napoleon* (1909).

Trafalgar has been studied by Desbrière (1907), Thomazi (1932), Chack (1938), Maine (1957). Read also Jurien de la Gravière, *Guerres maritimes sous le Consulat et l'Empire* (1881), Mahan, *Influence of the Sea Power on the French Revolution* (1919) Tramond, *Manuel d'Histoire Maritime* (1927), Thomazi, *Napoléon et ses Marins* (1950), Masson and Muracciole, *Napoléon et la Marine* (1968). Good analysis in Dufestre, 'La Manoeuvre de Boulogne', *Revue des Études napoléoniennes*, Sept. 1922, pp. 81–109, and P. Guiot, 'Le Camp de Boulogne' (series of articles published by *Neptunia*). From Boulogne to Austerlitz the reconversion of the Grande Armée is well evoked by Burton, *From Boulogne to Austerlitz* (1912).

The military history of the third coalition is described by Alombert and Colin *La Campagne de 1805 en Allemagne* (6 vols. 1902–8, fundamental) on the French side (to be complemented by *Le Corps d'armée aux ordres du Maréchal Mortier* by the same authors, and, by Colin alone, 'La question des étangs d'Austerlitz', *Revue historique de l'Armée*, 1908), and by Meyerhoffer von Vedropolje, *Die Schlacht bei Austerlitz* (Vienna, 1912) from the Austrian side. There is a picturesque account by Henry Lachouque in *Napoléon à Austerlitz* (1961). C. Manceron's *Austerlitz* (1960), on the other hand, draws from Epinal's picture. Thiry places the battle in its general order, *Ulm, Trafalgar, Austerlitz* (1962), and Vachée *Napoléon en campagne* (1913).

The following works on the fourth coalition cannot be overlooked: P. Foucart, *Campagne de Prusse*, 1806 (2 vols. 1887–90), *Campagne de Pologne*

1806–1807 (2 vols., 1882), Le Petre, 1906, and Clausewitz's *Notes* (1903). There are excellent studies of Jena by H. Houssaye (1912), Rousset, *Revue des Études napoléoniennes* 1912, Vol. II, pp. 321–34, and a lively account by H. Lachouque (1961) and by Thiry, *Iena* (1964). General Bonnal's work is more strategic, *La Manoeuvre d'Iena* (1904). On the entry into Berlin, G. Lacour-Gayet, 'Napoléon à Berlin', *Revue des Études napoléoniennes* 1922, pp. 29–48. P. Grenier's work, *Les Manoeuvres d'Eylau et de Friedland* (1901) has not been superseded by Petre, *Napoleon's Campaign in Poland* (1907), and Vidal de la Blache, 'La campagne de 1807', *Revue d'Histoire,* 1939. Precious details are to be found in the biographies of some generals and marshals who distinguished themselves in the campaigns: D. Reichel, *Davout ou l'art de la guerre* (1975, quite remarkable on Jena) which can be complemented with G. Rivollet, *Le Général de bataille Morand, les généraux Friant et Gudin . . .* (1963); Thoumas, *Le Maréchal Lannes* (1891); H. Bonnal, *La vie militaire du Maréchal Ney* (1910–14, 3 vols. Precise descriptions but aiming at an apologia; to be complemented by S. de Saint-Exupéry and C. de Tourtier, *Les Archives du Maréchal Ney,* 1962; on the other hand the works of Lucas-Dubreton, 1941 and L. Garros, 1955 can be ignored); L. Moreel, *Le Maréchal Mortier* (1957), R. Lehmann, *Augereau* (1945, inadequate); P. Saint-Marc, *Le Maréchal Marmont* (1957, hardly an improvement on a previous biography by R. Christophe published in 1955); Derrecagaix, *Le Maréchal Berthier* (1905) and J. S. Watson, *The Life of the Marshal Berthier* (London, 1957; mediocre); Giron de l'Ain, *Bernadotte chef de guerre et chef d'État* (1968, acquits him of the charge of having remained inactive at Jena, by recalling the Emperor's instructions on 13 October at 3 p.m. to wait where he was for further orders). There has been no serious work on Soult; on Bacler d'Albe, Troude (1954). Biographies of Murat and Masséna will be mentioned later. Much has been written about the European consequences of the campaign. On Naples, whence the Bourbons were removed 'by a simple decree', C. Auriol, *La France, l'Angleterre et Naples de 1803 à 1806* (1905); the campaign is dealt with by E. Gachot, *La Troisième Campagne d'Italie, 1805–1806* (1911); the coming to power of the new king and his government is very well described by J. Rambaud, *Naples sous Joseph Bonaparte* (1911). How Louis became King of Holland: Jorissen, *Napoléon I et le roi de Hollande* (1898), Rocquain, *Napoléon I et le Roi Louis* (1875), Dubosq, *Louis Bonaparte en Hollande* (1911), Labarre de Raillicourt, *Louis Bonaparte* (1963) have published numerous documents which throw a more or less favourable light on the unfortunate king who has been so abused by F. Masson in *Napoléon et sa Famille.*

The repercussions in Poland of the Prussian and Russian defeats have been well handled by Handelsman, *Napoléon et la Pologne, 1806–1807* (1909), and Askenazy, *Napoléon et la Pologne* (1925). On Switzerland note the excellent study by J. Courvoisier, *Le Maréchal Berthier et sa principauté de Neuchâtel* (1959). But Germany was subject to the greatest alterations. Excellent general studies by A. Rambaud, *La France sur le Rhin* and *L'Allemagne française sous Napoléon I* (1897); M. Dunan *L'Allemagne de la Révolution et de l'Empire* (Part II, roneotyped, 1954), and M. Freund, *Napoleon und die Deutschen*

(1969). On the new states: C. Schmidt, *Le Grand Duché de Berg* (1905, essential); A. Martinet, *Jérôme Napoléon, roi de Westphalie* (1902, which has not been superseded by Fabre, *Jérôme Bonaparte, roi de Westphalie*, (1952). On the new kings: M. Dunan, *Le Système continental et les débuts du royaume de Bavière* (1943, a fundamental book which goes beyond the bounds of its subject to create a real history of Germany and the Continental Blockade): Bonnefons, *Frédéric-Auguste, premier roi de Saxe et Grand-duc de Varsovie* (1902). On the Confederation of the Rhine: Beaulieu-Marconay, *Karl von Dalberg und Seine Zeit* (1879). On the debts imposed on Prussia: Lesage, *Napoléon I, créancier de la Prusse* (1924), and Ernouf, *Les Français en Prusse en 1807 et 1808* (1875). The papers of Estève who was Treasurer-General of the countries beyond the Elbe should make it possible, once they are made public, to determine the conditions of payment.

Eastern affairs played an important if not decisive role in the development of Franco-Russian relations, as is well shown by B. Mouravieff, *L'Alliance russo-turque au milieu des guerres napoléoniennes* (1954); N. Saül, *Russia and the Mediterranean, 1797–1807* (1970). On this matter E. Driault's book is fascinating, *La Politique Orientale de Napoléon—Les Missions de Sabastiani et de Gardanne* (1904). This oriental policy aimed at two objectives: the destruction of British power in India and the carving up of the Turkish Empire prepared by the separatist schemings of Pasvan-Oglou in Bavaria, Kara-Georges in Serbia, Ali Pasha of Janina and the Wahabites in Arabia. Remember the Boutin mission to Algiers.

There have been important studies of Tilsit which marked Napoleon's apogee: S. Tatistcheff, *Alexandre I et Napoléon* (with numerous documents taken from Russian archives which are today inaccessible, 1891); A. Vandal, *Napoléon I et Alexandre* (Vol. I, 1893,); Driault, *Tilsit* (1917); M. Dunan, 'Les deux grands à Tilsit' in *Napoléon* ('Génies et réalités' 1961); J. Thiry, *Eylau, Friedland, Tilsit* (1965).

On Napoleonic strategy: Colin, *L'Éducation militaire de Napoleon* (1900, shows the influence of Feuquières Guibert, Lloyd, Bourcet and du Teil on Napoleonic thought); Camon, *Quand et comment Napoléon a conçu son système de bataille* (1935). Cf., by the same author, *Quand et comment Napoléon a conçu son systeme de manoeuvre (1931);* Bonnal, *Psychologie militaire de Napoléon*, Yorck de Wartenbourg, *Napoléon Chef d'Armée* (1899); Druene, 'Napoléon Chef de guerre', *Revue de l'Institut Napoléon* (1967, pp. 97–116). Quimby in *The Background of Napoleonic Warfare* (1957), has renewed the problem. Cf. also Chandler, *The Campaigns of Napoleon* (1966). Some good studies of the soldiers: Morvan, *Le Soldat Impérial* (1904, excellent); M. Dupont, *Napoléon et ses Grognards*: M. Baldet, *La Vie quotidienne dans les armées de Napoléon* (1964); M. Choury, *Les Grognards et Napoléon* (1968). On the Guard: Lachouque, *Napoléon et la Garde impériale* (1957). Picard, *La Cavalerie dans les guerres de la Révolution et de l'Empire* (Vol. II, 1895). On services: Philip, *Études sur le service d'État-Major pendant les guerres du Premier Empire* (1900), Lechartier, *Les Services de l'arrière à la Grande Armée* (1910); La Barre de Nanteuil, *Le Comte Daru* (1966, on the war commissioners and the commissariat); J.

Bourdon, 'L'administration militaire sous Napoléon I', *Revue des Études napoléoniennes*, 1917, pp. 17–47 (excellent on the supply of munitions, arms, numbers of horses—80,000 were needed per annum—etc.). A. Soubiran, *Larrey* (1966) on health services. On the aides-de-camp: Gillot, *Le Général Marois* (1957). A good study of the generals by Six in 1947 (synthesis of his dictionary). On those whom 'glory passed by', Rivollet's book (1969), and the biography of an unknown man, Hurel, by M. Le Clère, *Revue de l'Institut Napoléon* (1972). Mention must be made of the special numbers of *Souvenir Napoléon* on 'Napoléon et le service de santé', under the direction of Alain Gérard (1976). For the signals (dispatch riders, drums or trumpets, the firing of blanks): Quennevat, *ibid.*, March 1975, pp. 12–16. The cryptography was mediocre; according to Alexandre I, the Russians could easily read the dispatches which Napoleon exchanged with his marshals, (R. Ceillier, *La Cryptographie*, 1948). On the imperial headquarters: M. Doher, 'Napoléon en campagne', *Souvenir napoléonien*, Nov. 1974. Note also Regnault, *Les Aigles Impériales, 1804–1815* (1967).

There is no overall study of the system of recruitment by conscription, except for G. Vallée's general account of the Hargenvilliers conscription (1937). Essential regional monographs: P. Viard for the North (*La Revue du Nord*, 1924, pp. 287–304; 1926, pp. 273–302);G. Vallée, *La Conscription dans le département de la Charente, 1798_1807* (1973; remarkable); M. Lantier, 'L'Opposition à la conscription dans le département de la Manche de 1808 à 1815', *Revue. Dep. Manche* (1960, pp. 23–47); R. Legrand, *Le Recruitement et les Desertions en Picardie* (1957); Vidalenc, 'La désertion dans le Calvados sous le Premier Empire', *Revue d'Histoire Moderne* (1959, pp. 60–72). J. Imbert, 'Économie et Guerre, 1806', *Mélanges Jacquemyns* (1967), stresses the inequality between town and country in matters of conscription. J. Waquet, 'La Société civile devant l'insoumission et la désertion, 1798–1814', *Bibl. École des Chartes* (1968, pp. 187–222). Note that Paris and the West were spared (Tulard, 'Guerre et expansion démographique à Paris' in *Contributions à l'histoire démographique de la Révolution*, 1970, pp. 254–63). The demography has been discussed by G. Vallée, 'Population et Constription de 1798 à 1814', *Revue de l'Institut Napoléon* (1958, pp. 152–9, 212–24, and 1939, pp. 17–23). The levies did not endanger the population rise in France, Vallée considers quite rightly. But they were unfair. The Ariège with a population of 196,454 supplied 444 soldiers in 1805 as against 956 from Paris, and 1,105 in 1811 as against 1,086 from the capital (Dessat and l'Estoile, *Aux origines des armées révolutionnaires et impériales* (1906) Cf. also Darquenne on the department of Jemmapes. On replacement: Desert (*Rev. Hist. Econ et Soc.* 1965) and Mareau (*Rev. Inst. Nap.* 1975).

Open Questions

Who was responsible for the renewal of war? Historians have long been fascinated by the problem. A. Lévy (*Napoléon et la Paix*, 1902) defends the theory of a pacifist Napoleon, reiterated by Cassagnac, *Napoleon pacifiste* (1932). Equally, Sorel in *L'Europe et la Révolution française* sees the spirit of all wars residing in England. J. Dechamps also sees England as responsible,

'La rupture de la paix d'Amiens', *Revue des Études napoléoniennes*, 1939, pp. 172–207. English historians rather tend to see Napoleon as the initiator of war (cf. Vol. XII of *The Oxford History of England*, by Sir George Clark, 1960).

The negotiations of 1806 have been well explained by P. Coquelle, *Napoléon et l'Angleterre, 1803–1813* (1904), especially Napoleon's double dealing with England and Russia. M. Bruguière has brought out the role of financial forces in this bargaining: 'Hambourg et "le parti de la paix",' *Francia*, 1973, pp. 467–81.

What role did Talleyrand play and how was he motivated? The bibliography which concerns him is vast. Disregard the very numerous anecdotal works: Vivent (1940), Savant (1960), Orieux (1970, Talleyrand apparently always acted in the interests of the nation!), Carrière (1975) and the very out-dated books of Bulwer (1868), Loliée (1910), Saint Aulaire (1936) and Duff Cooper (1937). On the other hand, works devoted to aspects of his life cannot be ignored: Greenbaum, *Talleyrand, Statesman, Priest, the Agent General of the Clergy* (1970); Poniatowski, *Talleyrand aux États Unis* (1967); L. Noël, *Talleyrand* (1975, main chapters: was Talleyrand Delacroix's father; the religious marriage of the former priest; the sinister Maubreuil affair); M. Missoffe, *Le Coeur Secret de Talleyrand* (1966, chapter VIII is interesting on financial investments); Martinie–Dubousquet, 'Talleyrand et d'illustres goutteux', *Information médicale* (Feb. 1974, pp. 3–18). But the fundamental work remains G. Lacour-Gayet, *Talleyrand* (4 vols., 1930–34) which is completed by E. Dard, *Napoléon et Talleyrand* (1937, using the Vienna archives where proof can be found of Talleyrand's betrayal at Erfurt, documents which had already been discovered by M. Dunan and which he used in Chapter VI of the joint *Talleyrand* of 'Génies et Réalités', 1964). Summarizing the above works, L. Madelin (*Talleyrand*, 1944) insists on the Austrian policies of the man whom Tarlé saw as 'the diplomat of the bourgeoisie, in the ascendant', (*Talleyrand*, trad. Champenois): 'Austria is the only power in Europe which can be alarmed as much by the enlargement of France as by the designs of Russia and England on the Ottoman Empire— designs which become more obvious every day. She is also the only power which can be annoyed by the constant undermining of the Hapsburgs by the Hohenzollerns in Germany.' Therefore a Vienna–Paris axis had to be established in order to maintain the balance of power in Europe. France had to be made to recognize her natural frontiers and to demand nothing more, neither in Italy (where the crown would be given to a successor designated by Napoleon), nor in Germany. L. Madelin gives credit to this opinion. In fact Talleyrand expressed the fears of the bourgeoisie, 'The Emperor, by taking provinces from Austria and by enlarging the Kingdom of Italy which his minister would have had him renounce, embarked on 'the endless career' of which Talleyrand had spoken with concern under the Consulate, and catastrophe lay at the end of the adventure on which he had in vain attempted to put a brake at the end of 1805.'

How was the transfer of the Grande Armée from Boulogne to Ulm carried out? P. A. Wimet has disputed Napoleon's famous dictation to Daru in which he exposed all at once the whole plan of campaign which he was going to undertake against Austria, and the itineraries of the seven corps of the Grande Armée: it is a matter of an invention of the 'all too lyrical Ségur' ('Napoléon a-t-il dicté à Daru le plan de la campagne de 1805?', *Revue de l'Institut Napoléon*, 1971, pp. 173–82). Colonel Daru, backing himself up with the evidence of Joseph and of de Monge, refuted Wimet's arguments ('A propos de la dictée de Boulogne', *Revue de l'Institut Napoléon*, 1972, pp. 113–15). In an unpublished thesis on *Daru et l'Intendance militaire* (typed 1977), from which we have taken the figures quoted in the chapter, M. Bergerot minimizes Daru's role: 'The Emperor expected Daru to concern himself principally with the civil list; the Imperial headquarters were at Boulogne with Berthier; a plan of campaign lies more within the jurisdiction of a military headquarters than of a deputy quatermaster-general even if it were Daru; the stopping places are determined by headquarters, and administration follows if the orders can be carried out. It is conceivable that Pierre Daru was in the know about the campaign of 1805, but that he should have been the secret and almost unique planner with Dejean, is hardly compatible with established fact and military custom.' And the author recalls the part played by commissariat officer, Petiet. It was he who, on 5 September, although unwell, asked, at Berthier's command, the prefects to make the roads leading to the Rhine passable.

Were there leaks about the naval manoeuvre which lead to Trafalgar? L. Pingaud in his biography of the comte d'Antraigues (ch. VI) has shown that this counter-revolutionary agent was informed about France by 'the friend's son', a mysterious correspondent whom people have attempted to identify as Daru, Stendhal's relation and protector. Colonel Daru denied this accusation and showed that in any case the information furnished by 'the friend's son' could not have advantaged Nelson at Trafalgar ('La bataille de Trafalgar et le fils de l'ami', *Annales historiques de la Révolution française*, 1973, pp. 128–33). For the opposite opinion to Pingaud's read J. Godechot, 'D'Antraigues et les Daru', *ibid.*, 1965, pp. 401–49; very convincing.

Did espionage play an important role? Bonaparte had already employed a double agent, Mehée de la Touche, in 1803, to discredit Drake's English network. Read P. Muller (*L'Espionnage militaire sous Napoléon*, 1896) and J. Savant (*Les Espions de Napoléon*, 1957) which claim that Mack was villified by the well-known spy Schulmeister, the true victor of Ulm. He takes up A. Elmer's theory expressed in *L'Agent Secret de Napoléon* (1932) which can be complemented by Harsany, 'Schulmeister, citoyen de Strasbourg et espion de Napoléon', *Saisons d'Alsace*, No. 51, pp. 84–99. But many of the assertions cannot be taken at their face value. On various adventurers: L. Grasilier, *Le baron de Kolli, le comte Pagowski* (1902).

There is doubt about what finally happened to some generals: Dorsenne probably died as a result of wounds in 1812, like Ordener or Rochambeau. But what about Nansouty? Did Boudet commit suicide after having lost his artillery at Aspern? It would be interesting to know more about some of the obscurer generals, (Rey, Jalras) or those who are still awaiting a biographer (Espagne, Marchand, Haxo, Gazan and the Faucher brothers who were shot in 1815). Cf. P. Conard, 'Napoléon et les vocations militaires', *Revue de Paris*, 1902. There is abundant information on the French prisoners of war in

Spain, notably at Cabrera (Wagré, Gille . . .) treated again by Geisendorf des Gouttes (1932). The lot of the English prisoners in France was more agreeable: M. Lewis, *Napoleon and his British Captives* (1962). On munitions factories J. Rousseau's thesis, summarized in *Souvenir napoléonien* (1971), points out that in 1806, 265,800 firearms were produced compared to 216,258 in 1811. The smooth-bore flintlock gun, with muzzle-loading, had a useful range of 600 metres. Three shots could be fired per minute. Cannon balls ranged from one to twenty-four pounds. Grape-shot was also used but there is some doubt about its accuracy.

On the exploitation of victory: M. Reinhard, 'L'Historiographie militaire officielle sous Napoléon I', (*Revue historique*, 1946); Mathews, 'Napoleon's bulletin' (*Journal of Modern History,* 1960); J. Tulard, 'Napoleon et l'arrière' (*Rev. de Défense nationale*, 1969).

The social class of the generals has been dealt with well by L. Chardigny, *Les maréchaux de Napoléon* (1977), who avoids the hagiographical excesses of Stendhal's *Journal* whilst varying the tone of Stendhal's ferocious attacks. Napoleon's opinions of his marshals are collected in Damas Hinard's celebrated dictionary (1854). It is to be remembered that the Emperor forbade the publication of *L'État militaire de l'Empire* after Year XIII for obvious reasons. Chandler's *Dictionary of the Napoleonic Wars* (1979) is to be highly recommended.

II. 6   THE CONTINENTAL BLOCKADE

Sources
Foreign policy and the Chambers of Commerce archives, series F^7 and F^{12} of the National Archives; *Mémoires* of Gaudin and Mollien (the real Minister for the Economy), Chaptal, Miot de Melito, Bourrienne (on Hamburg), Talleyrand and the points of view of the customs officers given by Boucher de Perthes and above all Gruyer (*Souvenirs d'un gabelou de Napoléon*, reissued 1947). Napoleon's *Correspondance* (Vol XIII) contains the essential texts, especially the Berlin Decree. In addition L. P. May, 'Une version inédite d'une allocution de Napoléon au sujet du Blocus continental', *Revue historique*, 1939, pp. 264–72 (a vigorous condemnation of the speculators) and *Napoléon I, Lettres au comte Mollien*, ed. Arnna and Gille (1959). The numerous brochures of Montbrion should also be consulted, *De la Prépondérance maritime et commerciale de l'Angleterre* (1805); André, *Analyse fondamentale de la puissance de l'Angleterre* (1805); the works of Montgaillard reiterated in his *Mémoires diplomatiques* (1896). On the opposite side, Gentz, *Essai sur l'état actuel . . . de la Grande Bretagne* (1800) and F. d'Ivernois, *Effets du Blocus continental* (1809).

Works
With an interval of some fifty years, two articles have offered an evaluation of the research on the Continental Blockade. In 1913, Marcel Dunan published in *Revue des Études napoléoniennes* an article which attracted great attention,

'Le Système Continental, Bulletin d'histoire économique'; in 1966, Roger Dufraisse presented a new evaluation in the *Revue d'Histoire économique et sociale*: 'Régime douanier, blocus, système continental' (pp. 518–43).

There are several syntheses on the Continental Blockade: Kiesselbach, *Die continentalsperre in ihrer ökonomischpolitischen Bedeutung* (1850, outdated but prophetic); Lumbroso *Napoleone I e l'Inghilterra* (1897); Bertin, *Le Blocus continental* (1901); J. Holland Rose, 'Napoleon and British Commerce' in *Napoleon Studies* (1906); Tarlé, *Kontinental' naja blokada* (Moscow 1913); Melvin, *Napoleon's Navigation System* (New York, 1919); Heckscher, *The Continental System* (Oxford, 1922);B. de Jouvenel, *Napoléon et l'économie dirigée. Le Blocus continental* (1942); M. Dunan, *Le Système continental et les débuts du royaume de Bavière* (1943, important chapters on the blockade with an extensive bibliography up to this date); Lacour-Gayet, *Histoire du Commerce*, Vol. IV (1961); Louaisil, 'Le Blocus continental', *Information historique*, 1949, pp. 32–5 (a useful summary). Among specialized studies: F. Crouzet's essential, *L'Économie britannique et le Blocus continental* (1958), a remarkable study of the repercussions of the blockade on British industry and commerce; D. Heils, *Les Rapports économiques franco-danois sous le Directoire, le Consulat et l'Empire* (1958) and Ulane Bonnel, *La France, les États-Unis et la guerre de course 1797–1815* (1961; illustrates the difficulties of remaining neutral). The situation of allies or of annexed countries was not in the least enviable: Tarlé, *Le Blocus continental et le royaume d'Italie* (1928); Cerenville, *Le Système continental et la Suisse, 1803–1813* (Lausanne, 1906); Mercader Riba, 'España en el Bloquero continental', *Estudios de Historia moderna*; Macedo, *O Bloqueio continental* (1962; deals with Portugal only). In M. Dunan's work mentioned above there is a bibliography relative to the consequences of the Blockade in the German states (p. 675). Its role in the maritime war has been dealt with in a masterly fashion by Mahan, *The Influence of Sea Power on the French Revolution and Empire* (1892).

Open Questions

Continental Blockade or Continental System? Marcel Dunan has made the necessary distinction in *Napoléon, l'Italie et le système continental*, a paper read to the Académie des Sciences morales et politiques and reiterated in the *Revue de l'Institut Napoléon*, 1965, pp. 176–90. 'The Continental System is an expression invented by Napoleon and was used, before historians used it, by contemporaries who understood the precise meaning which he had given to it, and it should not be confused with the Continental Blockade.' Whilst war on the Continent was being carried on in a traditional way, the Franco-British struggle was of an economic nature. Napoleon wished to strike at the proud British power, founded on her advanced industrial and commercial techniques, by closing all European outlets to her. This was the Continental Blockade proclaimed by the decree and of which the Continental System or Coastal System is an extension. 'The Coastal System which became the Continental System by an extension of the name blockade, takes its definite form when the Blockade, in the guise of an economic undertaking against the

British fortune, developed into an industrial and economic imperialism for the benefit of the holders of hegemony in Europe.'

How did England survive? A. Cunningham in *British Credit in the Last Napoleonic War* (1910) had evaluated the role played by credit, F. Crouzet has tackled the problem again in 'La Formation du capital en Grande Bretagne pendant la Révolution industrielle', *Deuxième Conférence internationale d'Histoire économique*, Aix-en-Provence, 1962. The same author has shown the limits of this resistance. The Blockade was unquestionably a factor in determining the devaluation of the pound sterling. British financial resources were not inexhaustible. Inflation, far from allowing the war effort to continue, paralysed it. It was the cause of the failure of the fifth coalition ('La crise monétaire britannique et la cinquième coalition', *Bulletin de la Société d'Histoire moderne*, Oct.–Dec. 1955, pp. 14–19). An excellent study of the influence of the crisis is to be found in Clive Emsley's *British Society and the French Wars* (1979).

In 1815 Great Britain's national debt was to be enormous whereas France was in possession of vast reserves of gold.

Was the alliance with Russia solid? Much has been written about the behaviour of Alexander I: Waliszewski (1923), Paleologue (1937), C. de Grunwald (1955), Valloton (1966), Palmer (in English, 1974) and above all Ley, *Alexandre I et sa Sainte-Alliance* which throws light on the role played by Russian mystics (Kochelev and Galitzine) in the imperial politics.

III. 1   THE BALANCE

Sources
The statistical works (there was one in 1808 by Pazzis on the Vaucluse, studied by A. Maureau, *Études vauclusiennes*, 1973) and the memoirs of the prefects quoted in chapter I of Part II (cf. A. de Saint-Léger, 'Les mémoires statistiques des départements pendant le Directoire, le Consulat et l'Empire', *Le Bibliographe moderne*, 1918–19; B. Gille, *Les Sources statistiques de l'Histoire de France* (1964) and J.-C. Perrot, *L'Age d'or de la statistique régionale* (Year IV–1894) give useful descriptions which can be complemented by the departmental *annuaire* (cf. for the Seine, Allard's excellent *annuaire* and the articles in the *Annales de statistique*). For communications: *État général des postes et relais de l'Empire français*. Travellers' accounts are also of considerable interest. Lequinio with his *Voyage dans le Jura* (Year IX), another former Conventional, Camus, with his *Voyage* in the East and the North (Year IX) and Raymond de Carbonnières with his famous *Voyage au Mont-Perdu et . . . Hautes Pyrénées* (Year IX) had opened the way for the much noticed *Voyage dans les départements du Midi de la France* by Millin (1807), plagiarized later by Stendhal in his *Mémoires d'un touriste* (Monglond, 'Millin', *Revue des Études napoléoniennes*, 1940, pp. 81–107 and 161–88) and in the *Dictionnaire topographique des environs de Paris*, by Oudiette. Among foreigners, Nemnich in 1809 (ed. O. Viennet, 1947) is particularly interesting as is Prince Clary and Aldringen (*Trois Mois à Paris*,

1912). Travel guides are very numerous, the best being *l'Itinéraire de l'Empire français* by Langlois (3 vols. and a supplement), reissued several times. We must be grateful to the fashion for topography for the remarkable *Topographie de Paris* by Maire (1st ed. 1808). Scenes of manners in Jouy, *L'Hermite de la Chaussée d'Antin* (1914), and Fortia de Piles, *L'Ermite du Faubourg-Saint-Honoré* (1914) and in the Parisian pictures and chronicles of Nougaret, Pujoulx, Prudhomme and Salgues. On Italy, the magnificent statistics of Montenotte by Chabrol (1824).

Works

As the capital of the Empire, Paris was the subject of numerous works. We merely mention the syntheses of Lanzac du Laborie (*Paris sous Napoléon*, 8 vols., 1905–11), M.-L. Biver (*Le Paris de Napoléon*, 1963), G. Poisson, *Napoléon et Paris* (1964), M. Guerini, *Napoléon et Paris* (1967) and J. Tulard, *Nouvelle Histoire de Paris: le Consulat et l'Empire* (1970).

The bibliography for the provinces is enormous, buried in every regional review. Some histories of large towns should be remembered: Trenard, *Lyon, de l'Encyclopédie au Préromantisme* (1958); *Histoire de Bordeaux* (Vol. V, 1968); C. Fohlen, *Histoire de Besançon*, Vol. II (1965); A. Vion, *La Vie calaisienne sous le Consulat et l'Empire* (1972), and on particular matters: Gaffarel for Marseille (*Revue des Études napoléoniennes*, 1916, pp. 65–93) or Villat, 'Napoléon à Nantes' (*Ibid.*, 1912, pp. 335–65). Mention should also be made with regard to Pontivy (Napoléonville) of P. Lavedan's article in the *Bul. Soc. Art. Fr.*, 1950, pp. 186–98. Regional studies: Rocal, *Du 18 Brumaire à Waterloo en Périgord* (1943), F. L'Huillier, *Recherches sur L'Alsace napoléonienne* (1947) which can be complemented by the special number of *Saisons d'Alsace* (1963), A. Maureau, *Souvenirs du Consulat et de l'Empire dans le Vaucluse* (1976) or J. de Vidalenc, *Textes sur l'histoire de la Seine-Inférieure à l'époque napoléonienne* (1976). *La Vie sociale en Provence intérieure au lendemain de la Révolution,* by Agulhon (1970), should also be mentioned. There is much to be learnt from the volumes of *l'Univers de la France* (Languedoc under Wolff's directions, *Bretagne* by Delumeau, *Île-de-France* by Mollat . . .) which contain important chapters on the Napoleonic period.

The annexed countries have been subjects of close study. For Belgium: S. Balau, *La Belgique sous l'Empire* (1894), Lanzac de Laborie, *La Domination française en Belgique* (Vol. II, 1895), P. Verhaegen, *La Belgique sous la domination française* (5 vols., 1922–9), Pirenne, *Histoire de la Belgique,* (Vols. VI, 1926), J. Cathelin, *La Vie quotidienne en Belgique* (1966), R. Devleeshouwer, 'La Belgique annexée à la France' in *Les Pays sous domination française* (roneoed 1968), J. Puraye's edition of General Dumonceau's *Mémoires* should not be forgotten (Vol. I, 1958; a Belgian in the service of France). On the left bank of the Rhine, Sagnac's *Le Rhin français* (1917), Capot-Rey's *Quand la Sarre était française* (1928), and the biography of the Prefect of Mont-Tonnerre, Jean Bon Saint-Abdré, by Levy Schneider (1901) are all out-dated and have been replaced by R. Dufraisse's remarkable synthesis, 'Les Départements du Rhin sous le régime napoléonien' in *Les Pays sous domination française* (roneoed 1968, with bibliography; and by the same author, 'Le Soulèvement des gardes nationales de la Sarre en 1809', *Bull. Soc. d'Histoire moderne*, 1969, pp. 1–6: the discontent had been caused by the unpopular institution of the National Guard and by the numerous convictions for offences against forestry laws. There was no patriotic movement connected to agitation in Germany.

For Illyria, see: Pisani, *La Dalmatie de 1797 à 1815* (1893; a good study of the administrations of Marmont, Junot and Fouché); Pivec-Stellé, *La Vie économique des provinces illyriennes, 1809–1813* (1931). On the Ionian islands which were occupied from 1807 and where General Donzelot was to hold on until 1814: J. Baeyens, *Les Français à Corton* (1973) which supplants Rodocanachi's *Bonaparte et les îles Ioniennes* (1899). J. Savant throws light on Napoleon and Greece, *Napoléon et les Grecs* (1945), also see Boppe, *l'Albanie et Napoléon* (1914).

As for dependent nations, for Westphalia, read: H. Berding, *Napoleonische Herrschafts und Gesellschaftspolitik* (1973); J. Tulard, 'Siméon et l'organisation du royaume de Westphalie', *Francia*, 1973, pp. 557–68; on Berg: C. Schmidt, *Le Grand-Duché de Berg* (1905). With regard to Switzerland, consult Suratteau, 'La Suisse dans le système français' in *Les Pays sous domination française* (1968). The case of Geneva has been dealt with clearly by Chapuisat in *Le Commerce et l'industrie de Genève pendant la domination française* (1908). On Neufchâtel, see Courvoisier's study (1961). For matters concerning Italy and Holland, refer to works quoted in other chapters. For the Grand Duchy of Warsaw: H. Grynwasser, 'Le Code Napoléon dans le duché de Varsovie', *Revue des Études napoléoniennes* 1917, pp. 129–70, the special number of the *Annales historiques de la Revue française*, 1964 (especially B. Grochulska's article on economic structures and M. Senkowska's on French *majorats*)' A. Soboùl, 'Le Duché de Varsovie' in *Les Pays sous domination française* (1968). On Italy: Fugier, *Napoléon et l'Italie* (1947); the records of the academy dei Lincei, *Napoléon et l'Italie* (1973, fundamental); Zaghi, *Il regno d'Italia* (1965); Roberti, *Milano, capitale napoleonica* (1946); Borel, *Gênes sous Napoléon* (1929). The road as a factor of unity: Cavaillès, *La Route française* (1946); J. Petot, *L'Administration des Ponts et Chaussés* (1958); the Civil Code was a further element of unity. Also the Napoleonic cult (W. Zajewski, 'Le Culte de Napoléon à Dantzig', *Revue d'Histoire moderne*, 1976, pp. 556–72).

Open Questions

At the moment in which France ruled Europe, contemporaries were questioning the French identity. Elements of a reply are to be found in M. N. Bourguet, 'Race et folklore, l'image officielle de la France en 1800', *Annales*, 1976, pp. 802–23, which analyses the official statistics, 'distributing the French throughout the nation according to their size, their physiognomy and their character'. Is a physical description of these Frenchmen possible? J. Houdaille, depending on statistics, army medical boards and passports, has produced two descriptive articles: 'La taille des Français au début du XIXe siècle', *Population*, 1970, and 'La couleur des yeux à l'époque du Premier

Empire', *Annales,* 1976. What about women? Y. Knibiehler ('La nature féminine au temps du Code civil', *Annales,* 1976) explains the regression of the female condition (women were not educated and were excluded from politics) in terms of medical influence (Moreau de la Sarthe, Virey) which stressed two physical aspects of women—their weakness in comparison to men and the fact of their being destined for maternity.

A linguistic atlas of the Empire would be indispensable. French was the official language, the language of administration, but even in France it had to compete with patois and dialects. Was it an instrument of bourgeois domination as Balibart and Laporte claim in *Politique et pratique de la langue nationale sous la Révolution* (1974)? It is a possibility, but this role of dominance, if not of unification, seems arguable in annexed and dependent countries. Reinhard, the Representative of France in Westphalia, questioned several councillors of state on the official language in Jerome's kingdom: 'They answered that it was the German language since it was used in law-courts and in administration, as the German text of the Code Napoleon had been declared the kingdom's code. Nevertheless in at least three ministries all affairs are dealt with in French, discussions in the Council of State take place in French, decrees are drawn up in French, German translations are frequently inaccurate.' Elsewhere bills and proclamations were in two languages. In Italy, where 'the French language is little known', according to Thiard in his *Mémoires,* p. 67, portable dictionaires such as Cormon et Manni (1802) were used. It is to be remembered that French was the everyday language of the chancelleries (for instance Vienna). There was the same problem over weights and measures. Unification in France was not yet completed. There were equally great difficulties over coinage. Rates of exchange were published regularly. It is well known how the Rothschilds built their fortune from the fruitful transference of guineas from England to France (B. Gille, *Histoire de la maison Rothschild,* Vol. I, 1965).

Note the existence of a feeling which favoured a customs union in the states under Imperial rule (J.-B. Dubois, Catineau-Laroche) and which was always rejected by Napoleon. This rejection played a decisive role in the failure of the 'Great Empire'.

III. 2   THE RULE OF THE NOTABLES

Sources
The sub-series F^{20} of the National Archives (migration of workers, investigation into diet), the lists of the 600 most highly taxed (cf. Agulhon, 'Les sources statistiques de l'histoire des notables au début du XIXe siècle dans les archives d'un département: Le Var', *84e Congrès des Soc. Sav.,* 1959, pp. 453–9), registers of statistics (Bottin, *Annuaire statistique du Nord*) and statistical surveys (for instance, Dartonne's for the *arrondissement* of Gien, published by B. Gitton in 1963; Abbé Marchand's memoirs on the communes of Rahay and Valennes in Year IX, edited in 1908 by J. L'Hermitte) are essential. The most interesting among the *Mémoires* are Hue, *Journal d'un*

Paysan, published by Vueclin in 1886 (document of rare value on life in the countryside), Lamartine (1870, life in Milly at the beginning of the Empire), Poumiès de la Siboutie (*Souvenirs d'un Médecin de Paris,* 1910), Agricole Perdiguier (*Mémoires d'un Compagnon,* 1854–5, rural conditions in the last years of the Empire), Ouvrard (1826), Vidocq (1828 reissued by J. Savant, 1950: the uncertain boundaries between workers and the criminal world), Véron (*Mémoires d'un Bourgeois de Paris,* Vol. I, 1853), Moitte (wife of the sculptor; excellent on everyday life), Stendhal (*Journal,* ed. Martineau, 1955), Pierre Foucher (by Victor Hugo's father-in-law, the life of a ministerial employee, ed. Guimbaud, 1929). There are many interesting observations on society in Fiévée's *Correspondance* (1836), in Jouy's chronicles, collected in *L'Hermite de la Chaussée-d'Antin* and in the *Itinéraire parisien* by Alletz, a commissioner of police during the Revolution and the Empire.

Works

The old general studies are out of date: Bondois, *Napoléon et la Société de son temps,* 1895; F. Corréard, *La France sous le Consulat;* G. Stenger, *La Société Française pendant le Consulat* (1902–8, 6 vols.) Hanotaux, 'Les transformations sociales à l'époque napoléonienne' (*La Revue des Deux Mondes, 1926, pp. 89–123, 526–77*), with the exception of Brousse and Thurot, *Le Consulat et l'Empire,* Vol. VI of the *Histoire socialiste de Jaurès* (1905), where numerous documents preserved in the National Archives have been gone through. Among recent syntheses: Jacques Godechot's contribution in the *Histoire de la société française* by Halphen and Doucet, and Bertrand Gille's in *Napoléon et l'Empire* by J. Mistler; A. Soboul's report, *Bilan social en 1815* (International Committee of historical sciences, XIIᵉ congress, 1965, pp. 517–45) and that of J. Tulard, 'Problèmes sociaux de la France impériale', *Revue d'Histoire moderne et contemporaine* (1970, pp. 639–63). On a particular region: M. Agulhon, *La Vie sociale en Provence intérieure au lendemain de la Révolution* (1971).

The system of property has been well analysed by M. Garaud, *La Révolution et la Propriété foncière* (1960). On the 'survival of feudal rights' in the west, cf. P. Massé's article in the *Annales historiques de la Révolution française,* 1965, pp. 270–98 (examines the case of feudal rents made over to commoners and the new tithe). On the sale of national property under the Empire, apart from M. Marion's observations (*La Vente des Biens nationaux pendant la Révolution,* 1908) and G. Lefebvre ('La vente des biens nationaux' in *Études sur la Révolution française,* 1963, pp. 307–37), the numerous regional studies, the best example of which remains Dubreuil, *La Vente des Biens nationaux dans le département des Côtes-du-Nord* (1911). On the role played by national property in the building up of a fortune: Barral, *Les Perier dans l'Isère au XIX siècle* (1964). On the notables, E. Beau de Loménie, *Les Responsabilités des Dynasties bourgeoises,* Vol. I (1943); C. Morazé, *La France bourgeoise* (1946); G. Chaussinand-Nogaret, L. Bergeron and R. Forster, 'Les notables du grand Empire en 1810', *Annales,* 1971, pp. 1,052–75 ('The notable is a man of riper years who belongs to professions which assure him of moral prestige, official authority or economic power.') Regional cases studied by F. Spannel, 'Les éléments de la fortune des grands notables marseillais au début du XIXe siècle', *La Provence historique* (1957), Vitte, 'La société mâconnaise à la fin du Premier Empire', *Cashiers d'Histoire* (1956), Bouyoux, 'Les six cents plus imposés du département de la Haute-Garonne en l'an X', *Annales du Midi* (1958, pp. 317–27), and in the *Revue d'Histoire moderne* of 1970, a series of studies by A. Palluel ('Les notables dans les Alpes du Nord', pp. 741–57), Agulhon 'Les notables du Var', pp. 720–25), J. M. Lévy ('Les Notables de l'Ain', pp. 726–40), Dufraisse ("'Les notables de la rive gauche du Rhin', pp. 758–76), J. Vidalenc ('Les notables des départements hanséatiques', pp. 777–92), Nicolas ('Le ralliement des notables au régime impérial dans le département du Mont-Blanc', *ibid.* 1972). N. Célestin deals with a particular case, 'Le Notariat parisien sous le Consulate et l'Empire', *ibid. (pp. 649–708).* On urban landlords: A. Daumard, *Maisons de Paris et propriétaires parisiens, 1809–1880* (1965). Beau de Loménie has drawn attention to the birth of bourgeois dynasties which were to dominate the nineteenth century, Fiévée deals separately with the world of banking, the best studies: Lhomer, *Le Banquier Perrégaux et sa fille, la duchesse de Raguse* (1926); J. Stern, *Le Mari de Mlle Lange, Michel-Jean Simons (1933);* M. Payard, 'Bonaparte et le fournisseur Collot' (*Revue des Études napoléoniennes*, 1935, pp. 129–43); Palmade, *Capitalisme et Capitalistes français au XIXe siècle* (1961); Gille, *Histoire de la Maison Rothschild* (1967); Gérard, *Messieurs Hottinguer banquiers à Paris* (1968); L. Bergeron, *Banquiers, négociants et manufacturiers parisiens du Directoire à l'Empire* (1975). Ouvrard has been the subject of several studies, by A. Lévy, J. Savant and Payard all mentioned above. Equally R. Szramkiewicz, *Les Régents et censeurs de la Banque de France* (1974) should not be forgotten.

Works concerning the peasant world are few and generally treat the entire nineteenth century (cases in point are Desert's thesis on Normandy, Merley on the Haute-Loire or Garrier for Beaujolais). Note, however, Berland, 'Les cultures et la vie paysanne dans la Vienne à l'époque napoléonienne' in the *Mémoires publiés par la commission de recherche des documents relatifs à la vie économique de la Révolution français* (1937, pp. 189–230). 'La lutte pour l'individualisme agraire dans la France du Premier Empire' is treated by Laurent (*Annales de Bourgogne*, 1950).

There is far more information about workers, although most of the observations which have been collected refer to Paris. This is true of Gerando's old book, *Des Progrès de l'industrie considérés dans leurs rapports avec la moralité de la classe ouvrière* (1841) and of the figures collected by Duchatellier, *Essai sur les salaires et les prix de consommation de 1202 à 1830* (1830). E. Levassuer's work *Histoire des classes ouvrières en France depuis 1789 jusqu'à nos jours* (Vol. I, 1867) remains useful despite certain obvious prejudices; complement it with Vol. VI of *Paris sous Napoléon* by Laborie (1910) and G. Vauthier, 'Les ouvriers de Paris sous l'Empire', *Revue des Études napoléoniennes,* 1913, Vol. II, pp. 426–51. Seasonal migrations have been studied by G. Mauco, *Les Migrations ouvrières en France au début du XIXe siècle* (1932); Arbos, 'Un rapport sur l'émigration saisonnière dans le Puy-de-Dome en 1808', *Revue d'Auvergne* (1934); A. Chatelain's 'Les migrations temporaires en France au XIXe siècle', *Annales de démographie historique,* 1967; also his 'résistance à la conscription et migrations temporaires sous le Premier Empire,' *Annales hist. Rev. Fr.,* 1972, pp. 606–25; R. Beteille, 'Les Migrations saisonnières en France sous l'Empire', *Revue d'Histoire moderne,* 1970, pp. 424–41, and above all, L. Chevalier, *La Formation de la Population parisienne au XIXe siècle* (1950). For the provincial centres: G. Clause, *Les Cardeurs et Fileurs de laine en 1812* (conference of the *Association inter-universitaire de l'Est,* 1972). R. Marquant has applied himself to the 'Bureaux de placement en France sous l'Empire et la Restauration', *Revue d'Histoire économique et sociale* (1962), pp. 200–237. The transition from the 'hard-working class' to the 'dangerous class' has been well elucidated by L. Chevalier, *Classes labourieuses et Classes dangereuses* (1958). The resurgence of 'compagnonnage' is analysed by E. Coornaert, *Les Compagnonnages en France, du Moyen Age à nos jours* (1966). On the problem of the *livret,* H. Sazerac de Forge, 'La législation ouvrière sous l'Empire', *Bulletin de l'Institut Napoléon,* 1949 (defends Napoleon's motives against the opinionof G. Bourgin, 'Contribution à l'histoire du placement et du livret en France', *Revue politique et parlementaire,* 1912).

The wages evolution has been reconstructed by J. Rougière, 'Remarques sur l'histoire des salaires à Paris au xixe siècle', *Mouvement Social,* 1968, pp. 71–108. Some strikes have been studied: P. Viard, 'Une grève sous le Premier Empire au Tregueil', *Mélanges Pirenne,* 1926, pp. 663–68; Lorenzi, 'Une grève parisienne en 1810', *Miroir de l'Histoire,* Dec. 1954, pp. 643–748 (makes use of notebooks of the works supervisor at the Arc de Triomphe at the Étoile, Héricart de Thury); J. Bruhat, 'Le mouvement ouvrier français du début du XIXe siècle et les survivances d'Ancien Régime', *La Pensée,* Dec., 1968, pp. 44–56.

There is little to be gained on the subject of social history from Broc, *La Vie en France sous le Premier Empire* (1895); J. Bertaut, *La Vie à Paris sous le Premier Empire* (1943); J. Robiquet, *La Vie quotidienne au temps de Napoléon* (1944); F. Darle, *Au temps de Napoléon Bonaparte* (1961), and H. d'Almeras, *La Vie parisienne sous le consulat et l'Empire* (no date); but to be recommended are Z. Harsany, *La vie quotidienne à Strasbourg* (1976); Rousseaux-Berrens, 'La Gastronomie à Paris', *Rev. Inst. Nap.,* 1961; J. Tulard, *La vie quotidienne des Français sous Napoléon* (1978).

Open questions
What were the population trends under the Consulate and the Empire? Marcel Reinhard is the first to have orientated research in this field ('La statistique de la population sous la Révolution et l'Empire', *Population,* 1950, pp. 103–20; 'Étude de la population pendant la Révolution et l'Empire', *Bulletin d'Histoire économique et sociale de la Révolution française;* 1959–60, pp. 20–28; 'Supplément', *ibid.,* 1962, pp. 19–20; 'Bilan démographique de l'Europe, 1789–1815', *Rapport au XIIe congrès international des sciences historiques,* Vienna, 1965) with Michel Fleury and Louis Henry ('Pour connaitre la population de la France depuis Louis XIV—Plan de travaux par sondages', *Population,* 1958, pp. 663–86).

The Empire had no policy of demography, but nevertheless it did not ignore the problems attendant on it. Peuchet interested himself in it in his *Essai d'une statistique générale de la France* (Year IX) and in his *Statistique élémentaire* (1805) as did Duquesnoy, but an essential role was played, until its suppression in 1812, by the Minister of the Interior's Bureau of Statistics, under Duvillard, Alexandre de Ferrière, then Coquebert de Montbret (B. Gille, *Les sources statistiques de l'Histoire de France,* 1964; Biraben, 'La statistique de population sous le consulat et l'Empire', *Revue d'Histoire moderne et contemporaine,* 1970, pp. 339–72).

There were three important censuses: 1801 (unreliable, gives a population of 27.9 million inhabitants for France with the boundaries of 1861), 1806 (29.5 million inhabitants, more accurate) and 1811. For their interpretation see J. Dupaquier, 'Problèmes démographiques de la France napoléonienne', *Revue d'Histoire moderne* 1970, pp. 339–58, and R. LeMée, 'population agglomérée, population éparse au début de XIXe siècle', *Annales de Démographie Historique,* 1971, pp. 455–510 (the survey of 1809 sets the threshold of the agglomerated population at 2,000 souls).

The proportion of urban population was particularly high in the Seine (89%) the south-east (Bouches-du-Rhône, 67%; Var, Hérault and Vaucluse, 41%), the Rhône (38%), the Nord (34%). At the time there were 45 million inhabitants in Russia, 29 million in Austria and 20 million in Great Britain.

An undoubted drop in the birth rate is to be seen as a result of progress in contraception which may have been tied to dechristianization (it fell from 34.6 per 1000 to 31.8 for the period 1806–10, according to Armengaud, 'Mariages et naissances sous le consulat et l'Empire', *Revue d'Histoire moderne,* 1970, pp. 373–89) but there was an increase in illegitimate births (4.6% in Year X, 6.5% in 1812). A parallel and marked decrease in mortality is to be noted. Can this be attributed to vaccination which was only invented by Jenner in 1796 and the effects of which were still limited under the Empire. No doubt the improved living conditions were a determining factor.

With reference to the conclusions of a vast investigation carried out by the I.N.E.D. in the special number of *Population* of November 1975, L. Henry and Y. Blayo give the following figures for France with the political frontiers of 1861:

Population in millions	Births in thousands	Marriages in thousands	Deaths in thousands	Period
29.29	4,824	874	4,475	1800–1804
29.73	4,812	1,180	4,270	1805–1809
30.15	4,913	1,305	4,624	1810–1814

It can be seen that the demographic balance remains positive; marriages continued to increase, perhaps due to the system of conscription which dispensed married men from service, so did births, although less markedly. If the number of deaths appears especially high, particularly after 1809, it is because war took an increasingly heavy toll from the time of the Spanish expedition.

Passy had spoken of 1,700,000 deaths, a figure taken from Hargenvilliers, assistant director of conscription, and repeated by Taine. Vacher de Lapouge put forward 2,600,000 men for France and 3,500,000 for abroad. In 1930, Albert Meynier, using information provide by Martinien, *Officiers tués et blessés, 1805–1815*, decreased the above estimates to 427,500 dead on the battlefield in *La Revue des Études napoléoniennes* of 1930 (pp. 26–51) 'Levées et pertes d'hommes sous le consulat et l'Empire'. But he did not account for the soldiers who died of sickness, or prisoners who did not return. In 1932, in a reissue of his article, in the form of an off-print (*Une Erreur historique, les morts de la Grande Armée et des armées ennemies*), he admits that the number of losses should be fixed at a million for the period 1800–1815. The figure has been adopted by G. Lefebvre. Returning to the problem and judging from the census of 1851 (which gives distribution by age), Bourgeois Pichat in *Population* (1951) gives 860,000 mission, presumed dead. Jacques Houdaille, using the registers kept in the War Ministry archives reaches a total of 916,000 killed for their country ('Le problème des pertes de guerre', *Revue d'Histoire moderne*, 1970, pp. 411–23). There was no question of a real population drain because of there being more births than deaths and because of foreign immigration on which Houdaille has thrown light.

Another factor in mortality: epidemics were on the decline under the Empire from 1813, with the exception of typhus. To be read with interest is R. Darquenne, 'La dysenterie en Belgique à la fin de l'Empire', *La Revue du Nord*, 1970, pp. 367–73, while awaiting a history of illness from 1800–15 (cf. G. Thuillier, 'Pour une histoire du médicament en Nivernais au XIXe siècle', *Revue d'Histoire économique*, 1975, pp. 73–98). Nosographies used by Biraben ('Les causes de décès sous la Révolution et l'Empire' in *Mélanges Reinhard*, 1973, pp. 59–71) throw light on the overwhelming majority of deaths due to organic lesions (syphilis, cancer, gangrene . . .)

With regard to the town or village, read the studies on Nancy, Toulouse, Strasburg and Caen in *Contributions à l'Histoire démographique de la Revolution française*, 2nd series (1965). For Paris, J. Tulard, 'Guerre et expansion démographique à Paris sous le Consulat et l'Empire', and L. Bergeron, 'Recrutement et engagements volontaires à Paris sous le Consulat et l'Empire', *ibid.* 3rd series (1970).

Balzac explains Napoleon's popularity with the peasants as springing from the assurance he gave them concerning the sale of national property. This is equally the idea developed by G. Lefebvre and Chabert (*Essai sur le mouvement des prix et des revenus en France de 1789 à 1820*, 1949). On the other hand, Tocqueville, M. Bloch (*Caractères originaux de l'Histoire rurale française*, 1952), and Godechot (*Les Institutions de la France sous la Révolution et l'Empire*) minimize the social significance of the sale of this property. Blandine Morel has returned to the question: 'Vente des biens nationaux et popularité de l'Empereur', *Revue d'Histoire économique et sociale*, 1975, p. 428. To be sure, she asserts, Foville in *Le Morcellement* (1885), points to the appearance of 500,000 new landowners between 1789 and 1816. But the establishment of a property register, and the sale of property by aristocrats in need of money, play a large part in this increase. National property was bought above all by well-to-do bourgeois. 'Even if the share of land owned by peasants, the working class and artisans, rose from 16,000 million in 1789 to 16,700 million after the sale of national property, this increase of 4.3% cannot be considered as a transfer of landed capital in favour of the people . . . in reality, apart from the clever profiteering politicians of the new regime, the sale of national property was a great advantage to the wealthy bourgeois, and very little to the peasants, the most interested of whom had to make do with odds and ends which had been turned down by others.' But the author does not mention the abolition of feudalism, maintained by Napoleon, nor the rise in wages by the day, both decisive factors in the Emperor's popularity.

Little is as yet known of contemporary crime. Several notorious cases of counterfeit money-makers and smuggling, and the horrible crime of the grocer of Trumeau, have diverted attention from realities. In Paris thirty per cent of delinquents were women; sixty-two per cent came from the provinces. Sixty-five per cent were workers and only eight per cent were servants; nineteen per cent were under twenty years of age. The Prefect of Police, Pasquier, indicates bands of well-organized children.

Napoleon attached considerable importance to the rate of government stock—the famous Five per cent (cf. Lanzac de Laborie, *Paris sous Napoléon*, Vol. VI, 1910) negotiated at the Bourse. In fact the *rentier* world seems to have preferred mortgages, mutual insurance societies, speculation in newly conquered countries, or even privateering. Hence the poor condition of the Bourse (cf. A. Colling, *Histoire de la Bourse*). On the law of 21 Nivôse, Year VIII: G. Massa-Gille, 'Les rentes foncières sous le Consulat et l'Empire', *Bibl. École des Chartes*, 1975.

A problem of vocabulary: the word 'bourgeois' whose meaning has changed since the Middle Ages. Under the Empire *propriétaire* (landlord) is more usually used to denote the bourgeois class, and the notables represented an élite (Vovelle et Roche, 'Bourgeois, rentiers et propriétaires' *84e Congrès des Sociétés savants*, 1959, pp. 419–52). This meaning continued to apply in towns: P. Delpuech, 'Une institution de Napoléon I, les bonnes villes', *Rev. Institut Napoléon*, 1971. For Normandy: J. Vidalenc, 'Sociétés urbaines et villes de la Seine inférieure sous le Premier Empire', *Annales de Nice*, 1969, pp. 291–314, and the *Journal d'un bourgeois d'Évreux* 1850).

Should Napoleon's contempt for tradespeople be relegated to the realms of legend? C. Durand varies his tone ('Les intérêts commerciaux et le recrutement du conseil d'État pendant le Consulat et l'Empire', *Études et documents, Conseil d'État*, 1961); so does Begouën-Demeaux in his biography of Jacques-François Begouën (Vol. II, 1958), an important merchant from Le Havre who was called to the Council of State but who was never able to enter the Senate. A significant fact is that most of the councillors of state who were called upon to deal with financial affairs (Jaubert at the Bank of France, Berenger of the Sinking Fund . . .) were sons of bourgeois but not confidants of Napoleon in the style of Louis XI's councillors (Olivier le Daim, Tristan l'Hermite). Narbonne (the natural son of Louis XV), and perhaps before him Roederer, was one of the few vaguely to fulfil this role (cf. Dard, *Le comte de Narbonne*, 1943).

Recruitment for the new army cadres was bourgeois-dominated as P. Carles pointed out in the case of the Hérault (fifty per cent of landowners' sons among officer cadets) at the conference on military history at Montpellier (1974). The tuition fees at the Polytechnic, the special military academy instituted in 1802, and at the Cavalry academy at St Germain, created in 1809, were so high as to be afforded only by well-to-do parents in spite of scholarships. This did not alleviate the conflict between civil and military society (cf. examples by G. Canton, *Napoléon antimilitariste*, 1902).

III. 3   A WARTIME ECONOMY

Sources
Sub-entries F^{10} (agriculture), F^{11} (provisions), F^{12} (commerce and industry), F^{14} (public works) and above all F^{20} (statistics) at the National Archives. Use can also be made of the archives of the Chambers of Commerce. The minutes of the General Council of manufacturers have been published by B. Gille (1961) as have the surveys concerning Paris (*Documents pour l'état de l'industrie et du commerce de Paris et du département de la Seine, 1778–1810* (1963). *La Description topographique et statistique de la France* by Peuchet and Chanlaire (1810) contains some valuable information. As an addendum to Festy's *L'Agriculture française sous le Consulat* (1952) there is a useful list of yearbooks and statistics classified according to departments. *La statistique du département du Nord* by Dieudonné has been reprinted. For Paris, consult La Tynna's *Almanach du Commerce* and Chabrol's *Recherches statistiques*. Official information (therefore unreliable) in *Exposés de la situation de l'Empire*, especially that of 1813 by Montalivet which draws up a balance sheet of the economic evolution with figures. For all the important surveys of the time: B. Gille, *Les sources statistiques de l'Histoire de France* (1964, to be complemented by B. Desgrey, 'Montalivet et la statistique au temps de l'Empire', *Revue de l'Institut Napoléon*, 1968, pp. 103–8). Among contemporary writings on agriculture: Pradt, *De l'État de la culture en France et des améliorations* (Year X); François de Neufchâteau, *L'Art de multiplier les grains* (1809); *Voyage agronomique dans la sénatorerie de Dijon* (1806) as well as his numerous reports printed by the agricultural society of the department of the Seine; Héron de Villefosse, *De la Richesse minérale* (1810); Rougier de la Bergerie, *Mémoires sur les abus des défrichements et la destruction des bois et forêts* (Year IX), and even better his *Histoire de l'Agriculture française* (1815); add, *Les Forêts de la France* (1817); Costaz, *Essai sur l'administration de l'agriculture suivi de l'historique des moyens qui ont amené le grand essor pris par les arts depuis 1793 jusqu'à 1815* (1818); Chaptal, *Mémoires sur la culture de la vigne* (1820); C. Sonnini, *Manuel des propriétaires ruraux et de tous les habitants de la campagne* (1808). On industry: the jury reports on products on show at the exhibitions were published at the time (cf. especially Costaz report in 1806). An essential

source: Chaptal, *De l'Industrie française* (reviews with figures all branches of industry, 1819). The works of certain economists cannot be overlooked: Ganilh, *Des Systèmes d'économie politique* (1802); Sismondi, *Nouveaux Principes d'économie politique* (1819); Say, *Principales causes de la richesse ou de la misère des peuples et des particuliers* (1818), and especially d'Ivernois, *Napoléon administrateur et financier* (1814) which was preceded by *Des causes qui ont amené l'usurpation du général Bonaparte et qui préparent sa chute* (1800). The *Mémoires* of Richard-Lenoir (Vol. I only appeared in 1873) are apocryphal. There is little to be gained from Laffitte's *Mémoires* (1932). For transport, the *Almanachs des postes* supply valuable information. Read also the *Code du Commerce* annotated by Fournel (1807); Dupré Saint-Maur on commerce in the Aude (1808).

Works

Excellent syntheses which we owe to Brousse and Thurot, *Histoire socialiste de Jaurès*, Vol. VI (old-fashioned but with numerous documents); H. See (*Histoire économique et sociale de la France*, Vol. II, 1939); Chabert, (*Essai sur le mouvement des revenus et de l'activite économique en France de 1798 à 1820*, 1949, a first attempt to apply serial history methods to the period); Palmade, *Capitalisme et Capitalistes français au XIXe siècle* (1961); F. Labrousse, 'Éléments d'un bilan économique: la croissance dans la guerre', *XIIe Congrès international des sciences historiques* (1965), pp. 473–96; Bergeron, 'Problèmes économiques de la France napoléonienne', *Revue d'Histoire Moderne*, 1970, pp. 469–505; the pages devoted to the Empire by A. Saboul in Volume III of the *Histoire économique et sociale de la France* (1976). An example of a local monograph: J. Vidalenc, 'La vie économique des départements méditerranéens pendant le Premier Empire,' *Revue d'Histoire Moderne* 1954, pp. 164–98.

Note on the subject of agriculture Festy's remarkable synthesis, *L'Agriculture française sous le Consulat* (1952) which is to be complemented by 'Les progrès de l'agriculture sous l'Empire', *Revue d'Histoire économique et sociale*, 1957. Certain regions have been the subject of monographs: R. Laurent, *L'Agriculture en Côte-d'Or pendant la première motié du XIXe siècle* (1931); R. Berland, 'Les cultures et la vie paysanne dans la Vienne à l'époque napoléonienne' (*Com. recherche et publ. de documents économiques*, 1937, pp. 189–231); Roque, *Aspects économiques de la vie niçoise* (1957); J. Vidalenc, 'L'agriculture et l'industrie dans les départements Normands à la fin du Premier Empire', *Annales de Normandie* (1957, pp. 281–307). The forests have only been the subject of a few fragmentary works: A. Granger, 'Notes sur l'administration des forêts sous la Consulat et l'Empire', *Revue forestière*, 1930, pp. 541–58; Cointat and Choulet, 'La forêt haute-marnaise sous l'Empire', *ibid.*, 1952, pp. 453–9; Dufraisse, 'La forêt de Haguenau sous la Révolution et l'Empire', *Études haguenoviennes*, 1958, pp. 145–84. On the vine a good comprehensive view by P. Boussel, *Napoléon au royaume des vins de France* (1951). About champagne, G. Clause, 'Notes sur la viticulture et le vignoble champenois au début du XIXe siècle', *Mémoires Soc. Agr. Dep. Marne*, 1965, pp. 137–47. There being no synthesis on stock farming, M. Rebouillat's monograph, *Les Progrès de l'élevage dans la Saône-et-Loire sous le Premier Empire* (Congrès National des sociétés savantes, 1967) and P. Percevaux's excellent study, 'La Dombes sous la Révolution et l'Empire', *Cahiers d'Histoire*, 1971, pp. 371–91, puts the vicious circle in its context: stock is badly fed, and since such produce is hard to sell well, even the slightest improvements in fodder cannot financed.

Much has been written about industry. Good comprehensive studies by A. Meynier, 'L'Industrie française de 1800 à 1814', *Revue de l'Institut Napoléon*, 1938, pp. 65–80; A. Viennet, *Napoléon et l'Industrie française* (1947, a work which concentrates particularly on the crisis of 1811), 'Napoléon et l'industrie' (remarkable special number of *Souvenir napoléonien*, January 1971). Several regional studies: P. Léon, *La Naissance de la Grande Industrie en Dauphiné (Vol. I, 1954)*, F. Crouzet, 'Les origines du sous-développement économique du Sud-Ouest', *Annales du Midi*, 1959, pp. 71–9 (shows the de-industrialization of the South), G. Thuillier, *Aspects de l'économie nivernaise au XIXe siècle* (1966), Brandt, 'L'Alsace napoléonienne et la Révolution industrielle' (*Saisons d'Alsace*, 1963). L. Bergeron, *Banquiers, Négociants et Manufacturiers à Paris* (1975), underlines the leading role played by Paris. M. Lévy-Leboyer brings light to bear on the re-financing of the economy and more particularly of the textile industry, *Les Banques européennes et l'Industrialisation de l'Europe au début du XIXe siècle* (1964). The privileged section remained the textile industry: Pinkney, 'Paris, capitale du coton sous le Premier Empire', *Annales*, 1950, pp. 56–60; Dhondt, 'L'industrie cotonnière gantoise à l'époque française', *Revue d'Histoire moderne* (1955, pp. 233–79); Dornic, L'Industrie textile dans le Maine (1955); Labasse, *Le Commerce des soies à Lyon sous Napoléon et la crise de 1811* (1957); E. Baux, 'Les draperies audoises sous le Premier Empire', *Revue d'Histoire moderne* (1937, insists on the difficulties of credit; interest loans reached 8 to 10 per cent); Clause, 'L'industrie rémoise lainière a l'époque napoléonienne', *Revue d'Histoire moderne*, 1970, pp. 574–95: Bergeron, 'Douglas, Ternaux, Cockerill: aux origines de la mécanisation de l'industrie lainière en France', *Revue historique*, 1972. Some industrial figures: A. Laboucherie, *Oberkampf* (1884); H. Causse, 'Un industriel toulousain au temps de la Révolution et de l'Empire: Boyer-Fonfrède', *Annales du Midi*, 1957; F. Leleux, *Lievin Bauwens, industriel gantois* (1969); Collignon, *Ternaux, manufacturier français*.

Important works have also been written on the subject of metallurgy: B. Gille, *Les Origines de la Grande Industrie métallurgique en France* (1947); G. Thuillier, *G. Dufaud et les débuts du grand capitalisme dans la métallurgie en Nivernais au XIXe siècle* (1954); H.-J. Favier, 'Forges du centre vues par un maître de forges vosgien', *Revue Hist. de la Sidérurgië* (1965, pp. 103–22); same author, 'La psychologie d'un maître de forges au début du XIXe siècle', *ibid.*, 1965, pp. 61—72. Woronoff, 'Tradition et innovation dans la sidérurgie', *Revue d'Histoire moderne et contemporaine*, 1970, pp. 559–73 (the case of the Haute-Marne under the First Empire). On the coal industry in its early stages: G. Thuillier, 'Les houillères de la Ruhr', *Annales*, 1950, pp. 882–97. A leading industry, the chemical industry (R. Tinthouin, 'Chaptal, créateur de l'industrie chimique française', *Fed. hist. du Languedoc Médit. et du Roussillon*, 1956, pp. 195–206; A. Thépot, 'Le système continental et les débuts de l'industrie chimique en France', *Revue de l'Institut Napoléon*, 1966, pp. 79–84).

A propos of state intervention: Ballot, 'Les prêts aux manufacturiers sous le Premier Empire', *Revue des Études napoléoniennes*, 1912, pp. 45–7; A. Lorion, 'Les expositions de l'industrie française à Paris', *Revue de l'Institut Napoléon* 1968, pp. 125–30 (complements Vol. VI of *Paris sous Napoléon* by Lanzac de Laborie); A. Thépot, *La direction des mines* in *Les directeurs de ministère en France au XIXe siècle* (1976; stresses the role of Laumont after 1810 and that of the mining engineers).

The activity of the different ports is not equally well-known. Bordeaux has now been thoroughly studied: besides Vol. V of the *Histoire de Bordeaux* (1968) and F. Crouzet's very close study, 'Les importations d'eau de vie et de vins français en Grande Bretagne pendant le Blocus continental', *Annales du Midi*, 1953, read P. Butel's articles, 'Le Commerce maritime de la France sous le Consulat et l'Empire: l'example du négoce bordelais', *Informations historique*, 1968, pp. 211–15 and especially 'Crise et mutation de l'activité économique à Bordeaux sous le Consulat et l'Empire', *Revue d'Histoire moderne*, 1970, pp. 540–58, which throws light on the progressions and crises of trade in Bordeaux at that time. *L'Histoire du Commerce de Marseille* may be useful and can replace P. Masson, 'Le commerce de Marseilles de 1789 à 1814', *Annales de l'Universite d'Aix*, 1916. On Calais: A. Vion, *La Vie calaisienne sous le consulat et l'Empire*, 1972. On the other hand, there is nothing on Le Havre, Nantes or La Rochelle. On the chambers of commerce: P. Cayez, 'La chambre de commerce de Lyon et le régime impérial', *Cahiers d'histoire* 1971, pp. 403–408 (it had more conservative leanings than in Paris).

As for the roads, read M. Blanchard, *Les Routes des Alpes occidentales à l'époque napoléonienne* (1920, fundamental); A. Palluel, 'Le Consulat et l'aménagement des cols alpins', *Revue de l'Institut Napoléon*, 1969, pp. 139–48. J. Sermet, 'Les routes transpyrénéennes', *Soc. Hist. Communication Midi de la France*, 1963 (Napoleon had arranged the opening of the Somport road in 1808). Somewhat confused, but rich in information: A. Remond, *Études sur la circulation marchande*, Vol. I, *Les Prix des transports marchands de la Révolution au Premier Empire* (1956). On the upkeep of the roads the *Histoire de l'Administration des Ponts-et-Chaussées* (1958) by Petot. Here again local monographs are extremely useful albeit regional (Vidalenc, 'Les relations économiques et la circulation en Normandie à la fin du Premier Empire', *Annales de Normandie*, 1957; R. Dufraisse, 'Les fonctions commerciales de l'Alsace napoléonienne', *Saisons d'Alsace*, 1963, others concern a product (Evrard, 'Le commerce des laines d'Espagne sous le Premier Empire', *Revue d'Histoire moderne*, 1937, pp. 197–226). Also revealing: Cottez, *L'octroi de Lyon* (1938).

Open Questions
Does the take-off of the industrial revolution in France date from the Empire? It is a point of view which has been defended by Marczewski and Toutain,

notably in the *Histoire quantitative de l'Économie française* (1961) and Markovitch, *L'Industrie française de 1789 à 1859*, Vol. I (1965): the increased rates of production (three per cent every year from 1796 to 1812), the development of leading industries and the accelerated introduction of machinery (Ballot, *L'Introduction du Machinisme dans l'Industrie française*, 1923) would be the main pointers in this direction. François Crouzet has contested this opinion: 'The growth which took place from 1800 to 1810 was partly only a recuperation of losses experienced during the Revolution and only a very small proportion of industries were modernized' (foreword to the special number of *Souvenir napoléonien*, 1971, 'Napoléon et l'Industrie'). For the even more radical Pierre Chaunu, the eighteenth-century boom which was interrupted by the Revolution did not continue under the Empire (*La Civilisation de l'Europe classique*, 1965). According to Albert Soboul, on the other hand, 'even if the absence of any real technological revolution and the modest nature of the annual rate of growth make it impossible to speak of a true industrial take-off', the boom of the years 1800–10 cannot be concealed, nor can the attendant prosperity (*Le Premier Empire*, 1973). E. Labrousse speaks of the 'wartime growth'. The Blockade may have had a decelerating effect but not an inhibiting one, it was able to delay world growth rather than to brake it; it 'effectively helped the accumulation of capital which after the peace was to be the source for public borrowing and private investment' (*Rapport au XIIᵉ Congrès international des Sciences historiques*, 1965).

In 'Wars, Blockade and Economic Change in Europe 1792–1815', *Journal of Economic History*, Dec. 1964, pp. 567–88, François Crouzet has put into relief the phenomena of 'de-industrialization' and of 'pasturization' of the land behind the big ports, especially Bordeaux, which worked for foreign countries. On the other hand industries were developing in the centre of the Continent (cotton in Saxony and in the east of France). It follows that, contrary to the opinion of Tarlé, ('Napoleon et les intérêts économiques de la France', *Revue des Études napoléoniennes*, 1926, pp. 117–37), who shows Napoleon sacrificing the annexed countries to the 'national interest', there was unquestionable industrial progress in Belgium and on the left bank of the Rhine, the implications of which were certainly varied, but which was nevertheless real: R. Devleeshouwer, 'Le Consulat et l'Empire, période de *take-off* pour l'économie belge?'. *Revue d'Histoire Moderne*, 1970, p. 610; the author stresses here that in 1807 industry in Belgium was relatively more important than in the rest of the Empire, and its growth was the largest in 'the whole from which she stood out'; R. Dufraisse, 'L'industrialisation de la rive gauche du Rhin', *Souvenir napoléonien*, 1970, pp. 28–33. So the shift of the vital economic European centres towards the Rhine valley favoured what is still today the 'golden triangle', Paris–Hamburg–Milan.

Does economic thought during the Empire deserve the discredit in which it is held? Émile James has drawn attention to the great currents into which it divides. 'Napoléon et la pensée économique de son temps', *Revue de l'Institut Napoléon*, 1966, pp. 113–23. In an unpublished memorandum M. Michael Chelini has drawn up a crucial bibliography of works which appeared in this field between 1800 and 1815, which bears witness to the richness of these currents. As early as 1801, Guer showed in his *Essai sur le crédit commercial* that France was richer than England; only the absence of a good credit system explained how France was behind England. Guer devoted himself to refuting Gentz (*Essai sur l'état actuel de l'administration des finances et de la richesse nationale de la Grande-Bretagne*) and like Bosc and Sabatier (other unjustly forgotten economists) he presented a method of calculating the national income (G. Thuillier, 'Les essais de calcul du revenu national de 1800 à 1808', *Revue de l'Institut Napoléon*, 1976, pp. 41–53) which counter-balanced the evaluations of Francis d'Ivernois, the Genevan economist who served England (O. Karmin, *Sir Francis d'Ivernois*, 1920).

The crisis of 1805 has given rise to much writing: Lanzac de Laborie, *Paris sous Napoléon*, Vol. VI (1910); Marion, *Histoire financière*, Vol. IV (1927); A. Fugier, *Napoléon et l'Espagne* (1930); A. Duchêne, *Guerre et Finances: une crise du Trésor sous le Premier Empire* (1940); J. Gabillard, 'Le financement des guerres napolóniennes et la conjoncture du Premier Empier', *Revue économique*, 1953, pp. 548–72 (takes the opposite view to Chabert, who in his *Essai sur l'activité économique* mentioned above, blamed too rapid industrialization and a slump in textiles; for Gabillard the crisis is explained rather by an essentially urban phenomenon of hoarding which caused deflation). B. Gille in his 'Contribution à l'étude de la crise de 1805', *Bulletin du Centre de recherches sur l'histoire des entreprises*, 1954, equally insists on this phenomenon of deflation. For J. Bouvier, 'A propos de la crise de 1805', *Revue d'Histoire moderne*, 1970, pp. 506–13, it was a crisis typical of the First Empire: a crisis of deflation brought about by the financing of the war and by financial behaviour which accompanied the lack of confidence. 'Should Barbé-Marbois be rehabilitated?' Escombe asks in the *Revue de l'Institut Napoléon*, 1975, pp. 101–19. For him the essential cause was the absence of any systematic recourse to public credit. Napoleon wanted war to provide for war; he condemned himself to being without the finances demanded of his politics.

III. 4 THE EMPIRE STYLE: BOURGEOIS OR NAPOLEONIC?

Sources

Series O², F⁷ (censorship) and F¹⁸ (bulletins concerning the conditions of bookselling and printing) of the National Archives are still to be explored. Among *Mémoires*: Mme de Staël, *Dix ans d'exil* (many editions, of which the most recent is by S. Balayé, 1966). Mme de Staël's correspondence has been published by A. Jasinski (since 1960); failing that O. Solovieff, *Mme. de Staël, ses amis, ses correspondants* (1970) could be read. For Chateaubriand consult the *Memoires d'outre-tombe* in Levaillant's centenary edition (1948). The correspondence is soon to be published. Among personal diaries: Sade (1970, shows that internment conditions in Charenton were not too severe), Stendhal (ed. Martineau, 1955), Constant (preferably ed. Mistler, 1945), Maine de Biran (ed. Lavalette-Monbrun, 1927 or H. Gouhier, 1954), Chênedollé (no date), Ginguené (ed. P. Hazard, 1910), Villenave (*Revue rétrospective*, 1893 and 1894). The *Mémoires* of Mme de Genlis (10 vols., 1825) are as unreliable as those of the duchesse d'Abrantès. There is nothing to be gained from the souvenirs of the bookseller Barba (1846). Other more useful *Mémoires*: Culmann (1862), Bavante (1890–91), Villemain (1853), Alissan de Chazet (1837), Brifaut (ed. Cabanès, 1920–21), Béranger (*Ma biographie,* 1857), Bausset (1827–9), Rémusat (1879). Consult also Brillat-Savarin, *Physiologie du Goût* (1825) and the baron de Gerando's *Lettres inédites* (1868). The general correspondence of Paul-Louis Courier is in the process of publication (Vol. I by G. Viollet-le-Duc, 1976). An exhaustive bibliography can be found in A. Monglond, *La France révolutionnaire et impériale,* Vols. V–IX (reprinted 1976). For the fine arts Mme Moitte's evidence on the life of the artists (1932) is essential. Hennequin's *Mémoires* (1893) evoke the *salons,* Vivant Denon and David. David is also evoked by Delécluze in *Louis David, son école et son temps* (1866). Delacroix's diary recalls the influence of the *Musée Napoléon* on the formation of Romanticism.

With regard to the monuments: Percier et Fontaine, *Residences de souverains* (1833) and above all the *Journal des monuments de Paris envoyé par Fontaine à l'Empereur de Russie dans les années 1809, 1810, 1811, 1814 et 1815* (ed. by A. Vueflart, 1892), not forgetting Claude-Nicolas Ledoux's famous treatise, *L'Architecture considérée sous le rapport des arts, des moeurs et de la législation* (1804).

Works
Little has been written about the literature of the Napoleonic era since M.-J. Chénier's famous *Tableau historique* (1816). Consult M. Albert, *La Littérature française sous la Révolution, l'Empire et la Restauration* (1898); J. Charpentier, *Napoléon et les Hommes de lettres* (1935); G. Vauthier, 'Napoléon et les encouragements à la littérature', *Revue historique de la Révolution française et de l'Empire,* January 1917; J. Mistler, 'La littérature' in *Napoléon et l'Empire* (1969, pp. 247–59; excellent and complete restatement of the question); the special number of *Europe,* April—May 1969: 'Napoléon et la littérature'. Very profitable are: A. Monglond, *Histoire intérieure du préromantisme français* (1970), and C. Dedeyan, *Le Cosmopolitisme européen sous la révolution et l'Empire,* Paris 1975 (studies on Schlegel, Humboldt, Fauriel). On language the *Histoire de la langue française* by F. Brunot (Vols. IX and X, 1943) are essential.

Many monographs have been written about the writers. For instance on Chateaubriand, Sainte-Beuve, *Chateaubriand et son groupe littéraire sous l'Empire* (1861), Maurois (1938), H. Guillemin (*L'Homme des Mémoires d'outre-tombe,* critical, (1964), Tapié (1965), duc de Castries (1976). For Mme de Staël the essential book is P. Gautier, *Mme de Staël et Napoléon* (1903); cf. also comtesse de Pange, *Schlegel et Mme de Staël* (1938), M. Levaillant, *Une amitié amoureuse: Mme de Staël et Mme Récamier* (1956) and the articles in the *Cahiers staëliens* since 1962. With regard to Benjamin Constant, note M. Levaillant, *Les Amours de Benjamin Constant* (1958), H. Guillemin, *Mme de Staël, Benjamin Constant et Napoléon* (1959), and P. Bastid, *Benjamin Constant et sa doctrine* (1967). On Sade, G. Lély's biography (1957) is very useful without being definitive. Complement it with J. Tulard, 'Sade et la censure sous le Premier Empire', *Actes du colloque Sade*, pp. 209–18 (1968). Other writers: *Fontanes* by A. Wilson (1928), *Alexandre Duval et son oeuvre dramatique* by Bellier-Dumaine (1905); *Restif de la Bretonne* by M. Chadourne (1958; does not, however, replace J. Rives Childs, *Restif de la Bretonne* 1949); *Collin d'Harleville*, by A. Tissier (1964–5); *Mme de Genlis* by J. Harmand (1912); *Mercier* by L. Béclard (Vol. I only appeared in 1903); *Senancour*, by J. Grenier (1968); *Geoffroy et la critique dramatique*, by C. M. Des Granges (1897, very important for the study of the serial); 'Delille est-il mort?' *Actes du colloque de Clermont-Ferrand* (1967).

The ideologues are the subject of a classic study by Picavet, *Les Idéologues* (1891), to be complemented by the works of J. Gaulmier (two biographies of Volnay, in 1951 and 1959); of Henri Gouhier (*Maine de Biran par lui-même* and current research by Regaldo ('Matériaux pour une biographie de l'idéologie', *Repertoire analytique de littérature française*, January 1970, pp. 35–49; March, pp. 27–41), also his thesis on *La Décade philosophique* (1977), E. Kennedy, *Destutt de Tracy and the origins of Ideology* (1978). Connected to the above is Constance de Salm's *salon* which was frequented by Jussieu, Lalande, Prony, Theis, Humboldt and Courier (R. Bied, 'Le rôle d'un salon littéraire au début du XIXe siècle' (*Rev. Institut Nap.*, 1977), and *Madame Récamier et ses Amis* by E. Herriot (1934).

On the theatre, Lecomte, *Napoléon et le monde dramatique* (1912, very useful); Lanzac de Laborie, *Le Théâtre français* (Vol. VII of *Paris sous Napoléon*, 1911); P. Ginisty, *Le Mélodrame* (no date), and the numerous biographies of Talma (A. Copin, *Talma et l'Empire*; Augustin-Thierry, *Le Tragédien de Napoléon*, etc.) Michèle Jones's study, *Le Théâtre national en France de 1800 à 1830* (1975) is mediocre.

The influence of the black novel on popular literature has been brought out very well by Alice M. Killen, *Le Roman terrifiant* (new edition 1967). Read also M. Leroy, *Histoire des idées sociales* (Vol. II, 1950), and E. Brehier, *Histoire de la philosophie* (Vol. II, 1948).

The esoteric current has been studied in a fundamental work by A. Viatte, *Les Sources occultes du Romantisme* (1928, new edition 1965). For further detail, A. Faivre, *L'Ésotérisme au XVIIIe siècle* (1973), and on a particular aspect Léon Cellier, *Fabre d'Olivet* (1953).

Among the general works on the fine arts, the following should be mentioned: Guizot, 'De l'état des Beaux-Arts en France et du Salon de 1810' in *Études sur les Beaux-Arts* (1852, pp. 3–100); F. Benoît, *L'Art français sous la Révolution et l'Empire* (1897; excellent analysis of aesthetic theories and a good view of the whole of painting; vast documentation—list of decennial prices, bibliography of publications, attendance at the *salons*); E. Bourgeois, *Le Style Empire* (1930); P. Francastel, *Le Style Empire* (1939, practical); L. Hautecoeur, *L'Art sous la Révolution et l'Empire en France* (1953); G. Janneau, *L'Empire* (1965, excellent view of the whole, copious iconography); M. Jullian, *L'Art en France sous la Révolution et l'Empire* (Sorbonne lecture, roneoed, 1964); F. Pariset *L'Art néo-classique* (1974). A more general view in F. Boyer, *Le Monde des Arts en Italie et la France, de la*

Révolution à l'Empire (Turin 1969, collected articles and the special number 'Les arts à l'époque napoléonienne' (1969, of the Société d'Histoire de l'Art français).

On painting consult the monumental catalogue of the exhibition *De David à Delacroix* (1974) and Bénézit, *Dictionnaire des peintres, sculpteurs, dessinateurs et graveurs* (fundamental, new edition, 1976). Add Marmottan's old book, *L'École française de peinture, 1789–1830* (1886). There have been several studies of the *salons*: G. Wildenstein, 'Table alphabétique des portraits, peints, sculptés, dessinés et gravés exposés à Paris au salon entre 1800 et 1826', *Gazette des Beaux-Arts,* January 1963, pp. 9–60; P. Riberette, 'Napoléon au Salon de 1810', *Revue de l'Institut Napoléon,* 1966, pp. 37–43; B. Foucart, 'Les salons sous l'Empire et les diverses représentations de Bonaparte', *ibid.,* 1969, pp. 113–19 (development of the Napoleonic cult).

Vivant Denon's role as director-general of museums is now well known, thanks to the studies of Lelièvre (1942) and, above all, of J. Chatelain (*Vivant Denon et le Louvre de Napoléon,* 1973). Museums took on a new importance: M. Hoog, 'La politique du Premier Consul à l'égard des musées de provinces', *Société d'Histoire de l'Art français,* 1969, pp. 353–63, and F. Boyer, 'Le musée de Mayence, création du consulat', *Revue de l'Institut Napoléon,* 1971, pp. 5–10, add some useful details to Clément de Ris's old book. On Paris, Lanzac de Laborie, *Paris sous Napoléon,* Vol. VIII, 1913 (important chapters on the *Musée Napoléon* and *Musée des Monuments français* . . . Add, with regard to the latter Courajod's edition of Alexandre Lenoir's *Journal*).

Private collections were developing. Schommer, 'L'Impératrice Joséphine et ses tableaux', *Revue de l'Institut Napoléon,* 1962; Davout collected Flemish paintings (Van den Bossche); lacking Bosch, Soult collected Spanish paintings. Among theorists, R. Schneider, *Quatremère de Quincy* (1910).

The influence of the poems by Macpherson ('Ossian') was enormous and has been analysed by P. van Thieghem, *Ossin en France* (1917); D. Ternois, 'Ossian et les peintres', *Actes du colloque Ingres* (1969); by the same author, 'Addition à Ossian et les peintres', *Bulletin du musée Ingres* (1972); H. Toussaint, *Catalogue de l'exposition Ossian* (1974); P. Vaisse, 'Ossian et les peintres du XIXe siècle', *Information d'Histoire de l'art,* 1974, pp. 81–8.

It is not surprising that much has been written about David. After the evidence of Hennequin, Delécluze and David's son (1880), the following should be mentioned: Saunier (1903), Cantinelli (1930), Holma (1940), Maret (1943), Huyghe (Preface to catalogue of the David exhibition, 1948) and, above all, Hautecoeur (1954). The list of authentic works by David and false attributions can be found at the end of Verbraeken, *David jugé par ses contemporains et la postérité* (1973); add D. and G. Wildenstein, *Documents complémentaires au catalogue de l'oeuvre de Louis David* (1973).

Numerous biographies of Gros, by Delestre (1867), Tripier-Lefranc (1880), Lemonnier (1905), Escholier (1936), Lelièvre ('Gros, peintre d'Histoire', *Gazette des Beaux-Arts,* May 1936, pp. 289–304).

The same applies to Ingres: Lapauze (1911), G. Wildenstein (1954), *Actes du colloque Ingres* (Montauban 1968). To be preferred to these is D. Ternois,

Tout l'oeuvre peint d'Ingres (1971, all Ingres paintings are listed and reproduced in the addendum).

On Girodet, apart from the memoirs of Delécluze and Delacroix, consult Levitine: 'L'Ossian de Girodet et l'actualité politique sous le Consulat', *Gazette des Beaux-Arts,* 1956, pp. 39–56; by the same author, 'Quelques aspects peu connus de Girodet', *ibid.,* 1965, pp. 231–46; the catalogue of the Girodet exhibition (Montargis 1967) and G. Bernier's useful synthesis, *Anne-Louis Girodet, prix de Rome 1789* (1975). For Gérard: Lenormant, *François Gérard, peintre d'histoire* (1847); G. Hubert, 'L'Ossian de Gérard et ses variantes', *Revue du Louvre* 1967, pp. 239–48. Prud'hon has been more favoured: a biography, by Clément (1872), Guiffrey (*L'Oeuvre de Prud'hon,* 1924) and Grappe (1958). The Goncourts made a catalogue of his work in 1876. There have also been several studies of Géricault (note especially K. Berger, *Géricault et son oeuvre,* 1968 and, at a stretch, Aragon's novel, *La Semaine Sainte*). On Isabey: W. Osmond, *Isabey, the Painter* (London 1947). With regard to the minor painters Marmottan's excellent work on Boilly (1913) should be pointed out, also those by Portalis on *Danloux* (1910), by G. Wildenstein on *Louis Moreau* (1923), by Levitine on 'Jean Broc' (*Gazette des Beaux Arts,* Nov. 1972, pp. 285–94), by F. Beaucamp on *Wicar* (1939), and by K. Simons on 'Fragonard fils' (*Revue de l'Institut Napoléon,* 1976, pp. 55–65). For military painting and more particularly the baron Lejeune, Y. Cantarel, *Recherches sur les petits maîtres français de la peinture militaire à l'époque napoléonienne* (typed thesis, École du Louvre, 1974). Other fashionable styles: G. and C. Ledoux-Lebard, 'L'Impératrice Joséphine et le retour au gothique sous l'Empire', *Revue de l'Institut Napoléon,* 1964, pp. 117–24; Zieseniss, 'Les portraits des ministres et des grands officiers à l'époque napoléonienne', *Société d'Histoire de l'Art français,* 1969, pp. 133–58. Popular imagery is also worthy of interest: J. Mistler, *Épinal et l'Imagerie populaire* (1961).

Less has been written on sculpture. Our knowledge has been refreshed by C. Hubert, *La Sculpture dans l'Italie napoléonienne* (1964). To be noted with regard to Canova, F. Boyer, 'Nouveaux documents sur Canova et Napoléon Ier', *Revue des Études italiennes,* 1949, and R. Schneider's older article, 'L'Art de Canova et la France impériale', *Revue des Études napoléoniennes,* 1912.

A knowledge of imperial architecture implies the study of the large collections: Legrand and Landon, *Description de Paris et de ses monuments* (1806–9); Krafft and Ransonnette, *Plans, coupes, élévations des plus belles maisons et des hotels construits à Paris et dans les environs* (1801–2); Marmottan and Vacquier, *Le Style Empire. Architecture et décor d'intérieur* (no date). Generalities to be found in Hautecoeur, *Histoire de l'Architecture classique en France,* Vol. V (1953, important), and Driault, *Napoléon architecte* (no date). A few monographs: Marmottan, *Le Pont d'Iéna* (1917); by the same author, *Le Palais de l'archevêché sous Napoléon de 1809 et 1815* (1921); E. Driault, *L'Hotel Beauharnais à Paris* (1926); M. Tartary, 'Le Louvre et les Tuileries sous Napoleon', *Recueil de l'Institut Napoléon,* 1945, pp. 43–59; R. Wahl, *Un projet de Napoléon, le palais du Roi de Rome* (1955). Works by Chalgrin at the Senate are described in Hirschfeld, *Le Palais du*

Luxembourg (pp. 42–57). Principal biographies: Silvestre de Sacy, *Brongniart* (no date); M. L. Biver, *Fontaine* (1964, excellent, uses the architect's unpublished diary); Stern, *François-Joseph Bélanger* (1932); Fouché, *Percier et Fontaine* (no date).

The whole aspect of decorative art changed Percier and Fontaine defined its 'canons' in a *Recueil de décorations intérieures comprenant tout ce qui a rapport à l'ameublement comme vases, trépides, candélabres, lustres, tables* (1812). Other collections: F. Contet, *Intérieurs Directoire et Empire* (1932); H. Lefuel, *Boutiques parisiennes du Premier Empire* (1926); J. Mottheau, *Meubles et Ensembles Directoire et Empire* (1958). P. Lafond's study, *L'Art décoratif et le Mobilier sous la Republique et l'Empire* (1900). Much is to be learnt about imperial orders in Maze-Sencier, *Les Fournisseurs de Napoléon et des deux impératrices* (1893). With regard to furniture, the older works of Dumonthier (*Les Sièges de Jacob frères, Les Sièges de Jacob Desmalter*) are still of interest, but the essential work is Lefuel's *François-Honoré-Georges-Jacob Desmalter* (1925). D. Ledoux-Lebard's works are fundamental, especially *Les Ébénistes parisiens du XIXᵉ siècle 1795–1870* (1965). On fabrics and wallpapers: Dumonthier, *Étoffes d'ameublement de l'époque napoléonienne* (1909) and *Étoffes d'ameublement style Empire* (1914); H. Clouzot, *Histoire de la manufacture de Jouy et de la toile imprimée en France* (1928). The gold and silversmith's art has been studied by H. Bouilhet, *Orfèvreries françaises aux XVIIIᵉ and XIXᵉ siècles* (1911, mainly Vols. II and III); J. Niclausse, *Thomire, fondeur-ciseleur* (1947). Generalities in S. Grandjean, *l'Orfèvrerie du XIXᵉ siècle en Europe.* Read Arizzoli-Clemental, 'Les surtouts impériaux en porcelaine de Sèvres, 1804–1814', *Bulletin Amis Suisses de la céramique,* 1976. With regard to medals, the regime saw them primarily as an excellent weapon for propaganda as it did painting. P. Poindessault ('Napoleon était-il l'héritier de César?' *Revue de l'Institut Napoléon,* 1973, pp. 81–6) compares French coins of the Napoleonic era to those of the Roman Empire: identical emblems, concern with propaganda. The Emperor's brothers and sisters had coins struck with their likeness: cf. J. de Mey and B. Poindessault, *Répertoire des Monnaies napoléonides* (1971), and Gassmann's articles in *Archéonumis.*

Theo Fleischman has written a good, if somewhat anecdotal synthesis on music, *Napoléon et la musique* (1965) which makes recourse to the general histories of Combarieu (1925) and Rebatet (1969) unnecessary. There have been few studies of the musicians of the period apart from the long typed thesis by J. Mongredien on Lesueur (1976). Rossini's beginnings are discussed in Stendhal's *Vie de Rossini.* Beethoven must be kept in a category of his own. The old works by R. Rolland (1928) and Herriot (1929) have been replaced by J. and B. Massin's *Beethoven* (1967). For other musicians, Fetis's old dictionary, *Biographie universelle des musiciens* will be useful. Remember that Wagner was born in 1813 in a Germany under French influence. For ballet: Marcelle Michel, 'La danse à Paris sous l'Empire', *Revue de l'Institut Napoléon* 1962, pp. 97–104. On song: P. Barbier and F. Vernillat, *Histoire de la France par les Chansons* (Vol. V, 1958).

Military music has been treated in a concrete fashion by Philippe-René

Girault in *Les Compagnes d'un musicien d'État-major pendant la Révolution et l'Empire* (1901), full of very lively accounts and showing the role of music in battle.

Technical problems such as the transition from the harpsichord to the piano have been analysed by A. de Place, *Le Piano forte sous l'Empire* (typed thesis of the *Hautes Études*, 1975, giving an exhaustive list of works for the piano of the Napoleonic period).

A good picture of scientific development has been supplied by A. George in J. Mistler, *Napoléon et l'Empire* (Vol. I, pp. 282–6). Of the scientists, Monge has attracted most attention: Jomard, *Souvenirs sur Gaspard Monge et ses rapports avec Napoléon* (1853); Aubry, *Monge, le savant ami de Napoléon Bonaparte* (1954). The fundamental work on medicine and pharmacy is P. Huard's *Sciences, Médecine, Pharmacie, de la Révolution à l'Empire* (1970 with an enormous bibliography and a remarkable iconography, with a documentary richness of the first order). Some useful biographies of doctors: *Corvisart* by Ganière (1951); *Laënnec*, by E. Rist (*La Jeunesse de Laënnec*, 1955) or by R. Kervan (1955). On archaeology, R. Dauvergne, 'L'archéologie gallo-romaine sous le Premier Empire', *Le Vieux papier* (1975).

Open Questions

It cannot be denied that Napoleon used the arts of his time with a view to personal propaganda. Holtman in *Napoleonic Propaganda* (1950) showed it very convincingly, and B. Monteano has pointed out the consequences to literature in *Une theorie de la littérature dirigée sous la Révolution et l'Empire* which has been taken up in *Constantes dialectiques en littérature et en histoire* (1967).

Another 'stifling' element was censorship which was entrusted to the writers, Esmenard, Lemontey, Fiévée, Lacretelle . . . The mechanics of censorship have been very well described by H. Welschinger, *La Censure sous le Premier Empire* (1882).

Should one, then, speak of a total decline in literature? Brunetière has attempted, without much reaction, to rehabilitate it in 'La littérature française sous le Premier Empire' (*Etudes critiques sur l'Histoire de la littérature française* 1911, pp. 255–82): 'Imperial literature deserves neither oblivion nor the sublime disdain of the critic and of history. It is worthy of being known.'

Have persecutions been exaggerated? The case of Desorgues, interned for having written lines against Napoleon can be explained. Sade was kept in Charenton with the agreement of his family. Even if Mme de Staël suffered under the Empire, what about Chateaubriand? H. Guillemin (*L'Homme des Mémoires d'outre-tombe*) has thrown light on the affair of the appointment to the Valais republic: Mme de Chateaubriand's health was in question and not the duc d'Enghien. Besides the author compares Mme de Staël's ambiguous attitude (page 81, note 1) to this execution and reduces Chateaubriand's opposition to a more accurate level.

Although the advance of science was incontestable, Napoleon has been labelled 'anti-science' because of the Fulton affair. Marmont was one of the first to write about this affair in his *Mémoires* (Vol. II, pp. 210–12):

'Bonaparte who was prejudiced against innovations, rejected Fulton's propositions.' These affirmations have been contested by a letter from Napoleon to Champagny, dated 21 July 1804, in which Napoleon is said to have written: 'Citizen Fulton's plan can change the face of the world.' The letter is indisputably a forgery. It only remains to determine the practical usefulness of Fulton's plans for an invasion of England: it is highly debatable.

On a minor matter, it should be pointed out that Guy Beaujouan, after Fayol (*Philippe Lebon,* 1943) has destroyed the legend of the murder of the inventor of lighting gas in 1804.

P. Gerbod (*L'Europe culturelle et religieuse de 1815 à nos jours,* 1977) underlines the laicization of culture but also stresses that culture, from 1809, became more and more nationalistic: Fichte, Schlegel, Arnim, Hoffmann and Schilling in Germany, Alfieri and Leopardi in Italy, Wordsworth in England. A popular literature was also born which was quite different from the popular works distributed by hawkers. Ducray-Dumenil and Arlincourt heralded Gaboriau, Boisgobey, Leroux and Fantômas (The serialized novel, *Europe,* 1974).

Noir brings the Emperor and the convict together in his *Vidocq* (1889). Weber (born in 1786) like Marschener (1795) prepare the way not for the stirring Suppé but for the Germanic opera from Wagner to Orff.

IV. 1. FROM SAVIOUR TO DESPOT

Sources

Sub-series AF^{iv} of the National Archives is fundamental, it regroups the papers of the Secretariat of State, the government turn-table. Add to that F^7 (police) and BB (justice) and for the Church, the Artaud de Montor bequest in the Institut Napoléon. Napoleon I's correspondence, Cambacérès letters, the *Almanachs impériaux, Le Moniteur,* the *Bulletin des Lois* and collections of circulars from certain ministries (Interior and Justice) make it possible to follow the activities of the government. Police bulletins published by E. d'Hauterive (*La Police secrète du Premier Empire,* Vol. V, 1964) end in 1810 with the dismissal of Fouché. It would be useful to add to this publication, Savary's bulletins which were by no means devoid of interest. Among *Mémoires* note Fain (essential for the workings of the machinery of government), Pasquier, Molé and Broglie (notably on the Council of State), de Bausset (Prefect of the Palace, 1827; perhaps touched up by Balzac), de Barral (on papers) and the prefects Thibaudeau, Plancy and Vaublanc. On the other hand little can be gained from the memoirs of Fouché, Talleyrand, Champagny and Savary. Desmaret (on the police, ed. Grasilier) should not be overlooked. Neither should Méneval (on the imperial entourage), Pontécoulant, Stanislas de Girardin, but Bourrienne should not be trusted. The *mémoires* of the imperial family (Joseph, 1856–8; Jerome, 1861–6; Eugène de Beauharnais, 1858–60) are in fact collections of letters. On the other hand Queen Hortense's are real *Mémoires* and Vol. I is particularly interesting. *Documents historiques et réflexions sur le Gouvernement de la*

Hollande (1820) by Louis Bonaparte could also be read. Entirely lacking in seriousness are the *Mémoires* of the valet Constant (1830–31) and of Roustam (1911). Ali's (1926) are above all interesting about Saint Helena (cf. Savant, Les *Mamelouks de Napoléon*, 1949).

Works

An immense amount has been written about the imperial family. Apart from natural descendants studied by J. Valynseele (1964), Ducasse, *Les Rois frères de Napoléon I* (1883); F. Masson, *Napoléon et sa famille* (13 vols. 1897–1919, famous but biased work in which the author systematically says the Emperor was right); Lumbroso, *Napoleone, la sua corte, la sua famiglia* (1921); A. Lévy, *Les Dissentiments de la Famille impériale* (1931); T. Aronson, *The Story of the Bonapartes* (1967). Many often satisfactory biographies have been written about Napoleon's brothers. On Joseph: Marmottan, *Joseph Bonaparte à Mortefontaine*, 1929; B. Nabonne, *Le Roi Philosophe*, 1949; Connely, *The Gentle Bonaparte* 1968; Girod de l'Ain, *Le Roi malgré lui*, 1970; on Louis: F. Rocquain, *Napoléon I et le Roi Louis*, 1875; Labarre de Raillecourt, *Louis Bonaparte*, 1963; on Jerome: A. Martinet, *Jérôme Napoléon, roi de Westphalie*, 1863; M. A. Fabre, *Jérôme Bonaparte, roi de Westphalie*, 1952; Bertaut, *Le Roi Jérôme*, 1954. Note Pietri's study of Lucien. The output on the sisters is not so good: Elisa (P. Marmottan, *Elisa Bonaparte*, 1898, well documented but ending in 1804); Caroline (J. Turquan, *Caroline Murat*, 1899; J. Bertaut, *Le Ménage Murat*, 1958); and Pauline (Fleuriot de Langle, *La Paolina, soeur de Napoléon*, 1946; M. Gobineau, *Pauline Borghèse, soeur fidèle*, 1958; Kuhn, *Pauline*, 1963; B. Nabonne, *La Vénus impériale*, 1963); on Pauline's first husband: J. Poulet, 'Montgobert, le général Leclerc et les Bonaparte', *Fédération des Sociétés d'histoire et d'archéologie de l'Aisne*, 1972. On the most important brother-in-law, Murat, besides *Les Archives Murat aux Archives nationales* (1967), the biographies by Chevanon and Saint-Yves (1905), Marcel Dupont (1934), Lucas-Dubreton (1944) and Garnier (1959), also the precious bulletin *Cavalier et Roi* published by J. Vanel. On the Emperor's stepson: Arthur Lévy, *Napoléon et Eugène de Beauharnais* (1926); F. de Bernardy, *Eugène de Beauharnais* (1973). On the court: *Cérémonial de l'Empire français* (1805) and G. Vauthier, 'La Maison de l'Empereur et les pages', and 'Voitures et chevaux de Napoléon', *Revue des Études Napoléoniennes*, 1917, pp. 230–42. Everything which bears at all on the court is very anecdotal. For Napoleon's political ideas at the time of his apogee, besides the precious anthologies by Dansette (1940) and Palluel (*Dictionnaire de l'Empereur*, 1969), read the preface to the *Correspondance officielle* of Napoleon (ed. Dufraisse, Club du Livre, 1969) and A. Cabanis 'Contribution à l'étude des idées politiques de Napoléon I', *Res publica*, 1975, pp. 121–44. Note that Cavoty's series, *Drames inconnus de la cour de Napoléon* (1962–4), does not fulfil its promise. Napoleon's day has been excellently conjured up by F. Masson, *Napoléon chez lui* (1894).

The machine of government is described by C. Durand: 'Conseils privés, Conseils des ministres, Conseils d'administration 1800–1814', *Revue d'Histoire moderne* 1970, pp. 814–28; by the same author: *Le Régime de l'activité gouvernemental pendant les campagnes de Napoléon* (1957); J. Tulard, 'Le fonctionnement des institutions impériales en l'absence de Napoléon d'après les lettres inédites de Cambacérès', *Revue des Travaux de l'Académie des Sciences morales et politiques*, March 1973, pp. 231–46. Despite Ernouf's work, *Maret, duc de Bassano* (1893), there is no thorough study of the Secretariat of State. In André de Montalivet, *Les Bachasson de Montalivet* (1955), can be found notes taken by Montalivet during ministers' meetings. These notes give the impression that they consisted of long monologues by the Emperor.

The decline of the Council of State? C. Durand (*La Fin du Conseil d'Etat*, 1959, and above all 'Napoléon et le Conseil d'Etat', *Revue de l'Institut Napoléon*, 1962, pp. 145–56) disputes the theory that after 1810 the Council suffered the downfall claimed by Thibaudeau and Stendhal; he observes however, that 'since 1807 and more especially 1809, Napoleon gives way in his mind to the argument of authority and the permanent nature of certain positions'. The fading out of the Senate has been gone into by J. Thiry, *Le Rôle du Sénat de Napoléon dans l'organisation militaire dans la France impériale* (1932), and C. Durand, 'Les présidents du Senat sous le Premier Empire', *Mélanges Jacquemyns*, pp. 75–99. On the Audit Office which included a certain number of former tribunes: U. Todisco, *Le Personnel de la Cour des Comptes* (1969); cf. also Duvergier de Hauranne's *Histoire parlementaire*.

Following on from Vautier in the *Revue des Études napoléoniennes* of 1919, pp. 218–23, Jean Bourdon has outlined 'L'épuration de la magistrature en 1807–1808' in the *Revue d'Histoire moderne*, 1970, pp. 329–36. Can one speak of a purging of the Prefecture? A new personnel was employed in a spirit defined by Savary in 1813 (C. Durand, *Quelques aspects de l'Administration préfectorale sous le Consulat et l'Empire*, 1962).

The police have attracted considerable attention. *Savary, duc de Rovigo, un policier dans l'ombre de Napoléon* by B. Melchior-Bennet (1962) compares to Madelin's *Fouché* (several new editions) which has not been superseded by Despaty's *Un ami de Fouché, d'après les mémoires de Gaillard* (1911), Zweig, *Fouché* (1931), J. Savant, *Tel fut Fouché* (1955), L. Kammacher, *Joseph Fouché* (1963), H. Buisson, *Qui était Fouché?* (1968), H. Cole, *Fouché, the Unprincipled Patriot* (1971). The workings of the police have been described in a superficial fashion by Hauterive, *Napoléon et sa Police* (1943), and more thoroughly by M. Clère, *Histoire de la Police* (1964). On a particular point: L. Deriès, 'Le régime des fiches sous le Premier Empire', *Revue des Études historiques*, 1926, and P. Lefanc, 'Conscription dorée, conscription des filles', *Revue de l'Institut Napoleon*, 1977, which shows the Empire's mania for indexing people. On Pasquier's appointment to the Prefecture of Police: J. Tulard, 'Une nomination de préfet sous l'Empire', *Revue de l'Institut Napoléon*, 1959. Chouannerie was still thriving in the West: E. Daudet, *La Police et les Chouans* (1895); Gabory, *Napoléon et la Vendée*, 1932; E. Herpin, *Armand de Chateaubriand*, 1910; Langlois, 'Complot, propagande et répression policière en Bretagne sous l'Empire, 1805–1807' (concerns the kidnapping of the Bishop of Vannes), *Annales de Bretagne,* 1971, pp. 369–421; Hutt, 'Spies in France, 1793–1808', *History Today,* 1962; P. Summerscale, 'Puisaye et les royalistes', *Revue de l'Institut Napoléon* 1977. On the unpopularity of the police read Proudhon's comments in *Mémoires de Fouché.* The reappearance of state prisons which had been denounced in 1814 by Demaillot, in a pamphlet which caused a stir, was significant: L. Deriès, 'Les prisons d'État en 1812', *Revue historique de la Révolution et de l'Empire,* 1916, pp. 84–94. On the affair of Werbrouck, the mayor of Antwerp whose acquittal was quashed by the Senate: R. Warlomont, 'L'affaire Werbrouck et le régime impériale', *Revue d'Histoire du Droit français et étranger,* 1963.

Historians' interest in the University is not surprising. Did Napoleon not see it as one of the foundations of his authority? To the general works by Prost, *Histoire de l'Enseignement en France* (1968), and Ponteil, *Histoire de l'Enseignement* (1966), add Aulard's classic study, *Napoléon I^e et le Monopole universitaire* (1911). Complement it with Lanzac de Laborie, 'La Haute Administration de l'enseignement sous le Consulat et l'Empire' (Roederer, Fourcroy, Fontanes) in *Revue des Études napoléoniennes,* 1916, Vol. X, pp. 186–219, and G. Vauthier, 'Fontanes et les débuts de l'Université', *Nouvelle Revue,* 1 and 15 March 1808 (A. Wilson's work is only about the author). E. Rendu throws light on the role of a councillor like Rendu, *Ambroise Rendu et l'Université de France* (1861). The recruitment of heads of schools was mediocre if L. Villat is to be believed. 'J. J. Ordinaire, premier recteur de l'Académie de Besançon', *Mémoires de l'Académie de Besançon,* 1928, pp. 117–51. Lanzac de Laborie's research (*Revue des Études napoléoniennes,* 1917) mostly concerned the beginnings of *lycées.* There have been few good studies of the faculties with the exception of one on the Faculty of Arts in Paris by Guigue (1935). On the formation of masters: Joxe, 'L'École normale en 1812', *Revue de l'Institut Napoléon,* 1963, pp. 27–34. Note also R. Palmer, *A Documentary History of the College Louis-le-Grand and its Director, Jean-François Champagne 1762–1814,* (1975).

The conflict with the Church has been studied in a masterly way from the regional point of view by R. Durand, 'Le Monopole universitaire et la concurrence ecclésiastique dans les Côtes-du-Nord', *Revue d'Histoire moderne,* 1934, pp. 16–47. It is known how Napoleon was annoyed by this competition and by the success with which the Church schools met. The decree of 15 November 1811 strengthened the monopoly by putting the Church schools under the authority of the University: cf. C. Schmidt, *La Réforme de l'Université impériale en 1811* (1905). Technical education was less neglected than has been sometimes claimed, according to A. Léon, 'Promesses et ambiguïtés de l'Oeuvre d'enseignement technique en France de 1800 à 1815', *Revue d'Histoire moderne,* 1970, pp. 846–59. A good synthesis on primary education which was, perhaps, less ignored than has been claimed: M. Gontard, *L'Enseignement primaire en France, de la Révolution à la loi Guizot 1789–1833* (1959).

Open Questions

To the Royalists a usurper, and to the Jacobins a tyrant, Napoleon founded a regime the definition of which divides political scientists. For René Rémond (*La Vie Politique en France*, Vol. I. 1965), the Empire marks a break in French parliamentary evolution: the idea of elections vanished, the role of the assemblies was reduced to nothing, the press was destroyed. For Pietri, on the other hand (*Napoléon et le Parlement*, 1955), the Emperor respected parliamentary prerogatives until the very end. He sees the suppression of the Tribunate as a strengthening of the assemblies' power—the Tribunate was not suppressed but incorporated into the Legislative Body. At the same time the legislators were no longer silent, they received the right to speak which they had long been demanding; equally, the twenty-seven tribunes who had become part of the Legislative Body were finally able to vote definitely on matters which they had formerly only discussed. Irene Collins' *Napoleon and his Parliaments* (1979) is excellent.

In fact, there appears to be no doubt about the dictatorial nature of the regime. The primacy of the executive was absolute (cf. Duverger, *La Dictature*, 1961, and the works of his pupils, among them J.-P. Daviet). Military dictatorship, say Mathiez and Lefebvre, but although the army was in fact the decisive factor in the success of Brumaire, it did not intervene again over internal politics except to put down the riots in Caen in 1812. Enlightened despotism? But the ideologues, the descendants of the *philosophes*, were removed from power from the beginning of the Consulate. Napoleon has frequently been represented as the forerunner of the Fascist dictators of the twentieth century. But the regime was established neither on a basis of racism (only the Bohemians had some trouble in the name of order: cf. Vaux de Foletier, 'La Grande rafle des Bohémiens du Pays basque sous le Consulat', *Études tsiganes*, 1968, pp. 13–22), nor of violence ('The blood of victims does not encourage the growth of roots, it kills them, the Terror killed the Republic,' Napoleon was to say to Montholon). The Napoleonic dictatorship was basically the Caesarism of Ancient Rome, a compromise between the necessities of a government of public safety at war with Europe, and the susceptibilities inherited from the Revolution with regard to monarchical power. Caesarism? More precisely 'Bonapartism', for one merit of the victor of Marengo is to have substituted his name for that of the victor of Alesia (cf. Jean Tulard in 'Actes du colloque d'Augsbourg sur le bonapartisme', *Francia*, 1977). Everything stems from Napoleon's personal charisma. The regime is identified with an individual.

It is hardly surprising that this individual continues to fascinate. It is, however, regrettable that his height (1 metre-68 according to M. Dunan, *Revue de l'Institut Napoléon*, 1963, p. 178), his illnesses (Cabanès, *Au chevet de l'Empereur*; Hillemand, *Pathologie de Napoléon*) and above all his love affairs have attracted more attention than his political ideas. For his love affairs F. Masson has been especially plagiarized, *Napoléon et les Femmes* (1894). J. Savant has drawn up a roll of honour of those who 'resisted' (*Cahiers de l'Académie d'Histoire*, 1970, No. 4): Mme Tallien, Mme Récamier, Alexandrine de Bleschamp, comtesse de Regnault de Saint-Jean-d'Angély, etc.—the most beautiful women of the day: something to make one reflect on the limits of Napoleon's dictatorship.

IV. 2 A MISTAKE: THE *NOBLESSE DE L'EMPIRE*

Sources

Sub-series AF[IV] of the National Archives (decrees dealing with endowments, especially AF[IV] 308 which contains a valuable dictionary of recipients, documents from the Council of the Great Seal for Titles) BB[30] 965–1120 (*Majorats*); O[2] (Domaine extraordinaire), AP (private archives: Davout, Ney, Caulaincourt, Maison, Watier . . .). Considerable information in the *Lettres de Cambacérès à Napoléon* (ed. Tulard, Vol. II). Consult the *Mémoires* of Pasquier, Molé, de Broglie, Miot de Melito, Roederer, Caulaincourt and above all the *Correspondances et relations avec Bonaparte* by Fiévée, particularly rich in information, though orientated towards public feeling. On those who were not won over: the memoirs of Frénilly.

Two fundamental sources: Campardon: *Liste des membres de la noblesse impériale dressée d'après les registres de lettres patentes conservées aux Archives nationales* (1889) and Révérend, *Armorial du Premier Empire* (new ed. by J. Tulard, 1974, gives the arms and the genealogy). Complement it with Labarre de Raillicourt, *Armorial des Cent Jours* (1961). For genealogy, the works of J. Valynseele contain important elements: *Les Maréchaux du Premier Empire, leur famille et leur descendance* (1957); *Les Princes et Ducs du Premier Empire non maréchaux, leur famille et leur descendance* (1959).

Works

For an exhaustive bibliography, see Saffroy, *Bibliographie généalogique, héraldique et nobiliaire de la France* (1968). There is only one synthesis on the *noblesse de l'Empire*: E. Pierson, *Étude de la noblesse de l'Empire crée par Napoléon Ier* (1910). Batjin, *Histoire de la Noblesse depuis 1789* (1862) is useful. Fugier has re-created well the spirit in which the Légion d'honneur was instituted, 'La Signification sociale et politique des décorations napoléoniennes', *Cahiers d'Histoire*, 1959, pp. 340–46. The administrative organization of the Légion has been described by L. Soulajon, *Les Cohortes de la Légion d'honneur* (1890) and by P. Codechèvre, 'Le Général Mathieu Dumas et l'organisation de la Légion d'honneur', *Revue de l'Institut Napoléon*, 1965, pp. 193–210. The members of the Légion are known to us through the *Fastes de la Légion d'honneur* by Lievyns, Verdot and Bégat (5 vols., 1842–7), and Testu (ed.), *État de la Légion d'honneur* (1814). Also consult the special numbers of *Souvenir napoléonien* (March and May 1973) under the editorship of Claude Ducourtial, and above all, the special number of *La Cohorte* (1968), 'Napoléon et la Légion d'honneur' (detailed catalogue of an important exhibition). See also 'La Légion d'honneur' (*Toute l'histoire de Napoléon*, 1956). Presentations have been described by A. Chatelle, *Napoléon et la Légion d'honneur au camp de Boulogne* (1956).

Two good works on the *sénatoreries*: L'Hommedé, 'Les sénatoreries', *Revue des études historiques*, 1933, pp. 19–40; F. Ponteil, 'Une nouvelle forme d'artistocratie au temps de Napoléon: les sénatoreries' (Paris, 1947, in *Études historiques* published by the *Faculté des lettres* of Strasbourg. Read also L. de Brotonne, *Les Sénateurs du Consulat et de l'Empire* (1895), genealogical study).

Attitudes towards the nobility have varied: M. Reinhard, 'Élite et noblesse', *Revue d'Histoire moderne et contemporaine*, 1956, pp. 1–37; C. Brelot, *La Noblesse en Franche-Comte de 1789 à 1808* (1972, good regional study of the old nobility). M. Bruguière, 'Finance et noblesse, l'entrée des financiers dans la noblesse d'Empire', *Revue d'Histoire moderne*, 1970, pp. 664–79 (throws light on the reserve in banking circles). P. Durye has drawn attention to 'Les Chevaliers dans la noblesse impériale', *Revue d'Histoire moderne*, 1970, pp. 671–9 (sixteen hundred knights were created by Napoleon. 'It seems that by limiting accession to the nobility with this title, the Emperor discouraged requests.' The knights' descendants 'never really mixed with the *grand bourgeois* and the old nobility'). Read also Labarre de Raillicourt, *Les Chevaliers de l'Empire et de la Restauration à lettres-patentes* (1968).

Napoleon wanted *majorats* instituted in order to avoid loss of privilege: Frain de la Gaulayrie, *Les Majorats depuis le Premier Empire* (1909), E. l'Hommedé, 'La question des majorats', *Revue des Études historiques*, 1924, pp. 45–70. Imperial endowments are linked to the same problem: the book of endowments has been preserved and has been analysed by C. Emmanuel Brousse in the *Revue des Études napoléoniennes*, 1935, pp. 168–73. The question has been taken up again by Senkowska-Gluck, 'Les donataires de Napoléon', *Revue d'Histoire moderne*, 1970, pp. 680–93, (many small endowments were in fact retirement or disability pensions).

On Napoleon's efforts to rally the Ancien régime nobility, there is a good local study by C. Alleaume, 'Napoleon Ier et l'ancienne classe nobiliaire, l'enquête de 1810 dans le département du Var', *Société d'études scientifiques et arch. de Draguignan* (1935, pp. 5–48). J. Bertaut, *Le Faubourg Saint-Germain* (1949), G. de Broglie, *Ségur sans cérémonies* (1977), J. Stalins, *L'ordre impérial de Réunion* (1959).

Open Questions

The problem of the integration of the two nobilities can only be clarified through a study of the Empire's matrimonial politics, a study which has been made easy by Révérend's *Armorial* and Valynseele's researches. Integration seems to have been slow. The first alliances were made, above all, with rich banking circles: J. Lhomer, *Le Banquier Perrégaux et sa fille, la duchesse de Raguse* (1926). On 5 April 1802, at the Château de Grignon, Ney married the second daughter of Auguié, quartermaster-general to the army and then guard-room administrator.

Did imperial endowments constitute an important contribution? We know of them through the works (in Polish) by M. Senkowska-Gluck (Warsaw, 1968), Berding ('Les dotations impériales dans le royaume de Westphalie', *Revue de l'Institut Napoléon*, 1976, pp. 91–101), Ingold (*Bénévent sous la domination de Talleyrand*, 1916), J. Courvoisier (*Le maréchal Berthier et sa principauté de Neufchâtel*, 1959) and H. de Grimouard's article, 'Les origines du Domaine extraordinaire', *Revue des Questions historiques* (1908, pp.

160–92). The income which they guaranteed was, finally, mediocre (J. Tulard, 'Les composants d'une fortune; le cas de la noblesse de l'Empire', *Revue historique*, 1975, pp. 119–38): they were too spread out, there were exchange problems, ill-will from local authorities, flaws in leases. For recipients of large endowments, losses were in the region of forty per cent (ninety per cent in 1813). Salaries and allowances were paid irregularly at the end of the Empire. Gratuities given directly by the Emperor (town houses, sums of money), private enterprise (privateering attracted Soult, Andreossy or Caffarelli for example), speculation (Bourrienne, Brune, Bernadotte), looting (Masséna and Soult) and corruption (F. Boyer, 'Oeuvres d'art pour les généraux français', *Revue de l'Institut Napoleon*, 1965, pp. 15–23) were the foundations of certain fortunes. An example of a great fortune built up under the Revolution and the Empire: R. Marquant 'La fortune de Cambacérès', *Bulletin d'Histoire économique et sociale de la Révolution française*, 1971, pp. 169–251. Less is known of the rebuilding of old fortunes. Among the old nobility rallied to Napoleon, the courtiers had all the favours. It was better to be a chamberlain than a general or a prefect. 'Yet another chamber pot on the heads of the nobility,' jeered Pommereul after the nomination of several chamberlains. Formerly a chamberlain himself, Pommereul, had become a prefect and in 1811 was called to replace Portalis (the younger) at the head of the direction of printing, Portalis not having denounced his cousin the abbé d'Astros to the police. On the ambassadors, see Whitcomb: *Napoleon's Diplomatic Service* (1979).

IV. 3   A DEVIATION IN FOREIGN POLICY: THE SPANISH HORNETS' NEST

Sources
Foreign Affairs Archives (Spain), series AF^{IV} of the National Archives, the Archivo historico nacionale of Madrid and the Public Record Office in London. The treaties were reproduced by J. de Clercq (1880). Numerous *Mémoires*: Abrantès, Azanza (1815), Escoiquiz (*Memorias*, 1915), Bacler d'Albe (important illustrations in Vol. II, 1892), Belliard, Bigarré (Joseph's entourage in Madrid), Billon, Blayney (English prisoner of war), Blaze (1828, pharmacist in the health service), Brun, Chevillard (*La Revue de Paris*, 1906), Chlapowski, Coignet, Daudebard (Saragossa, evidence published in 1812), Dellard, Delroeux (Baylen and Cabrera), Duhesme, Fantin des Odoards, Fée (*Souvenirs de la Guerre d'Espagne*, 1856, excellent), Fleuret, Godoy (*Mémoires du prince de la Paix* trans. into French by Esménard, 1836), Gouvion Saint-Cyr, Grivel, Guitard (1934), d'Hautpoul, Hugo (ed. Guimbaud, 1934), Hulot (1886), Jomini (*Guerre d'Espagne*, 1892), Jovellanas (Diarios), Joseph Bonaparte (*Mémoires*, Vols. IV–VIII), Jourdan, Lavaux, Lawrence (the point of view of an English grenadier), Lejeune, Marbot, Marmont, Masséna, Miot de Melito (fundamental for Joseph's entourage), Manière (Somo-Sierra and the Siege of Cadiz), Palafox (*Autobiografia*), Martins Pamplona (*Aperçus nouveaux sur les campagnes des*

français au Portugal, 1818), Ratton, Rocca (*Mémoires sur la guerre des Français en Espagne*, 1814), Saint-Chamans, Soult, Suchet, Talleyrand, Maurice de Tascher (1933; excellent), Thiébault, Vedel (1828; in defence of Baylen), Vigo-Roussillon (*La Revue de Deux-Mondes*, 1890–91). Pradt's historical memoirs are very suspect (1816). But the *Voyage pittoresque et historique en Espagne* (1807–18) and the *Itinéraire descriptif* by A. de Laborde are very interesting. Neither the *Catéchisme espagnol* nor the *Mémoire* by Cevallos should be overlooked, they are among the most important pamphlets inspired by the war in Spain. Several have been reproduced by Beauchamp, *Mémoires relatifs aux Révolutions d'Espagne*, 1824. A knowledge of Goya's work, especially *Los desastres de la guerra*, is indispensable. In his fine novel, *Le Flagellant de Séville*, Paul Morand has managed to re-create the state of mind of an *afrancesado*. The text of the Constitution of Bayonne is given by P. Conard in a critical edition (1909), the correspondence of La Forest, French ambassador to Spain, 1808–13, was published in 1905–7 by G. de Grandmaison. Wellington's dispatches are to be found in the edition of *Dispatches*, Vol VI (1834). Documents on the meeting in Bayonne in A. Savine, *L'Abdication de Bayonne* (1908).

Works

The origins of the Spanish affair have been dealt with in a masterly way by A. Fugier, *Napoléon en Espagne, 1799–1808* (1930). Add to it the pages by Miguel Artola in Vol. XXVI of the *Historia de España* edited by Menendez Pidal. The character of Godoy, who played the part of sorcerer's apprentice, has been treated with more indulgence by the French (Desdevises du Dezert, 1895; Chastenet, 1961) than by the Spanish (Corona, *Revolución y reacción en el reinado de Carlos IV*, 1957; Seco Serrano, preface to the *Memorias* of the Prince of the Peace, 1956). The economic situation has been well illuminated by P. Vilar, *La Catalogne et l'Espagne moderne* (1962), and R. Herr, *The Eighteenth Century Revolution in Spain* (1958).

The pro-French element has been the subject of considerable study: the basic work is Artola's *Los Afrancesados* (1953) which is complemented by Hans Juretschke's *Die Franzosenpartei in spanischen unabhanggigkeits Krieg* (1961). Consult on some important characters: Demerson, *Don Juan Meléndez Valdès et son temps* (1962); A. Dérozier, *Manuel Josef Quintana et la naissance du libéralisme en Espagne* (1968); M. Defourneaux, *Pablo de Olavide ou l'afrancesado* (1959); Dermigny, 'Carrion-Nisas et l'Espagne', *29ᵉ Congrès Fed. hist Languedoc*, 1955. Interesting points of view by C. Martin, 'Les Afrancesados', *Ecrits de Paris*, June 1965, pp. 68–80. J. Sarrailh, *L'Espagne éclairée de la seconde moitié du XVIIIᵉ siècle* (1964).

The war and the politics concerning it have been dealt with in several works: Napier, *History of the War in the Peninsula* (13 vols. trans. into French 1828); Oman, *History of the Peninsula War* (7 vols. 1902–30); G. de Grandmaison, *L'Espagne et Napoléon*, (3 vols., 1908–31; excellent); Grasset, *La Guerre d'Espagne* 3 vols., 1914–32 (detailed study of military operations); J. Lucas-Dubreton, *Napoléon devant l'Espagne* (1947); Artola, *Las Origines de la España contemporanea* (Vol. I, 1959); J. Thiry, *La Guerre d'Espagne*

(1966); P. Vilar, 'L'Espagne devant Napoléon', in *Les Pays sous domination française* (1968, pp. 128–58); by the same author, 'Quelques aspects de l'occupation et de la résistance en Espagne en 1794 et au temps de Napoléon' in *Occupants-Occupés* (1969, pp. 221–52); Charles-Roux, *Le Guêpier Espagnol* (1970); J. R. Aymes, *La Guerre d'independance espagnol* (1973). In addition the *Diccionario bibliograficol de la guerra de la independencia española (1808–1814)* (3 vols., 1944–52). The old works by Foy, the Count of Toreno and Gomez de Arteche can be discounted. Literary aspects and pamphlets have been well described by L. Trenard, 'La résistance espagnole à l'invasion française', *94ᵉ Congrès des Soc. Sav.* (1971, pp. 243–82). Add Balagny, *Campagne de l'Empereur Napoléon en Espagne* (5 vols., 1902–7); Glover, *Wellington's Army* (1977) and *The Peninsular War* (1974); R. Parkinson, *Moore of Corunna* (1976) and *Peninsular War* (1973); Tranié and Carmigniani, *La Guerre d'Espagne* (1978).

Among special studies: Perez de Guzman, *El 2 de Mayo 1808* (1908, fundamental); Titeaux, *Une Erreur historique; le général Dupont* (3 vols., 1903–4), and M. Leproux *Le Général Dupont* (1934) are rehabilitations of Baylen of which Clerc has made a detailed study (1903). A considerable amount has been written about the Siege of Saragossa: *La Guerra de la Independencia española y los sitios de Zaragoza* (1958). Joseph's behaviour as King of Spain has been analysed by P. Gaffarel, 'Deux années de royauté en Espagne', *Revue des Études napoléoniennes* (1919, pp. 113–45), and Giron de l'Ain, *Le Roi Joseph* (1970). Anti-French resistance varied according to the region: in Catalonia 'la embrolla' was rife, (P. Conard, *Napoléon et la Catalogne*, 1909), terror was the method adopted by 'el Empecinado' (Sanchez Diana, 'Burgos en la Guerra de la Independencia', *Hispania* 1970). In Cadiz resistance became confused with lawfulness (Solis, *El Cadiz de la Cortes*, 1958). On the English action: J. Weller, *Wellington in the Peninsula* (1962). For the Cortes: A. Fugier, *La Junte supérieure des Asturies et l'Invasion des Français* (1930). As for the formulae of the resistance: P. Vilar, 'Patrie et nation dans le vocabulaire de la guerre d'indépendance espagnole', *Annales historiques de la Révolution française* (1971).

The Portuguese problems are inseparable from the Spanish affair. On the diplomatic origins: Fugier, 'Napoléon et le Portugal jusqu'au traité de Fontainebleau', *Bulletin de l'Institut français au Portugal*, 1931, pp. 1–5 (throws light on the double game played by Spain in Hispano-Portuguese relations), M. Lhéritier, 'Napoléon et le Portugal', *Congresso do Mundo portugues*, Vol. VIII, pp. 279–98. On the resistance: Silbert, 'Le Portugal et l'étranger', in *Patriotisme et nationalisme en Europe à l'époque de la Révolution* (1973). On the francophile elements: Daupias d'Alcochete: 'La Terreur blanche à Lisbonne, 1808–1810', *Annales historiques de la Révolution française*, 1965, pp. 299–331 (studies the case of a manufacturer of French origin, Ratton, and that of the economist Acursio das Neves); on economic questions: Macedo, *O Bloqueio continental Economia e guerra peninsular* (1962). A general view by J. Godechot, 'Le Portugal et la Révolution, 1789–1814', *Arquivos do Centro cultural portuguès*, 1974, pp. 279–97).

There are few biographies of Junot except Lucas-Dubreton's rudimentary book and the older one by Brandao, *El rei Junot* (1917).

For a comprehensive view of the Portuguese problem, see Silbert's excellent restatement of the question, 'le Portugal devant la politique française' in *Les Pays sous domination française* (1968, pp. 193–227).

Open Questions

Although Godoy's double game has been the subject of much study, Barca's in Portugal was neglected until J. de Pin's article 'Le comte de Barca 1754–1817', *Revue de l'Institut Napoléon,* 1976, pp. 103–40. The author wishes to show that he attempted to apply a policy of neutrality for which he did not have the means, but he managed, under cover of the Portuguese monarchy's Brazilian odyssey (Oliveira Lima, *D. Joao VI no Brazil, 1808–1821,* Vol. I, 1945) to right his personal situation which was highly comprised. Was he one of the architects of the development of Brazil? (N. Daupias d'Alcochete, 'Lettres de Jacques Ratton à Araujo de Azevedo, comte de Barca, 1812–1817', *Bulletin des Études portugaises,* 1964, pp. 137–256, shows how his initiatives finally disturbed the cabinet in London, despite the Anglo-Portuguese treaty of 19 February 1810.)

In the *Mémorial,* Napoleon denounced Talleyrand as responsible, the fact that the Prince of Benevento denies this in his *Mémoires* has always fascinated historians, from Henri Welschinger in 'Talleyrand et la guerre d'Espagne' (*Comptes rendus de l'Académie des Sciences morales,* Dec. 1808, pp. 499–510) to André Fugier in *Napoléon et l'Espagne* (Vol. II, p. 316), it has been admitted that Talleyrand was constantly hostile to Spain and that he approved the establishment of Joseph in Madrid. No new document has turned up to invalidate this point of view. Murat's part in the decision to intervene in the peninsula was no less important. Connected with the banker, Michel Jeune, and introduced into Godoy's entourage, he was searching for compensation for the disappointing Grand Duchy of Berg which he had been given. The comte Murat, (*Murat, lieutenant de l'Empereur en Espagne,* 1897) does not deny that Murat coveted the throne of Spain, but states that he submitted without difficulty to Joseph, and he clears him of Napoleon's accusation: 'Murat spoiled it all for me.' Cf. also Vol. V of Murat's letters (ed. Le Brethon).

Marx in his articles in the *New York Daily Tribune* of 1854, collected in *Revolution in Spain* (London, 1939), is very hard on the central junta which he describes as counter-revolutionary, and indirectly admits the *afrancesados* were right. L. Dupuis has drawn attention to the necessary distinction between cultural and political *afrancesamiento,* which do not really overlap (*Caravelle, 1963*). There are even considerable shades of difference within political *afrancesamiento*: a comparative study of Espoz y Mina's *Memorias* (reissued 1952), of Azanza and O'Farril (*Memoria justificativa,* reissued 1957) and Reinoso (*Examen de los delitos de infidelidad a la patria,* 1818) would be revealing. It has merely been outlined, although in a masterly manner, by Artola in his introduction to the *Memorias de tiempos de Fernando VII,* and by Crawley, 'French and English influences in the Cortes of Cadiz', *Cambridge Historical Journal,* 1939, pp. 176–208.

Other subjects of debate: the importance of economic factors in the 'resistance' and the 'collaboration'. The effects of the Continental Blockade were more limited in Spain than in Portugal: cf. Mescader Riba, 'España en el bloqueo continental', *Estudios de Historia moderna*, 1952. A general picture of Spanish economy at the time of the war of independence can be found in Vicens Vives, *Historia social y economica de España y America*, Vol. IV, 1957.

Artola has thrown light on the reasons for the guerrillas' success: collaboration of the civilian population, knowledge of the country and, paradoxically, inferiority in numbers ('La guerra de guerrillas', *Revista de Occidente*, 1964). Compare these opinions with J. Godechot, 'Caractères généraux des soulèvements contre-révolutionnaires en Europe au début du XIXe siècle', *Mélanges Vicens Vives* (1967, pp. 169–81), which stresses the general shortage of French strength in the peninsula.

With regard to the problems of the independence of Spanish colonies, besides P. Chaunu's thought-provoking article, 'Interprétation de l'indépendance de l'Amérique latine' (*Tilas*, 1963), a foretaste of many more works by the same author, consult J. Godechot *L'Europe et l'Amérique à l'époque napoléonienne*, which gives the essential bibliography.

IV. 4 THE AWAKENING OF NATIONALISM

Sources

There are many *Mémoires* concerning the 1809 campaign: Boulart (1812), Cadet de Gassicourt (1818), Chevalier (1970 ed. Mistler), Chevillet (1906), Chlapovski (1908), Coignet (1968, ed. Mistler), Comeau (1900), Dupuy (1892), Eugène de Beauharnais (Vol. IV, 1858), Gervais (1939), Jerome Bonaparte (Vol. III, 1861), Lejeune (1851), Lorencez (1902), Macdonald (1892), Marbot (1891), Marmont (1856), Masséna (1849), Oudinot (1894), Parquin (1892), Percy (1904), Pils (1895), Pouget (1895), Rapp (1823), Seruzier (1823), Talleyrand (1891). On the other side: Metternich (1880) and Grüber (1909). Besides Napoleon's *Correspondance*, cf. P. Bertrand, *Lettres inédites de Talleyrand à Napoléon* (1889). See the bulletins of the Grande Armée (ed. Tulard, 1963) and the documents published by W. de Fedorowicz *1809, La Campagne de Pologne*.

Works

Dunan's *Napoléon et l'Allemagne, le système continental et les débuts du royaume de Bavière* (1942) is the fundamental work. A whole chapter is devoted to the 1809 campaign. The campaign is also the subject of a very outdated account by Pelet (*Mémoires sur la guerre de 1809 en Allemagne*, 4 vols. 1824–6). More recent discussions: Saski, *Campagne de 1809* (1899–1902), C. de Renémont, *Campagne de 1809* (1903); Gachot, *Napoléon en Allemagne* (1913). There are several works on Archduke Charles which are difficult to consult in France (W. John, *Erzherzog Karl, der Felder und seine Armee*, 1913). On particular points: Bonnal, *La Manoeuvre de Landshut*, continued by Buat, *De Ratisbonne à Znaïm* (1909, 2 vols. and atlas) in a critical spirit. More eulogistic are Ferry, *1809, la marche sur Vienne* (1909); Camon, *La Manoeuvre de Wagram* (1926); Dupont, *Napoléon en Campagne* (Vols. II and III, 1951–5). On the protagonists: Derrécagaix, *Berthier* (1904–5); Blocqueville, *Le Maréchal Davout* (1879) (cf. also his correspondence published by Mazade in 1885); L. Wirth, *Le Maréchal Lefebvre* (1904). The German uprisings are the subject of a solid, but one-sided study by H. Heitzer, *Insurrektionem zwischen Weser und Elbe—Volksbewegungen gegen die französische Fremdherrschaft in Königreich Westfalen 1806–1813* (1959). For the Tyrol: C. Clair, *André Hofer et l'insurrection du Tyrol en 1809* (1880); Derrécagaix, *Nos campagne au Tyrol* (1910). Staps's attempt illustrates this movement of national resistance: E. Gachot, 'Un régicide allemand, Frédéric Staps', *Revue des Études napoléoniennes*, 1922, pp. 181–203. Staps was not part of the 'enlightenment' sect in which the following figured, Metternich, Montgelas, the Bavarian statesman, Dalberg, J.-P. Richter and Brentano (R. Leforestier, *Les Illuminés de Bavière et la Franc-Maçonnerie allemande* 1914); He had a rival in La Sahla (Desmarest, *Quinze Ans de Haute Police*, ch. XVI). On the effects in Hungary of the Napoleonic wars: E. Balazs, 'Berzevickzy et Napoléon' (a plan for the constitution of Hungary was addressed to Napoleon), *Annales hist. de la Révolution française*, 1973, pp. 245–62. On Walcheren, where the English landing endangered the Empire: A. Fischer, *Napoléon et Anvers* (1933); L. Madelin, *Fouché*, Vol. II; Girod de l'Ain, *Bernadotte* (1968); Théo Fleischman, *L'Expédition anglaise sur le Continent en 1809* (1973).

Well-known, but outdated: Petre: *Napoleon and the Archduke Charles* (1909).

Open Questions

Between the two wars a great deal of interest was taken in the awakening of German nationalism. A. Robert's thesis, *L'idée nationale autrichienne et les guerres de Napoléon—l'apostolat du baron de Hormayr et le salon de Caroline Pichler* (1933), dwells on the personality of the dramatic poet and compiler, Hormayr (1781–1848). Was he the ancestor of pan-Germanism and the herald of the Anschluss? W. C. Langsman, *The Napoleonic Wars and German Nationalism in Austria* (1933) thinks so; A. Robert is more reserved. A. Fugier, *La Révolution et l'Empire* (1954) sees him above all as a procursor of Romanticism. By his desire to found 'the Austrian national idea' on history, particularly on the 'Hapsburg Middle Ages' he does, in fact, herald Romanticism. J. Droz expresses the same point of view in *Le Romantisme allemand et l'État* (1966; he dwells on the currents of resistance and collaboration in Napoleonic Germany). Also see H. Hammer, *Österreichs Propaganda zum Feldzug, 1800* (1935). On the Austrian minister, Stadion, Rossler's work (1957) and Falk, 'Stadion adversaire de Napoléon 1806–1809', *Annales historiques de la Révolution française* (1962, pp. 288–305).

Another instigator of the resistance to Napoleon: Gentz (Robert de Clery, *Frédéric de Gentz*, 1917; Sweet, *Gentz, Old Defender of the Old Order*, 1941; Albert Garreau, *Saint-Empire*, 1954). Note also Schlegel: Comtesse de Pange, *Schlegel et Mme de Staël*, 1938; L. Wittmer, *Le Prince de Ligne, Jean de Muller, Frédéric de Gentz et l'Autriche,* 1925; J. Mistler, *Mme de Staël et Maurice O'Donnel* (1926).

On the other hand, R. Dufraisse in *Patriotisme et nationalisme en Europe* (symposium, 1973, pp. 103–41) explains the failure of the movement on the left bank of the Rhine by the fact that the peasant classes were satisfied by the suppression of seigniorial rights and of unpaid labour and did not want a return to the past.

A small detail, but one which plays an important part in the legend—how was Napoleon wounded at Ratisbon? A rifle bullet (Méneval, Marbot), or a spent bullet (d'Espinchal)? Was he hit in the heel (Berthezène, Lejeune, Pils, Bourrienne)? In the big toe of the left foot (Savary)? In the right ankle (Reiset)? A discussion of these hypotheses can be found in Dunan, *Napoléon et l'Allemagne,* p. 642. 'The bullet which touched me did not wound me,' Napoleon wrote to Josephine.

The marriage to Marie-Louise which resulted from Wagram and which had no psychological effect on Europe (apart from the Tsar's contempt) but which had a disastrous effect on France where Austrian women were not loved, has been studied by F. Masson, *L'Impératrice Marie-Louise, 1809–1815* (1902). Unlike Marie-Antoinette, Marie-Louise, of whom at the time of her marriage Clary-et-Aldringen has left a vivid portrait, played no part in politics.

IV. 5   RELIGIOUS DISCONTENT

Sources

On the Roman archives, A. Latreille and J. Leflon, 'Répertoire des fonds napoléoniens aux Archives vaticanes', *Revue historique,* 1950, pp. 59–63, sub-series F^{19} of the National Archives; the *Papiers inédits d'Artaud de Montor,* the *Correspondance* of Napoleon I, the *Mémoires* of Jauffret (1819, very well informed), Pacca (1840, hostile to Napoleon), Consalvi (1864), Maury (*Correspondance diplomatique et Mémoires inédits* published by Mgr. Ricard, 1891); *Correspondance de la Cour de Rome avec la France* (1814); Mgr. de Barral, *Fragments relatifs à l'histoire ecclésiastique des premières années du XIXe siècle* (1814); Mgr. d'Aviau, *Lettres* (1903) Inventory of the Caprara foundation at the National Archives (1975). On the Congregation: the memoirs of Father de Gobineau (1955).

Works

An excellent bibliography is to be found in Plongeron and Godel, 'Un quart de siècle d'histoire religieuse', *Annales historique de la Révolution française,* 1972, pp. 181–203, 252–389. The fundamental works are those which have already been mentioned by Haussonville, *L'Église et le Premier Empire* (1868–70, important documents); H. Welschinger, *Le Pape et l'Empereur* (1905), A. Latreille, *Napoléon et le Saint Siège, 1801–1808, l'Ambassade du Cardinal Fesch à Rome* (1935, throws a new light on the personality of Napoleon's uncle who was able to show his independence under the influence of M. Émery); V. Bindel, *Histoire religieuse de Napoléon I* (Vols. II and III,

1940–42); A. Dansette, *Histoire religieuse de la France contemporaine* (Vol. I, 1948); A. Latreille, *L'Église catholique et la Révolution* (Vol. II, 1950); Mgr. Leflon, *La Crise révolutionnaire* (1951); these last four books present brilliant and well documented syntheses. There is no biography of Portalis's successor, Bigot de Préameneu.

On the orders: John Carven, *Napoleon and the Lazarists* (1974; the conflict with the Pope and the impossibility of sending the Lazarists to the East brought about the suppression of the order in 1809). The problem of the divorce which had hitherto been studied from the legal point of view by H. Welschinger (1889) and Colmet de Santerre (*Le Divorce de l'Empereur et le Code Napoléon*, 1894), has been treated anew by L. Grégoire, *Le Divorce de Napoléon et de l'Impératrice Joséphine, Étude du Dossier canonique* (1957), in which he refutes the servility of the Napoleonic clergy: the diocese of Paris conformed to the Gallican tradition. The Roman point of view is given, on the other hand, by G. Grandmaison, *Napoléon et les Cardinaux noirs* (1895).

A. Latreille has made a very thorough study in the *Catéchisme impérial* (1935) of the foundations of religious instruction under the Empire. On the Church's attitude to war: J.-P. Bertho, 'Naissance et élaboration d'une théologie de la guerre chez les évêques de Napoléon', in *Civilisation chrétienne* under the editorship of B. Plongeron (1975). With regard to the Church and politics, read the pages devoted to the imperial clergy by B. Plongeron in his important but difficult thesis, *Théologie et politique au siècle des Lumières, 1770–1820* (1973) and C. Langlois's highly perceptive remarks, 'Religion et politique dans la France napoléonienne' in *Christianisme et Pouvoirs politiques* (1974).

The occupation of Rome has been dealt with by H. Aureas, *Miollis* (1961), and L. Madelin, *La Rome de Napoléon* (1906). A good monograph on the Pope's captivity by Mayol de Luppé (1912) could be brought up to date by the impending publication of the *Mémoires* of Chabrol who was Pius VII's 'goaler' at Savona. Consult also the best specialist on Pius VII, J. Leflon, 'Face à Napoléon: Pie VII', *Revue de l'Institut Napoléon*, 1975, pp. 1–19.

On the 1809 and 1811 commissions and on the 1811 council there is only the old book by Mgr Ricard (1894) which has been renewed by A. Latreille, 'Le Gallicanisme ecclésiastique sous le Premier Empire—vers le Concile national de 1811', *Revue historique*, 1944. By the same author, 'Le Clergé du Sud-Est et l'occupation de Rome par Napoleon' in the *Mélanges Fugier*, pp. 163–77. On the feelings of the Belgian clergy: L. Lefebvre, 'La crise religieuse dans la région de Bastogne', *Mémorial Bertrang* (1964), pp. 127–58. Leflon, *Eugène de Mazenod* (Vol. I).

More is becoming known about the secret societies under the Empire. The admirable work of G. de Bertier de Sauvigny, *Le Comte Ferdinand de Bertier et l'énigme de la Congregation* (1948) reveals the role played under cover of the pious association of the Congregation, by the Chevaliers de la Foi in the broadcasting of the excommunication Bull. This fine thesis answers the questions posed by G. de Grandmaison in *La Congrégation* (1890). The works of A. Lestra, *Histoire secrète de la Congrégation de Lyon* (1967) and *Le Père Condrin, fondateur de Picpus* (Vol. I, 1952) cannot be overlooked. On the Aa, cf. Godechot's discussion in the *Mélanges André Latreille* (Lyons, 1972). Remember that Paul Claudel has presented a masterly picture of the Pope's captivity in *L'Otage*.

Open Questions
B. Plongeron's works which carry on from Mgr Jean Leflon, dwell on the new clergy who have been so ignored by historians, from the sociological and theological point of view, ('Le fait religieux' in the 'Nouvelle Histoire de la France contemporaine: Révolution-Empire', *Revue hist. de l'Église de France*, 1972). Along the same lines, consider J. Godel's remarks, 'L'Église selon Napoleon', *Revue d'Histoire moderne* (1970, pp. 837–45). Napoleon's religious politics were less innovative than they may have seemed. Without a doubt he strengthened the principle of authority within the Church (by ecclesiastical organization which was parallel to the civil administration; the authority of bishops over priests and revocability of office; finally, and unintentionally, by the Pope's authority over the Church of France resulting from the exceptional powers given him for the negotiation of the Concordat and by organizing a Church for him in which there were no longer intermediaries). Napoleon had wanted a Gallican Church but created an Ultramontane one. In the conflict between the Pope and the Emperor, the Pope was the winner all the way.

IV. 6   THE ECONOMIC CRISIS

Sources
At the National Archives sub-series AF^{IV} (1058–1059, subsistence, and 1355, general results of the licensing system, have been made little use of), F^7 (police reports on the crises), F^{11} (subsistences), F^{12} (industrial crisis), F^{20} (statistics). Many documents on the depression in the departmental archives. Napoleon's correspondence with Mollien is fundamental, *Napoleon, Lettres au Comte Mollien* (1959). To be completed with Mollien's *Mémoires* the following *Memoires* may be consulted: Chaptal, Gaudin, Laffitte (mediocre), Ouvrard, Pasquier (essential for Paris and matters of supplies), Réal (very inadequate), Savary and above all Thibaudeau (clearly explains the policies followed by the Prefect of the Bouches-du-Rhône). Among the numerous brochures which throw light on the crisis, once again attention must be especially drawn to F. d'Ivernois, *Exposé de l'exposé de la situation de l'Empire publié à Paris en fevrier-mars 1813* (1814) and *Napoléon administrateur et financier* (1814). It is interesting to consult Magnien, *Tarif des droits de douane et de navigation maritime de l'Empire français* (ed. 1808, 1811 and 1813) and the *Tableau des prix moyens mensuels et annuels du froment en France depuis 1er vendémiaire an IX jusqu'an 31 décembre 1870* (1872).

Works
It would be suitable to add to the books quoted in the chapter on the Continental Blockade: M. Dunan, 'Napoléon et le système continental en

1810', *Revue d'Histoire diplomatique*, 1946, pp. 71–98 (throws light on the change in conception of Napoleon's foreign and anti-English policies); by the same author, for the application of these policies, *L'Allemagne de la Révolution et de l'Empire* Vol. I, section 2, 1800–1815 (1954), and 'Napoleon, l'Italie et le système continental', *Revue de l'Institut Napoléon*, 1965, pp. 176–90; F. L'Huillier, *Étude sur le Blocus continental. La mise en oeuvre des décrets de Trianon et de Fontainebleau dans le Grande-Duché de Bade* (1951); G. Sevières, *L'Allemagne française sous Napoléon I* (1904; in fact Hamburg and the Blockade) and B. Groshulska: 'L'économie polonaise et le renverse-ment de la conjoncture', *Revue d'Histoire moderne* 1970, pp. 620–30.

The American implications have been picked out well by P. A. Heath, *Napoleon I and the origins of the Anglo-American War of 1812* (1929), U. Bonnel, *La France, et les États-Units et la guerre de course* (1961). On the other hand, Schalk de la Faverie, *Napoléon et l'Amérique* (1917), is completely out of date. R. Dufraisse's article is essential, 'La politique douanière de Napoléon', *Revue de l'Institut Napoléon*, 1974, pp. 3–25. Whilst awaiting the publication of the large work on smuggling by the same author, read F. Ponteil, 'La contrebande sur le Rhin au temps de l'Empire', *Revue historique*, 1935, pp. 257–86; J. Bertrand, 'La contrebande à la frontière du Nord en 1811, 1812 and 1813', *Annales de l'Est*, 1951, pp. 276–306; J. Tulard, 'La contrabande au Danemark', *Revue de l'Institut Napoléon*, 1966, pp. 94–5; R. Dufraisse, 'Contrabandiers normands sur les bords du Rhin', *Annales de Normandie*, 1961, pp. 209–31.

The crisis has been made the subject of an excellent analysis by Chabert, *Essai sur le mouvement des revenus et de l'activité économique en France de 1798 à 1820* (1949) and O. Viennet's more detailed study, *Napoléon et l'Industrie française la crise de 1810–1811* (1947). Among regional researches: Lavalley, *Napoléon et la disette de 1812. À propos d'une émeute aux halles de Caen* (1895); R. Levy, 'La disette au Havre en 1812', *Revue des Études napoléoniennes*, July 1915, pp. 5–43; L. Boniface, 'La disette de 1811–1812 dans de département des Alpes-Maritimes', *Annales Soc. Lettres, Sciences et Arts des Alpes-Maritimes*, 1936, pp. 266–84; F. L'Huillier, 'Une crise de subsistances dans le Bas-Rhin', *Annales d'Histoire de la Révolution française*, 1937, pp. 518–36; P. Léon, 'La crise des subsistances de 1810–1812 dans de département de l'Isère', *Ibid.*, 1952, pp. 289–309; J. Vidalenc, 'La vie économique des départements méditerranéens pendant l'Empire', *Revue d'Histoire moderne*, 1954, pp. 165–98; J. Labasse, *Le Commerce des soies à Lyon sous Napoléon et la crise de 1811* (1957); J. Vidalenc, 'La crise des subsistances et les troubles de 1812 dans le Calvados', *Actes du 84ᵉ Congrès des Sociétés savantes*; Gaillard, 'La crise économique de 1810 à 1811 à Saint-Omer', *La Revue du Nord*, 1957, pp. 153–86 (from the papers of Saint-Omer which, although very much subjected to the imperial power reveal the difficulties in the commune of Thérouanne); Lantier, 'La crise alimentaire de 1812', *Revue du Département de la Manche* (1961, pp. 130–47); Hemardinquer, 'Document sur les crises de 1805 à 1815 à Lyon' (89ᵉ *Congrès des Sociétés Savantes* (1964), pp. 239–63); R. Cobb, *Police and the People: French popular Protest, 1789–1820* (1970, the first study in depth of the 1812 rebellious movement). For Marseilles consult R. Caty's excellent monograph, 'Jean-Louis Bethfort et le commerce des blés à Marseille de 1801 à 1820, *Provence historique*, 1973, pp. 164–216. On supplies for Paris: Passy: 'Napoléon, l'approvisionnement de Paris et la question des subsistances', *Séances et travaux de l'académie des Sciences morales et politiques* 1897, pp. 558–616, 777–820; L. de Lanzac de Laborie, *Paris sous Napoleon*, Vol. V (1908); J. Tulard, *Nouvelle Histoire de Paris: le Consulat et l'Empire* (1969). On substitute products: R. Pascal, *Une Industrie disparue à Albi: l'indigopastel* (1954). For industry, C. Ballot, 'Les prêts aux manufactures sous le Premier Empire', *Revue des Études napoléoniennes*, 1912, pp. 45–77. On the English crisis, besides F. Crouzet's thesis, W. Galpin, *The Grain Supply of England during the Napoleonic Period* (1925).

Open Questions

The Continental Blockade caused an alteration in the great international routes, especially to the East, as the sea-routes had been cut off (Échinard, *Grecs et Philhellènes à Marseille de la Révolution à l'Indépendance de la Grèce*, 1973). At the end of 1810, C. Schmidt points out ('Napoléon et les routes balkaniques', *Revue de Paris*, 1912, pp. 335–52), the French frontiers to the south-east touched the Ottoman Empire. 'Henceforth a traveller could go from Paris to the States of the Grand Seigneur without leaving French territory or at least countries under French domination.' This splendid continuity, 'this continent whose barriers are the sea, closed by gates of bronze', in Montalivet's words disguised, the deepest of cracks. In place of the Rhine, the Danube, in 1810, became the canal which supplied the German States with English goods. 'During Napoleon's reign, ships laden with sugar, coffee, tobacco and yarn were sent out from London to Salonika where these goods were loaded on to horses or mules and carried across Serbia and Hungary to be distributed throughout Germany, and even in France.'

Jean-Baptiste Say derived ideas of free trade from this picture. (Schmidt, 'Jean-Baptiste Say et le Blocus Continental', *Revue d'Histoire des Doctrines économiques et sociales*, 1911). J. Bouvier ('Les crises économiques sous l'Empire', *Revue d'Histoire moderne*, 1970, p. 512) discerns in the origins of the great depression of 1810–15, an independent industrial crisis, that of 1810, tied to difficulties in the supply of raw materials due to the Blockade; an agricultural crisis in 1811, a deflation in 1812 brought about by the cost of war and by a crisis of confidence. Perhaps in the collapse of 1810 he underestimates banking difficulties (B. Gille, *La Banque et le Credit en France de 1815 à 1848*, 1959) and monetary problems (G. Thuillier, 'La crise monétaire de l'automne 1810', *Revue historique*, Sept. 1967, pp. 51–84). In E. Labrousse's classic distinction between crises of the old kind (where the crisis is set off by the agricultural sector) and modern types of crises (which are provoked by banking or industry), the 1810–15 depression occupies a special place. It combined both types (Chabert *op. cit.* and Gabillard, 'Le financement des guerres napoléoniennes', *Revue économique* 1953, pp. 548–72) and even took on a worldwide dimension (England and the United States).

The licensing system, an infringement of the Blockade, is particularly complex. The first licences signed in 1809 authorized the export of commodities from France in exchange for iron and naval furnishings; colonial produce and goods manufactured in England were still prohibited (F. Crouzet, 'Importations d'eaux-de-vie et de vins français en Angleterre pendant le Blocus continental', *Annales du Midi*, 1953; P. Butel, 'Le commerce maritime de la France sous le Consulat et l'Empire', *Information historique*, 1968; Viard, 'Les conséquences économiques du Blocus continental en Ille-et-Vilaine', *Rev. Études napoléoniennes*, 1926). The first licences then must be distinguished from the 'new system' of licences defined by the decree of 3 July 1810 and the 1812–13 licences which permitted the exchange of wine and silk for all colonial commodities like coffee, sugar or indigo.

IV. 7 THE DEFEATS

Sources
On the Russian archives refer to Serge Goriaïnow's old article, 'Documents russes sur 1812', *Revue des Études Napoléoniennes*, 1912, pp. 276–95 (which also published the plans of the 1st Russian corps, August–December 1812, and some extracts from the correspondence between the Tsar Alexander I and the Grand Duchess Catherine from the work of the Grand Duke Nicholas Michailovitch). Volumes V, VI and VII of the *Vnyechnaya politika Rossy* cannot be overlooked (1967–72; cf. M. Spivak's report, *Revue de l'Institut Napoléon*, 1976, pp. 222–3). Consult Nesselrode's letters and papers (1904). Finally consult G. de Grandmaison, 'Napoléon en Russie d'après les documents des archives espagnoles', *Revue de Questions historiques* (1902). From the English point of view consult volumes VIII–X of *Correspondence, Dispatches and Other Papers* by Castlereagh; *British and Foreign State Papers* (1841); Wellington, *Dispatches* Vols. VI and VII and the documents published by C. Webster, *British Diplomacy, 1813–1815* (1921). Metternich's memoirs are a mixture of documents and personal reminiscences. The same can be said of Lebzeltern's (1949). Many diplomatic papers can be found in the addendum to W. Oncken's *Osterreich und Preussen im Befreiungskriege* (1880).

Memoirs of the campaign in Russia are numerous: Aubry (1889), Bangofsky (1905), Margrave of Baden (1912), Bennigsen (Vol. III, 1908), Biot (1901), Bourgogne (1898), the Pole, Brandt (1917), Caulaincourt (fundamental, the best *Mémoires* of the period, 1933), Chevalier (1970), Coignet (ed. Mistler, 1968), Dedem (1900), Domergue (director of the French theatre in Moscow, 1835), Dutheillet (interesting on the illnesses which struck the soldiers, 1899), Duverger, Faber du Faur (1895, illustrated), Galitzin (translated from the souvenirs of a Russian officer, 1844), Grüber (1909, the point of view of Schwarzenberg's Austrian corps), Guitard (1934), Hogendorp (1887), Labaume (1814, which had a great success under the Restoration), Langeron (1902; the Russian point of view), Montesquoiu de Férenzac (1863; excellent), Paixhans (1868), Pils (1895), Pion des Loches

(1889), Pisani (1942; the Italian point of view), Pouget (1895), Roos (doctor, 1913), Ségur (his *Histoire de Napoléon et de la Grande Armée pendant l'année 1812*, 1824; a classic), Séruzier (1823), Soltyck (1836), Suckow (a native of Württemberg, 1901), Surugues (1821), Tascher (1938), Uxkull (1961; a Russian officer, gives curious details), Villemain (1853), Wilson (1860). Read the same on the German campaign, also Berthezène (1855), Lowenstein (Russia, 1903), Odeleben (1817; a German officer attached to Napoleon's headquarters), Parquin (1843). On Spain: Jourdan (1899), Marmont (1856), Masséna (1850, Vol. VII), Noël (1895; an account of Torres Vedras), Jean-Jacques Pelet (in English, ed. Howard; on 1811 in Portugal), Soult (Spain and Portugal, 1955), Sprünglin (*Revue hispanique*, 1904; important for Portugal), Suchet, (1828; excellent); in addition, the campaigns of Captain Marcel (1913). On Italy: Eugène de Beauharnais (Vols. VIII and IX). For Bernadotte's defection: Suremain (1902) and Vaudoncourt (1817). On Holland: Jacquin (1960). On public feeling, Maine de Biran's letters to the Prefect, Maurice (1963).

Clausewitz's analysis of the 1812 and 1813 campaigns falls into the category of *Mémoires*, as does Jomini's: *Précis politique et militaire des campagnes de 1812 à 1814* (1886). Read also A. Chuquet, *Lettres de 1812* (1911), Norvins, *Le Porte-feuille de 1813* (1825), *La Guerre nationale de 1812* (on Russia; 7 vols.) and Colomb's campaign notes on the German partisans (1914).

Besides Napoleon's *Correspondance*, consult the *Lettres Personelles* of the sovereigns to Napoleon (unfinished), and on the Emperor's state of mind, the *Lettres à Marie Louise* (1935).

Works
The Russian campaign has given rise to a wealth of literature, particularly at the time of the centenary in 1912. Some syntheses on the whole campaign: Jacoby, *Napoléon en Russie* (1938); Tarlé, *La Campagne de Russie* (French trans. 1938); G. Bertin, *La Campagne de Russie d'après les Témoins oculaires*; C. de Grunwald; *La Campagne de Russie* (1963, collection of texts); Palmer, *Napoleon in Russia*; J. Thiry, *La Campagne de Russie* (1969).

The diplomatic atmosphere has been well presented by A. Vandal, *Napoléon et Alexandre I* (Vol. III, 1896), J. Mansuy, *Jérôme Napoléon et la Pologne en 1812* (1931), which enables the correction of Pradt's inaccuracies in his *Histoire de l'ambassade dans le grand-duché de Varsovie* (1815), Dundulis, *Napoléon et la Lithuanie en 1812* (1940). On military preparations: Tulard, 'Le dépôt de guerre et la préparation de la campagne de Russie", *Revue historique de l'armée* (1969); L. Hastier, 'Napoléon faussaire', *Vieilles Histoires* (1961, pp. 63–103); Villatte des Prugnes, 'Les effectifs de la Grande Armée pour la campagne de Russie', *Revue des Études historiques* (1913); R. Bielecki, 'L'effort militaire polonais, 1806–1815', *Revue de l'Institut Napoléon* (1976). Details of the operation are given by Margueron, *Campagne de Russie. Préliminaires, 1810–1812* (1898–1906), and by Fabry, *Campagne de Russie. Opérations* (5 vols. 1900–3). Read also B. de Baye, *Smolensk* (1912), and Gronski, 'L'administration civile des gouvernements russes occupés en 1812', *Revue d'Histoire moderne* (1928, pp. 401–12). Van

Vlijmen, *Vers la Bérésina* (1908), sees, in what is generally considered a disaster, a masterpiece of strategy. For the Russian historiographer, Kutuzov's role and that of his partisans was determining (Jiline, *Le Désastre de l'armée napoléonienne en Russie*, in Russian, 1968). On the foreign contingents: Sauzey, *Les Allemands sous les aigles françaises* (1902–12), and Boppe, *Les Espagnols à la Grande Armée* (1899), Le Gall-Torrance, 'Mémoires russes sur l'époque napoléonienne', *Revue de l'Institut Napoléon* (1979), M. Holden *Napoleon in Russia* (1974).

The Prussian war effort from the point of view of 'the revenge', a multitude of works in France: Cavaignac, *La Formation de la Prusse contemporaine* (1897–8, principally Vol. II); Vidal de la Blache, *La Regénération de la Prusse après Jéna* (1910); Gromaire, *La Littérature patriotique en Allemagne* (1911); by the same author 'Arndt et Napoléon', *Revue des Études napoléoniennes* (1913, IV, pp. 372–401); C. de Grunwald, *Stein* (1936). The former accounts of events by Charras (1870) and Rousset (1871) should be replaced by J. d'Ussel, *La Défection de la Prusse* (1907); *L'Intervention de l'Autriche* (1912). For Clausewitz, Vol. I of the copious study by R. Aron (*Penser la guerre*, 1976) is essential. The influence of Spain's example is analysed by R. Wohlfeil, *Spanien und die deutsche Erbehung, 1808–1814* (1965). Read also Bouvier, *Le Redressement de la Prusse* (1941), Paret, *York and the Era of Prussian Reform* (1966) and *Clausewitz and the State* (1976); Straube, *Das Jahr 1813* (1963); Max Lehmen *Scharnhorst* (1887; old-fashioned but useful); Unger, *Gneisenau* (1914); Ranke, *Hardenberg* (1874). Hoffman has left a striking description of the battlefield at Leipzig. The pro-Napoleon element did not disappear for all that. Hegel wrote: 'One day Germany, through the power of a conqueror will be united in one mass.'

For details of the operations—before Napoleon's arrival: Reboul, *La Campagne de 1813* (1910–12); Clément, *La Campagne de 1813* (1904); Lanrezac, *La Manoeuvre de Lützen* (1904); Tournés, *Lützen* (1931); P. Foucart, *Bautzen* (1893) and *La Poursuite* (1901); Lefebvre de Behaine, *La Campagne de France*, Vol. I, entitled *Napoléon et les Alliés sur la Rhin* (1913); Thiry, *Lützen et Bautzen* (1971); by the same author, *Leipzig* (1972). On the Frankish corps, Spivak, 'Le corps franc du Major Adolphe von Lutzow', *Revue de l'Institut Napoléon* (1974).

Bernadotte's attitude has been well explained and severely judged by L. Pingaud, *Bernadotte, Napoléon et les Bourbons* (1901).

On Italy and the importance of its role: H. Weil, *Le Prince Eugène et Murat, opérations militaires, négociations diplomatiques* (1905); Rath, *The Fall of the Napoleonic Kingdom in Italy* (1941) and especially Fugier, *Napoléon et l'Italie* (1947). On Lagarde, Director of Police in Tuscany, the biographical note by F. Boyer (*Rassegna storica del Rissorgimento*, 1957, pp. 88–95). For Florence, R. Boudard (*Rassegna Storica Toscana*, 1974, pp. 47–61). As for Rome and the end of the French domination, Vol. II of J. Moulard's thesis is essential, *Le Comte Camille de Tournon* (1930). The English attitude in Sicily is dealt with by J. Rossetti, *Lord W. Bentinck and the British Occupation of Sicily, 1811–1821* (1956). Add to the bibliography on Murat quoted above, A. Valente *Gioacchino Murat e l'Italia Meridionale*

(1956); Johnston, *The Napoleonic Empire in Southern Italy* (1904); H. Weil, *Joachim Murat, roi de Naples, la dernière année du règne* (1909).

The fall of Holland is studied at first hand by Caumont de la Force, *L'Architrésorier Lebrun, gouverneur de la Hollande, 1810–1813* (1907). For Hamburg, J. Mistler, "Hambourg sous l'occupation française', *Francia*, 1973, pp. 451–67 (from d'Aubignosc's reports).

The best account of Spain is G. de Grandmaison's *L'Espagne et Napoléon*, Vol. III (1931). On the particular organization of Catalonia: P. Conard, *Napoléon et la Catalogne* (1910). The operations in which Wellington confronted Masséna have especially been the subject of interest: E. Gachot, 'Les lignes de Torres Vedras' (*Revue des Études napoléoniennes*, 1918, XIV, pp. 225–39) is favourable to Masséna and blames Bessières, Soult and Marmont. Views in favour of Masséna by Valentin (1960), Marshall-Cornwall (1965) and D. Horward, *The Battle of Bussaco, Masséna against Wellington* (1965). On what followed: Weller, *Wellington in the Peninsula* (1962). On the refugee *afrancesados* in France after Vitoria: *Revue des Études napoléoniennes* 1915, Vol. VII, pp. 276–8. On Suchet, one of the best marshals: F. Rousseau, *Le Carrière du maréchal Suchet* (1898); on Jourdan, R. Valentin's very objective biography (1956); for Bessières, A. Bessière's biography (1952) and the bulletin, *Les Amis de Bessières* (1969–1976); Sarramon, *La Batille des Arapiles* (1978).

The collapse of the colonies is recounted by C. Parkinson, *War in the Eastern Seas, 1783–1815* (1954); H. Prentout, *L'Île de France sous Decaen* (1901); J. Eymeret, 'L'Administration napoléonienne en Indonésie', *Revue française d'Histoire d'outre mer* (1973, pp. 27–44); by the same author, 'Java sous Daendels', *Archipel* (1972, pp. 151–68) which takes the place of Collet's old thesis. On Napoleon's indifference (opposite point of view in Besson and Chauvelot), *Napoléon colonial* (1939). On America: Gandia, *Napoléon et l'indépendance de l'Amérique latine* (1955); Pardo de Leygonier, 'Napoléon et les libérateurs de l'Amérique latine', *Revue de l'Institut Napoléon* (1962, pp. 29–33); O. Baulny, 'La Naissance de l'Argentine et l'entreprise ibérique de Napoléon', *Ibid.* (1970, pp. 169–80); C. de Sassenay, *Napoléon I et la fondation de la République Argentine* (1892). The maritime war in the West Indies has been well described by H. de Poyen (1896).

Open Questions

What were the real causes of Napoleon's defeat in Russia? The Emperor blamed the climate. Russian historians claim that action by the partisans was decisive. In his essay, *Est-ce le gel qui a detruit l'armée française en 1812?* Davydor criticizes French evidence, among which Chambray's *Histoire de l'Expedition de Russie*, 1823. They confuse two different aspects of the retreat—from Moscow to the Beresina and from the Beresina to the Niemen. During the first part there were only three days of frost out of twenty-five, during which the French lost sixty-five thousand men. How can the winter alone be blamed? At Eylau or in Spain, conditions were no better. It was only during the second part that there were twenty-two days of continuous frost. For the Russians (and it is not necessary to bring in Tolstoy and Borodino) the

French defeat was prepared by Kutuzov cutting off the Grande Armée's route from Smolensk; it was precipitated after the battles at Taroutino (6 October), Malojovski (12 October) and Krasno (6 November), by the joining up of the three armies from Moscow, Finland and Moldavia.

Can the French losses be counted? Martinien's estimates only concern officers. According to Mehliss, 16,000 French soldiers, or soldiers in the service of France, were taken prisoner from 1810 to 1814, or died in Russia, Poland and Germany. This list, drawn up in 1826 is not reliable. Disagreement is already considerable concerning the number of soldiers who entered Russia: 517,000 according to M. Bergerot's estimate in his unpublished thesis on Daru, based on the ordnance officer, Robert; Marbot says 325,900 of whom 155,400 were French and 170,500 allies (but he is unreliable); Ségur says 444,700 soldiers, the *Mémorial* says 400,000, of whom 140,000 were French speaking. The loss of commissariat papers in the 'Orcha burning' (20 November) at the crossing of the Beresina, does not help. Prisoners and deaths from exhaustion in Germany must be taken into account, (Lariboisière, Eblé). Only figures concerning certain corps can be put forward: the average then being between forty and fifty per cent of officers, and eighty to ninety per cent of soldiers.

A legend destroyed: T. Sauvel ('Le décret de Moscou mérite-t-il son nom?', *Revue historique Droit français et etranger,* July 1975, pp. 436–40) shows that the famous decree organizing the Comédie-Française was neither signed in Moscow nor on the retreat but back in Paris. It was dated from Moscow for reasons of propaganda and in order to 'save face' and reassure the public with regard to the extent of the disaster.

What part did the fire in Moscow play in the final disaster? It did not determine the retreat, but nevertheless compromised the French situation (D. Olivier, *L'Incendie de Moscou,* 1964). Although he denied it and accused the French, Rostopchine was largely responsible for the fire, part of which was proably caused accidentally, Ségur, *Rostopchine* 1873; La Füye, 'Rostopchine et Kutusov', *Revue des Questions historiques,* 1936.

Metternich's attitude in 1813 has been variously judged. Bibl, *Metternich der Dämon Osterreich's* (1936) gives a very hostile portrait, since Bibl joins the liberal school and judges the diplomatist far more severely than do French historians (Sorel, *Essais d'Histoire et de Critique,* 1883; M. Paléologue, *Romantisme et Diplomatie,* 1924; Bertier de Sauvigny, *Metternich et son Temps,* 1959). H. von Srbik is more favourable (*Metternich der Staatsman und der Mensch,* 1925) and makes him out as an enlightened despot of the Age of Reason. H. Kissinger in *A World Restored* (1957) introduces an often neglected element, legitimacy, into his analysis of Metternich's politics. Chapters IV to VII are among the most enlightening to have been devoted to Austrian diplomacy. But England's weight in the formation of the sixth coalition cannot be under-estimated (C. Webster, *The Foreign Policy of Castlereagh,* Vol. I, 1931, and Buckland, *Metternich and the British Government,* 1932; dwells on Austria's difficult financial situation). A good summing up in Krache, *Metternich's German Policy* (Vol. I, 1963).

Napoleon was not uninterested in the navy as has often been so hastily said.

He organized it into prefectures, militarized it (conscription made up for deficiencies in enrolment in the navy), rebuilt it (witness the development of the dockyard at Antwerp and the boom in Cherbourg), rejuvenated its cadres (Baudin, Hamelin, Duperré, Roussin). 'Louis XIV had only Brest,' he stated on 24 March 1811, 'I have all the coasts of Europe. In four years I will have my navy.' Meanwhile the superiority of the Royal Navy remained uncontested, making it possible for Great Britain to avoid the obstacle of the Blockade by keeping the Danish straits open (1,678 ships reached Göthenburg in 1810), to have a presence in Lisbon, Gibraltar, the Balearic Islands, Sardinia and Sicily and to control the sea route to the East Indies via the Cape. It also enabled her to form ties with sultanates at the entrance to the Red Sea (thus compensating for the 1807 failure in Egypt against Muhammad Ali), and finally, through the intermediary of the unrivalled East India Company, to concentrate on trade with China. Was it this naval superiority which finally allowed England to prevail? Mahan (*Influence of Sea Power upon French Revolution and Empire*, 1892) saw the key to the English victory in her mastery of the seas; F. Crouzet, on the other hand, in J. Mistler's *Napoléon et l'Empire* (1968) shows that this naval superiority served no purpose in the Continental war, except in Spain: English naval support in the Adriatic was no help to Austria at the time of the fifth coalition; the landings in Naples in 1805 and Walcheren in 1809 were failures, like Maida in 1806. Finally the upkeep of a fleet to block the French coasts was extremely expensive. According to F. Crouzet, England could not have won without the Russian disaster. As for the Anglo-American war (T. Roosevelt, *The Naval War of 1812*, 1882) even if it inconvenienced Great Britain, it had no serious effect on the conflict with France. Thus the Royal Navy protected Sicily from Murat's attempts at landings better than Maria Carolina's court or the somewhat degenerate Sicilian aristocracy could (cf. the villa Palagonia derived from Bonarzo).

IV. 8 THE FALL

Sources
The military *Mémoires* of Belliard (1842), Biot, Bro (1914), Brun (1953), Clausewitz (*La Campagne de 1814*, Fr. trans. 1900), Langeron (1902), Macdonald (1892), Marmont (Vol. VI, 1857), Parquin (1892) and the political *Mémoires* of Barante (1901), Beugnot (1866), Caulaincourt (1933, fundamental), Chateaubriand, Baron de Damas (1922) Count de Damas (Vol. II, 1914), Frénilly (1909), Gain-Montagnac (1817), Maine de Biran (ed. Lavalette-Monbrun, 1927), Pasquier (important; Vol. II, 1893), Portal (1846), Rochechouart (1933), Savary (1828), Semallé (1898), Talleyrand, Villèle (1888), Baron Vincent (*Le Pays Lorrain*, 1929), Vitrolles (ed. Forgues, 1884). Foreigners are often more impartial, for instance Underwood (published with Mme de Marigny's *Journal* in 1907). Read also Bellart (*Oeuvres*, 1827), *Le Manuscrit de 1814* by Fain (1823), Lainé's papers, published by Perceval in 1929. Napoleon's *Correspondance* should be complemented by L. Madelin's edition of Napoleon's *Lettres* to Marie-

Louise and by Palmastierna's edition of Marie-Louise's letters to the Emperor (1955). The press became interesting again; add, for the study of public opinion, the correspondence of the *commissaires extraordinaires* by Benaerts (1915) and above all the pamphlets of Pichon (*De l'état de la France . . .*), Rougemaître (*L'Ogre de Corse*), Goldsmith (*Histoire secrète du Cabinet de Bonaparte*), Massé and Doris, etc., to which Germond de la Vigne drew attention in 1879, and extracts of which can be found in J. Tulard, *L'Anti-Napoléon* (1964). For pictures, J. Grand-Carteret, *Napoléon en images* (1895). *Le Moniteur* published the essential texts: the text of the Charter can be found in J. Godechot, *Les Constitutions de la France* (1970). Two useful works of reference on politicians: Bourloton, Robert et Cougny, *Dictionnaire des Parlementaires français* (5 vols. 1889–91), and above all M. Fleury and B. Gille, *Dictionnaire biographique du conseil municipal de Paris et du conseil général de la Seine* (1972; with a very important preface by M. Fleury on the 1814 crisis).

On the Congress of Châtillon, M. Escoffier has published some interesting documents in the *Revue des Études napoléoniennes,* 1914, Vol. VI, pp. 85–99.

Works
The Malet affair in 1812 certainly heralded 'the beginning of the end'. It is not surprising that an enormous amount has been written about it: Lafon (a participant) in 1814, then in the same year, Lemare, d'Aubignosc, former director-general of police in Hamburg in 1824, then, in 1834, Saulnier who was secretary-general of police under Fouché, and finally Peuchet in his *Mémoires tirés des archives de la police* in 1838. More serious syntheses are by: Hamel (1873), Billard (1907), Gigon (1915), Masson (1921), Lort de Sérignan (1925), Garros (1936), J. Bourdon ('Conspirateurs et gouvernants', *Le Mercure de France* November 1948), B. Melchior-Bonnet (1963), J. Tulard (in J. Mistler, *Napoléon et l'Empire*, 1968). The role of the *Chevaliers de la Foi* is brought to light by Bertier de Sauvigny, *Le comte Ferdinand de Bertier et l'énigme de la Congrégation* (1948) and the ramifications in the south denounced by Pelet de Lozère are well explained by M. Agulhon, 'Le rôle politique des artisans dans le département du Var de la Révolution à la IIe République' (*8e Colloque d'Histoire sur l'Artisanat*, Aix, 1965, pp. 82–99, mostly from the reports of the Commissioner Caillemer).

Several syntheses have been written about the crisis of 1814: H. Houssaye, *1814* (1888, a classic), A. Chuquet, *L'Année 1814* (1914), J. Thiry, *La Campagne de France* (1938) and *La Première Abdication* (1939), F. Ponteuil, *La Chute de Napoléon I* (1943).

On the military operations, Lefebvre de Behaine's important work, *La Campagne de France* (4 vols., 1913–35, unfinished), and Bertin, *La Campagne de France d'après les témoins oculaires* (no date); Lachouque, *Napoléon en 1814* (1960). The battle of Montmirail has been described by J. Colin in the *Revue des Études napoléoniennes,* 1914, Vol. V, pp. 326–58, and by M. R. Mathieu, *Dernières Victoires, 1814. La Campagne de France aux alentours de Montmirail* (1964).

The situation in the south cannot be overlooked: C. Clerc, *Campagne du*

Marechal Soult dans les Pyrénées occidentales en 1813–1814 (1894); L. Batcave, *La Bataille d'Orthez* (1914); C. Portal, 'Note sur la bataille de Toulouse' (*Bulletin de la Société des Sciences et Belles-Lettres du Tarn,* Vol. I); Geschwind et Gelis, *La Bataille de Toulouse* (1914).

The war effort is analysed by Lévy-Schneider, 'Napoléon et la Garde nationale' (*Rev. fr.,* 1909, pp. 131–5); L. Girard, *La Garde nationale* (1964); Lomier, *Histoire des Régiments des Gardes d'honneur, 1813–1814* (1924; excellent); J. Durieux, 'Soldats de 1814', *Revue des Études napoléoniennes,* 1933, pp. 202–11. On the desertions, Lantier and Vidalenc's articles quoted on p. 393; Waquet, 'L'essai de levée du quarantième dans l'arrondissement d'Amiens en Mars 1814', *Revue de l'Institut Napoléon,* 1967, pp. 1–14 (it was a failure). Read also P. Benaerts, *Les Commissaires extraordinaires de Napoléon en 1814* (1915), taken up by J. Thiry, *Le rôle du Sénat dans l'organisation militaire de la France impériale* (1932).

The country had to face up to an invasion which has been admirably evoked by Erckmann-Chatrian. Among the numerous regional works, the following should be noted: Steenackers *L'Invasion de 1814 dans la Haute-Marne* (1868); P. Gaffarel, *Dijon en 1814–1815* (1897); A. Chuquet, *L'Alsace en 1814* (1900); P. Fauchille, *Une Chouannerie Flamande 1813–1814* (1905; the Royalist uprising led by Fruchart, so-called Louis XVIII, from Bellemare's reports); F. Borrey, *La Franche-Comté en 1814* (1912); J. Vidal de la Blanche, *L'Évacuation de l'Espagne et l'Invasion dans le Midi* (2 vols. 1912–14; remarkable); Perrin, *L'Esprit public dans la Meurthe de 1814–1816* (1913); A. Vovard, 'Les Anglais à Bordeaux en 1814' (*Revue des Études napoléoniennes 1914, Vol. VI, pp. 259—85); C. Pfister, 'Nancy en 1814' (Acad. Stanislas,* 1914, pp. 147–214); H. Contamine, *Metz et la Moselle de 1814 à 1870* (1932). On Napoleon's desertion by his marshals: M. Dupont, *Napoléon et la Trahison des Maréchaux* (1939). The clergy's attitude is analysed by F. Borrey, *L'Esprit public chez les prêtres franc-comtois pendant la crise de 1812–1815* (1912). On the politicians: E. de Perceval, *Un Adversaire de Napoleon, Lainé* (1926); C. Pouthas, *Guizot pendant la Restauration* (1923); Beau de Loménie, *La Carrière politique de Chateaubriand de 1814 à 1830* (1929).

Lefebvre de Behaine in *Le Comte d'Artois sur la route de Paris en 1814* (1921) throws light on the complicity of mayors and prefects from which the Royalists profited. Reference can also be made to L. Madelin, *La Contre-Revolution sous la Revolution, 1789–1815* (1935).

Open Questions

What were the principal causes of the Bourbon restoration? Surely not Chateaubriand's *De Buonaparte et des Bourbons* despite the affirmations of the author. Although this pamphlet was announced on 31 March, it only appeared on 4 April after the die was cast. (cf. H. Guillemin, *L'Homme des Memoires d'outre-tombe,* 1964). Even less by *De l'esprit de conquête et de l'usurpation dans leurs rapports avec la civilisation européenne,* perhaps written by Benjamin Constant to support the claims of Bernadotte, and published on 30 January 1814. It caused a great stir in Europe at the time, but none in France (cf. Constant, *Oeuvres* ed. Roulin, Bibl. Pléiade, 1957). Did treachery play a part—Marmont's 'Ragusade'? In his *Mémoires* Marmont blamed the unfortunate movement of Souham's corps on the subalterns, which is hardly chic. Napoleon blames him in the *Mémorial* but he has found an indulgent biographer in Saint-Marc (1957). His underhand dealings with Schwarzenberg cannot, however, be denied, nor the effect of Souham's defection on the Tsar. From 1857, Laurent de l'Ardèche undertook to refute Marmont's *Mémoires*.

Before the publication of Berthier de Savigny's thesis on *Ferdinand de Bertier et l'Énigme de la Congrégation* (1948), it was difficult to judge the different royalist agents. He tends to reduce Vitrolle's role (Vitrolle somewhat exaggerated his part in his *Mémoires*) and underline, on the other hand, the part played by the *chevaliers de la Foi* in the events of 12 March at Bordeaux and 12 April at Toulouse. In his biography, *Désiré Monnier* (1974), R. Fonville points out the role of the chevaliers of Cy in the Franche-Comté under the marquis de Champagne, mayor of Lons-le-Saulnier. As for Oudet's *Philadelphes* (Oudet died at Wagram), it is difficult to believe their 'inventor', Nodier.

What about public opinion? Collected information is contradictory. According to F. Rude, 'a reawakening of revolutinary patriotism in 1814 in the Rhône-Alps region' was noticed in Lyons. (*Cahiers d'Histoire*, 1971, pp. 433–55), but numerous dissertations for masters' degrees directed by the University of Paris IV or Section IV of the *École Pratique des Hautes Études* give a very different version. At Caen the duc de Berry was welcomed with enthusiasm. Although soldiers from Bergerac attempted some anti-Royalist demonstrations at Agen, when the news of the re-establishment of the monarchy was known on 17 April, the Prefect, Villeneuve-Bargemont noted in his *Journal*: 'It is impossible to describe the joy which is manifested everywhere.' The General Council of the Haute-Marne affirmed: 'The valour and the generosity of the allied sovereigns have finally broken the yoke under which we were suffering in silence, a yoke which had been made insupportable in this department.' But the reason for this enthusiasm in the Hautes-Alpes sprang from the hope of seeing the abolition of the *droits réunis* which had given rise to violent riots at Manosque. There was the same enthusiasm and the same subsequent disappointment in the Creuse, according to a report from Sémonville. In the Landes, the comte d'Angosse detected the key note of the popular joy: 'One sentiment dominates all others, it is the desire for peace, the need for rest.'

A point of detail: on Napoleon's suicide attempt at Fontainbleau, Constant, Marchand, Fain and Caulaincourt give contradictory evidence. The doctor Hillemand ('Napoleon a-t-il tenté de se suicider à Fontainebleau?' *Revue de l'Institut Napoléon* 1971, pp. 70–78) tends to think that it was a question of an accidental overdose of opium supposed to relieve abdominal pain. Napoleon would then have dramatized the accident when confiding in Caulaincourt.

Did Talleyrand inspire an assassination attempt on Napleon by the mercenary Maubreuil in April 1814? F. Masson (*L'Affaire Maubreuil* 1907) thought so. M. Gasson (*La tumulteuse existence de Maubreuil* 1954) lays the blame for the plot on Roux-Laborie, the Prince of Benevento's confidant.

Talleyrand would then have attempted to cover up the affair despite Maubreuil's tenaciousness.

In spite of Daumesnil's heroism (H. de Clairval, *Daumesnil,* 1970) and the qualities of Moncey (biography by the Duke of Conegliano 1901) and of Mortier (Morcel, *Le Maréchal Mortier* 1957), the defence of Paris was difficult because of lack of fortifications and the low morale of the population. The betrayal was merely an accessory. Dessolle had no problem in maintaining order in the capital with the National Guard after the 'fall' of Napoleon.

Rousselot, *Napoléon à Bordeaux* (1909) clearly shows that the defection of the port cannot only be explained by the Blockade, but also by requisitions and by troops passing through to Spain. Civilians here suffered directly from war.

IV. 9   1815: THE LAST CHOICE

Sources
The Additional Act is published by Godechot, *Les Constitutions de la France* (1970). The debates of the Chambers are in Vol. XIII of the *Archives parlementaires*. The principal police reports for the period preceding Napoleon's return have been published by E. Welvert, *Napoléon et la Police* (1913), and Firmin-Didot, *Royauté ou Empire* (no date, Anglès's reports). With the disappearance of Napoleonic censorship, many pamphlets and brochures appeared, recensions of which can be found in the *Catalogue de l'Histoire de France* at the *Bibliothèque nationale*. Besides Napoleon's *Correspondance* read Pélissier, *Le Registre de l'île d'Elbe* (1897), there are numerous *Mémoires*: Autichamp (1815), Beugnot (1866; for the First Restoration police), Lucien Bonaparte (ed. Jung, 1882, Vol. III), Bourrienne, Campbell (in Pichot, *Chronique des Évènements de 1814–1815,* 1873), Canuel (1817, on the Vendée), Mme de Chastenay, Chateaubriand, Constant (*Mémoires sur les Cent Jours,* ed. Pozzo di Borgo, 1961), Cournot (1913), baron de Damas (1923), Ferrand (1897), Fleury de Chaboulon (1901; to be rectified with Napoleon's annotations), Fouché, Gaudin, Guizot (Vol. I, 1858), Hobhouse (*Lettres écrites de Paris,* 1819; interesting eye-witness), the Queen Hortense (Vol. II, 1927), La Fayette (1838, Vol. V), Lamarque (1835), Louis-Philippe (the events of 1815, 1849), Michelet (*Ma jeunesse,* 1884), Molé (ed. Noailles, Vol. I, 1922), Pasquier, Peyrusse (1869), Poli (1954), Pons de l'Hérault (1897; essential for the Island of Elba), Puymaigre (1884), Rochechouart (1889), Réal (1835), Savary, Sers (1906), Talleyrand, Thibaudeau (1913; remarkable on the Hundred Days), Viennet (1929), Vitrolles (1884), Ussher (1906; for Elba). Add for Waterloo: Berthezène, Canler (1862), Chevalier, Coignet, Grouchy (publication of personal papers, 1873), Levasseur (1914), Marbot, Ney (personal papers, 1833), Pontécoulant (*Napoléon à Waterloo,* 1866), Scheltens (1880) and Trefcon; from the English

point of view, the *Dispatches of the Duke of Wellington* (Vol. VIII, 1852), Cavalié Mercer (1833), Lawrence (1897) and Woodberry (1896). Cf. *The British Soldier in the Napoleonic Wars,* compiled, ed. and trans. by A. Brett-James. There is a lot to be learnt from Jaucourt's correspondence with Talleyrand (1905) and from the Swiss: Sismondi, 'Lettres écrites pendant les Cent Jours' (*Revue historique,* 1877–8), and Pictet de Rochemont, *Correspondance diplomatique* (1892). Glance at Alexandre de Tilly's curious brochure, *Du Retour de Bonaparte* (London 1815), the *Lettres sur les Cent Jours* by Cauchois-Lemaire (1822), and *Les desordres de la France et des moyens d'y remédier,* by Montlosier (1815). An attractive picture of Marseilles in 1815 by V. Gelu (ed. Guiral, 1971). Cf. also Schoelle's compilation.

Works
General syntheses by Vaulabelle (*Histoire des deux Restaurations,* 1845; well-known but unreliable), Houssaye, 1815 (*Les Cent jours,* 1896; *Waterloo,* 1899; brilliant, documented, but written from the point of view of 'the revenge'); Stenger, *Le Retour de Napoléon* (1908); E. Le Gallo, *Les Cent Jours* (1924; solid thesis but not always objective); F. Ponteil, *La Chute de Napoléon I et la crise française de 1814–1815* (1943; good); J. Thiry, *Les Cent Jours* (1943), F. Sieburg, *Napoléon. Les Cent Jours* (1957); R. Margerit, *Waterloo* (1964, excellent; goes beyond the limited history of the battle to study events on the whole). E. Hubert's rapid study *Cent Jours* may be ignored.

Much is to be learnt from works of regional history. Rather old are: L. Pingaud, *La Franche-Comté en 1815* (1894); Gaffarel, *Les Cent Jours à Marseille* (1906); Gonnet, 'Les Cent Jours à Lyon', *Revue d'Histoire de Lyon* (1908); Contamine, *Metz et la Moselle de 1814 à 1870* (1932); G. de Manteyer, *La Fin de l'Empire dans les Alpes* (1942); Avezou, 'Les Cent Jours en Isère', *Bull. Soc. Delphinale* (1951) and, above all, the fundamental studies: J. Vidalenc, *Le Département de l'Eure sous la monarchie constitutionnelle* (1952), and P. Leuilliot, *La Première Restauration et les cent jours en Alsace* (1958). Several books have been written about Elba: Pellet, *Napoléon à l'île d'Elbe* (1888); P. Gruyer, *Napoléon à l'île d'Elbe* (1906); P. Bartel, *Napoléon à l'île d'Elbe* (1947; maintains the conspiracy theory); R. Christophe, *Napoléon empereur de l'île d'Elbe* (1959); G. Godlewski, *Trois Cent Jours d'Exil* (1961; more serious than the preceding ones); F. Beaucour, *Sari un fidèle de l'Empereur* (typed thesis, very well documented). Cf. also J. Tulard, 'L'Île d'Elbe en l'an X', *Revue de l'Institut Napoléon,* 1964, pp. 64–8.

The return is now well known. On the intrigues which preceded it: A. Espitalier, *Deux artisans du retour de l'île d'Elbe* (Émery et Dumoulin, 1934); Ernouf, *Maret, duc de Bassano* (1878); E. Bonnal, *Les Royalistes contre l'Armée* (1906); L. Guillot, 'Le general Lefebvre-Desnoëttes', *Revue de l'Institut Napoléon,* 1963, pp. 145–51. On the concern which the Restoration caused to the buyers of national property: cain, *La Restauration et les biens des émigrés* (1929). On the return itself: J. Thiry, *Le Vol de l'Aigle* (1942); A. Chollier, *La Vraie Route Napoléon* (1946) and S. & A. Troussier, *La*

Chevauchée héroïque du retour de l'île d'Elbe (1965). On Sisteron: Gombert (1968). The Additional Act has been analysed by Deslandres, *Histoire constitutionnelle*, Vol. I (1932); L. Radiguet, *L'Acte aditionnel* (1911), and above all P. Bastid, *Benjamin Constant et sa doctrine* (excellent study of the ideas of the author of *La Benjamine*). An excellent study of the plebiscite which wipes away all preconceived ideas is by F. Bluche, *Le Plébiscite des Cent Jours* (1974). For the elections: see in *Rev. fr.* (1913) an article on the elections to the Chamber of Representatives, but for the attitudes of mind of the deputies see Rodocanachi, *Sébastien Bottin* (1926) the addendum of letters from the well-known writer of yearbooks who was a deputy in 1815. The financial heritage of the Revolution can be seen in M. Bruguière, *La Première Restauration et son Budget* (1969), and Gignoux, *La Vie du Baron Louis* (1928).

On Napoleon's entourage: M. Reinhard, *Le Grand Carnot* (Vol. II, 1952); F. Pietri, *Lucien Bonaparte* (1939); Blocqueville, *Davout* (1879); L. Madelin, *Fouché* (Vol. II); Serieyx, *Drouot et Napoléon* (1931).

For the other side: Duc de Castries, *Louis XVIII* (1969; excellent biography). Read the documents collected by E. Romberg and A. Malet, *Louis XVIII et les cent jours à Gand* (1898–1902). Lasserre has dealt with the resistance in the Vendée in *Le Général Lamarque et l'Insurrection royaliste en Vendée* (1906), and so has R. Grand in *La Chouannerie de 1815* (1942). G. Lavalley, *Le Duc d'Aumont et les Cent Jours en Normandie* (no date) is useful. On dealings between the two sides: H. Malo, *Le Beau Montrond* (1926, Talleyrand's agent).

A. Sorel, *L'Europe et la Révolution française* (Vol. VIII, 1904) and P. Rain, *L'Europe et la Restauration des Bourbons, 1814–1818* (1908) deal well with diplomacy. For the Congress of Vienna: Webster, *The Congress of Vienna* (1934); Nicolson, *The Congress of Vienna* (1917), and the collective work *Le Congrès de Vienne et l'Europe* (1964). Lagarde-Chambonas's critical edition of the *Souvenirs du Congrès de Vienne* (1901) cannot be ignored, nor can Talleyrand's letters to the duchesse de Courlande, published by G. Palewski (*Le Miroir de Talleyrand*, 1976).

Volumes have been written about the Battle of Waterloo, from Clausewitz (*La Campagne de 1815*, Fr. trans. 1900), Jomini (*Précis de la Campagne de 1815*, 1939) and Charras (*Histoire de la Campagne de 1815*, 1869). The Belgian point of view is given by Couvreur, *Le Drame belge de Waterloo* (1959) and by the articles in the *Bulletin de la Société belge d'études napoléoniennes* (1950–1975) indices in the December 1975 number) and *Waterloo illustré* (16 numbers published) which deal with every aspect of the battle. The Dutch point of view: Van Loben Sels, *Précis de la campagne de 1815* (interesting). On the Prussians: Müffling, *Aus meinem Leben* (1851); cf. on this subject Vigo-Roussillon, 'Le général von Müffling, principal artisan de la victoire des Alliés', *Rev. hist. de l'Armée*, 1970, pp. 43–64, which confirms the general's souvenirs. Blücher, for his part, has found an excellent biography in Blasendorff, *Gebhard Leberecht von Blücher* (1887). Also possible are: Damitz, *Histoire de la campagne de 1815*, von Ollech, *Geschichte des Feldzuges* and Plotho, *Der Krieg in Jahre 1815*, although they are all very old-fashioned. For the English: Siborne (*History of the War of 1815*, 1845), Ropes (*The Campaign of Waterloo*, with an atlas, 1892), H. F. Becke, *Napoleon and Waterloo* (1914), and J. Holland-Rose's article, 'Wellington dans la campagne de Waterloo,' *Revue des Études napoléoniennes*, 1915, Vol. VIII, pp. 44–55: Waller, *Wellington at Waterloo* (1967). For American historiography read above all, *Waterloo, Day of Battle* (1968). Finally, the French have been equally verbose: besides Houssaye and Margerit quoted above and E. Lenient (*La Solution des Énigmes de Waterloo*, 1915), Lachouque's *Waterloo* (1972, preface by J.-F. Chiappe) is essential. The special numbers of *La Revue des Études napoléoniennes* of June 1932 and June 1933 will be useful, as will J. Regnault, *La Campagne de 1815* (1935), not forgetting J. Thiry, *Waterloo* (1943). The end of the Empire is evoked by J. Thiry, *La Seconde Abdication*, and especially J. Duhamel, *Les Cinquante Jours de Waterloo à Plymouth* (1963). So ends what Spengler calls 'the twenty years' war' between the English aristocracy and the French bourgeoisie. On the federal movements, there being no general history, read: J. Vanel, 'Le mouvement fédératif de 1815 dans le Tarn' (*Gaillac et pays tarnais*, Fed. Languedoc, Pyr. Gascogne, 1977, pp. 387–95).

Open Questions

Can one speak of a purge under the First Restoration? Pouthas (*Guizot pendant la Restauration*, 1923) does not think so. Louis XVIII had undertaken 'to eliminate all bitter memories'. Most of the prefects with the exception of well-known regicides (Thibaudeau, De Bry) were kept on. The notables had to be carefully handled. But N. Richardson (*The French Prefectoral Corps 1814–1830*, 1966) shows that the part played by the nobility gradually increased: thirty in March 1814, fifty-eight in March 1815. At the Supreme Court of Appeal, in the reorganization of 15 February 1815, the first president, Muraire (Decazes's father-in-law) made way for De Sèze, Louis XVI's former lawyer, while the Attorney-General, Merlin de Douai, and his deputies, Pons and Thuriot—all regicides—were ousted. The Prefecture of Police and the Ministry of Police were amalgamated, which provided an excuse for some dismissals (Foudras replaced Veyrat as inspector-general of the prefecture); cf. Lenotre, *Dossiers de Police*, 1935; Dossonville became Commissioner, cf. Guyon, *Biographie des commissaires*, 1826). But there was no violence and no purging procedure. It was with the return from Elba, and despite the amnesty promised at Lyons on 12 March, that the purge took the form of punishment. Only six prefects (Camille Périer, Casimir's brother, Petit de Beauverger, Bossi, Bourgeois de Jessaint, Plancy and Girardin) kept their positions. Many preferred to resign (Flavigny, Vaublanc, Lavieuville). The Parisian administration was purged, as was the Ministry of the Interior. A new purge in the shape of the 'White terror' followed the King's return. The changes of opinion which accompanied the changes of regime gave rise to Émery's famous *Dictionnaire des Girouettes*. There has been much discussion of the reasons for Napoleon's return from Elba—from the assassination plot elaborated by the governor of Corsica, Bruslart (A. Chuquet, 'Le départ de l'île d'Elbe', *Revue de Paris*, 1 February 1920) to the plan to deport Napoleon to a far-away island (*Correspondance de Talleyrand et de Louis XVIII*, 13 and 21 October, 7 December, 1814). Jean Massin ('Waterloo', *Le Monde*, 19 June 1965) thinks that Napoleon returned because of 'patriotism' in the revolutionary sense which the word adopted from 1789 to 1815, and to put down the 'counter-revolution'. He thinks that there is no reason to doubt his sincerity in saying to Las Cases: 'I did not come back to collect a throne, but to pay off a great debt; the cries of the French people reached me, could I remain deaf to them? How then can this refusal of all popular support during the Hundred Days be explained? According to Massin, he must have been a 'Girondin who borrowed his methods of government from the Montagne. Sincerely revolutionary in a limited sense, but not at all democratic.' He must then belong to the notables to whom he granted so many concessions. But they did not call him back from Elba, and his return was therefore, above all, a personal adventure in which this master of strategy knew how to choose the right moment to exploit popular irritation with the monarchy, although this irritation was not universal. In fact it was the legitimacy of Napoleonic power which established itself by this return (C. Durand, 'Le pouvoir napoléonien et ses légitimités' in *Annales Fac. Droit et Sc. polit, d'Aix-Marseille*, 1972, pp. 7–33). F. Bluche takes up the problem in 'Les Cent Jours, aspects du pouvoir', *Revue. hist. Droit fr. et étranger*, 1973, pp. 627–34. He shows that the Bonapartist electorate was to the left in 1815, the conservatives and the 'silent majority' abandoned him. Hence the low poll at the plebiscite for the Additional Act: study of the regions shows how unpopular Napoleon was in the south and the west—both Royalist bastions. On the other hand, favourable votes were considerable in frontier regions: Burgundy, Champagne, Alsace, Lorraine and the Nord. Officials voted in Paris, but the loss of popularity was enormous: from 120,000 votes in 1804 to less than 20,000 in 1815. Popular disappointment caused by the Additional Act when a dictatorship of public safety was expected, explains the sudden waning of enthusiasm in Grenoble and Lyons, unless the acclamations in March have been greatly exaggerated. Read, too, J. Chaumié, 'Les Girondins et les Cent Jours', *Annales hist. Rev. fr.* 1971, pp. 329–65.

Specialists in strategy still disagree about Waterloo. Let us remember the incredible polemic which divided Lenient (*La Solution des Énigmes de Waterloo*, 1915) and Colonel Grouard ('Les derniers historiens de 1815', *Revue des Études napoléoniennes* 1917, Vol. XI, pp. 163–98). Napoleon's mistakes cannot be denied, they were perhaps due to ill health (an attack of haemorrhoids) but surely not to treachery (Bourmont's defection preceded the disaster, but it did, nevertheless create an atmosphere of uncertainty which Napoleon acknowledged in his *Campagne de 1815, Correspondance*, Vol. XXXI). He made mistakes in his choice of men (Ney instead of Murat, Soult instead of Davout); he underestimated Blücher's strength after Ligny; he lost time and made a frontal assault on Wellington instead of manoeuvring. These mistakes are admitted neither in the bulletin of the Grande Armée nor in the account dictated on St Helena.

Finally, for those who would like to know what Cambronne said on the battlefield: C. Pitollet, *La Verité sur le mot de Cambronne* (1921) which destroys H. Houssaye, *Le Garde meurt et ne se rend pas* (1907).

The effect of Napoleon's return was to upset Talleyrand's politics in Vienna where the latter was trying to bring France together with Austria and England in the face of the Russo-Prussian axis. M. Maurice Schumann ('Talleyrand, un prophète de l'Entente cordiale', *La Revue des Deux Mondes*, Dec. 1976, pp. 541–56) appears to have a certain nostalgia for this lost balance of power—the allies put an end to their quarrel and re-established the Treaty of Chaumont, of which France bore the cost at the second Treaty of Paris. As a result of the new Treaty of Paris, works of art taken from conquered countries had to be returned, although they had been kept in 1814: F. Boyer, 'Metternich et la restitution par la France des oeuvres d'art de l'étranger', *Rev. Hist. diplomatique*, 1970, pp. 65–79; by the same author, 'Le Retour des oeuvres d'art enlevées en Lombardie, en Venétie et à Modène', *Revue des Études italiennes,* 1970, pp. 91–103 (there were pictures by Luini, Titian, 'Velvet' Breughel, Veronese, Guerchin and Bassano), 'Le retour en 1815 à Florence des oeuvres d'art emportées en France', *Rivista italiana di studi napoleonici,* 1970, pp. 114–23. More serious still was the division of the country into two camps. Bertier de Sauvigny (*La Restauration,* 1955) shows that Napoleon's return, 'by reawakening Jacobin passions against the nobility and the clergy', detached the liberals from their 1814 alliance with the Royalists, and precipitated them into the Bonapartist camp. 'France will be for many years divided into two enemy peoples.'

IV. 10 THE LEGEND

Sources

Mémoires on the last phase are abundant: Beker has left an account of his mission with Napoleon (1841), the log-book of the *Saale* was published in the *Revue des Études napoléoniennes* in 1933; Savary, Planat, La Faye (1895), Bonnefoux (1900), Lallemand (diary in *French-American Review,* April 1949), Bonneau (*Revue rétrospective,* 1895), Jackson (Fr. trans. 1921), Nichols (*La Sabretache,* 1912), Keith (1882) and Maitland (*Relation,* 1825, reissued in 1934 with Home's evidence by Borjane; also by Borjane, *Napoléon à bord du 'Northumberland'* after some English accounts, among them Glover, and in addition Lord Lyttleton (1936) which throws light on what followed.

Waterloo. Two excellent witnesses on St Helena: Las Cases, *Le Mémorial de Sainte-Hélène* (ed. Dunan, 1951, because of his critical apparatus, rather than the Pléiade edition by Walter, the Garnier edition by Fugier or that of Seuil with a preface by J. Tulard) which only goes up to 1816, and Bertrand, *Cahiers de Sainte-Hélène,* which covers the whole period (ed. Fleuriot de Langle, 1949–51, no index). Other eye-witnesses: Ali (1926), Antommarchi (1825, many reissues), Arnott (1822), Balcombe (Fr. trans., 1898), Bouges (*Souvenir napoléonien,* 1976), Gorrequer (Kemble, *Gorrequer's Diary,* 1969), Gourgaud (ed. Aubry 1947), Hudson Lowe (Paul Frémeaux, *Dans la chambre de Napoléon mourant,* unpublished diary of Hudson Lowe, 1910),

Marchand (ed. Bourguignon-Lachouque, 1952–55), Montholon (*Récits de la captivité*, 1847), comtesse de Montholon (1901), O'Meara (1822, many editions), Santini (1853), Stockoë (1901), Verling (doctor, *Carnet de la Sabretache*, 1921), Warden (ed. Cabanès, 1931). The presence on the island of a representative of Louis XVIII's government should not be forgotten: Firmin Didot, *La Captivité de Sainte-Hélène d'après les rapports du Marquis de Montchenu* (1894). Mougins-Roquefort, *Napoléon prisonnier par les Anglais* (1978). Do not overlook the reports of Sturmer, the Austrian commissioner, nor those of the Russian commissioner, Balmain (*Revue bleue*, 1897) nor the *Hudson Lowe Papers*. Numerous documents in the five volumes of the *Captif de Sainte-Hélène* (1821). On plans to escape: *La Belle-Jenny* by Gautier.

Works

There are two bibliographies on St Helena, one at the end of the collective work, *Sainte-Hélène, terre d'exil* (1971), the other by C. Albert-Samuel in the *Revue de l'Institut Napoléon*, 1971, pp. 151–7.

On the surrender to the English, rather than Silvestre, *De Waterloo à Sainte-Hélène* (1904), R. Chandeau, *Napoléon à Fouras* (1958), the numerous books on the *Île d'Aix* and C. Manceron, *Le Dernier Choix de Napoléon* (1960), read the excellent studies by Duhamel, *Les Cinquante Jours* (1963), G. Martineau, *Napoléon se rend aux Anglais* (1969), and G. Hubert, 'Napoléon de Rochefort au *Bellerophon*' in *Souvenir napoléonien*, Sept. 1975, and Bordonove, *Vers Sainte-Hélène* (1977).

Among the general works on St Helena: Forsythe, *History of the Captivity* (1850); Rosebery, *La Dernière Phase* (1901); F. Masson, *Autour de Sainte-Hélène* (1935); Brice, *Les Espoirs de Napoléon à Sainte-Hélène* (1938); Paul Ganière, *Napoléon à Sainte-Hélène* (1957–1962); Korngold, *Les Dernières Années de Napoléon* (1926); G. Martineau, *La Vie quotidienne à Sainte Hélène* (1966; excellent). Jean Thiry, *Sainte-Hélène* (1976). A fundamental work of reference: A. Chaplin, *A St. Helena Who's Who* (1919, a biographical dictionary of everyone of interest on St Helena). The following can be usefully consulted: Hauterive, *Sainte-Hélène au temps de Napoleon et aujourd'hui* (1933), René Bouvier, *Sainte-Hélène avant Napoléon* (1938), and on a particular point: Healey, 'La bibliothèque de Napoléon à Sainte-Hélène', *Revue de l'Institut Napoléon* 1959–61, and A. Lorion, 'Le vrai visage des aumôniers de Sainte-Hélène' (Bonavita and Vignali), *Revue de l'Institut Napoléon*, 1972, pp. 75–8. A. Cahuet, *Retours de Sainte-Hélène* (1932) deals with the dispersal of the companions in exile after the Emperor's death. On the will, J. Savant's study in *Toute l'Histoire de Napoléon*, 1951, pp. 1–98, J. Lemaire, *Le Testament de Napoléon* (1975), and F. Beaucour, *Le Codicille secret du Testament de Napoléon* (1976; concerning the seventh codicil which contains different bequests). J. Bourguignon has written a thoroughly documented book about the return of the ashes, 1943, and J. Boisson has written a more recent one.

Numerous partisans kept the memory of Napoleon alive in France: J. Lucas-Dubreton, *Le Culte de Napoléon 1815–1848* (1959), to which add

Tudesq, 'La légende napoléonienne en France en 1848' (*Revue historique,* 1957). By way of comparison: Lee Kennet, 'Le culte de Napoléon aux États-Unis jusqu'à la guerre de Secession', *Revue de l'Institut Napoléon,* 1972, pp. 145–56; and on the role of the exiles: I. Murat, *Napoléon et le Rêve américain* (1976). G. Lote, 'La mort de Napoléon et l'opinion bonapartiste en 1821', *Revue des Études napoléoniennes,* 1930, Vol. XXXI, pp. 19–58, is interesting.

P. Gonnard, in *Les Origines de la Légende napoléonienne* (1906), has insisted on the part played by writings coming from St Helena in the building up of this legend. Other elements have been brought to the fore by J. Dechamps, *Sur la Légende de Napoléon* (1931). On the other hand the role of soldiers on half-pay has been minimized by J. Vidalenc, *Les Demi-Solde* (1955). The influence of literature has been examined by M. Descotes, *La Légende de Napoléon et les Écrivains français du XIXᵉ siècle* (1967). To Balzac, Hugo and Stendhal, should be added Béranger (J. Touchard, *La Gloire de Béranger,* (1968) and *Barthélemy et Mery* (by J. Garsou, 1899); do not overlook Erckmann-Chatrian (J. Braun, *Saisons d'Alsace,* 1963) nor the father of *The Three Musketeers.*

On the transformation of the legend into myth: the special number of *Yale French Studies* (1969); P. Barbéris, 'Napoléon, structure et signification d'un mythe', *Rev. Hist. Lit. France,* Sept. 1970, pp. 1031–58; J. Tulard, *Le Mythe de Napoléon* (1971).

Open Questions

Many details of Napoleon's surrender to the English remain obscure. Napoleon no doubt, deluded himself about the fate which awaited him. But the activity of the partisans is undeniable: M. Dunan, 'Napoléon et *l'habeas corpus* en 1815', *Revue de l'Institut Napoléon,* 1955, pp. 89–92, and J. Dechamps, 'Les défenseurs de Napoléon en Grande-Bretagne de 1815 à 1830', *Revue de l'Institut Napoléon,* 1958, pp. 129–40. But in *England and the St Helena Decision* (1968) M. Thornton shows the weakness of their position, and the necessity for them of ruses which are analysed by J. Duhamel in the *Revue de Paris,* 1962, No. 7, pp. 46–59. If he was not deceived, Napoleon certainly made a mistake.

Who wrote the famous *Manuscrit venu de Sainte-Hélène* which brought Napoleon back to everyone's attention? Despite the hesitations of the anonymous writer of the preface to the edition of 1974 (which is not as good as Driault's old edition or Rumilly's 1947 edition), the problem of attribution seems to have been decided in favour of Lullin de Chateauvieux by A. Eberwein-Rochat in Volume X of the *Bulletin Soc. Hist. et d'archéologie.*

Of what value are the St Helena eye-witnesses? Las Cases has been studied by E. de Las Cases, 1959. He wrote his *Mémorial* from a liberal point of view and introduced much that was apocryphal, including Murat's pseudo-letter of 29 March 1808 on Spanish affairs. As padding for his work he has drawn from documents in the *Bibliothèque historique,* a collection of texts published by one of Maret's men, A. V. Benoit, and of which P. Gonnard has made a study, 'La légende napoléonienne et la presse libérale, 1817–1820' in *Revue des*

Études napoléoniennes, March 1912, pp. 235–58. So the *Mémorial* aroused mistrust and should be compared with other eye-witness accounts. But Montholon is even more unreliable although Hélène Michaud's judgement is qualified ('Que vaut le témoignage de Montholon à la lumière de fonds Masson?', *Revue de l'Institut Napoléon*, 1971, pp. 113–20). Antommarchi has a bad reputation; at least J. Poulet rehabilitates him from the medical point of view ('Le cas Antommarchi', *Revue de l'Institut Napoléon*, 1971, pp. 130–38). The most accurate and the most complete source in the long run is Bertrand's *Cahiers* which Fleuriot de Langle deciphered, not without some mistakes. Vasson's study of Bertrand (1935) preceded the publication of the *Cahiers*. Among those who left no memoirs: Archambault, whose biography is suggested by Rustan in the *Revue du Tarn*, 1957, pp. 147–51, and Piontkowski ('Un aventurier ou un missionnaire?' by S. Kirkov, *Revue de l'Institut Napoléon*, 1976, pp. 185–93). What did Napoleon die of? Sven Forshuvud has written a veritable detective novel based on arsenic poisoning and he has pointed to the guilty man: Montholon (*Napoléon a-t-il été empoisonné?* 1961). Godlewski rejects the cancer theory and tends towards hepatitis of which Napoleon was cured and a gastric lesion of which he died (*Revue de l'Institut Napoléon*, 1960, pp. 145–51). P. Ganière thinks it was cancer developing from an old ulcer in *Sainte-Hélène, terre d'exil* (1971).

Pages have been written about Napoleon's death masks. Read E. de Veauce, *L'Affaire du Masque de Napoléon* (1957), and J. Jousset, 'L'Affaire du Masque de Napoléon', *Revue de l'Institut Napoléon*, 1957, pp. 100–106. Little is to be gained by history from the arguments over Napoleon's deathbed: J. and G. Rétif de la Bretonne, *La Vérité sur le Lit de mort de Napoléon* (1960). Finally the same G. Rétif de la Bretonne has maintained in *Anglais, rendez-nous Napoléon* (1969) that Napoleon was buried in Westminster. The butler, Cipriani, is apparently under the dome of the *Invalides*. This is refuted by D. MacCarthy in the *Revue de la Société des Amis du Musée de l'Armée*, 1971, pp. 31–43. The most recent manifestation of the myth: Cavanna, *Les Aventures de Napoléon* (1976).

On the political posterity, the best book is William Smith's *Napoleon III* (London, 1972).

GENERAL BIBLIOGRAPHY

The hero of this adventure has inspired more books than there have been days since his death. This is not a strictly national nor even European phenomenon. It has reached Asia—in 1837 Ozeki San'ei wrote a biography of Napoleon in Japanese.

According to Lois Villat, the first complete biography of the Emperor dates from 1821, the year of his death: *Napoléon, sa naissance, son education, sa carrière militaire, son gouvernement, sa chute, son exil et sa mort,* by M. C. But Napoleonic biography was already colossal, made up of pamphlets and official eulogy. Arnault in 1822 undertook *Une vie politique et militaire de Napoléon.* Laurent de l'Ardèche in 1826, Norvins in 1827, Jomini and Thibaudeau in the same year, and even Walter Scott hastened to follow suit. All these attempts have been eclipsed by the monumental work, *Histoire de Consulat et de l'Empire* which Thiers completed in 1862, making way for Michelet (*Histoire du XIXe siècle,* 1875) and for Taine (*Les origines de la France contemporaine: le régime moderne,* 1887) which heralded Frédéric Masson's long series (*Napoléon et sa famille,* 13 volumes, 1897–1919), Driault (*Napoléon et l'Europe,* 5 vols. 1912–1927, which takes up Albert Sorel's *L'Europe et la Révolution française*), Lanzac de Laborie (*Paris sous Napoleon,* 8 vols. 1905–1911), L. Madelin (*Histoire du Consulat et de l'Empire,* 16 vols., 1936–54), Jean Thiry (*Napoléon Bonaparte,* 28 vols., 1938–75). The Second Empire undertook the publication in 32 vols. of the *Correspondance;* the collection was incomplete and at times falsified but gave a picture of the Emperor's prodigious activity; Palluel's *Dictionnaire de l'Empereur,* 1969 makes it possible to use it without an index). More was to be added by Lecestre, L. de Brotonne, Lumbroso, Masson, d'Huart, Teutey and Picard, etc. 'His glory will be spoken of under the thatch for a very long time,' Béranger predicted. There was a deluge of work from Capefigue (1831) to Lanfrey (1867) and Peyre (1887).

There are some Napoleons of 'the left' (Jaurès, *Histoire Socialiste,* Vol. VI, 1905; Tersen, *Naploléon,* 1959; Soboul, *Le Premier Empire,* 1973) and some of the right (J. Bainville, *Napoléon,* 1931; C. Maurras, *Jeanne d'Arc, Louis XIV et Napoléon,* 1938; L. Daudet, *Deux idoles sanglantes, la Révolution et son fils Bonaparte,* 1939; F. Olivier Martin, *L'Inconnu Napoléon Bonaparte,* 1952), all excellent. The pamphlet (Iung, *Bonaparte et son temps,* 1880–1; J. Savant, *Tel fut Napoleon,* 1953; H. Guillemin, *Napoléon tel quel,* 1969) borders on hagiography (M. Tartary, *Sur les traces de Napoleon,* 1956). G. Lenotre's *Napoléon, croquis de l'epopée* (1932), and A. Castelot's *Bonaparte et Napoléon* (1968) are anecdotal; the following are learned: Pariset, *Le Consulat et L'Empire* (Vol. III of *l'Histoire de France contemporaine* by Lavisse, 1921), G. Lefebvre, *Napoléon* (1935, reissued by Sobone), Fr. Dreyfus, *Le Temps des Revolutions* (1968), Godechot, *Napoleon* (1969), Furet and Bergeron (1973), Sussel, *Napoléon* (1970), Bergeron Lovie and Palluel, *L'Episode napoléonien* (1972), A. Latreille, *L'Ève napoléonienne* (1974), L. Genet, *La Révolution et l'Empire* (1975). There are Napoleons in small format (Lucas-Debreton, 1942; M. Vox, 1959) and large ones (G. Lacour-Gayet, 1921). There are Russian Napoleons (Merejkowski, 1930, Tarle, several editions; Manfred, 1977), German ones (Kircheisen, 1911–34; Ludwig, 1924), English ones (Seely; Rosebery, 1900; Holland Rose, 1901; Thompson, 1952; Markham, 1963; Cronin, 1971), American ones (Dowd, 1957) and Italian ones (Lumbroso, 1921) or Dutch. He can be followed from day to day: Schuermans, *Itinéraire général de Napoléon* (1911); L. Garros, *Quel roman que ma vie* (1947); J. Massin, *Almanach du Premier Empire* (1965). Thiers's *Atlas,* J. C. Quennevat, *l'Atlas de la grande armée* (1966) and the *Atlas administratif du Premier Empire* by F. Dainville and J. Tulard (1973) will be very useful. All writers have been fascinated by Napoleon (Chateaubriand, Hugo, Balzac, Stendhal, Senancour and also L. Bloy, Élie Faure (1921), Delteil (1929), Rosny Aîné (1931), Saurès (1933), J. Romains (1963), A. Maurois (1964), P. Morand (*Napoléon homme pressé,* 1969), A. Malraux (*Les Chênes qu'on abat*), not to forget the scenarios of the films by A. Gance and S. Guitry. But the historian will profit little from these writings. There are innumerable reviews: *Revue de l'Empire* (1842–8), *Revue napoléonienne* (Lumbroso, mainly from 1901–9), *Revue des Études napoléoniennes* (1912–39); dazzling until about 1930; thereafter superficial and hagiographical; index); *Revue de l'Institut Napoléon* (has been appearing since 1938; and under M. Dunan's influence it has taken over from the *Revue des Études napoléoniennes*: index); *Le Souvenir napoléon* (seems since 1970 to produce hagiography in special editions); *Toute l'histoire de Napoléon* (had published general excellent special editions between 1951 and 52); *Bulletin de la Société belge d'études napoléoniennes* (92 numbers between 1950 and 1975, concentrating particularly on Waterloo; indexes in No. 92); *Rivista italiana di studi napoleonici* (of uneven merit and published irregularly, but often attractive); *Het Nederlands genootschap voor Nopoleontische studien* (in Dutch); *Annales historiques de la Révolution française* (since 1908) should not be forgotten.

Dominating the whole collection by virtue of its text and extraordinary iconography which eclipses even Dayot's old albums and Bourguignon's *Napoléon* (1936) is Jean Mistler & Coll., *Napoléon et l'Empire* (1968). Iconography also in Grand-Carteret (1895) and Broadley, *Napoleon in Caricature* (1911).

The careful reader who is keen to know more should refer to the excellent bibliographical guides: G. Davois, *Bibliographie napoléonienne française* (1909; very complete until that date); L. Villat, *Napoléon* (1936) and J. Godechot, *L'Europe et l'Amérique à l'époque napoléonienne* (1967). Lumbroso, Kircheisen and Monglond's mammoth bibliographies have remained unfinished. On specific points: E. Hatin, *Bibliographie de la presse périodique française* (repub. 1965); *Guide bibliographique sommaire d'histoire militaire* (1969); J. Tulard, *Bibliographie critique des mémoirs sur le Consulat et l'Empire* (1971) recalls that many memoirs were the work of dyers, Saint-Edme, Lamothe-Langon, Villemarest, Beauchamp, Marco Saint-Hilaire, even Balzac. Every year the *Bibliographie de l'Histoire de France* published by the C.N.R.S. gives works and articles which have appeared in the period 1800–1815. There are several useful dictionaries: *Biographie des hommes vivants* (1816); Arnault, Jay, Jony and Norvins, *Biographie nouvelle des contemporains* (1921); P. Larousse, *Grand dictionnaire universel du XIXe siècle* (exceptionally rich); B. Melchior-Bonnet, *Dictionnaire de la Révolution et de l'Empire* (1965). Robert, Bourloton and Cougny, *Dictionnaire des Parlementaires* (1889–1891) and Six, *Dictionnaires des Généraux et amiraux de la Révolution et de l'Empire* (1934) are specialized works. Consult at the *École pratique des Hautes Études* (section IV) H. Robert's thesis on the diplomatic staff, D. Duchesne on the staff of the *Cour de Cassation*. Pinaud on Napoleon's bishops, U. Todisco on the *Cour des Comptes* and Szramkiewicz on the regents and censors of the Bank of France, the two last being for the most part biographical dictionaries. The history of the period was to be given a new dimension by the opening of private archives. On this subject read the annual reports of C. de Tourtier in the *Revue de l'Institut Napoléon*. Texts in Burnat (1963), Bertaud (1973) and Ravignant (1969).

The whole stretches from the collection *Que sais-je?* (*Napoleon* by Calvet, 1943) to the uninteresting 'academic' biography (L. Bertrand, O. Aubry, J. Calmette) by way of the syntheses of universal history)*Histoire Générale* by Lavasse and Rambaud, Vol. IX, 1897; *New Cambridge Modern History,* Vol. IX, 1965; *Le Monde et son histoire,* Vol. VII, 1968) and the useful articles in the *Encyclopaedia Universalis*; European evaluation in the Acts of the XII international congress of historical sciences (Vienna, 1965); Holtman, *Napoleonic Revolution* (1967); Zaghi, *Napoleone e l'Europa* (1969); *Napoleon und die Staatenwelt seiner Zeit* (1969); Ben Jones, *Napoleon, Man and Myth* (1977). On the histriographical debate, Geyl, *Napoléon, For and Against* (1949) would have been better brought up to date. After such a wealth of literature Georges Lefebvre's *Napoléon* and *Napoléon et l'Empire* under the direction of Jean Mistler must be mentioned again. This book owes a lot to them, to Villat and Godechot's biographical works and to memoranda of the bicentenary of Napoleon's birth published in 1970 by the *Revue d'Histoire moderne et contemporaine*.

INDEX